The PC Multimedia Handbook

WITHDRAWN

Technology

and

Techniques

By David Dick

Dumbreck Publishing

The P.C. Multimedia Handbook
© 2000 by Dumbreck Publishing
ISBN 0-9521484-8-X

The book cover was designed by Kenny Cullen (kenny.cullen@virgin.net)

Introduction

M ultimedia - where art meets technology

Multimedia on CDs and on the web is a huge growth area and the hardware and software to create multimedia productions is now at an affordable level.

This book attempts to explain the technology that makes it possible - the digitization of graphics, audio and video, and the supporting computer hardware.

It also examines the techniques involved in multimedia production - from initial design through to web and CD implementations.

It explains the theory of audio, video and hardware and also covers the practical steps in creating graphics, capturing audio and video, and video editing.

It is sometimes hard to say where technology ends and artistic flair begins. Design, photography, video editing, computer graphics and animation involve both practical and creative skills. The book is intended as a useful guide to both the technology and techniques of creating multimedia productions.

My first book, the P.C. Support Handbook, was designed around specific computing courses.

With multimedia, there is a wide range of different subject matter covered in different courses. I hope that I have covered the essentials and that the content is useful to students, hobbyists and media professionals.

The P.C. Support Handbook has developed over the last eight editions due to the feedback from its readers. Feedback on this book is similarly welcomed. Comments, ideas and suggestions can be e-mailed to me at (davy@dumbreck.demon.co.uk).

David Dick

Contents

Multimedia Basics

Multimedia - where art meets technology

There are many definitions of the term *'multimedia'*. At its simplest it refers to multiple forms of media. In practice, it is the convergence of graphics, audio, video, animation, and programming skills with imaginative and creative skills.

Multimedia is different from all communication mediums that have gone before.   At a visit to the cinema, the material is watched as a continuous sequence; the film has a start and a finish and the viewer watches the material in the order that the filmmakers decided. Watching television is similar. Although the viewer can flick channels, the content of any one channel is fixed and the order of the material is printed in television schedules in newspapers.   Similarly, books and videotapes are designed for sequential use.   Audiocassettes, audio CDs and magazines are a little better, in that the user can jump between tracks or flick between pages, providing some control over the content.

Multimedia, on the other hand, is the combination of all of the above.   It contains audio, video, graphics, animations, video and text - and it is all under the control of the user.

Multimedia is not just the repackaging of existing material. Early multimedia CD-ROMs made this mistake and used the large storage space of CD-ROM disks to store the entire text of books to CD, or place photographic albums on CD, and such.   While they undoubtedly help archive material, they were not true multimedia products. They missed out on the true value of multimedia authoring.

A distinguishing feature of multimedia is the ability of the user to <u>interact</u> with the media. This may be through choosing menu options or clicking the mouse on icons or areas of the screen. The vast amounts of data are usually linked through hypertext systems or authoring packages.

Multimedia should use the various types of screen output to more effectively communicate with the user or viewer.   The kinds of facilities expected in a final multimedia package include:

- still graphic images
- animated graphics
- moving video images
- digitised sound/music
- synthesised sound/music
- plain text
- digitised photographs

This interaction is the key to the success of a multimedia product.   The experts vary slightly, but generally agree that we recall 10% of what we read, 20% of what we see and 30% of what we both see and hear.   However, because we learn more from taking part in active learning, we recall a massive 70% of what we see, hear and do.   Multimedia packages allow the user to control the viewing process and decide what they want to see/do, how long they want to see/do it and what they want to see/do next.

Applications for multimedia

New uses are constantly being found for multimedia and these can be generally categorised as:

Training

Training is concerned with the acquisition of specific skills, of the mind or the hand.   Examples are learning a foreign language or playing the guitar.   Boeing use multimedia material to train their ground personnel. CBT (Computer Based Training) means that the knowledge of lecturer/teacher/trainer/instructor can be embedded into a training package and used anywhere at any time.

Education

Education is *'knowledge based'*; specific skills may not flow from the absorption of this knowledge.   The theories of evolution, politics, religion, pure science, mathematics, etc. may be learned for their own sake rather than to be practised. The Educational Software & CD-ROM Yearbook by REM is jam-packed with details of 1000 different educational CD-ROMs on subjects such as history, science, geography, art and architecture, economics and media studies, etc.

Distance learning

Distance learning assumes that the student is remote from the educational establishment. This could be for any of a variety of reasons, such as disability, family commitments, working overseas, shift working, etc.   Those undertaking study communicate via downloading material, uploading exercises and carrying on e-mail dialogues with support lecturers.   Students often use educational CDs where a teacher/lecturer is present to answer specific questions or to clear up any vagueness in the application's presentation.   This immediate help is less available with distance learning students and the multimedia material has to reflect this.   It must anticipate possible student problems, provide adequate help and guided support.   The package should have facilities for student self-assessment, to reinforce students in their learning.   Many establishments have, or are preparing, distance learning multimedia-based courses.

Edutainment

Edutainment combines elements of education and entertainment in a manner that imparts knowledge to a user while wrapping the material up as an entertaining experience.   Packages featuring the adventures of Peter Rabbit or Barney Bear provide children with animated stories.   The text of the story is displayed on screen and each word is highlighted as the story is read out.   Children can activate parts of the screen and can control the flow of the story by mouse clicks.   Serious learning is taking place in conjunction with the attractive activities. Adult edutainment equivalents are CD with conducted tours of *'The Louvre'*, investigating *'Great Artists'* and exploring *'The Ultimate Human Body'*.

Entertainment

These are solely aimed at providing fun with no attempt at any serious education, although in some packages a little general knowledge may be picked up along the way.   Applications include the *'Cinemania'* and *'Music Central'* multimedia databases on films and music, interactive music CDs such as *'Explora'* by Peter Gabriel and *'Jump'* by David Bowie, and the guide to *'Wines, Spirits and Beers'*.   Other well-known applications of multimedia are the effects produced in films such as *'Toy Story'*, *'The Mask'* and *'Jurassic Park'*, *'Antz'* and the huge range of games that now exist on CD-ROM.

Simulation

Simulation provides a computer replica of a living or supposed situation and there are applications for use in both entertainment and industry.   Leisure applications cover both the real world (e.g. flight simulators) and the imagined world (e.g. fighting the aliens on the planet Zog).   Industry has many serious uses for simulations in situations where training staff can be hazardous both to the trainees and to real equipment.   Typical applications are training French train drivers using simulations of railway routes and British firefighters learning to handle dangerous situations.   Users can learn from their mistakes without any harm being done.

Marketing

Marketing covers the promotion of both opinions and products; it is aimed at altering the views and preferences of those who use the application.   After viewing the application, users are hoped to desire certain products, holiday at a particular location, study at a particular university, etc.   Example marketing applications are the *'virtual kitchens'* demonstrated by Matsushita, unattended public information displays (known as kiosks) promoting clothes or holidays, and CD-ROM travel guides covering from the *'AA Days Out in Britain and Ireland'* to *'Travel Mexico'* and *'Voyage in Spain'*.   Multimedia marketing has a large growth potential, both in CD-ROM format and over the Internet.

Presentations

This is a specific form of marketing where the salesperson is present and is using the multimedia presentation to enhance the effect of his/her delivery.   The material is projected on to screens or video walls (see the chapter on electronic presentations).

Home shopping

This also overlaps with marketing activities.   While marketing promotes the demand for the product, home shopping provides the convenience to place the order.   A growing number of product catalogues are provided on CD or many more are available on the World Wide Web.   Users can log into a company's web site and use the search facilities to bring up details of desired products.   The user can read the text descriptions and view the images.   The product range is huge covering from computers to books and clothes. In the case of music CDs, the user is also allowed to hear short clips from albums. The user can instantly place an order and can pay with a credit card.

Reference

Reference material is readily available in book format but multimedia versions provide many extra facilities such as very quick subject searching and cross-referencing, the use of animations to aid explanations and sound and video clips of famous people and events.   Examples of reference material are BOOKBANK (British books in print), specifications, dictionaries (e.g. the Oxford Compendium), the Guinness Book of Records and a range of impressive annually updated multimedia encyclopaedias (e.g. Compton's, Grolier, Hutchinson, Microsoft and Britannica).   Archiving of reference material is another popular use, where the ability to quickly move around material and have easy search facilities provides added value.   This allows for huge databases of material such as research results, specifications, legal documents, etc.   These may include diagrams, personal signatures, scanned documents and even voiceprints.

There is currently a huge growth in electronic publishing in the shape of news, books, technical manuals, public information, and promotional brochures.

Delivery methods

The finished multimedia products are supplied to the user in a number of different formats. Multimedia is often spoken of in the same breath as CD-ROM. However the CD-ROM is not always used for multimedia purposes, and multimedia does not necessarily require the use of a CD-ROM.

It is true that projects that are rich in video and photographic content requires lots of storage space and these are often best met by the capacity offered by CD-ROM.   However, much effort has been put into making multimedia suitable for Internet distribution and the relative merits of these and other methods are discussed below.

The delivery of multimedia products can be either offline or online. The offline version is usually self-contained. All the project's elements are included on the CD-ROM or within the kiosk's hard disk.   The online version allows access to the material over local area networks, wide area networks or the Internet.

CD-ROM features

- Works on any multimedia PC, with predictable results.
- Available to PC users who have no Internet connection.
- Stores large amounts of information in a variety of formats (i.e. text, video, sound, animation).
- Allows fast user access.
- No ongoing costs to the user, after purchase, to access the information.
- Expensive for the producer to update regularly, due to production costs.
- Contents are always available, undisturbed by telephone breakdown, busy periods, etc.

Internet features

- Can be potentially accessed by a huge audience.
- Provides two-way traffic (i.e. e-mail, form-filling, voting).
- The contents are dynamic - i.e. they are easily updated (daily, hourly, instantly as necessary).
- Poses potential problems of security. The site can be hacked into and the data can be altered.
- Slow for supplying large graphics and video to users, even though streaming techniques help to reduce the problem.
- A huge web site is required to store the same amount of data as a CD-ROM.
- Providers are charged by bandwidth usage. The more popular the site, the more the Internet provider charges the web site owner, (unless they have their own equally expensive web server).
- Many users will incur telephone charges or standing charges every time they access the material.
- Provides additional commercial opportunities (e.g. credit card transactions, auctions, gathering mailing lists, etc).

Some CD-ROM products now have web links, so that the viewer can get his/her modem to dial up a specific web site and fetch current data.   This allows, for example, educational institutions to produce CD-ROMs that can be updated less regularly, since the users can fetch any new material via the institution's web site.   Similarly, a manufacturer can create a CD-ROM catalogue of products and customers can click a hyperlink to fetch the current pricing and availability.

Intranet features

An intranet is a local area network serving a single organisation, with its own web server.   The only computers connected to the intranet are the ones used by the company's employees and the multimedia content stored on the web server is only available to this limited set of users.   There is no connection to the outside world and no one else can access the web server.   It is like the Internet in miniature. Companies can use intranets to store and distribute company training and it also becoming more popular in educational establishments.

Kiosk features

These are standalone applications designed for stores, museums, trade fairs, information points, etc.   The computer equipment is housed in a sealed unit and interacts with the public through its monitor and input device (usually a touch sensitive screen). The project is stored on hard disks and is potentially available 24-hours, 7 days a week.

Electronic presentations

The material is usually stored on a laptop computer and displayed via a projector on to a screen.   With large presentations, extra bright projectors, rear projectors or video walls may be used.

The origins of multimedia

Current multimedia systems have their roots in the development of interactive video, CBT (computer based training) and hypertext systems and this page examines these pioneering systems.

Interactive video

The system comprised the following components:

- A TV monitor.
- A videodisk player (usually the Philips laservision player which used larger versions of our current CD-ROM disks). The player had a normal TV output and had a computer or microprocessor built in.

The disks were larger than modern CD disks and contained previously recorded video sequences that could be viewed by choosing options from the keyboard. Examples of use are Lloyds Bank's training staff in till, cash and cheque transactions; McDonell Douglas staff training manuals on aircraft maintenance and repair. Some used an actions/consequences approach, where a video displayed an activity and the play was suspended while the user (often in groups) considered and choose from a selection of responses. The chosen response ran another video clip that displayed the consequences resulting from the selection. This method was also adopted for early arcade video games. These were radical applications in the early 1980's and the programmes were very expensive to produce. The user content was mostly video sequences linked together by text and user responses, reflecting the state of technology at that stage. Nevertheless, these elements are in common use in modern multimedia applications.

CBT/CAL

With the growing popularity of desktop PCs, the drive towards interactive systems moved to centre round the computer and its programs. This removed the requirement for specialist apparatus and early CAL/CBT was distributed on ordinary floppy disks. The system provided new levels of user support. Computer Based Training (CBT) developed specific skills (e.g. typing tutors) while Computer Aided Learning (CAL) explored ideas (e.g. science and philosophy). Both applications provided user options and stored user responses in variables. In this way, a user's progress was monitored and appropriate advice given. Users could be given assessments and told their scores. Users could be given a certain number of attempts at a multi-choice question. The support given for a wrong answer could depend on what incorrect choice was entered and the previous experience of the user as judged by previous responses.

CBT/CAL provided an *'intelligent'* system which users enjoyed as they had more control over the learning experience. They could work at their own pace, reviewing a page, changing direction and stopping for a break. Early applications tended to have a linear format within each lesson and they lacked the visual impact of interactive video. Again, most of the elements of CBT can be found in current multimedia systems an specially on the Internet.

Hypertext

Both interactive video and CBT tended to require the user to follow a fixed training pattern with clear end objectives. Options were allowed but they were temporary detours from the main path to be treaded by the user. Although this had distinct advantages in certain situations, and is still implemented in some packages today, it did not follow the way humans think and approach issues. Few people learn a subject by systematically working through a linear path of material. Only fiction is read linearly. People learn by association; having grasped a concept it leads them to one or more linked concepts. For example, reading a car repair manual on fixing carburettors may inspire a reader to find out more about how the ignition systems works, what a catalytic converter is, or how to use a double-grommeted nut wrench. Hypertext builds a system that supports that way of thinking. Users can leave a particular subject area and explore something linked - or completely different; they can choose to return to the previous theme or can move onwards or sideways if they wish. Each person will use the system in a different way.

Users move from one subject to another by selecting menu options or by clicking the mouse on a highlighted word (a hypertext link) or on a particular area of the screen (a hotspot). Early systems were solely text based and graphical interfaces followed later. The best definition of hypertext is that it:

> *"produces large, complex, richly connected*
> *and cross-referenced bodies of information"*

Hypertext is widely implemented in Windows applications' help systems and this *'navigation'* process is one of the cornerstones of multimedia packages. The largest example of hypertext is, of course, the World Wide Web. Hypertext's benefits include good browsing abilities, rapid navigation, the ability to annotate results and the ability to save results and queries for later use.

Reported problems with hypertext are disorientation (it is much easier to get lost than when page-hopping with a printed book) and *'cognitive overhead'* (the large variety of options stuns the brain's ability to easily consider alternatives).

The multimedia machine

Most computers are capable of playing multimedia titles but the equipment for creating high-end multimedia products requires more power and more hardware.

The authoring computer

The requirements for the computers that create multimedia products are much more demanding than those for simply playing multimedia titles.

It is certainly possible to create basic multimedia projects with the simplest of computer systems, using little or no specialised hardware.   A simple presentation involving text, graphics and limited animation, can be created on a basic computer without any extra hardware add-ons whatsoever.

Of course, the more sophisticated presentations use sound clips, video sequences, complex animations, etc. and therefore require a high performance machine and special equipment to capture video, edit video, create multi-track sound, and so on.

The photograph shows the likely hardware requirements for a single computer used for producing multimedia products. In a large multimedia company, there will be many machines and they will share resources through networking.   One computer may be equipped to carry out all the sound tasks of the project, while another is used for video editing, another for scanning and graphics creation, another for planning and managing the project, and so on.

Description of hardware components

Computer	The main processing chip (the CPU) should run at a minimum of 400MHz and preferably as fast as possible. This is the main engine of the whole process and a slow CPU will increase the time taken to complete processor-intensive tasks such as video editing and graphics rendering.
Monitor(s)	A large monitor size, 19" or preferably 21", is required to get the best from some software packages. Programs such as Director, Premiere or PhotoShop use many pop-up windows and these will obscure some of the main working area (i.e. the main window where the objects and images are being worked on). Having more screen space allows an uncluttered layout. The photograph shows two monitors in use. The 21" monitor is used for the main activities while the 19" monitor is used display the various toolbars. The second monitor could also be used to run a second application. The contents can be cut from one application and pasted into the other application. Or the second application could be a word processor, so that the developer can write notes while working, or read test specifications while testing an application.

	This technique requires two graphics cards; one for each monitor, and this is easily set up in Windows 98 onwards (see the chapter on using Windows).
Memory	The memory stores parts of the multimedia software, as well as the project being worked on. Increasing the amount of memory in the computer allows more application components and project elements to be instantly available from memory, thus speeding up processing. While 64MB is a tolerable amount, 128MB is a more realistic minimum and 256MB is preferable.
Hard Disks	Multimedia files are huge, with video clips requiring up to 2GB of storage each. There can never be enough disk storage space. A 20GB hard drive is realistically the minimum size and larger drives are preferable, with several drives providing more capacity and flexibility. For video work, in particular, the drives need to be fast and of consistent performance. UDMA-66 drives are a minimum, with SCSI types being preferable.
Video Capture Card	This card usually fits inside the computer and may have an external connecting box as shown in the photograph. The output from a camcorder is connected to the card and it converts it into a video file for integration into a multimedia project. The poorest systems use VHS connections, the middle range use S-VHS connections and the recommended cards use a digital interface (known as IEEE 13494 or 'FireWire'). The first two connectors will accept output from normal analogue camcorders, while FireWire cards have to be fed by a digital camcorder.
Digital Camera Reader	Digital cameras capture photographs in computer format and have to be copied from the camera on to the computer's hard disk. Many methods are used. Some connect to the computer's serial port, while some connect to the USB port. Many cameras save their images on memory cards and these can be unplugged from the camera and inserted into a special card reader. The card reader connects to the computer and carries out the file transfers.
Sound card/MIDI	The sound card allows a range of audio devices to be connected (e.g. microphone, output from a cassette player or VCR, etc.). The card converts these audio passages into computer files for use in multimedia projects. The card should also have a MIDI socket, for connecting an electronic keyboard. This allows electronic music to be composed, recorded and saved to disk. Some sound cards provide multiple audio inputs, so that multi-track recording can be carried out in real time. A high-quality card will produce less background noise and will improve the sound clip's quality.
MIDI keyboard	Connects to the sound card's MIDI connector and is used to record musical compositions. Requires additional music sequencer software.
CD-ROM player	Required to install applications, copy over files from clip art collections, etc. Since the player is only being used for occasional file transfers, its specification need not be demanding.
CD writer	Used to 'burn' (i.e. record) CD copies of the project on to Recordable CD disks. In a commercial setting, these may be copies for internal testing, or may be the master copy used for creating the glass master for mass production. Since these are generally one-offs, there is no requirement for a particularly fast writing speed.
Mouse	Used for all normal Windows operations.
Tablet	Used as a mouse replacement for graphics and photo-retouch activities, where the mouse does not provide accurate enough control. The tablet connects to the computer (usually through the USB port) and the pen or stylus is used in place of the mouse. The pen has buttons on the side of its body so that it can emulate the buttons on the mouse.

Modem	Used when the multimedia project is a web site. The web site pages are written and tested on the computer and then copied on to the web site. If the web site is one that is regularly updated, a fast modem should be used. The fastest current modem is a 56kbps model and consideration should be given to using the ISDN, or preferably ADSL system. Of course, the modem provides additional facilities such as conducting searches and research on the web, keeping in touch with clients via e-mail and joining user groups who have specialist knowledge in multimedia activities.
Royalty-free collections of graphics, clip art, photographs, music, and sound effects	Many CDs are available that supply collections of clip art or photographs. These can be inserted into multimedia projects and save a lot of time creating them from new. But commercial multimedia products have to avoid using any photographs, images, sound clips, etc. without permission of the owners of the copyright. This is got round by purchasing special collections where there are no restrictions on the use of the images or sounds.

Items not in picture

Microphone	Connects to the sound card and is used to capture audio into the computer. The types and quality are discussed in detail in the chapter on digital audio.
Headphones	Connects to the sound card and is used to monitor all audio output in the project. A home user may use a set of speakers but this is not suitable in an office where many computers are being used.
Flatbed Scanner	Connects to the computer (usually through the USB or parallel port) and scans in photographs, images signatures, etc. and converts them into computer graphic images. Since multimedia projects are designed for viewing on a screen (rather than the printed page) there is no need for a high-resolution scanner. However, the scanner should produce true colour representations of the image being scanned.
Digital Camera	Used to capture photographs as digital images for later transfer to the computer. Like the scanner, high-resolution images are less important than the colour reproduction of the camera.
Video camcorder	Used to capture video sequences. Video is the most demanding of all elements in multimedia and poor equipment results in dropped frames (i.e. jerky video). The highest performers are FireWire camcorders and these should be used for serious work. Older analogue systems are adequate for home and hobby use.
Touch-Sensitive Screens	Its main use is in places where a keyboard is not practical, such as an unattended information point or other kiosk. They might also be used in training children and the handicapped - those who would find difficulty in using a keyboard.
Voice-operated software	A useful tool where the user is physically handicapped or where the multimedia package expects the trainee to leave their hands free from the keyboard or mouse as much as possible, for use with other activities. Driving test simulations may be an example of such an application. It could also be used for teaching foreign languages.
Network card	If the computers in a multimedia company require access to a common pool of material, they could be connected via a local area network. There is a cost for fitting a network card in each computer and the cost of the main network server and cabling of the office.

Home users who have an older computer should not be discouraged.   Most of the activities described in the book can still be carried out, although they may take a lot longer to complete.

Computer measurements

Computers use three measurements of volume and efficiency:

Measurement	Unit	Components	Explanation
Computer's Processing Speed	MHz	CPU chip	The computer's CPU clock speed is measured in *MegaHertz* (A MegaHertz, or MHz, being one million cycles per second). The clock speeds quoted for CPUs are their <u>actual</u> speeds - e.g. 500MHz means 500,000,000 pulses per second.
Capacity	Bytes, Kilobytes (KB) Megabytes (MB) Gigabytes (GB)	Memory, Disks	Measures how much data can be stored. A kilobyte is 1024 bytes, a megabyte is 1,0485,76 bytes and a gigabyte is 1,073,741,824 bytes.
Transfer rates	Bits per second, kilobits per second, megabits per second.	Modem, disk, scanner, capture card and network interfaces.	Measures how quickly data can be moved between components in the system. Usually shown as bps, kbps and mbps.

Although memory size and disk capacity are measured in bytes, other devices transmit data serially and are measured in bits per second. Some magazines, books, brochures, web sites, etc. use the terms Mb and MB, or MBps and Mbps as if they were the same measurement. To avoid confusion, this book uses an upper-case *'B'* to denote Bytes and a lower-case *'b'* to denote bits.   So, for example, a card may transfer data in MBps while a modem may transmit data in Mbps.

The ins and outs

The diagram shows that some of the add-on devices are input devices (they bring data into the main computer) and others are output devices (they receive data from the main computer systems).

For example, the video capture card, CD drive, mouse, keyboard, tablet and touch screen are all input devices, while the CD writer and DVD writer are output devices (although they could be used as reading devices).

Other devices, such as memory, hard disks, modems and sound cards are both input and output devices.

At one moment they may be sending information to the computer, while at other times they may be receiving information from the computer.

The playback computer

The Multimedia PC Marketing Council have produced standards for computer components that they think are required for the satisfactory playback of multimedia products. These specifications are detailed in the following chapter on technology.

Level 1 of the standard required a 386SX main processor chip and Level 2 required a 486SX main processor.   Both of these chips are extinct, making the standards redundant.   The Level 3 standard requires a Pentium processor running at 75MHz.   Since it is difficult to buy a new computer with a Pentium chip slower than 500MHz, it follows that all modern computers can play back multimedia material to the Level 3 standard.   Even the joint Intel/Microsoft PC 99 Guide (which predicts the specification for forthcoming computers) only specifies a 300MHz Pentium, 32MB of memory, AGP video card with 3D acceleration and hardware acceleration for video playback.

In other words, most users have computer systems that are easily capable of handling the minimum specifications for multimedia products.

Multimedia software

The hardware allows the multimedia components to be captured and saved.

These files usually require editing before being used (to shorten them, remove mistakes or to add effects). Special software to edit sound, video and graphic files is available, as is a range of packages to create graphics, animations, etc.   Most importantly, software is required to merge all these elements into a single multimedia project.

The range of software to support the creation of multimedia products includes:

	Typical Examples	Purpose
Audio Editing	CoolEdit, Software Audio Workshop, Xing MP3 Encoder	Audio files can be manipulated in many ways to create the final clip to be included in a production. These include cut and paste, mixing, merging, filtering out frequencies, adding echo effects, looping, muting, reversing, pitch altering, volume altering, panning, fading and waveform editing. Other utilities convert audio files into compressed MP3 versions.
Video Editing and effects	Adobe Premiere, Avid Cinema Adobe After Effects, Elastic Reality, Morph2, LSX-MPEG2 Encoder	Most packages use 'Non-Linear Editing' where the video clips are digitised and individual sections of the clip (right down to a single frame) are easily accessed for editing and the application of effects. Typical facilities are cut and paste, adding filters, transitions between scenes such as fades and wipes, titling, warping and morphing (gradually transforming one object into another object). The clips are organised into the correct running order and saved as the finished video clip. Other utilities convert video files into compressed MPEG versions.
Graphic Creation Photo Retouch	PhotoShop, Paint Shop Pro, Paintbrush, Corel Draw, Freehand	These packages are used to create drawings, charts, cartoons, etc from graphic elements such as lines, boxes, circles and polygons. The line widths, styles (e.g. dotted, arrowed) and colour are alterable and a variety of fill patterns are provided. Text of various sizes, types styles and colours can be added. Packages such as Paintbrush produce bitmap files while upmarket products produce vector images (although these can be converted to bitmaps).
Animation Graphic Effects	3D Studio, Visual Reality, Ray Dream Studio	The most common effects are 3D objects using wireframes and rendered fills and animations. Many authoring packages provide animation facilities but these are not as sophisticated as dedicated animation packages.
Image Editing	Photoshop, Picture Publisher, PhotoStudio	These packages are used to manipulate the contents of a photographic image. This includes altering the colours, altering contrast and brightness, and zooming, scaling and cropping of the image. It may also include special effects such as quantizing (producing an oil painting effect) and altering the data masks (producing a pop video effect). These packages are often used to alter the image's main contents (e.g. removing a blemish from someone's face, or removing the telegraph pole that seems to stick out of someone's head).
Authoring Packages	Director, Authorware, Icon Author, MasterClass, Toolbook	This is the key piece of software that integrates all the sound, video, graphic and text components into a meaningful order to achieve a prescribed effect.
Web Authoring	HTML editors, Dreamweaver JavaScript, Flash	These packages are designed for creating web-based multimedia material. They may be the web equivalent of the authoring package (i.e. they integrate all the components into a set of interlinked web pages) or they provide animations and effects that are optimised for web use.
Music Software	Audio Architect Cubase Cakewalk Steinberg B Box drum kit	These packages provide facilities to compose, record, edit and mix music tracks. The audio tracks can be real world audio, recording via microphones or can be synthesised MIDI tracks.

Multimedia Skills

The first two essential ingredients for creating multimedia have been covered.   The third ingredient, the one that makes the hardware and software useful, is the skills of the individual or team producing the multimedia project.

At the end of the day, it is the skills of the designers, programmers, artists, etc. that decide whether a masterpiece or a monster are created.

This page attempts to outline the variety of skills that are involved.   For convenience, it places skills in groups.   This does not minimise the contribution of any group in the team. All the skills are required for a successful outcome.   It is also readily acknowledged that there is some overlapping of skills For example, a photographer may be told what scene to shoot but still uses his/her skills to get the best shot, or a video camera operator may spot an unusual activity and shoot it for later consideration).

The aim is not to start a debate about the relative merits of individual jobs or their boundaries. The aim is to lay out the spread of skills employed by large multimedia companies and to consider the complex set of tasks and relationships involved in creating large multimedia titles.

Creative skills

This group of skills covers those who come up with the original ideas, or have the flair to advise on changes, additions and improvements.

Title	Job Description
Designers	There are two main design specialists: Instructional designer - ensures that the subject is clearly presented. Preferably an expert in the subject contained in the project. User interface designer - constructs the structure of screens that make up the project and the links between screens.
Copywriter	Also called content writers. They write all headings, body text, and the material for the voiceovers.
Graphic Artist	Deals with all that is visual in the project. This will involve creating original graphics and editing photographs supplied by the photographer.
Composer	Composes the music for the project.

Technical skills

This covers those who use their knowledge of their discipline and their equipment to achieve the tasks set for them.

Title	Job Description
Video Specialist	Captures the project's video sequences. May work on his/her own or may be in charge of a team of cameramen, lighting specialists, set designers, production assistants and actors.
Sound Specialist	Captures original audio clips and gathers existing available audio clips (from copyright free collections). May work on his/her own or may work with audio engineers, composers and musicians.
Photographer	Captures original photographs, often from a shooting list provided by the project manager. May be a permanent employee or may be a freelance brought in on a contract basis.
Video editor	Modifies video clips to fit allocated time, applies video effects, adds voiceovers, dubbing, background music, etc.
Animator	Creates animated sequences to the supplied specification.
Technical writer	Creates the installation instructions, user manual, database maintenance instructions, etc, as necessary.

Software skills

This covers all those who use their programming experience to implement the structures and screen contents that tie all the elements into a cohesive body of work.

Title	Job Description
Programmer	Usually creates projects using authoring packages such as Director, Authorware, Toolbook, or Icon Author. Builds up the project according to the
Web Site Producer	Specialises in the production of multimedia for web sites. Usually has a wide knowledge of HTML, JavaScript, Perl, ASP, CGI, and can implement databases and e-commerce facilities such as shopping carts and secure transaction processing.
Tester	Subjects the project to exhaustive testing to discover errors and bugs before the project is shown to the wider world.

Management skills

This covers those who ensure that the multimedia project sticks true to its original aims and finishes on time and within budget.

Title	Job Description
Project manager	Also known as the team leader, this job controls overall design and management. He/she is also the key figure in the day-to-day management of people and resources.
Document manager	Keeps track of all the media files, authoring scripts and specification documents, to ensure that the most recent versions are the ones supplied to developers and that the previous versions are backed up for returning to in the event of a catastrophe. This is also sometimes referred to as version management.
Account Manager	Interfaces between the client and the production team. He/she sets up meetings with the client and maintains contact throughout the production schedule.
Researcher	Carries out additional research on behalf of the copywriter, artists and designers.

The above skills concentrate on those required for the successful completion of the final product. Other staff are obviously involved in a looser way - e.g. marketing staff, proofreaders, accounting staff, media distributors and so on.

In a large company, a large number of staff will be employed to carry out these tasks listed above.

In a small company, many of the jobs will be rolled together - e.g. one person may both shoot and edit the video material, while another person may carry out all the design tasks.

For those working from home - you are the team!

Overview of production

A complex multimedia project is carried out in distinct phases.

- Work out the main aims of the project.
- Create an outline working prototype.
- Work out the project's technical requirements, navigation requirements, and screen layout specifications.
- Produce a storyboard.
- Produce a navigation map.
- Work out a project plan for handling people, time and resources.
- Assemble all the multimedia components (i.e. record all the sound and video clips, photograph all the pictures, draw all the graphics).
- Use an authoring package to tie all the elements together.
- Test the project and correct any errors.
- Distribute the project (i.e. put it on a web site, burn a CD-R, or create a CD master).

These are covered in more detail in other chapters.

Colour theory

This section is included here as it contains valuable insights into the working of the human eye and brain. This is worth knowing in its own right. From a multimedia perspective, it applies to graphics, photography, video, multimedia project design, web page design, etc.

It explains how we perceive colours and how digital cameras, camcorders, TV screens, and computer monitors work.

It also explains why certain colours work better than others and why certain colour combinations are more powerful than others.

How the eye works

Electromagnetic radiation has a wide spectrum that covers from radio signals to cosmic rays. Within that spectrum lies a small frequency range known as the visible spectrum.

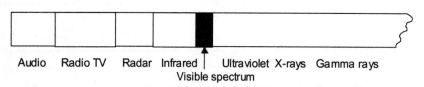

The visible spectrum is that portion of the spectrum that produces visual sensations. The eye is sensitive to the energy from a broad band of wavelengths extending from around 350nM to 700nM. Immediately below the visible spectrum is the infrared spectrum, which is used in television and camera remote controls, and for the transfer of digitised pictures from cameras to computers fitted with IrDa ports. Above the visible spectrum is ultraviolet, which can be damaging to the eyes and skin.

The diagram below shows a graph whose horizontal axis is measured in wavelength. To avoid confusion, it is best to remember that as a wavelength gets longer, its frequency goes down, and vice versa. So, the wavelength of 430nM has a higher frequency than the wavelength at 560nM.

The colours of the rainbow are simply the frequencies of the visible light spectrum, in ascending order. These colours are red, orange, yellow, green, blue, indigo and violet.

The eyeball's interior, known as the *'retina'*, is lined with a collection of photoreceptors (i.e. photosensitive cells). Light enters the eye through the cornea (to achieve focus) and the iris (to control the amount of light) before being beamed on to the retina.

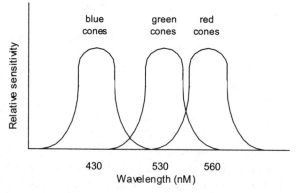

The retina contains two types of photosensitive cell, known as *'cones'* and *'rods'*. When these are struck by light photons, they release electrical energy that is processed by the brain as visual information.

The rods are very light sensitive and contribute to the perception of movement and to the detection of objects at very low light levels (i.e. 'seeing in the dark'). They still detect light when the cones have stopped responding.

The cones are of three distinct types, each having their maximum sensitivity at different points on the visible spectrum, as shown in the diagram.

These are called the blue, green and red cones and the signals from these three collections of cones are mixed in the brain to arrive at the particular colour being perceived. Although we often refer to 'seeing' colours, the perception of colour exists only within the brain. Any possible colour is arrived at by the evaluating the relative levels of signal coming from the different sets of cones.

Limitations of the eye

The ability to detect colours is known as *'photopic vision'*. The inability to successfully process light of different wavelengths (particularly between the red and green areas of the spectrum) produces *'colour confusion'* which affects around 10% of the population. The total inability to differentiate any colour differences is known as *'scotopic vision'* and results in a monochromatic view of the world. This is full colour-blindness.

So, the eye contains four different types of receptor - three for colour information and one for light levels.

Note: This is exactly how a colour television works. The TV station transmits four different pictures - one for the red components, one for the green components, one for the blue components and a monochrome picture to provide the light levels. These four pictures are superimposed on each other on the TV screen to produce the television picture.

As the diagram on the previous page shows, the peak responses for the different cones are not evenly spaced.   The red and green cones are closer together in the spectrum.   The eye optimally focuses light from the upper-end of the visible spectrum on to the retina (somewhere around 560nM).   This means that the blue cones produce a slightly more blurred image than the red and green cones.   Therefore, they do not need the same spatial resolution as the other cones and this is reflected in the allocation of the number of cones on the retina of each type.   There are about 40 red cones and 20 green cones for every blue cone on the retina.

The rods and cones are not spread evenly over the retina.   The retina's central area, the *'fovea'*, is covered only in cones, with the surrounding areas being a mixture of cones and rods.   The cones are tightly packed in the fovea and these provide spatial resolution in normal light conditions (i.e. details and patterns).

Colour processing

Light from the sun and from fluorescent tubes is *'white light'* - it contains all the colours of the spectrum. Domestic light bulbs produce light with a slight yellow cast, while sodium street lamps produce light with an orange cast.

'White' light is the combination of all colours, while 'black' indicates the absence of all colour sources.

The human eye perceives rays of light that are directly produced and fired into the eye (TV screen, computer monitor, torch, light bulb).   Most day-to-day light is not direct light, but the light that is reflected from an object.

White light is shone on an object and some of the light is absorbed, the remainder being reflected into the eye of the viewer.

The human eye reacts to light by processing various light sources that are either:

* Reflected from an object (known as *'subtractive mixing'*)
* Directly targeted at the eye (known as *'additive mixing'*).

Subtractive Mixing

Objects have no colour of their own; they only have abilities to absorb or reflect parts of the visible spectrum. We see what is reflected and don't see what is absorbed. Natural daylight reflecting off non light-absorbent paper (i.e. white) allows the full light spectrum to be reflected.   These reflected wavelengths are mixed inside the eye and interpreted as white.   Adding ink or paint pigment to the paper surface results in the area affected selectively absorbing some of the wavelengths from the white light source. The viewer sees the resultant colour reflection from the mix.   Since the introduction of the pigment has taken away some of the wavelengths, the process is termed *'subtractive mixing'*.   An object is seen to be 'blue' because it reflects blue light and absorbs all other light.   For convenience, we refer to an object as being red, rather than saying that the object reflects wavelengths that are in the visible red spectrum.   Similarly, we say that an object is cyan, rather than saying that it absorbs most red wavelengths and reflects most blue and green wavelengths. This shorthand makes life easier, as long as we know how light really works.   White objects reflect all light, while black objects absorb all light.

Additive Mixing

The colour monitor exploits the fact that the three main colours, as detected by the eye, are red, green and blue.   In this case, the light is not reflected but is directly transmitted from the monitor screen to the eye. Any other colour of light can be obtained from mixing the three primary colours of light - red, green and blue - in the appropriate ratios.   For example, mixing red and green light produces yellow light, while mixing red, green and blue in the same full proportions produces white light.   Since the monitor's CRT (cathode ray tube) uses three different light sources to produce the colours, the process is termed *'additive mixing'*.   If no light sources are added to the mix, no wavelengths reach the eye and the screen is perceived as being black.

The diagrams show the effects of colour mixing.

Additive mixing is shown in the left diagram.   Imagine three torches being shone into an eye, in a darkened room. If only the red torch is switched on, the eye sees a red pool of light. If only the green torch is switched on, the eye sees a green pool of light.   If the red and green torches are switched on together, the eye sees a red pool and a green pool of light. But, where these pools overlap, the user sees a yellow patch of light.

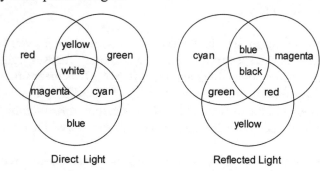

Direct Light   Reflected Light

If the blue torch is now switched on, it will seen as a pool of blue light, with a cyan patch where it overlaps the green light and magenta patch where it overlaps the red light.   In the middle, where all the lights overlap, the eye sees a white patch of light. The monitor screen works in this way, replacing torches with illuminated coloured dots on the screen surface (see the chapter on display technology for full details).

Subtractive mixing is shown in the right diagram.   Imagine an eye looking at a white sheet of paper in bright sunlight.   All the light is being reflected and the eye sees a large white area.   Imagine the sheet of paper is now run through a printer so that a circular area is printed filled with cyan ink.   The cyan ink prevents light at that wavelength from being reflected and the eye sees a pool of cyan. If the paper were run through the printer a second time to print a magenta-coloured circle on the sheet, all light in the magenta areas of the spectrum would also be absorbed. The eye would now see a pool of cyan and a pool of magenta.   Where the two areas overlap, the eye would see a patch of blue. If the paper were run through the printer one more time, printing a yellow filled circle on the sheet, the yellow ink would absorb light in that part of the spectrum.   The eye would now see a yellow pool of light.   Where the yellow pool overlapped the magenta pool, a patch of red would be seen.   Where the yellow pool overlapped the cyan pool, a patch of green would be seen.   Where all three inks overlap, all light in the spectrum is absorbed and the eye would see a patch of black.

A full-colour version of these diagrams is on our web site.

Colour range

Research shows that individuals can distinguish around 256 different levels for each colour.   This happily coincides with the range of values stored in a single byte of storage.   Therefore, a single byte can store 256 different levels of blue (or red, or green).

Since a monitor uses a light source for red, green and blue, and each colour need only be represented by 256 different levels, the maximum colours produced is

$$256 \times 256 \times 256 = 16,777,216$$

These 16.7 million colours are sufficient to provide all possible colours that can be perceived by the human eye.   For this reason, schemes using 16.7 million colours are known as *'true colour'*.

Each colour value is stored in a single byte, which is the equivalent of 8 bits.   Since there are three guns a total of 3 bytes or 24-bits stores all possible colours.   This explains why true colour systems are also described as having *'24-bit colour depth'*.

Intensity

The human eye, and digital cameras/camcorders, record information about objects by the wavelength of the reflected light (i.e. its colour) and the brightness of the light.

White objects reflect nearly all the light that shines upon them while darker objects reflect around 10% of the light.   So, a dark blue object and a dark green object both reflect different light wavelengths into the eye. However, they both reflect light at low levels.   When the general light conditions are poor, such as at dusk, there is even less light to reflect.   This is part of the explanation for the inability to distinguish between dark colours at night.   Witness statements at an evening crime scene often show confusion about the colour of the robber's jacket, the colour of the getaway car and so on.   This is because the colour-sensitive cones have ceased to respond to the low light levels, while the rods are still processing illumination information, with their maximum sensitivity being in the 510nM region (the green part of the spectrum).

Computer Technology

This chapter is in the book because the efficiency and reliability of the computer hardware is as important to multimedia production as the efficiency of the multimedia software. The graphics cards, monitors, video capture cards and sound cards are covered in other chapters in detail. This chapter looks at the CPU, memory and hard disk systems.

Many everyday applications can be used on machines with fairly low specifications. Users can carry out word processing, web browsing, sending e-mail, and so on, with a computer with a slow processor, little memory and not much in the way of hard disk space. Multimedia systems are different. They require lots of power. They are ask to shift and stores huge amounts of data. Sound and video files can be huge and this makes it difficult to move them around the system fast enough.

This is a key difference between multimedia files and other files. If a user finds that his/her Internet connection slows down, it just means that the web page takes longer to download. The web page is sitting on the web site and can be retrieved in small bursts until it is all fetched. This is not the case with, for example, capturing audio or video in real time. There is only one chance to capture the audio or video source. If the system is not up to the job, chunks of the source are left unrecorded and this appears as gaps in a sound clip or jerkiness in a video clip. The multimedia computer system is only as good as its weakest link. With multimedia, the concern is with the DTR (data transfer rate) of all the components in the chain.

Consider the diagram below. It shows how video data moves from the camera to storage on a hard disk.

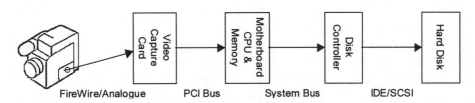

The following factors affect how efficiently a computer can handle multimedia data:

- Camcorders can have either analogue (VHS or S-VHS) outputs or digital (FireWire) outputs, with the latter requiring the fastest performance from the other components in the chain.
- The video capture card performance determines whether the data coming from the camcorder can be digitised fast enough, at a big enough resolution, in enough colours, without losing any of the data.
- The video capture card can connect into the main computer via a slower ISA slot, a faster PCI slot, or even a parallel port or USB port. All these have different rates of handling data.
- The computer's motherboard components, processor and memory all have different performances.
- The data, once it has been processed by the computer's CPU chip, has to be sent to a disk controller for writing away to the hard disk. The controller can be an older IDE type, a fast UDMA type or the most reliable SCSI type. Each has different abilities for shifting data to the disk.
- The last link in the chain is the hard disk. Even disks of the same type (i.e. UDMA or SCSI) have different specifications. For example, one disk may be manufactured to run at a faster speed than another. A disk may also provide a more reliable flow of data, free from sudden drops in data flow.

For all these reasons, the machine used for multimedia editing and authoring has to be chosen carefully.

Overview of computer systems

The main components in the computer system are:

CPU (Central Processing Unit)

The heart of any computer system is the Central Processing Unit. It is a silicon microchip and its function is to interpret and execute the program instructions. The speed and design of this chip largely determines the overall speed of the computer. Early PCs used a chip known as the 8088 and this was followed by a range of chips through to the present Pentium and Xeon chips. Early machines ran at a speed of 4.77MHz while the Pentium III runs as fast as 1000MHz. Apart from improvements to their raw clock speeds, modern chips have other in-built improvements over earlier models.

Memory

To work, the computer has to temporarily store the program and data in an area where it can be used by the computer's processor. This area is known as the computer's *'memory'*. Memory consists of computer chips that are capable of storing information. That information may be:

- The program that keeps the computer running (e.g. Windows).
- The instructions of the program that the user wants to run (e.g. an authoring or graphics program).
- The data that is used or created (e.g. multimedia scripts or graphic images).

Disks

These are used for the long-term storage of data. The bulk of the information (programs and data) used by computer applications is stored on disk and must be transferred to main memory before it can be processed by the CPU. Storage devices include magnetic disks (removable floppy disks and built-in hard disks), CD-ROM disks and magnetic tape.

Monitors

Programs send the output from their calculations to a screen via a graphics card. The screen is contained in a unit called the *'monitor'* - sometimes also called the VDU (*'visual display unit'*) and these devices are covered fully in the chapter on display technology.

The power of the machine

The power of the machine is usually indicated by the speed of the processor. The faster the speed of the chip, the more instructions it can process in any given time.

The following measurements of time are used:

Millisecond	=	1/1,000th of a second
Microsecond	=	1/1,000,000th of a second
Nanosecond	=	1/1,000,000,000th of a second

These measurements are used to describe the time taken for the computer processor to process one unit of data, usually one byte. Different models of computer are designed to run at different speeds. Of course, the faster the machine, the greater the purchase price. One measure of speed of a machine is the number of cycles per second at which it can operate (measured in MHz - MegaHertz - millions of cycles per second). The slowest PC was just under 5MHz. The fastest speed is always being improved upon and is currently 1000MHz, with even faster machines on the way.

The choice of machine depends very much upon its expected use. If the machine were used entirely for word processing, a lower speed machine is perfectly satisfactory. Since the slowest part of the process is the typist's thinking and typing time, there is little to be gained by having very fast processing in between long pauses at the keyboard. On the other hand, where there is going to be a great deal of machine processing, such as graphics calculations, video editing and other multimedia number crunching tasks, a faster machine becomes essential.

Of course, the raw speed of the CPU is not the only factor in determining the machine's overall speed. Other factors, such as the speed of the disk and video card, the amount of RAM available, whether the machine has an efficient caching system, etc., also determine the machine's performance.

Units of measurement

All computer data and program instructions (e.g. between the camcorder and the capture card, or between the CPU and memory) comprise movements of binary 0's and 1's. To make sense of the stream of 0's and 1's, the system must break the stream up into manageable groups and process data a group at a time. The standard ways of organising binary information are given below:

BIT - this is the single binary digit and stores only two conditions (ON or OFF). This is the basic unit on which the system works.

NIBBLE - this is a group of four bits. It can store 16 different combinations (from 0 through to 15) and is not in common use. It is used in some parallel printer modes.

BYTE - this is group of eight bits. It can store 256 different combinations (from 0 through to 255) and is the standard method of representing a single character.

WORD - A word is a group of bits that is treated by the computer as a single unit for retrieving, processing and storing. So, if a data bus happens to be 8 bits wide, it can process 8 bits at a time (i.e. the computer's word size is a single byte. If the data bus happened to be 16 bits wide, its word size would be 16 bits.

Measurement of capacity

When measuring data (either as disk capacity, memory, bus widths or as speed of transfer) it is always referred to in its binary state - e.g. One Bit, One Byte, One Kilobyte, One Megabyte, etc.

Memory or disk capacity describes the amount of data a device can hold at any one time and is measured in bytes. One byte can store a single character. A character can be a letter or a number, or any of the many special characters found on the keyboard. A byte may also store part of program instruction, part of a graphic image, part of an audio clip, etc.

In computing, where operations are often considered in units of 2, the Kilo or K actually means 1,024 characters with similar definitions for the larger numbers.

Kilo is 2 raised to the power of 10, or 2 x 2 x 2 x 2 x 2 x 2 x 2 x 2 x 2 x 2. Tera is 2 multiplied by itself 40 times, or exactly 1,099,511,627,776.

A rough measure of memory requirements is:

> 1 byte can store 1 character
> 1 KB can store a few paragraphs of text
> 1 MB can store the text of a reasonably sized book

The table shows the numbers that result from the binary numbering method. Since each number increases by a factor of two, no number can ever be an exact thousand or an exact million. In order to maintain the convenience of expressing size in thousands and millions, sizes have to be rounded to the binary number nearest to the wanted number.

Amount	Calculation (2 raised to the power of n)	Actual Amount
1 kilobyte (KB)	2^{10}	1,024 bytes
1 megabyte (MB)	2^{20}	1,048,576 bytes
1 gigabyte (GB)	2^{30}	1,073,741,824 bytes
1 terabyte (TB)	2^{40}	1,099,511,627,776 bytes

The range of Intel CPUs

From the beginning of the PC range of computers, the main CPU has been from the Intel range, supplemented by other manufacturers with *'clones'* or improved versions of each chip in the series.

The most recent series consists of the following chips:

Pentium It replaced the 486 chip and had a 256-bit internal bus and a 64-bit external data bus. On most occasions, it allowed two instructions to be executed in parallel, greatly speeding up throughput. The chip also had the main mathematical operations (i.e. add, divide and multiply) hard-wired into the chip.

Pentium Pro This chip used six different pipelines and 40 general-purpose registers. All the pipelines operated simultaneously, offering greatly improved processing capability. The chip used 16k of level 1 cache. There was also 256k or 512k of second level cache built into the chip and directly connected to the CPU itself. This meant that the cache operated at the full CPU speed (at that time, external caches on other systems operated at only half speed). This made the Pro's caching much more efficient.

Pentium MMX This is a version of the Pentium with 57 additional instructions in the CPU instruction set. These are multimedia and communications extensions to the CPU giving them the title *'MMX'* - multimedia extensions. The new instructions use a technique known as SIMD - Single Instruction, Multiple Data. One instruction can work on up to 8 bytes of data simultaneously. This provides very fast repetitive processing of data - ideal for video decompression, sound synthesis, multimedia, 3D rendering and other graphics-intensive activities. MMX aware programs - ie those using the new MMX instructions produce speed improvement in these areas. These facilities are now incorporated into current Pentium models.

Pentium II It was an improved Pentium Pro with MMX additions. It was released with a 100MHz processor/cache interface and a 66MHz system bus. The built in second level cache was taken out of CPU and was mounted, along with CPU, on a plug-in card. This card plugged into a special connection slot known as *'Slot One'*, which meant that the Pentium II needed a completely re-designed motherboard. The external second level cache only ran at half the CPU speed, which meant that the performance was diminished. However, the 32-bit performance, coupled with MMX capabilities, placed Pentium II machines in the lower multimedia and graphics workstations market. The newer Slot 1 Deschutes chip used the same slot as the standard Pentium II and operated at faster speeds. It also ran at system bus speeds of 100MHz (compared to 66MHz). A version aimed at the budget PC market, known as the Celeron, has a 66MHz bus.

Pentium Xeon   The Xeon is intended for high performance workstations and network servers.   It requires yet another new motherboard with a *'Slot 2'* connection.   It requires a higher specification motherboard with faster memory and a different chipset (the 450NX).   The Level 2 cache runs at the same speed as the clock and is available in 512KB, 1MB and 2MB sizes.

Pentium III   The Pentium III uses the Slot 1 connection with a bus speed of 100MHz, 133MHz or 200MHz. The internal second level cache is 512k but still runs at only half the CPU clock speed.

The Pentium III introduces *'KNI'*, Katmai New Instructions, comprising 70 new machine code instructions aimed at 3D graphics, MPEG2 video encoding/decoding, AC3 audio and image processing.   These work on the same principle as the MMX (Single Instruction Multiple Data) moving large amounts of data with a single instruction.   The PIII has a separate set of 128 registers for SIMD operations, thereby speeding up both SIMD and normal register activities.

The Pentium III Xeon is essentially the Pentium II Xeon with the added KNI instructions.

Alternatives to Intel

The main challenge to the Intel line comes form AMD.   The K7 chip uses its own proprietary slot connector, requiring a specially designed motherboard.   It has a clock speed of 600MHz and a bus speed of 200MHz. Like the K6, it provides its own set of 21 SIMD instructions, known as 3DNow!.   However, these are incompatible with KNI instructions.

Summary of P.C. Processors

	The first PC	Pentium	Pentium Pro	Pentium II	Xeon	Pentium III
Introduced	1978	1993	1995	1997	1998	1999
Number of Pins	40	273	387	Slot 1	Slot 2	Slot 1
Transistors	29,000	3.1m	5.5m	7.5m	7.5m	9.5m
Addressable Memory	1MB	4GB	64GB	64GB	64GB	64GB
Clock Speed (MHz)	4.77 / 8	60/233	150/266	166/450	400/450	450/1000

Speeding up processing

If each new instruction was fetched from memory after the previous instruction has been fully executed, the only way to increase the computer's efficiency would be to increase the rate at which the CPU was clocked.   Already, clock speeds have been raised from the original 4.77MHz to 1GHz and beyond. However, the laws of physics and the cost of manufacture restrict the ability to continually raise machine clock speeds.   Very fast CPUs, for example, require very fast address buses and data buses to keep up with the demands of the CPU, adding to the cost of the motherboard.   In practice, other methods are used to speed up the CPU's efficiency.

These include:

- Using two or more CPUs, so that several instructions can be processed simultaneously. Many Pentium motherboards have all the necessary logic on board to allow four CPUs to be connected for parallel running.   This is known as *'symmetric multiprocessing'* and is ideal for heavy multimedia processing such as video handling, as the multiple CPUs even out the processing load and prevents time glitches that might result in dropped video frames.
- Clock multiplying - making the operations inside the CPU chip run faster while maintaining the existing speeds for the main buses and motherboard devices.
- Introducing efficient memory caching systems, either built in to the CPU chip and/or as external secondary cache.

Clock-multiplying

All Pentium CPUs are run faster than the main computer bus speeds.   This is termed *'clock multiplying'*. By having extra memory, *'cache memory'*, built in to the chip, the CPU pre-fetches data and program instructions.   This way, the amount of traffic between the chip and the bus is reduced.   Consequently, the internal speed of the CPU can be multiplied by some factor (e.g. doubled, tripled, and so on) without straining the CPU/bus interface. For example, the overall system can be running at 100MHz while the CPU runs at 700MHz.

The *'clock'* frequency (i.e. number of pulses per second) is divided down and supplies the timing pulses on the PCI bus.   The same clock frequency is also multiplied by a chosen factor and clocks the internal operation of the CPU.   The setting of links on jumper blocks determines the clock's working frequency; other jumpers set the multiplication factor.

A Pentium with a 66MHz clock speed and a multiplier of 3.5 produces a CPU speed of approx 200MHz. Similarly, a 100MHz clock speed and a multiplier of 4 produces a 400MHz CPU clock speed. Operations via the separate memory bus are processed at the basic clock rate. This is 60MHz for older Pentium and Pentium Pro CPUs, 66MHz for newer Pentiums, Pentium Pros and Pentium IIs, 100MHz for Pentium II CPUs (running at 350 MHz and above), and 100MHz or 133MHz for Pentium IIIs.

Maths co-processors

The Pentium range of chips have their own *'maths co-processors'* built in to the CPU. The computer's main CPU is best at handling integer calculations; its speed drops dramatically when confronted with floating point (i.e. fractions) calculations. Mathematical tasks normally undertaken by the CPU are delegated to the co-processor. The maths co-processor chip, unlike the main CPU, is not designed for a general-purpose role; it is tailored to carrying out its functions in the most efficient way possible. This provides great potential advantages:

- The co-processor is much quicker at mathematical calculations.
- The main CPU is freed to carry out other tasks.

However, there are a number of other considerations:

- This great improvement only occurs for a <u>proportion</u> of the machine time, since the computer only spends a proportion of its time on mathematical calculations.
- Some applications benefit much more from the maths co-processor than others. For example, there is no advantage for word processing, as the number crunching element is almost non-existent. There is also little benefit for database operation, as most database activity requires file accesses, which are very slow compared to any processing activity. However, dramatic performance increases can normally be expected with computer-aided design and animation packages. These rely heavily on the calculation of curves, etc. and are all equipped to use a maths co-processor to best advantage. Similarly, graphics, Desk Top Publishing and other graphic-oriented applications also rely on substantial amounts of number crunching to calculate arcs, vector co-ordinates, etc.

CPU cache memory

Standard memory speeds have not progressed at the same rate as processor speeds. As a result, the CPU can process data faster than the data can be fetched from memory or placed in memory. Consider that a 1GHz CPU cycles every 1ns while the access time for main memory is usually 60ns. This means that the CPU has to stand idle while the required location in memory is accessed for data to be transferred. This waiting is enforced by *'wait states'* which prolong the CPU's access cycle time. While this matches the performance of the CPU to that of the computer memory, it slows down the effective CPU operating speed. This bottleneck could be overcome if the much faster Static RAM was used as main memory. However, the cost of using SRAM for many megabytes of machine memory is entirely prohibitive at the present time. It would also be extremely wasteful to have expensive RAM sitting doing little, while most of the computer activity centres round only a small portion of the memory at any one time.

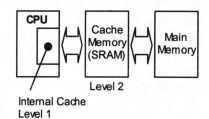

A favoured solution is to use a small block of fast RAM between the CPU and the main memory. This is known as *'cache memory'*. Any data held in the cache memory can be transferred to the CPU at greater speeds, due to its faster access time of between 2ns and 10ns. This means that the CPU can access memory without the need for wait states. The result of using cache memory is to dispense with wasted CPU time and to increase computer efficiency. Since the block of fast SRAM is likely to be substantially smaller than the computer's main memory, the cache memory can only hold a portion of the data that is resident in main memory. The aim is to ensure that only the data most likely to be required is stored in cache memory.

This relies on two established facts, collectively known as the *'principle of locality'*.

- The running of applications programs involves jumping and looping through different parts of the long list of program instructions. Despite this, most program activities are sequential - an instruction follows from a previous program instruction, with occasional jumps to other program areas. When arrived at the new program area, the machine then progresses sequentially through the new area. Often, the same few instructions are repeated over and over again as part of some iterative process.

- The data for programs is often grouped together in sequential fashion. For example, multimedia files are often huge and needs to be read in sequential order (e.g. from the beginning of the video clip to the end of the video clip).

If the data is often accessed sequentially, then a group of data is transferred from main memory into cache memory. This one-off transfer will take place at the slowest speed - i.e. that of the main memory, wait states and all. Any subsequent requests for data are transferred to the CPU at the higher cache memory speed. Concentrating the program's main data into the fast memory ensures that the performance is optimised. When another area of data is requested - one not already stored in cache - the data is transferred from main memory into cache memory, along with the contiguous data in main memory. The fetch of the first piece of data, in this case, is actually slower than normal, since an entire block of data was transferred at a wait-state speed. However, since subsequent fetches from that memory block are faster, the overall effect is to speed up processing.

Primary/secondary cache

Pentium chips already have a small area of cache memory built in to the CPU chip. This is known as *'Primary Caching'* or *'Level 1 Caching'*. This is often considered inadequate and can be supplemented with the addition of extra *'Secondary' or 'Level 2'* caching. The Pentium II has two 16k L1 caches but reverts to an external cache that runs at half the speed of the CPU. The Celeron Pentium II has 128KB of cache while the Xeon has a 512KB, 1MB or a 2MB L2 cache, both types running at full CPU speed.

The table shows some common memory speeds:

	486DX	Pentium	Pentium Pro	Pentium II	Xeon	Pentium III
System	33MHz	66MHz	66MHz	100MHz	100MHz	100MHz
CPU	100MHz	233MHz	200MHz	450MHz	400MHz	550MHz
L1	10ns	4ns	5ns	2ns	2ns	2ns
L2	30ns	15ns	5ns	4ns	2ns	4ns
Main Memory	60ns	60ns	60ns	10ns	10ns	10ns

PC bus architectures

To maximise the computer's efficiency, it is essential that data be transferred between the processor and memory (and vice versa) as quickly as possible. When a user wishes to use a slow speed card in the computer, this should not be allowed to slow down these CPU/memory transfers. The solution is to provide a separate high-speed bus linking the processor and memory. All the communication between CPU and memory is carried over this bus. The normal ISA bus remains to handle disk, video, expansion slots, etc.

ADVANTAGES:

- The memory chips runs as fast as the CPU allows, while slower speed cards are catered for on the separate slower bus. The system runs at its maximum speed.
- Now that the memory has its own separate bus, a block of even faster memory (cache memory) can be introduced between the main memory and the CPU. The cache memory is used to handle pages of memory data at a time. (see notes on memory)

The local bus

All current computers use *'local bus'* architectures, where the expansion bus is clocked more slowly than the CPU, for the benefit of slower add-on boards. However, a *'local bus'* connects the memory, video and disk controllers to the CPU on a full 32-bit or 64-bit bus. This bus is clocked at a much higher rate - up to that of the CPU - for maximum data transfer. Consequently, all cards that run on the local bus outperform their equivalent ISA card versions. Video performance, in particular, can be spectacularly speeded up but the benefits are also available to disk controllers and other local bus cards. The local bus boards still run ordinary application software and require no special operating system arrangements. Currently, the technology appears both in add-on cards and implemented on the motherboard.

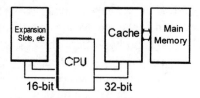

Memory Bus Architecture

There are two major variations in local bus technology - the extinct VESA Local Bus and the current Intel PCI bus.

PCI Bus

Current computer systems use the Intel PCI ('*Peripheral Component Interconnect*') Bus.   Initially designed as a 32-bit connection system for motherboard components, it developed into a full expansion bus system.   The diagram shows a typical PCI configuration, although the details vary slightly with

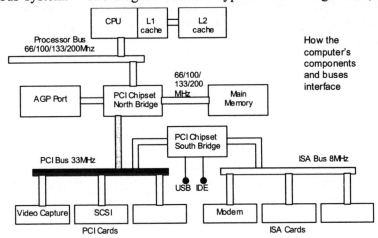

How the computer's components and buses interface

different CPUs and different memory systems.   The PCI bus exists as a local fast bus, separate from the slower ISA bus.   A bridge controller (the '*South Bridge*') allows the use of older ISA cards on a normal ISA bus. However, it decouples the CPU clock and data path from the bus and interfaces to them through another chip in the PCI chipset (the '*North Bridge*').   The PCI bus is therefore independent of the machine's CPU.   It works equally well with the 486, the Pentium or any future chips and is used with the DEC Alpha workstation and the PowerPC.   All that is required is that each CPU has its own CPU-PCI chipset.

The chipset comprises two chips.   The North Bridge handles the CPU, memory, cache and the PCI bus, while the South Bridge handles USB, IDE drives and the ISA bus.

Current PCI buses run at 33MHz, even though motherboards run at up to 200MHz. The PCI bus is synchronised to the system bus but is reduced to a proportion of its speed.   Early systems used a 66MHz front side bus, while current Pentium systems use 100MHz or 133MHz.   Athlon-based motherboards currently run up to 200MHz.

Comparison of Bus Systems		
Bus Type	Clock Speed	Max Data Rate
ISA	8MHz	7.629MB/s
PC Card	8MHz	20MB/s
CardBus	33MHz	133MB/s
PCI	33MHz	133MB/s
AGP	66MHz	266MB/s
AGP 2x	66MHz	533MB/s
AGP 4x	66MHz	1066MB/s

Plug and play

Another potentially big benefit of the PCI system is its '*Plug and Play*' facility, known as '*PnP*'.
Plug and Play needs three key elements:
- The PC must support it (this is provided in all new computers).
- The adapter cards must support it (almost all new cards and devices have this feature).
- The operating system must support it (Windows 95/98 does; NT, OS/2 and DOS don't).

PCI systems have a PnP-specific BIOS, which extends the normal BIOS POST operations to include device configuration.   This auto-configuring of cards, makes alterations and additions to hardware a simpler process.   With all other buses, the addition or swapping of cards involves ensuring that there is no clash of memory addresses, IRQs and DMA channels between the existing and the new devices.

These problems are intended to be eliminated with PCI since the BIOS will maintain a list of all memory addresses, IRQs and DMAs in use and provide non-conflicting allocations for new cards.   Each of the new PCI plug-and-play cards has its own '*configuration space*' - usually a set of memory registers that are solely devoted to storing configuration information.   The Plug and Play BIOS chip interrogates these registers to determine the card manufacturer and type and the range of options it can handle.   The cards are all capable of working with a range of different memory addresses, IRQs, etc. The BIOS determines the best settings for the cards and sends data to be stored in each card's configuration space detailing what the specific settings for the card are.

With Windows 3.1, the basic plug and play services were supplemented by providing '*BIOS extensions*' (software to link the BIOS facilities and the extra facilities).   Windows, from version 95 onwards, has the additional services designed into the operating system.

Plug and play is fully implemented when users have the required combination of PnP BIOS conforming to the PPA BIOS 1.0a specification, PCI motherboard, PnP operating system or BIOS extensions and all add-on cards being of the PnP variety. Additionally, some software still ignores best practice and bypasses some BIOS routines. True full PnP depends upon all the required features being present although partial benefits can be gained from a lesser specification although this will still involve some manual installation. PnP still functions when the computer has some older (non PnP) cards installed, as the PnP BIOS assigns the PnP cards' configurations around those of the existing non-PnP cards.

Interface methods

All connections to the computer and its adapter cards use one of these interface methods:

PARALLEL

Data is sent with all the byte's bits being transmitted simultaneously over a set of wires. Used by most printers, disk drives, etc.

SERIAL

The data is transmitted one bit at a time over a single connector wire. This is slower than parallel transmission but is much cheaper (particularly over long distances). Keyboards, monochrome monitors, some printers, the mouse, and LAN cabling use this method.

ANALOGUE

Analogue signals have an infinite number of different states, as would be expected from real-world audio or video sources. They require special adapters to interface to the computer and examples are modems, microphones and video sources such as cameras and VCRs.

External ports

To facilitate the connection of external devices, PCs have a number of external ports at the rear of the machine. Normally, a PC will have at least a parallel port and a serial port, although some machines may have more. All machines will have a keyboard interface and an outlet for attaching a monitor. Some motherboards also have joystick ports or USB sockets.

Parallel port

Also known as the 'Centronics', 'LPT' or 'Printer' port. With the advent of improved ports, the conventional port is also now known as the SPP ('Standard Parallel Port'). By convention, the whole cable is described as a Centronics cable. Apart from its obvious use with printers, the parallel port is used as a means of connecting scanners and some video capture devices to the computer.

In parallel transmission, the data port has eight separate wires connecting the computer to the external device. There is a separate pin in the socket for each data wire, plus other pins for the control information. Five volts on a wire represents logic 1, while zero volts represents logic 0. In this way, an entire byte of data can be transmitted at a time.

Whereas the serial port has its own chip to carry out data transmission, the Standard Parallel Port requires these tasks to be carried out by the computer's CPU.

Standard mode

The Standard Mode, also known as the 'Centronics' or 'Compatibility' Mode, is purely an output system. It is used with printers and does not expect any input other than status information (e.g. out-of-paper or paper-jam information). No user data enters the computer using this mode.

Byte mode

Four-bit working is inadequate for fast data transfer and a full bi-directional parallel port was first introduced in 1987. Here, the eight data lines are capable of both reading and writing data, allowing the port to be an input as well as an output device. This significantly speeded up data transfers to a maximum of 300Kb per second. However, the system was still hampered by the CPU having to carry out all the port's handshaking and flow control activities.

EPP

In 1992, the IEEE 1284 standard was brought in. This has become known as the Enhanced Parallel Port (EPP). Like the normal bi-directional ports, the EPPs are capable of either sending or receiving data on the data pins.   The main advantage of the EPPs is that they do not require the CPU for flow control as the chips on the cards carry out these tasks.   The EPP performance is a major advance, with typical data transfer rates of 800MB per second (a 2MB/s maximum).

Enhanced Parallel Ports are also *'backward compatible'* with older, non-EPP devices.   This means that a computer with an EPP will have the following characteristics:

- Any device that is EPP compatible device will attach to an Enhanced Port and will detect that the port is of the EPP type.   Subsequent data transfers will be at the maximum rate allowed by the port.   This allows the newer printers and network adapters to operate at their best potential.
- Any device that is not EPP compatible will still attach to an Enhanced Port but the port will operate in standard mode.

If an EPP compatible device is attached to a standard Parallel Port, the device will work in standard mode.   For the user, this should be an automatic process as the device software is able to test the port type and configure itself accordingly.   The EPP was designed for use with hard drives, CD-ROMs, LAN cards, etc.

ECP

The Enhanced Capability Port was promoted by Microsoft and Hewlett Packard and is designed for interfacing to the modern range of printers and scanners.   While it is capable of operating in other modes, the ECP mode provides added features such as DMA operation and RLE (Run Length Encoding) compression of data.   Compression ratios of up to about 64:1 are supported, making it an ideal interface for the transferring of scanned bitmaps.

Windows 95/98 has built-in support for ECP ports and the IRQ and DMA can be set up in the *'Device Manager'* menu.   Naturally, the device must also be ECP capable.

Serial port

A serial transmission system is cheaper to provide, since it only requires a single channel between the PC and the external device.

In a serial system, data that arrives in parallel format from the bus is converted into a stream of bits that is sent sequentially along the single cable.   A chip called UART (Universal Asynchronous Receiver Transmitter) carries out this conversion task. The PC uses a standard known as RS232C and is implemented as COM1 and, if fitted, COM2, COM3 and COM4.

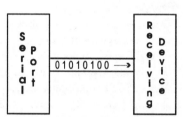
The letter 'T' being sent down a serial cable

Common devices to be found on a serial port are printers, plotters, modems, and card readers for digital cameras.   Although the above example shows data being transmitted out of the port to a device, it should be stressed that the RS232 port is essentially a bi-directional port.   This means that data can also be passed in to the port from an external device.

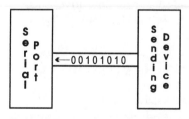
The letter 'T' being received into the serial port

A good example of an input device is a serial mouse.   Other examples are bar code readers, electronic tills and remote monitoring equipment. In the case of a modem, the port will transfer data both in and out of the PC.

PC Cards (PCMCIA) & CardBus

Announced in 1990, the PCMCIA standard (Personal Computer Memory Card International Association) appeared as a standard interface for portable computer users. All major hardware and software suppliers support the standard.   The standard aims to allow the easy connection of a range of add-ons.   PCMCIA products are now referred to as *'PC Cards'*.   The PCMCIA connection is the portable's equivalent of the ISA expansion slots on a desktop machine.   Each add-on card is about the size of a credit card and the original intention was to provide the easy connection of additional memory chips.

Memory cards

The cards, some of which are also sometimes described as *'Flash memory'*, have a 68 pin plug at one end and connect to sockets inside palmtop/notebook computers and digital cameras.   Once inserted, they act like a normal bank of memory configured as a RamDisc. When a card is withdrawn, it retains the data stored in its chips until it is required again. This also provides portability, as the card can be pulled out of one machine and inserted in another machine, just like a floppy disk. The cards mostly use static RAM as the storage medium with a small lithium battery maintaining the data contents. Flash RAM handles larger capacities but has some problems in ensuring that the programming voltages to set the memory contents are the same on all machines using the PCMCIA interface. Memory cards are available in sizes from 128kB to 64MB although they are very expensive at the high capacity sizes.

PCMCIA interface

PCMCIA is now used mainly as a hardware I/O standard, allowing the connection of a whole range of devices already associated with desktop PCs. These include disk drives, CD-ROMs, sound cards, digital cameras, video capture cards, data acquisition cards, modems, faxes, and LAN interface cards. These connect through the PCMCIA interface and ignore any ISA, MCA or EISA bus that might be on the machine. The system dynamically assigns I/O addresses and IRQs to the cards during the boot-up or when cards are inserted.

ADVANTAGES

- Speed. Intel claims that flash RAM has an access time that is 10,000 times faster than a hard disk.
- Software will appear in this credit-card format.
- Easy change of cards, while the computer is still running - known as 'hot plugging' or 'hot swapping'. The new card should be automatically detected and recognised by the interface, based on the information stored and supplied by the card. The functions of some of the pins on the interface are re-mapped according to the device detected. By default, the card is assumed to be a memory card. Since the process is automatic, there is no need to re-boot the computer each time a card is changed.

DISADVANTAGE

- The range of add-ons remains much more expensive then their desktop counterparts.

Physical versions

- Type 1 of the standard covers the use of the card as a memory storage device. This defines the physical thickness of the card as 3.3mm and size 54mm by 85mm.
- Type 2 announced in 1992, expanded the PCMCIA standard use to cover the connection between card and machine as the basis for designing a range of I/O (input/output) add-on cards for LAN adapters, SCSI controllers, modems, sound cards, video capture cards, etc. This card is 5mm thick and has a size of 48mm by 75mm. This is type most commonly fitted to portable computers and digital cameras.
- Extended versions of Version 1 and Version 2 standards are available. These have the same width and thickness as the normal version but allow for extra long cards to be used. This allows even more complex circuitry to be mounted on the cards but means that the cards will protrude from the computer's casing by up to 135mm.
- Type 3 is 10.5mm thick to allow for the inclusion of larger peripherals and small hard disk drives such as the 170MB Maxtor drive, the 270MB SyQuest drive and the Hitachi MP-EG1A 260MB digital camcorder's drive.
- Type 4 is 16mm thick to allow for the inclusion of larger capacity hard disk drives. IBM, Western Digital and Hewlett Packard have already produced hard disks to this format, the first two being 1.8" and the HP being only 1.3". Other models are available from Maxtor and Conner.
- Type 5 is 18mm thick and was announced by Toshiba for its wireless network cards.

All types plug into the same 68-pin interface socket, arranged as two rows of 34 pins. While cards can be inserted upside down, the interface ensures that this will not harm the card or the computer (although it will naturally prevent the card from working).

Data compression techniques can be used to store data on PC Cards, increasing their effective capacity.

Standards

The Personal Computer Memory Card International Association has evolved the following set of PCMCIA standards:

- PCMCIA 1.0 specified the minimum specification for early cards.
- PCMCIA 2.1 specified the interfaces used with the 16-bit cards.
- PCMCIA 3.0 is the new CardBus system and supports 32-bit working, DMA and 3.3volt working (older cards require 5 volts while newer portables work on 3.3volts). It has a 32-bit address bus and a 32-bit data bus. It supports bus mastering and runs at 33MHz, providing a throughput of 132MBps. Windows, from version 95 Release 2 onwards, has built-in CardBus card and socket services.

Universal serial bus

The Universal Serial Bus (USB) was developed by Intel and it promises to be the new general-purpose PC port. It could eventually replace serial ports, parallel ports and internal interface cards as the means of connecting slow to medium speed external devices such as keyboards, mice, modems, scanners, etc. Unlike the large 9/25 pin serial connections and the 25/36 pin parallel connections, the USB requires only four wires in a light flex cable. There is one wire for the common ground, two to identify data in each direction and a 5v power supply wire.

It has many distinct advantages:

- The bus is relatively fast with a maximum date transfer rate of 12Mbps and a lower rate of 1.5Mbps for slow devices such as keyboards and mice.
- USB is Plug and Play compliant. So, devices can be *'hot swapped'* - i.e. fitted and removed without rebooting or reconfiguring the machine. The configuration problems previously associated with adding and altering equipment is eliminated. If a new device is fitted while the computer is switched on, it is automatically configured.
- Since one entire USB system requires a single IRQ, problems of running out of machine IRQs will disappear.
- The bus provides its own power supply to any low-power devices that connect to it. There is no longer any need for each external device to have its own power unit. This should make peripherals cheaper and eliminates the tangle of power connections at the rear of machines. However, adding multiple devices may place a strain on the computer's own power supply.
- Devices were once designed to only work their own manufacturer's interface cards (e.g. scanners, some mice). USB devices do not have this restriction. This should make the new USB models of the devices cheaper and easier to connect.

USB allows a single port to connect many devices together is in daisy chain. Up to 127 devices can connect to a single USB port if hubs are used to expand the system. A hub is a star-like connector that connects a group of devices to a single connection point.

The diagram shows a PC with two USB ports. Port 2 connects directly to a hub and this has three outlets connected to USB devices. Typical USB hubs support four, five or seven port outlets.

Port 1 connects to two devices that are daisy chained to the port. One of these devices also acts as a hub and has two further devices connected to it.

Hyundai 17B+ and 15G+ monitors are available with three USB ports mounted on the base. So, a PC port may connect to a monitor with the speakers, headphones and microphones connecting directly to the monitor. Or a keyboard could be designed as a hub, with a mouse, joystick and light pen attaching to a connection at the rear of the keyboard.

Many USB devices are now available (e.g. Canon and Kodak digital cameras, Logitech mice, Genius joystick, Samsung, Philips, Sony and Iiyama monitors, Cherry keyboards).

USB is supported by all modern PCI chipsets (i.e. HX, VX, TX, LX, BX, 8) but is only supported in Windows 95 Release 2, Windows 98 and Windows 2000. All Windows 3.1 users, and many Windows 95 users cannot currently access USB facilities.

USB2

The current standard for Universal Serial Bus is USB 1.1. This specifies the data rate of up to 12Mb/s, with low speed signalling at 1.5Mb/s, on the same interface as mentioned earlier. The consortium developing USB includes companies such as Intel, Microsoft, Hewlett Packard, Lucent and Philips. It released a new standard (USB2) at the start of the year 2000. USB2 is entirely compatible with the existing cables and plugs, but runs at up to 480MHz. This frequency was chosen after calculations showed that it was as high as could be achieved on the existing cabling. The consortium foresee USB2 co-existing with the IEEE 1394 FireWire (see below).

Generally, USB2 will connect computer peripherals like printers, scanners, and so on, while FireWire connects Audio/Visual and multimedia applications like digital camcorders, digital TV equipment etc. They hope to see USB2 sockets alongside FireWire sockets on future equipment. The first USB2 devices to be announced were purely of 'industrial' interest, being chipset extensions, protocol analysers etc. It is expected that mainstream USB2 equipment will start to appear early in 2001, and because of the compatibility mentioned above, will be easily integrated with existing USB systems.

Firewire

Another high-performance serial bus is IEEE-1394, commonly known as *'Firewire'*.   This was developed from the Apple computer range and is also known as the *'Multimedia Connection'* since it allows camcorders, scanners, disk drives, DVD players, CD-ROMs and printers to share a common connecting bus.   The common interface means that it is also suitable for the home networking of PCs.
Like the USB system, it supports up to 63 devices.   However, FireWire does not require the use of hubs as each device has a common connection to all other devices - including the PC.   The standard connecting cables are 6-wire; two for the power and four used to connect to consumer audio and video products (TV sets, VCRs, amplifiers, etc).   The four bus wires are configured as two twisted pairs, crossed between ends to provide transmit and receive pairs.   FireWire devices have several sockets and a 1394 cable plugs into the sockets of the devices to be connected.   There are no cable length restrictions (as with LANS) and no need to set device ID numbers (as with SCSI). The only restriction is that the devices must not be cabled in a way that wires the system as a loop.

Sony uses a four-wire variant (known as *'I-link'*) for its products, using the IEEE-1394.1 standard.
Despite its simplicity, FireWire is an extremely fast interface that can move data at 100Mbps, 200Mbps or 400Mbps.   800Mbps and 1.2Gbps versions are being discussed.   Even the slowest speed is capable of simultaneously delivering two full-motion video channels running at the high video rate of 30fps, accompanied by CD quality stereo sound.   It multiplexes data such as compressed video and digitised audio along with device control commands on the common bus.

DVC (Digital Video Cassette) systems made by Sony already use FireWire on their camcorders.   The other major players such as JVC, Hitachi and Philips will also have FireWire systems on their D-VHS (Digital VHS) recorders.   Since DVC requires 3.5Mb per sec (i.e. 28Mbps), it cannot be handled by USB (12Mbps limit) but is well within FireWire's capabilities.   On the other hand, a 90-minute video could require almost 19GB of hard disk space.   This places this aspect of FireWire at the professional end of the video market.
FireWire devices, like USB devices, are hot swappable.
FireWire is fully supported from Windows 98 onwards and as an upgrade to Windows 95.

Relative uses
Both FireWire and USB are competing with Ultra SCSI and Fibre Channel for the high-speed bus market.   The likely uses of USB and FireWire are complementary rather than competing.
- USB remains the option for input devices (mouse/keyboard/joystick), audio (sound/music/ telephone), printers, scanners, storage devices (floppy, tape) and slow speed communications (modems, ISDN)
- FireWire offers a higher performance for top-end devices such as DVD drives, DVC cameras, D-VHS recorders and wide-band networking.

Infrared

Sending data by infrared is widespread and is the method used in most TV and video remote control handsets.   The beam of light is just below the visible part of the spectrum and data is transmitted by pulsing the light beam on and off.   It is a very useful low-power short-range system.
It is now finding its way into the computing field and is being developed by a group of manufacturers known as the Infrared Data Association (IrDA). Uses for IrDA include:
- Wireless keyboards and mice.
- Wireless printers.
- Wireless LAN adapters.
- Wireless peer-to-peer computer networks.

The initial IrDA implementation, introduced in 1994, was seen as a direct replacement for the serial port and had a data rate of 115kbps. It uses RZI (Return-to-Zero Invert) modulation. This means that a light pulse is transmitted for each logic *'zero'* in the data stream; a logic *'one'* will not produce a light pulse. By 1995, a faster 4Mbps version had been introduced.   It uses PPM (Pulse Position Modulation) where a constant stream of light pulses is transmitted.   The time between each pulse is not evenly spaced and the exact position in time for the pulse indicates one of four binary values from 00 to 11.   The transmission of these 4-bits has named the system 4PPM.

115kbps systems are common in applications such as wireless printer connection whereas the 4Mbps system is commonly implemented in portable computers.

Bluetooth

Bluetooth is an open interconnection standard that has been in preparation for a number of years but is yet to make significant impact. Bluetooth capable equipment will offer short-range digital voice and data transmission by radio signals, for both point-to-point and multicast applications. Point-to-point transmission is useful for personal applications, where cables and infra red light links are currently used. Multicast will allow the use of networking, email, World Wide Web and no doubt other yet to be developed technologies.   The use of radio links presents interesting problems.   Higher frequencies only work between antennae that can see each other, so called "line of sight", whilst lower frequencies are subject to fading and interference. The Bluetooth standard overcomes these problems and incorporates encryption technology to ensure privacy where it is needed.   At the time of writing the current Bluetooth equipment is still in the experimental stages and capable of 720kbps at a range of some 10m, or 100m with a booster.   By the year 2005, the consortium developing Bluetooth technology hopes to see 10Mbps, which is a data rate equivalent to that used in many mainstream office networks. As third generation mobile telephony drives technology development in the area, Bluetooth connections and the Wireless Application Protocol (WAP) are expected to become very popular.

Comparison of serial interface performances		
Interface	**Cabling**	**Max Data Rate**
Serial (RS232)	Twisted Pair	115kbps
Infrared (IrDA)	Optical Beam	4Mbps
USB	4-wire Cable	12Mbps
USB2	4 wire Cable	480Mbps
Firewire(IEEE 1394)	6 wire Cable	800Mbps
Bluetooth (now)	Wireless	720kbps
Bluetooth (full implementation)	Wireless	10Mbps

Computer Memory

When the user wishes to run a program (e.g. a sound editor), a copy of the program is loaded from the user's disk and placed in the computer memory. The program is then run from the computer memory.

This makes it possible for the computer to be a word processor, graphics package, Internet browser, video editor and many other functions. The computer, in fact, will run whatever program is currently in memory. If another program is loaded, that becomes the new function of the machine. This is what makes the computer so versatile - it is not tied to any one activity.

The memory inside a computer stores a variety of information.

- A computer loads a program into its main memory, from where it can be run.   A computer program is a list of instructions for the CPU, each instruction being stored as a numeric code.
- Computer programs exist to manipulate data. The data may be loaded from disk or CD, entered from the keyboard, downloaded via a modem - and a range of other input devices. The data may be in the form of video clips, audio data, etc.   Whatever its format, the data will always be held in the form of numeric values.
- The computer stores some of its own system programs (such as Windows components) and its own system information (such as the nationality of the keyboard in use, screen display information, etc.).

All of these must share the same pool of memory held inside the computer.   In addition, the machine stores much of the code it requires to handle its hardware in programs that are permanently blown on to chips.   If the computer is to avoid getting into utter confusion, it must allocate these activities to separate areas, each with its own distinct boundaries within the machine's addressable memory.

The memory chips themselves consist of a large number of cells, each cell having a fixed capacity for storing data and each has a unique location or address.

This type of memory is known as RAM (Random Access Memory) and its contents are *'volatile'*. This means that the program and the data held in the memory is lost when the machine is switched off. This is not a problem for the program as it is only a copy - the original program is still stored on disk. However, any data created is only sitting in the memory and will be lost, unless it is saved to disk before the computer is switched off. The term *'random access'* is used to distinguish it from serial access devices. With serial access devices, such as tapes, the data is read in with one item following the other. The last item takes longer to fetch than the first item. Random access means that any cell address in the entire memory area can be accessed with a uniform time overhead.

ROM

The other type of memory, known as ROM, *'Read Only Memory'*, chips are *'non-volatile'* (i.e. the program code exists even when the machine has been switched off). These chips are used in a wide range of electronic control circuits, from industrial machine tools to domestic washing machines. They are also the ideal choice for computer control. A computer's control programs require to be non-volatile. The computer's basic functions are controlled by system software and there is a potential Catch-22 situation, in that

"the computer needs a program to be loaded, so that the computer can load a program"

By placing part of the operating system software into a ROM chip, the system BIOS, the basic machine control programs are available to be run as soon as the computer is switched on. The programs in the ROM provide the machine's basic input and output functions, to allow application programs to be loaded and run. Unfortunately, if the system is to be updated, the BIOS chip has to be replaced with a new chip that contains the new program routines. This requires opening the computer case and is a job for experienced support staff or technicians. As a result ROM BIOS chips have been replaced by EEPROM, or *'Flash ROM'* which allow BIOS updates to be carried out in software.

This type of chip is used to store chunks of the system's own programs (e.g. to check for the user typing at the keyboard, or to handle disk activities. When the computer is powered up and running, some of the system programs are run directly from ROM. Most system programs are loaded into the computer memory from the hard disk when the machine is first switched on.

NOTE　　　Confusingly, ROM chips are also random access devices. The difference between ROM and
　　　　　RAM variants is not in their access methods, but in their volatility (or lack of it) and speed.

The operating system takes up some of the computer's available memory, so not all of the memory is actually available to the user. Sophisticated software packages such as Macromedia Director and Microsoft Word take up large amounts of RAM and the user may create large projects and documents using these packages that can use up the rest of the available memory. This means that the more memory in a machine the more efficient the computer runs. Each year, machines are supplied with more memory and users can usually add extra memory to an existing computer.

Memory access

The machine has to separate one program instruction from the next. This is achieved by storing the machine instructions in different memory locations. This means having each consecutive instruction stored in its next consecutive memory address. It is important to differentiate between an address and its contents. The address is a unique location in memory. The contents of this address may be part of an application program or system program, or may be data.

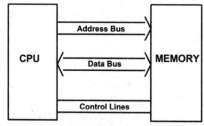

The CPU will fetch an instruction from the memory by placing the instruction's memory address on the Address Bus and a Read signal on one of the Control Lines. The memory chip places the address's contents on to the Data Bus and this is picked up by the CPU. The CPU then carries out the instruction. If the instruction involves writing a piece of data to memory, the appropriate location is placed on the Address Bus, the value to be written is placed on the Data Bus and a Write signal is placed on one of the Control Lines. Once the instruction is completed, the CPU can fetch the next instruction, often stored in the next consecutive program memory address. The simplified diagram uses a single bus for both data and program instructions. This is very common and is called the *'Von Neumann'* architecture.

Memory categories

A summary of the main memory definitions is given below; these are explained in greater detail later.

Type	Where used
DRAM (Dynamic Random Access Memory	Once was the only type used for main memory. It is used for the User Area, System Area and both Extended and Expanded Memory.
EDO	Extended Data Out. A new, faster alternative to DRAM chips. These have access times of 50ns, 60ns or 70ns.
BEDO	Burst Mode EDO memory. Sends a group of data bytes to the CPU without involving the CPU in much of the process. Faster than ordinary EDO memory.
SDRAM	Synchronous DRAM. Keeps the CPU and memory timed in step, thereby minimising the control signals between them and greatly increasing data transfer rates compared to both DRAM and EDO.
SGRAM	An even faster version of SDRAM which can operate in burst mode for both write and read operations (SDRAM can only read in burst mode).
SRAM (Static RAM)	Fast access memory normally used for caching the CPU (see below).
VRAM (Video RAM)	Latest dual-port memory technology used in newer video cards to speed up screen updates.
WRAM	Windows RAM. Developed by Samsung for video cards. It is dual-ported like VRAM but supports a block write mode for faster data rates.
Multibank DRAM (MDRAM)	20ns access time. A cheaper alternative to SRAM for caching and a faster alternative to DRAM for video cards.
Rambus (RDRAM)	2ns access time. Synchronised to the bus clock and provides data on both edges of the signal.
RIMM	The Rambus In-line Memory Module is a high-performance version of the Rambus, cable of operating at up to 1GHz, compared to the Rambus 800MHz capability.
PC100 Modules	New faster memory DIMMs are required to cope with the shorter 8ns access time demanded by 100MHz bus motherboards.
Cache RAM (Level 1)	Memory built in to a CPU and sitting between the CPU and external memory to speed up data access. Access times are from 2ns to 10ns.
Cache RAM (Level 2)	Memory normally on the motherboard between the CPU and main memory to speed up data access. L2 cache is built in to the Xeon processor module.
CMOS RAM	Small block of additional memory is used to store information about the computer (e.g. type of drives in use, amount of memory in the machine, etc.).
Environment	Part of main memory that is set aside for storing information about the current prompt, search paths and user-defined variables.
User Area	Also known as Base Memory and Conventional Memory. All DOS programs and parts of Windows applications run in this area. Extends from address 0 to 640k.
UMA (Upper Memory Area)	Also known as the System Area and the High DOS area. Extends from 640k to 1MB and is used by the ROM BIOS chip and the ROM chips that are fitted on expansion cards. The parts not used by ROMs are available to provide the window into Expanded Memory, with unused areas being called Upper Memory Blocks (see below).
UMBs (Upper Memory Blocks)	Unused areas of the UMA. Can be used to store device drivers and TSRs if the machine has been memory managed.
EMS (Expanded Memory)	The original way to create extra memory beyond the 1MB limit. A block of memory (often chips on a separate card) can have a part of its contents viewed at any one time through a 'window' in the UMA. Mostly used by games.
HMA (High Memory Area)	The first 64k block of memory above the 1MB boundary. Used to store part of DOS when the system is memory managed.
XMS(Extended Memory)	The area of memory above 1MB. Used by Windows and by a wide range of utilities such as disk caches, ram drives, print spooling, etc.
ROM BIOS	The ROM chip fitted in every PC. When the machine is switched on, it tests the system and loads DOS.
BIOS Extensions	The ROM chips that are fitted to add-on cards to control their operations (e.g. video cards or disk controller cards).

RAM types

Computers use two types of RAM. These are termed Dynamic Ram and Static RAM and they have differing constructions and characteristics.   These characteristics include, speed, complexity and cost. The speed of the chip is termed its *'Access time'* and is measured in nano-seconds (i.e. 10 to the power minus 9).   Both types use arrays of transistor switches to store the binary data.   The main difference lies in how the transistors are switched and it is this that affects the chips' characteristics.

NOTE :

> Both types use different circuitry and are therefore not interchangeable.   Static RAM
> cannot be plugged into sockets intended for Dynamic RAM and vice versa.

DRAM

Dynamic Ram, or DRAM, is commonly used for the computer's main memory.   An incoming data signal with logic level *'on'* (i.e. logic 1) to a cell is used to charge a capacitor, which holds the transistor in its switched state.   The charge in this capacitor quickly leaks away and the transistor would lose its information.   To prevent this, the capacitor has to be constantly *'refreshed'*.   The contents of the capacitor have to be read on a regular basis. If it contains a value, the capacitor is fully re-charged to maintain its *'on'* state.   When an incoming logic level wishes to store an *'off'* state (i.e. logic level 0), the capacitor is discharged. With a main memory of 640k, and 8 cells to every byte, this involves reading and writing to 5,120,000 different cells.   If the machine has a 128MB memory, then over 1,024 million cells have to be refreshed regularly.   For this reason, DRAM - despite technological improvements - is a relatively slow memory system.

120ns or 150ns would be considered as slow access times for modern DRAM, while 70ns or 80ns would be average and 60ns would be considered fast.

SRAM

Static RAM, or SRAM, does not use the capacitive method.   Each cell represents a single bit and the value is held by a more complex set of transistors that are configured as a bistable (commonly called a *'flip-flop'*).   The output of this flip-flop can be 'set' or 'reset', to store either a binary 0 or a binary 1.   In this chip, the cell's state will maintain itself, until it is either altered by a new value, or has its power removed.   There is no need to constantly refresh the cells' contents.   The result is that the static RAM chip is significantly faster than dynamic RAM.   An access time of 20ns to 45ns would be considered slow, while 15ns would be average and 10ns would be considered fast.

Static RAMs have one major drawback.   They require a more complex structure, with a greater component count for each cell.   As a result, the fastest static RAM is larger and much more expensive than dynamic RAM.   For this reason, it is not used for the main memory chips of the computer.   They are, instead, used for fast cache memory (see later section).   Most SRAM chips are of the DIL (dual in line) or SIL (single in-line) type and are of the SIMM (single in-line memory module) or SIP (single in-line package) variety.

Special very fast SRAM is used for cache memory.

Fast access memory types

Ranges of memory chips take advantage of the above techniques, and others, to improve memory performance.   These memory types currently are:

EDO RAM

> This stands for *'Extended Data Out'* memory and is used both for main memory and in video cards as a replacement for VRAM (see below). It is an extended version of page-mode working.   With normal page-access memory, the data is removed from the chip's output buffer when the Column Address line is de-activated.   With EDO, the data stays available while the chip is getting set up for the next access.   Access delays are reduced in this way and a complete memory transaction can take place in a single clock cycle instead of the normal two clock cycles.   This will not double the chip's overall speed, since it only improves sequential access times. Overall, typical speed improvements of 5% to 10% are expected. Can't be used in 386s, 486s or older Pentiums.   Available as 72-pin SIMMs or 168-pin DIMM versions (at 3.3v or 5v).

BEDO

> Burst Mode EDO memory was essentially EDO with the addition of burst mode operation plus some tweaks to the memory access cycle. Only supported by the FX chipset.

VRAM

This is a variation on DRAM chips, where normal data write operations and constant sequential reads occur at the same time. This is especially useful for video memory (see the chapter on Screen Technology).

SDRAM

Synchronous DRAM uses synchronous working as outlined earlier. For even faster working, it also uses both interleaving and burst mode techniques. This ensures speeds up to 100MHz, in burst mode, compared to EDO's 50MHz maximum speed and BEDO's 66MHz maximum. Because of its reliance on its clock speed, SDRAM performance is measured in MHz. Current chips are roughly equivalent to 10-12ns access times.

WRAM

Windows RAM was developed by Samsung especially for use in video cards. It is dual-ported like VRAM but supports a block write mode for faster data rates.

MDRAM

Multibank RAM applies the interleaving technique for main memory to second level cache memory to provide a cheaper and faster alternative to SRAM. The chip splits its memory capacity into small blocks of 256k and allows operations to two different banks in a single clock cycle.

SGRAM

The *'Synchronous Graphics Ram'* is an even faster version of SDRAM that can operate in burst mode for both write and read operations (SDRAM can only read in burst mode). This increased writing speed is very important in graphics applications. They have 10ns, 12ns and 15ns access times.

RDRAM

Dispenses with the page mode type of interface in favour of a very fast serial interface operating at 800Mbps. This *'Rambus'* interface is a fast local bus between CPUs, graphics controllers and block-oriented memory.

SIMMs

The *'Single In-line Memory Module'* is the standard for most machines and consists of a set of memory chips mounted on a small printed circuit board. There may be eight or nine chips on the board, dependent on whether parity checking is in use. The board has an edge connector similar, although smaller, to that used on add-on cards. The memory 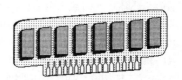 board plugs into a special set of slots on the motherboard. Since the board is clipped into place, it provides a more secure connection than earlier DIP chips. The constant heating and cooling of memory chips made them regularly expand and contract until they sometimes popped out of their holders - an effect known as *'chip creep'*. This is avoided with SIMMs, making their use more reliable. SIMMs are available in two basic types - 30-pin and 72-pin; this refers to the numbers of pads on the edge connector.

SIMM banks

Motherboards provide slots for inserting SIMMs and these groups of slots are known as *'SIMM banks'*. The motherboard manual should be consulted, as different configurations are possible.

The Pentium has a 64-bit data bus and requires two 32-bit SIMMs be fitted at a time. The two SIMMs must be of the same capacity - i.e. using two 16MB SIMMs provides 32MB of main memory. Although all Pentiums support 72-pin SIMMs, there are variations in the type of memory supported by particular motherboards. Try to avoid mixing parity and non-parity SIMMs. Fitting parity SIMMs to non-parity motherboards will probably crash the system; fitting non-parity SIMMs to a parity system will probably disable the parity checking of existing parity SIMMs. Try to avoid mixing memory speeds as adding a slower SIMM usually brings the whole bank down to its access speeds. It is usually possible to mix pairs of SIMMs- e.g. one pair of 16MB and a pair of 4MB. VX and HX chipsets allow each bank to have different memory types (e.g. FPM in one bank and EDO in another bank) and run each bank at its best speed. FX chipsets allow the mixing of EDO and FPM in the same bank, with all SIMMs being treated as FPM. Some early Pentiums used 30-pin SIMMs.

DIMMs

Standard now in many computers is the *'Dual In-line Memory Module'*. It is a 168-pin module that has electrical contacts on both side of the board. It has a greater reliability than SIMMs and is available as a non-parity 64 bit part or as a 72 bit parity device. This data width directly matches the Pentium's data bus width, allowing a single DIMM to be fitted. Newer motherboards only support DIMMs, requiring less memory banks and providing a more compact layout. DIMM boards are available with FPM, EDO or SDRAM fitted. Using DIMMs does not in itself lead to any speed improvement, as it is only a connection type. It is the use of SDRAM on DIMMs with interleaving that makes these particular DIMMs faster. DIMMs are available in both rare 5v and common 3.3v versions. The voltage of the

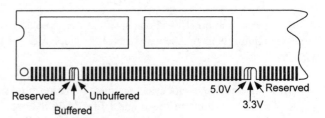

component, along with whether or not it is buffered, can be ascertained by measuring the exact position of the keyway slots on the DIMM.

Most motherboards are fussy over the use of DIMMs with SIMMs and the manual should be consulted; some or all of the SIMMs may have to be removed to allow the DIMM to function.

As the speed of DRAM and in particular SDRAM increased the manufacturers stopped referring to the speed of memory parts in nanoseconds (nS). A series of standard memory speeds was proposed by Intel and adopted by the industry for SDRAM . These are outlined in the table below.

Standard	Speed	Equivalent Period	Comments
PC 66	66 MHz	15nS	Already obsolete
PC 100	100 MHz	10nS	Current (2000)
PC 133	133 MHz	7.5nS	Current (2000)
PC 200	200 MHz	5nS	Emergent

It is expected that the emergence of Rambus & RIMMS will mean that the speed of conventional SDRAM is unlikely to go beyond the PC200 specification.

RIMMs

The *'Rambus In-line Memory Module'* is very similar to a DIMM connection. It is also a 168-pin module that has electrical contacts on both side of the board. It is specifically designed for RDRAM and DIMMs and RIMMs are not interchangeable - a RIMM will not fit in a DIMM slot and vice versa.

The first RIMMs are being supplied in newer boards (e.g. i810/820 chipset boards) to support the latest generation of processors such as Coppermine/ Williamette.

RIMMs use RAMBUS technology. This is an extremely fast but essentially serial technology, as opposed to the more usual parallel arrangement. This is because it was originally developed for to suit the setup of Nintendo games machines. The typical RIMM setup comprises say 3 RIMM sockets. Each socket must contain either a RIMM module or a so-called RIMM continuity module. This continuity module is just a short circuit to allow serial memory signals to pass through. New motherboards that have RIMM sockets fitted come with RIMM continuity modules as part of the supplied hardware kit.

Disks & Drives

A computer needs somewhere to store its programs and data when they are not in the machine's memory. The most common storage medium is the disk system. The computer's disk systems are designed for the long-term storage of programs and user data. When the power is removed from a machine, the contents are lost from memory, so the hard disks are used for their preservation. In addition, almost all PCs allow data to be stored on removable disks called *'floppies' or 'Zip discs'*. This allows data to be moved around by carrying disks from machine to machine, or sending a disk through the mail. Hard disks, on the other hand, are permanently built-in to the machine and are not normally accessible by the user. Floppy disks are not a suitable method of storing multimedia files and are not examined.

How disks work

The physical characteristics of all magnetic disks are similar. Thin, non-magnetic plates are coated on both sides with magnetic recording material. A special set of heads is used to both record data on to the disk and to read data from the disk. The method is identical to that used for recording videotapes or audio cassettes. The only real differences are that the medium is a disk instead of a long strip; and the information being transferred is digital data, instead of audio or video information. So, the disk is a direct access device, which means that the reading/writing heads can move directly to the track and sector where the desired information is stored (unlike tape, which is a serial device, where you have to search from one end of the tape to find the information).

Hard disks

Hard disks hold an incredible amount of information, anything from early 10 Megabyte models to current 73 Gbytes and over models. It is known as a *'hard disk'* because it is made from a solid sheet of aluminium. It is coated with ferric oxide or cobalt oxide and a number of such disks are stacked on top of each other and placed in an airtight casing. Each extra disk boost the drive's storage capacity and each of these disks is known as a *'platter'*. The term covers both sides of that particular disk. So, if a drive had three platters, it would contain 6 sides. Areas of the hard disk's coating are magnetised and demagnetised to store the data. Modern drives can have many platters, depending on the capacity of the drive. For example, IBM's 32.8GB model uses ten platters.

The disks are mounted on a vertical shaft and are slightly separated from each other to provide space for the movement of read/write heads. The shaft revolves, spinning the disks. Data is stored as magnetised spots in concentric circles called *'tracks'* on each surface of the disks.
Each disk surface has its own read/write head and they are linked so that they will all move in unison.

The disks spin at a constant speed. The slowest models ran at 3600 rpm (12 times faster than a floppy disk) and current models range up to 10,000rpm. Apart from their large capacities, hard disks have a much better access time than a floppy disk. A hard disk's mechanism allows it to read in data, write a file and find files much faster than a floppy disk.
Hard disk systems are composed of:
- A sealed drive unit.
- Disk controller electronics, either on a controller card or built in to the drive.
- Connecting cables between the drive and the computer motherboard.

The older models of hard disk drives were 5.25" and newer models are 3.5" in diameter. There is no relationship between the size of the disk and its capacity. The 3.5" models are generally faster and quieter than the 5.25" version. A full-height drive is about 3.25" high, while a half-height drive is about 1.63" high. Nearly all 3.5" drives are half-height models.

Tracks

Data is written to a disk magnetically in a similar way to recording on audio tape or videotape. In this case, however, the media used is not a long continuous cassette of tape but the same type of surface material in the shape of a disk. The disk is rotated to allow access to all parts of its surface. So, data is written in circles round the disk. The data is organised on the disk in concentric circles known as *'tracks'*. The tracks number from the outside of the disk to the inside, with the outermost track being called track 0. The number of tracks on a disk varies from 40 or 80 on floppy disks to about 1000 on some hard disks. The *'density'* of a disk is the number of tracks that the disk can handle.

Writing/reading data

A disk is coated on both sides with a magnetisable material, to allow it to store a magnetic pattern that will represent the computer's data. Iron-oxide coatings were universally used in older drives, with improved cobalt-oxide coatings appearing in newer models. The coating is magnetised under the influence of a coil of wire called the read/write head (the same coil that writes data is also used to read back data when required). The disk is mounted on a vertical shaft that spins it at 300 rpm in the case of floppy drives and from 4000 rpm to over 10,000rpm for hard disk drives. The read/write head can be moved to any track on the disk by an electric actuator and it floats just above the surface of the disk. This movement is organised by electronic circuitry known as the *'disk controller'*.
So, by moving the head to the desired track and waiting until the desired portion of the track rotates under the head, any part of the disk can be accessed for reading or writing. Writing involves energising the coil to create a magnetic field, which in turn creates an altering magnetic pattern on the disk surface. At a later date, when the magnetised area of the disk is passed under the head, the magnetic fields on the disk induce a current in the read coil. These pulses of current are cleaned up and used to convert back to the binary data that was originally recorded.
The dimensions of the read/write head areas are dependent on the number of tracks that are used on that disk. On a large capacity hard disk with many hundreds of tracks, the head dimensions are extremely finely engineered. The heads commence their numbering from head 0.

Sectors

A hard disk holds from 30kB to over 50kB of data on a single track. To make the most economical use of tracks, they are divided into compartments known as *'sectors'*. Sectors number from 1 upwards and each sector normally holds 512 bytes, i.e. 1/2kB, of user data. Therefore, a 36-sector track on a hard disk stores 18k of data. The number of sides and the maximum number of tracks are determined by the hardware of the disk drive and are outwith the control of the user. However, the size and number of sectors are set under software control (hence the description *'soft-sectored'*)

Clusters

In practice, sectors are mostly grouped in a unit called a *'cluster'*. The cluster is the smallest area of disk that can be used to store an independent item of data. So, if a particular disk used 4 sectors to a cluster, a batch file of only a few hundred bytes would still consume 2k of disk space. If a program or a piece of data requires more than one cluster's worth of space, it can be stored in subsequent unused clusters.

Formatting

All disks, floppy or hard, have to be formatted. This lays down data on the disk that is never seen by users; it is solely used to distinguish between one track and another and between one sector and another. The read/write head is moved to the desired track and sector before reading or writing data in that sector. So, every block of data can be uniquely addressed by the read/write head used, the track used and the sector used to store it. Before any read or write operation is started, the system ensures that it has really arrived at the correct track and sector. A mechanical or electronic glitch may position the head over the wrong sector, resulting in either reading the wrong data or overwriting data. To overcome this, the data sections laid down on a disk are preceded by a Sector ID which contains the track number, the sector number and the sector size. If the information in the sector ID matches the desired location, the read or write operation proceeds normally. In the event of an incorrect head movement, the sector ID will not match the wanted location and the head is returned to track zero for another attempt.

Preparing a hard disk with sector IDs is known as *'low level formatting'*. A complimentary *'high level formatting'* process consists of preparing the disk for use by DOS. A low level format is carried out by the disk controller card and results in a disk that has its sectors identified and organised according to the required interleave. A high level format uses some of these sectors to set up the structures needed to store details of the fields and their whereabouts. Some hard disks allow a low-level format using a special utility and a high level format is carried out by giving the DOS FORMAT command. With floppy disks, the FORMAT command carries out both low and high level formatting.

Protecting hard disks

Hard disks require most of the safety precautions already mentioned concerning floppy disks to be observed. The need to keep the disk unit away from strong magnetic fields, avoiding smoke and dust, etc. apply as much to hard disks as floppy disks. On the one hand, the hard disk is in a sealed unit and therefore has a better chance of surviving a hostile climate. On the other hand, the repercussions of disk failure are much more serious. If a floppy disk is damaged, it can be thrown in the waste bin at little financial loss. If a hard disk is damaged, it is a very costly item to replace. In addition, a damaged floppy disk should have its backup copy immediately to hand and so productivity is not affected. With a hard disk failure, a new disk has to be ordered up, fitted and have all the backup files restored before the machine is ready for use.

Apart from the above environmental problems, hard disks are particularly vulnerable to knocks and jolts. If the case of the machine should be jolted while the machine is powered up, the head may make contact with the surface of the disk and scrape off some of the coating from the tracks. If this happens, the data in these sectors is lost and considerable permanent damage can be caused to the disk surface. This is termed a *'head crash'* and it takes out sectors from the system. If the head crash happens when the head is positioned over the system areas, the disk can be rendered unusable. Since the system files cannot be relocated to any other sector, they must be found in specified tracks and sectors of the disk.

To minimise possible damage, modern drives have auto-park mechanics; that means that the read/write head is positioned out of the way of the data tracks when it is not involved in read or write operations.

Disk speed

The speed of a disk drive is based on
- The time to get to the required data (known as the *'access time'*)
- The time taken to read that data from the disk (known as the *'data transfer rate'*)

Access time

The time taken to reach the required data is based on two factors:
1. The time that the head takes to get to the wanted track (seek time) measured in milliseconds. Each track-to-track jump time may be different, since some head movements will wish to move across a larger amount of the disk than other movements. Due to the way that files are written, most track-to-track movements are not very distant. So, the average access time is calculated on the basis of 1/3rd of the tracks, instead of the expected half of the tracks. A poor seek time would be 25ms and a fast seek time would be 8ms. Drives with seek times lower than around 25ms are using voice coil actuators rather than stepper motor actuators.
2. The time taken to get to the wanted sector (latency period). This is the time spent waiting for the wanted sector to rotate to the position directly under the read/write head. On average, this is half a disk revolution. At 3600 rpm, this would be 8.33ms, at 4500 rpm this would be 6.67ms and at 10,000 rpm it would be 3ms.

The access time of modern drives range from about 16ms to under 8ms.

Data transfer rate

The rate at which a small amount of data (e.g. a single sector) is transferred is determined by the above factors and is a physical restriction that cannot be adjusted by the user. When a number of sectors require to be read, the most common case, the way that the disk is low-level formatted plays a large part in achieving the maximum data transfer rate. Low level formatting separates each sector with *'sector IDs'* that determine the sector boundaries. The maximum data transfer rate is reached when the head reads from a contiguous set of sectors, without having to move the head to another track. In such a case, the rate would be determined by the sector size, the number of sectors per track and the speed at which the data passes under the read head.

With a floppy drive, the disk rotates at 300 rpm and so the 18 sectors on a 1.44 MB floppy would be read in 0.2 secs. The transfer rate would be:

$$0.5k \times 18 / 0.2 = 45k \text{ bytes/second or } 360 \text{Kbits/sec}$$

With a hard disk rotating at 4500 rpm the track reading time is 13.33 and the data transfer rate for a drive with 63 sectors/track would be:

$$0.5k \times 63 / 0.01333 = 17.3 \text{MB/second or } 138 \text{Mbits/sec}$$

So, reading a 1MB file from a large hard disk can be over four hundred times faster than reading from a floppy disk. Of course, the access time for both drives has to be included and this slightly reduces the overall performance of the drives. Most controllers also have to decode various timing pulses before sending the data to the computer. Dependent on the type of card used, this produces various levels of delay and affects the overall data transfer rate. The above figures are maximums, in that they assume that all the data is read in one contiguous read, with no additional track-to-track movements.

Another major factor in determining data transfer rate is the efficiency of the electronics in the disk controller card. A very fast disk requires that the controller be able to transfer the data to the motherboard at the same rate.

Interfaces

The *'controller'* is the electronic circuitry used to control the operations of the drive mechanism and the head read/write activities. In most machines, this circuitry is built on to the machine's motherboard.

In early systems, manufacturers produced their own interface arrangements and this meant that users had to always use the manufacturer's specific card and drive components. One group of manufacturers produce the disk controllers while other manufacturers, like Seagate and Maxtor, produce the hard drives. Consequently, a number of standard interfaces have been arrived at, to allow the devices to communicate. The mechanics of drives mostly work in the same way but there are differences in the way that the drive communicates with the motherboard.

The most common interfaces are described next.

EIDE

The rapid development of the other parts of the computer system has left the disk subsystem as the bottleneck for many activities. 1995 saw the more widespread use of an interface, known as EIDE (Enhanced IDE), capable of handling four devices. The devices are mostly disk drives but the interface easily handles CD- ROMs and ZIP drives. It is also cheaper than the other alternative fast interface - the SCSI interface.The EIDE interface offers significant improvement in speed over the previous IDE interface. An EIDE disk drive remains compatible with the older IDE system. Such a drive can be connected to an IDE controller and will work happily, although its transfer rate will slow down to that of the normal IDE performance. It is this compatibility that gives the Enhanced IDE its name.

This originated the current range of improved non-SCSI drive systems that remain backward compatible with older computers. So, for example, a UDMA/66 drive produces a full data transfer rate of 66.6MBps when connected to a motherboard and BIOS that are both ATA/66 compatible. However, its 40-pin plug still connects to an older motherboard IDE connection (the extra 40 wires in the cable are shields for the 40 pins) - although, of course, it runs at the reduced data transfer rate.

ATA interface

ATA (AT Attachment) is the general standard for connecting disk drives and currently has four flavours:
- ATA-1 describes the original normal IDE working.
- ATA-2 is the foundation of a range of EIDE interfaces. It also incorporates ATAPI (ATA Packet Interface) which describes the ability of the interface to work with other devices beyond disk drives. If a scanner or CD-ROM is described as having an ATAPI standard, it means that it connects to the IDE controller.
- ATA-3 is the upgraded specification which introduced PIO Mode 4 and Multiple Word DMA 2. It also brought in power management - particularly useful for portable computers.
- ATA-4 is the specification which encompasses the newer Ultra DMA drives, also known as Ultra-ATA, Ultra DMA/33 and Ultra DMA/66.

ATA devices cover a wide range of transfer times, using different data transfer methods.

The most common data transfer methods are:

DMA	With the Direct Memory Access method, the circuitry on the disk controller card relieves the CPU of much of its memory read/write activities. The CPU tells the DMA controller which disk to access and what memory area to read/write and the DMA controller handles all the data transfers. This is termed *'Bus Mastering'* since the CPU controls all data transfers during this period. During this time, the CPU is freed to carry out other tasks. These tasks cannot involve memory access but can be computer calculations. There are six variants of DMA transfers: | DMA Mode	Speed	Standard
---	---	---
Single Word 0	1.04MBps	ATA
Single Word 1	2.08MBps	ATA
Single Word 2	4.17MBps	ATA
Multiple Word 0	4.7MBps	ATA
Multiple Word 1	13.3MBps	ATA-2
Multiple Word 2	16.7MBps	ATA-3	
ULTRA-DMA	Ultra DMA uses techniques such as improved timing and data pipelining to double the maximum data transfer rate achieved by the standard DMA method. It also introduces CRC (Cyclic Redundancy Checking) error testing to ensure the integrity of data moving on the bus. This is in addition to the normal sector CRC checks, relating to integrity checking when writing to the disk surface. Ultra-DMA drives will connect to existing IDE motherboards but will not provide the higher transfer rates. Motherboards using LX and TX chipsets onwards support Ultra-DMA drives. There are three variants of Ultra-DMA transfers: | DMA Mode	Speed	Standard
---	---	---
0	16MBps	ATA-4
1	24MBps	ATA-4
2 (UDMA/33)	33MBps	ATA-4
4 (UDMA/66)	66MBps	ATA-4	

SCSI

The SCSI interface standard is the Small Computer Systems Interface (pronounced *'scuzzy'*).   The SCSI drive has the controller circuitry built-in. The drive is connected via a 50-wire or 68-wire cable to an adapter card that connects to one of the computer's expansion slots.   Since the controller circuitry is on the drive, the card is described as a *'host adapter'* rather than a controller card. Its only real job is to allow SCSI devices to connect to the computer bus.   Since it is a simple device, it is able to connect up to seven or sixteen different devices.   The connecting cable can have a number of connector plugs along its length, to connect to a number of internally fitted SCSI devices.   External devices, such as DAT drives and external CD-ROMs, can connect to the bus via a D-shell connector on the SCSI adapter card.

When several devices are connected, the system is described as being *'daisy chained'*.   The total length of the chain must not exceed 19 feet (reducing to 9 feet for Wide SCSI and only 5 feet for SCSI-3), to minimise transmission errors.   Each end of the chain must also be fitted with terminating resistors. These terminate the cable and prevent signals being reflected back down the cable as noise.   The terminators may consist of resistors built in to the device and activated by DIP switches, or they may be separate terminating plugs or *'blocks'*.   Each external device has two connectors - one for connecting to the existing chain and one for either extending the chain or terminating the chain.

The intelligence built in to the host adapter is designed to relieve the machine's CPU from the tasks of organising the control of the various devices attached to it.   The machine CPU can transfer these responsibilities to the circuitry of the host adapter card so that it can carry out other activities.

The generalised nature of this interface means that it is able to connect more than just disk drives to the motherboard. A range of devices, such as CD-ROMs, tape drives, scanners, etc. can be connected to the SCSI interface with ease.   Each device must be given a different ID number. With SCSI-1 and SCSI-2, these range from 0 to 7 and the host adapter usually defaults to ID 7.   Wide SCSI-2 and SCSI-3 support up to 16 devices. The ID number is set in each device with the DIP switches or jumpers on the cards.

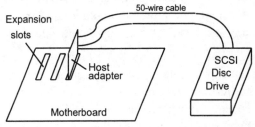

SCSI versions

A range of different SCSI standards has evolved with the following data transfer rates from the device to the adapter card.   These use different data bus widths and different electronic controls.

Bus widths are either 8-bit or 16-bit. This is the bus between the controller and the drive; the controller may well have a 32-bit interface via the PCI connector.

Fast SCSI doubles the transfer rate by using more stringent electronic parameters that allow timings to be altered and overheads reduced.   Ultra SCSI's electronics run at double the normal clock frequency and this produces transfer rates that are double that of Fast SCSI.

Since the data transfer rate between the adapter and an ISA based computer works out at around 2Mb/sec; a SCSI adapter that connects to PCI bus produces far better results.

Type	Data Rate	Data Path	Comments
SCSI-1/ SCSI-2	5MB/sec	8-bit	50-pin connector. Asynchronous
SCSI-2 Fast	10MB/sec	8-bit	50-pin connector. Synchronous
SCSI-2 Fast Wide	20MB/sec	16-bit	68-pin connector
SCSI-3 Ultra	20MB/sec	8-bit	50-pin connector. Also called Fast 20.
SCSI-3 Ultra-Wide	40MB/sec	16-bit	68-pin connector
Ultra-2	40MB/sec	8-bit	Also called Fast 40.
Ultra-2 Wide	80MB/sec	16-bit	68-pin connector
Ultra 80	80MB/sec	serial	Also called Fast 80

SCSI systems do not use the machine's BIOS, having placed a device driver in the CONFIG.SYS file to install the necessary control software.   This means that a SCSI drive can cohabit with an ST506 or an IDE system in the same machine without any conflicts.   In addition, since devices of different transfer rates can work with the same adapter, upgrading to a faster SCSI hard disk will involve no changes to the SCSI adapter.   Many CD-ROMs, scanners and Postscript printers now have SCSI-2 interfaces.

NOTES:

- The best UDMA performances compete with the middle/top SCSI performance but SCSI systems also have an edge on performance in multitasking environments. The CPU can send an instruction to a SCSI device and carry on with other tasks until the device responds. With EIDE, the CPU has to wait until the device responds before carrying out other tasks thereby slowing down throughput, particularly in situations of multiple I/O requests. This explains SCSI's popularity in multimedia systems.
- The performance of the interfaces has outstripped the speed of most current drives, which run at about a 10MB/sec sustained data transfer rate. Even the most modern and fastest drives (such as the 10,000 rpm Seagate Cheetah) can only provide a sustained transfer rate of up to 30Mb/sec.
- An ultra-wide controller card, such as the Adaptec 2940UW, has both 68-pin connectors (for ultra-wide devices) and 50-pin connectors (for SCSI-2 devices).

Disk cache

The speed of a computer's throughput is not solely determined by the raw speed of the CPU. Many applications are disk based and large database applications are especially disk-intensive in their operations. So, a large proportion of the time is spent in disk activities rather than processing activities. Windows also makes heavy use of disk operations, particularly if machine memory is small and swap files are in operation. Additionally, Windows uses many DLL (Dynamic Link Library) files. These sub-programs are usable by various applications and function like overlay files. However, this technique also increases the number of disk accesses required to run applications.

There has been continual progress in CPU development from the days of the 8088 processor. Disk development, although making rapid progress of late, has remained the main bottleneck in the system as it is still largely limited by the mechanical nature of its operations.

Disk caching has proved a highly successful method of improving disk access times. They work on the same principle as memory cache systems explained previously. Memory cache acts as a high-speed buffer between the fast CPU and slower memory. With disk caching, memory chips are used as a high-speed buffer between the fast CPU and very much slower disk devices. It is also argued that the reduced need for disk accesses results in reduced disk wear, prolonging the disk's life

Full disk caching can be implemented in two ways:

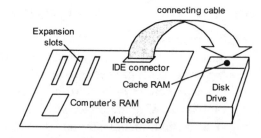

1. Using memory chips that are not part of the PC's normal memory map. The cache memory chips are now located inside the disk drive case, as shown in the diagram. Modern drives have from 512k up to 16MB of this built-in cache memory.
   In both cases, they provide extra memory that is dedicated to interfacing slow disk access with fast CPU access.
2. Using a chunk of the computer's memory, usually extended memory, under the control of the DOS or Windows 3.1 SMARTDRV utility, or Windows 95/98 VCACHE utility.

Both caching systems work in the same way. The CPU demands data at a much faster rate than the disk mechanism can fetch it. The cache memory in the disk drive - or in the computer memory - stores copies of the data that was previously read or written. It also reads ahead - it reads in data from sectors beyond that requested. If the machine wishes to read a file, there is a fair chance that the data is already stored in the cache memory. If so, then it can be transferred at a much faster rate than would be the case with reading directly from disk. If the data is found in cache, then it is described as a *'hit'*; if it has to be fetched from disk, then it is a *'miss'*. To improve the *'hit rate'*, the controller predicts the next data to be read (see notes on the principle of locality) and pre-loads this data into cache memory.

Windows caching

Windows 3.1 and DOS use SMARTDRV as the cache controlling software. Windows 95 onwards uses a new system called VCACHE. SMARTDRV has minimum and maximum values set during configuration. VCACHE is more intelligent and is able to use the available memory to best advantage. The amount of memory used depends on the demand on the systems resources and the application packages. Depending upon the amount of RAM available at any time, it allocates the amount it needs for cache at that time. If the system demands change, then VCACHE automatically reallocates the amount allocated to caching. Another benefit of VCACHE is that it caches CD-ROMs.

Fragmentation

Often, a file is stored as one contiguous block of disk space. However, files can end up occupying several non-contiguous areas of the disk when:

- An existing file is added to. Unless it is the last file in the FAT table (very unlikely), the extra data will have to be placed in the first free clusters.
- A new file is allocated the space of a smaller erased file. Again, the extra data is forced to overflow into a non-contiguous area of the hard disk.

The continual movement of the head from one area of the disk to another slows data retrieval by up to 25%. Fragmentation can be eliminated with utilities such as the DOS DEFRAG command, Windows *'Disk Defragmenter'*, or Norton's *`Speed Disk'*. These re-order the allocations to achieve contiguous space for files. The result of defragmenting is to have each file occupying consecutive disk clusters.

Using Disk Defragmenter

Windows 95/98 have built-in defragmenters, reached through Programs/ Accessories/ System Tools/ Disk Defragmenter. These offer a choice of disk to defragment, give a report on the current state of fragmentation and can show the details of the defragmenting process.

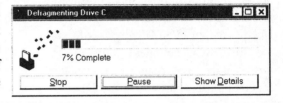

Windows 2000 disk defragmenter

The Windows 2000 version is a total rewrite, to accommodate FAT, FAT 32, FAT32X, and NTFS. Defragmentation is, as it has always been, a two-stage process. Firstly, the existing file system is analysed for fragmentation, then the fragmentation is removed by shuffling the contents of disk clusters to put fragments of the same file next to each other. In Windows 2000, this two-stage process can be controlled. Analysis can take place without defragmentation and an analysis report can be produced, detailing how much fragmentation has been discovered.

In a new departure, the report gives details of exactly which files are the most fragmented and how. This allows the user to decide whether to undertake the process of defragmentation.

Two *'spectrum'* style graphs are produced. One is from the analysis phase, which shows the state of the disk. The other is from the defragmentation phase, which initially looks just like the analysis display but which gradually changes with the defragmentation process, to show how much of the defragmentation process has been carried out.

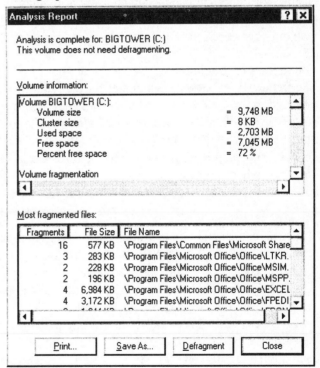

Disk problems

The user's data isalways at risk of corruption through hardware, software or power problems.

Windows provides the SCANDISK utility as diagnostic aid for detecting problems with files and folders. When run, it compares the size of each file as given in the directory entry. It then checks whether there is the correct number of clusters in the file's chain to accommodate the file.

In making these checks, a number of problems are detected along the way. These problems are rarely hardware faults. They are usually software glitches that have made rogue writes to the FAT, or users switching off the power before a program has completed its disk housekeeping, or users pressing Alt-Ctrl-Del to escape from a problem they don't understand.

Protecting files

Computers are susceptible to temperature extremes, power cuts or fluctuations and magnetic fields. This can lead to a sudden machine breakdown and the collapse of the program it is running. Worse still, it can lead to the loss or corruption of important data. In most organisations, the data held in the machine is more important than the machine itself. If a hard disk crashes, it is a simple matter of purchasing and fitting another disk. However, if scores of Megabytes, or even Gigabytes, of data are lost, then countless amounts of person-hours are required to replace this data. In many cases, the data can be reconstituted from paperwork (e.g.

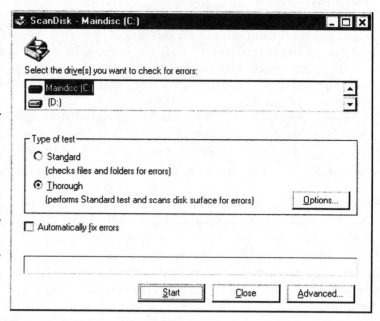

customer forms, order forms, etc.). In other cases, the data has no paperwork equivalent (e.g. telephone orders or data that was automatically gathered in real time from remote stations) and can be lost forever. Despite all efforts to achieve reliability, these losses remain a distinct possibility. The only defence is to ensure that important data is copied away at regular intervals, thus creating backup copies. In the event of machine failure and data loss, the user can reconstitute the data using the backup version. The user then only has to add the changes that have occurred to the data since the date and time of the backup.

Frequency of backups

The frequency of backups is a matter for the individual organisation and is decided by asking *"how much extra effort would be required to reconstitute lost data if backups were carried out weekly instead of daily?"* or *"is there any data that can afford to be lost at all?"*. If data changes slowly on a particular machine, there is less need to carry out frequent backups. Where the data on a machine regularly changes, the degree of change should be reflected in the frequency of backing up. There are occasions, however, when frequent backups are important even for slowly changing data. Where the data being added contains vital information, a more frequent backup ensures that this information is not lost.

Backup strategy

Organisations should conduct their backup activities in a way that minimises duplicated effort. When the disk is backed up for the first time, a full backup is carried out requiring much storage space to store the hard disk's data. With large amounts of data, tape streamer backup drives, ZIP drives or writeable CD-ROMs are used. In general, there is little need to back up application programs since they are readily available from the original installation disks or CDs. The only exception may be where an application is heavily customised at installation time and backing up would save these settings.

When the second backup is due, a great deal of time is saved if only new files and those files that have been altered are backed up to disk. This saves wasted time and disks backing up data that has not been changed since the last backup. This second, smaller, set is called an *'incremental'* backup. When the third backup is carried out, even fewer files are involved in the backup. The disks are grouped and labelled for an incremental restore, if required. Every so often, say monthly, a complete system backup would be instigated to freshen the set of backup disks, the older sets of disks being recycled.

Backup for Windows 95

The Windows 95 version is accessed through the
          Start/Programs/Accessories/System Tools/Backup
options and the main screen is as shown in the illustration. It offers an additional option to compare the files in the backup set with the files on the hard disk. Entire drives, folders or individual files are selectable.

The example show the entire C: drive being backed up, along with parts of the *'export'* folder of the F: drive. Components are selected for backup by checking the box of the desired drive, folder or file.

When *'Next Step'* is clicked, the user can choose which device to copy the backup files to.

When the *'Start Backup'* option is clicked, the user is asked to enter a name for the backup set of files. The files are saved with this name and the *'QIC'* file extension (e.g. *'SALES.QIC'*)

If a particular set of files is regularly backed up, the settings for that set of files can be saved. This saves the trouble of selecting the same set of folders and files every time the backup needs to be carried out. Once the files and the backup destination are selected, the *'SaveAs'* option is selected from the *'File'* menu. The backup set name is entered and *'Save'* is selected.

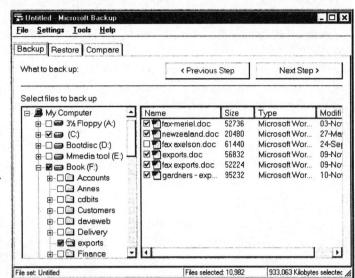

Restoring

If the files ever need to be restored, the *'Restore'* tab of the *'Backup'* utility is selected. From the left windowpane, select the drive that holds the backup file. From the files displayed in the right pane, select the desired backup set (e.g. *'SALES.QIC'*). Clicking the *'Next Step'* button provides the option to restore all or selected parts of the backup set. Clicking the *'Start Restore'* button restores the selected files to the original drives and folders from which they were backed up. Using the

> Settings/Restore/Alternate Location

options allows the user to specify different destination folders for the restore process.

Backup for Windows 98

The Windows 98 version is also accessed through the *'Start'* menu's

> Programs/Accessories/System Tools/Backup

options and the backup window is as shown. The left panel displays the computer's directory and file structure and the right panel displays the files that have been selected for backup. Entire drives, folders or individual files are selectable.

The example shows that certain files in the *'zips'* folder of the C: drive have been selected. Components are selected for backup by checking the box of the desired drive, folder or file.

Clicking the *'Options'* button provides a number of facilities, including:

TYPE

The choices of backup type are:

All selected files

This is a full backup of every file selected.

Incremental backup

Backs up those files that have been modified since the last backup. The archive bit is reset for each file that is backed up. This means that a full restoration requires the files from the initial full backup and the files from every subsequent incremental backup. This requires the storage of the set of all backups and is recommended where different files on a disk tend to be used and altered.

Differential backup

This also backs up of all files that have been modified since the previous full backup. The

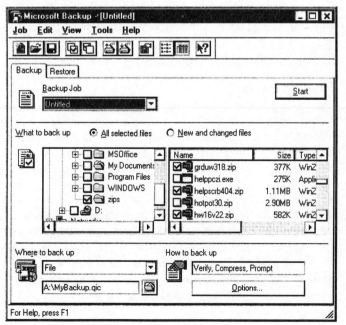

difference with this method is that backups after the initial full backup do <u>not</u> result in archive bits being reset. This option backs up all files that have been altered since the full backup, even if these files were backed up in a previous differential backup. Thus, the new differential backup supersedes all previous differential backup files. This option only requires the storage of the full backup plus the last differential backup and is recommended where the same files are regularly being modified - e.g. budget files, price lists.

ADVANCED

This automatically backs up the Windows Registry along with files. For this option to work, the user has to previously select the *'Preferences'* option from the *'Tools'* menu and check the *'Backup or Restore System Registry When Backing Up or Restoring the Windows Directory'* box.

The bottom left of the window displays a *'Where to back up'* dialog allowing the user to choose which device to copy the backup files to. The *'SaveAs'* option from the *'File'* menu allows the user to name the backup set of files. When the *'Start'* option is clicked, the files are saved with this name and the *'QIC'* file extension (e.g. *'LETTERS.QIC'*)

Restoring

If the files ever need to be restored, the *'Restore'* tab of the *'Backup'* utility is selected. The set of files to

be restored is chosen from those listed in the *'Restore from'* box. Clicking the *'Refresh'* button displays the folder and files structure of the backup set in the left panel.

Clicking any folder in the left panel results in its contents being displayed in the right panel. This way, individual files can be selected for backup, if desired. The bottom left dialog box allows the choice of backing up files to their original folders, or selecting a new drive or folder for the backup.

Clicking the *'Options'* button provides extra control such as:

ADVANCED

Restores the saved Registry settings.

GENERAL

The choices allow the restoring of all files, even over existing copies, only

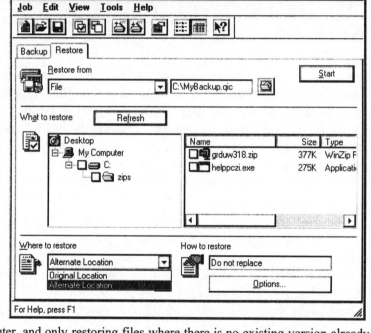

restoring over older versions on the computer, and only restoring files where there is no existing version already on the computer.

Clicking the *'Start'* button restores the selected files to the chosen destination drives and folders.

Other storage options

Floptical disks

The disk surface is still magnetised to store the data. There are extra optical servo tracks to the disk surface to ensure very accurate alignment. These extra tracks appear between magnetic tracks and are used to ensure that the read/write head positions itself exactly in the middle of the desired track. This increased accuracy allows more tracks to be place on thea 3.5" disk and this results in higher capacity disks. The most popular floptical drive is the 120MB Panasonic LS-120. It is backward compatible - i.e. it can also read standard floppy disks.

Removable cartridges

Large capacity disks using conventional magnetised surfaces are available, each with their own particular drive mechanism. This means that disks cannot be exchanged between different cartridge drives. The Iomega 'Zip' drive has a capacity of 100MB capacity, while their 'Jaz' model has a capacities of 1GB and 2GB. The Zip drive has a seek time of 29ms and the Jaz seek time is 12ms. The Zip has an inferior performance compared to IDE or SCSI hard disks, while the Jaz is almost comparable. Interface types used are the SCSI, IDE or proprietary card, with the parallel port being used for external models.

Display Technology

The term *'Computer Video'* was used for many years to describe the techniques used to transfer computer images to the monitor. These images could be mainly static (as in the case of databases or word processing) or could be animated (as in the case of games, graphic simulations, etc). Now, computer video describes the specific technique of showing real-life video footage for multimedia presentations. This chapter examines the technology of monitors and computer graphics cards and discusses the technical and operational factors to be considered when choosing - and using - such devices.

The visual output of the early mainframe computers was only plain text and numbers. Usually this output was directed to a line printer. Even when screens became more common, they were mostly used to *'monitor'* the computing process. The introduction of the personal computers brought the first moves towards a more attractive presentation. IBM machines introduced its *'IBM character set'* for screen and printer and this provided some line and box graphics. There was no need for sophisticated screens and early monitors were crude, low-definition devices.

Two main developments have led to greatly improved monitor design:

- Programs have become increasingly more graphics based (desktop publishing, graphic design, photo retouch, video editing, multimedia authoring, etc.). These programs required monitors that could display ever more detailed output.
- Users were spending much longer periods in front of the monitor, as the computer developed into more of a personal tool. This raised questions of eyestrain, fatigue and other harmful effects that had to be addressed.

The monitor, and its hardware and software drivers, are becoming increasingly complex devices. There is a wide choice of specifications, techniques, performances and prices. There is no overall *'correct'* choice; there is only an appropriate choice for a particular use. For multimedia in particular, a large screen monitor with high resolution and high colour depth is essential.

Monitor Construction

Monochrome Monitors

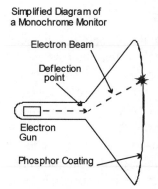

Simplified Diagram of a Monochrome Monitor

Electron Beam

Deflection point

Electron Gun

Phosphor Coating

Although no multimedia is developed on monochrome monitors, an understanding of how they work leads on to an appreciation of the further complexities of colour monitors. The construction of computer monitors is identical to that of television screens. The monitor is based around a CRT (cathode ray tube) which contains the main elements shown in the diagram, plus control and amplifier circuitry. The electron gun, or *'cathode'*, produces an electron cloud that is then drawn as an accelerated stream towards the front screen of the CRT which is held at a very high voltage. When the electrons strike the coating on the inside of the tube they cause a temporary phosphorescence of that area of the tube surface. This causes a bright spot to appear in the middle of the monitor screen.

To produce a picture from this system, the two other requirements are:

- The whole of the screen should be covered by the beam.
- The beam should be modulated, to provide a grey scale.

SCANNING

The CRT monitor is a serial device. Each individual area of the screen has to be illuminated to different degrees to provide a picture. It is not practical to have a separate gun for each spot on the screen. The one gun has to handle the whole screen surface. The process of ensuring that the electron beam systematically covers each part of the monitor screen is known as *'scanning'*.

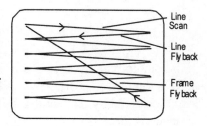

Line Scan

Line Fly back

Frame Fly back

The screen scanning process executes in the same way that a book page is read - from left to right and from top to bottom, one line at a time. The finished picture is, in effect, composed of a set of parallel lines, called a *'raster'*.

To achieve this, electronic circuitry is introduced to deflect the electron beam in both the horizontal and vertical directions.   The movement from left to right, and the accompanying rapid *'line flyback'* from right to left is carried out by the *'line scan'* circuitry.   The slower movement down the screen and the final rapid *'frame flyback'* is carried out by the *'frame scan'* circuitry.   These scans are synchronised by line and frame scan oscillators.

Commencing from the top, left corner of the screen, the beam is moved rightwards at a constant, pre-determined speed.   When it reaches the rightmost edge, the electron stream is switched off, while the deflection circuits 'fly back' the position to the left edge of the screen, ready for the next line of scan. The period when the stream is switched off is known as the *'line blanking'* period.   This process is repeated hundreds of times, until the entire screen is covered. The exact amount of lines depends on the resolution of the screen standard in use - anywhere between 200 lines and 1000 lines or over.   When the last line is traced on the screen, the electron stream is again switched off - the *'frame blanking'* period, while the beam is returned to the top left corner of the screen.

MODULATION

In a TV receiver, the intensity of the beam can be varied continuously across the scan of the line, limited only by the quality of the controlling electronics.   For computer monitors, each line is considered to have a certain amount of elements along its length.   Each element can then be illuminated or not, to produce the picture intelligence.   Each of the picture elements is known as a *'pixel'*.   The number of picture lines and the number of pixels across each line are a measure of the *'resolution'* of the screen picture.   A SVGA screen, for example, has a resolution of 800 x 600 - i.e. is has a matrix of 800 pixels across by 600 pixels down.

If a monitor were to have a modulating input signal that was TTL (transistor-transistor logic) the input voltage would switch between +5 volts and 0 volts.   The electron stream would either be completely on or completely off.   Such a monitor would not be able to provide shades of grey.   If the flow of electrons can be stepped in discrete stages, then a grey scale can be implemented.   The input here would be an analogue signal, which is capable of providing degrees of modulation of the electron beam.   In an ideal world, the modulating signal would vary in infinitely small steps, to display a huge amount of picture detail.   While the monitor can cope with fairly small changes, the memory that would be required to store such variations is currently prohibitive (see later section on memory).

FRAME REFRESH SPEEDS

The screen produced by the above process has only a short life, as the glow from the phosphoresced areas will rapidly die away.   The whole process has to be repeated regularly enough so that the persistence of vision of the human eye perceives the screen as a continuous display, with no detectable flicker. Where the picture has a dark background, any flicker is less noticeable.   Where there is a white background, the constant cycle of lighting a pixel, letting the pixel illumination dull, followed by again fully illuminating the pixel causes the most pronounced flicker.   This can be particularly noticeable with Windows, since most backgrounds are light-coloured.   Initially, 40 frames per second was considered adequate and a refresh rate of 50Hz (cycles per second) was used.   This was discovered to be too slow, as it still produced enough flicker to cause eyestrain and headaches.   40Hz is the rate at which most people can detect flicker.   Many people are capable of detecting and being bothered by flicker at up to 70Hz. At 72Hz, flicker ceases to be a factor.

Over the years, the frame refresh speeds - i.e. the vertical scanning frequency - has gradually increased. At the end of 1997, VESA recommended 85Hz as the refresh rate for 14" monitors.   VESA has set 70Hz as the lowest acceptable rate for SVGA graphics adapters, with 72Hz as the acceptable standard. With 1024 x 768, VESA has set the rate at 70Hz, although larger screen sizes often use 76Hz.   Modern monitors commonly have a top frame refresh speed exceeding 100Hz and some of the Philips models have a top rate of 160Hz.   These figures are for non-interlaced systems. The pace of improvement has been tempered by the fact that faster frame speeds increase the system bandwidth and thereby cost more to manufacture.

The frame refresh speed is also commonly known as the *'vertical scan range'*.

LINE REFRESH SPEEDS

The frame refresh speeds and screen resolutions have a direct bearing on the required speed from the line scan circuitry.   Consider the frame refresh time being kept constant and the resolution being increased. The system has to produce more horizontal lines in the same time, so the line scan time has to be shortened, to get each line drawn faster.   This results in a higher line scan frequency.   Similarly, if the resolution remains constant but the frame refresh is speeded up, there will still be more lines drawn in the same time - the line frequency has to be increased.   A VGA monitor has a line frequency of 31.5KHz. This means that 31,500 screen lines have to be traced out every second.   For a SVGA screen, 48,000 screen lines may be required to be produced each second.   Monitors have a lower line refresh rate of around 30KHz and maximum refresh rates depend upon the quality of the product.   Typical upper rates are around 100KHz for older models and up to 160KHz for top quality models.

The line refresh speed is also commonly known as the 'horizontal scan range'.

BANDWIDTH

When a monitor is driven at a high resolution with high frame refresh speeds, much data has to be placed on the screen in a very short time.   The ability of a system to achieve high throughput is measured by its 'bandwidth'.   The bandwidth is measured in MegaHertz (millions of cycles per second) and describes how quickly the electronic circuitry can change from the system voltage state to a zero voltage state; this in turn determines how many pixels can be handled per second.   A high resolution screen will have more dots along each screen line.   This will demand a greater throughput and hence a higher bandwidth. Similarly, a high frame refresh rates involves writing to the screen more often which also increases the data moved in any one time period - i.e. the bandwidth is increased.

Typical VGA colour monitors have bandwidths between 30MHz and 100MHz, dependent on price. SVGA monitors range as high as 200MHz.   Low resolution, slow refresh speeds require a lower system bandwidth than superior specifications.   The higher the system bandwidth, the more demanding is the monitor circuitry.   This partly explains why a high-performance monitor is more expensive than poorer models.

Simply lowering the frame refresh rate would lower bandwidth and reduce monitor costs. This is an unacceptable solution, since it produces severe flicker problems.   Incompatible cards and monitors may be easily connected, resulting in driving a monitor with a signal that is changing at a pace beyond its bandwidth capabilities.   This would result in the signal not responding fast enough to changes and adjacent unwanted pixels being lit, with the consequent downgrading of clarity.

INTERLACING

To provide high-resolution screens at lower cost, a system of 'interlacing' is contrived.   Here, the picture is built up in two halves.   Firstly, all the odd lines are built up.   This is immediately followed by filling in all the even lines.   If the frame speed is unchanged, then the whole picture takes twice as long to build up as a non-interlaced model.   This reduces the required bandwidth and hence cost.   The problems of a jerky picture at low refresh speeds are reduced, since each frame 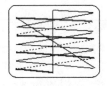 refresh manages to update the whole screen, albeit only every other line.   This used to be an acceptable compromise, although non-interlaced monitors are the best performers and are now universally sold. Non-interlaced models are also sometimes referred to as 'sequential' systems.   They draw every line, both odd and even, in a straight sequence until the whole screen is painted before returning to the top of the screen.

SYNCHRONISATION

The internal circuitry of the monitor contains oscillators to produce the necessary line and field scans. The start of these line and field scans must coincide with that required by the computer's graphics output. The cable between the computer and monitor carries the modulation information.   It also carries line and frame synchronising pulses from the computer.   These pulses are used to keep the oscillators in the monitor running at the correct timing.   Without these synchronising pulses, the screen would soon suffer from 'line tear' and 'frame roll' as the slight timing differences between the two units became aggregated.   The sync signals are usually two different TTL lines varying from 0v and 5v, one each for the line and frame pulses.

ASPECT RATIO

This is the ratio of the screen's width to the screen's height.   Monitor CRTs, like conventional TV screens, are built with a ratio of 4:3.   To maintain a uniform screen display, the screen must be driven at the same rate - i.e. there should be 4 pixels across the screen for each three pixels down the screen. If this is achieved, then all the pixels on the screen are square and graphics drawing is simplified.   This was not the case with earlier screen standards.   For example, the CGA standard produced a screen grid of 640 pixels by 200 pixels.   To fill the screen area, the 200 horizontal lines are spaced further apart than with a higher resolution.   This distorts the horizontal to vertical ratio and results in the pixels not being 'square'.   Drawing a box whose dimensions was 20 pixels by 20 pixels would not produce a box, but a rectangle.   Similarly, a circle would produce an ellipse.   These problems could be overcome - at the expense of further complexity (i.e. more calculations, more time).   Later standards do not suffer from this problem.   The SVGA standard, for example, is 800 x 600, which is exactly a 4:3 ratio.   Whilst no manufacturer produces video monitors to native widescreen video standards, such as 16:9 and 2.23:1, these standards are starting to appear in games and DVD presentations. They are generally accommodated by *"letterboxing"* the displayed image on a standard 4:3 screen. A band above and below the image is unlit.

Colour Monitors

There are many good reasons why users wish, or need, to use colour monitors:

- Art and graphic packages really require colour if they are to be used to the maximum effect. Professional packages allow for *'colour separations'*.   The various coloured components of the picture create their own separate printouts on a printer.   The masters are taken to a commercial printer, where a separate print run is made for each colour.   Each run overlays on the same sheet, to reproduce the original artwork.
- Multimedia and video almost always require colour for maximum realism and impact.
- Computer Aided Design packages make use of colour to represent different elements of the design. A street plan, for example, might show water routes in a different colour from electricity supply routes. Also, when technologists design a printed circuit board, each layer of connecting tracks are a different colour, with the silk screen layer being a different colour again.   These jobs could be accomplished with a monochrome screen, but the viewing would be much more difficult, therefore less productive.
- Sales and business presentations are greatly enhanced by colour.

The colour monitor exploits the fact that the three main colours, as detected by the eye - are red, green and blue.   In this case the light is not reflected but is directly transmitted from the CRT screen to the eye.   Any other colour of light can be obtained from mixing the three primary colours of light - red, green and blue - in the appropriate ratios.   For example, mixing red and green light produces yellow light, while mixing red, green and blue in the same proportions produces white light.   Since the monitor CRT uses three different light <u>sources</u> to produce the colours, the process is termed *'additive mixing'*. If no light sources are added to the mix, no wavelengths reach the eye and the screen is perceived as being black.

CRT Construction

The monochrome monitor screen was only concerned with *'luminance'* - i.e. how bright a particular pixel on the screen should be. Screen brightness might vary from being off (i.e. black) through to fully on (i.e. white) and shades of grey (i.e. guns partly on).   The colour monitor is concerned with luminance - but it is also concerned with the <u>colour</u> of each pixel - known as the *'chrominance'* information.   The colour output from the PC is sent out as three separate signals - one each for the red, green and blue components.   Other outputs carry the vertical and horizontal synchronisation signals.   These video outputs are produced by the graphics card of the computer. A specially constructed monitor is required to produce the colour display.

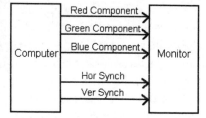

The Shadow Mask Tube

The diagram shows the most commonly used model of colour tube, which is called the *'shadow mask tube'*. The tube was originally invented by the Radio Corporation of America and first demonstrated as early as 1950. Although originally produced for colour TV tubes, the same technology is used in most current computer monitors. More modern, improved, and more expensive alternatives now exist in the *'Trinitron'* tube.

The shadow mask tube is really three tubes in one and has three electron guns, one each for the red, green and blue components of the screen. Each of these guns produces an electron beam that can be either switched off and on (as in the RGB monitors) or have its intensity varied (as in analogue monitors).

The inside of the tube is coated with many thousands of tiny dots of red, green and blue phosphor. These dots are arranged in triangles comprising a dot of each colour. It is this cluster of dots, referred to as *'triads'* or *'dot trios'*, which provides the luminance and chrominance for a single pixel. When a colour phosphor is hit by an electron beam it emits a beam of coloured light and the mixing of the various beams of colour takes place in the viewer's eyes to produce the final perceived colour for each triad.

It is the job of each gun to emit, modulate, focus and accelerate its own electron beam towards its own set of phosphor dots. However, as a single beam scans, it would illuminate dots that were part of another colour set. To prevent this, a metal sheet is placed inside the tube, between the guns and the screen, about 1cm from the screen.

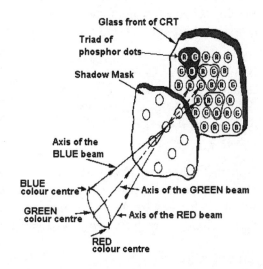

This screen is perforated with tiny holes and these are aligned so that only the 'red' beam will ever be able to illuminate the red phosphors, the 'green' beam will only ever illuminate the green phosphors and the blue phosphors are only ever illuminated by the electron beam from the 'blue' gun. There is a single hole in the mask for each triangle of dots. The rest of the screen is *'shadowed'* off from the beam by the mask - hence the name *'shadow mask tube'*. Since the holes only occupy a minority of the area of the mask, the mask absorbs the vast majority of the emitted electrons. As a result, colour tubes need much greater beam currents and a higher final anode voltage than a monochrome tube.

SIGNAL			COLOUR
R	G	B	
0	0	0	Black
0	0	1	Blue
0	1	0	Green
0	1	1	Cyan
1	0	0	Red
1	0	1	Magenta
1	1	0	Yellow
1	1	1	White

COLOURS AVAILABLE WITH RGB

To obtain a pure white screen, all the guns are driven at the same amplitude. If any of the guns suffers partial or total failure, the picture will have a *'colour cast'*. A total failure of the red gun, for example, would result in a cyan cast (the complementary colour of green and blue). A partial failure of the blue gun produces a yellowish tinge to the display. Changing character-istics of components might lead to colour casts and these are usually eliminated by altering variable controls on the printed circuit board. A monitor model may provide external controls to allow the drive of each gun to be altered.

COLOUR PURITY

Colour purity confirms that a pure red (or green or blue) video drive produces a screen that is uniformly red (or green or blue) all over the screen area. Achieving and maintaining the alignment of each beam with its corresponding set of mask holes and phosphor dots is a tricky business. This work is carried out by trained staff, who have to open up the monitor case to carry out the adjustments.

The first adjustment is CENTRE PURITY, which ensures that the beams pass through the colour centres. If centre purity is incorrectly adjusted, then a pure red picture would begin by producing red at the left side of the screen. It would then drift away to other colours. Another adjustment is EDGE PURITY, which tackles the more common problem of obtaining purity in the corners of the monitor screen. Here a red picture would produce pure red at the screen centre, with loss of purity at the extremities. These tests are carried out by using a test screen of solid red, followed by the same tests for the other guns. In practice, loss of colour purity is not normally sufficiently severe to produce other than *'hot spots'* - area where the solid colour suffers a change in tone.

NOTE: This effect can also be caused by shadow mask magnetisation (see next section).   The purity should only be adjusted if de-gaussing proves ineffective.

CONVERGENCE

Any picture on a colour monitor is a mixture of three separate pictures. Even a monochrome display on a colour monitor is only a mixture of the red, green and blue pictures, in equal quantities.   It is essential that the three pictures be correctly aligned with each other. This involves ensuring that any one graphics pixel is achieved by illuminating the phosphors in the same triad. Failures to align are normally at their worst away from the screen centre.   For example a screen filled with a white grid might display properly

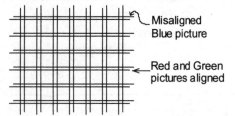

Misaligned Blue picture

Red and Green pictures aligned

at the centre while the vertical lines at the edges may be yellow (red + green) with a blue edge (known as *'colour fringing'*). Such misconvergence can vary by 0.5mm to 1.5mm across the screen and is a major cause of eyestrain.   Static Deflection is concerned with aligning the undeflected beams (i.e. converging the triad in the centre of the screen).   Dynamic Convergence is concerned with the total area covered by the beam travel.

Note that a tube may have perfect colour purity and still be badly misconverged.   Convergence tends to alter with age. At least one model has external controls for convergence - all the others have internal variables for use by trained technicians. Misconvergence is not a problem with Trinitron tubes or monochrome tubes, which only have a single gun.

DEGAUSSING

The electron beams are easily deflected by magnetic fields. The shadow mask is metal and therefore able to be magnetised. If this happens, the unwanted magnetic fields will distort the beam - causing problems with purity.   Likely sources of unwanted magnetic fields are loudspeakers and power supplies. In monitors, as in TV sets, a coil surrounds the tube.   When the monitor is first switched on, the coil is automatically energised.   A high alternating field is produced by the coil, which is gradually reduced over a period of seconds.   This removes any residual magnetic field that may have been present on the shadow mask.

In adverse conditions, such as using computers on production lines, near heavy machinery, etc., the excessive local magnetic fields may render the automatic degaussing apparatus only partially effective. In these circumstances, the technician can manually degauss the screen using a degaussing coil or wand. These are plugged in to the mains supply and gradually moved in a circular motion over the face of the shadow mask tube for about a minute.   Still maintaining this movement, the coil or wand should be slowly moved away from the face of the screen. At about 6 - 10 feet distance, the degaussing device can be switched off.   Do <u>not</u> switch the device off close to the screen, otherwise the device acts as a <u>gaussing</u> device, instead of a degaussing device!   All monitors provide degaussing at switch-on as standard. An extra refinement is to have a degaussing button that will carry out the function at any time during the running of the system.

Trinitron construction

The Sony Corporation of Japan developed the Trinitron CRT in 1968. Although the tube's construction follows similar principles to the shadow mask tube, its approach produces a significantly different performance. The screen area (the part seen by the user) of a shadow mask tube resembles part of the

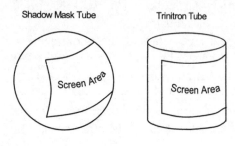

Shadow Mask Tube   Trinitron Tube

Screen Area   Screen Area

surface of a sphere. The screen is curved in both the vertical and horizontal directions. This system provides for easy focusing of the electron beams on to the phosphor inner coating. The screen area of a Trinitron tube looks like part of the rounded surface of a cylinder.

The vertical direction is flat although the horizontal direction remains curved in most models.   Sony has recently introduced the Multiscan F500 which is flat in both the horizontal and

vertical planes.   The Trinitron tube has the following advantages over the shadow mask variety:
- distortion of displayed lines is minimised
- screen corners are sharper
- suffers less glare from lighting

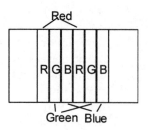

Another major departure is in the distribution of the tube's phosphor coating. The Trinitron tube moves away from the triad cluster of coloured phosphors. Instead, the phosphors are arranged in vertical strips in alternating colours. These strips stretch continuously from the top to the bottom of the screen.   A set of three colours is called a *'triplet'* instead of a triad.   Their construction sometimes covers a greater area than a triad, resulting in a poorer horizontal resolution than a shadow mask tube.   To overcome this, Hitachi has introduced an *'Enhanced Dot Pitch'* tube that is more densely coated in the horizontal direction, resulting in more horizontal triplets.

Because the screen is composed of stripes of colour, instead of independent clusters, the quality of the final picture is regarded as being superior - although some have not found it to their tastes.   The shadow mask is replaced with an aperture grill that has a vertical slot for each vertical phosphor triad.

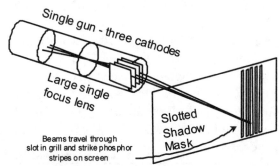

The third important difference is in the construction of the guns.   Instead of having three separate colour guns, as in the shadow mask, the Trinitron employs a single gun with three cathodes - it produces three beams.   The three beams have a common focus plane, which results in a sharper image and better focusing over the entire screen area.   The use of a single focusing lens allows a larger gun dimension than the individual guns of the shadow mask tube. This results in higher beam density.   This, together with fewer losses in the mask, results in a much brighter picture.   Trinitron quality is measured in *'slot pitch'* or *'grill pitch'* instead of dot pitch.   A 0.26mm slot pitch is about 0.28mm or 0.29mm dot pitch. The aperture grille is held in place by two fine supporting wires that run across the screen. This results in two fine horizontal lines appearing on the screen but this generally does not present problems to users. The Trinitron tube is now used in a range of Sony, Taxan, Philips and Eizo monitors.

ENERGY SAVING

The *'green'* machines currently being marketed are ones where positive steps have been taken to protect the environment by reducing the power consumption of the computer, the monitor, or both, during periods of inactivity.   A typical 14" monitor consumes between 65 Watts and 100 Watts of power, while a 17" monitor will consume around 150 Watts.

Power-saving efforts centre round:

The Energy Star Programme - this is the voluntary code of practice agreed between the American Environmental Protection Agency and manufacturers.   The code stipulates that units should be capable of entering a *'low power'* state of 30W maximum.

The DPMS System - this is the power-saving method recommended by VESA and can be used to meet the Energy Star standard.   It is known as the *'Display Power Management Signalling'* system and depends upon the monitor and the graphics card both being DPMS compatible.   Spare lines on the monitor connecting lead are used to carry the control signals from the PC to the monitor. The graphics card signals to the monitor how to control its energy-consuming components - i.e. the HOR and VER drive circuitry, the very high CRT voltages and the current to the tube's cathode. Differing power savings can be made, dependent upon the time required to bring the monitor back to full operation.   The *'Suspend'* operation lowers power consumption to about 10-20% of its normal level and allows for a fairly fast recovery time. The *'Active Off'* operation lowers power consumption to about 5% but has a slower recovery time.

TCO-92 - this is a more stringent standard from Sweden that requires a 30W maximum on standby and 8W maximum on power down.

Meanwhile, Hitachi has produced its own power saving system that is not VESA compatible.   It uses a serial port connection between the monitor and the computer. The provided Windows software allows the serial connection to power down the monitor when it is not in use. The software also provides control over the normal monitor settings.

NOTE

Although the main unit consumes less power than the monitor, steps can be taken to save energy by closing down the disk drive power or reducing the disk speed and by running the CPU at a reduced speed.   Most computers are now available with the energy-saving techniques implemented either in software or in the BIOS. The facilities range from a single power-down facility to independent power-down times for CPU slow-down, hard disk power-down, monitor power-down and system power-down; intervals can be from one or two minutes up to one or two hours.   Major manufacturers such as AMI and Phoenix incorporate these features in their new BIOS chips.   VESA introduced a standard for implementing power management via the BIOS (known as VBE/PM, the VESA BIOS Extension for Power Management) in 1994.   EIZO monitors already switch themselves off if no incoming signal is detected.

RESOLUTION

The quality of a screen picture, in terms of its detail, can be defined by its *'resolution'*.

The screen resolution is measured by the number of pixels across the screen, by the number of pixels that can be displayed in the vertical direction. The amount of colours for each resolution in the table is merely the most commonly used figures; the colours available for the higher resolutions are really only limited by financial, rather than technical considerations.

Even these high resolutions are unable to fully meet modern needs. Advertisers used to talk a lot about WYSIWYG (What You See Is What You Get). This meant that the screen would display the image in the exact size and detail as would be expected in the final printed output.   The higher resolutions of modern printers place an increasing demand on WYSIWYG DTP and graphics systems.

Mode	Resolution
VGA	640 x 480
SVGA	800 x 600
8514/A	1024 x 768
XGA	1024 x 768
EVGA/SVGA	1024 x 768
Unnamed	1280 x 1024
Unnamed	1600 x 1200

Consider that an A4 sheet is approximately 97 square inches - say 80 square inches printable area after taking borders into consideration.   A typical laser printer or inkjet printer has an output at 600 dpi (dots per inch), or 360,000 dots per square inch.   So, to display a full A4 sheet on screen - at printer resolution - would require 80 x 360,000, or a full 28,800,000 dots.   Clearly, even the highest screen resolution is incapable of fully displaying detailed DTP and CAD work.   With current printers having 1200dpi or higher capability, the problem is greatly worsened.

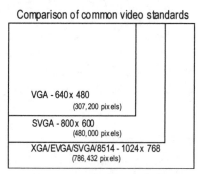

Comparison of common video standards

VGA - 640 x 480
(307,200 pixels)

SVGA - 800 x 600
(480,000 pixels)

XGA/EVGA/SVGA/8514 - 1024 x 768
(786,432 pixels)

These limitations are minimised by the *'zoom'* facility offered by many packages; this allows a close up view of a small area of the printed output.   While zooming allows the fine detail to be inspected, it is no longer at the correct physical size.   Many would argue that this is not a problem since users could not visually resolve 360,000 individual dots on a one inch square in any case.

DOT PITCH

In a shadow mask tube, the holes in the mask are set at pre-defined intervals across its surface.   The triads of colour phosphors are laid on the inner screen at a matching pitch.   The distance between the centre of one triad to the centre of the next nearest triad is known as the *'dot pitch'*.   The dot pitch, therefore, is a measure of the finest quality possible in the picture from that particular monitor.   The dot pitch is measured in fractions of a millimetre.   The lower the dot pitch value, the more closely spaced are the individual illuminated spots - hence the better picture detail.   Since adjacent triangles are offset, the dot pitch value is usually a diagonal measurement.

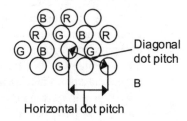

Diagonal dot pitch

B

Horizontal dot pitch

Users, however, view their monitors in terms of the screen resolution mentioned earlier.   The dot pitch requires to be converted into the maximum horizontal resolution that the particular monitor can support.

The value of the horizontal *'dots per inch'* is a more useful measure when deciding the quality of a monitor.

The horizontal dot pitch normally works out at a factor of around .866 times the manufacturers quoted diagonal dot pitch.

The table shows the <u>maximum</u> number of dots that can appear across different screen sizes.

Advertised screen size			14"	15"	17"	19"	21"
Theoretical width of screen			11.2"	12"	13.6"	15.2"	16.8"
Diagonal dot pitch	Horizontal pitch	Dots per inch	Maximum theoretical number of horizontal dots				
0.22mm	0.19mm	133	1492	1599	1812	2025	2238
0.25mm	0.22mm	117	1313	1407	1595	1782	1970
0.26mm	0.23mm	112	1263	1353	1533	1714	1894
0.28mm	0.24mm	104	1172	1256	1424	1591	1759
0.31mm	0.26mm	97	1094	1172	1329	1485	1641

The exact figures will vary by manufacturer and those in the table are working approximations. Manufacturers tend to err on the side of over-estimating the active image area of their screens.   An inspection of a range of 17" monitors reveals that the actual screen diagonal size varies from 16.34" down to as little as 15.25".   If the actual viewable area is less than the calculated area, then it follows that the actual number of viewable pixels is also likewise reduced.   This means that the above table significantly overestimates the specification of the monitors. The real world performance is less than that shown.   In the case of the 15.25" view from a 17" monitor, it means that the number of viewable pixels is less than 90% of the figure shown in the table.

As can be seen, there is a direct relationship between dot pitch, screen size and the maximum screen resolution.   A .28mm dot pitch monitor has around 1424 dots per line on a 17" screen but has only around 1172 dots per line on a 14" screen.   The 17" monitor in this case is capable of handling 1280 x 1024 mode with ease.   The 14", on the other hand, has fewer dots on the screen than the number of individual pixels required by the 1280 x 1024 picture.   The result is a marked loss of detail and the blurring of small characters.   Since even the table shows idealised figures, the 14" monitor is best run at no more 800 x 600.

Although the smallest dot pitch is more desirable, they are more costly to manufacture. .21mm and even .2mm dot pitch monitors are available but are expensive.   Typical dot pitch sizes for colour SVGA monitors are 0.26mm and 0.28mm.   VGA monitors and large-size SVGA monitors normally have up to 0.31mm dot pitch.   Some manufacturers claim that a .28mm 14" monitor is a 1024 x 768 model and this is only true if an inferior picture is acceptable, since each individual pixel cannot possibly be separately displayed.   For large-screen monitors, the dot pitch can be greater without any loss of detail. Alternatively, the dot pitch can be reduced to .28mm; in this case, more detail can be crammed on the screen (e.g. more columns of a worksheet).

Even where a screen's construction quality allows for the reproduction of high resolution, the higher resolution modes may not be able to be used.   A 14" monitor, for example, would display tiny icons and extra small text if it were driven at high resolutions.   The table shows the most likely resolutions to be used with a particular screen size.

VIDEO STANDARDS

VESA

The Video Electronics Standards Association was formed out of a group of independent vendors of graphics controllers, who were unprepared to allow IBM to continue to set the standards.   Members include Intel, Orchid, Taxan, Tseng Labs and Video 7. The slowness of IBM in developing beyond VGA and its eventual production of an IBM-bound product in XGA, led VESA to produce their own advanced 800 x 600 standard in 1989; this became known as the Super VGA Standard (see below).   IBM is now a member of VESA, as are over 200 companies internationally.   VESA has gone on to tackle the problems caused by different manufacturers having different standards, by establishing a set of mode numbers that provide a common reference point for all graphics adapters.

Resolution	Best Monitor Size
640 x 480	14"
800 x 600	15"
1024 x 768	17"
1280 x 1024	19"
1600 x1200	21"

Common Graphics Modes

Below is a brief description of the most popular graphics modes currently to be found in use.   Earlier ranges, such as MDA, Hercules, CGA and EGA, are no longer manufactured and are out of use.

VGA

Video Graphics Array.   Introduced by IBM in 1987 and remains a popular mode.   It introduced the first screen with square pixels, i.e. a 4:3 aspect ratio. It was also the first standard to dispense with TTL levels of screen drive and introduce varying levels of colour intensity. It handles a palette of 256 colours, with a resolution up to 640 x 480.   It also supported refresh rates of 60Hz or 70 Hz.   The 16-colour version quickly became the industry standard.   Now overtaken by superior resolutions.

SVGA

Super VGA. The original VESA specification was for a 16-colour 800x600 screen. This produced over 50% more dots than VGA, for the same screen area.   This allowed for example, spreadsheets to display more worksheets columns on the screen, by displaying 132 characters instead of the usual 80 characters. It was also very useful for Windows and its applications, since the user could see more icons on the screen at any one time as well as having improved resolution. This was the most common standard supplied with new models.   Later VESA standards allowed for 1024x768 and 1280x1024 resolutions in 16 colour and 256 colour versions. It covers refresh rates of 56Hz, 60Hz or 72 Hz.   Modern SVGA cards produce 16,777,216 colours.

8514/A

An IBM top-end product which does not use the memory-mapped method of other graphics cards.   It was mainly aimed at the CAD market and has its own separate processor for graphics activities. (See later notes)

EVGA

Enhanced VGA.   Introduced by VESA in 1991. A non-interlaced, 70 Hz refresh rate 8514/A standard which is only common in large-size screens.

XGA

Extended Graphics Array. Originally an interlaced standard from IBM which is more versatile than the 8514/A. The 8514/A and the XGA systems failed to replace VGA as IBM hoped.   (See later)

NOTES

- There is a certain amount of uncertainty in dealers' specifications.   Not all suppliers subscribe to the VESA coding. Often, the term SVGA simply means 'better than VGA'.   A 1024 x 768 card is sometimes called Ultra VGA.   Often, the higher resolution (1280 x 1024 and upwards) models are referred to as 'Workstation' monitors.
- This confusion also involved VESA members, since they were producing graphics products before they came together to create common standards.   As a result, a large range of goods produced by VESA members was outwith their own standards. These lower specification products are 'unofficial' VESA standards and products. Many of these units will remain in use for some time.
- Some monitors are incapable of working down to 800x600 but are still marketed as 'SVGA'.
- A monitor advert that states 'up to 32,767 colours' may only apply to a low resolution with higher resolutions only supporting 256 colours.
- The specification of a monitor should be checked, rather than relying on its title in an advertisement.

Screen Sizes

Higher resolution monitors allow more information to be simultaneously displayed on the screen - more of a worksheet, more of a database record, an entire A4 page of DTP.

ADVANTAGES

- Less time is spent on scrolling a window on the output.
- More data visible on screen at the same time means fewer errors.

DISADVANTAGES

- Putting more information on the same size of screen means that text, icons and graphics are all smaller than before - and therefore more difficulty to read.   A 14" model of SVGA monitor, for example, is only useful to those with gifted eyesight.

- To maintain the required readability requires a bigger, and therefore more expensive, monitor.   The user is forced to move from a 14" model to a 17" or even 20" model.   Unfortunately, there appears to be a geometric ratio between screen size and cost.
- Bigger screens have problems maintaining an even resolution over the entire screen area.   Some extreme areas become slightly fuzzy, due to convergence problems.   An even quality can be maintained using *'dynamic beam focusing'*, but this involves extra, costly, construction complexities.

The average monitor is a 15" or 17" model with 19" becoming popular.   20" and 21" models are becoming widespread for DTP and CAD use.   For specialist work, multimedia and other presentations, monitors are available up to 43", at staggering prices.

NOTES:

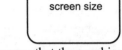
screen size

- When a manufacturer's specification refers to the screen size, it is describing the measurement between any two diagonal corners.
- This measurement usually does not describe the <u>actual</u> screen area.   It is common for the phosphor coating to only extend over a proportion of the front screen, resulting in a permanent, unlit border round the screen.
- The unused area of the screen does not result in any loss of resolution; it just means that the graphics detail is compressed into a smaller area than the screen dimension suggests.
- Although a small size monitor is capable of displaying a high-resolution screen, it is often not a practical situation, since the size of the text can be too small to be readable.   This is being countered by the introduction of *'anti-aliasing'*, a technique in the video card that adds artificial shading to lines and letters, to give an appearance of added sharpness.

Screen Drives

RGB

This is the most straight forward of the colour drive methods and is the method used for the older CGA and EGA standards.   For CGA, four connections are used to convey the picture information from the computer to the monitor (other connections are used for the signal ground and the horizontal and vertical synchronisation signals).   The RGB system operated by switching the red, green and blue guns off and on from zero volts to around one volt.   Any gun, at any time, is either fully switched on or fully switched off.   The fourth connection allows any of the eight colours to be displayed in one of two intensities (i.e. - red appears pinkish, etc.).   EGA systems provided two wires for each gun - one for on/off and one for intensity.   This resulted in 64 possible colours.   These drives were described as *'TTL'* types (<u>T</u>ransistor to <u>T</u>ransistor <u>L</u>ogic).

ANALOGUE

For accurate design work, a monitor with sharp images in a range of colours is perfectly adequate. However, for artwork, a greater degree of diversity of colours is required.   After all, a 'real' picture has many shades and hues. With RGB drive, any gun, at any time, was either fully on or fully off.   This is unable to meet more sophisticated needs.   Ideally, each of the guns should be able to have its intensity varied from fully off to fully on - and <u>every</u> intensity in between.   The permutations provided would provide the rich variety encountered in normal life.   It is argued that, for art and graphic work, a greater <u>variety</u> of colours on screen has a greater impact on the viewer than increased screen <u>resolution</u>.

If a video card runs the three colour drives at 64 different intensity levels, the possible colours produced are 64 to the power 3, which is 64x64x64 = 262,144 colours.   When the drives are 256 different levels, the result is 256x256x256= 16,777,216 different colours.

NOTE   The construction of some monitors may not allow the display of much more than about 256,000 different colours.   The computer system - its memory, its graphics hardware and its software drivers - can now handle over 16 million colours.   The drive variations to provide the 16 million colours will still be sent to the monitor but, mainly due to the characteristics of the phosphors, the full range of colours may not be reproduced.

COMPOSITE VIDEO

In this method, the output from the PC is a single signal that combines the three colour components and the synchronisation signals.   The monitor has to separate these signals, before applying them to the monitor circuitry.   Some PCs have a composite output as well as a RGB output.   This allows these models to use some TVs as monitors, which can be useful.   However, they suffer from poorer quality, as the extra signal processing circuitry introduces more noise and more signal distortion.   For these reasons, this method is only common on home games computers and is not often found as an option for PCs.   A 'VGA to TV PAL' card is available that provides a composite video output to connect a PC computer to a domestic TV but results are obviously inferior to a proper monitor.

Display Data Channel

VESA has developed a system, known as DDC, whereby the graphics card and monitor can communicate with each other using one of the unused pins on the video connector cable.   This is of special significance when used with the Plug and Play facilities of Windows 95 or Windows 98.   The monitor holds information on its specification and this 128-bit information block is continually transmitted to the graphics card.   The data block is called the *'Extended Display Identification'* - EDID.   The graphics card can then adjust to the best drive for that monitor.   For example, graphics cards will always automatically use the maximum refresh rates supported by the monitor for a particular resolution.   It will also automatically use the best screen mode available.   These changes take place without any activity on the part of the user although the user is still free to choose the setup if desired.

The current standard has two levels - DDC1 and DDC2.   DDC1 describes the basic operation and DDC2 is further split into B and AB categories.   The B specification supports a larger range of video modes DDC1 while the AB specification supports a new bus, termed the ACCESS.BUS to control the monitor/graphic card communication.   The ACCESS.BUS is a serial system that rivals USB.   Almost all new monitors are both DDC1 and DDC2 compliant.

Physical Layout

The layout of keyboard, monitor and documents in relation to the user's vision and easy physical reach is of great importance.   Prolonged periods of body inactivity, particularly in bad seating, can itself result in backache and neckache.   Add uncomfortable seats and badly laid out desks and the situation is worsened.   Bad desk layouts not only contribute to back problems - they are also a source of eye problems, as users strain to read monitors and documents in adverse conditions.   In a normal day, the human eye experiences a variety of muscle movements.   The eye normally moves rapidly from one object to another, with the vertical, horizontal and focusing changes that are entailed.   In contrast, prolonged viewing of a VDU involves prolonged muscle tension, to maintain concentration on a relatively small flickering viewing area.   VDU users complain of a range of symptoms from redness, watering and ache through to focusing difficulties, loss of clarity and double vision.

A range of measures to improve user conditions includes:
- Size of desk.   An inadequate desk surface usually results in an unmanageable clutter, loss of productivity and user stress.   Consider placing the CPU unit under the desk, or using mini-tower CPU units.   Most desks are about 70cm high, which satisfies the average user.
- Seating position. The seat should be comfortable and be of the swivel type, preferably on castors. The seat height and backrest should be adjustable.   Certain users may require footrests to maintain adequate posture.
- Size and type of monitor screen.   The screen size should be adequate for the job being carried out.   Detailed CAD or DTP work on a small screen is a sure way to cause eyestrain and lost working days.
- Position of monitor. The monitor should be moved to suit the user and not the other way round.   EU regulations require that monitors have positional adjustment (e.g. a tilt and swivel base or adjustable monitor arm).   The VDU user should be able to rotate the display from side to side as well as tilt the screen up and down.   Many users prefer to stand the monitor directly on the desk surface, rather than on top of the computer case.   Some desks have glass top so that the VDU can be situated under the glass.   This frees the desk space but may introduce extra reflections from office lighting.   A preferred position would involve the user being stationed about 30" from the monitor and looking down on it from a small angle.   Flickering first affects the edges of a user's vision.   If a user sits close to a monitor, the effects of flicker is more pronounced.
- Position of monitor controls.   These should be front-mounted for ease of access. Thumbwheel controls provide greater precision setting than tiny knobs.
- Protection of monitor controls. Ideally, the controls should be covered by a flap, to prevent accidental changes to settings.

- Regular breaks - necks suffer most when forced to maintain a fixed position for long periods; eyes suffer from maintaining a fixed focal distance.   Those employees on permanent screen operations - data entry workers, database operators, program coders, etc. - should have scheduled breaks in their working day.
- Use of document holders - these can be adjusted for the most comfortable reading position. This avoids the continual refocusing involved when reading documents that are left on the desk.

Screen Glare

The aim is to minimise the amount of office light that reflects from the screen surface of the monitor. Screen glare makes reading the screen data extremely difficult and is very tiring to user eyes.   The aim is to have as little contrast as possible between the screen and its surroundings.   Preventative measures include both lighting and environment changes and choice of monitors.

- Avoid fluorescent lighting completely.   The room lighting should be diffused.   Both the Lighting Industry Federation and the Chartered Institute of Building Service Engineers provide booklets that cover the problems of poor lighting and the lighting required for areas where VDUs are in use.
- Don't place a monitor in front of windows or other bright light sources.   If there is no alternative to having a monitor face a window, use blinds or curtains.
- The room walls and furnishings should have matt surfaces with neutral colouring.
- Use monitors with FST tubes, as they suffer less glare than conventional tubes.
- High quality monochrome VGA grey-scale monitors produce high contrast results and are preferable to a higher resolution colour monitors with fuzzy areas.
- Use monitors whose screens have anti-glare silica coatings.   The screen can also be etched to refract the light.   A smooth panel can be bonded to the surface of the screen.   This lets light out, but minimises glare by breaking up light that strikes the screen. By preventing light entering the tube, the picture contrast is improved - as in Trinitron tubes.
- Use monitors with fast refresh rates as this minimises flicker effects.   Some monitor tubes use long-persistence phosphors to minimise flicker, but they also tend to blur movement.
- Fit a non-glare filter in front of the monitor screen.   These are mostly made from glass, although some are plastic.   But beware, the Association of Optometrists believe that filters reduce glare - at the expense of making the screen more difficult to read.   Keep the screen clean, with an anti-static cleaning compound.
- Use VDU spectacles when working at screens; these are specially tinted and can include prescription lenses.
- Where the application allows user-defined screen colours, choose screen colours carefully.   There is evidence that dark lettering on a light background aids readability. It is more protective to the eyes when using handling text as there is no need for the user to constantly adapt to differing contrasts. On the other hand, dark backgrounds suffer less from the effects of flicker.

Adjustments/Controls

Many of the reported monitor problems of users are easy to resolve. Often, a monitor is simply badly adjusted, or has gone out of adjustment over time.   A few simple tweaks may be all that is required to restore normal working.   Most monitors provide the basic control over its operations in the form of adjustable knobs or thumbwheels; a few controls require a screwdriver adjustment.

Common Controls

Most quality monitors allow a fair degree of additional trimming of monitor performance, as follows:

BRIGHTNESS

This varies the density of the electron beam(s) and hence the amount of screen illumination.   In monitors with poor power regulation, an increase in brightness might lead to a shrinking of the picture size.   This may appear with manual alterations to the brightness control - or may occur when the screen content switches from a mainly black content to a mainly white content.   The monitor power supply cannot cope with the increased current demands and the voltage to the screen scanning circuitry drops.   The reduced voltage means that the scan drive is reduced and the picture occupies a smaller proportion of the screen area.   At the extremes, this cannot be cured by user adjustment and the monitor has to be sent for repair or be replaced.

CONTRAST

This control increases the amplitude of the drive to the gun(s) and hence increases the ratio between different levels of screen brightness. Too much contrast drives the light grey details into displaying as white, thereby losing detail. Too little contrast makes all colours tend to grey, producing a wishy-washy screen.

HOR/VER POSITION

These controls adjust the starting points, and hence the stopping points of both the horizontal scan and vertical scan.   The effect of these adjustments is to move the picture vertically or horizontally along the screen and this is used to centre the picture.

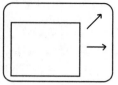

HOR/VER SIZE

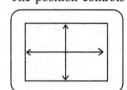

The position controls determine the commencing point of the scans. The size controls vary the <u>amplitude</u> of the beam swing in the horizontal and vertical planes and this determines the actual size of the illuminated portion of the screen.   Some monitor models can be adjusted so that the scans fill the entire screen area, eliminating the black border. This increases the effective viewing area and aids readability. However, with shadow mask tubes particularly, this may result in the loss of menu options at the corners (this is particularly a Windows problem, where icons like the minimise/maximise icon sit in the extreme top left-hand corner of the screen).

Pre-Set Controls

Monitors come with the following different approaches to their controls:
- Entirely manual - the user has to make adjustments each time the monitor is used for a different mode. This is thankfully now uncommon.
- Auto-sensing . This works entirely automatically and is the most common approach.
- User choice from either a set of in-built stored settings or from a set of user-entered settings that were digitally set and stored.   If none of these options are taken, the system works in auto-sensing mode.

Where digital controls are used, there are usually 8 or 9 settings, although there can be up to 30 predefined modes & user-defined settings. Now, the monitor circuitry automatically sizes and places images as it switches between resolutions.   A block of built-in memory is used to store size and positional information for different analogue and digital sources.

Less Common Controls

VER/HOR CONVERGENCE CONTROLS

Some monitors, such as the Iiyama Vision Master, allow the user to adjust the convergence of the three colour elements of the picture.   In most monitors these are internal controls, as best results are obtained using test equipment.   A signal which comprises three colour grids, is injected into the monitor, so that the alignment of the colours is achieved more easily.   Without a test generator, the adjustment is a more hit-and-miss affair.

PINCUSHION CONTROL

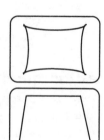

Like the control above, this control is also concerned about the picture's shape, as opposed to its size or position.   It is difficult to maintain linearity at the extremes of the picture area and the result is 'pin*cushion distortion'* as shown in an exaggerated form in the diagram.   The Compaq V70 monitor, for example, allows the user some control over the screen's beam linearity.

TRAPEZOIDAL DISTORTION

With trapezoidal distortion, the edges of the screen remain straight but the scan length at the top of the screen is progressively lengthened with each successive line scanned.   This produces a trapezoidal shape as shown in the diagram.   Again, the shape has been exaggerated for clarity. Available with the Hitachi CM6111ET.

HOR/VER LOCK

This is also called horizontal and vertical phase.   Controls are often marked as HSYNC and VSYNC. These controls vary the lock between the incoming sync signals from the computer video circuits and the monitor's internal oscillators.   The adjustment ensures that the monitor's oscillators maintain synchronisation.

CONTROL OF INDIVIDUAL GUNS BRIGHTNESS

This degree of control allows the user to set the screen colours to match printer colours, where the user has a colour printer. Used in the Mitsubishi Diamond Pro and Philips Brilliance monitors.

Flat Display Panels

In the past couple of years, CRT replacements in the form of flat LCD / TFT panels have started to appear. Other technologies include Gas Plasma displays and IBM's HPA. The technology used in these displays has been perfected in laptop computers over the years and is based on individual pixels being addressed in an array. Such displays may either use a standard video card or may be based on a specialist proprietary digital card (DVI).

The principal differences between flat panel displays and CRTs are:

- As explained earlier, the actual viewing surface of a CRT is less than its quoted screen size. With Flat displays, the entire viewing area is visible and exactly corresponds to the quoted screen size.
- CRT displays have to be constantly refreshed to avoid flicker effects, as explained earlier. Pixels on a flat panel display do not fade between refreshes, such that a frame rate of around 60Hz produces a flicker-free picture. Increasing the frame rate above about 60Hz produces no perceived improvement, while increasing the systems' bandwidth requirements.
- Because flat panels are built from a fixed matrix, they have a native resolution. Driving the display at a different resolution involves scaling (interpolation) of the incoming signal to either shrink it or expand before using it to drive the display. Scaling up may cause pixellation making the image chunky and difficult to read. Alternatively, a signal of smaller resolution can be displayed as a small image in the centre of the screen. Scaling down may result in the loss of some important detail. CRT displays always use the entire screen area for display and cannot scale down.
- Some flat panels need a proprietary adapter card that is not compatible with other displays (CRT or Flat Panel). Some use DVI interfaces, which are expensive and complex. Others are compatible with standard analogue SVGA outputs but require expensive internal electronics to digitise the signal.
- Viewing angles are smaller, and output brightness is usually less than the equivalent CRT display.
- There are only a very few manufacturing plants for large LCD "blanks" and the etched glass screens. Therefore, the only commercially available LCD screens have an absolute maximum diagonal of 19". (experimental and Gas Plasma displays excluded) .
- Because of the low manufacturing yield and scarcity, flat panels tend to be expensive.

While flat panel displays are a tantalising and interesting technology, they do not currently offer the flexibility of the CRT. However, flat panel technologies are only a few years old, whereas CRT technology is over a century old. There can be little doubt that as flat panel technology matures, they will become cheaper and more common. In the meantime, they are useful in certain areas where space, privacy or subliminal flicker are issues.

The principle of operation of each of the major types of flat panel displays is explained below:

Liquid Crystal Displays

The Liquid Crystal Display is one of the most popular alternatives to cathode ray tube monitors and is widely used in portable and notebook PCs. It employs the following principles:

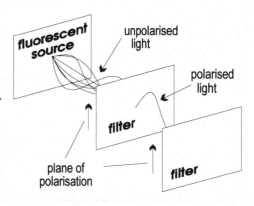

Light is only a very high frequency radiated wave. In fact, light is *'unpolarised'* - it is composed of waves in angles of every plane. In an LCD display, the source of this light is usually a fluorescent source behind the screen - such models being described as having a *'backlit'* display. This light is passed through a polarising filter. Only the waves in a single plane will pass through this filter. This single plane is known as the *'plane of polarisation'*.

This polarised light is then presented with another polarising filter. If the second filter has the same plane of polarisation as the first filter, then the light is able to pass through and be viewed by the user. If the plane of polarisation is opposed to that of the first filter, then no light wave is able to pass through.

It follows, then, that if the second filter can alter its plane of polarisation, it will control the flow of light waves to the user. If the diagram was considered as a single pixel and was repeated thousands of times over, as a matrix, then it would constitute a VDU screen.

In practice, it is not possible to continually alter the plane of polarisation of the second filters. Instead, a cell is composed of a piece of *'nematic'* liquid crystal between the filters. The planes of polarisation of the two filters differ by 90 degrees. Now, the light from the fluorescent source still passes through the first filter in a single plane only. This time, the effect of passing through the liquid crystal is to twist the wave 90 degrees, along the crystal's plane. When the wave reaches the second filter, it is at the correct angle to pass through since they are both aligned.   So, the normal state is to pass light.   That is why most LCDs have a lit screen as default.

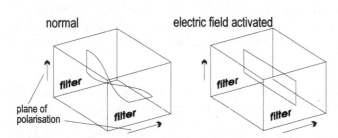

The second diagram shows the effect of applying an electric field to the cell.   The molecules of the liquid crystal will line up, its plane will become straight and there will be no 90-degree twist to the light wave as it passes through.   The light's plane is now different from the second filter and no light will pass through the filter.   So, if each pixel area has its electric field switched on or off, pixels are lit or unlit - i.e. a functioning VDU has been created.   If the two filters are given the same planes of polarisation, then pixels will remain unlit until the electric field is energised.

LCD construction

In practice, the display is not constructed pixel by pixel.   Instead, the screen is manufactured as a single entity, with a layer of liquid crystal sandwiched between layers of glass.   This, in turn, is sandwiched between polarising sheets.   A grid of wires is used to access any particular area of the screen surface.   A voltage is applied to the appropriate vertical and horizontal co-ordinates, to activate that particular pixel. This is called *'direct multiplexing'* and although relatively easy to manufacture, it is difficult to control drive of the cells.

The main problems are:

- The voltage on the control wires cannot be too high, otherwise there is a likelihood of turning on cells adjacent to the wanted cell.
- The small allowable voltage swings do not provide enough control to achieve satisfactory grey scales and good contrast.
- The scanning arrangements are inadequate.   The data on every pixel in a line can be stored and applied to the vertical wires at the same time.   However, It is only possible to address a single row at any one time.   So, for example, a VGA screen of 480 lines would result in each line only having its pixels set every 1/480th of the time.   The greater the vertical resolution the less time is available for holding a particular cell in the 'dark' state.   During the rest of the time, the cell is reverting to its 'light' state, with a consequent deterioration of picture contrast.

TFT displays

To solve these problems, an *'active matrix'* is employed.   This uses TFT (thin film transistors) in a matrix, with a single transistor located at the junction of each vertical and horizontal control wire.   The voltage at each cell can now be increased, since smaller level signals can be placed on the control wires that are amplified by the transistor.   Since this higher voltage now only occurs right at the cell, there is little chance of activating adjacent cells. The result is a sharper picture.   Additionally, the higher voltage swings result in faster cell changes and therefore greater contrast.   Finally, the higher voltage range available allows much greater control over grey scales.   TFT LCDs also improve on scanning difficulties.   The short time available for each cell remains unavoidable.   However, the construction of the TFT screen results in a capacitance effect on each cell.   This maintains the desired charge while the cell is not being addressed and maintains the desired 'dark' state longer, improving screen contrast.

Colour LCDs

LCDs are also available in colour versions.   These are expensive, since they have even greater production quality control problems than monochrome versions.

They are available in both passive-matrix and active-matrix versions.

ADVANTAGES OF LCDs

- No electron beams, thereby eliminating problems with linearity, misconvergence, pincushion distortion, and sizing/positioning.
- Low power consumption and low voltages.
- Light weight - ideal for portables.
- No radiation or flicker problems, unlike CRTs.
- Flat displays - hang on wall / easy to locate in work area.

DISADVANTAGES

- Restricted viewing angle.
- Poor contrast.   Supertwist displays give more contrast but introduce a certain tinge. This is correctable with special film coatings and extra construction complexity. It is called *'triple supertwist'*. It is more expensive to manufacture and is used in the best LCD displays.
- Slow speed.   When the liquid crystal structure has been pulled into a straight configuration, under the influence of the electric field, it takes a relatively long time to restore to its former state. This explains why LCD screens often 'smear' when scrolling or attempting other fast screen updating.
- Costly to manufacture, due to difficulties of quality control.

PASSIVE MATRIX

The cheaper of the versions, this screen is effectively a sandwich of three LCD screens, each screen emitting red, green or blue.   All modern systems increase efficiency by using *'dual scan'* displays. These split the screen in two vertically and each half is simultaneously scanned and lit.   So, a single screen is painted in half the time - i.e. the refresh rate is doubled and flicker is halved.

ACTIVE MATRIX

Each colour triad is comprises the necessary red, green and blue LCD elements and each is activated by its own switching transistor.   In this way, the TFT mechanisms described above take place on light waves of pre-determined colour.   Since each element is individually switched, the *'ghousting'* associated with older screens is eliminated.   In addition, TFT elements are less sensitive to heat and brighter backlights can be used.

Unfortunately, these screen are expensive to produce, since even a VGA monitor would require almost a million transistors to be assembled on the one screen.   A single non-working transistor means that a pixel has lost one of its colour elements. Too many defects means that the screen has to be scrapped. About a third of all units produced are unable to meet this very demanding quality control.

PLASMA DISPLAYS

Gas plasma displays are produced by filling the space between two glass plates with neon /xenon gas and then exciting it with a suitable voltage, usually greater than 80V. The exciting electrode is etched onto the glass. The original gas plasma displays were orange and black and had high power consumption. Recently however various companies have resurrected the technology, extended it to full colour and are using it for display panels, High Definition Television (HDTV) displays and desktop monitors. Among the prime movers of this technology in Europe are Philips BV whose FlatTV is plasma based.

DEVELOPMENTS

A number of alternative technologies have been promised, only to fail to live up to their early promise. Current developments include:

- Improved resolutions from plasma displays.
- Reflective LCDs. There is no backlighting source. Instead, a mirror is placed behind the display and this allows room light to be reflected back or blocked, dependent on the controlling electric field.
- Field Emissive Devices. FEDs promise to be as slim as LCD panels but are cheaper to produce and impose no restrictions in maximum screen size.

Graphics Cards

The rapid development of computer applications such as video, animations, walkthroughs and photorealistic graphics has stretched both the demands on the computer monitor and the video card technology.   Graphics cards have undergone significant improvements from the early versions that only supported text and crude chunky graphics.

The electronics to drive the monitor is mounted on a separate graphics card that slots into the expansion bus on the computer's motherboard. The monitor cable plugs into a socket on the video card.

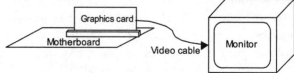

Graphic Card Performance

There are a number of factors to be considered when purchasing a graphics card. Such a purchase might be as part of an entire system. It is also possible to buy a matching graphics card and monitor, to upgrade the graphics facilities of an existing system.

The main considerations are:

- RAM size/Resolution/Colour Depth
- RAM type
- Internal bus size
- Chip Set used
- Extra facilities (e.g. video handling, 3D, TV)
- Bandwidth
- External bus type
- Refresh rates
- RAMDAC used

GRAPHICS RAM SIZE

SCREEN MEMORY

The number of colours that a monitor can produce is theoretically endless. Tiny voltage changes to any of the monitor's guns will alter that colour and hence the mix perceived by the viewer. The limitation is in the ability of the computer graphics card to store all the possible colour permutations (in the form of a large range of voltage levels) for each screen pixel. All graphics standards use a 'memory mapped' method of handling screen output. An area of computer memory is reserved for holding the individual pixels that comprise the screen picture. This screen memory is <u>additional</u> to the computer's 640k user area. In all but the lowest resolutions, extra memory for storing the screen's composition is located on the graphics controller card. The data in this memory area is used to regularly update the picture. The computer's CPU (or co-processor chip on 8514/XGA cards) has the task of constantly updating the screen memory area. The electronics on the graphics card reads this information and uses it to control the drive to the monitor. For a simple, monochrome system the storage may only require a single bit per pixel. If the bit is 0, the pixel is left unlit; if the bit is 1 then the pixel is illuminated. In colour systems, extra pixels are required, to store the colour and hue of the pixel.

In text modes, the bit pattern for each displayable character (i.e. the alphanumeric set, punctuation and the IBM extended character set) is pre-stored and is copied into the screen memory area. It is a much more complex task in graphics mode. To place a straight line on the screen, the CPU must calculate the position of every pixel in that line and write this information to the appropriate screen memory locations. For an arc, there is the added time required to calculate the curve's co-ordinates. The main memory of the PC was not designed for the current high-resolution screens. The amount of memory put aside to hold the screen information is totally inadequate by today's standards. Out of the 1MB memory area, a maximum of 128KB is laid aside for graphics memory. This would directly address a 640 x200 screen of 256 colours. To go beyond this specification, the machine has the additional graphics information stored in <u>extra</u> memory with special software routines to access this extra hardware. Consequently, graphics cards have their own memory chips to store graphics information. The RAM size required is determined by the maximum screen resolution and the maximum colour depth (i.e. how many colours to be displayed).

The formula to calculate the amount of memory required for a particular screen standard is:

$$\text{HORIZONTAL RESOLUTION} \times \text{VERTICAL RESOLUTION} \times \text{COLOUR BITS} / 8$$

The number of bits for each pixel depends on the number of colours that the pixel has to display. For monochrome, only one bit per pixel is required (pixel is either lit or unlit). For 4 colours, 2 bits per pixel are required, providing 2 to the power of 2 combinations. For 16 colours, 4 bits are required, providing 2 to the power 4 combinations. For 256 colours, 8 bits are required (i.e. 2 to the power 8 combinations). A 16-bit system can provide 65,536 different colours for each pixel (called 'high colour'), while a 24-bit system provides 16.7million colours (often termed 'true colour'). Some cards offer 30-bit depth producing 1,073,741,824 colours! Other cards use 32-bits to handle true colour at faster rates.

The equation given produces a memory requirement specified in bytes. Dividing the result by 1024 gives a requirement measured in Kilobytes (KB). There are 1024 bytes to a kilobyte. Dividing by a further 1024 produces a measurement in MB (MegaBytes).

EXAMPLES
A 16-colour VGA screen would require
>640 x 480 x 4 / 8 = 150 Kbytes

A 16-colour SVGA screen would require
>800 x 600 x 4/8 = 234Kbytes (i.e. at least a 256k card)

A 256-colour VGA screen would require
>640 x 480 x 8 / 8 = 300 Kbytes (i.e. at least a 512k card)

A 256- colour SVGA screen would require
>800 x 600 x 8/ 8 = 469 Kbytes (i.e. at least a 512k card)

A 256-colour 1024 x 768 screen would require
>1024 x 768 x 8 / 8 = 768 KB (i.e. a full 1MB card)

A 24-bit, true colour 1024 x 768 screen with 16.7 million colours would require
>1024 x 768 x 24 / 8 = 2.25MB (ie a 4MB card)

Finally, a top of the range system with true colour at 1600 x 1200 would require
>1600 x 1200 x 24 / 8 = 5.49MB (ie an 8MB card)

SVGA cards used to be supplied in 256KB and 512KB versions; they now come from 1MB to 16MB.

Bits per pixel	Colour Depth
4	16
8	256
16	65,536
24	16.7m

NOTES:
- If a board's design allows for future expansion, then extra memory can be fitted to the card to allow it to cope with greater resolutions.   Many cards allow up to 8MB of memory to be fitted while some cards allow up to 40MB to be fitted.
- Where the fitted RAM size is vastly greater than is currently required for a particular mode, the memory can be divided into *'pages'* - each page containing the data for a full graphics screen.   This allows rapid switching between screens, since the second screen can have its pixel pattern built up in memory, while the first screen is being displayed.   This is the basis of on-screen animation.
- Most cards can display a number of colours from a larger possible palette (e.g. 16 colours from 64 or 256 from 32,767).   A piece of software may wish to use more colours than the card is capable of displaying at any one time.   The 'extra' colours are displayed by *'dithering'* using the existing colours, producing a rather coarse hatching effect.   This allows cards with poorer specifications to still run the application. This may be acceptable in some applications but photo-realistic graphics, video clips and multimedia applications would demand a wider displayable colour range.

BANDWIDTH
The term *'bandwidth'* describes both memory and graphics needs and there are important differences. The general description of monitor bandwidth was given earlier.   With colour monitors, the graphics data is sent in parallel to three separate guns and the amount of colours being used is not relevant to the bandwidth calculation.   The restriction on any one channel's capabilities is measured by the resolution required and the refresh rate.   The formula to calculate the required graphics bandwidth is:
>HORIZONTAL RESOLUTION x VERTICAL RESOLUTION x REFRESH RATE / 8

So, a 640 x 480 display with a 70Hz refresh rate requires to cope with
>640 X 480 X 70 / 8 = 2.56MB /sec, i.e. over 20 million different pixel values per sec

while a 1600 x 1200 display with a 75Hz refresh rate requires to handle
>1600 X 1200 x 75 / 8 = 17.17MB /sec, i.e. over 135 million different pixel values per sec

Memory bandwidth is much greater than graphics bandwidth for the same screen because it has to store and transfer the colour details for each pixel.

So, a 640 x 480 display, with a refresh rate of 70Hz and 256 colours requires to transfer
>640 X 480 X 70 X 8 / 8 = 20.2MB /sec, i.e. over 160 million different pixel values per sec

while a 1600 x 1200 display with a 75Hz refresh rate and 16m colours requires to transfer
>1600 X 1200 x 75 X 24 / 8 = 137.36MB /sec, i.e. over 432 million different pixel values per sec

Where a card is intended for multimedia and video use, the bandwidth capability of both the monitor and the graphics card become crucial factors.

RAM TYPE
At one stage all graphics cards used standard DRAM (Dynamic RAM) chips as a frame buffer to store the graphics information about that frame.   In this *'Single Port'* system, the CPU has to write to the DRAM using the same data and address buses as that used to get data from the DRAM to the VDU driver circuitry.   Since these transfers in and out cannot be simultaneous, a bottleneck existed.   The logic value on a single pin on the DRAM chips controlled whether the memory was in read or write mode.

When toggled to write mode, the CPU updated the screen information. When in read mode, the chips on the graphics card read the information and processed it to drive the monitor.

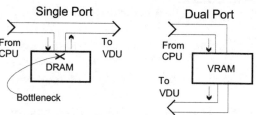

The last few years saw the introduction of cards using VRAM (video RAM) which overcame the speed limitation imposed by conventional DRAM. With the VRAM *'Dual Port'* system, separate address and data buses were provided for the in an out transfers. Hence, this memory block was capable of being both read and written to simultaneously, with the system preventing attempts to read and write to the exact same memory areas at the same time. Writing was carried out with random access - i.e. only those pixels that need updating were accessed and altered. Since the stream of data to the monitor was in serial format, the read process was always a complete sequential read of the frame buffer. This greatly speeded up the screen handling process and the extra cost was justified where fast screen updates were required. VRAM systems required their own dedicated controller.

A development on VRAM is Windows RAM (WRAM). This is a modified dual-ported system and is faster then VRAM and up to 50% faster than DRAM. It carries out some of the tasks (e.g. blitting) normally placed on the graphics controller, thereby speeding up processing. It is manufactured by Samsung and can be found in high performance systems such as the Matrox Millenium II card.

Other memory options are EDO RAM as found in the Orchid Righteous 3DII card and SGRam as found in the ATI All-In-Wonder Pro and STB Velocity 128 cards. See the chapter on Memory for details of these memory chips.

DDR SDRAM

A recent innovation is Dual Data Rate or DDR SDRAM. Conventional SDRAM is synchronised with the bus, by carrying out transfers on the rising or falling edge of the bus's clock signal. DDR SDRAM is triggered by both the rising and falling edge of the bus clock. Thus it should optimally perform at twice the speed of conventional SDRAM. In practice, however, such extreme gains are never seen.

External bus type

A very wide range of graphics cards is available, using every type of data bus system. Since the fastest data buses have the greatest throughput, the graphics card should be matched to the fastest bus. So, a PCI computer is able to accommodate a graphics card on either its ISA expansion slot or its PCI expansion slot. Although an older ISA or PCI graphics card will work in the system, an card would provide a better performance. Similarly, a VESA card should be used in a VESA local bus machine, although an ISA can be used. PCI cards and VL cards are not interchangeable.

Old ISA graphics cards are supplied in 8-bit and 16-bit data bus models. Since the width of the data bus affects the speed of data transfer into the graphics card, users should avoid older 8-bit models. Users with 8-bit XT machines have no choice, since their machines only have 8-bit buses. Most standard ISA PCs use of the 16-bit model. The 32-bit models are for use with the *'local bus'* architectures, where greater data transfer rates between the system and the graphics card can be gained. Graphics cards for PCI Pentium boards use a full external 64-bit data bus. AGP cards use their own high-speed 32-bit bus.

Internal bus size

The bus size in a graphics card's specification refers to its internal architecture, the path between the card's RAM and the card's graphics processor. The most critical element in graphics performance is not data flow into the graphics board; it is how the board organises and manages the frame buffer held in memory inside the graphics board. Having a 64-bit internal bus greatly speeds up throughput, enhancing the card's performance. It also allows some cards to use cheaper DRAM instead of VRAM. The card's memory is organised into interleaved banks, allowing one bank to be written to while the other is being read. This increases throughput without the expense of VRAM. However, with increasing resolution, even 64-bit buses can act as a bottleneck and 128-bit versions are now common. The Imagine 128 Series 2 chip from Number Nine has a 128-bit bus with memory interleaved as three banks and a data rate of 500Mbps. Other examples of 128-bit bus cards are the STB Velocity 128ZX and the Matrox Millenium G200.

Refresh rates

Greater resolution and greater colour depth (i.e. bits per pixel) both mean that the card has to move more data for a single frame. This means that cards commonly have lower refresh rates at higher resolutions and at greater colour depths. For example, even a high performance card like the ATI Xpert@Work PCI card has a wide variation in refresh rates. It handles 200Hz at VGA and SVGA, 150Hz at 1024x768, 100Hz at 1280x1024 but is only 85Hz at 1600x1200.   An older S3-based ISA card from 1992 fares much worse with respective rates of 70Hz for VGA, 60Hz for SVGA and 1024x768 and an unacceptable 45Hz interlaced format at 1280x1024.

Chip set used

To reduce costs, all SVGA graphics cards are based round a limited range of different VLSI chips, sometimes referred to as the *'graphics engine'*. These chips are dedicated to the one task and different manufacturers produce a range of chips with different performances. Example chips are the Tseng Labs range (from the basic ET4000 to the new ET6000), the S3 range (from the early 86C911 to the 928, 964, Trio64V to the new Virge), the Weitek range (from the 5186 to the new P9100), the ATI range (from the Mach8 to the 3D Rage Pro) and the Cirrus Logic range (from the 5426 to the GD5480).

All these chips, and others, provide varying performances. It is best to compare the working speeds of the chipsets as used on various cards. This may use *'Wintach'* readings, measuring how cards cope with actual applications packages or general card tests may be used, measuring the bit manipulation features. Example chip/card features are:

Chip	Graphics Card	Memory Type	Refresh rate at 24-bit SVGA	RAMDAC
Matrox MGA-2164	Millenium II	WRAM	200Hz	250MHz
S3 Virge	Diamond Stealth 3D2000	EDO RAM	120Hz	220MHz
Tseng ET6000	Hercules Dynamite	SDRAM	90Hz	250MHz
ATI 3D Rage Pro	ATI Xpert@Work	SGRAM	200Hz	230MHz
Cirrus Logic GD5465	VideoLogic GrafixStar 560	RDRAM	150Hz	230MHz
Alliance 3dfx Voodoo	Hercules Stingray 128/3D	EDO	150Hz	180Mhz

Method of screen writing

As soon as the PC progressed beyond the CGA standard, the standard machine BIOS (Basic Input/Output System) was inadequate and required extension. The added graphics functionality is provided by an extra EPROM (Erasable Programmable Read Only Memory) chip on the graphics card.   The efficiency of this BIOS extension affects the screen writing speed. Some SVGA cards copy the extension software into an area of RAM to speed up screen handling. This technique is known as *'ROM shadowing'*.

Currently, there are three approaches to screen handling:

- Leave the computer's CPU to do all the screen handling.   This is the simplest and cheapest method but it is also the slowest. Watch a screen update in Windows - around 15% of the CPU time is used up in updating the screen cursor alone!   The problems worsen if the system is upgraded. Adding a 1600x1200 card, for example, means the CPU has to handle an even bigger amount of screen data - with no extra computing power to process it.
- Use a Co-Processor to take on the graphics work and relieve the CPU. This is fast but expensive and is usually found in CAD environments.
- Use a graphics accelerator card, which is also a quick method and generally found in most modern high performance PCs.

When extra cards take over the graphics, the main machine has to have special software drivers installed, to allow communication to the cards.   For example, Texas uses a memory-resident driver known as TIGA (Texas Instruments Graphics Architecture) to translate Windows drawing commands into the specific commands required by the graphics boards which use their graphics chips (the TI 30410 and the TI 30420).   This is now a *'standard'* in the sense that many boards are now manufactured which are TIGA compatible.

3D CARDS

Games and animations such as walkthroughs and flybys show a quick succession of frames with each frame showing the viewer a different viewpoint on the scene.   As the viewpoint is moved, so the shading, shadowing and fine detail will alter.   Each scene comprises a range of objects (buildings, people, etc) and each object is made up from many individual graphics polygons, usually triangles.   Each triangle has its own colour and surface detail (e.g. grains of sand, bricks, leaves).   The scene will have one or more supposed sources of illumination; this could be the sun, streetlights, etc.   As the viewpoint is moved the light source will illuminate the triangles differently.   To produce a 3D effect, the user is shown perspective (i.e. distant objects are made smaller than close objects) and defocussing (i.e. distant object are not as clear as close objects; they are usually dimmed or 'fogged').

The commonly implemented features in 3D cards are:

Facility	Explanation
Z-Buffering	Since x and y describe the horizontal and vertical co-ordinates, 'z' refers to depth. A Z-buffer stores the depth information of objects (e.g. the dog is behind the tree). This allows *hidden surface removal* - i.e. time is saved by not drawing parts of an object that are obscured by foreground objects.
Flat shading	The polygons are filled with a uniform colour, which is not as effective but is very quick. Flat shading can be implemented to improve frame rates.
Gouraud shading	Obscures the boundaries between polygons by drawing realistic colour gradients; produces smoother and more natural shapes.
Phong shading	Achieves better results than Gouraud shading but is more demanding of processing power.
Texture mapping	Filling polygons with the same graphics bitmap (e.g. woodgrain or feathers).
Anti-aliasing	Curved and diagonal edges produce a 'staircase' effect known as *jaggies*. If the colours of the boundary's surrounding edges are blended, the effect is minimised.
Perspective correction	If an object is receding into the distance, the bit maps used to texture should also gradually diminish. So, a brick wall bitmap would draw smaller and smaller bricks as the wall shrunk towards the horizon.
Mip mapping	Similar to the above, except that new patterns are rendered for distant polygons.
Bilinear/trilinear filtering	Large areas when rendered can appear like a patchwork quilt, with blocks of slightly differing colouring. Filtering determines a pixel's colour on the colour of the surrounding pixels thereby producing a more uniform transition.
Alpha blending	Controls an object's translucency, thereby providing water or glass effects. It is also used to mask out areas of the screen.
Logarithmic fogging	More distance objects are fogged to grey.

The routines to constantly calculate all of these objects and display them on the screen (typically at 20 pictures per second) require a great deal of computational power.   This is called *'rendering'* and it strains even the most powerful PC.   To overcome this problem, many of these computational routines are embedded in graphics card's chipset and called by special software drivers.   Initially these drivers, known as APIs (Application Programming Interface), were written by graphics card manufacturers for their own range of cards.   The routines for a Matrox card would not work with a VideoLogic card, and so on.   As a consequence, games supplied with one card would not work with another graphics card, as the games were specially written to use the card manufacturer's APIs. Games bundled with the Diamond Stealth 3D 200, for example, are specially written for the card's VIRGE chipset.

There was a need for standard interfaces and this has been met by Silicon Graphic's OpenGL and Microsoft's Direct 3D.   OpenGL is not designed for the games market. Windows 95 Release 2 and Windows 98 provide DirectX facilities, which includes Direct3D.   Card manufacturers only have to write drivers to interface their cards to the Direct3D API's functions.

Microsoft's DirectX

Microsoft has produced a number of APIs under the title DirectX.   These are:

Direct 3D	Provides a standard interface for 3D object display and rendering.
Direct Draw	Reduces CPU time by allowing software direct access to alter video memory.
Direct Sound	Reduces CPU time by allowing software direct access to sound hardware. Also provides synchronisation of video and sound data.
Direct Play	Aids running applications over networks or communications lines.
Direct Input	Speeds up mouse and joystick responses.

RAMDAC used

The graphics information is stored in memory in digital format and has to be converted into analogue values to drive the gun(s) of the monitor. A chip, known as a RAMDAC (RAM digital/analogue converter) carries out the conversion function. The frame buffer data for each pixel is read in the order that it is sent to the monitor for display. This data is passed to the RAMDAC for conversion. With 24-bit colour, the numbers stored in memory exactly relate to the intensity of the red, green and blue elements of each pixel. This makes the digital to analogue conversion simple. However, this is not the method with lower colour depths. It is common that a card can only handle a subset of its full range of colours at any one time. For example, a card capable of 65,536 different colours may only be using 256 colours in a particular mode. This subset of colours is known as the *'palette'* and is stored in a look-up table in memory. During normal activities, the screen's pixel colour information is stored as a sequence of logical colour numbers. The colour number for each pixel is read from memory, translated into the values for each gun and these values are given to the RAMDAC to produce the actual colour that will appear on the monitor. Each Windows application package stores information about the palette it uses. When the application is run, Windows sets the RAMDAC to use that palette. When several applications are open at the same time, each application may have different sets of colour numbers in their required palettes. This can result in unexpected colour changes, as the range of colours supported by the card is less than the range of colours requested by the applications. RAMDAC performance is measured both in resolution (e.g. 24-bit) and conversion speed (up to 250MHz).

Card Connections

The output from the graphics card appears on a socket at the rear of the computer case.
The diagram shows the two types of connector used with PCs.

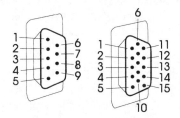

The CGA connector and EGA connector are identical and each has two rows of pins while the VGA/SVGA/XGA connector has three rows of pins. The chart shows the use of the pins.

Pin	Mono	CGA	EGA	VGA/SVGA/XGA
1	Ground	Ground	Ground	Red
2	Ground	Ground	Red Intensity	Green
3	Not Used	Red	Red	Blue
4	Not Used	Green	Green	Not Used
5	Not Used	Blue	Blue	Not Used
6	Intensity	Intensity	Green Intensity	Red Return
7	Video	Not Used	Blue Intensity	Green Return
8	Horizontal Synch	Horizontal Synch	Horizontal Synch	Blue Return
9	Vertical Synch	Vertical Synch	Vertical Synch	No Pin (used as key)
10				Ground
11				Not Used
12				Not Used
13				Horizontal Synch
14				Vertical Synch
15				Not Used

Many cards also offer other connections to extension devices. The range of connections includes:

VESA Feature Connector	This is a set of 26 pins on the graphics board that allows the connection of other video add-on cards e.g. video capture facilities. Unfortunately, the connection only supports VGA and 256 colours.
VAFC	The VESA Advanced Feature Connector is an 80-pin connector that overcomes the limitation of the standard VESA connector. It works up to 1024x768 and has a throughput of 150Mb per second.
VMC	The VESA Media Channel (VMC) is an edge connector on the graphics card. It is designed to handle up to fifteen different audio and video sources on a single channel, allowing a great flexibility in connecting together sound cards, video capture cards, MPEG systems, video conferencing systems and anything that the future may throw at it. Its first appearance is in the Video Logic 928Movie and PCIMovie cards.
Video Input	The ability to display input from live video sources such as VCRs and camcorders, as provided in the Media Vision 1024 card. An extra daughterboard may have to be fitted for this.
TV Aerial Input	A number of graphics cards, such as the ATI Wonder Pro, now have a built-in TV tuner, allowing both viewing of television programmes on the monitor and the capture of television programmes to hard disk.
RGB output	Used for connecting to high-quality monitors and other video devices that use RGB connectors.

AGP

The Accelerated Graphics Port was developed in response to the huge memory and consequent data transfer overheads required for 3D graphics.   A large number of texture maps require to be stored in memory. This allows rapid access to the texture data for the rapid rendering of 3D objects.   Fetching directly from disk would be far too slow to maintain the frame refresh rates. However, 3D rendering produces two main problems:

- The memory requirements of these maps can exceed the actual amount of memory fitted in the graphics card.
- Very large amounts of data need to be transferred to produce rendered screens at up to 30 frames per second.

The solution is twofold - use some of the computer's existing memory and access it at far faster data

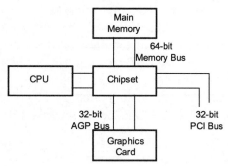

rates.   This requires a new motherboard with an entirely new bus system - the Accelerated Graphics Port.

The Accelerated Graphics Port is currently only available on newer Pentium II and Pentium III systems and these motherboards have their own AGP card slots and use the 440LX chipset onwards.   The graphics card no longer sits on the 33Mhz PCI bus.

As the diagram shows, the card is plugged directly into the separate AGP 66MHz bus that connects, via the chipset, to the CPU and memory.   This is called 'x1 mode' and provides a maximum throughput of 264MBps - double that of the PCI bus.   This data rate is still half of that travelling over the 64-bit connection between the CPU and memory.   To compensate, the 440BX chipset provides an 'x2 mode'. This transfers data on both the rising and falling edge of the clock pulse, which doubles the theoretical throughput to 528MBps.   The computer's memory is shared between the application program's usage and the graphics card usage.

100MHz bus system push the data rate up to 800MBps and a new 4x chipset is expected soon.

Normal 2D graphics do not require this extra performance and normal applications will not particularly benefit from this new technique.   Since support for AGP did not appear until a new DirectDraw in Windows 98, the shared memory usage ability of AGP cards were inactive until then.   In the short-term, AGP provides a faster data transfer rate. In the long term, it offers a cheap and fast video system.

Other facilities

The preceding pages outline some of the more important features of graphics cards.   However, many more factors may prove important for a particular user or for a particular activity.   These might include:

- Support for DPMS power saving. The ability of the graphics card to control the power usage of the monitor at times when there is no user activity.
- Virtual Screen or virtual desktop. A user may wish to display a great deal of detail on the screen (e.g. many Windows groups or many Windows applications open at the same time). This would normally require a large screen monitor otherwise each window would be too small for comfortable viewing. An alternative is to use a normal monitor screen size and only view a part of the full screen at any one time. Moving the mouse to an edge of the screen scrolls the display in that direction.   Thus a 640x480 screen can act as a window on a larger 1280x1024 display held in screen memory.
- Zoom. The virtual desktop provides a scrolling window on a larger screen.   The zoom facility allows the user to magnify any portion of the screen, usually to allow detailed editing of graphics or DTP.   There is no scrolling in this case.   The Number 9 GXE64 Pro card, for example, magnifies the screen up to 5 times normal size.
- Support for the connection of multiple monitors - either through installing multiple graphics cards or fitting the new graphics cards that have twin video outputs. This allows separate multitasking programs to be run on separate monitors.
- Drivers to allow the user to switch resolutions without having to reboot the machine to activate the new screen mode.
- Drivers for a wide range of monitors, applications (particularly AutoCAD and 3D Studio) and operating systems such as Windows 95, Windows 98, Windows NT and OS/2.
- MPEG-2 players, to handle DVD drives.

Video handling

Many graphics cards support a range of full motion video options, including MPEG, QuickTime, Video for Windows and Intel Indeo formats.   Video playback is often achieved by fitting an extra daughter board or using additional video handling software.   Video for Windows (AVI) is the most common PC video format although MPEG systems are becoming very popular.   MPEG requires special hardware to decode the compressed files, although it can use a software method to decode if the computer has a fast CPU.   Modern cards should be capable of supporting both of these video standards. See the chapter on multimedia for more details.

Since video playback places the greatest strain on CPU resources, CPU usage tests are a valuable indication of a card's performance.   A low CPU percentage usage is desired and large variations can be measured between cards. The Matrox MGA Millenium cards requires almost 25% of the CPU's time to play a 16-bit AVI file, while the Miro 20SD card requires less than 6% to play the same file.

Co-processor cards

Co-processor cards use a second processor to carry out the graphics tasks. The computer CPU passes brief instructions to the CPU on the co-processor graphics board and the co-processor board carries out the graphics calculations and board memory updates. Typical functions given to a co-processor would be text display, line drawing, rectangles, ellipses and area colour fills.

The 8514/A boards and the VESA XGA boards initiated this method and other co-processor systems are based around the Texas TI-34000 series.

Accelerator cards

Like co-processor boards, the accelerator board is designed to relieve the computer's main CPU of valuable graphics processing time.   In a co-processor system, a second processor chip is employed for the graphics tasks.   In an accelerator system, the main graphics tasks are implemented in hardware. These main tasks are line and box drawing and *'bitblitting'* (bit-to-block transfers - i.e. memory flooding). Since these operations are implemented in hardware, there is no need for a processor to determine what needs to be done - the tasks are pre-defined.   This results in the graphics functions being carried out more quickly.   Most graphics cards on sale currently use some form of graphics acceleration.

A number of hardware-based 3D accelerator cards are produced, based on the 3DFX Voodoo or the VideoLogic PowerVR PCX2 chipsets.   The trend, however, seems to be towards producing combined 2D/3D chipsets such as the 3D Labs Permedia 2.

NOTE

There can be significance variations in the efficiency of each card's method of handling graphics functions.   For example, one particular card may need less information passed to it, in order to carry out a particular graphics function, compared to another card.   Some cards will carry out a smaller range of graphics functions, the remaining functions being left for the computer's main CPU to process.

Card performance

There is no doubt that graphics accelerator cards substantially improve a system's performance. However, manufacturers' claims should be put in perspective:
- The claims only consider the graphics functions being tested in isolation.
- When considered as <u>part</u> of the overall activities of an application program, the performance is nowhere near so spectacular.

Their figures, although significant, don't begin to approach the raw performance figures.   When in the higher 1024 x 768 modes, the cards tended to perform significantly better for certain applications. Word for Windows, for example, showed improvements of between 160% and 490%.   Corel Draw, on the other, showed a slightly worse performance compared to SVGA. As expected, the performance of VL-Bus and PCI bus is appreciably better than ISA versions.   Not every application can make the maximum use of a graphics card.   Improvements tend to be greater at the higher resolution end of their use. Generally, very high resolutions are only usable on larger sized monitor screens, from 15" upwards.

Using Windows

All modern multimedia software applications, such as PhotoShop, Adobe Premiere, Sound Forge, etc. are designed for use under Windows. Of course, applications such as Sound Recorder, Media Player, PowerPoint, etc. are Microsoft products and as such are also built for Windows use.   Before using applications, therefore, it is best to get an understanding of the structures and methods used by Windows - as these methods are used in any Windows application.   For example, all applications will load and save files in the same way, and they will all create files that are understood by Windows (for copying, e-mailing and so on).

An operating system is a set of programs to control the hardware and manage the computer's resources. For many years, the only major operating systems for PCs was Microsoft's MSDOS (Microsoft Disk Operating System).   Although it is still in use, many new users have never seen or used it, since they have been brought up using the Windows family of operating systems.

Even if machines are Windows based, they still use many of the original DOS concepts such as file extensions, sub-directories (folders) and paths.

Windows and DOS

The main characteristics of any operating system are:
  - They conceal the difficulties of handling the hardware.
  - They present the user with a relatively simple interface.
  - They communicate with the user, carrying out valid commands and giving error messages when incorrect commands are attempted.
  - They relieve users from requiring a detailed knowledge of how the computer hardware works.

With the earliest computers, users required a great knowledge of each item of hardware.   When DOS appeared, computers became available to ordinary users.   The user could carry out a range of activities by giving simple commands, in the knowledge that the operating system would translate the simple user command into the set of hardware tasks needed to carry it out.   The operating system could be considered as the foreman of an organisation.   When the manager (i.e. the user) gave an order for work to be carried out, the foreman took on the job of ensuring that the actual physical task was carried out. The manager need not know where the resources are kept and what activities are involved - that is the job of the foreman.

Windows 3.1, 95, 98 and Millennium Edition all base themselves on core DOS structures. Windows NT and 2000 use a different model, although they still use the idea of filenames, folders and paths.

Filenames and extensions

All programs and data are held on a storage device until they are ready to be used. The most common storage device is the magnetic disk, although CD disks, ZIP disks, and memory 'flash cards' are also in use.   A file is collection of related data.   The data may be instructions to the computer (program files) or graphic images, sound clips or similar information (data files).   Hard disks are likely to be storing scores of thousands of such files at any one time.   Each file has a unique name; no two files are allowed to have exactly the same name in the same disk folder. This unique name is used by the computer to later find the file and carry out activities such as loading it, printing it, copying it, etc.   If a file is saved with the same name as an existing file of that name, the new file's contents replace the existing file contents.

To aid future recognition of files, there are certain conventions followed by DOS and Windows for the naming of files.

Firstly, all file names may have three parts:

REPORT.DOC

File Name   Dot   File Extension

FILENAME

DOS and Windows 3.1 allowed file names consisting of alphanumeric characters and certain other characters. The file name had to be a maximum of eight characters and with a minimum of 1 character. With Windows 95 onwards, file names can be up to 255 characters and spaces, full stops, commas, semi-colons and brackets was introduced. The following characters, however, are not allowed to be included in file descriptions:

> " \ / ' ? : * |

The filename part is compulsory and Windows will not accept a file without a name.

While a filename of *'G'* is valid, the file name used should describe the contents of the file. A file given the name of *'HH'* or *'Z1'* may have significance when it was first saved - but will probably not convey much six months later. More meaningful names such as *'BUDGET99'* or *'NOV_MEMO'* should be used with DOS and Windows 3.1, while fuller descriptions such as *'Final Budget figures for 1999'* and *'Departmental memo for November 2000'* can be used with Windows 95 onwards.

FILE EXTENSIONS

On most occasions, the user has no control over the name given to a file's extension. Since most multimedia work is carried out using application packages, the extensions are automatically supplied by the package (see below). Occasionally, the user has control over the name of the file extension. In these cases the use of an extension is optional but is recommended.

DOS and Windows 3.1 allowed a file to have up to a three-letter extension. So files called *'MEMO'*, *'MEMO.99'* and *'MEMO.TXT'* were all valid filenames.

From Windows 95 onwards, this restriction was lifted and files could be called, for example:

> project 2000.the results of the feasibility study

Here, the extension has been chosen to provide further detail about the file. It is best, however, to use the file extension to describe the <u>format</u> of the file's contents. Files can have differing types of contents:

- The **programs** themselves; i.e. applications such as graphics creation, audio sampling, video editing and authoring packages. Most large commercial packages are comprised, not of a single file, but of a collection of linked files.
- The **data** used by applications; i.e. audio samples, video clips and web pages. These are stored in special formats used by the particular package. Data files used in one package cannot be used in another package, although sometimes file formats can be converted. It is therefore important to know the format in which data is stored.
- **Text** files that are in plain English; i.e. files that can be read via DOS, e-mail, Notepad, HTML readers, etc. Note, however, that most word-processors allow the text to be underlined, italicised, emboldened, etc. and this involves including special codes into these files, thus making them less readable by text-based applications.

DOT

When a file extension is used, a dot must be used to separate the filename and extension.

PRE-DEFINED FILE EXTENSIONS

Where the user has a choice, files can be given any file extension that helps convey the file's internal format. However, a number of file extensions are commonly used and these have to be avoided. Examples of these extensions are:

PROGRAM EXTENSIONS

There are a number of extensions that are claimed by Windows and DOS applications. The most important of these are the COM, EXE and BAT extensions, since any file with one of these extensions is regarded by the system as being a program file. This means that the program can be run in Windows simply by double-clicking on the filename in Windows Explorer, or by entering its name in the Windows *'Run'* box. The application's name can be entered without the dot or extension and is still recognised.

The Paint Shop Pro application program, for example, is called *'PSP.EXE'*, while the Windows Media Player program is called *MPLAYER.EXE'*.

COM and EXE files are composed of many thousands or millions of instructions, in the special 'machine code' recognisable by the computer's CPU but unreadable by humans.

Note that simply giving a file a COM or EXE extension does not convert that file into a program file.

If a file called REPORT.DOC contained a company report in plain English, changing the file name to REPORT.EXE would have no effect on the file's internal contents.   Any attempt to run the file as an application would result in an error message.   Each of the three program extensions has a different meaning to DOS, since it has to handle each type differently.

WINDOWS EXTENSIONS

Microsoft Windows also claims a number of extensions to itself.   These are in addition to the program extensions that it also uses.   Typical Windows extensions are BMP (Bit Mapped Pictures) used for creating background wallpaper effects, INI (initialisation files) used for storing details of Windows configurations and Windows application details, and other Windows extensions such as DRV, TMP, PIF, VXD and TTF.

APPLICATION DATA EXTENSIONS

Individual applications claim extensions for their own use.   This makes the use of a program easier, since the housekeeping is then carried out by the program itself.   If the user wishes to open up a file called REPORT, there may be various files with that same file name but different extensions.   There may be REPORT.DOC, REPORT.XLS, REPORT.DBF and so on.   The word-processing application created the text file with the extension .DOC.   The user only entered the file name as REPORT and the application automatically added the .DOC extension.   Similarly, the Excel spreadsheet program added the .XLS extension to the worksheet saved by the user as REPORT.   The database package also automatically added the .DBF extension to the file of records that the user saved simply as REPORT. Now, when the user is in a particular application and requests to open the REPORT file, the application will know which file to open by the extension on the end.   The Spreadsheet package will ignore the other files named REPORT and only work with the file called REPORT.XLS.   The same is true of the word-processing and database packages.   The technicalities of this are hidden from the user, who need never even know that the files have been given any extensions.

There is a wide range of application extensions and some are even used by more than one application. This can confuse matters unless files of the same type are kept in their own particular compartments (see later).   Example extensions are:

BARK.WAV	A sound sample file.
FOOTBALL.AVI	A movie file.
SCREEN.HLP	A help file (common with many applications).
CAR.JPG	A graphics file.
SALES.DOC	A word-processed file created in Word.

OTHER EXTENSIONS

A number of other extensions are commonly in use and are regarded as a standard between packages.   In other words, every package recognises the file as being of the same format.   Examples are:

READ.ME	A text file usually included on the program disk, containing last-minute information about the release.
MEMO.TXT	A file containing plain English text.
JENNIFER.PCX	A graphics file in Paintbrush format, recognised by most word-processing, DTP and graphics packages.
MARGARET.GIF	A graphics file in Graphics Interchange Format, used regularly on the Internet.
STREETS.LST	A list containing related items, such as names or addresses.
NAMES.SRT	A file containing a list of items in a sorted order (e.g. names in ascending order or debts in descending order).

Directories / Folders

A floppy disk can contain hundreds of files; a hard disk can contain tens or hundreds of thousands of files.   This would make finding and operating on a file very difficult, as each file would be mixed in with the thousands of others.   It is essential, therefore, that files are stored in a logical way, so that they are easy to retrieve and manipulate.   DOS and Windows have an electronic disk filing system that is derived from an office manual filing system, where every file is kept in a filing cabinet under a different name or heading.   Files could be stored by office department or function.

Consider, for example, searching for the discipline record of John Smith, the repair worker.   The office may have six filing cabinets but only the one labelled *'Personnel'* will need to be searched, thus removing five-sixths of the data from the search.   The Personnel filing cabinet will have three drawers and only the one labelled *'Discipline'* need be opened - the others are labelled as *'Promotion'* and *'Sick Records'* and are thus ignored in the search.   When the drawer is opened, three wallets are found, labelled as *'Clerical'*, *'Production'* and *'Maintenance'*.   Only the Maintenance wallet need be opened, again narrowing down the search.   Finally, an alphabetical search is made of the files in the Maintenance wallet, until the file of John Smith is found.   The above process provides a very speedy access to any individual file - assuming that files have been stored in a logical order in the first place.

Users of computer systems need to have the same ease of access to their computer data files as they have with their manual paper system.   This is the role of the filing system.   This provides an electronic equivalent to the manual system. It holds its files in different compartments (called *'directories'* or *'folders'*) on the disk, just as the manual system holds files in

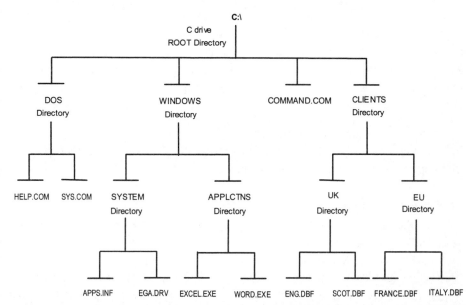

different physical compartments.   If a graphics package is in use, a folder can be created to hold the graphics files; if a word-processor is being used, then a folder can be created to store all word-processed files, and so on.

The creation of DOS compartments (folders or directories) containing other compartments (sub-folders or sub-directories) results in a structure called the *'tree'*.

The diagram only represents a small fraction of an actual structure; a real hard disk may have hundreds of folders, each containing many different files.

Although the structure is called a tree, it is actually drawn as an inverted tree.   At the top of the structure is the ROOT folder.   This is the compartment that the user sees when the machine is first switched on (i.e. the root of the whole structure).   When the user opens the Windows Explorer application, the files first displayed are those in the root folder.   In the example in the diagram, there will be only one single file displayed - COMMAND.COM, since all the other files reside inside other compartments.

Spreading from the root folder are branches (folders and sub-folders) and leaves (the data files and program files).   Each branch of the tree (i.e. each folder) may contain leaves (i.e. files) or other branches (i.e. sub-folders).   In the example, the root folder contains one file and three sub-folders called DOS, WINDOWS and CLIENTS.   The folder names can describe the application contained within it (e.g. WINDOWS) or can describe the function or organisational structure of the company (e.g. CLIENTS). The rules for folder construction are:

- The number of folders and their structure should mirror the needs of the organisation.
- Each folder and file should be named to clearly label its contents.
- Only the relevant files for a folder should be stored in that folder.
- Do regular housekeeping to ensure that folders are kept up-to-date.   Ensure that only relevant files are being stored in each folder; move files to other folders where appropriate; remove files that are no longer used to prevent the disk becoming clogged up with old unwanted files.

Paths

To get to any file, a path is taken from the root folder, through any other folders and sub-folders until the file is reached.   So, each file can be fully described in terms of its name and where it is stored.   The full file description consists of three parts:

- What disk is it on.
- What folders is it in.
- What the file is called.

Here are a few examples of files included in the example diagram on the preceding page:

        C:\COMMAND.COM
        C:\DOS\HELP.COM
        C:\WINDOWS\SYSTEM\APPS.INF
        C:\CLIENTS\UK\SCOT.DBF
        C:\CLIENTS\EU\ITALY.DBF

If the same files resided on a floppy disk, filenames might be

        A:\COMMAND.COM
        A:\DOS\HELP.COM
        etc.

Since each file can be described in terms of its path as well as its name, files with the same name and extension can now exist on the same disk - as long as they are stored in separate folders.   For example, two files called REPORT.DOC could exist on the same disk in different parts of the folder structure as shown:

        C:\CLIENTS\UK\REPORT.DOC
        C:\CLIENTS\EU\REPORT.DOC

Where this happens, the two files can have exactly the same contents or can be completely different files that happen to use the same filename and extension.

Microsoft Windows

One of the most successful and comprehensive of DOS environments has been Windows 3.1 from Microsoft.   It was as a *'GUI'* - a graphical user interface - and it used a range of icons (miniature pictures) to represent computing functions, so simplifying activities.   For example, if the user was word processing and clicked the printer icon, the document would be sent to the printer.   In this way, it is hoped to reduce the time users spend trying to <u>understand</u> the machine, providing more time actually <u>using</u> the machine.   Later versions, such as Windows 95, 98, 2000 and ME, use improved programming to speed operations and provide new facilities - but they all retain the same basic GUI methods.

Microsoft Windows versions use a WIMP environment.   That means they use <u>W</u>indows, <u>I</u>cons, <u>M</u>enus and <u>P</u>ointers (or <u>W</u>indows, <u>I</u>cons, <u>M</u>ouse and <u>P</u>ull-down menus).   Windows allows files to be clicked on by the mouse and deleted, moved, copied, renamed, printed, etc.   It has many additional features, such as:

- Supports multi-tasking - this means that more than one program can be running in memory at the same time.   If desired, one application can be seen on the screen while the other application is working away in the background.   Alternatively, both applications can be seen on the screen at the same time, each application occupying a different portion of the screen, or '*Window*'.
- Allows easy copying of data between programs.
- Has its own set of extra utilities, such as Paint (paint program), WordPad (small word processor), Cardfile (small database), Terminal (for connecting the computer to a modem), Calculator, etc.
- Full on-line help system.   This includes a full hypertext system where the user can type in a search entry, find out about that item and be provided options to view items of a similar category.   So, for example, if the user is reading help on *'Copying a Help Topic Onto the Clipboard'*, the screen will display a line offering help on *'Annotating a Help Topic'*; if this line is clicked on with the mouse pointer, the user is taken to a further page of information on that topic.
- Provides a set of common features and techniques for all Windows applications; this means that every application written to be used under Windows will use the same techniques (e.g. the same way to load and save files, the same way to import a picture, etc.).   This results in users being able to adapt to a new Windows application quickly, since activities learned in a previous package are re-used.   With DOS-based applications, each package would do the same job in a different way; one package would expect a particular function key, another would require a particular key combination using Alt and Ctrl keys, while yet another would expect the operation to be achieved through menu options.

The Windows environment allows for extensive configuration to meet the needs of the user (e.g. screen colours, use of memory, background wallpaper, choice of printers, sensitivity of the mouse, etc.); this is covered in the chapter on Windows configuration.   Windows can be keyboard-operated but it is really designed for mouse operation and is certainly much easier and quicker to use with a mouse.

Windows 95

Windows 3.1 was not a full operating system, as it required DOS to be installed. Most of its activities were directed through DOS drivers and software. It was more correctly described as an *'environment'*. Windows 95 is not really an environment in the sense of simply being an add-on interface to DOS. Indeed, there is no need for DOS to be installed on the machine, unless these facilities are required for running older DOS-only applications.   Windows 95 has its own drivers for memory management, CD handling, etc. This makes it an operating system and graphical user interface in one package.

Windows 95 can run all the old Windows 3.1 and DOS programs.   However, Windows 3.1 is unable to run programs that are specially written for Windows 95.

BENEFITS OF WINDOWS 95

- The *'Documents'* option from the *'Start'* menu stores and displays a list of the last 15 files used on the computer, allowing simple recall of commonly used files. Single click on any of the file names and the file is opened inside its appropriate application. So, if a file called 'REPORT.DOC' is clicked, the system loads Microsoft Word and then opens the REPORT.DOC file within it.
- Provides pop-up help windows.   If the user allows the mouse pointer to linger over a command button, a pop-up window displays the function of that button.
- Allows the user to allocate long filenames of up to 255 characters.   It should be understood that Windows 3.1 and DOS programs still use the old eight-dot-three naming system.   So, any files created under Windows 95 that are saved under DOS or Windows 3.1 will have their files names truncated.   A Word file called *'Consumer Report on Beef'* would probably be re-saved as *'CONSUM~1.DOC'*.
- Plays video much more efficiently.   The improvement is dramatic and is of the order of two to three times.
- Supports plug-and-play - the system recognises p-n-p components and automatically assigns resources. Newly installed p-n-p compatible cards are automatically recognised by Windows 95.
- Provides a *'Recycle Bin'* as an improvement over Windows 3.1's undelete facility. Files that the user decides to delete appear to be deleted but are, in fact stored in their complete form and can be accessed at any time via the Recycle Bin.   The user can decide to recover a file from the Bin or can permanently empty the Bin's contents.
- Provides more extensive *'Help'* facilities.
- Adds new communications features such as The Microsoft Network, Microsoft Fax, HyperTerminal and Phone Dialler.
- Adds extra diagnostic facilities through the provision of a *'Hardware Wizard'*.
- Easy handling of applications through an *'Add/Remove Programs'* facility.

PROBLEMS WITH WINDOWS 95

- More complex to maintain.
- Not as stable an environment as was hoped for.   Users requiring maximum stability have upgraded from Windows 3.1 directly to NT or Windows 2000, skipping over Windows 95 and 98 altogether.   Such users expect a more sophisticated and reliable product, while ensuring the benefits of the Windows 95/98 interface.
- Retained some 16-bit components along with new 32-bit components.
- More demanding hardware requirements than with Windows 3.1.
  The hardware requirements for Windows 95 are:

	Minimum	Realistic Minimum
CPU	386DX	486/Pentium
Memory	4MB	8MB, preferably 16MB.
Video card	VGA	SVGA
Bus	ISA	PCI or Local Bus
Mouse	Normal	Mouse with right-hand button

  Since Windows 95 wants 4MB of memory for its own use, even more RAM is required to provide memory for use by the applications.
  Using a local bus or a PCI bus system will result in improved graphics handling.

Windows 98

The basic 32-bit architecture of Windows 98 is largely identical to that of Windows 95.   Many of Microsoft's additions to Windows 95 such as Internet Explorer, the OSR2 (Operating System Release 2) update pack, new drivers, etc are now included in Windows 98.   In that respect, existing users of Windows 95 who have already added these features will not find Windows 98 to be greatly altered.

BENEFITS OF WINDOWS 98

- Internet Explorer 4 or 5 built in.
- Includes Outlook Express, with e-mail and newsgroup facilities.
- Many more built-in device drivers for modems, printers, etc.
- Supports multiple monitors.   Up to eight video cards can be connected to the machine, each handling its own monitor.   This means that a much larger desktop size can be set, with each monitor displaying a different area of the desktop - or a different application.
- Support for USB and FireWire.
- Much more comprehensive system diagnostic tools.
- Improved Plug and Play.
- Much larger set of drivers available on the installation CD.
- FAT32 allows single disk partitions greater than 2GB and stores data in smaller clusters, minimising wasted disk space.
- Makes better use of AGP graphics cards and MMX processors.
- More comprehensive *'Help'* facilities including many troubleshooting guides.

The hardware requirements for Windows 98 are:

	Minimum	Realistic Minimum
CPU	486DX	Pentium
Memory	16MB	32MB or more
Video card	VGA	SVGA
Bus	ISA	PCI
Mouse	Normal	Mouse with right-hand button

Since the software is only supplied on CD-ROM, a CD-ROM drive is essential to both initially install the main Windows 98 program and to later install any extra features supplied on the CD.

Windows 2000

Released in February 2000, the interface of this operating system is essentially a slightly upgraded version of the Windows 98 interface. It is, however, designed for use as a corporate desktop platform, and consequently a lot of effort has been put into making it easy to administer.

Points that are worthy of note in Windows 2000 from the user point of view include:

- Menus now *'fade into view'.*
- Little used menu items disappear behind a slightly raised panel with a chevron on it.
- Users who print to network printers now receive a notification as their print job is done.
- Network Neighbourhood has been replaced by My Network Places.
- Each individual user has a personalised desktop.
- Individually customised and personalised menus.
- Individually customised toolbars for each user.
- Enhanced Accessibility for people with disabilities. New *'Narrator'* applet reads your screen back to you, and on screen keyboard available for mouse only use. Apart from being useful for people with disabilities, these can solve problems for able-bodied users in unusual environments.
- Web pages can be stored on the hard disk to make them available offline. This technology was introduced in later editions of Win98, and is now mainstream.
- Built in support for multiple languages, switchable in the task bar.
- Easier upgrades, as long as the machine to be upgraded satisfies the compatibility lists.
- More wizard-based administration, including a wizard to connect to a network.
- Significant improvements to the Help System, which is now HTML based.
- There are more error messages, and they are easier to understand.
- The safe start-up system, which is used when machines are badly configured, now has the best of Win98's options and the best of NT's options.
- Unicode is now used throughout, and the new European currency symbol is fully supported.
- Support for multiple processor motherboards, DVD, infrared and FireWire have been added, while support for colour printers and multiple monitors has been enhanced.

- Windows 2000 uses either Fat32 or NTFS. Fat32 is compatible with prior versions of Windows, but supports large volumes and is less wasteful of partial sector space. NTFS, the NT File system is incompatible with earlier windows versions, but is better suited to multiple access use as it gives users individual rights to read, write, modify and execute files, like UNIX (see chapter on Unix).

System requirements for Windows 2000 are outlined below.

	Minimum	Realistic Minimum
CPU	200MHz Pentium	300MHz Pentium
Memory	32MB	64MB
Hard disk	600MB	1GB
Video Card	VGA	SVGA
Bus	ISA	PCI
Mouse	Normal	Wheelmouse

The operating system needs about 600MB of hard disk space for its own files, before any user applications or data are added to the machine.

Win 98 ME

Microsoft is introducing the Win 98 Millennium Edition, or Win 98 ME for short. This is intended to be a personal Operating System and so lacks all of the groupware features of Windows 2000.

It is essentially an upgrade of Windows 98, with the added features listed below.

The interface is very similar to Windows 98, with only a few cosmetic changes.

- It has a more useable help system and extra wizards.
- It has a new *'System Restore'* utility.   Over time, with programs being added and deleted, components will have been added, deleted and modified.   With Windows ME, these changes are noted and saved. This allows a user to return the system to the state it was in on any previous point, before an alteration was made.
- A new *'System File Protection'* utility guards against any overwriting or deletion of important system files that may occur during the installation of other software.
- A new *'Hibernation'* utility allows the machine to be closed down, with the current active programs and files being noted.   When the machine is switched on later, the computer automatically opens these original programs and files.
- A new *'Windows Image Acquisition'* utility builds the downloading of images from digital cameras into Windows, rather than requiring the separate utility supplied with the camera.
- A new *'Movie Maker'* utility provides video capture facilities for those with video capture cards. It will automatically create separate clips for each scene in the video.   It also provides basic video editing facilities such as cropping, amalgamating clips, and adding fades and voiceovers.
- A new version of the *'Media Player'* includes the playing of CDs and the playing of streamed audio and video.   It also includes a 'CD ripper' that converts a track from an audio CD into a compressed WMA file (the Windows alternative to MP3).

Using Windows

Since Windows 95, 98 and 2000 share a great deal of common user interface, the following descriptions cover all systems.   Differences are highlighted within the text.

Using the mouse

The Windows interface and all applications that work within Windows use the mouse in the same way. The main mouse activities are listed below.

Point	The mouse is moved so that the screen pointer is positioned over the desired item - e.g. an icon or object.
Click	Click the left mouse button while the pointer is positioned over the desired item. This is most commonly used to select an object.
Double Click	Click the left mouse button twice in rapid succession while the pointer is positioned over the desired icon or object. This is most commonly used to execute an activity - e.g. open an icon or run a program.
Right Click	Brings up a *'context menu'* with options appropriate to the task being performed. For example, right-clicking on a word highlighted as incorrect within Word invokes the spell checker, while right-clicking an object in Paint Shop Pro brings up a menu of cut and paste options.
Drag	Move the mouse while holding down the left mouse button.
Shift Click	Hold down the *'Shift'* key while clicking on the desired item.
Shift Drag	Hold down the *'Shift'* key while dragging the mouse.

Closing vs Minimising

When the user is finished using an application, that application can be closed by clicking on the *'Exit'* option in the *'File'* drop-down menu. The top right-hand corner of applications for Windows 95 and later has a set of buttons as shown in the diagram. Clicking the *'Close'* button will also close and exit the application. On the other hand, the user can click on the minimise button that appears on the leftmost button of that set. The application is reduced to an entry on the Task Bar at the bottom of the screen. This is known as *'minimising'* and the application remains active, frozen at the point at which it was minimised. If the application is later clicked on the Task Bar, it is restored to full-screen, ready to proceed at the same stage it is was at when it was minimised. The illustration shows Microsoft Word and the Lexmark Printer Utility being held in a minimised state.

Accessing Programs

An opening screen similar to that shown below provides alternative methods of accessing applications.

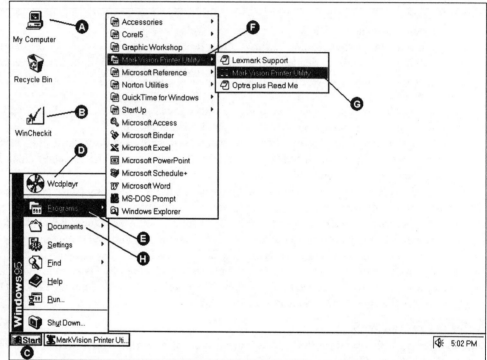

1. The *'My Computer'* icon, marked as **(A)**, opens a window that displays all the files and sub-folders on the computer's disks, plus access to the computer's printers, networking and the Control Panel.

2. **(B)** shows an icon for a user's application that has been placed directly on to the Windows desktop. This is a *'shortcut'* to the application and the program can be run simply by clicking on the icon. In this way, the user's most commonly used programs can be displayed as soon as Windows is loaded.

3. The button **(C)** is labelled *'Start'* and clicking this button displays the menu shown on the left of the screen. The menu option **(D)** displays an application that has been placed on the start menu as an alternative means of accessing often used programs. Clicking on its menu bar loads and runs the program.

4. One of the *'Start'* menu options is titled *'Programs'* and moving the mouse pointer over the button, marked as **(E)**, displays a menu showing all the programs available on the computer. Clicking one of the menu options, such as the item marked *'Microsoft Excel'* in the example, loads and runs that particular program.

5. In some cases, an entry in the Programs menu is not a single program but a collection of similar programs. For example, the *'Corel 5'* option contains a suite of different drawing, tracing and presentation utilities. Similarly, the menu bar option marked as **(F)** contains three supporting components. Placing the mouse pointer on that menu option reveals another sub-menu that allows access to the sub-options. Clicking menu bar **(G)** in the example shown runs the Lexmark printer utility.

6. Clicking option **(H)** on the *'Start'* menu reveals the last 15 documents opened by the user. Clicking any of these documents opens the corresponding application and then the document.

7. Clicking on the file name when in Windows Explorer.

8. Clicking on the program name on the bottom Task Bar.

9. Using the *'Run'* option from the *'Start'* menu. Only useful where the user knows the exact name of the file and the exact sub-folder path in which it is stored, or wishes to run a program that was recently used.

In all cases, when the application is exited the user is returned to menu screens as shown above. Windows 95 onwards allows for extensive configuration to meet the needs of the user (e.g. screen colours, use of memory, background wallpaper, choice of printers, sensitivity of the mouse, etc.).

'Start' Menu Options

Apart from running applications, the *'Start'* menu offers a number of useful facilities.   These are:

Settings	This has three sub-options: Control Panel - Provides similar functions to Windows 3.1 for setting keyboard and mouse characteristics, etc. Extra functions include adding new hardware, adding and removing software, and configuring network facilities. Printer - Provides options to add new printers, to set printer ports and to set the configuration of printers. Taskbar - Sets the options for the Taskbar and the Start Menu.
Find	Searches the computer's disk drives (and network drives if on a network) for specific files. Searches can be for specific names, specific contents, specific dates or specific sizes.
Help	Provides comprehensive help in three ways: Contents - Help is organised in a systematic way providing information in a hierarchical fashion with the user delving deeper if he/she wants more information on a subject. Index - The user can scroll through a long list of help topics or can search by entering a word or phrase. Find - Every word used in every help file can be scrolled through or searched for.
Run	A pull-down menu lists the programs that were recently loaded via the *'Run'* facility. One of these can be selected or the user can click the *'Browse'* option to search for a specific program to be run.
Shut Down	Provides options to close down the computer or to restart in DOS mode.
Favorites	Provides quick access to commonly used files, folders and webs sites. (Windows 98/2000 only).

Other Accessories

One of the options in the *'Programs'* menu is a collection of utilities under the heading *'Accessories'*. These are supplied as standard with Windows 95 onwards and include:

Available to most Windows 95 users and all Windows 98/2000 users	
Multimedia Utilities	Media Player, CD Player, Sound Recorder and Volume Control.
System Tools	System Monitor, and Disk utilities - Backup, Disk Defragmenter, DriveSpace (not with Windows 2000) and ScanDisk.
Calculator	A calculator providing scientific functions and conversion between different number bases.
Clipboard Viewer	Facilities to view, save and delete the contents of the Clipboard.
Dial-Up Networking	Uses a modem to connect a computer to a network, or to another computer with a modem.
HyperTerminal	An improved version of Terminal, transferring files between two computers over the telephone network. Requires the computers to be connected to modems.
Phone Dialer	A utility allowing users with modems to place telephone calls from the keyboard or from a stored pick list.
Direct Cable Connection	A utility to allow two computers to share their resources. One computer can access the files and printers of the other computer.
Paint	A more basic version of Paintbrush, with facilities to create and edit bitmap pictures. Provides line drawing, box drawing, text overlay, fills, etc.
Imaging	A simple tool to add lines, boxes and text to an existing image. Also provides facilities to scan images and documents, when a scanner is fitted to the computer.
Notepad	A simple word-processing program for small files, less than 64k.
WordPad	An improved version of the Windows 3.1 Write word processing program
Available with Windows 98	
DVD Player	Used to play DVD disks where the computer has a DVD drive.
Disk Cleanup	Detects temporary file, internet cache files, etc that are using up valuable disk space.
System Info	A very powerful utility for testing the computer's system files, Registry, etc.
Maintenance Wizard	A utility to automate checks for disk errors, etc, at times set by the user (e.g. overnight).
Available with Windows 2000	
Fax	Used to send, receive and organise faxes.
Accessibility Options	Improved usability and readability for the visually or physically impaired.
Synchronise	Used to keep the contents of a desktop machine synchronised with laptops, PDA's etc.

The actual applications appearing on the list will depend upon how the user's machine is configured. This will depend on the version of software installed and the number of items installed onto the hard disk from the installation CD.

Windows Explorer

Windows Explorer allows access to disk operations at file and directory (folder) level.

Explorer has two screen panels. The left panel is the *'folder tree window'* and it displays a graphic representation of the folder structure of the currently chosen disk drive with an icon of a folder for each folder. It also allows access to the Control Panel and the Printer utilities. The right panel is the *'folder window'* and it displays icons and names representing the files and folders within a selected folder. In the folder tree window, the currently chosen folder is highlighted. To select a new folder to view, the user clicks the mouse pointer on the folder name or its folder icon. A plus sign on a folder indicates that it contains sub-folders that are not being currently displayed. The terms *'expanding'* and *'collapsing'* are used to describe the display or non-display of folders. In the example shown, the *'mmbook'* folder

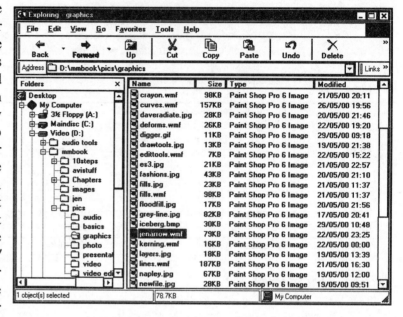

has been expanded and all the sub-folders at the next level are revealed. In turn, the *'pics'* folder has been expanded and all sub-folders within *'pics'* are listed. The *'graphics'* sub-folder has been selected and its contents are viewable in the right hand panel.

Windows 98 provides two display options:

<u>View in Classic Mode.</u>
This provides the standard interface as provided with Windows 95.

<u>View as a Web Page.</u>
The right-hand panel displays the folder's files and highlighting a file provides file details (type, size, date created/modified). If the file is a graphic file, it is displayed (as with the globe example shown).

The main Explorer activities are carried out using the mouse and keyboard and these are:

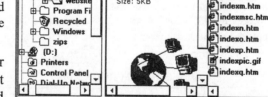

EXPANDING A FOLDER
Double click the mouse pointer on the desired folder or single click on the plus icon to its left; if using the keyboard, highlight the desired sub-folder with the cursor keys then press the plus key.

COLLAPSING A FOLDER
Double click the mouse pointer on the desired folder; if using the keyboard, highlight the desired sub-folder with the cursor keys then press the minus key.

DELETING A FILE

Highlight the desired file in the right panel by clicking the mouse pointer on it; press the Delete key; when prompted, confirm the file's transfer to the Recycle Bin.

DELETING A FOLDER

Highlight the desired folder icon and press the delete key; when prompted, confirm the transfer of the folder and all its files and sub-folders to the Recycle Bin. Deleting files and folders, in fact, only sends them to the Recycle Bin area where they can either be recovered or permanently deleted.

UNDELETING

Since files and folders that are 'deleted' are actually sent to a folder called the 'Recycle Bin', they are available for recovery. Double-clicking the Recycle Bin icon on the desktop opens a window that displays all the items available for recovering. The desired files can be selected and the 'Restore' option on the 'File' menu restores them to the folder from where they were deleted. If a file came from a folder that has since been deleted, the folder is also restored. To permanently delete a file or group of files, the file(s) should be selected and the 'Delete' option chosen from the 'File' menu. The file(s) are deleted and the disk space is recovered for future use. Choosing the 'Empty Recycle Bin' option deletes all the files currently in the Bin.

CREATING A FOLDER

Highlight the folder into which the new folder is to be added; choose the 'New' option from the 'File' menu and the 'Folder' option from the 'New' menu. An unnamed sub-folder is created and it must immediately be given a name.

MOVING A FILE

Click the pointer on the desired file in the right panel so that the file is highlighted. Go to the 'Edit' menu and choose the 'Cut' option. The file is now removed from the source folder. Open the folder that is the intended destination for the file. Go to the 'Edit' menu and choose the 'Paste' option. The file is now resident in the destination folder. Another technique involves dragging a file from the right panel to a folder in the left panel. This works for data files that are moved between folders in the same drive. For program files, it will not move the file but will place a 'shortcut' in the destination folder. In this way, the program can be loaded and run from the destination folder as well as from the source folder where the program file remains. Dragging any file into a folder on another disk drive will copy that file into that folder, whether it is a program or data file.

COPYING A FILE

Click the pointer on the desired file in the right panel so that the file is highlighted. Go to the 'Edit' menu and choose the 'Copy' option. The file remains in the source folder. Open the folder which is the intended destination for the file. Go to the 'Edit' menu and choose the 'Paste' option. The copy of the file now resides in the destination folder.

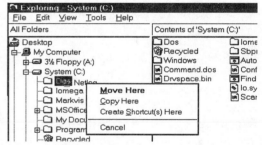

Alternatively, dragging the file with the right mouse button pressed will present the user with a menu of choices as shown. This provides for the copying or moving of a file into the destination folder. It can also create a 'shortcut' to a program file. A quick way to copy a file to a floppy disk is to highlight the file and click the right mouse button. A menu opens and clicking the 'Send To' option offers the user the opportunity to copy to the A: drive.

MOVING/COPYING GROUPS OF FILES

Files can be moved or copied as a group in a single operation. If the group of files are contiguous (next to each other) in the file list, click on the first file in the desired group, hold down the 'Shift' key and click on the last file in the group. This will highlight the entire group of files, which can then be moved or copied. If the desired files are not contiguous, hold down the Ctrl key while clicking on each desired file. An addition in Explorer is the ability to click and drag a rectangle around the files to be used. Any unwanted files within the rectangle can be deselected by holding down the Ctrl key and clicking on them.

COPYING/MOVING A FOLDER

The technique is identical to moving/copying files except the folder is highlighted instead of a file.

RENAMING A FILE

Highlight the desired file in the right panel. Choose the 'Rename' option from the 'File' menu. When prompted, type in new file name. The file remains in its current folder but is renamed.

RENAMING A FOLDER

Click the pointer on the desired file in the <u>right</u> panel, wait a moment (so that it is not perceived as a double-click) then click again. A box appears around the folder name and the name can be changed.

PRINTING A FILE

Highlight the desired file in the right panel. Choose the *'Print'* option from the *'File'* menu. The *'Print'* option will only appear on the *'File'* menu if the file is capable of being printed.

Searching for files

Windows Explorer has a tool to help find files on a disk.   The tool is accessed by selecting *'Files and Folders'* from the *'Find'* option of the of the *'Tools'* drop-down menu.

This allows comprehensive searches for files. The user decides:

- What drive(s) to search.
- The name of the wanted file (or group of files as described in *'wildcards'* below)
- If a particular word is being looked for (e.g. the file must contain the word *'camcorder'*)
- To look for files modified at certain times (e.g. during the last seven days, last four months, or between two specific dates).
- To look for files created at certain times.
- To look for files of a certain size (e.g. only find files larger than 100MB or files smaller than 5kB).

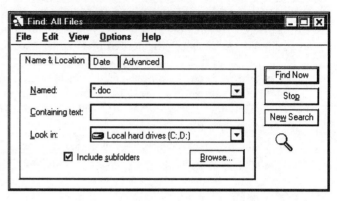

These options can be used on their own or together (e.g. find all document files on the 'C' drive created in the last month that are larger than 10MB and contain the word *'camcorder'*).

Wildcards

A name of a file can be entered in the *'Named'* dialog box above and the search will look for that specific filename.   Often, however, the user requires to find a list of files. This requires a method of handling files in groups, such that it only displays a desired subset (say all .DOC files) from a drive.

This facility is known as *'wildcards'*.   A wildcard is a character or set of characters incorporated into a search. Wildcards use the question mark (?) and asterisk (*) characters.

THE * WILDCARD

The * wildcard is used to replace a group of characters.   It can replace anything from zero to 255 characters.   The example in the illustration uses *.doc to search for Word document files.   Other examples are:

*.WAV	will display only those files that have the .WAV extension.
MUSIC.*	will display all files with the name MUSIC, regardless of the extension.
G*.*	will display all files that start with the letter 'G', regardless of the extension.
M*.WAV	will display all WAV files that start with the letter 'M'.

THE ? WILDCARD

The ? character is used to replace any single character in a filename.   Unlike the * character, the ? character does not represent a group of characters. If a number of characters are to be wildcarded, then there will have to be multiple occurrences of the ? character. The length and structure of files have to be known to use this option.   For example:

MEM???99.DAT

will find the files MEMJAN99.DAT, MEMFEB99.DAT, MEMAPR99.DAT, etc.   Any memos written before or after 1999 are ignored in the search.   The * wildcard option could not be used here, as MEM*99.DAT would display all files beginning with MEM and using the DAT extension - the 99 part of the command would be ignored, since the * wildcard takes precedence and replaces the last letters of the filename.

File attributes

Every file on a disk has a set of *'attributes'*.   These are flags that indicate the current status of the file (e.g. whether it is a hidden file or not).

The file's attributes are normally hidden from users but can be viewed in Windows Explorer by right-clicking on the file name and choosing *'Properties'* to display attribute information and other file information.

As the illustration shows, there are four attributes and their status can be altered using this window.

These attribute options are:

READ-ONLY

One of the attribute flags stores whether a file can be both read and written to (known as READ/WRITE) or can only be read (known as READ ONLY). If a file is read-only it can still be accessed by users and can appear in folder listings, can have its data extracted and used for calculations, can have its text printed out, etc. However, it cannot be deleted and cannot have its contents altered. Any attempt to delete a read-only file is disallowed and an error message will result. Similarly, any attempt to alter the contents of a file, such as a word-processed file, would be disallowed. This means that files can be set to prevent accidental erasure, by ticking the *'Read-only'* check box.

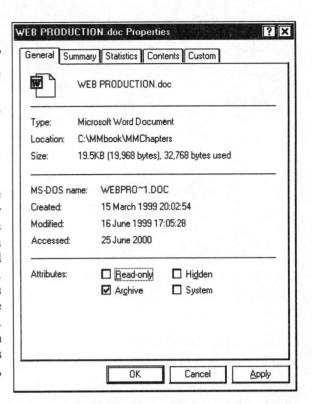

ARCHIVE

A file's archive bit can also be set by the user and is mostly used in conjunction with the BACKUP command, to control which files are selectively backed up. The BACKUP command can make a backup copy of all files or can be set to only make a copy of files that have not been previously backed up. The way that the BACKUP command knows whether a file has been previously backed up is via the archive flag. When a file is created or modified, its archive bit is set to on (indicating that it should be backed up). When a file is backed up, its archive bit is automatically set to off (indicating that it has been backed up). A future backup process will only select the files with archive bits set on and will ignore files with archive bits set off.

HIDDEN/SYSTEM

These flags hide the file from the normal view of the user and so it does not appear in folder listings, cannot be copied and cannot be deleted. The user should not normally adjust these flags.

Formatting a floppy disk

Floppy disks are normally supplied pre-formatted and ready to use. However, the user may decide to clean up a disk by formatting it. This removes all files and folders on the disk. The format utility is accessed by selecting the floppy disk drive in the Windows Explorer left panel and clicking the right mouse button. This produces a menu from which the *'Format'* option can be selected. A *'Format'* dialog box is opened as shown. This allows the user to set up the process to match the size of the floppy disk placed in the drive. The user can choose to give the disk a name by typing an entry in the data entry box provided. The *'Copy system files'* option will, if checked, create a disk that is capable of starting up the computer. These system files use up valuable disk space and the box should only be checked if a boot disk is required.

The dialog box provides for three types of formatting:

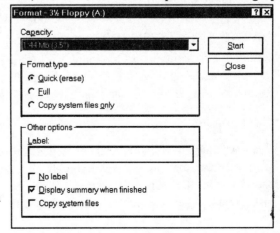

Type	Purpose
Quick (erase)	Can only be used with disks that were previously formatted. Saves time by not checking for errors on the disk surface.
Full	Checks for surface errors and marks them as bad sectors.
Copy System Files Only	Does not actually format the disk. It turns a working disk into a boot disk.

When the options are chosen, clicking the *'Start'* button begins the formatting.

Copying A Disk

This utility makes an exact replica of one disk on to another disk; any previous contents on the destination disk are lost. The utility is accessed by selecting the floppy disk drive in the Windows 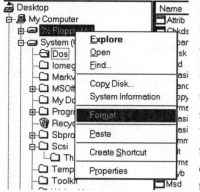 Explorer left panel and clicking the right mouse button. This produces a menu from which the *'Copy Disk'* option can be selected. A *'Copy Disk'* dialog box is opened as shown. If the machine has a single floppy drive, that drive letter will be highlighted in both windows. Where a machine has several floppy drives, they will appear in both windows and the user can choose the source and destination drives for the copy. Clicking the *'Start'* button initiates the copying process.

Where two different drives are involved, the user only has to wait until 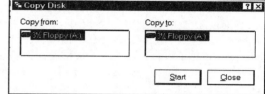 the process is completed. Where the user nominates the same drive as both the source and destination drives, the program prompts for the switching of the disks when required.

Using The Clipboard

A big advantage of using Windows is that information in one document can be copied or transferred into another document.   This could involve the copying or transferring of data from within the same application - e.g. copying or transferring a paragraph of text from one Word document to another Word Document.   It could also involve the copying of data from one application to a different application - e.g. copying a picture from a Word document into Paint Shop Pro for editing. The stages are:

- Move to the application that contains the desired information.
- Highlight the information to be copied/transferred.
- Use the *'Copy'* or *'Cut'* option to fetch the information from the source application. If the information is cut, it is removed from the source document; if it is copied, a replica of the information is used.   In both cases, the information is placed in a temporary store, known as the *'Clipboard'*.
- Move to the application that is the destination for the data.
- Move the cursor to the spot in the destination document where the information is to be placed.
- Use the *'Paste'* option to place the information into the document at the cursor position.

The contents of the Clipboard can be pasted as many times as required - into different parts of the same document or into different documents.   While the machine remains in Windows and no further information cuts are carried out, the Clipboard will store the information.   This is automatic, unless leaving an application results in a particularly large piece of information being left in the Clipboard. In that event, the user is asked to confirm that the information should be left in the Clipboard.

COPYING WINDOWS TO THE CLIPBOARD

It is also possible to copy the entire Windows screen, or any individual window on the screen, to the Clipboard.   The two options are:

- Pressing the *'Print Screen'* key while in Windows results in the entire monitor screen area being saved to the Clipboard.
- Pressing the *'Alt'* and *'PrintScreen'* keys results in the active window area being saved to the Clipboard.

SAVING THE CLIPBOARD

Windows also contains a Clipboard Viewer, allowing users to examine the current Clipboard contents. The current contents of the Clipboard can also be given a filename and saved as a file with a .CLP extension.   These files can be recalled to the Clipboard at any time for future pasting into documents.

Taskbar

When working in Windows, there will often be a number of applications running at the same time. Some of these may have been automatically loaded at the startup of Windows or they may have been loaded during the Windows session.   Each time an application is loaded, it is added as a button to the Taskbar and when the application is closed the button is removed from the Taskbar.   The Taskbar usually sits along the bottom of the screen and the buttons show every application that is currently open. Switching between applications only requires the appropriate button on the Taskbar to be clicked.

Windows 95 and later operating systems provide additional access, since pressing the Windows key or the CTRL and ESC keys brings up the *'Start'* menu, superimposed over the current application window.

Leaving Windows 95/98

Choosing the *'Shut Down'* option from the *'Start'* menu displays a dialog box that allows the user to leave Windows 95/98 in one of three ways, as shown.

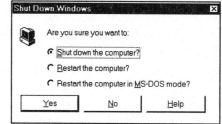

Option	Function
Shut down the computer	Saves data or changes to applications before closing down.
Restart the computer	Closes down then restarts so that any new settings may take effect.
Restart the computer in MS-DOS mode	Allows the user to have a prolonged DOS session.

Leaving Windows 2000

Choosing the *'Shut Down'* option from the *'Start'* menu displays a slightly different dialog box that allows the user to leave Windows 2000 in one of three ways, as before, only this time the choice is on a pull down combo box. In addition, pressing CTRL+ALT+DEL brings up the Windows 2000 task manager, which is based on the NT task manager and allows the shutdown options as well as the option to "kill" an individual task.

Configuring Windows

All Windows versions are multitasking systems. From version 95 onwards, Windows applications only load in components when they are required, resulting in less memory overheads and more applications effectively multitasking. They also support multithreading, which allows different parts of the same application to run at the same time. A user, for example, can carry on using a word processor while it carries out a spell check or a file search.

Installing/deleting software

During an upgrade, existing applications from the previous operating system may have been added to the *'Programs'* sub-menu of the *'Start'* menu. Most recent application packages will begin their installation procedures automatically upon insertion of the installation CD in the CD drive.

Windows 95/98 applications can also be added via the following steps:

1. Open the *'Start'* menu.
2. Choose the *'Settings'* option.
3. Choose the *'Control Panel'* option.
4. Choose the *'Add/Remove Programs'* option.
5. Choose the *'Install'* option from the *'Install/Uninstall'* option.

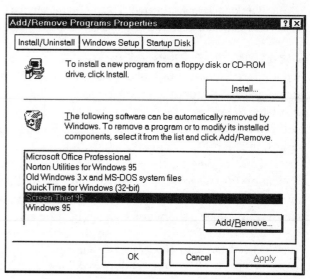

The Install Wizard then carries out the required installation activities. Windows 95/98 applications provide uninstall facilities and may be removed by highlighting the application name on the pick list and choosing the *'Remove'* option. Older Windows 3.1 applications can also be installed using the Wizard but since they have no built-in uninstall facilities, they cannot be automatically removed later.

An alternative method involves running the application's Setup program via the *'Run'* option on the *'Start'* menu. Windows 95 onwards intercepts Windows 3.1 applications installed with this method and converts some of the normal installation activities into its own format. For example, additions to Program Manager are converted into the later version's Start Menu shortcuts and INI entries are entered in the Registry.

Adding/Deleting Windows Components

Since the *'Typical Setup'* only installs a selection of the available Windows components, extra components can be added later, using the *'Windows Setup'* option within the *'Add/Remove Programs'* window. A list of linked components is displayed by category.

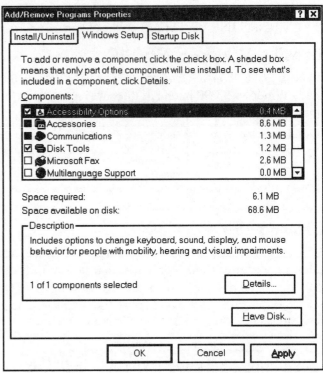

In the example shown, the *'Microsoft Fax'* box is unchecked indicating that it is not currently installed on the computer.

The *'Disk Tools'* box is checked indicating that all these components are installed.

The *'Accessories'* box is checked but is also greyed.   This indicates that only some of this category's components are installed.

Extra components can be installed by making its box active (i.e. a tick will appear in the box) and clicking the *'Apply'* button.   Similarly, components can be removed by making their boxes inactive (the tick is removed from the appropriate boxes) and clicking the *'Apply'* button.   Highlighting a category and clicking the *'Details'* button displays the list of components within that category.   This allows individual components to be selected or deselected.

Windows 95 categories cover:

> Accessibility, Accessories, Communications, Disk Tools, Fax, Multilingual Support,
> Multimedia, Microsoft Network, Windows Messaging.

In addition, Windows 98 includes the following the categories:

> Desktop Themes, Internet Tools, Online Services, System Tools, WebTV.

A text box explains the meaning of each category and each component as it is selected.

Creating Windows Shortcuts

When applications are installed on a Windows 95 or later system, they appear as an entry in one of the menus displayed from the *'Start'* button.   Windows 3.1 applications and DOS applications will install onto later Windows machines but will probably not appear in these menus.   In addition, it might be useful to allow a particular application to be called up from a variety of places such as several different folders, the Start Menu and even the Desktop.

These facilities, and others, are achieved with the use of *'shortcuts'* - small files that acts as links to an application file, wherever it is stored.   So, an application program file is stored once on the hard disk but can be pointed to by many different shortcut links in different areas of the menu system.

The steps to create a shortcut for an application are:

- Select the *'Taskbar'* option from the *'Settings'* menu.
- Select the *'Start Menu Programs'* option following by the *'Advanced'* option.
- From the folder structure displayed, highlight the folder where the shortcut is to appear.
- Choose the *'New'* option from the *'File'* menu.
- Select the *'Shortcut'* option and enter the file's name, including the path where it is stored. If this is not known, use the *'Browse'* option to locate the correct folder and filename.
- Select the *'Next'* option and enter the name of the program, as it is to appear on the screen menu.

DOCUMENT SHORTCUTS

If a machine regularly uses a few data files (e.g. a database, an accounts main sheet, or a graphics template) these files can also be pointed to by shortcuts.   The steps are identical to those above.   This feature allows a regularly used data file to rest on the StartUp menu and be used by clicking on - without first having to run the application package and search for the file.

The Startup Group

Windows 95 onwards contains a *'StartUp'* folder.   Any programs added to this folder are run automatically when Windows is started.   This allows utilities such as virus checkers and printer monitoring software to run in the background.   It also allows an application program to be run.   For instance, if a computer was used mainly for graphics editing, the machine could be configured to boot up straight into PhotoShop.   A shortcut that points to PhotoShop is placed in the StartUp folder and this will run PhotoShop.   If the user wishes to run another package, exiting PhotoShop takes the machine into the normal Windows interface.

Customising the Start Menu

When the computer boots into Windows 95 or later version of Windows, it displays a *'Start'* button on the bottom taskbar.   Clicking this button displays a menu similar to that on the right.   The bottom seven entries on the menu are the standard choices.   Where an entry has an arrowhead, clicking the entry produces another menu.

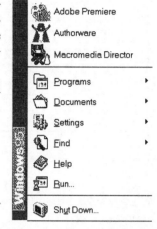

The top three entries have been added later by the user so that commonly used applications can be quickly accessed without hunting through sub-menus. This is achieved by:

- Choosing the *'Settings'* option from the *'Start'* menu.
- Choosing the *'Taskbar'* option from the *'Settings'* menu.
- Choosing the *'Start Menu Programs'* option from the *'Taskbar'* menu'.
- Choosing the *'Add'* option from the *'Start Menu Programs'* menu.
- Typing in the full name of the application file (i.e. drive, path and filename) or using the *'Browse'* utility to search for the file on the disk.
- A screen such as that below displays the user's disk structure and the wanted folder should be highlighted

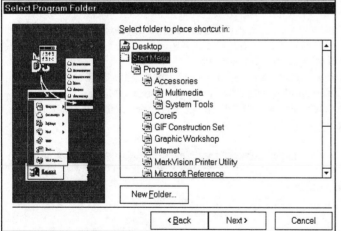

before clicking the *'Next'* button.   If required, a new folder can be created at this stage.

- If the *'Start Menu'* is chosen as the destination option, the application will appear on the Start Menu on bootup.   If the *'Programs'* option is chosen, the application will appear in the Programs menu.   If a sub-folder is chosen (e.g. *'Internet'* in the example shown) then the application can be run by opening that particular folder.
- When a folder has been selected, the application name as it will appear in the menu, can be entered.

An existing application can be deleted using the *'Remove'* option in the Taskbar properties menu.

Altering the Setup

The main configuration options as determined by the Windows Setup routine can be altered to suit personal choice or to accommodate changing hardware and software demands. This can range from adding and deleting programs as already described, through to altering the configuration of hardware such as keyboard, monitor, modem, printers, mouse and sound cards. It includes the system settings such as date and time, fonts to be used, user passwords, etc.   These alterations are made via the *'Control Panel'*, which is accessed as an option from the *'Settings'* option on the *'Start'* menu.   The diagram gives an example of the alterations that may be available and some of the most common alterations are described next.

Display

Choosing the *'Display'* option in the *'Control Panel'* offers four choices for altering display properties. The *'Settings'* menu, as shown in the diagram, alters the main display characteristics. These are:

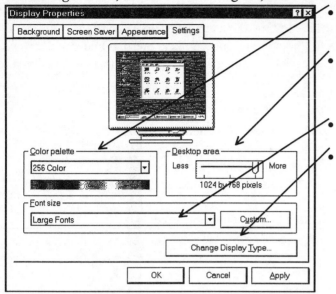

- Selecting the number of colours to be used (this depends on the maximum number of colours offered by the video card).
- Setting the screen resolution by clicking on the slider and moving it to the required setting (the maximum resolution depends on that supported by the screen and by the video card).
- Selecting large or small fonts for use with text to be displayed on the desktop.
- Selecting the video card and monitor to be used. This option allows both the video card type and the monitor type to be changed. In each case, a list of manufacturers' types is displayed and the desired choice can be highlighted and the *'OK'* button clicked. Where the desired type is not in the list (probably because it has been introduced since Windows 95/98 was written) the *'Have Disk'* option can be clicked. This allows the appropriate software to be loaded from the disk supplied by the manufacturer of the video card or monitor.

Windows 98 onwards has a different *'Settings'* layout with an *'Advanced'* button providing five sub-options:

General	Select large or small fonts for use with text to be displayed on the desktop.
Monitor	Select the driver for the monitor in use (might require the floppy disk that came with the monitor, if Windows does not have the correct one in its stored list).
Adapter	Select the driver for the graphics card in use (might require the floppy disk that came with the card, if Windows does not have the correct one in its stored list). Also allows user selection of the card's refresh rate.
Performance	Select the maximum rate at which the graphics card can handle data. This is also accessed through the *'Advanced Graphics Settings'* feature covered later.
Color Management	Select the colour profile that makes the monitor display colours exactly as they will be when they are used for colour prints.

The *'Appearance'* option allows the screen display to be set to the user's preferences. This includes the colours for Window text, message boxes, etc. Alternatively, the user can choose from a number of default colours schemes.

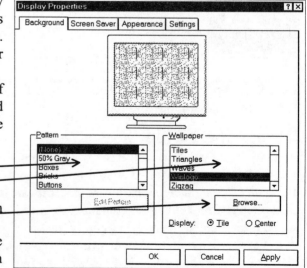

The *'Screen Saver'* option lists a selection of possible screen savers and these can be previewed before one is selected. A *'Wait'* text box sets the time delay before activating the screen saver.

The *'Background'* option allows the setting of:
- a background pattern.
- a background wallpaper.
- a background wallpaper using any other graphic on the hard disk, selected via the *'Browse'* option.

In addition, Windows 98 onwards allows the desktop to display an HTML page, which can be an existing document, or a user-created page.

The *'Display'* configuration within Windows 98 onwards provides two other tabs:

Effects	Selects the size of icons, smoothing of screen fonts, etc.
Web	Creates an *'Active Desktop'* where elements of the web are displayed on the desktop. These could be output from web channels, web site tickertapes, etc.

PERSONALISED BACKGROUNDS

The Windows background can use any .BMP file as wallpaper, such as those supplied as Windows background images, or those scanned or drawn by the user.   To maximise system resources, the wallpaper file used should be as small as possible.   A small graphic displayed using the *'Tiled'* option uses the same amount of system memory as one displayed with the *'Centred'* option, but much less than a large graphic displayed using the *'Centred'* option.

GRAPHICS ACCELERATION

The graphics card has to be able to keep up with the rate at which graphics data is being sent to it.   As of version 95, Windows provides control over the rate of sending data to the graphics card.   This is known as the *'Advanced Graphics Settings'* feature and is accessed by clicking on *'Control Panel'* followed by clicking the *'System'*, *'Performance'* and *'Graphics'* buttons.   Four settings are available. The lowest setting, called *'None'*, ignores the graphics card's drawing functions and uses Windows own drawing functions.   The highest setting, called *'Full'*, assumes that the system works normally and sends data at the highest rate.   The intermediate settings provide more limited card functions.

'95 Mouse Customisation

From the *'Mouse'* option in *'Control Panel'*, the response of the mouse can be altered as shown.

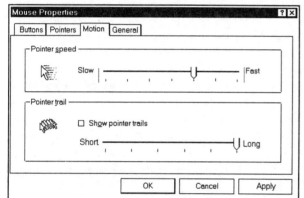

The *'Motion'* sub-menu provides for:

- dragging a slider control to set the speed at which the pointer moves across the screen.
- dragging a slider control to set the length of trails from the moving pointer. A mouse used with an LCD screen or large screen monitor is made more visible if the movement of the pointer leaves a trail behind it, the trail rapidly fading away. The machine can have mouse trails enabled or disabled by clicking the box to contain a check or be empty respectively.

The *'Buttons'* sub-menu sets up the mouse for left or right-handed use.   If the user of a machine is left-handed, the mouse is manipulated by the fingers of that user's left hand. The role of the mouse buttons can be reversed, so that the left button carries out the functions of the right button and vice versa, to make for more natural use of the mouse.

The *'Double Click Speed'* is determined by dragging the slider control to the desired setting.   There is a test box below the speed bar.

The *'Pointers'* sub-menu offers choices on the shape of the mouse cursor or pointer during operations such as *'Busy'* or *'Select'*.

The *'General'* sub-menu allows the selection of the mouse type currently in use. Most makes of mouse are Microsoft compatible but other common mouse drivers can be chosen from a pick list.

'98 Mouse Customisation

The Windows 98 Mouse Properties dialog offers six categories of settings:

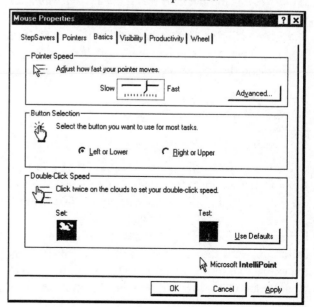

Basics	Sets the speed at which the pointer moves across the screen and the double-click speed.
Pointers	Sets the shape of the mouse cursor or pointer during various operations.
Productivity	Enables an odometer to count the miles/km that the mouse travels.
Visibility	Displays mouse pointer trails.
StepSavers	Replaces the double-click with a single-click.
Wheel	Assigns the wheel button on an Intellimouse to equate to a double click, fetch Help, run Explorer, etc.

Keyboard customisation

If the *'Keyboard'* option is chosen from the *'Control Panel'*, the response of the keyboard can be altered via the options shown.   The *'Language'* sub-menu, as shown, provides for:

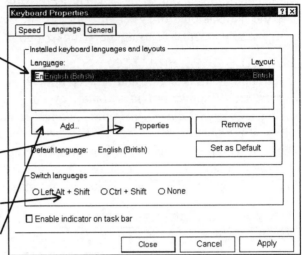

- Determining the keyboard layout. Different countries place different characters and symbols on the keycaps.   To ensure that key presses correspond to the language of the country in which it used, the keyboard layout has to be configured in Windows. In the United Kingdom, that would mean choosing an English (British) setting as opposed to the English (American) setting, which places certain symbols on the keyboard in a different layout from British users.
- Determining the keyboard variations within certain counties.   This does not apply to Britain and the standard *'British'* option would be chosen.
- Setting up hot-key switching between languages, where the same machine is used in a multi-lingual environment.   The *'Add'* option allows extra keyboard options to be added to the selection list.

The *'Speed'* sub-menu provides for:

- Setting the *'Repeat Delay'*.   A slider control determines how long a key has to be depressed before it begins to auto-repeat the character; dragging the slider to a faster or slower setting along a speed bar sets the value.
- Setting the *'Repeat Rate'*.   This determines the speed at which the key will auto-repeat the character.   This setting is also achieved by dragging the slider to a faster or slower setting along a bar.   Below the speed bar there is a test box to test the settings, before exiting the window by clicking on the *'OK'* button.
- Setting the *'Cursor Blink Rate'*.   This determines the cursor's flash speed and is also set by dragging a slider.

The *'General'* sub-menu provides for matching the software to the physical keyboard in use. Most keyboards are covered by the *'Standard 101 or 102 key or Microsoft Natural Keyboard'* category, but the option can be changed by clicking the *'Change'* option and selecting the keyboard type currently in use.

SETTING THE DATE AND TIME

The computer's real-time clock can be set within Windows. It has exactly the same effect as using the DATE and TIME commands under DOS.   The date and time settings within *'Regional Settings'* only control the way they are displayed; they do not alter the computer's internal clock.   This facility is called up via the *'Date/Time'* option in *'Control Panel'*.

CD AUTOPLAY

From version 95 onwards, Windows is able to automatically play CDs when they are inserted into the CD-ROM drive. These can be normal audio CDs or the growing number of applications (including the Windows installation CD) that have an *'autorun.inf'* file that commences the running of the application.

This facility can be enabled and disabled through the *'Start/Settings/Control Panel/System/Device Manager'*.   The CD should be highlighted from the list of devices and the *'Properties'* and *'Settings'* options selected.   Ticking the *'Auto Insert Notification'* box allows CDs to be automatically detected. Unchecking the box means that the CD's contents are viewed and run in the same way as any disk drive.

AUDIO CDs

The default situation in Windows is that Audio CDs are automatically played by the CDPLAYER.EXE program.

This can be altered using the *'View'* option within Explorer. Choose the *'View'* then *'File Types'* options to display a list of file types.   Highlight *'Audio CD'* from the list and click the *'Edit'* button.   The new panel displayed includes an *'Action'* box that shows a *'play'* option.   Highlight the *'play'* option and click the *'Edit'* button.   This will display the following command line:

```
cdplayer.exe /play
```

Deleting the '/play' from the line results in the audio CD being detected and the CD player software being called up - but the music will not begin until the user presses the 'play' button on the player. Deleting the entire line results in audio CDs not being detected. If the shift key is held down while an audio CD or an autoplay CD is inserted into the CD-ROM drive, then the disk will not automatically play.

Windows Fonts

Fonts are collections of alphabetic, numeric, punctuation and symbol characters as seen on the computer monitor or printed to paper. Fonts have three characteristics:

TYPE FACE -   the actual *shape* of the characters, such as Arial (a sans serif face i.e. plain outline with no feet or twirls), Times Roman (a serifed face used in many publications) and Gothic.

TYPE SIZE -   the actual *height* of the characters as measured in points, there being 72 points to an inch.   A 36-point headline, then, is half an inch high.

TYPE STYLE -   such as bold, italics or underlined.

In addition, Windows handles fonts in two ways:

BITMAP

A bitmap font holds an actual picture of each character, composed of a collection of pixels.   This means that each point size must either have a different bitmap or an existing bitmap has to be scaled up or down.   In addition, each type style has to be independently stored.   So, there is a bitmap for the normal version, the bold version, the italicised version and the underlined version - not to mention the bold underlined, etc.   Bitmap fonts occupy lots of disk space, particularly for the larger point sizes. They are faster than True Type since the image can be dumped to the printer without any translation.

TRUE TYPE

True Type fonts do not store an exact bitmap picture of every typeface, size and style.   Instead, it stores a <u>description</u> of a typeface.   This description is stored as geometric mathematical formulae that outline the shape of the various parts of the character in normal, bold, italic and bold italic modes. When an application chooses to use a particular font, the font description is fetched and scaled to the required type size.   Windows then generates a bitmap of the font for use with the screen or printer. This process is known as *'rasterising'*. A slight manipulation of the factors in the formulae allows the faces to be scaled to any size.

This has two distinct advantages:

- The computer need only store the set of four descriptions for each typeface, compared to a set for every font size with bitmaps.
- The mathematical formulae of true type fonts maintain smooth curves even with large type sizes, whereas bitmaps tend to become very 'blocky' and ugly at larger sizes.

SETTING UP FONTS

The management of fonts is carried out from the *'Fonts'* option in the *'Control Panel'*.   This displays a list of the fonts that are already installed in Windows. These are the fonts that are available within Windows applications such as Word, Excel, etc.

The *'File'* sub-menu allows:

- The addition of new fonts via the *'Install New Font'* option on the *'File'* menu.   This opens an *'Add Fonts'* window where the location of the new font can be given and the name of the font highlighted before clicking the *'OK'* button. The location can be a floppy disk and a box can be checked to copy the font(s) from the original location into the Windows fonts folder.

- The deletion of existing fonts from the system.   Highlight the font from the pick list and choose the *'Delete'* option from the *'File'* menu.

Font Name	Filename	Size
Aardvark Bold	aardvrkb.ttf	27K
Adelaide	adelaidn.ttf	36K
Alefbet	alefbetn.ttf	20K
Algerian	Alger.ttf	68K
Algiers	algiersn.ttf	83K
Arabia	arabian.ttf	47K
Architecture	architen.ttf	33K
Arial	ARIAL.TTF	65K
Arial Black	Ariblk.ttf	47K
Arial Bold	ARIALBD.TTF	65K
Arial Bold Italic	ARIALBI.TTF	71K
Arial Italic	ARIALI.TTF	61K
Arial Narrow	Arialn.ttf	61K

336 font(s)

MAINTAINING FONTS

Over a period of time, the number of fonts will grow as many applications add their own fonts into Windows.   In many cases, the new fonts look very similar to existing fonts. As a result, no new facilities are added and yet the hard disk - and Windows' fonts menus - becomes rapidly expanded.

The following fonts should always remain on the computer, as they are the standard Windows set and are used by many application packages and by Windows itself:

Font Name	Example
Arial	I am Arial
Courier New	I am Courier New
Symbol	α σ δ φ γ η φ κ λ
Times New Roman	I am Times New Roman
Wingdings	☞ • ♎ ⚐ ♑ ♒ ♌ &

In addition, Microsoft uses fonts whose names start with MS - e.g. MS San Serif - for screen writing and these should also remain in Windows.

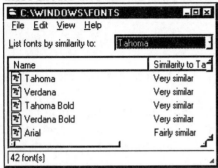

In a very full system, there may be many fonts that are almost identical.   This can be checked by choosing the *'List Fonts by Similarity'* option in the *'View'* menu of the *'Fonts'* with *'Control Panel'*.

It will produce a screen similar to that shown.   In the example it can be seen that the Verdana and Tahoma fonts are very similar, while the Arial font is only fairly similar to Tahoma.

An inspection of these lists allows decisions to be made on which fonts are almost duplicates and can be removed from the system.

Printers

Printer options can be set up using the *'Printers'* option from the *'Settings'* option in the *'Start'* menu.   This produces the screen shown on the right. Clicking the *'Add Printer'* icon runs the Add Printer Wizard which steps the user through the installation options.

Clicking on a particular printer icon produces a status window for that printer. Clicking the *'Properties'* option in the *'Printer'* menu produces the screen shown on the right.   The *'General'* sub-menu allows a test page to be printed to check that the printer is functioning properly.

The *'Details'* sub-menu offers the following:

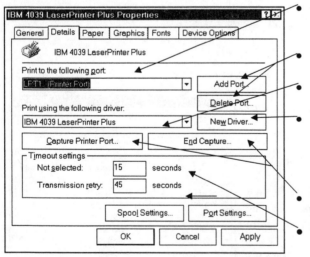

- Set the printer port to be used for the printer connection.   The pick list displays the possible ports to choose from (e.g. LPT1, LPT2, COM1, and COM2).
- This list can be altered by adding extra ports or deleting existing ports.
- Set the printer driver to be used with the printer.   The pick list displays any drivers that are already installed.
- New drivers can be installed by clicking the *'New Driver'* button.   This displays a pick list of all available Windows printer drivers. If the required driver is not in the list but is supplied with a printer, then it is installed by choosing the *'Have Disk'* option.
- Direct printing to a remote printer on the network or to the local printer attached to the computer.
- Set the amounts of time that will expire before a *'Not Selected'* message is displayed or before attempting to re-send a document to the printer.

- The *'Spool Settings'* button opens a sub-menu to configure print spooling arrangements.   Windows 95/98 speeds up operations by creating a temporary file for a file that is to be printed.   The temporary file provides the source for the printer allowing printing in the *'background'* - the user can carry on with other processing.   There are options to commence printing as soon as the first page of a document is spooled or after the entire document is spooled.   The first option is faster but the second option provides smoother background printing.   The sub-menu also provides selection of two data formats for the spool file.   EMF is the normal choice with RAW being used for Postscript printers.   A final option allows printers that have bi-directional ports to be configured.
- The *'Port Settings'* button opens a sub-menu that allows for the spooling of MS-DOS print jobs.

The *'Paper'* sub-menu offers:

- Setting the paper size to be used in the printer.
- Setting printing to portrait or landscape mode.
- Setting the way paper is handled (e.g. hand-fed single sheets or automatically from paper trays).
- Setting the number of copies that are to be printed.
- Determining whether to print in duplex mode (i.e. on both sides of the paper); only available if the printer is a duplex machine.

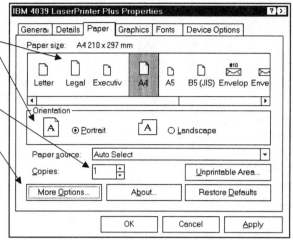

The *'Graphics'* sub-menu sets the printing resolution in dots-per-inch (if the printer supports high resolutions, the graphics are clearer), the method of dithering to print colour graphics as greyscales and the intensity of shading to be used.

The *'Fonts'* sub-menu allows printers that have add-on fonts cartridges to be recognised. It also allows True Type fonts to be downloaded as bitmap soft fonts or to be printed as graphics; the latter option is useful where a document uses many typefaces.

The *'Device Options'* sub-menu allows Windows 95 onwards to recognise extra memory that has been added into a printer. It also allows control over the printer memory usage so that large files do not cause the printer to run out of memory.

DEFAULT PRINTER

The default printer is the one that is used when a job is printed without first specifically mentioning which printer should be used. It follows that the default printer should be the one that is mostly commonly used. If there is only one installed printer then it is automatically the default printer. The default printer choice is set using the *'Set as Default'* option within the *'Printers'* sub-menu of the *'Settings'* option in the *'Start'* menu.

VOLUME CONTROL

Windows, from version 95 onwards, provides control over the audio volume from the desktop. The following steps install this facility to the desktop:

- From the *'Start'* button choose the *'Settings'*, *'Control Panel'* and *'Multimedia'* options.
- Check the box marked *'Show volume control in the taskbar'*.

A loudspeaker icon is added to the Windows taskbar.

Clicking on this icon displays a mouse-controlled volume control slider that adjusts the audio volume. Checking the *'Mute'* box completely disables all audio output.

This effectively provides a 'master' volume control and its settings affect the output of all audio devices. If the volume is set low then the audio outputs of the microphone, line-in (e.g. tape deck) or MIDI device are all reduced. If the *'Mute'* box is checked, all devices are silenced.

However, there are times when a more detailed control over the audio levels of individual audio sources is required. For example, it may be necessary to disable a microphone input when the sound card is recording from a tape deck, as the sound from the loudspeaker may be picked up by the microphone

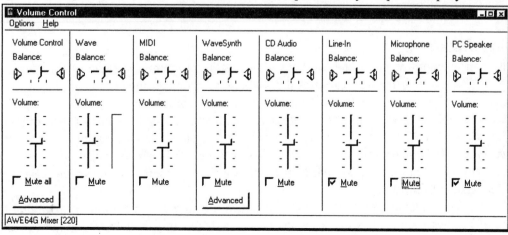

causing 'howling'.   Alternatively, if both the microphone and tape deck sources are required, it may be necessary to mute the loudspeaker.

Windows, from 95 onwards, provides a facility for mixing the volume levels of a range of audio input devices. From the *'Start'* button, choose the *'Programs'*, *'Accessories'*, *'Multimedia'* (or the *'Entertainment'* option in Windows 98/2000) and finally *'Volume Control'* options.

Alternatively, double click the loudspeaker icon on the taskbar.   This displays the panel shown on the previous page.   Each device can be individually muted or have its volume level set.   This proves useful when creating multimedia productions and when working with audio recordings.

File associations

Users can use applications to work on data in two ways:

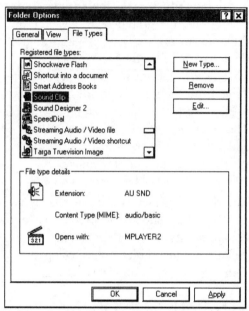

1. Open the application (e.g. word processor, paint program, etc) and, once in the application, open the file to be worked on (e.g. letter, graphics file, etc).
2. Find a file within Windows Explorer and double-click on it. This opens the application, followed by opening the file.

The second method makes use of *'file associations'*.   A file's extension is linked to a corresponding application.   As new applications are added to the computer, the file extensions used by the new application is added to the database of associations.

Where more than one application can process a file with a particular extension, only one application can be the default association - i.e. the one activated when the file is double-clicked in Explorer.   Of course, this does not prevent the other application processing the file using method 1 above.

These default associations can be viewed and altered within Windows Explorer by pulling down the *'View'* menu.

In Windows 95, the *'Options'* choice and in Windows 98, the *'Folder Options'* choice both provide a *'File Types'* tab as shown in the example.   In the example, files with the *'AU'* and *'SND'* extension are played using the *'MPLAYER2'* application.

The *'Edit'* option allows the default application to be altered.

Recycle Bin

The Recycle Bin is a useful addition to Windows 95 and later versions but it can easily clog hard disk space with old files if not controlled.   The space allocated to the Recycle Bin can be individually set for each disk drive, or a maximum figure can be specified for all drives.   A third option is not to use the Recycle Bin and to lose all files on deletion.

The steps to optimise the Recycle Bin allocations are:

- Right-click on the Recycle Bin icon or folder in the Explorer listing.
- Choose the *'Use one setting for all drives'* option.
- Move the slider to the required allocation (usually around 5%).

Managing Memory

A computer can use both memory and the hard disk to store programs, or parts of programs, that are running.   The chapter on technology explains that a chunk of computer memory is used as a *'disk cache'* (a temporary store) to speed up data transfers from the disk to the processor.

Conversely, when the computer runs out of memory, it can temporarily store bits of the program on the hard disk (an area known as *'virtual memory'*).   Although this slows down programs, it allows them to carry on working.   So, large data files benefit from disk caching, while large applications or multi-tasking make use of virtual memory.   The system has to balance these resources to make the best use of the computer's time and resources.

Windows 95/98 automatically grabs all available physical memory in the computer, intending to use it for a range of utilities such as disk cache, fonts, etc.   This memory is held by Windows 95/98 even when it is not in use. So, even a newly switched on machine will show that all the available memory is allocated. As the program runs, Windows dynamically shares the memory between the system's resources and the user's applications. This does not always work out very efficiently and can leave a user's application being swapped to the *'virtual memory'* on the disk drive, while the memory set aside for disk caching is not being fully utilised.

Windows automatically detects the amount of memory available for disk caching and sizes the cache to that value. However, as the program tasks and sub-tasks are regularly being switched in and out of memory, the constant resizing of the cache leads to extra processing as everything is moved around in the memory to fit the new size. The wasted processing time can be minimised by setting the maximum and minimum values of the disk cache. The following lines can be added to the SYSTEM.INI file:

```
[vcache]
MinFileCache =2048
MaxFileCache=8192
```

The maximum value depends upon the actual amount of physical memory present. About half the actual memory is a reasonable figure for the setting. These settings speed up normal processing as more of the application is in memory. Where users are carrying out heavy database, video or imaging work, the settings may be increased to reflect the greater reliance on sustained data throughput.

Virtual Memory

Windows, from version 95 onwards, detects how much disk space is available for virtual memory and

automatically resizes the virtual memory amount when required. Windows is often left to organise its own management but user configuration can be achieved via the *'System'* icon in *'Control Panel'*. Clicking the *'Performance'* option followed by the *'Virtual Memory'* option reveals dialogue boxes to set the drive to be used along with minimum and maximum sizes.

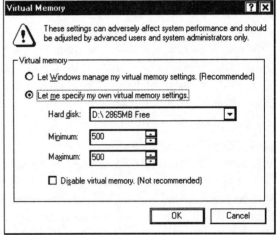

Setting a high value minimises the number of times that the area will have to be resized. If the minimum value is set to the same value as the maximum value, the swap file size remains constant and saves Windows from managing the file.

Before creating a swap file, ensure that the disk is defragmented and the surface in checked with ScanDisk. Even better, create a separate partition for the swap file. Where there is more than one disk drive in the computer, the drive with the fastest access times and the highest data rate should be used for the swap file. This will improve overall performance

NOTE:

There is a balance between disk cache size, swap file size and performance. If the disk cache minimum size is too large, there is not sufficient physical memory for processing and more is saved to slower virtual memory. If the maximum value is too small, handling of large files is slowed down. These problems mainly affect computers with small RAM sizes. The larger the amount of memory installed, the less the problems, and the smaller the size of the swap file needed.

System Monitor

Windows 95/98 provides comprehensive reporting on the demands of the system and pinpointing system bottlenecks. The *'System Monitor'* and is accessed from the *'System Tools'* menu of the *'Accessories'* option within the *'Programs'* option. If it is not present in the System Tools menu, use the *Settings/ Control Panel/Add*

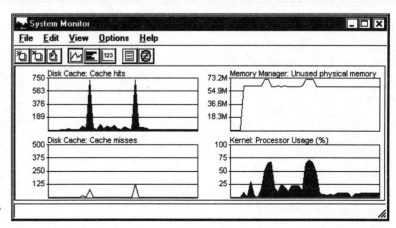

Programs/ Windows Setup/Accessories buttons to install this feature.   The Windows 95/98 installation CD may be required for this.

The '*Edit*' pull-down menu offers options to add, delete and modify the items that appear in the report window.   The example shows a Pentium III 500MHz computer running a movie file while carrying out various file and other activities.   The Pentium III chip can easily handle the video processing, never exceeding 75% CPU usage.   The disk caching is working well, with a large amount of cache hits, and the amount of available main memory is large enough to avoid much disk swapping.   In addition, a range of other activities, such as swap file information, disk cache size and free memory can be monitored.   Windows 2000 provides an even wider range of monitoring options.

Additional Windows 98 facilities
The following facilities are supplied with Windows 98 and are not available in Windows 95.

DVD
Windows 98 has a built-in DVD software player.   This is reached through the '*Programs*', '*Entertainment*' and '*DVD Player*' options from the '*Start*' button.   DVD players with hardware decoders will also offer their own interface.

MAGNIFIER
This utility opens an extra screen window where the main screen contents are magnified around the area pointed to by the mouse cursor.   This is primarily aimed at visually impaired but is also useful for viewing graphics or fine detail in a large spreadsheet, etc.
This utility can be added by choosing the '*Settings*', '*Control Panel*', '*Add/Remove Programs*', '*Windows Setup*', '*Accessibility*' and '*Accessibility Tools*' options from the '*Start*' button.
The utility is invoked using '*Programs*', '*Accessories*', '*Accessibility*' and '*Magnifier*' options from the '*Start*' button.   The user can control the amount of screen space devoted to the magnified view and can set the degree of magnification.

MULTIPLE MONITORS
Windows 98 can handle up to eight PCI graphics cards and eight monitors.   In practice, motherboards will not have that many spare PCI slots.   However, setting up a second monitor is an easy task.   First, a second graphic card is installed and a monitor attached (see the chapter on Upgrading).
When the computer is switched back on, the '*Settings*', '*Control Panel*', '*Display*', and '*Settings*' options are chosen from the '*Start*' button.   This will open a window like the one shown earlier in the chapter (see 'Display').   However, the window will display two monitor icons instead of the normal single icon.
Each icon will have a number, with monitor 1 being the one that will display the right side of the desktop and monitor 2 displaying the left side.   The icons can be moved around with the mouse to alter the arrangement. Thus, monitor 2 can be switched to display the right side.   If desired, the icons can even be positioned vertically if monitors are to be stacked.   When the Monitor 2 icon is positioned, it should be clicked to highlight it, followed by clicking the '*Extend my Windows desktop onto this monitor*' box. Once set up, objects can be dragged from the main screen to the secondary screen.
For example, if Monitor 2 is the one on the right, dragging an object off the right hand side of Monitor 1 places the object into the secondary monitor.

Multimedia Design

The message - not the medium

Before venturing into the detailed requirements for designing multimedia projects, the starting point is a recognition that *'Content is King'*.   Projects are undertaken to satisfy a particular educational, promotional or leisure need.   The design and content support this primary need.   Poorly designed and badly laid out content will spoil an otherwise worthy project.   On the other hand, clever and innovative use of graphics, video, etc will not save a project whose content was flawed from the start.

This chapter covers all design aspects - for kiosks, CDs, web sites, etc.   In this chapter, the overall work is termed the *'project'* and this is intended to cover all distribution formats.   Similarly, all independent user views are termed *'screens'*.   When the chapter is being read with a view to creating web content, the *'screen'* refers to an individual web page and the *'project'* refers to the collection of pages that make up the web site.   The chapters on web site creation look at the additional special factors that apply to design for that medium.   The term *'home screen'* is used to describe the main screen of any project.

The best projects are *'user-centred'*.   That means that the project, from beginning to end, is focussed on the needs of the end users.   Matters such as screen design and layout are secondary to making the project easy to use, easy to understand and enjoyable.   It is a case of function over form.

Design is . . . what works

There are many approaches to project design and layout.   There are many heavy books that examine the human mind in detail and advise on design approaches.   Their work is very important and has produced studies on how humans learn and interact with their environment.   The lessons for designers are covered in the concepts of HCI (Human-Computer Interaction) and the many observations are embodied in all design guides.   Ultimately, designers are concerned with results - design is what works.   That is not to say that extremely valuable lessons cannot be learned from the theoretical work and practical examples of others. It's just that there are added ingredients, such as flair and imagination, which use these principles and practices to better effect than using a simple checklist approach to design.
The bottom line is that design is what is effective, efficient, easy to use, and solves problems.

An effective project is the result of effective design and this is characterised by two factors.
- Content   - what the project will contain and how it its pitched.
- Presentation   - how the contents will be displayed.
These headings over-simplify the process and both are looked at separately in this chapter.

Overview of projects

Good projects don't just 'grow' at the keyboard. They are planned. The larger the project, the more people and resources are involved in its creation and more planning and co-ordination is required. The aim is to:
- Meet schedules
- Manage complexity
- Conform to specs
- Maintain quality
- Control costs

As the simple diagram shows, there are three major competing factors in a project.   These are the time, the resources (ultimately the budget) and quality. Throughout the creation of the project, these three factors have to be kept in balance. For example, the quality can be increased by spending more time and using up more resources, but there are always budget restraints.
Alternatively, it is always possible to save on the budget by reducing time at the expense of quality, but the final product may not reach an acceptable standard.
The aim is to meet the client's expectations in time, on budget and at the required quality. This requires the construction of detailed plans, as explained next.

Stages in a multimedia project

The main steps in designing projects for multimedia are similar to those for any software project, although there are extra considerations.

The main phases are:

Project brief
This states the main aims of the project and is supplied by the organisation commissioning the work.

Requirements analysis
This clarifies the brief and provides the specification of the project requirements.

Create/test prototype
This is a skeletal version of the project and is used to clear up any misunderstandings regarding their needs.   The lessons from this stage are used to create the requirements specification.

Requirements specification
This states the project's technical requirements, detailed aims, navigation requirements, and screen layout specifications.

Design document
This provides a detailed overview, showing all navigational paths and sketches of screen content (showing media components, user interactions and screen layout).   This should also include the creation of a storyboard and navigation maps.

Project plan
This states the financial and operational tasks in producing the project. It allocates individual responsibilities and creates the running order for events (e.g. shooting lists). Often a Gantt chart is used to plan the sequence of activities and milestones (dates for the completion of significant stages).

Test document
This includes the test specification, which in turn includes tests for usability and functionality, fitness for purpose and consistency. After testing, the test results are added, for comparison with the expected results.

Implementation
This is the main phase of the project, covering the capture/creation of material and integration into a complete piece of work.

Project testing
This checks the project, to ensure that it passes all the tests specified in the test document.

Development report
This records the approach taken to the project, any assumptions made, any problems encountered, and any suggestions for future improvements.

Project assessment
This is a critical analysis of the project, noting its strengths and weaknesses and making comparisons between it and any other similar applications.

Development Techniques

Just as in developing any software products, there are many techniques that can be used to assist in the development of multimedia projects. Many of the experiences of software designers and programmers are used in creating robust and cost-efficient projects.

Waterfall method

This is a tried and tested technique in software development.   It outlines the main stages of the development process.

Progress to the next stage is only permitted when the current stage is satisfactorily completed.

As the diagram shows, it is usually an iterative process. That means that some of the stages may have to be repeated. Any mistakes or inadequacies in the requirements stage, for example, may not become apparent until the unit testing stage.   This would require modifications to the original requirements specification, which in turn leads to design changes that need to be implemented and tested yet again.   The thick lines show the main flow, while the thinner lines indicate iterative steps. Experience shows that the stages frequently overlap, causing extra iterations and complicating the planning and documenting process.

Exploratory programming

This is similar to the way that many individual users develop projects. An outline specification is used as a guide to the implementation of the project. When the project is completed, it is tested and any flaws or inadequacies are addressed at that stage. This usually requires much iteration, as there are often many alterations required.

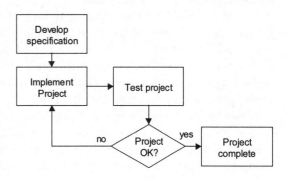

In a commercial environment, it is really only suitable for small projects or for projects where it is difficult to define the specification requirement in detail. It also requires software that supports rapid system alterations.

Re-usable components

This technique builds projects from modules and components that have already been designed - for stock use or more usually for previous projects. The aim is to use a 'building block' approach to a project, selecting the required components and making the minimum of alterations.

Clearly, this is of limited use, as most projects are quite different from each other. Of course, there are exceptions; such as creating a series of tutorials that all use the same basic interface and navigation. An example might be a set of CDs covering car maintenance. Although each CD will cover a different vehicle, all projects will have the same basic structure and menus (e.g. they will all have sections on *'changing spark plugs'* or *'changing tyres'*). A new CD can be quickly assembled from the existing material, with changes to the photographs, diagrams and text where appropriate.

Prototyping

Prototyping is an excellent, although time-consuming, way to develop an understanding and a client agreement on a project. A prototype is a partial implementation of a project, showing the key structural and layout details. It would have the structure, navigational controls and front end implemented. In addition, one or two other sections may be completed, to show how the finished project would look. The prototype is shown to the client and used as a means of sharpening up the definition of their needs. Misunderstandings and extra features can be picked up and settled at this stage, before a great deal of expensive and possibly wasted effort has been expended.

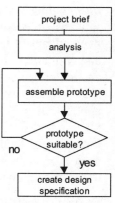

Video production analogy

Some approaches are based on techniques used for video production and the terms used are those expected in film studios.

This includes concepts such as:

'the pitch'	The basic summary of the idea, production costs and timescales are used to attract financial support/approval for the project.
'the proposal'	A production overview including themes, elements or characters, and activities.
'the treatment'	The development of the proposal to include style and plot development.
'the script'	The comprehensive guide to the entire production. This will include the breakdown of the script into sub-sections, which include all details such as text content and camera angles.
'the storyboard'	The set of sketches and notes that shows the location and movement of elements within each scene (see later).

Iterative methods

Many of the above models are based on iteration, with earlier stages being returned to so that changes and additions can be made. Although this is regarded as the best approach in maximising a project's final effectiveness, it can also produce extra problems. In particular, where the client is involved in the continued evaluation and testing process, it provides endless opportunities for the client to redefine needs and query previous decisions. While a mutually agreed comprehensive project specification and design document will minimise disputes and clarify who is financially responsible for the costs of the changes, it will still introduce delays in completing the final project.

Requirements analysis

It is vital that a clear understanding of the project is achieved before any other work is undertaken. This prevents many wasted hours and potential disputes with the client commissioning the project. The client will provide a project brief, which is a short summary of the aims of the project. The task of systems analysis is to convert the project brief into a project plan that can be implemented.

A thorough set of discussions clarifies the detailed aims of the project. This would include issues such as the general content (e.g. education, training, entertainment), the target audience (the likely age, sex, previous knowledge/experience of those using the multimedia) and the mood (serious, light-hearted).

It may also involve market research, to confirm that the project assumptions are correct (e.g. is there really a market for a Spice Girls CD game any more? Just how many small companies would be prepared to buy an interactive tutorial on completing VAT returns? etc.). These discussions and investigations lead to the production of a project specification.

The aim of the analysis phase is to produce precise statements, which can act as a checklist in the later testing phase. Example statements might be that all menus should in a bottom panel, or that every screen should provide *'Help'* and *'Exit'* options.

Requirements Specification

This document covers the educational requirements and technical requirements and should be as factual as possible. Refer to the following sections on *'Design principles'* and *'Design requirements'* for further details. The main elements in the requirements specification are:

Aim

This specifies the educational/entertainment requirements of the project and identifies the target audience. It also lists the assumptions of the target audience. For example, a tutorial on *'computers for beginners'* makes different assumptions from a tutorial on *'advanced networking techniques'*. In the first case, the users may not even know how to use mouse, while the other set of users will understand even advanced terminology used in the text. The project has to take into account the likely abilities and limitations of the users, understanding what they will want to do and what problems they may encounter using the package.

This section may also detail any educational requirements and tools. For example, a teaching application may begin by listing the expected learning outcomes from using the package and may include self-test questions at the end of each section. The package may supplement the learning of those doing badly in the self-assessments by supplying additional material and references for the subject areas in which the user scored less well. Educational packages may also include a glossary of terms or explanations of acronyms.

Technical requirements

This specifies all hardware requirements, including the specification of the computer and all peripherals. This is dependent upon the delivery method (CD, web, intranet, or kiosk). For example, projects designed for standalone kiosks can have a specific set of requirements- such as the need for a touch screen or large screen monitor. Other possible factors in the requirements list are particular video/audio CODECs or add-ons (e.g. QuickTime), specialist drivers, a sound card, and a particular amount of memory or hard disk space. The specification may also lay down performance requirements such as the speed of computer, the screen resolution, the colour depth and frame handling rates of graphics cards, or the lowest acceptable version of the operating system.

Navigation requirements

This specifies the general interface look (e.g. web-style, windows-style, image maps, etc.) It also details the specific navigational requirements of the project (see the later section on this topic).

Screen layout specification

This specifies the position of all the project's main elements and may include menus, buttons, active screen areas, video display areas, etc.

Some of these sections are inter-related. For example, if the technical requirements specify the use of a touch screen, then the screen layout specification will have to reflect this by stating that menu buttons have to be spaced slightly further apart. Similarly, designing the project for use on an intranet may mean that the project is designed to set and assess student performance is examinations or training exercises.

Design principles

The requirements specification leads the project into the last main design stage - the creation of the Design Document. This document fills in all the important details and is used as the set of tasks that face the team. The tasks are then worked into a Project Plan for implementation.

Before tackling the Design Document, there is a need to discuss the difference between general design principles and specific design requirements.

Design principles are general principles that require interpretation for a particular project, to take into account the nature of the content and its intended audience. They are independent of any existing technology and seek to stress the principles upon which the project is based. Understanding these principles helps designers adopt a more user-centred approach and produce a more usable product.

Examples of design principles are that the system is:

Recognisable	The user can easily recognise the current state of the system and can clearly identify the alternative possible actions (e.g. the user is informed about his/her location in the project and the navigation choices are easily understood).
Predictable	The user knows the result of a future action based on experience of previous actions (e.g. clicking the backwards arrow always returns to the previous screen; users who are familiar with Windows already understand how pull-down menus work).
Traceable	The user can assess the effect of past operations on the current state (e.g. the user has passed five self-assessment tests and knows that he/she is on the final test that moves him/her to the next learning outcome).
Familiar	The user can employ knowledge and experience from the real world (e.g. an icon of a dustbin symbolises deletions, while an icon of an open door symbolises entry to another area of the project).
Consistent	The user is comfortable with a consistent look to screens/buttons/backgrounds, and consistent feedback (e.g. buttons may always have rollovers or may click when depressed).
Controllable	The user controls the system and not the other way round. (e.g. the user controls the pace of events, the user can by-pass animation/videos, the user may be provided with video playback controls/volume control/etc.)
Adaptive	The system assesses user understanding and adapts to that level. The content and/or the interface is altered to suit the capabilities of the user. (e.g. the user may choose from beginner/average/expert level when entering the project, or may be provided with specially chosen content that accords with his/her answer to previous questions).
Responsive	The user is provided with full and continuous feedback. All responses are given in context (e.g. unhelpful 'incorrect response' messages are out and are replaced by messages giving help on what the user is doing wrong.
Supportive	The system should anticipate user problems in knowledge and in navigation (e.g. it may provide wizards or pop-up help)

These are principles. That means that they are applied to real situations and will result in differing design requirements for different projects. For example, some training packages may provide less user control than others. An employer may decide that the employee must review all parts of the training course and specify that users will not have the ability to skip sections of the project. Or a college/university package may prevent a user from moving out of a section until it is successfully completed. On the other hand, this approach would be counter productive in, say, an encyclopaedia.

Applying design principles to the project should lead to the production of a set of design requirements.

Design requirements

Unlike design principles, design requirements are unambiguous. They require no interpretation by the programmer. The items in the Design Document can be evaluated with a checklist. That is the whole idea. The designer creates a set of requirements that are so specific that there is little room for errors or ambiguities during the implementation stage. The larger the team working on the project, the more scope there is for errors between members.

NOTE:
> Even the multi-billion big boys get it seriously wrong. The 1999 Mars Climate Orbiter crashed on the back of Mars because one NASA team was using imperial measurements while the other was using metric units. The result was that the spacecraft was put into too low an orbit and crashed!

A few examples of design requirements are:
- Always place forward/backward/home/quit buttons in the same place.
- Always issue a warning message before changing or deleting any data.
- Always display a site map in the lower left corner of the screen.
- All icons should have a caption under them.

These requirements focus upon <u>users</u> and their <u>tasks</u> and the requirements may be clarified by encouraging client and user participation.   The appearance of the screens, in terms of colour schemes, etc., is not considered at this stage. That is because aesthetic appeal is not an end in itself.   It is more important at this stage to get the logical visual design correct, with screen design issues coming later.

Developers make use of *'paradigms'*. These are extensions from earlier successful examples and may provide experience and expertise in both design requirements and the creative use of technology.

It is important, however, that developers don't design for the computer or the technology - they design for the user. They should only add features when they are required - not because it can be done.

Deciding the design requirements may be time-consuming but shortcuts should be avoided. If the design requirements are not fully developed, the whole project may be flawed as a result. Never attempt to fix problems in the project documentation. Don't tell users how to get round your problem - fix the problem at this stage.   Equally, don't decide to fix problems in the next release. If this project is poor, there won't be a next release!

Design document

The design phase lays out how the project will work in detail.   A number of methods are used by different developers, but a top-down approach (where the main functions are outlined followed by subsidiary functions, continuing to the end of the outline) and flowcharts (showing the links between screen pages) are common development methods. The design phase produces all the content details. This will cover all internal resources (i.e. the company's own talent, hardware and raw material) and requirements for buying in skills (e.g. commissioning photographers, video camera teams, sound studios, graphics artists, animators, voice-over artists, etc).   Details of copyright would also be addressed at this stage.

Structure design

The structure of the project is dependent upon the size and nature of the project.   Larger projects will have more individual screens than smaller projects and some projects are better implemented with a particular structure. For example, a free-running presentation for an exhibition may simply cycle through a series of screens in an entirely linear fashion, while a CD for a travel agent may require direct entry to any topic from anywhere in the structure. The structure design breaks down the project material into meaningful chunks and decides how they relate to each other.

Project content

Clients often have a lot to say and this message must be efficiently structured. The key points are:
- Split the project contents into main topics.
- Split over-general topics into sub-topics.
- Merge small topics into a single topic. This avoids having too many screens with little content.
- Don't split a single topic over several screens. This causes confusion (particularly on web sites, where a user may jump from another site straight into the second screen of a series of linked pages).
- If the content is too large for a single screen, consider reorganising content to create sub-topics, rather than having scrolling screens.
- Contents should be concise, without over-elaboration that clogs the screen and wears down the viewer.
- Avoid designing a project with too deep a structure. This results in navigating through too many levels to get to the desired material. As a result, it deters users from exploring.

- Avoid designing a project with too shallow a structure. This creates too many menu options at each level, and individual screens contain too much material (overcrowding the screen or requiring scrolling of screen material).
- Too few screens result in redundant data (see section on linear structure) and long download times (for web sites), while too many screens result in the user spending more time jumping around than reading.

Presentation structures

Thought has to be given on how screens are linked, which screens are linked and how the user is likely to view and use the project. Above all, navigation must be obvious and intuitive. For example if the project is an electronic book, screens could use a page metaphor. Individual screens would be displayed like book pages, with page turning arrows.

The most likely structures to be implemented are:

Hierarchical structure

The project content is broken down into different sections and each section, in turn, sub-divides its information into more detailed options. Generally, moving down provides more specific information while moving upwards provides more generalised information. The diagram shows links moving <u>down</u> the structure. When the user clicks the link (i.e. menu button, hyperlink, etc) the screen pointed to by the link is displayed. In practice, there will be links allowing the

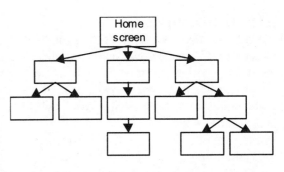

user to move back <u>up</u> to a previous screen and probably move straight back to the home screen.

Linear structure

Some projects benefit from a linear structure where the user is prevented from jumping around the project. These projects present ideas in a progressive fashion (i.e. the user requires to acquire one piece of information

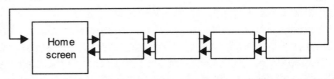

before the next piece makes any sense). Example projects are those where order is important (e.g. step-by step cookery or car maintenance instructions) or where ideas build on previous ideas (e.g. telling a story or developing certain training programmes). A linear structure only provides links that step the user forwards or backwards through the project to allow the user to review information. The project will also provide a link in the last screen to return the user to the home screen.

A web site variation on linear structures is a single large web page with links pointing to sections within that page. This is common on pages with large text content. The advantage for the site designer is that one large file is easier to update than a collection of files. It also allows existing text documents to be quickly converted into hypertext pages. From the user's point of view, a single large web page is easier to print out than a collection of smaller files.

There are also a number of disadvantages for users in this method. The file is large and takes a long time to download. The user spends time and telephone costs downloading whole chunks of the page that may be of no particular interest, just to get to the one required item. Once the page is downloaded, it can be difficult to navigate.

In the example shown, the top of the page provides all the links to the sections of the document. But once a user jumps halfway down a long document, there is no further navigation apart from links to return to the top of the page. Adding links to point to other sections of the document is impractical in a document with lots of sections. Imagine if the example document had 50 sections instead of three. While it may just be acceptable to have 50 links in the top menu, repeating the 50 links after every section makes the page extremely cumbersome. However, this method is commonly used in reference works, where users are expected to be more patient and diligent.

Web structure

This web, or *'network'*, structure has an opening home screen with some initial links.   The user is

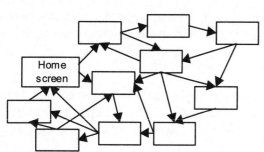

encouraged to wander round the screen without any particular order.   This is useful for projects where there is no evident strong link between one screen and another and there is no hierarchy of information.   An example of this type of project is one promoting a particular holiday resort.   The project may have many screens with information on travel, climate, currency, historical sites, restaurants, entertainment and so on.   Each screen can be read without having any special relevance to any other screen.

It is also used for playing games such as dungeons and dragons.

Hybrid structures

An entirely hierarchical structure is cumbersome to use, since the user has to go all the way back up the structure to navigate down another path.   It is more user-friendly to provide links that allow the user to

move <u>across</u> the structure as well as up and down.   Since this combines elements of linear and hierarchical structures, it is call a hybrid or composite structure.

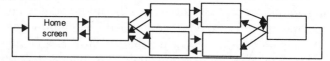

In the case of a linear structure, an element of choice can be built into the serial links.   For example, a tutorial on upgrading a computer's hard disk has many logical steps.   However, there are different steps for fitting an IDE drive compared to fitting a SCSI drive. The user chooses which path to follow.   After the steps for that choice are navigated through, the user joins the main common linear path again.

A further variant is the *'menu structure'*. This is a simplification of the hierarchical structure, with linear elements.

A number of routes are displayed in an opening menu.   Each route consists of a linear set of screens.   When the set of screens is completed, the user is automatically returned to the opening menu.

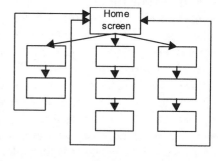

This is different from the hierarchical structure, which allows further sub-routes at each lower level.   While the hierarchical structure is useful for further detailed information at each lower level, the menu structure is useful for taking a user through a collection of tasks.   For example, a project on financial investments may have an opening menu's opening screen that offer options on different investment schemes (ISAs, TESSAs, Bonds, etc.).   Choosing a particular menu option results in the user being taken through a linear presentation on that subject.

Orientation problems

It is important that the user feels comfortable using the project.   That involves the user knowing where he/she is in the project and being able to take logical decisions to move round the structure.

Loss of control or loss of orientation is a desired feature in some web structures used for mazes and dungeons and dragons.   For all other projects, it is to be avoided.

Loss of orientation is caused by:

Poorly designed structures, resulting from:

- Creating confusing web structures through lack of preparation.
- Mixing hierarchical and linear structures.   This practice is fine in some instances (e.g. it is widely used for FAQ (Frequently Asked Questions) and similar text-based web sites).   However, care has to be taken in the provision of links. If a user goes down a level, across a linear path and comes back up a level they are not returned to their original point in the site, causing confusion.

Poorly worded links

- Links titled *'Forward'* and *'Back'* are fine for linear structures, as the user understands their meaning.
- Links called *'Up'* and *'Down'* have little meaning in mixed hierarchical and linear structures.

There are a number of ways to ensure that the user is in control:

- Avoid bad design (e.g. sending a viewer away, mid-thought, to another screen or another web site).
- Avoid unnecessary mixing of hierarchies.

- Provide logical links (e.g. *'Return to Home Screen'*).
- Provide understandable link titles (e.g. *'Disk Specifications'*).
- Provide a project map.   This is not usually a graphical map but a list of the main screens on the project. This could simply be a set of links placed along the bottom of the screen. Better still is placing them in the map in a *'frame'* that is continually displayed as the user navigates the project.   Even better, provide information about where the user is on the map.   This can be achieved by titling each screen.

For web sites, each web page should be able to stand on its own because:

- Another site may provide a link to your site, not by pointing to your home page but by pointing to any page in your site.
- A user's search may take him/her into any page on your site.

The project should attract users to look at the other screens.   It is important that each screen makes sense on its own - even when it constitutes part of a linear series of screens. References to the contents of other screens should be kept to a minimum.   Above all, ensure that each screen has a link to the rest of the project, even if only to the home screen. Best of all, place a site map on each screen.

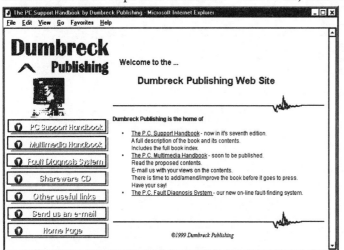

In the example web page shown, the hierarchical menu on the left links to a lower set of pages in the hierarchy. In some cases, such as the *'E-Mail'* and *'CD Offer'* options, the lower web page has no lower level.   In the case of the *'Contents'* option the lower web page has links to 18 other lower-level web pages - one for each book chapter.   In the case of the *'Index'* option there are 26 lower-level web pages - one for each letter of the alphabet.   There are no orientation problems, since a left panel displays a map of the site layout at all times.

Navigational requirements

The navigational requirements is that part of the design requirements that deals with the specifics of how the user negotiates the project.   The methods may be different for each project.   Some may use a web-style interface with hyperlinks, while others may use a windows-style interface with pull-down menus and dialogue boxes.   Others may use image maps or other navigation methods.

Examples of typical navigational requirements are:

- Access to all main project sections is from a set of pull-down menus/ side menu of buttons.
- The main menu bar/ side menu will appear in all screens.
- Access to all navigation options is by mouse click.
- A single mouse click will activate any option.
- The menu bar will include a *'help'* facility.
- The menu bar will include a *'quit'* option (not required for web sites).
- Within each section, the user should be able to navigate backwards and forwards through the screens.
- The cursor will change shape/colour when it is over an active area.
- The shape/colour of an active area will alter when the cursor is over it.

This example list provides some key features such as allowing the user to control the pace of the project material, allowing the user to access any main section at any time, and allowing the user to seek help or to quit an any time.   This is not a shopping list or a checklist.   It is NOT a list of recommendations.   It presents examples that may act as a guide to constructing a list that is appropriate to a particular project.

Output from Design phase

The three main documents that are produced from the design phase are:

Navigation map - the map showing how individual screens are connected by buttons or hyperlinks.

Storyboard - the drawings and descriptions of screen contents.

Screen design - the specification of screen elements (e.g. fonts, point sizes, colours, etc.).

Navigation maps

This is required for all but the very simplest of projects. It details every connection between one part of the project and another.   Users navigate (i.e. move round) the application by choosing menu options, clicking on icons, buttons or hypertext entries, or clicking on *'hotspots'* (active areas of the screen - e.g. a county on a map).   The map shows where the user is taken on activating one of the navigation tools.

Navigation maps can be hand-drawn, or they can be created using drafting packages such as Visio, or even using Word's Flowchart AutoShapes.   Ideally, the method should allow quick and easy alterations and additions to the structure and this would favour a dedicated drafting package.

There is no preferred method or layout for creating navigation maps (unless an organisation has set its own internal standards). The over-riding requirement is that the map be legible and complete.

The diagram below illustrates part of a navigation map for a tutorial on data communications.

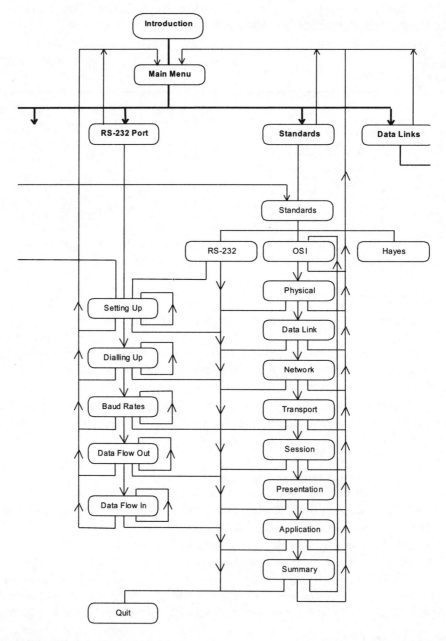

Notes:

Each screen has a direct link back to the main menu.

Each screen has a direct link to quit.

The *'Summary'* screen has a link back to the *'OSI'* sub-menu.

Some screens show internal loops as shown on the right.   These screens contain animations and the user can opt to re-run the animations as often as required, before moving on.

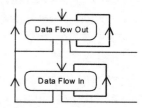

Storyboards

A project consists of many separate, but linked, screens. The navigation map describes how each screen is linked and the storyboard describes what happens inside each screen.

A single storyboard might be enough to describe a small project whose screens are made up of static, or largely static material. Its purpose here is to document the layout and features of each screen (fonts, colours, navigation buttons, etc.).

Most often, though, there is a collection of storyboards, with some storyboards describing a particular set of screens, while others describe animations or video clip contents. They derive their name from the fact that a project is interactive; the user navigates round the project and - in doing so - is told a story. In addition, individual screens may contain their own dynamic content, such as video clips and animations. Since the use of a project is a dynamic activity, the storyboard has to chart this movement.

The essential features of a storyboard are:

- It is a set of sketches and notes.
- It can be a rough sketch or can be finely detailed (see below).
- It can convey the main points or can be thoroughly documented (see below).
- It shows the interface at different points in the interaction.
- It provides snapshots of the intended sequence to convey the impression of the final result.
- It provides key frames to show clients.
- It provides a useful tool in user-centred design.
- It describes the mood to be set.
- It can be hand-drawn or can be created using storyboard software.
- It combines with the navigation maps to define the entire project.
- It is not a static set of documents. It may require redrafting several times before agreement and understanding is reached between the client, the designer and those who will implement the project.
- Used correctly, it shortens the time taken to agree the project with the client, and also speeds up production time.

There are many systems that have been developed for creating storyboards and there are two main approaches:

Schematic approach

This is basically just a rough sketch or outline of the project. The entire storyboard could be drawn and hand-written. The aim is get over the essential elements of the project. This takes less preparation time than the detailed method, but the savings may be lost again because of additional changes and additions at a later stage.

Consider the rough sketch in the illustration. It gets over the way that the opening screens will unfold.

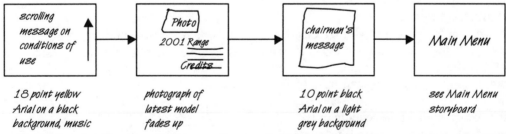

However, without the detail under the boxes, there would be considerable scope for wasted time and wasted resources, as the output from the programmers is found not to match the expectations of the client. Storyboards that are more of a rough guide sometimes require more versions to be produced to even adequately define the overall parameters of the project.

Detailed approach

This approach provides full details of every screen, including descriptions of the text, fonts, graphics, images, sounds, animations, videos, button shapes and sizes, user responses, etc.

While this takes much longer to prepare, it eliminates most ambiguities at an early stage.

It leaves less margin for error at the implementation stage and less scope for client misunderstanding.

It sketches and describes each scene, image, video clip, audio clip, text, and navigation icon.

Each screen of the storyboard is accompanied by a full description, containing:
- Title and general description.
- Name and description, or description of function, of each object appearing on the screen.

Example

A college project displays course information to potential new students. After choosing a subject area (e.g. computing, media studies, applied science, etc), the viewer is presented with information on the courses on offer. The example below is the description of computing courses descriptions screen.

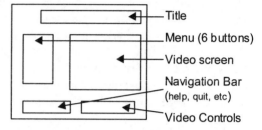

Title
Menu (6 buttons)
Video screen
Navigation Bar (help, quit, etc)
Video Controls

Title	*Computing Courses Descriptions Screen*
Description	*The user chooses a course from the menu and is shown a short video showing the college's computing facilities and class activities.*
Background	*A light grey embossed image of the college main building.*
Screen title	*Displays the name of the computing department. Animates in from the left. Arial Bold Italic 36 point blue.*
Menu button 1	*Runs the video describing the HNC course in computing. Rollover button 100x30, chiselled 12 point text on dark marble face.*
Menu button 2	*Runs the video describing the HND course in information technology. Rollover button 100x30, chiselled 12 point text on dark marble face.*
Menu button 3	*Runs the video describing the HNC in multimedia. Rollover button 100x30, chiselled 12 point text on dark marble face.*
Menu button 4	*Runs the video describing the HND in networking. Rollover button 100x30, chiselled 12 point text on dark marble face.*
Menu button 5	*Runs the video describing the HNC in graphic design. Rollover button 100x30, chiselled 12 point text on dark marble face.*
Menu button 6	*Runs the video describing the HND in hardware support. Rollover button 100x30, chiselled 12 point text on dark marble face.*
Video screen	*Displays the video chosen from the menu bar. 320x 240 full-colour AVI.*
Video controls	*Provides user control over the play of the video clip. Stop/Pause/Replay.*
Navigation bar	*Provides user control over project navigation. Quit/Return to Main Screen/ Go to Enrolment Screen*

Animation example

The above example works fine with screens that are static or have simple moving elements.

The storyboards for animations and video clips are more complex, in that they have to show the positions of objects at different points in time.

The example on the right shows the steps for an animation that shows one way that numbers can be sorted into ascending order.

It shows movements and the resulting states for each stage of the animation.

A hand-drawn representation is perfectly satisfactory for this. There is no need to spend extra time producing perfect images. The aim is to show the <u>order</u> that events take place and the <u>movements</u> in the animation.

This animation would likely run in a window of the main screen. The main

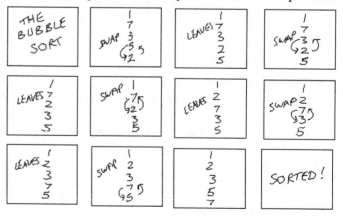

screen details (background, buttons, colours, etc.) would already have been described in a separate document. This sketch would therefore be accompanied with details of the animation's timing, along with the colour/content of the background and the size, font style and colour of the numeric elements.

It is helpful if a template is created containing the empty boxes that will contain the animation. The little time spent of preparing a master template is repaid later. The result is a cleaner presentation where the elements inside the boxes become the focus of attention.

Video Storyboard example

Video Storyboard

Project . . . .   Clip Number . . . .

Clip Description . . . .

View	Shot No.	Description	Audio, Effects, Other Information
	89	Over the shoulder shot Time: length of dialogue.	"I'm glad you could come over. It's nice to see a new neighbour. I notice that you look a bit anaemic".
	90	Medium Close Up Time: length of dialogue.	"Can I get you a drink?"
	91	Extreme Close Up of teeth. Time: length of dialogue.	"I'll just help myself, thanks"
	92	Extreme Close Up on eyes. Time: 3 seconds	"Gulp"
	93	Mid Shot of vampire slowly closing in on victim.	Dramatic music.
	94	Extreme Close Up of hand producing a crucifix. Time: 4 seconds	Fanfare. "Arghh"
	95	Long Shot of vampire retreating out of frame. Time: 6 seconds	"I'll be back"

Once again, creating a template similar to that above speeds up future storyboards, as the blank template can be printed and copied fot future use.

Rough drawings are all that is necessary for this storyboard.   The screen sketches and the screen descriptions are adequate for all but the largest productions - those with huge detail and a cast of thousands.

This is probably not the shooting order or production order of the final project. This is taken care of with project management tools, which may result in more efficient shooting lists and lists that maintain continuity (see the notes in the chapter on digital video).

These storyboard outlines are suggested approaches.

Organisations may have their own internal systems and standards and may use storyboarding software.

Once the storyboard is finalised, it is used as the model for creating the project prototype.

H.C.I.

Human-Computer Interaction (HCI) is the study of how computers and people communicate with each other and how the computer interface can be improved. In this context, the *'interface'* does not just mean the look and feel of the screens. It also covers how tasks are performed, how information is presented, what kind of questions are asked, etc. In other words, computer programs (including multimedia applications) have to be modelled around the physical and psychological characteristics of the human beings that use them. The programs must adapt to the users, and not the other way round.

HCI takes into account how people learn, including what aids learning and what inhibits learning. HCI is applied to all computer programs, since they all have some degree of user control. Multimedia titles, in particular, are created so that users have a high degree of control over what is seen and what is done. This makes HCI an even more important discipline for multimedia designers and developers.

Some HCI issues revolve round the physical world (e.g. don't use dark green letters on a black background because the eye will not sufficiently distinguish the text).

Most HCI questions examine how the human brain functions, how we understand external stimuli, how we store experiences, how we recall and use knowledge, and so on. An understanding of these processes allows software programs to adapt to these general rules of behaviour.

This chapter adopts many of the lessons from these studies and these are embodied in the many suggestions in the chapter.

Human Memory

As the diagram shows, the memory process occurs in stages. Short term memory helps the user understand how to navigate or make informed choices, while long term memory is used to educate, etc.

Perception

The human senses are continually receiving information from the outside world. Sight, sound, touch, taste and smell all process information that has to be categorised by the brain. For example, walking down the street may produce sights (other pedestrians, cars, shops), sounds (mobile phone ringing, police siren), touch (rain on face) and smells (hamburger stand). The brain constantly filters out less important information. Of course, what is regarded as important is dependent on the human's condition at the time. If the person is hungry, the smell of hamburgers may predominate, whereas the sound of a phone is only meaningful if the person owns a mobile phone. The process of filtering unwanted information and identifying required information is shown as *'perception'* in the diagram.

Important HCI issues arising are:

- Any movement attracts attention - also alerts peripheral vision. Messages/flying text.
- Temporal media (video, animation, sound) dominates over static media (text, graphics, tables).

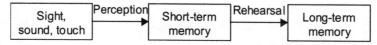

The designer has to prevent *'sensory overload'*, where there are too many screen stimuli competing for the viewer's attention. The main points here are:

- A user can look and listen at the same time.
- A user can't look and look at the same time.
- In multiples windows, only have activity in one window at a time.
- Don't show multiple graphics, videos, and photographs all at the same time.
- Don't overdo strong stimuli. Excessive bright colours and sound warnings/feedback cause stress/fatigue.
- Minimise distractions during memorisation tasks (no pop-up *'well done'* messages/fanfares).

Short Term Memory

Short-term memory acts as the temporary store for information. If the information is really significant, it will be processed into long-term memory.

Examples of short-term memory are:

- Someone consults a telephone directory and recalls the number just long enough to dial it.
- Someone carries out a mathematical calculation in their head, memorising interim calculations just long enough to complete the calculation.
- Someone is introduced to twenty people at a party, and each name is stored long enough to say *"Hello Kris", "Hello Danielle",* etc.

Once the information has been used, it is quickly forgotten.

The working memory can be easily overloaded. For instance, a person will recall a local telephone number long enough to dial it, but will have great difficulty in memorising a number that includes a long international code.

Important HCI issues arising are:

- Don't expect users to store a great deal of information.
- Users can handle around seven items at any one time.
- The number of options in a menu should not exceed seven (see above).
- Don't ask multiple questions in the same screen.
- Images are best remembered if accompanied by text.
- Don't expect users to carry over much information from one task to the next.
- Structuring information, known as *'chunking'*, helps memorisation. For example, breaking a telephone number into the area code, the exchange code and the local number (e.g. 0141-775-2889 is easier to remember than 01417752889).
- Lower the task complexity by dividing a task into a sequence of smaller tasks (e.g. most software installation routines have separate screens for inputting user details, information on which folder to store the application, software serial number and site key, etc).

Long Term Memory

When an item is regarded as being significant, it will be committed to long-term memory. All our experience, knowledge and attitudes are stored in long-term memory.

<u>Getting it in</u>

If an item is considered to be of great importance, it is quickly processed into long-term memory. For example, if a patient is told that he/she has 143 days to live, the number is not forgotten! Similarly, if one person stands out in a crowd, that person's name is usually recalled from all the others.

The aim of most multimedia titles is to impart information and knowledge to the users. The information may be in the form of significant knowledge (e.g. quantum physics, mathematics, and electronics) or it may even be entertainment (e.g. trivia questions, holiday information or the rules for playing chess).

In many cases, the information is processed and stored because the user <u>wants</u> to retain the information. In other cases, such as preparation for examinations or learning a programming language, the user may lack motivation and has to force himself/herself to absorb the information. This is usually achieved through a process of *'rehearsal'*. If a piece of information is repeatedly spoken, written down, read over, practiced, then the information is likely to be stored in the long-term memory.

<u>Getting it out</u>

Unfortunately, humans are better at recognition than recall. They may not remember what Mr Jones the butcher looks like but they will know him when they meet him. The user's ability to recall information is improved by the user employing reasoning and understanding during learning. In other words, if the user is presented with a list of facts, they have less chance of being recalled than information obtained through on-screen activity (e.g. virtual experiments, exploration, searches, and other user tasks).

Important HCI issues arising are:

- Provide aids to user recall. These may be keywords or spatial memorisation (items are better remembered in groups).
- The use of analogies bases itself on the user's previous knowledge or experience to attach fresh memory links. Users learn by using previous knowledge. For example, everyone is familiar with the address on a letter containing a name, address, town and country. Similarly, an e-mail address has a name, host name, domain name and country. Making the comparison aids the appreciation of the concept.
- Consistency of associations creates better contexts for memorisation and recall
- Structuring information helps categorical memory by creating extra links for retrieval.
- Recall of video material can be poor if the content is too detailed or too much. The brain is forced to filter out most of the detail in the short time it has to process the material. Even the main points can be lost if complex material is presented over a short time. This also applies to audio material. Providing controls for the user to pause or rewind the material, although helpful, do not fully solve this problem. The real answer lies in adjusting the pace of the presentation and in chunking the material into separate items.
- Long continuous tasks should introduce a mental break (e.g. display a summary, quiz, etc.).

User Interaction Design

The user interaction design is that part of the design requirements that deals with the specifics of how the user interfaces with the project.   The aim is to make the system as usable as possible and to achieve the project's goals safely, effectively, efficiently and enjoyably.

The section is broken down into sub-headings for ease of reference.

In practice, there is some overlap between these sections and with other parts of the design requirements document.

Menus

- Each menu should have a clearly marked title (e.g. *'Orders Menu'*, *'Repairs menu'*, etc).
- Menu items should be grouped logically into menu blocks or even separate menu screens. Related buttons should be grouped together, with different groups located slightly apart or separated by a line.
- Menu options should be placed in logical order (e.g. operational sequence, frequency of use, importance)
- Every menu should include a clearly marked exit option.
- Menus should include the ability to return to the main menu or to return to a previous sub-menu.
- Menus should include shortcuts for experienced users, where appropriate.
- Menus should contain no more than seven items, to avoid information overload.
- The interface must be consistent (e.g. a button should not do different things in different screens; the controls should be in the same place on every screen).
- If a menu item is not active on a particular screen (e.g. the 'home' button on the 'home' screen), it should be removed or disabled and greyed out - rather than ignoring the user's clicks or giving error messages.
- Controls and feedback should look like their physical counterparts (e.g. switches, knobs, VU meters, etc.).
- Use real-world metaphors - dustbin, hourglass, loudspeaker, arrows for forward/backwards, flags of countries (for different languages), boats/planes for travel agent, etc.
- Test with users that the symbols are recognised. Don't use symbols that users have to learn or look up in a guide.
- Icons should have clear outlines for easy visual discrimination.
- Use appropriate controls (e.g. using a list box rather than requiring user entry).
- Where Toolbars are used, these should be limited to frequent operations and should only be available as a shortcut (i.e. they should also be in main menu).
- Toolbars should be under user control. They should be removable and user configurable.

Simplicity

- The project must be able to be used without an instruction manual (either printed or on-line).
- The project must be able to be used without special training.
- The project must use familiar terms. There should be no jargon, no irrelevant information, and no rarely needed information.
- Where unfamiliar terms are essential to the project, their meaning must be explained.
- If a screen uses image maps, indicate it.   Their use must be obvious.
- There must be no hidden links.   All navigation control must be easily distinguished. Users must not have to click on all screen objects, searching for links.
- Screens must not use graphic images that look like buttons but aren't.
- Screens must not use buttons that don't look like buttons.
- Still frames can be used as links to video clips.
- Dialogue should not need to be remembered from one screen to another.
- Task complexity should be reduced, by breaking the task into a sequence of smaller tasks.

Feedback

- The user must receive immediate feedback from mouse activities (e.g. 'key click' sound on clicking the mouse button or button rollovers when the cursor hover them).
- The user must be given appropriate error messages, in context, when an illegal operation is attempted.
- Where the system has a long response time (e.g. database activities or loading a large video clip), the user should be given update messages or a progress indicator (e.g. a bar that grows from 0% to 100%).
- The novice user should be given the option to enable information windows that automatically pop up when tackling complex options or tasks.
- The user should be informed of his/her position within the structure at all times, using navigation beacons (e.g. displaying an annotated site map or displaying the path already taken).

User support
- The user should have access to built-in help facilities.
- The novice user should have access to wizards, where appropriate.
- Further material should be available for those needing more learning support.
- Where appropriate, the user should be able to choose the difficulty level (e.g. beginner/average/expert) when entering a project.
- Slow learners should be easily able to repeat sections of the project.
- The user must be warned about options that may modify or delete data, and choices must be offered and clearly explained.

User control
- No action should take place without user initiation (see below).
- The user should be able to switch off the sound or adjust the volume control.
- The user should be able to replay videos/animations, or switch them off.
- The user should be able to by-pass project opening introductions.
- The user should be able to by-pass parts of a sequence.

These suggestions will not all apply to every project. For example, although most projects are based on user-initiated actions, there is some need for computer-initiated activities. Any form-filling or question-and-answer tasks in a project are computer-initiated and the user often has to complete the tasks before being allowed to proceed.

Screen design
Project content organises the project's message by volume, while screen design focuses on <u>how</u> it is said. The key issues here are:

Style issues
The content style is dependent on the intended audience. Projects won't all have music/video/ graphics on every screen just because the technology exists. An estate agent, for example, will have many properties and require many screens, each containing graphics. A project reporting law court proceedings, on the other hand, is likely to require large screens with lots of text.

The style has to reflect the knowledge, experience and tastes of the target viewer. A project for teenagers has an entirely different approach to a project aimed at young schoolchildren. Again, if the project was targeted at a mature/elderly audience, it would use yet another approach. Consider how a project on alcohol abuse would differ if written for each of these age groups.

Sometimes, the content is determined by user expectations (e.g. primary colours for children, clean line art for diagrams, rendered graphics for objects, digital photographs for real estate, etc.).

The project *'style'* describes the slant of the material - e.g. sober, trendy, or outrageous.

There is also the *'look and feel'* of the project. A project can be given the correct style and still not work because of the implementation of the elements. All the elements used in the project (e.g. logos, buttons, colour schemes, headlines, body text, etc.) should look like they belong as a family. A project is often spoiled by using different buttons or different colour schemes on different pages. This can be prevented by having a fully fleshing out screen layout details in the Requirements Specification document.

Cultural issues
There is no such thing as a cultureless, or cross-culture, product. Every designer carries his/her own background/preferences/prejudices. Laying aside stereotypes, there are huge cultural differences, even between nations with apparently similar cultures. American and UK citizens have very similar cultures. They speak a common language, have similar dress codes, eat similar foods and follow similar religious and political beliefs. Yet, the American fervour for the right to carry arms sends shivers down the spines of most UK citizens. On the other hand, they overwhelmingly respect speed restrictions, while the British treat speeding as their second national sport.

The differences between other countries are even more marked. There are different political cultures, different geographic cultures and different social cultures. There are co-existing cultures within any one country or market. These, for example, may be ethnic or religious. There are even different cultures <u>within</u> cultures. These may be differences of social class, of religion or of age.

The project's use of words and images should take into account cultural differences throughout the world. It is relatively easy to identify areas that might offend people from other cultures, but it is a lot more difficult to identify grey areas and to avoid the transmission of confusing messages.

Some words and phrases (e.g. *'using a rubber'*) have different meanings in different countries while certain images (e.g. nudity, alcohol, etc.) have differing levels of acceptability. When Vauxhall launched their *'Nova'* range of cars in Spain, they were at first unaware that the Spanish translation of *'Nova'* means *'Does not go'*.   Even colours have different symbolic meanings in different countries and this is covered later.

Of course, some projects are consciously designed to attract a particular culture (e.g. teenage fanzines or ethnic material).

Legal issues

Apart from copyright, which is covered later, there are a number of other important content issues:

- All the contents (text, video, graphics) must be legal.   Care must be taken over laws on Copyright, Pornography, Official Secrets, Privacy, etc.
- Contents must be accurate. Apart from the project losing credibility, the owners may fall foul of the laws of Libel, Trades Description, etc.
- While projects destined for web sites are viewed by an international audience, there would be great difficulty in another country trying to make the content subject to their laws. Nevertheless, respect for other cultures should be taken into account.   Even at its most base level, the thought of losing sales in that country should guide the decisions on screen content.
- Credit should be given to all works or references used on the screen.   This can be a verbal acknowledgement or, on web sites, by the provision of a link to the other's site.

Layout issues

The eye is drawn to temporal (moving) object before static objects.   This means that a video clip or an animation will dominate a screen.   The designer must ensure that any textual material on the same screen is not swamped by these images.

Less overpowering is the use of animated text. This has the benefit of drawing attention to itself without distracting from the screen message.   Indeed, the fact that the text dissolves/fades to introduce new text draws greater attention to the message.

With totally static screens, the eye is first drawn to photographic images, clip art and diagrams, etc.

There are preferred positions on the screen for placing information.   Corners and edges are regarded as areas of peripheral vision - the eye concentrates on the central area of the screen.   Screen layout should follow reading conventions.   Most cultures read text from left to right and from top to bottom.

What's good	What's bad
The use of contrasts (big/small, heavy/light, bright/dark, thick/thin, etc.).	Ugly colour clashes.
Lots of white space.	Using colours schemes that hinder viewing by users with colour confusion.
An uncluttered screen.	Busy, fussy screens.
Eye grabbers (e.g. a single brightly coloured object on a grey scale background, or a single photograph and elegant script text on a light embossed background),	Buttons that produce melodies, voices, bells, klaxons, drum rolls when pressed.
Shadows.	Frilly borders.
Gradients.	Too much text, too many numbers.
Shaded text.	Flashing images (consider potential epilepsy problems).
Projects that establish their presence quickly on startup, with a display title window.	Lame humour, regional humour, in-jokes.

Serious consideration should be given to the effective use of *'white space'*.   This term originated from the printed page and indicated those areas of the page that were not printed on.   In multimedia terms, it indicates those are of the screen on which there is no text, graphic or other object.   Some large web portals, such as Yahoo and AltaVista, completely cover the screen with text hyperlinks.   The text is usually well organised and is acceptable as a quick way to access other resources.   However, the screens are very crammed and this would not be effective on another type of web site or project.   White space allows the eye to rest a little and helps focus the eye on what is important on the page.   The key headings are not submerged in a morass of text and other objects.

The use of text and of colour are covered in their own sections later.

Backgrounds

Backgrounds are backgrounds; they are intended as a backdrop for the main screen content. They must not dominate the screen. For example, a piece of text with a small font size and grey or white colour is almost invisible with a background that is a brightly coloured, highly detailed photograph.

The backgrounds supplied with some applications are very elaborate and, although effective for an introductory screen that will have large bold headings, they obscure the text message when used for all the subsequent screens. It is best to use plainer backgrounds with the main project screens.

Graduated tints also make effective backgrounds. If a gradient fill is being used, the fill should be light at bottom and dark at top.

Using dark text and objects with a light background produces lower user errors and increased user completion times, compared to light objects on a dark background. Using black on a white background is universally acceptable, if not the most visually stunning.

Whatever backgrounds are chosen, there must be a large contrast between the text colour and the background colour, for maximum readability.

A constant background should be used in most projects. This provides consistency, a feeling of completeness/unity, and perhaps a corporate identity.

Occasionally, changing backgrounds can be used to good effect. Consider a project for a travel agent or an estate agent. Here, a different background could be used for each section of the project.

Also, subtle alterations to the shade of the background are effective in notifying viewers that they have entered a new area of the project.

Web site issues

Web pages could contain other useful information, apart from the main project content - e.g. the date the page was last updated.

Pages could also provide a link that allows the user to contact the site creator. This is a courtesy to allow user feedback to the designer and is also a marketing tool that encourages users to contact the site promoter.

Designing with colour

Before reading this section, it would be advisable to re-read the section on colour theory in the chapter on 'Multimedia Basics'. It explains how light and colour is processed by the eye and by the brain.

Colour has an instinctive appeal. Indeed, it has become so widespread that advertisers now use monochrome photographs in advertising so that they appear distinctive.

People respond to the colours on a screen before they respond to the actual visual elements on the screen. Colour can be used to convey mood and to convey information.

Colour associations

The eye operates according to strict physical properties but the brain's processing of the information imposes meaning upon the information. The cultural and personal experience of colours means that they may be perceived as being happy, sad, threatening, etc. Some interpretations may be cultural (e.g. black representing death) or may be personal (e.g. if all tax bills were printed on green paper, every green document would be viewed with suspicion by that person). Colours have been given subjective properties. For example, some colours are described as 'warm' while others are 'cold'. Colours have also entered our language to describe emotions. For example, being caught 'red-handed' or telling ' little white lies'. In the first case, red indicates negative attitudes, while the white in the second example indicates something harmless.

Some common colour associations are:

Colour	British Associations	Some Alternative Associations
Red	Anger, danger, heat, negative values	In China - festivity and joy
Green	Environment	In Muslim culture - holy
Blue	Cold, sea, sky	
White	Purity	In China, Japan and India - death, funerals, mourning
Black	Death, mourning, evil	
Purple	Luxury	In Latin America - death
Yellow	Sun, happiness	In Egypt - prosperity. In America - caution

In the real world, objects do not have a consistent colour, since they only reflect the light that illuminates them at the time.   For instance, brightly adorned streets may appear drab and grey in the twilight, just before the streetlights are switched on.   Also, the blue of the sky changes with the time of day.   This trait can be exploited by project designers and graphic artists, who can alter the colouring for objects to convey the time of day or the mood (e.g. New York's Central Park at night has a different mood from Central Park in the bright sunlight).

Colour coding

Colour has long been used to categorise information and this technique can be employed in multimedia projects.   It is called 'colour coding' and there are two types:

Ordinal Coding	The depth of a colour or set of colours is used to indicate relative values of a piece of information. For example, a map may use increasingly dark shades of blue to indicate the increasing depth of the seabed, while using ever-lighter shades of green to indicate ever-higher heights of land. Similarly, a scale from pink to deep red might indicate rising temperatures. There is no need to consult a chart, unless exact readings are required; a glance at the colours is sufficient to discover the relative height, depth, speed, temperature, sales, age, etc. of an object.
Nominal Coding	In this system, colours have been picked on an arbitrary basis to indicate an object. For example, the various lines on the London Underground are colour coded for ease of use. Similarly, maps use one colour for motorways and other colours for minor roads, rivers, etc.

Colour coding only works when the user is aware of the purpose of each code.   The meanings of colour codes have been learned over years (everyone understands that a red traffic light means stop).

In a multimedia project, care should be taken if the colour codes used are different from those that are commonly recognised.   Users will not be prepared to learn elaborate colour systems just to navigate the system or categorise information - unless they perceive that it is absolutely necessary and that the package is worth persevering with.   In other words, colour coding can be an advantage or a disincentive, depending upon how it is used.

Colour and learning

Colour should be used for accentuating a point, and not simply for adornment.

Learners prefer colour screens to black and white screens.   Their preference is for dark foreground objects on a light background.   In reality, the learner's immediate performance in using a package is similar with black and white or colour.   However, there is evidence that the use of colour can lead to greater retention and recall of information, as coloured material is recalled more accurately than black and white material.

- Colour is a useful way to emphasise learning cues. However, used indiscriminately, it distracts from the important learning cues.
- Also, viewers will tolerate more text on a screen if colour is used to highlight important sections of the text.
- Colour highlighting is more effective than shape highlighting, except for users who suffer from colour confusion.
- Projects aimed at children should use primary colours, as children only learn to distinguish between shades later.
- The number of colours used on a screen also impacts on the learning experience.
- Using up to seven different colours increases viewer interest, while increasing the number of colours beyond seven makes identifying information more difficult. People's short-term memory can only handle a limit of between five and nine colours. Using more than seven colours may actually reduce the amount of material accessed in a project.
- Projects should therefore use this limited set of colours for screens (excluding colours in photographs, of course).
- Finally, since colours have associative properties, the same colour should always be used for the same function.

Using Colour

The point should be repeated that colour should be used as an additive feature. Projects should not rely on colour unless it is an integral part of the project. For this reason, it is commonly advised that a project be initially designed in black & white. The slogan to *'get it right in black and white'* before considering colour slightly overstates the case but provides the correct emphasis. Of course, there are exceptions to this rule. Some projects may rely heavily on the use of colour in order to make the project's message effective. For example, detailed animations of chemical, electrical or mechanical processes may rely on the use of different colours to make the process legible.

Colour perceptions

As previously explained different colours produce different reactions. This is partly physical (how the eye processes) and partly psychological (how the brain translates colour).

- The yellow and red ends of the spectrum increase eye fatigue.
- Red produces the most fatigue, but is also the most stimulating.
- Blue produces the least fatigue, and is perceived as being the most cheerful.
- Green is perceived as the most restful to the eye.
- Brighter or larger areas of colour attract attention.
- Intense hues and light colours are perceived as foreground elements, while dull hues and dark colours are perceived as background elements. This mirrors the user's perceptions of the real world.
- Areas of high contrast between colours appear in the foreground.
- Areas of low contrast recede into the background.
- Viewers are attracted to bright colours.
- Bright colours quickly tire viewers' eyes.
- Save the brightest colours for the objects that viewers should look at first.
- Overusing bright coloured object confuses the viewer, who doesn't know which objects are meant to be the most important.
- Use the minimum number of colours on one screen. Too many colours, particularly bright colours, make the project look gaudy and cheap.
- A headline or caption that uses different colours for each letter almost always fails to impress and usually irks users.
- The basic colours (black, white, yellow, red, blue, green and grey) work best for text colours.
- Cluttered screens can handle fewer colours.
- Screens with relatively few items can handle more colours.
- Colour is more attention-grabbing than blinking or inverse video.

Colour combinations

Colours always appear along with other colours and care must be taken that the colours used are complementary to each other, and that they maximise the screen impact for the greatest number of viewers. Some guidelines are:

- Use appropriate combinations (e.g. grey for background).
- Avoid clashing colour schemes such as green/blue and red/blue.
- Avoid a red/green colour scheme, as around 10% of the population suffer from colour confusion.
- Colours look darker and smaller against a white background.
- Colours look brighter and larger against a black background.
- Consistent colour scheme - for text, hyperlinks, buttons (e.g. don't use red for exit on one screen and then green for exit on another screen).
- Colour schemes can be dependent upon the era. For example, house-decorating colours in the conservative 50's or the psychedelic 60's are at odds with current house paint colours. Certain colours are more popular at certain times and their use can set the intended mood for an era.
- Insufficient contrast between background and text colours increases eye fatigue.
- Over contrast (e.g. white text on black background) is also tiring. Use light grey on a black background.

Media requirements

The following pages consider the main media components of a multimedia presentation, outlining how they operate and considering the main factors affecting performance.

Text

A picture may be worth a thousand words, but certain ideas can only be expressed or summarised in text format.   For example, a scientific formula or a table of figures is difficult to represent in any other media.   The bandwidth restrictions on web sites also often push designs towards an emphasis on text content. A web site that describes a holiday resort rather than showing multiple photographs and video clips may be less exiting but is a lot smaller to store and a lot quicker to download.

There is little difference between user comprehension of words read on a screen and words read from a printed page.   However, users read around 25% slower from a monitor screen.

All multimedia applications employ text and their attributes used should reflect the nature of the application. The later section on fonts discusses typefaces and their attributes.

Text layout issues

Too much text on the screen repels viewers and the screen layout seeks to make the viewing experience both easier and more enjoyable. Of course, some projects of necessity use a great deal of text and the users know what to expect when they open such screens.   Viewers who wish to examine historical records, court transcripts, scientific papers, component lists, price lists, etc. expect to see a great deal of text on a screen. In fact, spreading the text over many separate pages makes the researcher's task more difficult.   For all other projects, however, the viewer may have much less motivation and the layout should be an invitation to browse and not a barrier.

Some recommendations for text layout are:

- Do not place all the text centred on the screen.
- Do not use text that is too small or too large, as it makes the viewer uncomfortable.
- Headings, subheadings and main points in a screen should be highlighted, to draw the audience's attention to the importance of that particular item.   This may be achieved by formatting the text to be bold, italicised or displayed in a prominent colour, or the text may be placed in a filled box.
- Don't use underlines on headings; instead, use a bold heading to summarise the screen.
- Avoid having more than 12 words on a line; 8 to 10 words is a more practical limit.
- Use the same point size for the body font throughout the project.
- Use the same point size for all headings and sub-headings in the project.
- Never rescale text to make it fit the screen.
- Screen text should be left justified and ragged on the right edge.   Block justified text may look better but is harder to read.
- Apart from necessary blocks of text, each line should make a single point. Each new concept should appear on its own new line/block/bullet.
- Avoid using all upper case letters, as lower case letters are easier to read. A mix of upper and lower case is acceptable.
- Using text that is all capitals makes reading more difficult for those who speed-read, day cut as they use word shapes to help identify words (see the illustration).
- Use underlining sparingly, as underlining words obscures their shape, making reading more difficult.
- Use serifed typefaces for quotes.

Text Effects

Designers are always looking for ways to make their projects more distinctive.   Some text effects work, while others make things worse.

- Avoid having text of many different colours on any one screen.
- Using colours to highlight titles or hypertext links is effective.
- Wipes and transitions can attract viewers' attention, if not overplayed.
- Users prefer fixed screens to scrolling screens.
- Scrolling is only suitable as an aid for browsing lists. It should not be used as a method of reading body text. If it's big enough to requiring scrolling, break it up into logical chunks on separate screens.
- Be careful of typestyle choices for web sites. If an uncommon font is used, it will not be recognised by other's browsers and they will substitute their own choice of font, losing the graphic effect intended by the designer. The only sure way to ensure viewers see the pages as they were intended is to create a graphic image of the text. Unfortunately, this results in large file sizes for the text graphics.
- Reversing letters is an eye-catching technique.
- Inverting letters is an eye-catching technique.

- Using letters sizes and shapes to produce the outline of an object such as a car, a house, etc. can be effective in some situations but requires a little imagination and a lot of patience.
- Initial capital letters at the start of a paragraph, known as *'drop caps'* can enhance text and draw the readers' attention. The first two words are generally capitalised, to prevent the drop cap effect being too overpowering.

> **M**ULTIMEDIA AUTHORING packages do not generally have spell-checking or grammar-checking features and the author has to be very careful that misspelled words do not slip through and mar an otherwise professional project. All packages allow

Language issues

The language used also develops a mood. The words used to review current youth music would not be very effective on a government project or a project for the over-70's. Similarly the choice of words used in the text is important; the grammar should suit the intended audience. Young children should not be bamboozled with complex words and older users should not be patronised. Jargon, abbreviations and acronyms should also be avoided, although some 'foreign' words or phrases are eye-catching and add glamour or mystery to the screen (just think of how many perfumes are given French names).

Grammar/punctuation checks

A well thought out presentation is spoiled if it contains typing errors, grammatical errors or other inconsistencies that detract from a professional feel. Points to bear in mind are:

- Always spell check the text. Bear in mind that a sentence will pass a spell check as long as the words exist. They might still be the wrong word for the sentence (e.g. compliment mixed up for complement). If in any doubt, consult a dictionary.
- Always grammar check sentences, preferably using both software and manual checking.
- Use active verbs.
- Always use the same tense within screens and between different screens.
- Avoid prepositions, adverbs and adjectives.
- Punctuation marks should be in the same format as the word it follows. For example, if words are in italics any commas, colons, semi-colons and full stops should also be in italics. Similarly, words in bold should be followed by bold punctuation marks.
- An ellipsis is a row of full stops and is used to effect in a number of ways. Each full stop in an ellipsis must have a space before and after it.

Text importation

Multimedia authoring packages do not generally have spell-checking or grammar-checking features and the author has to be very careful that misspelled words do not slip through and mar an otherwise professional project. All packages allow text to be imported into the project and this is the safest way to protect against typing or grammatical errors. Text can be entered into a word-processed file, which can be checked before being imported into the authoring package's project. The file types allowed by the authoring package should be checked and the text file should be saved in one of the acceptable formats. For example, this may mean converting a Word 2000 file, into an older Word 6 format.

Lists and Tables

Bullet points and numbered lists aid readability. Users, particularly those with reading difficulties, can be intimidated by the thought of tackling a large chunk of text. Breaking down information into smaller chunks allows the user to read as much or as little as they want. Lists are a convenient way to summarise a set of facts or arguments. It is best to use an odd total when numbering lists. When viewers see a heading such as *'10 reasons to buy our product'*, they assume the list has been padded to bring it to an even number. A heading such as *'9 reasons to buy our product'* is more acceptable.

Tables, on the other hand, are difficult to comprehend and large tables are only fully read by the dedicated viewer. Naturally, small charts are easier to read than large ones. There may be scope to reduce the table's content to show only the essential data (perhaps about four columns and four or five rows).

Where a lot of data has to be displayed, the key facts may be picked out in a different colour from the rest of the table entries. In addition, making each row a different colour aids scanning along the rows.

Consideration should be given to exposing one row of the table at a time, so that the information is explained as it is built up. This works where the table is a central part of the screen presentation.

Also, be careful that sans serif types are not confused in tables. The figure 1 and the capital I are almost identical. This is an even bigger problem when used in displaying formulae.

Lastly, if trends in numeric data are being displayed, it may be best to use a graph rather than a table.

Fonts

In the world of Windows and Windows applications, fonts are understood to be collections of alphabetic, numeric, punctuation and symbol characters as seen on the computer monitor or printed to paper. Windows fonts have four main characteristics:

TYPEFACE -   the actual *shape* of the characters, such as Arial, Times Roman and Univers.
TYPE FAMILY -   the collection of *variations* on the basic typeface, such as weight (e.g. bold, light, black), slant (e.g. italic or oblique), width (e.g. expanded, condensed, narrow), or combinations (e.g. bold-italic or normal-italic).
TYPE SIZE -   the *height* of the characters as measured in points, there being 72 points to an inch.
TYPE STYLE -   such as bold, italics or underlined.

From a printer's point of view, a font is a collection of the characters of one typeface, at one point size. So characters at 18 point Arial bold, regular and italic are all part of the same font, while these same Arial characters at 20 point make up another font.   Equally, a set of 18 point characters in Times New Roman would make up yet another font.   Since most multimedia applications handle fonts using the Microsoft definition rather than the printer's definition, designers are advised to adopt this approach.

Typeface definitions

The illustration shows the descriptions that are given to the different dimensions of a typeface.   The *'base line'* is the line on which the main body of a character sits.   The *'x height'* is

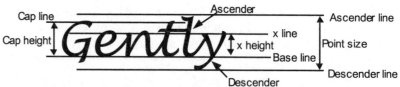

the height occupied by main body of each lower-case character.   The *'cap height'* is the height occupied by the main body of upper case characters.   Many lower-case characters, and even upper-case characters in certain faces, have extensions to their main body.   An *'ascender'* is an upward stroke, as in an *'l' 'd', 't'*, while a *'descender'* is a downward stroke as used in *'g'* and *'y'*.   Note that the font in the example has an ascender line that is significantly above the cap line (i.e. some lower-case letters are taller than capital letters).   In many cases, the ascender rises no further than the cap line and the full height is not used (see below).   A *'counter'* is the curved bowl of a character, such as in a 'b' or 'p'.

Point size

The height of text is measured in points.   There are 72 points to one inch and a 36-point headline might therefore be expected to be half an inch in height.   However, the point size is measured from the ascender line to the descender line and is not the same as the cap height.   If the text is entered in upper case, or a font contains only upper case characters, the space from the base line to the descender line is

lost.   There are normally no typefaces with a single character that touches both the ascender line and descender line.
Additionally, the typefaces rarely use the full height given to them and the displayed or printed text is less than expected.
The illustration shows the upper-case letter 'I' being displayed in a range of different typefaces.   It can be clearly seen that there are large differences in the cap height of each character - even though they are all formatted to the same type size!   There are also large variations in the x-height of different typefaces.

Bitmapped vs scaleable

The chapter on *'Computer Graphics'* examined the difference between bitmap graphics and vector graphics.   The same principles apply to text fonts.   Bitmap fonts contain the actual images of each character (i.e. the actual dot pattern that makes up the character's outline).   This requires a separate file for each point size, as rescaling a small type size to a larger size results in ugly *'jaggies'*, just as with other rescaled bitmap images.   Bitmapped fonts are now largely ignored in favour of TrueType fonts.
TrueType fonts contain the vector information for drawing each character at display time.   These instructions are used to create the rasterised version.   As each face has the same shape at all sizes, the same instructions are merely given different dimensions to create the face at any given point size.   They are *'scaleable'*.   Since TrueType fonts only contain descriptions, they have small file sizes - and they only require one description for each variation (i.e. there is a file containing a normal description, one containing an italic description, one containing a bold description, and so on).

Serif vs sans serif

A serifed font, such as Times Roman, has small details and strokes added at the top and bottom of characters. The added detail aids readability.   They keep individual letters apart while keeping words linked as a group.   They also make letters more distinctive (i.e. the lower-case letter 'l' is distinctly different from the upper-case letter 'I').   The serifs at the top of characters are used by readers to speed their recognition of words (to test this, cover the bottom of a line of text and see how readable the words are in serif and sans serif fonts). Serifed faces are used in almost all printed publications.

A sans serif font has a plain outline with no feet or twirls, the word *'sans'* being the French for *'without'*. It has a cleaner outline and is commonly used for titles, captions, labelling items in diagrams, and displaying scientific formulae.   It provides a good screen contrast with the main serifed body text, but its suitability for formatting large areas of body text is a matter of debate.

Proportional vs non-proportional

The output from typewriters is of fixed width. Every character occupies the same amount of space along the horizontal line. So, narrow characters like i, l, f, 1, etc take up the same space as wide characters such as w and m.   This makes the text much harder to

> This is an example of proportional spacing
> `This is an example of standard width printing`

```
9866   99.55   88
2311   18.11   28

9866 99.55 88
2311 18.11 28
```

read.   That is why typewritten notes always look inferior to book and newspaper print, which use proportional spacing of characters.

With proportional spacing, a character only occupies as much width of the screen as it actually needs.   So, the letter *'m'* uses more space than the letter *'i'*. As a result, proportional spacing results in more professional output, similar to typeset documents as seen in books.

However, one problem with proportional spacing is lining up data into columns as seen in this example. Since each digit occupies a different screen width (e.g. an eight is wider than a one), figures do not line up in neat columns. In this respect, a fixed-width character set produces more readable results.

Leading

Leading (pronounced as *'ledding'*), is the term used to describe the spacing between individual lines of text. In the early days of printers, thin slices of lead were inserted between lines of typeset characters, hence the name.   The technique is also termed *'line spacing'* or *'interlinear spacing'* and is a a feature available with web sites using Cascading Style Sheets. Generally, the leading is about 20% greater than the text size.   So, for example, a 20 point text would have a 24 point leading between lines of text.

serifs

Increasing the leading can be used to space out the lines of a screen quote. It can also be used to increase the space between scrolling lines of text, allowing the viewer more time to read the lines as they scroll. It is never a good idea to decrease line spacing as the lines start to merge, making the text unreadable.

Kerning

Proportional spacing ensures that each character does not occupy excessive screen width.   Nevertheless, each character occupies its own space; there is a distinct boundary between each character.

Kerning allows certain character combinations to overlap their boundaries, for a more snug fit and a more readable text.   For example, a lower case letter may partially sit under the previous letter's overhang, as in the example below.

Two WAV files   These words are unkerned. Notice the gaps between the letters.

Two WAV files   These words are kerned. Notice how the 'w' fits under the top of the 'T' and how the extremities of the 'W', 'A' and 'V' overlap each other's space.

Kerning facilities are common in DTP and word-processing packages such as Microsoft Word.

If the graphics/authoring package does not provide kerning facilities, this effect may have to be manually created in the graphics package (i.e. letters are cut and paste so that they kern).

Hinting

When typefaces are displayed at very small point sizes, it is difficult to define the character shapes accurately. For example, the stem (the vertical part of a character) may be displayed as one pixel wide on one character and two pixels wide on another character, or the pixels of a curve might merge into a single blob. Hinting uses instructions that ensure consistent displays at these lower point sizes.

Body text vs display text

Windows applications have a large range of typestyle available to them.

Some are designed to be used as the main text of screens and printed pages. These types are known as *'body'* typefaces.   Other typestyles are designed for their decorative or descriptive effect and these are known as *'display'* typestyles.

Examples of Display faces: **Arnold Bocklin**   **Army**   *Brush Script*   Space Toaster

Examples of Body faces: Baskerville   Times New Roman   Book Antiqua

Display faces are usually difficult to read at smaller point sizes and are rarely found used as a body text. Display typefaces are designed for headings and sub-headings and should be displayed no smaller than about 14 point.

Displaying web/screen fonts

At one time, font design was concentrated on achieving the most readable printed output.   To achieve WYSIWYG (What You See Is What You Get) results, the font destined for the printer was faithfully reproduced on the monitor screen.   This did not pay any regard to how readable the font might be on the screen, as the emphasis was on printed reproduction.

With the huge growth in reading information directly from the screen, printed output is a secondary issue. Indeed, for most multimedia work, the end user will not require printed output.

The aim is now to achieve the most readable <u>screen</u> output.   Fonts should be readable for longish periods without causing eyestrain.

The point was made earlier that most typefaces do not use the total allocated height.   In particular, a small x-height means that the main body of the text is using up a small proportion of the screen allocation.   The font size cannot be increased, as this makes the line width longer, resulting in fitting fewer words to a screen.

The answer lies in using typefaces with x-heights that make up a larger proportion of the height allocated by the point size.   Well-known typefaces that use this technique are Rockwell and Lucida.

V V   G G   Microsoft has produced two typefaces that are designed primarily for screen display. The serif version is called Georgia and the sans serif version is called Verdana.

e e   e e   If these are not already on the computer, they can be downloaded free from the Microsoft site (www.microsoft.com/truetype/) and installed.

r r   o o   The leftmost column displays the Verdana typeface, while the column next to it shows the same word displayed in Arial, at the same point size.

d d   r r   The third column displays the Georgia typeface while the last column displays the same word in Times New Roman, at the same point size.

a a   g g

n n   i i   In both cases, the x-height of the new Microsoft screen fonts is substantially larger than the other fonts, making them look like a larger point size.

a a   a a   The trick is to avoid increasing the x-height to the point where it is difficult to spot the difference between upper and lower case characters.   They are also designed so that the characters never touch, even at tiny point sizes (as low as 4 point).

In the longer term, higher-resolution screens will provide more screen pixels for each screen character. This will allow anti-aliasing techniques that result in clearer text displays at smaller point sizes.

Specifying web fonts

When designing web sites, there is no way of knowing what computer or browser is being used to read and interpret the web site's scripts.   If simple serifed and non-serifed body fonts are used in the design, there is a good chance that the site will be displayed at the receiving end in the same way, or a broadly similar way, as the designer intended.   The HTML code can, for example, instruct the computer to use Arial (for PCs), Helvetica (for Macs) or any other sans serif typeface.

When rare and exotic typestyles are required to be used for a web site, this raises serious problems.   It is highly unlikely that the site visitors will have the same fonts installed on their computers and they will not see the screen effect that was planned.

There are a number of ways that this problem is tackled and these are examined in the chapter on web site creation.

Using body fonts

The purpose of type is to make the text easy to read.   Fonts are a <u>medium</u>.   Therefore, body fonts should not draw attention to themselves.   The aim is to have the viewer read the text, not marvel at the fonts.   Most users do not like having to do a lot of reading from the monitor screen and anything that gets in the way of smooth and easy reading will deter the user from delving into the main text; instead he/she is more likely to skim over the screen headings and sub-headings.

The following advice is offered for using body text.
- Use the same font face and size on all body text throughout the project.
- Avoid using serifed fonts at small point sizes.
- Where the script specifies the font size, do not use less than 12 point for serifed fonts and 10 point for sans serif fonts.
- Bold typefaces at small point sizes tend to be difficult to read.
- Do not overuse capitals, bold face or italics in the text, as they tend to obscure the message.
- Bear in mind that underlined text can be used to provide emphasis - but is also used for text hyperlinks.
- Avoid using large fonts to emphasise parts of the main text.
- Use italics to emphasise a word in the text.
- Use a small graphic next to a block of text, or place the text between lines, to bring emphasis to the text.

Using decorative fonts

Decorative fonts are a different issue altogether.   They can be used very effectively to convey a mood Consider these examples:

ACE Builders Merchants	Wick Childrens Nursery
Chizzel & Robbem Accountants	Brenda's Hair Salon
Crossroads Coffee Shop	Bargain SuperStore
HENRI'S PICTURE GALLERY	Ajax Computer Repairs
Family Lawyers	HONG KONG RESTAURANT

Tradition and advertising have conditioned the public into certain visual expectations.   For example, many Chinese/ Cantonese restaurants use fonts like that shown above for their shop signs and printed menus.   And a *'trendy'* or *'whimsical'* font would not look too good on a project for funeral undertakers, while *'traditional'* and *'formal'* fonts would never be used on a teenage magazine or fanzine.

There is no formal categorisation of fonts and an examination of the surrounding environment quickly reveals current practice.   Magazines, advertising, catalogues, promotional leaflets, etc. are full of examples of the selection of fonts for different effects.

General descriptions of common fonts styles include:
- Traditional fonts use small x-heights and long ascenders and descenders.
- Elegant fonts use small x-heights, long ascenders and descenders, and have angled counters and hairline accents.
- Contemporary fonts use high x-heights and short ascenders and descenders.

Additional advice
- The aim of headings and sub-headings is to organise text information and present it in meaningful and readable chunks.
- Lots of subheadings help the viewer find information quickly and prevent the screen being one intimidating mass of text.
- Use larger spacing above a heading then below a heading.
- The importance of a piece of text can be indicated to the viewer by increasing its size and/or weight.
- Any typeface can be used as a heading, if the point size is big enough.
- A project should use a limited number of font styles.
- Do not use two different sans serif fonts in the same project.
- Do not use two different serifed fonts together in the same project.
- Many fonts will have similar outlines, but will have different typestyle names.   This is because typeface names can be legally protected, while the designs of typefaces are much harder to protect (after all, the letters of the alphabet are not copyrighted).
- It is OK to use a serifed and sans serif font in the same screen.

Graphics

Graphics tend to dominate the screen's text content, because images can be scanned much more quickly than text. This means that the use of graphics has to be carefully planned. The designer has to justify the use of every graphic used in a project. The purpose may be defined as decorative, educational, informational, or whatever - but they should not simply be inserted to fill a space.

The designer has to be aware that photographs and images are subject to misinterpretation. People use their own experience and knowledge to interpret a vague photograph or drawing. Users may be unintentionally offended by some material or be misled by taking the wrong meaning from it.

The purpose, type, colouring, use and positioning of graphics can all affect how well the project is received. These issues are dealt with below.

Graphics and learning

- Illustrations should be there for a distinct purpose.
- Using pictures generally is of more benefit to poor readers than good readers, who are more prone to appreciate concepts in written format.
- Using pictures displaying analogies is particularly helpful for slower learners. (e.g. using diagrams of shopping baskets and wallets to illustrate material on world economics).
- Viewers prefer illustrated text to viewing text on its own.
- Viewers are more drawn to a realistic drawing than to a basic sketch.
- Coloured pictures are recalled more accurately then black and white pictures.
- An organised layout of photographs is better understood and retained than a collage of photographs.
- Complex diagrams and illustrations may not produce the optimum results unless the text directs the reader's attention (e.g. in a series of steps relating to diagram annotations). The text must aid the reader, not hinder their absorption of the graphic information (e.g. if the text is too confusing, the diagram is largely ignored).
- Adding detail to an element on a drawing can improve comprehension, while adding too much detail can be counter-productive, as the essentials get lost in the detail.
- Pictures on their own (i.e. not linked to text) do not aid learning, although they may be decorative.
- Relevant pictures aid learning and recall.
- Diagrams are only useful if they are carefully constructed to ensure that they contain relevant and useful information.
- Although a picture can sometimes substitute for text, generally graphics do not replace text.
- A photograph or image should be placed close to the text that it relates to.
- A graphic in one part of the screen only helps the text it relates to - the other text is not improved on.
- Consider the cultural implications of including each image.

Graphics layout

- Take advantage of white space - don't fill every available space with the image.
- Do not place a border round the entire screen. Use borders above and below, or left and right, but not on all sides.
- Similarly, graphic images can be placed on two sides of a block of text, but there should not be images surrounding the entire text.
- Placing too many images on one screen is often a waste. Generally, there should be no more than three images per screen, excluding image maps and navigation buttons.
- Where many images are necessary on a screen (e.g. a project displaying the facilities of a hotel), small images should be used as links to larger images, rather than cramming the screen.
- Use a high contrast between graphics image and the background, as this maximises legibility.
- The shadows on buttons should not be too heavy (perhaps just one pixel wide) or they will be too overbearing.
- Captions should be positioned underneath or to the right of the graphic.
- For web sites, stick to traditional hyperlink colours. Although they can be set to whatever the designer decides, new colours schemes will confuse the user.

Finally, ensure that the source of all images is legal. This may mean purchasing royalty-free clip art libraries or royalty-free photographic collections. Alternatively, images can be created in-house or can be commissioned to freelance artists and photographers.

Video

The human eye is adapted to perceive movement better than uniform prolonged information. This means that moving material such as animations and video will predominate on a screen. The eye will roam around the screen if there is no movement to observe and will immediately detect and lock on to any screen movement.

Motion video can do what all the other media can't - provide realism to a project. Static photographs are very useful and are small in size, but video can convey mood much better than photographs. For example, the New Orleans Mardi Gras viewed on video and viewed as photographs are entirely different experiences. Unfortunately, video clips consume large amounts of disk space and have to be used in moderation. Therefore, the designer has to choose where they can be used to best effect. The question has to be asked whether the same learning or the same impact can be achieved by audio or graphic means.

There is a huge source of video material available. This may be original material (such as old videotapes, old cine film) or may be purchased or licenced from commercial sources. Alternatively new material can be shot or commissioned.

The designer must decide how a video is introduced into a screen. A clip may:

- play as soon as the screen is entered.
- only appear when the viewer opts to see the clip.

Video clips must be controllable. Viewers must not be forced to watch a long introductory video clip; there should be an option to by-pass the opening screen. Similarly, viewers should not be forced to watch other video clips. The screen should allow user controls to start the clip, stop the clip, replay the clip, freeze the action, play in slow motion, and play in a frame-by-frame mode.

The controls provided should have a familiar and intuitive appearance. They should be simple and look like typical VCR controls. Inventing new control symbols just confuses viewers.

Animations

Animations are a common and effective way to aid learning. They can display actions that cannot normally be viewed (e.g. the working of the heart or of the combustion engine) or are too small to see (e.g. the working of a watch mechanism).

Animations are often seen as being significant parts of a project and should be used for explaining key points. A long animation (e.g. showing the 25 steps involved in carrying out a particular task) is better broken into a set of shorter animations. The trick is to structure the set of sub-tasks so that the viewer does not stop after looking at the first few elements.

Animations often have a verbal narration, as this is more effective than just using accompanying text.

Some packages, such as Lotus ScreenCam, allow the designer to capture a computer session as a file than can be replayed later. This is ideal for teaching viewers how to use a particular software package. They also allow a voiceover to be added to the screen action, so that the entire animation can be used as a *'talk you through'* utility.

As with video, animations should be provided with user controls to stop, start, pause the animation and these controls should use the familiar VCR button icons.

Lastly, the designer must be aware of the dangers of flashing animation sequences. Photo-sensitive epilepsy affects 1 in 200 people between 3 and 18 years. The problems normally occur at around 10-20 flashes per second, but no more than 3 flashes per second is allowed on television. The dangers are worsened with high contrast black and white flashes. In 1997, almost 700 Japanese children were hospitalised with convulsions, vomiting and irritated eyes, after watching *'Pocket Monsters'* - a children's cartoon. The cartoon included a three-second scene of a bright flashing explosion.

Sound

Sound is an additive feature and must complement the screen content and not distract from it. The careful selection and inclusion of voice, music and sound effects adds to the experience of using the project. Typical uses of audio are:

- Verbal introductions (e.g. *"Welcome to the planet Zogg . . . . . "*. Can get tedious after repetition).
- Musical introductions. Don't have a long musical introduction that the user cannot bypass. Keep it short, or let the user by-pass the introduction.
- Aural warning (e.g. if the time limit for a self-assessed test is due to expire).
- Aural feedback (e.g. if correct/if wrong, clicking sound when the mouse key is pressed). Avoid having annoying fanfares, etc. every time a button is pressed.

- Verbal instructions.
- Reinforcement - encouraging words from the computer intended to *'humanise'* the project.
- Provide atmosphere, with sound effects, appropriate music and background vocals.
- Background music - intended to pass time or create an overall atmosphere. Remember, the user may have to listen to this music for hours. The designer has to decide whether background music is necessary, is atmospheric, or is just downright annoying. Particularly annoying are the MIDI clips that play throughout the browsing time of some web sites.
- Music in context - clips that are played at specific points in the project.

As with video and animations, sound should be controllable by the user. The user should be able to listen, pause, stop, rewind and alter the volume.

There is an even bigger source of audio material available than video.   This may be original material (sound removed from old cine film or old videotapes) that is owned or may be used with permission. Alternatively new material can be recorded or commissioned.   There are royalty-free collections of sounds covering a wide range of real world and synthesised sounds and music.   These will not cover all situations and specially recorded material will usually need to be gathered.

Sound and learning

Most audio content is not easily remembered.   Sound is therefore not very effective at conveying detailed information and should only be used for descriptions when accompanied by graphics or an animation. Similarly, sound should not be used as the only method of communication, as users may be deaf, hard of hearing, or viewing in a noisy environment.

Natural sounds (e.g. baby crying, water running, traffic noise) have more impact than artificial sounds (e.g. alien sounds, zaps and pings).

Some last layout thoughts

Screen design attempts to satisfy most of the people most of the time.   There is no 'correct' design, since all people are different and view the same material differently.   Design can, however, apply general rules.   For example, the page material (whether it is text, graphics, or whatever) does not have to be accurately centred on the screen.   Viewers often glance first at the area to the left of centre of the screen.

The eye also tends to ignore the screen extremities, with unequal weight given to the top and bottom of the screen area.   An examination of most books shows that they have a larger top margin than bottom margin.

A blank screen with a large block of text should be avoided, while a blank screen with a simple logo and button in the bottom right corner can be very effective.   There is plenty of scope for experiment.

—————Dumbreck

It pays to look around at other products and to examine web sites, to see what they get right and what they get wrong. Seeing what works and what doesn't provides very useful experience and should be recorded for future reference.

Copyright

There are two copyright issues to be considered when creating multimedia projects:

- The elements that are included in the project must be fairly and legally used.
- The finished work must be protected against abuse by another party.

Using other material

While professionals rarely react to their work being adopted for personal use, they will take action when their photographs, film clips, audio tracks, etc are re-used in a commercial product. Great care should be taken to protect against legal action.   The Copyright Licensing Agency run a *'Copywatch'* scheme to detect illegal copying and advice can be sought from them at 90 Tottenham Court Rd, London W1P 0LP (Tel 0207-631-5555).   If in doubt, seek written permission from those who own the rights of the copyright.   They may be prepared to give unconditional permission (after all, it is free publicity for their product), they may place conditions on its use or they may wish to charge some commission for its use.

An alternative is to stick to using copyright-free sound, pictures and clip-art collections. The original purchase price of the media should include a licence to reproduce it in any projects thereafter, without any further payments being required.   There are many stock photographs that can be purchased in this way, although getting the appropriate image may not always be so easy.

Of course, home-created material is generally copyright-free, with the following conditions:

- Audio/video recordings and photographs must be made after obtaining any necessary permissions.
- General photographs, such as crowd scenes or country villages, present no problems.
- Rock concerts have strict bans on recordings the live performance of their artists.
- Photographs and recordings of individuals, without permission, raise questions of invasion of privacy, if not legal repercussions.
- The rich and famous have the financial/political muscle to deter unapproved recording.
- Altering someone else's work does not free it from copyright. For example, downloading an item of clip art and altering some colours or adding on an extra piece here or there does not get round copyright. The original work remains and is the copyright of the person who created it.
- Making an exact copy or another piece of work, starting from scratch, does not make the image free from copyright. The original work is the intellectual property of its creator.
- While media representations of objects are strictly controlled, there is less of a problem with creating images of the original objects. For example, there is not problem in taking a photograph of the Eiffel Tower, or creating an original drawing of a particular brand of car.

Protecting material

Once the project is completed, the entire work and individual elements (i.e. the written words, drawing, animations, photographs, video clips, etc) should be copyright protected. The 1998 Copyright, Designs and Patents Act provides legal protection for computer material, as it is considered to be a *'literary'* work. The project does not have to be specially registered with any public body, filling in forms, etc. Copyright exists from the moment the work is produced. This may require proof of *'originality'*. In the event that there is a dispute over who first produced a particular image, photograph, video clip, or whatever, the judgement goes in favour of the individual who has the earliest proof of owning/using the material.

The UK is a member of four major international conventions on copyright and most countries of the world belong to at least one of them. This provides some measure of international copyright protection, although the legal and financial implications of copyright action deter many people.

The CLA points out a distinction between those who create material in their own right and those who create material for their employer. For example, if a lecturer writes student notes in college time, the material is commissioned, paid and owned by the college. Similarly, if a multimedia designer creates material during the working day, it belongs to the company. However, any work carried out in an employee's own time, using his/her own resources, is probably the property of the individual (unless the organisation's contract with the individual explicitly states otherwise).

Ensuring copyright

The work should contain the word *'copyright'*, followed by the name of the person or organisation and the date of origin. The use of the copyright symbol © is not compulsory in UK, but is recommended as it is required in some other countries.

This, of course, does not prove that the date stated is genuine. The traditional method is to post a copy of the work to one's self, using registered post (to get a dated receipt). The package remains sealed until it needs to be publicly opened to prove the date of originality. For very expensive projects, the work should be deposited with a solicitor.

The copyright on an idea is a little more complex. For example, if someone wrote an article describing a great idea for a project, someone else is entirely free to adopt the idea and turn it into a commercial work. However, if he/she writes another article repeating the idea, it is an infringement of the idea's copyright. Finally, designs are not copyright protected, although they may be registered at the Patent Office as a *'design right'*.

Implementation

The implementation phase is concerned with the production of the components (i.e. creating the graphics and animation, recording the interviews and voiceovers, filming/digitising/editing the video clips, writing the text copy) and integrating them into a project with an authoring package. It will involve using project management software, to manage time and resources. It may also require version management software to handle the masses of files involved in the project. These are constantly being added and altered and it is essential to ensure that there is no confusion over who is working with what version of what element at any one time.

Project management

The planning for a project begins at the earliest stage, with the detailed tasks being progressively identified.

Most projects should work on a time allocation of three thirds:

- One third design
- One third implementation
- One third testing

Many managers wish to concentrate on the middle stage, seen as *'getting the job done'*.   More enlightened, and usually more successful, managers realise that skimping on any one stage affects the quality of the final product.   A carefully planned design ensures that the project is successfully started and adequate testing ensures that it is successfully completed.

Large projects benefit from the use of project management software, to ensure that the most efficient use is made of resources and to achieve a working product in the shortest possible time.   A video crew might require a long advance booking, the well-known personality for the presenter/voice-over may only be in the country over a short time period, etc. and the activities have to be planned to prevent hold-ups. The illustration below shows a very basic Gantt chart.   It is illustrative only. It is not indeed to be used as model. A real working chart would have many more activities and more linkage between activities. Nevertheless, it shows how the software can be used to plan tasks, monitor tasks for slippage, alter tasks and produce reports for management information.

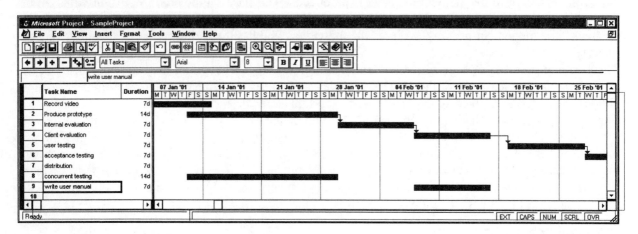

An alternative approach is the Pert Chart illustrated below. It contains the same information as the Gantt but displays the information in a different way.

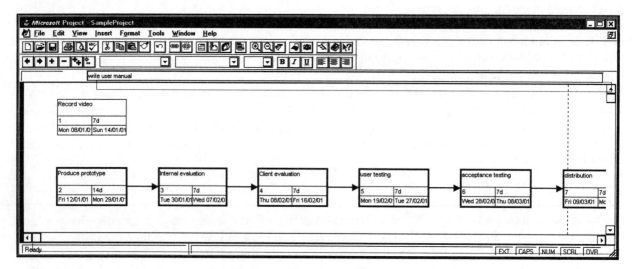

The creation of large projects using project management software is beyond the scope of this edition of the book.

Evaluation and testing

No projects work correctly first time. That is not a criticism of the team members or the team leaders. It is a result of the huge complexity arising from the size and scope of these projects. It is not an issue that only affects multimedia projects. All software suffers from the same problem (just how many bug fixes have Microsoft issued for their products?). The challenge is to recognise the inevitability of problems and to budget time and resources to tackle them.

Of course, prevention is better than cure and the organisation's culture should be one of minimising problems during the development process. A small design fault is easily fixed at the design stage. If it is missed and is allowed to shape the implementation of the project, it will be much more costly to put right at that later stage. The target of *'get it right first time'* minimises problems, reduces the hassle factor and saves a lot of money. Of course, extra money has to be spent on the testing but this is repaid many times over in the savings on bug fixing.

What can go wrong

To the question *'what can go wrong?'* there is only one answer - *'anything!'*

The problems are in three main categories:

Design flaws	These cover any mistakes made prior to commencing the implementation of the project. As such, they cover any shortcomings in the original specification. They could be learning issues (e.g. using the wrong criteria for self-assessment), navigation issues (e.g. poor module linkages) or omissions (e.g. forgetting to tell teams to use a particular font or colour).
Content errors	These cover any mistakes made on the actual screens of the project. Typical problems might include incorrect statements, misspellings, grammatical mistakes, poor quality images or video, or deviations from the design document criteria.
Programming errors	These cover any mistakes in the logic and operational flow of the project. Typical problems might include links that don't work, incorrect file handling, mistakes in calculations and running totals, and system crashes.

The testing stages are vital to ensure that the product meets the client's needs and to maintain the reputation of the company.   Testing is the process of locating errors in the project, with aim of eliminating them before the project is distributed.

Some of the tests cover errors in content and screen design - although a tightly worded design document should limit these types of problems.

Much of the testing concerns the detection of flaws in the functions of the project, mainly navigation errors, errors when passing information between modules and other errors (such as search engines, database activities, file handling, etc).

And, of course, there can be problems, even when the project meets the specification.   Flaws in the specification may result in an unsatisfactory final product, or the client may wish to alter the specification.

Multimedia companies put in place procedures to minimise the disruption to a project's completion and these centre round two types of check:

Evaluation

Evaluation checks that the project performs according to the users' requirements. Validation tests ensure that the project has been built to the original specification and has not moved away from the client's original intention.   These tests are on content, presentation and style, testing whether it addresses the agreed client group, and such issues.

Testing

These verification tests ensure that the project functions perform correctly.   This tests that all buttons work correctly, all navigation tools take the user to the intended destination, self-assessed tests provide correct marks, all video and audio clips play correctly, etc.   Functionality testing covers internal screen functions and navigation between screens and this is covered later.

Design evaluation

This is designed to reach clarification and agreement with the client on the requirements specification and design document.   The intention is to have agreement on a detailed set of specifications that the client will sign off as acceptable as the basis for the project implementation.   Increasing the specific details in these specifications reduces the scope for future controversy, a problem known as *'feature creep'*.   If the client wishes to change the project at a later date, they can be clearly identified as alterations to the agreed specifications and will have to be paid for by the client.

Before meetings the clients, the organisation's own experts would carry out their own design evaluation, This aims to correct problems before meeting the clients and to sharpen the terms of the specification. This may take the form of a *'cognitive walkthrough'*, where each task is compared against psychological criteria. This aims to identify the required cognitive processes and uncover any learning problems. Another approach is *'heuristic evaluation'*, where tasks are compared to usability criteria such as checking whether the system is predictable, consistent, contains task-oriented dialogue, provides feedback, does not produce memory overload, etc.

Concurrent testing

This approach recognises the need for continuous assessment by those developing the project's modules. The policy of *'Test early, Test often'* aims to identify and rectify errors during the development of each module.   Bear in mind that a module may contain programming script (e.g. for file handling, database operations, mathematical calculations, etc.) that has an effect on other modules in the project. Correcting errors at this stage is more efficient and prevents a possible knock-on effect in other modules.

Usability tests

Sometimes called an implementation evaluation, this takes place after a runnable system has been produced and is a user-centred activity.   Its task is to identify user perceptions, user satisfaction and user problems. It focuses on the project's tasks rather than its features and requires participants that match as closely as possible the customers who will use the final project.

Usability testing seeks to determine how typical users of the project will understand, use, interact with, comprehend and recall the project. The tests may be extended to collect reactions from a broader range of users. Participants are invited to use the project and their responses are evaluated.

Simple activities such as surveys and questionnaires can gather broad opinions, while laboratory observations or observing users in their own viewing environment produces more detailed information. User observations are less focussed on the opinions of the users and looks closely at the actual performance of users in navigating and using the project.   This take the form of a checklist that contains items on how quickly users can find a particular screen, if they can retrace their steps easily, if they can easily exit the system, etc.   It may also include tests on how well the material is comprehended.   This may only be as simple as asking the user questions at certain times. For example, a user may be asked to explain what he/she thinks a screen is about, after only reading the first couple of lines of screen text.

The process may be filmed and the observer would have a checklist of what tasks were required, what the user did, how the system reacted and the observer's comments.   The observer should remain in the background so that the process is not influenced by his/her presence.

Laboratory tests

Laboratory-based tests may involve recording equipment or two-way mirrors to closely observe the users' activities or may involve setting up logging computers that record every user activity (e.g. which screens they visited, how long they stayed on each screen, how often a screen was returned to, whether the help facilities were used, etc.).   Since all monitoring is hidden, there are no distractions for the user, but the environment is nevertheless artificial. Users often feel pressurised and feel the need to do and agree with what they think is wanted.

Tests in the field

These are conducted under more natural conditions. The advantages are that they are cheaper to run, and tend to uncover things not found in laboratory tests. Unfortunately, they are more difficult to observe.

In both settings, the user is allowed to carry on with the project uninterrupted, although help can be given when requested.   Both methods require preparation to get the maximum information from the tests. Experience has shown that conducting iterative tests with only small samples (around 6 to 10 people) will find 90% of problems.

Test specification

The testing of individual modules and their interactions is not a random activity. Every action that is included in the project has to be tested. Every screen, every button, every multimedia element, every piece of programming script has to be tested. This requires a systematic approach. The testers already have the navigation map that can be used to test navigational links. They also have to build up a set of other tests. Some are already available from the project specifications (layout, fonts, etc.). Other tests are developed as the implementation work proceeds. When a task is undertaken, the necessary future tests are recorded. Examples are:

- A project handles a database of 25 students for recording the results of student performance tests. Tests would include checking that the results were accurately stored and accurately recovered. It would also have to check what would result from a 26th student trying to join the group (e.g. error message, database corruption, system crash, etc.).

- A science project asks the user to enter a value between 5 and 15. Tests would ensure that the mathematical functions worked correctly (i.e. the value input by the user produces and displays the correct answer). It should also make *'boundary checks'*. This tests how the program responds to values that are at the boundaries of the acceptable/unacceptable range. It checks that the values of 5 or 15 accepted by the program, and checks what happens if the user enters 4 or 16.

- A web site uses a CGI script to check how often the site is visited. If the script is included on a splash page, the counter is incremented once for each visitor, as they only pass through the splash page once per visit. If the script is embedded in the home page, the counter can be incremented every time the user returns to the home page (depending on the user's web caching) - giving inaccurate results.

Testing stages

There are three main stages of project testing. The first two stages of testing are carried out in-house - within the organisation's own staff, while acceptance testing is carried out with the representative(s) of the client.

Unit testing

Often carried out by the programmer who created the screen or module (set of interlinked screens). This promotes *'quality at source'* - the programmer finds his/her own faults faster and clears them up quicker than an outside tester. The down side is that the programmer can often overlook the same fault, due to his/her familiarity with the work. It is almost universally true that everyone prefers programming to testing. This means that organisations have to create a climate that ensures that testing is carried out adequately.

Integration Testing

When the project is complete, all the screens and elements of the project are linked together. Integration testing checks that all the links work and that no errors have been introduced by the passing of information between modules.

Acceptance testing

When the project is finished its internal debugging stages, it is ready to be presented to the client. The aim is to get the client's agreement for a final sign-off. This allows the project to be installed or distributed. As mentioned before, it is vital to get the client's sign-off for design stage at an earlier time, so that acceptance tests concentrates on the search for operational errors. If not, the client may start raising issues and requesting amendments to design issues (usually requiring substantial extra work). The larger the number of client representatives at the acceptance testing, the more chance there is of new demands emerging.

Testing methods

In the commercial world, software developers produce two main testing stages. The *'alpha'* product is an early implementation of the product and is expected to contain lots of errors. It is intended for internal circulation only, so that these errors can be detected an eliminated. The testers are very thorough and very strict, so that the worst problems are eliminated before it goes out for more general testing. Once the alpha testing has eliminated the worst of the bugs, the *'beta'* version is provided to a selected audience outside the company, to people who have not been involved in its production. It is supplied on the basis that it will contain some errors and these new testers have not been party to any of the previous discussions and come to the product with a fresh eye.   Since they do have any preconceptions, they will detect problems that were overlooked by the company testers. The feedback from the beta stage is crucial in curing these problems, thus producing as reliable and useful a product as possible.

Internal screen tests
These tests are designed to check that the screen layout and all internal functions (i.e. those that carry out activities within the screen but do not take the user to another screen) work correctly.
Typical tests are:
- Do all the typestyles, font sizes, colours and positions match those specified in the design document?
- Does the background, button design and hyperlink colours match those in the design document?
- Has all text been spell checked and grammar checked?
- Do all users controls (e.g. mouse, keyboard, touch screen) function correctly?
- Do button rollovers roll over?
- Do image map components change when the pointer hovers them?
- Does a long text window scroll?
- Are non-functioning controls greyed out or hidden? Do they still function despite being greyed?
- Do the buttons that start video clips, animations, or audio clips fetch and run these components?   Do these components run smoothly, with no glitches?
- Do the user's media controls (e.g. volume control, video pause button) function as intended?
- If a web page, is the page size acceptable, or would it create problems with download times?

Navigation tests
These are designed to check that all controls that move the user around the project act in the way laid down in the navigation map.
The likely navigation elements in a project are:

Next screen	Previous screen
Next topic	Previous topic
Return to home screen	Exit
Return to top of this sub-menu	Move to new project area

The most efficient approach is to list all the areas of the project that function within their own boundaries. A typical example is a set of linear screens with a single access point to the first screen and one or more exit points that are all in the final screen.   These may be parts of main project content or may be subsidiary modules such as glossaries, search engines or help pages.   These modules can be tested on their own, as independent sub-programs.   The navigation through and back up the module's screens can be tested and the last screen should be tested to see that it does not include a 'next screen' button (since there is no next screen in the module).

Final thoughts on testing
If projects are subject to such prolonged testing, why are they still distributed containing errors?
The project undergoes concurrent testing, unit testing, integration testing, usability testing and acceptance testing, yet errors still manage to pass through the testing procedures.   A certain amount is inevitable, while other factors are predictable.   Developers are often pressurised to produce quantity and quality can suffer as a result. Early release dates leave little room for adequate testing. There may also be intense pressure to release a product before the competition complete theirs.   The only way to ensure the best quality product is to factor sufficient testing resources into the project budget.

Maintenance
The maintenance phase looks at making program changes after the completion and distribution of project. This could involve distributing patches to correct errors in the distributed product, or it could involve additions or alterations to the existing product. The correction of errors would be at the expense of the multimedia developer, if they were caused by the company's negligence. If the errors were caused by the client requesting the wrong specification, the cost is met by the client.
If the project was for a client, future changes may be made at the client's request, as an additional chargeable contract.
If the project is internal, it may involve adding new features for future updates (e.g. Internet linking, client databases, etc.).

Computer Graphics

By computer graphics, we mean all images that are artificially created, in contrast to images of the real world as captured by a camera (see the next chapter).

The image content may include drawings, text, and imported clip art. It may also be a hybrid image, combining drawn elements with real-world pictures imported from scanned photographs, pictures from digital cameras or still photographs captured from video sequences.

The use of images

Humankind has always used drawings and paintings to communicate - from the early cave paintings to the latest brand logo. We see graphic symbols every day and understand their meaning without thinking about them. Examples of everyday graphics include:

- Road signs (Stop, No Entry, etc.).
- Toilet signs (male and female outlines).
- *'No Smoking'* signs (a cigarette with a bar across it).
- The CND peace symbol.
- The nazi swastika.
- The communist hammer and sickle.

The list is endless, once it is given a little thought. No words have been used and sometimes the graphic is not particularly obvious - yet we are accustomed to responding to the symbolism of the graphic.

In other situations, graphics play an important informational or educational role:

- Street maps.
- The London underground map.
- Diagrams on how to assemble a model or kit furniture.
- Flowcharts for deciding on benefit entitlement.
- Car wiring diagrams.
- Cartoons demonstrating safer sex methods.

Other uses of graphics include making multimedia screens more readable (by breaking up large chunks of text) and providing brand identification (such as the Macdonalds logo.).

For all the reasons given above, graphics are a very important element in all multimedia productions. Some of the above examples use only black and white, while others use colour to add extra vitality to their message.

Image Properties

Although the content of images may vary widely, they all have some basic properties that describe them. Firstly, every image has resolution and colour depth. Resolution describes the size of the image while colour depth describes how many colours are in the image. An image can be quite large and have few colours, or even be in black and white, while a small image may contain many colours. They are only related in the effect that they have on the final file size. Larger images mean larger file sizes, with more colours also usually resulting in larger file sizes.

An image may also have other properties such as animation or transparency.

Resolution

As the chapter on screen technology explained, the screen display surface can be depicted as a grid of separate picture elements (pixels). At any one moment, each element is individually controlled to display a particular colour and intensity. Early monitor screens were constructed to display a smallish grid of a few hundred elements in each direction. Modern monitor screens can easily handle a grid size of at least a thousand elements in each direction. The monitor's resolution is a measure of its size when measured in pixels (i.e. how many pixels in the horizontal and vertical directions).

Similarly, the resolution of a graphic image is measured in terms of the number of pixels used for the image's width and height.

A VGA monitor screen has a resolution of 640 pixels x 480 pixels. Displaying an image of 640x480 would fill the screen. Similarly, an 800x600 image would fill an SVGA screen.

It is generally accepted that most monitor screens display around 70 to 90 pixels per inch, so all graphic images intended to be displayed on computer monitors (i.e. web sites, kiosks, multimedia CDs) should be created to this standard. Creating files to a larger resolution results in them being too large to be fully viewed on the screen and large resolution graphics should only be produced for printed output.

Colour Depth

The *'palette'* is the range of colours that the system is capable of displaying. In the past, graphics cards were unable to handle large screen resolutions and large palettes at the same time - due to the slow speed of the hardware and the lack of sufficient video memory. Even today, with faster cards and large amounts of memory on video cards, the user has to sometimes decide between having the high screen resolution screen (but only 16-bit colour) or having full colour (with less than the highest possible resolution). Most cards can cope with both demands at a reasonable frame refresh rate, but force the user to choose a lower specification when a faster refresh rate is selected.

The table shows the most common colour depths used with graphic images.

The 8-bit colour depth is commonly used for web graphics, while 16-bit and 24-bit depths are used for photo-realistic images. The 16-bit system is often described as *'high colour'* while the 24-bit system is described as *'true colour'*. All graphics packages provide facilities for reducing the colour depth of an image. Examples of reducing colour depth are:

Typical working colour schemes	
Bit Depth	Number of Colours
1-bit	2 colours (usually black and white)
2-bit	4 colours
4-bit	16 colours
8-bit greyscale	256 shades of grey
8-bit colour	256 colours
16-bit	65,536 colours
24-bit	16.7 million colours
32-bit	16.7m plus greyscale mask (alpha channel)

- Reducing a true colour image to 256 colours for placing on the Internet,
- Reducing a 256-colour image to 16 colours, where the image only contains a simple logo or cartoon.

The reduction in colour depth will shrink the final file size. In the first case, there will also be a reduction in quality. In the second case there is no loss of quality, since the image uses less colours than the range provided in the 256-colour palette. If the image, for example, was a web button or logo with seven different colours it could be reduced to a 4-bit scheme.

The 24-bit colour system handles the screen output in a straightforward manner. A 24-bit graphics card can vary the intensity of each primary colour (red, green and blue) to 256 different levels. Every pixel in the image requires three bytes (i.e. 24 bits), one for the intensity level of each primary colour. Each byte stores a value from 0 to 255, representing the 256 different intensity values. The monitor screen is displayed by three guns and each gun's intensity is controlled at any one moment by the value held in the corresponding byte. Therefore, if all three values are 255, each gun's intensity is at maximum and the pixel is perceived as being white. If all values are at zero, the guns are switched off and the pixel is perceived as being black. The setting of different values for each gun produces the 16.7 million colours (i.e. 256 x 256 x 256). This is known as *'RGB colour'* system and is used by JPEG files and other 24-bit file formats.

The 16-bit colour system only has 16 bits to store colour information on each pixel. Most commonly, it allocates 5 bits for red levels, 6 bits for green levels and 5 bits for blue levels. So the range of levels used to drive each monitor gun is less than with 24-bit systems and results in a set of 65,536 different colour combinations (i.e. 32 x 64 x 32).

CLUTs

The GIF format has a maximum colour depth of 256 colours and 256 different levels fit in a single byte (a third of the size of the 24-bit formats). This means that the image data cannot be directly used to control the monitor guns.

The solution used by GIF and other low colour range images, is to use a pre-defined set of colour values, stored in a table. Each colour has a colour number or *'index'*. This table is called a *'CLUT'* (Colour Look-Up Table) and it stores a maximum of 256 values. These values are used to set the proportions of red, green and blue to be used in each colour. Typically, zero would store white, while 255 would store black, 35 red, 210 blue and 185 for green. Since each colour is represented by a number, these numbers can be stored in the graphic file, along with a table that matches each colour to a table number. 256 values (ie 0 to 255) can be stored in a single byte, hence the name *'8-bit'*.

The diagram shows the process when the graphics file is read. Firstly, the lookup table is read from the file and stored in the computer's memory. Then each byte of the file (i.e. each pixel value) is read from the file and compared to the table. The corresponding red, green and blue values are used to control the monitor guns.

In the example, the third byte stores a value of 98. The values in the table switch the red and blue guns fully on, while the green gun is switched off. The result is that the pixel is displayed as a magenta colour. The two earlier pixels had a value of zero and these resulted in all the guns being switched on. This produced three white screen pixels.

The limit of 256 colours to a CLUT means that its smaller file size is gained at the expense of the colour range that it supports.

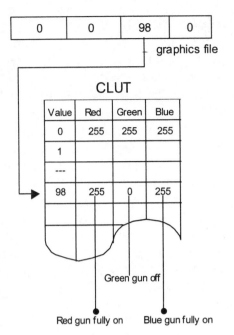

Notes:

- For simplicity, the example concentrates on how the lookup table works and does not show the effects of compression or of dithering.
- The range of colours currently stored in the table is called the *'palette'*.
- An image may not use all of the colours provided in the table. A CLUT may provide a palette of 256 colours but the image may only be designed using a few colours.
- Each image may use a different set of colour combinations. An image of a burning building may have a palette containing many shades of red, while an image of a gloomy dungeon may have a palette that contains mostly shades of brown and grey.
- If the hardware or software handles less colours than an image's palette, the colours not included in the palette are obtained by *'dithering'* (see below).
- Squeezing a 16.7 million colour image into a 256 colour version (e.g. converting a JPEG to a GIF) results in many colours being outside the palette's range and the colours not included in the palette may also be displayed through dithering (see below).

Dithering

When a palette of 16.7 million colours is used, all possible colours are catered for. When that same image is reduced to a lower colour depth (e.g. down to 256 colours for web use), it cannot contain the same range of colours as previously. Dithering is a method of representing other colours that are not included in the palette, so that the image appears to contain more colours than those allowed by the range stored in the palette. A colour <u>not</u> in the palette is displayed as mix of pixels of other colours that <u>are</u> included in the palette. Consider the case of pink not being included in the image's colour palette. Any pink areas could be represented by a checkerboard of white and red pixels. When viewed from a distance, these screen areas appear pink.

Note:

Since the colour is obtained from mixing pixel colours, a single pixel cannot be dithered; only an area can be dithered.

The problem with dithering arises when a colour requires several other colours to be included in the mix. This can easily result in a *'grainy'*, *'hatched'* or other patterned effect being evident in the dithered area.

The *'Bayer'* algorithm is fast but does not produce great results and most software packages use an *'error diffusion'* method of dithering. These use either the Floyd-Steinberg, Burkes, or Stucki method of dithering. The method recognises that the colours used to mix will not produce an ideal match for the colour being dithered. Therefore, it uses an error-adjusting method, where any deviation from the desired colour in a pixel are compensated for by a deviation in the opposite direction in the next pixel. This brings the dithered area closer to the desired colour and results in improved image quality.

'Screen dithering' is another form of dithering that is produced when the application package, or more commonly the hardware, is unable to handle the image's colour range. So, for example, if a 24-bit image were viewed with a graphics card that only supported 256 colours, the additional colours are dithered.

Colour schemes

From a hardware point of view, there is only one method of obtaining different colours on a monitor screen -and that is controlling the amount of emissions from the monitor tube's red, green and blue guns. From an artist or designer's point of view, other methods of controlling colour are preferable and more natural and the range of common colour schemes is outlined below.

RGB

The RGB model is based on setting the values that will directly drive the red, green and blue guns. Adjusting the value of one of the guns alters that gun's brightness and changes the pixel's colour. The RGB model is also sometimes called the *'additive primary model'* as it matches the way that the human eye perceives colour, and is the method used by scanners, digital cameras, camcorders and monitors.

HSL/HSB/HSV

Although the RGB model is easy to understand, it is quite difficult to make small colour adjustments with it. If the shade of a particular colour needs to be slightly altered, it might need the values of all three guns to be changed, and this can be a tricky process.

The HSL (Hue/Saturation/Lightness or Luminance or Value) model is also sometimes known as the HSB (Hue/Saturation /Brightness) model. As the name implies, it adjusts colours from three different standpoints:

Hue	the pure base colour (red, orange, yellow, green, blue and purple)
Saturation	the strength of the colour
Lightness	the brightness of the colour

There is sometimes confusion over the relationship between these factors. Each hue operates at a particular light wavelength. If the wavelength is altered, the hue changes. If light at all other wavelengths are added, the original wavelength is less dominant - i.e. its saturation level has been lowered. So, for example, pink is a red hue at a low saturation - not red at a high lightness level.

Software packages allow the user to control the image's HSB components, as an alternative to setting the RGB values. The value of the hue is often expressed (e.g. as in PhotoShop) in degrees on a colour wheel. The outer rim of the wheel starts at red, runs through to green, to blue, and back to red. Red sits at 0°, yellow at 60°, green at 120°, blue at 240° and magenta at 270°.

The values for saturation and lightness are expressed in percentages. A colour with 100% saturation is bright and vivid. The vividness diminishes as the saturation is lowered, until it appears as a shade of grey at 0% saturation. A colour with a lightness of 100% is pure white, while a 0% lightness is pure black. Intermediate values set the overall brightness of the image.

CMYK

This colour scheme is used for creating printed output, as commercial printers make a colour print based on plates that store the Cyan, Magenta, Yellow and Black (described as *'Key'*) components of an image. This colour model is not used in multimedia.

Graphic Images

A graphic can be stored as a bitmap, or as a vector image. Bitmaps are pixel-based, while vector images are description-based. For multimedia purposes, the majority of uses are filled by bitmap images, although Flash is a popular medium for vector animations on the web.

BITMAPS

A bitmapped image is one in which every pixel on the screen or in the image is *mapped* to a *bit* of data. With a monochrome image, there is a direct correlation between the number of screen pixels and the number of bits to store the picture. Each bit only stores whether the pixel is white or black. With colour pictures, each pixel is represented by a group of bits that determine the pixel's colour (more accurately described as *'pixel mapped'*). Either way, the image file contains information on every pixel in the image. Bitmap formats are used to store and manipulate photographic images, either scanned or imported from digital cameras.

VECTORS

A vector image is one where the data represents not pixels, but *objects*. These objects could be text, circles, squares or such. The image file does not contain data on every single image pixel. Instead, it contains a list of drawing instructions along the lines of
'go to 50 pixels in and 60 pixels down and draw a line to the point that is 120 pixels in and 200 pixels down'.

Of course, the instructions are more complex than that, as they may contain instructions to draw a curved line, a dotted line, a thick line, and so on. Vector formats are popular with freehand drawings, maps, diagrams, logos and cartoons, where the lines and filled areas are clearly defined.

Picture Scaling

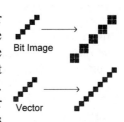

Bit Image

Vector

The benefit of vector files lie in their *'scalability'*. The user may wish to expand or shrink a picture so that it fits into a particular space in a document. This should be achieved with no loss of detail or picture distortion. The top diagram shows the result of scaling up a bitmap picture that contains a straight line to twice its height and width. Where there was a single pixel there is now a group of four pixels. Scaling the picture to four times its original size results in a group of 16 pixels for every original single pixel. The result is a very *'blocky'* image and the effect is known as *'pixellation'*. The vector file on the other hand represents the line as *'draw a row of pixels between point A and point B'*. Scaling the picture up still produces a single row of pixels, maintaining the fine detail. The illustration shows a magnification of a curve produced by a bitmap, compared to one created by a vector image.

Resizing a bitmap image to twice its height and twice its width results in four times as many pixels to describe the new contents. If the file is saved, it is now four times larger. With a vector image, resizing simply means changing the vector values, not adding in any extra data. This means that the new vector file displays a much larger image, without increasing its own file size. The vector file size will only increase if extra details are added to the picture, requiring extra data to be stored. Vector images are described as being *'resolution independent'*.

Depending on the image, either form could be more efficient. Bitmapping is far easier to use on complex coloured images such as digitised pictures, whereas a simple piece of computer-drawn clip-art would be much more efficiently stored as a vector oriented image.

However, if a large bitmapped graphic could be easily converted to a vector image without loss of quality (which is not often the case) then the vector image would most likely be smaller in size.

Graphics software

Application packages described as *'Paint'* software usually create and manipulate bitmap images, while those described as *'Draw'* packages usually work with vector images.

Corel Draw, Adobe Illustrator, Macromedia Freehand, and Serif Draw Plus are examples of high-quality vector packages. Adobe PhotoShop, Corel Photo-Paint, Paint Shop Pro and Microgafx's Picture Publisher are examples of high-quality bitmap packages. The *'Paint'* utility supplied with Windows is a typical lower-end basic facility, while many freeware and shareware packages sit between these in terms of facilities. Paint Shop Pro 6 can work with both vectors and bitmaps and most quality vector packages can *'rasterize'* (export their files in bitmap formats). However, due to the complexity of many bitmap images, particularly photographic images, it is unusual to effectively *'trace'* (convert a bitmap image into a vector format).

Aliasing

Software packages recognise the problem with scaling edges on bitmap images. It is not noticed on vertical and horizontal edges but can be very unpleasant on diagonal and circular edges. This applies to all objects including text.

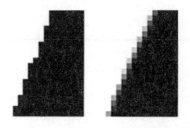

The effect is minimised by a technique known as *'anti-aliasing'*. The diagram shows two drawings of the same diagonal edge. The one on the left was drawn without using any anti-aliasing method and has crude steps along its edge, while the other looks much smoother. The anti-aliasing technique adds intermediate pixels of shades that merge between the two main colours. If the background was white and the object was black, anti-aliasing produces pixels of varying shades of grey, to remove the hard stepped edge. If the background was blue and the object was red, it would produce additional pixels of varying shades of magenta.

Using anti-aliasing to place objects or text into images with a large colour depth presents no problems and improves the overall image quality. However, it will present problems with file size with images of low colour depth. For instance, a simple two-colour title only requires a 1-bit colour depth (with the bit set on for the foreground colour and set to off for the background colour).   Since anti-aliasing introduces extra pixels with intermediate colours, the range of colours used has been increased.   A simple 2-colour text may now use, for example, 32 different colours.   This increase in colour depth results in a larger file size.   Another problem with anti-aliasing is its effect on transparent GIFs used for the web (see the chapter on web site creation).

File sizes

The final storage requirement for a bitmap image depends on its resolution and colour depth. The size of an uncompressed file is calculated thus:

$$\text{File Size} = \text{Bit Depth} \times \text{Screen Resolution} / 1024$$

Dividing by 1024 converts the answer into kilobytes.   For very large files, the answer can be divided by a further 1024 to get the answer in megabytes.

Some example file sizes are:

An 8-bit image that fills a VGA screen would require
$$1 \times 640 \times 480 = 307,200 \text{ bytes}$$

An uncompressed true colour image at 800x600 requires
$$3 \times 800 \times 600 / 1024 / 1024 = 1.373\text{MB}$$

An uncompressed 1280 x 960 true colour image requires
$$3 \times 1280 \times 960 = 3,686,400 \text{ bytes or } 3.515\text{MB}.$$

Compression

The file sizes are too big for practical use on web sites or in multimedia productions.   The files can be reduced in size by various compression techniques.   These attempt to store and convey the same image information using less bytes.   In some cases, a little of the image quality is sacrificed to achieve this smaller file size.   Files that degrade their quality are known as 'lossy' systems.

GIF files use a lossless string-table compression (LZW) method, while JPEG files use a lossy DCT (Discrete Cosine Transform) compression method.   Details of these algorithms are contained in the chapter on digital video.

FILE FORMATS

As for bitmapped images, the only difference between one file format and another is the way the data is compressed, and how much extra information is needed, such as height and width of the picture, number of colours, etc. This information is normally stored in a portion of the file called a 'header'.

The most common graphic file formats on a PC are:

GIF : The acronym 'GIF' is meant to be pronounced as 'jiff', but is usually pronounced 'giff'. GIF was designed for fast transfer of graphics data over modems, and stands for Graphics Interchange Format.   It uses a technique called LZW or String-table compression to compress graphic images, making them smaller for faster transfer over the Internet. Now a very common file format, GIF files can be found on web sites and graphics packages everywhere.

GIF files can have a colour range of any power of 2 - up to 2 to the power of 8. This means it could have 2, 4, 8, 16, etc. up to 256 colours. This does not mean that all those colours must be used, however.   The 256 colour limitation limits its ability to store photographic images with any realism, although GIFs containing photographic images are often used satisfactorily on the web.

There are two GIF formats - GIF87a and GIF89a. The GIF87a format is the most common and it supports transparency and interlacing.   In addition, the GIF89a format supports animation.

The type of compression used by GIF files is lossless, making it an ideal format for storing plain images such as logos, cartoons, etc.   On the other hand, photo-realistic images lose a lot of quality from being converted from 24-bit format to 8-bit format and JPEG is usually the better option in this case (see below). GIF files use a CLUT (colour lookup table) as explained earlier.

Interlaced GIFs and Transparent GIFs are covered in the chapter on web site creation.

PNG : Unisys owns the patent for the LZW compression used in GIF files and this produced a demand for royalties for the use of GIF files.   In response, the Portable Network Graphics standard was produced for transferring bitmap graphics files over CompuServe and the Internet.   It improves on GIFs by offering 8-bit, 24-bit and 32-bit colour and has its own 'zlib' lossless compression system.   Although a modern format, it surprisingly does not support animation.

PCX : Nobody seems to know what PCX stands for, other than that the first two letters are for 'Personal Computer'.   PCX files use run-length encoding (RLE), which means that simple computer-generated pictures are stored fairly efficiently.   It is comparatively inefficient at storing digitised or complicated pictures. Nonetheless, it has been around for some time and is now fairly common. PCX pictures may be found in monochrome (2 colours), 16 colours, 256 colours, 24-bit true colour, or even, rarely, in 4 colours. PCC files are PCX files by another name though they are usually smaller, intended for clipart.

TIFF : The Tagged Image File Format originated on the Mac computer, and was designed for use with desktop publishing. It is a complicated standard, so much so that some alleged TIFF-using packages may not import TIFFs from other packages. It can use a variety of compression schemes, and can have any number of colours, as well as a huge array of options, used by putting *'tags'* in the file header. The more exotic *'tags'* cause TIFF readers to occasionally *'screw up'* on TIFF files. TIFF files tend to be used more for DTP than multimedia.

BMP : BMP stands for Bit-Mapped Picture and is the Windows standard bitmap graphics file. BMP files are used for the background wallpaper in Windows. It is uncompressed, meaning that simple pictures will occupy much more file space than is necessary. It also means that complicated, true colour pictures do not require a sophisticated decoder to display them. A damaged BMP file means image distortion may occur, while corruption to most compressed files means complete unusability. There is also another format called the RLE format, which is a compressed version of BMP, but this is little used. Finally, a BMP file may be found with the extension DIB, for Device Independent Bitmap, but is basically the same as a BMP file.

JPEG : When the Joint Photographic Experts Group was appointed by the CCITT to design a graphic compression and storage scheme, the JPEG (pronounced *'jay-peg'*) file format was eventually created. It uses *'lossy'* compression, which means that slight detail is lost during compression. The level of detail loss is controllable, and a substantial space saving can be made even with very little detail loss. The JPEG compression standard is a complicated process involving several levels, and at first specialised hardware was needed to perform the process. There is a lossless version of JPEG, but this may require the extra hardware. JPEG files are stored in true 24-bit colour, and the JPEG scheme is much less efficient in storing images of any lower colour range. Although the system is lossy, it is better at storing photographic images than the GIF format, as the losses are small in comparison to the loss of quality in reducing the colour depth of photographs to fit the GIF 8-bit depth.

JPEG files are 24-bit, with a byte allocated to each of the three primary colours. This drops the need for a CLUT, as the red, green and blue monitor guns have a direct feed each of 256 different levels.

WMF : The Windows Meta-File format is a comparatively simple vector oriented format born through the Windows interface. It is very effective for DTP. Like most vector formats, it is little used for multimedia.

EPS : Encapsulated PostScript. This file format uses the standard PostScript language to talk to PostScript printers and is used for high-quality output. It is independent of the make of printer as all Postscript printers produce exactly the same text and graphic images when given the same PostScript commands. Most video cards are not equipped to display files in the PostScript language and it is common to embed pre-prepared EPS images into other applications such as DTP documents.

CDR : The vector file saved by the Corel Draw application package with a .CDR extension. Corel Draw is also capable of saving its files in a variety of formats such as EPS, PCX, etc.

CLP : The file saved in the Windows Clipboard when the user uses cut and paste operations or presses the PrintScreen button. The Windows Clipboard viewer allows the image to be saved away as a .CLP file. This file can be recovered from disk and placed back in the clipboard at any time.

TGA : The bit-mapped file format used by Fantavision's Targa systems. It is most commonly found in 24-bit colour, though it may also be 8-bit colour, or even monochrome. Targa files can be run-length compressed, which works well with monochrome and some 8-bit files, or uncompressed, which is most useful with 24-bit files.

HPGL : The Hewlett Packard Graphics Language is most common format for use with plotters.

GRAPHICS CREATION

This chapter does not attempt to be a tutorial for graphic artists. The issues of imagination, construction, perspective, etc are the subject of another book - or a college course. This chapter, however, looks at the main technical and practical issues involved in creating graphic images.

The main considerations when creating graphics are:

Format type Bitmaps can store photographic images while vector graphics consist of many drawn components. Bitmaps provide a range of manipulation options that are not available to vector images but lose much of their quality when scaled (see below). Vector images are scaleable with no loss of quality and would be the likely choice for creating symbols, line drawings and logos.

Elements Unless the image is from a real-world source (i.e. scanned photograph, picture from a digital camera, or other bit image), it is constructed from a collection of squares, rectangles, circles, polygons, lines, arcs or bezier curves.

Content   The elements have certain properties that can be altered for the maximum impact. These are element size (i.e. circle diameter, line width, rectangle dimensions) and appearance (e.g. box or circle, colour, line type - plain, dotted).

Location   Where the graphics appear on the screen and what proportion of the screen they occupy will depend on the nature of the final application.   Large graphics are suitable where they have a crucial role in the presentation (e.g. a car repair program would use large and clear diagrams).   Small graphics should be used where they should not distract the viewer from the main presentation.   Similarly, graphics backgrounds should not overpower the foreground message.

Perspective   The monitor screen is two-dimension; all screen content has only width and height.   To provide the illusion of depth, images can be made to appear as if they recede into the background. The left box in the diagram has a front panel and rear panel of the same size.   The rear panel in the right-hand box is smaller, which is perceived by the viewer as depth.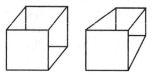

Layer   As in the example shown for text, graphics layering allows one item to partially obscure another.   In the boxes above, the front square is layered over the other lines and partially hides them from view.

Graphics importation

Multimedia authoring packages do not generally provide more than elementary painting features that are sufficient for basic boxes and lines.   For all other purposes, images are created in dedicated fully featured graphics packages and the finished item is imported into the authoring project.   The file types allowed by the authoring package should be checked, as it is unlikely that every file format is supported by the authoring package.   This may require, for example, exporting a Corel Draw image as a BMP file to be acceptable by the authoring package.

Graphics manipulation

The facilities offered by graphics packages vary and the most common manipulations are:

SCALING

The sides of the image can be pulled or squeezed so that it shrinks or expands to fill a given area.   While this poses no problems for vector images, bitmaps will lose detail on shrinking and will become *'blocky'* when expanded.

FILLING

The diagram shows a number of squares that have been filled with either a plain solid colour, a fountain fill (e.g. linear, radial or conical gradations) or a pre-determined pattern (e.g. bricks, curtains, granite).

TRANSITIONS

As with text transitions, the graphic can be written to the screen in a pre-defined way such as being drawn form the left or filling in from the centre outwards.

CLIPPING/CROPPING

Images often contain more detail than is required.   This distracts the viewer from the essential detail and occupies more disk space than is necessary.   The image can be clipped or cropped.   This brings the picture in from the top or bottom, or left and right borders.   The example shows the continent of Africa being taken from a map of the globe.

ROTATING

The text can be rotated from its normal horizontal axis to any degree and in any direction.   This can be used for visual effect or can be used to align the text along the outline of an object.

REFLECTIONS

A mirror image of an object can be in either the vertical plane, as in the example, or in the horizontal plane.   It is used for visual effect, or to save drawing time by drawing half of a symmetrical shape and creating an identical mirror image of the other half.

MORPHING

This takes two images and creates a set of intermediate images, showing the stages of transformation from one to the other.   Morphing can be applied to objects (e.g. swords are turned into ploughshares) or photographs (e.g. Tony Blair turns into Margaret Thatcher).

Getting started in Paint Shop Pro

The examples in this section use JASC Paint Shop Pro v6, although the techniques used are common to all packages, such as PhotoShop and others.

The application's interface is as shown in the illustration.

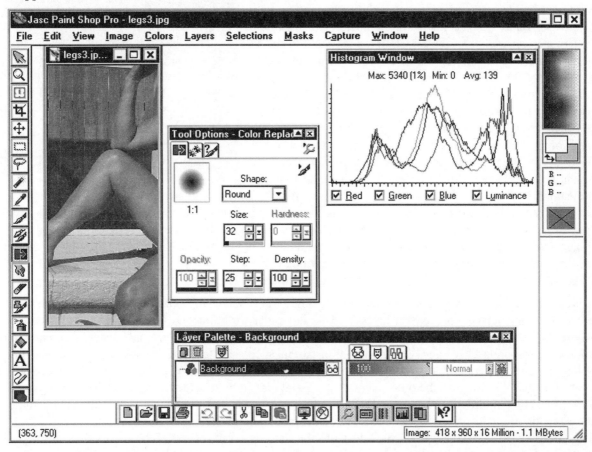

It has a large working area surrounded by various menu and tool palette option.   The main working area can contain one or more graphic images and extra tool or information windows can be added when required.   The example shows a single graphics file and three additional windows being opened.

Creating a new image

Choosing the *'New'* option from the *'File'* drop-down menu opens the dialog box shown in the illustration.

The Image Dimensions are usually entered as pixel values and the example shows a size that is one quarter of a VGA screen.

The Resolution value is usually set to 72dpi or 90dpi, being the common monitor resolutions. Higher figures are only necessary for obtaining more detailed graphics intended for printed output.

The *'Image Type'* menu sets the image's colour depth. 256 colours is adequate for all drawing needs but 16.7m colours should be chosen if a photographic image is to be included in the composition.   In addition, some of Paint Shop Pro's tools only work with 24-bit images. If necessary, the file can be created at this depth and reduced to 256 colours before saving.

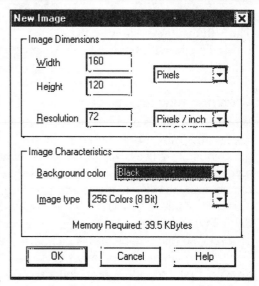

Clicking the *'OK'* button creates an *'active image area'* within the main work area. In the example above, a 418x960 image is sitting in the main work area.

This initial active image area becomes the default background layer of an image (see next).

Using layers

Before discussing all the objects and shapes that can be placed in the image editing area, it is best to understand some of the practical limitations of working with bitmaps.

Consider the image displayed here. It has a background photograph, a foreground photograph and some text.

The background image is loaded into Paint Shop Pro and the text is laid on top. As the text is fixed in position in the work frame, it permanently obscures the content underneath it. The data for the final picture only stores one colour value for each pixel. The white pixels of the text replace all previous values stored for those pixels. The user can move the text around, to find the best position but, once the text position is set, the user cannot go back and move it again. Similarly, if the font size needs to be increased or decreased or the type style needs to be changed, this can cause major adjustments. If the need for an adjustment is immediately spotted, the user can use the *'Undo'* facility, to revert to the layout before the text was fixed in position, and a second attempt at adding text can be made. However, the need for the alteration may only become apparent after a further series of additions to the image, such as the example of adding a face to the image. Now, the text can only be altered by initiating multiple undos, but these remove all the other additions.

Clearly, then, this is not satisfactory except for the simplest of graphics.

Major applications such as Paint Shop Pro and PhotoShop solve this problem by allowing the user to place different objects on separate layers. This is similar to the technique used in the early cartoons, where the background was painted on one sheet of transparent plastic, midground scenes were painted on another transparent sheet and yet another transparent sheet had the foreground figures painted on it. When the sheets were laid on top of each other, the entire picture was visible. Now, if one scene was altered, it had no effect on the other layers. Extra layers could be added, layers could be removed and layers could be modified - all independently of each other. The top-most layer will still obscure some of the contents of the lower layers, but the layer contents remain intact.

The computer application equivalent is to store the various layers of the picture as if they are separate pictures. Each layer can be viewed on its own, or along with one or more other layers. Now, each layer has its own values for every pixel and these can be changed within any one layer at any one time. When the entire design is finished, the layers are amalgamated to produce the final image file. This is known as *'flattening'* the image and it is only at this stage that the final decision is made on the value of each pixel in the final image. Where two layers have content in the same area of the screen, the values for the pixels at the upper layer are used in the final image.

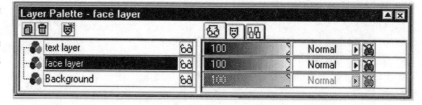

The illustration shows the Layer Palette with three layers being worked on.

Creating new layers

When a new file is opened, the software will create the first layer automatically. To add an extra layer, choose the *'New Raster Layer'* from the *'Layers'* menu or click the *'Toggle Layer Palette'* icon in the toolbar. Always name the layers when using multi-layered images, as this aids the later recognition of the layers. The layers Palette can be displayed at any time, by choosing the *'Toolbar'* option from the *'View'* menu and checking the *'Layer Palette'* box. Clicking the icon in the top-left corner also adds a new layer, while double-clicking on the layer in the Layer Palette, opens a dialog box that allows the layer to be named. A layer can be dragged and dropped into a new position in the order of layers, so that is contents take a higher precedence in the final flattening process.

The other main benefit of layers is the ability to blend the contents of the layers for added effects. Note how the first letter of *'Naples'* and a section of the face blend in the same space. This is a very powerful tool and is covered later.

Layers are essential for complex images but the user should get into the habit of always using them for all but the most simple of compositions.

Other aids

Before commencing to create graphics, there are two more points of support. The *'Help'* facilities are extensive and has an extensive Index and a very useful *'How Do I'* reference.

The other, indispensable, tool is the *'Undo'* button. This can be used for all kinds of purposes such as correcting mistakes and, when used in conjunction with the 'redo' button, switching back and forward to compare the effect of a particular modification (i.e. looking at the *'before'* and *'after'*).

The toolbar

This is a horizontal bar, at the top or bottom of the work area, displaying the most commonly used activities as a set of icons. Although the tools that appear are user configurable, the default set is as in the illustration.

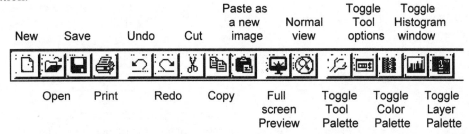

The first four icons provide the usual file functions - to create a new image, load an existing image, save an image (either a newly created image or one that was loaded and modified) and print the image.

The next two icons, undo and redo, are covered above, while the cut, copy and paste are covered later.

The *'Full Screen Preview'* icon displays the active image (the one highlighted, if there is more than one image in the work area) against a plain black background. All the tools and dialog boxes are removed from this view. Clicking anywhere on the preview screen restores the display to the state it was in before clicking the full screen preview.

The *'Normal View'* icon displays an image at its normal 1:1 magnification, to return to a view of the image before a reduction or magnification of the image was chosen.

The last five icons toggle various on-screen palettes. These can be hidden from view and only displayed when they need to be used. This lets the user see as much as possible of the image being worked on. Clicking an icon displays (toggles on) that palette, while a second click on the icon hides (toggles off) the palette. Hitting the *'Tab'* key hides all currently displayed floating palettes and these can be restored by again clicking the Tab key (this is handy when working with large images that are partly obscured).

The illustration printed two pages earlier, shows all the palettes being displayed. The Tool Palette is displayed down the left side of the application, while the Color Palette is displayed down the right side. The other palettes appear as information and dialog boxes within the work area and they can be dragged to positions that do not obscure the image or each other. The purpose of these palettes is discussed later.

Paint tools

A brief summary of the tools using for drawing and painting images is given below.

	Arrow tool	Used to decide which object is highlighted as the focus.
	Zoom tool	Used to zoom into the detail of an image.
	Mover tool	Used to move a layer by clicking on an object in the layer.
	Dropper tool	Picks up a colour from the image and to use as a foreground or background colour.
	Paint brushes	Used to paint on the screen.
	Eraser tool	Alters the image's pixels to the foreground/background colour or to transparent.
	Airbrush tool	Simulates the action of an airbrush or can of spray paint.
	Flood fill tool	Fills an area of the image with the background/foreground colour or with a gradient.
	Text tool	Adds text to the image in any type style, font size or colour.
	Draw tool	Draws freehand and point-to point lines, and bezier curves.
	Preset shapes	Adds outlined or filled shapes such as circles, squares and rectangles.

Adding preset shapes

This is the easiest way to get started with Paint Shop Pro, and many images employ basic shapes.

Clicking the *'Preset Shapes'* icon in the left-hand Tool Palette opens the dialog box shown.

It allows the selection of a basic shape from a drop-down list that offers a circle, square, rectangle, triangle, pentagon, hexagon, octagon and various star and arrow shapes.

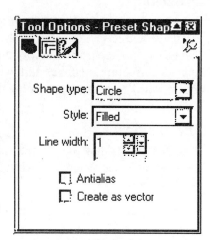

The *'Style'* menu allows the shape to be stroked (more aptly called *'Outline'* in early versions) where only the outline of the shape is drawn. It also provides a *'Filled'* option, where the shape is drawn and filled in the colour chosen.

The *'Line Width'* sets the width of the shape's outline and can be set to any value between 1 and 255 pixels.

Checking the *'Antialias'* box invokes anti-aliasing around the shape's edges (see earlier for an explanation of anti-aliasing).

Selecting colours

The drawing tools will draw in whatever colour is selected as the current foreground or background colour. The Colour Palette is displayed in the top-right of the screen. The top window displays all the colours that can be selected from.   The number of colours displayed depends upon the colour depth chosen by the user, when the new file was created (see earlier).   For example, if the user chose to create a 256-colour image, 256 colours are displayed in this box.   The two smaller boxes display the colours used for the foreground and background colours (the foreground colour is in the box that overlaps the other). These are known as the colour *'swatches'*.

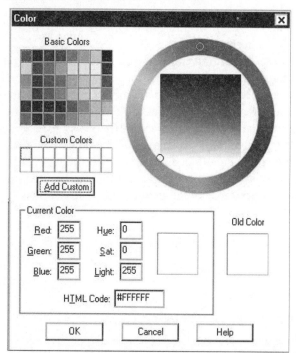

No matter what tool is currently selected, moving the pointer into the top box changes the pointer to the colour dropper.   Moving the pointer over a colour in the top box, displays the colour more fully in the bottom box. The numbers indicate what proportions of red, green and blue are included in any colour that the dropper is pointing at.

When the desired colour is found, clicking the left mouse button makes that colour the new foreground colour, while clicking the right mouse button makes that colour the new background colour.

If more precise control over colours is required, the user can click on a colour swatch to open the dialog box shown. Clicking the foreground swatch opens the dialog box to alter the foreground colour, while clicking the background swatch sets the background colour.

The dropper is moved around the square selection area and the required colour is selected by clicking the mouse.   Since it is impossible to show all 16.7m colours in the selection area, a colour from the *'Basic Colors'* selection, or a colour on the colour wheel can be selected. This results in a sub-set of the colours appearing in the square selection area.   For example, if blue was clicked in *'Basic Colors'* or on the colour wheel, the square selection area will only display the varieties of blue that are available.

Browser-safe colours

Internet Explorer and Netscape Navigator use the same set of 216 colours in their palette, with all other colours being dithered. If the final image is intended for web use, the image colours must be *'browser-safe'* - i.e. be made up from these 216 colours.   The safe colours are those made up from multiples of 51 and therefore suitable values for the Red, Green and Blue entry boxes are 0, 51, 102, 153, 204 and 255.

Using Colour Fills

At this stage, the image consists solely of bold, solid shapes against a solid colour background. Users often experiment with different colour options, deciding that the background colour or one of the object's colours should be changed. The flood fill tool, the one that looks a pot of paint being poured, is used to change and entire area of one colour to another colour. The area need not be painted with a single, uniform colour. The Flood Fill tool allows control over how colours are painted.

The steps for creating flood fills are:

- Set the foreground colour or background colour to the new colour.
- Click the Flood Fill icon to display the dialog box shown.
- From the *'Fill Style'* drop-down menu, select the type of fill required.

The illustration below shows just a few of the effects that can be achieved with fill styles. The middle tap of the dialog box provides control over factors such as the angle of the fill, fixing the centre for radiating fills, the amount of steps to reproduce in a pattern, and so on.

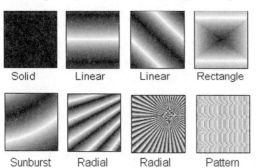

| Solid | Linear | Linear | Rectangle |

| Sunburst | Radial | Radial | Pattern |

Solid fills are useful for logos, cartoons, diagrams, etc, while gradient fills are useful for backgrounds, web buttons and special effects. When the fill style is selected, click the left mouse button over the area whose colour is to be changed. This will fill the area with the new pattern. If a solid colour is selected for the fill style, the area is flooded with the foreground colour, while clicking the right button floods with the background colour.

The examples show a linear fill and a radial fill being used as a background

Note:

The colour will flood into every adjacent pixel of the colour being replaced. This means that

if two adjoining areas overlap, the new colour fills both objects. For example, if a filled circle and a filled triangle of the same colour overlap, or even touch, both are changed to the new colour. Of course, if the objects are placed in different layers, they are treated separately. In this case, they can only both be changed by flooding them individually in their own layers.

Care must also be taken to avoid flooding areas that were not intended for alteration. For example, if an unfilled box, or other shape, sits in an area of a particular colour, clicking on the shape will only flood that area. However, if the boundaries of the shape are incomplete, the fill will leak out the gap and fill the entire area.

Flooding a selection.

Paint Shop Pro has a facility to make a *'selection'* (see later) which defines a shape on the screen. This shape is usually a part of the area of another object. The selection area can be defined and subjected to its own flood fill. The image of the cruise liner was obtained from IMSI's Master Photo Collection, (1895 Francisco Blvd. East, San Rafael, CA94901-5506, USA). The right-hand image shows the effect of defining some extra selections and filling them to represent the shadow of the hills, the reflection of the ship, etc. This technique is examined again in the chapter on digital photography, as its opacity and tolerance settings provide an ideal method for remodelling photographic images.

Drawing lines

The Draw tool, the one that looks like a pencil, is used to draw lines on the screen.   Clicking the icon opens a dialog box that allows the user to choose the type of line to be drawn, the width of the line and whether the line should be anti-aliased or clean.

With all lines, the colour of the line is determined by the mouse button that is used to place the starting point of the line. If the left mouse button places the first point, the line is drawn in the foreground colour, with the right button resulting in a line in the background colour.

If the *'Style'* option in the dialog box is set to *'filled'*, the area bounded by the lines is filled in the colour chosen for the line. If the last point laid down does not meet the first point, a line is automatically added between these points.   The filled option works with all types except *'single line'*.

The types of lines that can be drawn are:

Single Line

This draws a single line.   The mouse is moved to the start point of the line, the left or right mouse button is then pressed, depending on the colour of the line to be drawn.   The button is held down while the mouse is moved to the end point of the new line.   When the mouse button is released, the line is set in place.

Freehand Line

This draws an irregularly shaped line, under the control of the mouse or graphics tablet. It can be used to create hand-written effects, signatures and artist sketches.   The appropriate mouse button is clicked at the start of the line and held down while the shape is drawn.   When the button is released, the line is fixed. Given the difficulty in maintaining accurate control with a mouse, this option is used most effectively with a graphics tablet.

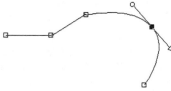

Point-to-point Line

This draws a set of joined-up lines from the nodes laid down by the user.   The lines can be straight or curved and can be used together in the same drawing.

The mouse is clicked at the first point and released.   As before, the left or right button is clicked to choose the foreground or background colour.   From then on, all other nodes are added using the left mouse button.

<u>Straight lines</u>

When the next point is clicked, a line is drawn between the two points (nodes).   This is continued until the shape is completed. During this time, the mouse can be clicked on any node and dragged into a new position.

<u>Curved lines</u>

To add a curve, click the left button and drag it slightly. This adds a curved segment node with adjustment handles, as shown in the illustration.

Clicking on a new position adds the other end of the curved line.

The curve's shape is altered by dragging the protruding adjustment handles (these do not appear in the final drawing).

When the completed shape is drawn, it can be fixed by clicking anywhere outside the drawing area, pressing the Ctrl-Q key combination, or right-clicking the mouse and choosing the *'Quit Node Editing'* option.

Bezier curves

This option draws very smooth curves but its operation takes a little getting used to.   Like the curved lines above, it provides handles to set the direction and amount of curve.

The first node is placed as before and the mouse button is held down while the mouse is dragged to the end position of the curve.   Two further points are clicked to place the control handles.   If both handles are clicked above, or below, the line an arc is drawn between the outer nodes.

The example shows control handles being placed above and below the line. This produces a sine waveform, as shown.

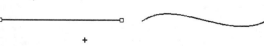

Paintbrush

The Draw facilities are useful for creating outlines shapes and adding detail to charts, diagrams and illustrations. The Paintbrush is a more artistic tool that works perfectly with a graphics tablet, where the tablet pen can be used almost like a paintbrush. The Paintbrush tool paints in the active image, using a larger range of effects than the draw tools. Clicking the Paintbrush icon brings up the dialog box shown. The options provided are:

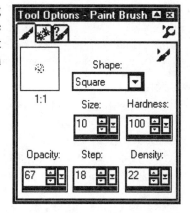

Shape

This drop-down menu offers a selection of different brush tip shapes. As shown in the illustration, they are horizontal, vertical, square, round, left slash and right slash.

The slash tips are useful in emulating handwriting, where the user may have a heavier vertical stroke than horizontal stroke.

Size

This sets the width of the brush tip and can be set from 1 pixel to 255 pixels.

Hardness

This sets how sharp the edges of the painted lines, with 100% producing very precise edges. As the percentage is lowered, the edges are progressively softened through increasing anti-aliasing.

Opacity

This sets the degree to which the paint is transparent, with 100% covering everything beneath it. As the percentage is lowered, the image from below shows through increasingly.

Step

This sets the spacing of the *'paint drops'*. The values that can be entered are percentages of the brush size. At 100%, the line is painted as a chain of adjacent dots (see example below). As the percentage is lowered, the dots are painted closer together, to the point where they appear as a continuous line.

Density

This sets the amount of paint that is applied with each brush stroke, with 100% covering the painted area completely. As the percentage is lowered, less of the paint is deposited on the image area with a brush stroke. As in real life, painting over the same surface again builds up the coverage. Note that this is different from the opacity setting. A low density percentage leaves unpainted spots that allow the image underneath to be visible. With a low opacity setting, an area can be completely covered with paint and the image underneath is visible over the entire painted area. These effects are not mutually exclusive - they can both be used together to produce added effects.

In addition, Paint Shop Pro provides some preset brushes that emulate the actions of painting with a piece of chalk, charcoal, crayon, marker, pen and pencil. These are accessed by clicking the paintbrush icon, just above the 'Shape' input box in the Tool Option dialog box. This opens a drop-down menu from which one of these options can be chosen.

Examples of the effects of different settings are shown in the table and illustrations below. The lines were drawn using a brush size of eight pixels.

Paint Brush Dialog Box Settings			
Hardness	Opacity	Step	Density
100%	100%	1%	100%
100%	100%	100%	100%
0%	100%	1%	100%
0%	100%	1%	33%
0%	40%	1%	100%

The three squiggly lines on the right are examples of painting in charcoal, chalk and crayon.

Like flood fills, the paintbrush can be used to paint inside selections. An area can be outlined as a selection (see later) and the painting will only affect the area. Any movements of the paint brush that stray outside of the selection are ignored.

Airbrush

The Airbrush tool is accessed by clicking on the icon that looks like a can of spray paint. It opens a dialog box that is identical to the one for the Paintbrush. It has the same options, which produce the same effects. The only difference is that it acts exactly like painting with an airbrush or aerosol of paint. The longer the can is left over an area, the more paint is deposited.

Zoom

The image that is displayed on the monitor workspace is initially shown at a 1:1 ratio. In other words, if the new file has been set to 320x240 pixels, that's how much space it will occupy on the workspace.

There are many occasions when the user will want to examine parts of the screen in more detail. This means zooming in on that part of the image, so that the area is enlarged.

For other tasks, such as applying filters, the user will want to look at the whole image, zooming back out once more.

Zooming in and out can be carried out in a number of ways:
- By clicking the Zoom icon, the one that looks like a magnifying glass and moving the pointer of the area to be the centre of attention. Clicking the left mouse button zooms in, while clicking the right button zooms out.
- By hitting the + key on the numeric keypad to zoom in, and hitting the - key to zoom out.
- By rolling the mouse wheel (if the mouse has a wheel) back and forward.

The zoom out will reduce the image up to one-twenty-fourth of its normal size, although the highest zoom out is only useful in an image of an immense resolution (one that is 24 times the size of the normal work area!).

The zoom in enlarges the image up to 32 times its normal size. As the zoom in becomes greater, the individual pixels that make up the image become visible.

This allows the user to carry out *'pixel editing'*.

Pixel editing

The illustration shows the effect of zooming in on a picture of the Empire State Building. When fully enlarged, as shown on the right, the individual pixels are easily identified and, more importantly, can be easily painted individually.

This allows the fine detail in drawings, maps, logos, etc. to be painted with the paintbrush. It also allows photograph images to be cleaned up or doctored, and this is covered in the chapter on digital photography. The width of the paintbrush is set to a size of a single pixel, so that the brush only accesses a single pixel at a time.

Eraser

The icon for the Eraser tool looks like the rubber on the end of a pencil. Clicking the icon opens a dialog box that is identical to the one used for the Paintbrush and Airbrush. It has the same options, which produce the same effects. The cursor is moved over the area for deletion, while a mouse button is held down. Holding down the left mouse button results in all the erased erases being painted the background colour. Erasing with the right button paints the affected area with the foreground colour. If the brush width is set to a value of one, the brush can erase down to single pixel accuracy.

Decreasing colour depth

The colour depth of an image, as explained earlier, can be reduced to decrease the final file size. There are two options that can be used and both are accessed from the *'Colors'* drop-down menu.

The *'Decrease Color Depth'* option opens a sub-menu with fixed choices such as 1-bit, 4-bit, 8-bit and so on. After choosing a new colour depth, a dialog box opens and the user is offered a choice of *'Nearest Color'* (replacing all colours outwith the palette to the nearest colour available in the palette) or *'Error Diffusion'* (i.e. dithering). The *'X Colors'* option also allows the image to be translated into web browser-safe colours. Although the error diffusion method may produce a larger file size, its quality is better than the nearest colour method, on all but simple block graphics.

Increasing colour depth

While decreasing the colour depth is commonly used, there are occasions when it is necessary to increase the colour depth of an image. This is achieved via the *'Increase Color Depth'* option of the *'Colors'* drop-down menu. This will not alter the colours used in the existing image. However, it will increase the number of colours in the available palette. This allows extra colours to be added to the image.

Examples of this are adding coloured captions to monochrome images and adding a true-colour photograph into an image that was previously 256 colours.

Adding text

Many graphic images will have text embedded in the image. For example, this may be used to add annotations to a diagram or to have a graphic background to a text message.

The text icon is the one with the capital *'A'* and clicking it opens the dialog box shown below.

Most of the entries will be familiar to users of word-processing and DTP packages.

The *'Name'* drop-down menu displays a list of all the type styles that are stored on the computer and the desired style can be selected from the list.

The *'Size'* drop-down menu allows the user to select the

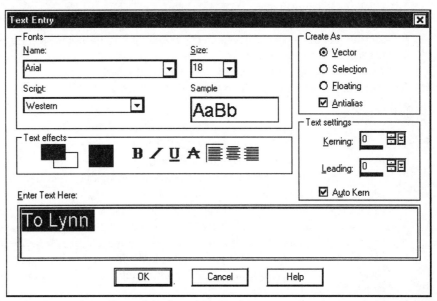

required font size for the text. The list offers a selection of common sizes in the range 8 point to 72 point. Any other value can be typed into the value box. The value can be an intermediate value between any two preset values, or it can be more than the maximum value of 72 points. There are 72 points to one inch.

The middle panel provides the controls over the font attributes (such as bold and italics) and alignment (such as centred or left-aligned)

The *'Leading'* values adjust how much space is inserted between lines of text.

The *'Kerning'* values adjust the level of kerning between letters on a line. The example shows the effects of kerning, with the upper sentence left unkerned. Each letter occupies its own horizontal space. The second sentence was produced with the *'Auto Kern'* box checked. Note how the *'o'* is tucked under the *'T'* and how the *'y'* protrudes into the space of the capital *'L'*, to produce a more natural look

The user enters text in the bottom box and, when finished, clicks the *'OK'* button. The text is then dragged into position and fixed by clicking the right mouse button.

Text Effects

Plain text is required for the body text of web sites, for annotating diagrams, etc.

The Headline text and web buttons are usually created with added effects for extra appeal.

The first two examples are of text created with Paint Shop Pro's own added effects. These are best used with the *'Floating'* and *'Antialias'* boxes checked.

The text is then dragged into position as before. Before the text is fixed in position, the effects are accessed through the *'Effects'* option of the 'Image' drop-down menu.

The desired effect (Drop Shadow and Chisel in the examples) is chosen and this effect is applied to the text. In both cases, the magnitude, opacity, etc of the effect is set by the user. More than one effect can be added, or the same effect can be repeated over again, before the text is fixed by clicking the right mouse button.

Apart from the effects built in to Paint Shop Pro, extra effects can be built up by the user, using other tools in combination.

Many of the tools provide a *'Feather'* option. This provides a smooth transition from the edges of the area being outlined. This provides a soft outline that helps a selection blend with its surroundings.

charcoal

The steps for achieving the charcoal text effect are:
- Make white the foreground colour for the text.
- Use the text entry dialog box to enter the required text, style, font size, etc.
- Check the *'Floating'* and *'Antialias'* boxes.
- Click the 'OK' button and position the text (do not click the right mouse button at this stage).
- Click the Paintbrush icon.
- Click the brush types icon in the dialog box (top right hand corner) and choose the charcoal option.
- Set the required opacity, density, etc., as required (will involve a little experimentation to get the particular effect desired).
- Paint over the text. Only the area inside the text letters is painted.
- Click the right mouse button to fix the text in place.

hot wax

The steps for achieving the hot wax text effect are:
- Make white the foreground colour for the text.
- Use the text entry dialog box to enter the required text, style, font size, etc.
- Check the *'Floating'* and *'Antialias'* boxes.
- Click the *'OK'* button and position the text (do not click the right mouse button at this stage).
- Choose the *'Emboss'* effect from the *'Other'* option of the *'Image'* drop-down menu.
- Choose the *'Feather'* option from the *'Modify'* sub-menu of the *'Selections'* drop-down menu. Set the value to a figure that is proportional to the font size (e.g. a value of 6 for 18 point text).
- Choose the *'Hot Wax'* effect from the *'Other'* option of the *'Image'* drop-down menu. Apply this effect twice.
- Choose the *'Emboss'* effect from the *'Other'* option of the *'Image'* drop-down menu. Apply this effect twice.
- Click the right mouse button to fix the text in place.

There is great scope for experimenting with different effects and different option settings. For example, the drop shadow is also effective when the main text colour is white rather than a dark colour.

Edit tools

Up to this point, the tools described have been used to create text and graphic objects. However, Paint Shop Pro, like all graphics packages, has a range of tools that allow extensive editing of these objects. This provides much greater control over the final graphic or photographic image.

A brief summary of the tools using for editing and manipulating images is given below.

Tool	Name	Description
	Deformation tool	Used to rotate, resize, skew and distort a piece of text, image or selection.
	Crop tool	Used to remove unwanted areas and borders from an image.
	Selection tool	Used to select a particular part of an image for separate processing.
	Freehand tool	As above but works with irregular shapes.
	Magic Wand	Used to select an area from an image, based on its colour.
	Clone Brush	Used to retouch photographic images (see the chapter on digital photography).
	Color Replacer	Used to replace all pixels of a certain colour to a new colour.
	Retouch tool	Used to retouch photographic images (see the chapter on digital photography).
	Picture tube	Adds chosen images at random as the brush paints.

Selection tool

The Selection tool, the icon that looks like a rectangle of dots, is used to mark out an area of the image. This area, known as the *'selection'* can then be treated separately from the rest of the image. The selection can be flood-filled, painted, deformed, and subjected to many other image manipulations.

Once outlined, the selection can be dragged to any part of the active image area. The selection can also be cut from the frame and pasted into a new layer or as a new image.

When the Selection tool icon is clicked, a dialog box displays a drop-down menu that offers a choice of rectangle, circle, ellipse, star, triangle, pentagon, etc., as the shape for the selection. The dialog box also provides control over the amount of feathering and the adoption of antialiasing.

The picture shown uses two layers. The background is a linear gradient fill. A photograph was loaded and the *'Arrow 3'* option of the Selection tool was used, with substantial feathering to obtain a soft outline. This selection was added to the gradient background as a new layer. The two layers were then flattened to produce the image shown.

Freehand tool

The Freehand tool, the icon that looks like a lasso, is used for the same purposes as the Selection tool, but offers more flexibility in outlining shapes. This makes the selection of irregular shapes much easier.

The earlier page in this chapter on colour fills showed an example of a cruise liner, with selected areas of

the picture being flood filled to add shadow and depth to the scene. These irregular shapes were first drawn with the Freehand tool in *'Freehand'* mode. The selections were then flood filled.

The Freehand tool provides three ways to make a selection. One of these is selected, along with any feathering and antialias options.

Freehand   **Point to Point**   **Smart Edge**

Freehand

The mouse cursor is moved to the point where the selection is to start. The left mouse button is held down while the mouse is used to trace the area to be included in the selection. This can be any shape and can include as much or as little of the image as required. As the cursor is moved, a line is displayed to show the boundaries drawn so far. When the button is released, a straight line is added to join the point where the cursor currently sits to first point of the selection. So, unless a straight edge is wanted, ensure that the mouse is moved as close to the starting point before releasing the mouse button. When the button is released, the selection is surrounded by *'crawling dots'* to mark the area that has been outlined.

Point-to-point

The mouse cursor is moved to the point where the selection is to start and the left mouse button is clicked. The mouse is moved to the next point and the button is clicked again. A straight line connects the two points. This is continued until the area is selected. When finished, the right mouse button is clicked and this adds a final straight line between the current cursor position and the first point added to the selection.

Smart edge

When a specific object is to be outlined as a selection, the above two methods are a little too crude. Consider the three example selections above. Attempting to outline all the details of the face and hair would be very difficult to achieve using freehand, even where the user has experience of controlling the mouse or graphics tablet. Attempting to use the point-to-point method would result in an image with multiple unnatural straight edges.

The *'smart edge'* option is designed for selecting objects with detailed outlines, with the minimum of effort. As the system detects the edges of objects, it works best where the object is clearly defined. The mouse cursor is moved to the point where the selection is to start and the left mouse button is clicked. The mouse is moved to the next point and the button is clicked again. A line is drawn to connect the two points but this line is not straight - it weaves out and in to follow the edge of the object. The selection is carried out as a series of such points.

Selections create a boundary around an object that can then be manipulated. There are occasions when the area <u>outside</u> the selection is the part to be processed. This can be achieved by choosing the *'Invert'* option from the *'Selections'* menu.   The outer area is now treated as the selection and can be dragged, copied, deformed, etc. This tool is known as the *'Magnetic Lasso'* in PhotoShop.

Deformations

The illustration shows a piece of text, followed by examples of rotation, skewing and distortion.   Deformations can be applied to text, clip art, photographic images or a selection

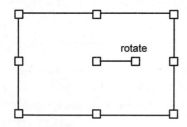

This effect only works with an object that is in a layer. If the object is in the background, it has to be promoted into being a layer. To do this, go to the Layer palette and right-click on the background entry. In the dialog box that opens, choose the *'Promote to Layer'* option.

Additionally, the only backgrounds that can be promoted to a layer are those that are either greyscale or are 24-bit colour.   This means that images of other colour depths (e.g. 32k colours or 256 colours) have to be converted to an acceptable format. This is achieved by choosing the *'Increase Color Depth'* option in the *'Colours'* drop-down menu.

To apply a deformation to an object, it is selected and the Deformation icon in the Tool Palette is clicked. The object is now surrounded by box-shaped tags as shown in the diagram.   Another tag appears at the centre of the object, with a horizontal line leading off to another tag on its right.

Resizing

If one of the tags on the vertical edge (i.e. between the corners) is dragged, the horizontal size of the image is shrunk or expanded, while dragging the tags on the horizontal edges changes the vertical size. Dragging a corner tag changes the size in the horizontal and vertical directions in a single operation.

Skewing

If an edge tag is dragged, while the shift key is held down, the image is skewed.   The direction in which the image is skewed is decided by which tag is dragged.   Dragging horizontal tags produced a horizontal skew, as shown in the above illustration.   A vertical skew is obtained by dragging a vertical edge tag.

Deformations

If a corner tag is dragged, while the shift key is held down, all other tags remain stationary and the image is distorted from that corner   The example in the above illustration shows that the text has been distorted from both lower corners, to produce a sense of perspective or shadow.

Rotating

If the rotate tag is dragged, the entire object is rotated in the direction of the tag movement.

These deformations can be used in combination, and in conjunction with other effects, to produce greater control over how objects are displayed.

Cropping

Where the required final image is smaller than the existing overall image size, the wanted section can be extracted by cropping.   This removes the unwanted section round the image, resulting in a more balanced image content - and a smaller file size.

The steps for cropping an image are:

*   Click the *'Crop'* icon in the Tool palette.
*   Move to one corner of the image to be retained and click the left mouse button.
*   Hold down the button, while dragging the cursor diagonally to other opposite corner.
*   Release the mouse button (the crop area is outlined).
*   Choose the 'Crop' option from the 'Image' drop-down menu, or click the *'Crop Image'* button in the Crop dialog box

This results in a smaller rectangular image.   The image can also be cropped to any of the pre-defined shapes offered with the Selection tool (e.g. stars, arrows, etc) or with the Freehand tool.   After defining the area, the *'Crop to Selection'* option is chosen from the *'Image'* drop-down menu.

Magic Wand

The Magic Wand tool also selects an area but does not use the mouse or graphics tablet to draw the area outline. Instead, the selection is made based on the colour within the image. The user clicks on the Magic Wand icon and clicks in an area of the image to be selected. The tool than automatically creates a selection that includes all the pixels of that colour. The tool's dialog box contains a 'Tolerance' input box, to control how close the pixel's colour must be to the chosen pixel, to be included in the selection. A zero tolerance results in a selection that only includes pixels of the exact same colour. Increasing the tolerance brings more pixels, of similar colour, into the presentation.

Color Replacer

The flood fill allows the colour of a specific area to be changed. However, if the same colour appears throughout an image, flood fills are a slow way to proceed. Imagine having to flood fill an intricate checked pattern with thousands of small square areas. It would be slow and prone to mistakes (click outside the desired area and the wrong area is altered).

The color replacer tool allows all instances of a colour to be changed in a single operation. It also allows selected areas to be altered to the new colour. The steps are:

- Select the colour to be replaced (usually using the dropper) as the foreground colour.
- Select the colour that will replace the original, as the background colour.
- Double-click the left mouse button to replace all pixels that are in the foreground colour with the new background colour. Double click the right mouse button to replace all pixels in the background colour with the foreground colour.
- For more selection replacements, hold down the left mouse button and move the mouse over the areas that should be replaced with the new background colour. All other colours that the mouse may move over are ignored. Holding down the right mouse button, paints out the background colour with the foreground colour.

Picture Tube

Clicking on the icon for this tool opens a dialog box whose 'Tube' drop-down menu offers a section of cars, spiders, leaves, etc as a painting image. The 'Scale' slider bar sets the size the objects will be when they are painted over the image. When the mouse left button is clicked, held down and painted over the main image. This facility, as provided, is of limited use. The range of tubes is quite small and is very well known. However, there are many additional tubes that can be downloaded from the Internet and the user can create his/her own tube designs and save them. This opens the opportunity for creating personalised backgrounds for multimedia productions.

Other Edit facilities

Apart from the options that are provided on the Tool palette, Paint Shop Pro offers other edit facilities that are accessed from the drop-down menus and some of these are covered below.

Flip

This facility does what it says - the object is flipped head over heels; what was the top of the picture is now the bottom, and vice versa. The effect can be applied to a layer or to a selection.

Mirror

This is another obvious facility. The image is reversed in the horizontal plane. The left hand side of the image is now the right hand side, and vice versa.

Canvas size

There are times when the image area is full of graphic objects and there is a need to add yet more to the image. The 'Canvas Size' option from the 'Image' pull-down menu provides an opportunity to increase the overall dimensions of the image without disturbing the existing image pixels. The dialog box reports on the current file dimensions and the user can enter new dimensions. If the new dimensions are greater than the existing dimensions, extra pixels are added around the existing image and the original image can be placed in any spot within the enlarged area.

If the new dimensions are less than the existing dimensions, the image is cropped to the new size. This is not shrinking the image (see the Resize option next) but removing some of the existing image information.

Resize

Cropping removes part of the image to produce a reduced image area, while Canvas Size adds extra pixels to enlarge the image area. In both cases, the remaining image details are represented by the same number of pixels as before.

The purpose of the Resize facility is to alter the resolution of the image, so that each detail is represented by less (or more) pixels than previously.

If the image is resized downwards, there are less pixels used to represent the same image. This produces a smaller file but has lost some detail consequently. This is a common method of reducing file sizes for use on web sites.

If the image is resized upwards, the image is enlarged and the extra pixels are interpolated (estimated).

The facility is reached by choosing the 'Resize' option from the 'Image' drop-down menu. This displays the dialog box shown. There are three options for resizing an image:

The 'Pixel Size' option has entry boxes for specifying the final pixel width and pixel height for the image.

The 'Percentage of Original' option has entry boxes for specifying the new size based on a percentage increase or decrease from the original

Checking the 'Maintain aspect ratio of' box ensures that a change to a 'width' entry box results in an automatic change in the 'height' entry box, to maintain the relationship between vertical and horizontal content. If the box is unchecked, the aspect ratio can be altered to any value, although care should be taken to ensure that the graphic content does not look elongated or squashed.

The 'Actual/Print Size' option specifies the actual size for printed output, which is not used for multimedia purposes.

Where an image is made up of several layers, an individual layer can be resized or the entire set of layers can be resized. To resize a single layer, the layer should be highlighted, the dialog box should be opened and the 'Resize All Layers' box should be unchecked before clicking the 'OK' button. To resize the entire image, check the 'Resize All Layers' box before clicking the 'OK' button.

The 'Resize' drop-down menu offers four methods for resizing the image:

Smart Size	Paint Shop Pro analyses the image and decides which algorithm to use.
Bicubic Resample	Uses interpolation techniques to minimise the 'blockiness' that often results from expanding a bitmap image. It is the best choice for enlarging photo-realistic images and images that are irregular or complex.
Bilinear Resample	As above, but used for shrinking an image.
Pixel Resize	Pixels are duplicated, or removed, until the specified width and height are achieved. The best choice for images that have hard edges (cartoons, diagrams).

After resizing, the effects of using the 'Sharpen' filter should be tested, as it often improves the image.

Bilinear and Bicubic resampling only work on grey scale images and 24-bit images. To resample an image with a different colour depth:
- Increase the image's colour depth to 24-bit. This is achieved by choosing the 'Increase Color Depth' option in the 'Colours' drop-down menu.
- Resize the image.
- Reduce the image's colour depth to the original depth. This is achieved by choosing the 'Decrease Color Depth' option in the 'Colours' drop-down menu.

Saving the image

Saving in Paint Shop Pro's own format (the PSP format) saves the image and all its properties. This allows a piece of unfinished work to be saved, complete with all its separate layers, etc. If the work is saved to a general format such as GIF, PCX, JPG, etc, the layers are flattened and lost.

ANIMATION

Animation, from the Latin *'anima'* meaning *'soul'*, is the computer modelling of movement.

At their simplest, animations use movement to draw the user's attention to the screen content. At their best, they use animation to explain processes that would be difficult to effectively get over with words alone. CD-ROM encyclopaedias are full of good examples of the effective use of animation - to demonstrate the workings of the petrol engine, the workings of the human ear, and so on.

Animation arises from a collection of graphic images being displayed on the screen one after the other in quick succession. The eye possesses a persistence of vision such that, if the images are images are updated quickly enough, the viewer does not detect the sequence as a set of different pictures. In this way, animation creates the illusion of movement. This is the technique used to show movies in the film theatre or on television. Ideally, an animation should display at 25 or 30 frames per second.

The animation software aids the designer to create animations quickly and with less pain and then exports the finished product in a format that can be used by other packages. Examples of output are AVI, MOV, and animated GIF formats.

Animation packages use two different approaches:

2D

These animations are drawn in two dimensions - width and height. There is no attempt to represent the third dimension -depth. They are used for simple animations such as animated logos and flying text. They are also used for more complex constructions, such as cartoons and animated sequences.

There is often no need to use more than two dimensions; indeed, trying to produce depth can sometimes make the presentation more obscure rather than clearer. An animation showing the stops that an aircraft would make on a route between Birmingham and Auckland only requires a 2D animation. Similarly, animation demonstrating a computer's memory management or a sort algorithm in software engineering is best shown as a 2D. In addition, of course, the public expects to see traditional cartoons displayed in two dimensions.

Application software for creating 2D animations include Macromedia Flash, Microsoft GIF Animator, Alchemy GIF Construction Set and Paint Shop Pro Animation Shop. These are aimed mainly at animations for web use, although they could be used in other multimedia applications. Macromedia Director also incorporates animation facilities, as do many authoring packages.

There are two techniques used in 2D animation.

Cel-based

The cel-based animation works on the same principle as the early film animators who painted a separate clear acetate sheet for every frame in the animation. This is the technique used in GIF Animator, GIF Construction Set and Animation Shop. The individual frames are created with a painting package and these packages compile them into an animated GIF (type 89a).

Microsoft PowerPoint and authoring packages such as MasterClass use a *'path following'* technique, where the application is instructed to create frames that move an object over a path drawn by the user.

Morphing

The morphing method uses the power of the computer to create many of the frames of the animation. The designer draws two key frames and the software creates the intermediate frames, a process known as *'tweening'*. Macromedia Flash uses a vector-based morphing approach and can output finished animations as animated GIFs, AVIs or QuickTime movies.

3D

Three-dimensional animations add the additional dimension of depth. At their simplest, they create animated logos that revolve, spin etc. At their most complex, they are complete 3D cartoons, such as Toy Story and Antz or objects merged into real-world movies (such as the prehistoric monsters in Jurassic Park). The objects may represent real-world or fictional characters, or they may represent inanimate objects (such the background in a flyby or walkthrough).

Since the objects are in three dimensions, they have curved and undulating surfaces, producing shadows as they move. The objects' surfaces have textures that have to be rendered. The texture may be skin, fur, scales, cloth, grass, wood, glass, leaves, and so on. As the object is moved, the texture of the object alters and the shadows are altered. This is a very complex operation compared to most 2D productions. With 2D, the object can simply be dragged a little way across the screen between each frame.

With 3D, every frame contains masses of new detail that have to be calculated and stored. This process, known as *'rendering'* can take a very long time. Of course, once calculated and stored, the animation plays back smoothly at normal speed.

Animation software aimed mostly at simple animations for the web include Cool3D and Simply 3D.

Powerful animation packages include LightWave 3D, Strata Studio Pro, 3D Studio, Bryce 3D and Poser.

Poser specialises in producing moving human and animal figures and has libraries of faces, hands, hair, etc. Figures can be assembled and organised to walk or run across the screen.

Bryce 3D specialises in creating landscapes where the user controls the map contours and the object surfaces. The iceberg in the illustration was created in a matter of seconds. Of course, creating and animating multiple objects takes a lot longer.

Animation formats

FLI

FLI, and its successor FLC, are both short for *Flick*, a file format used by Autodesk Animator. It is a very common animation format currently used on PCs, and uses a (comparatively) simple delta compression scheme.

GIF89a

This file type is really a collection of graphics images embedded into a single file. The file header contains specific playback information. If the viewing software cannot handle animated GIFs, it still reads and displays the first picture in the sequence. Otherwise, it plays back the file as a sequence of pictures at a pre-determined rate. This technique is used extensively on Internet web pages.

AVI/MOV

These have become very popular outputs format for animation software, as they can be easily integrated into so many other application packages. See the chapter on digital video for a full description of these formats.

Using Animation Shop

Animation Shop is supplied with Paint Shop Pro and works in a very similar way to all other simple animated GIF software, such as Microsoft GIF Animator or GIF Construction Set.

A set of graphic images is created with any drawing or painting package. Small changes are made in each successive image. In the example, the digger is slowed edged forward while the digger arm is lowered.

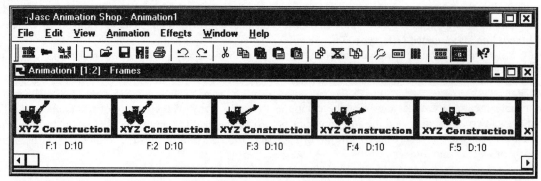

The illustration shows the interface of Animation Shop. The *'Animation Wizard'* is accessed from the *'File'* drop-down menu and its dialog box prompts for the names of the image files to be added. The files are added in the sequence that the animation will run and the user controls the delay between displaying each image. The package also provides for transitions to be added between frames. This provides effects such as wipes, dissolves and fades and these are covered in detail in the chapter on digital video. Every transition adds extra frames to the animation and increases the file size.

The package also provides a *'Banner Wizard'* that allows the creation of moving text effects. Text can be entered and be made to wave like a flag, move like a marquee, and so on.

The two wizards help to produce animations quickly, but the user can ignore the wizards and build the design from scratch.

Digital Photography

The power of the photograph

"A picture is worth a thousand words"

Like all clichés, it contains some truth.   A photograph can often sum up a mood or a situation far better than even the best advertising slogan, sound bite, or explanatory text. Like all photography, digital images can be used to accurately record details (e.g. pictures of machinery, accidents, etc) or to create or capture a mood (e.g. sunsets, weddings, goal-scoring, etc).

Digital processing offers the addition of easy picture manipulation and editing (e.g. removing red-eye, making the sunset warmer, removing drunken old uncle Bert from the wedding photographs, etc.).

Photojournalism

Photojournalism has produced many famous photographs recording significant events in history, or the state of a nation or technology throughout history.

Some classic photographs are:

- Youth standing in front of tank in Tiananman Square, China 1989 (Charlie Cole).
- President Kennedy slumped over in his open-top car after being assassinated in Dallas, Texas.
- Man chips at the Berlin Wall. 1989 (Anthony Suau).
- Starving Child in Sudan 1993 (Kevin Carter)
- The Loch Ness Monster.
- Winston Churchill giving his *'V for Victory'* hand sign.
- Pictures of the holocaust.
- Pictures of troops in First World War trenches.
- The execution of Ruth Snyder in New York State 1928 (the only known photograph of anyone dying in an electric chair).

Some pictures graphically report on events (photojournalism), while others have significantly altered public opinion.   One such photograph was of Vietnamese children running along a road, flesh melting, after a US napalm bombing run.   The revulsion against the US action helped shorten the Vietnam War. The lesson was well learned by governments when, in later conflicts, they sought to control information by replacing free-wandering reporters/photographers with selected military briefings to chosen journalists.

Advertising & promotion

The power of photographs for advertising is also well known, with many examples such as:

- The Che Guevara portrait that appeared on millions of bedroom posters, tee-shirts, etc.
- Government road safety campaign posters.
- The desperate pictures of starving children used by aid agencies to raise funds.
- The Benetton advertising billboards.
- The cover of the Beatles' *'Abbey Road'* album.

Advertising executives, sport and media personalities and politicians used to work to the old adage that says, *"there is no such thing as bad publicity"*.   Now they are less sure, as photographs of mad cows, the live exporting of livestock, brawling footballers and drunken personalities have harmed individuals and even entire industries.

Nevertheless, *'photo opportunities'* are regularly engineered to promote individuals, as in the following examples:

- The Royal Family, politicians and personalities parading their offspring.
- Government ministers kissing babies, visiting hospitals, opening prestigious events, and so on.
- Marilyn Munroe, with her dress blown up by a rush of air from a street vent.

Education & information

While the above examples may be well known or dramatic, the use of photographs in explaining issues is a long-established practice.   Consider how useful a manual on car repairs or a mail order catalogue would be without the photographs.

Getting the picture

There are four ways that real-world pictures can be captured for use in multimedia projects:

- Using a scanner to transfer copies of any photograph (either newly developed or old pictures).
- A 35mm or APS scanner, to digitise slides, negative strips or an APS (Advanced Photo System) adapter.
- Using a digital camera to capture directly as a computer file.
- Extracting a still image from a video clip.

The first three techniques are covered in this chapter and the chapter on digital video covers extracting stills from a video clip.

A quick guide to digital photographs

With a normal film camera, the light reflected from the subject being photographed is focussed on to a film that is covered in multiple coatings of a silver halide emulsion. Tiny particles of silver are created on the film in correspondence to the light intensity hitting different parts of the film surface. After processing, this forms the film negative from which the final prints are made.

With a digital camera, the light still passes through the lens but is shone on a complex digital device known as a CCD (see later). The CCD contains hundreds of thousands, or millions, of light sensitive sensors. The electrical charge in each sensor is proportional to the amount of light hitting it.

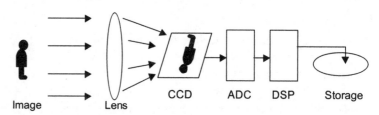

These analogue values are passed through an ADC (analogue to digital converter). This converts the picture information into a digital equivalent. The signal is then passed through a DSP (digital signal processor). This adjusts the signal for the optimum contrast range and can also compress the signal if desired. The signal is then saved to some storage medium as a computer file. This file can be loaded into any graphics editing package at any later date, optimised or edited, and integrated into multimedia projects.

Comparison of digital images and 35mm film

Inevitably, comparisons are made between conventional film quality and the quality from digital photographs. It is true that early models of digital cameras had very low resolutions and were totally unable to compete with emulsion film in terms of quality.

However, even the early digital cameras had some benefits over film cameras:

- The results of a photographic session can be reviewed immediately. The photographer can leave the location, knowing that the required images have been successfully captured.
- There are no time delays, waiting for the film to be processed, possibly to find that not all the images were usable.
- There are no ongoing costs in purchasing fresh rolls of film. The images can be downloaded into the computer and the memory can be re-used for other photographic sessions.
- There are no film processing costs (of course, the camera is much more expensive to buy initially).
- There is no wastage. Unwanted images can be deleted from the camera's memory and the memory capacity can be re-used to store other photographs.

The best current digital cameras rival the quality of conventional film. The silver halide coating on 35mm film has over 86 billion crystals per negative. These are contained in multiple (up to 17) layers of emulsion, each layer with different sensitivities. After removing the effects of lens error and focus error, it is roughly equivalent to a 4 million pixel CCD. Conventional 35mm film quality is the equivalent of 2400 lines per inch, which can be achieved with a digital camera using a 4 megapixel CCD.

Of course, the emulsion of a 35-mm print is evenly distributed over the film surface, while the sensors on CCD are regularly laid out in even lines and columns (due to the way they are produced). This subtle symmetry in the final output is noticeable to professional photographers. This effect is minimised in the new Fujitsu Super CCD which uses hexagonal elements arranged in a honeycomb pattern, to break up the regular lines and columns.

Scitex are developing a CMOS (Complementary Metal Oxide Semiconductor) sensor that is designed to fit into the back of a professional film camera, in place of the spool of film. This allows the existing professional photographer to get into digital photography without replacing all the camera equipment. The sensor has a claimed resolution of 6.6 megapixels.

How digital cameras work

Many of the principles, such as the operation of the lens, focal length, filters, etc apply to all cameras, whether they are digital or take standard rolls of film.

The Lens

Lenses are seen in many everyday objects such as spectacles, monocles, binoculars, telescopes and magnifying glasses.   They are made from a glass or transparent plastic material.

In a camera, its job is to focus the image of objects in the real world into the camera for processing and capture.   The larger the diameter of the lens, the more light it is capable of gathering.

Light from the image is gathered at the front of the lens and the light beams are concentrated on an area at the rear of the lens. With a film camera, the area focussed upon is the film; with a digital camera, it is a light-sensitive electronic device known as a CCD (see later).

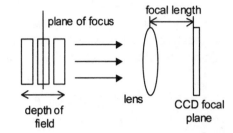

Depending upon the exact dimensions of the lens used in a camera, there is a point at which the image is sharply formed (i.e. in focus).   This distance is known as the *'focal length'* and is the measurement from the centre of the lens to the spot at the back of the camera (i.e. the camera film or the CCD) where the image is sharply focussed.   For cameras with a fixed focal length, the measurement is taken when viewing a distant object.   The spot where the incoming light hits the sensors is termed the *'focal plane'*.   The small size of CCDs means that they have a shorter focal length than those in 35mm film cameras.   It is typically about 8mm (somewhere between 6mm and 10mm).   This is equivalent to the 40mm to 55mm focal length found on a film camera, as the CCD area is much smaller than the frame of a 35mm film.   By convention, the specification of a digital camera's focal length is usually given as the equivalent figure for a film camera (presumably on the basis that most purchasers are ex-film camera users).

Optical zoom

When a camera has an optical zoom, the zoom lens can be physically moved in relation to the back plane. Altering the focal length alters the distance an object has to be from the lens to be in focus and alters the amount of the scene that enters the lens. The zoom lens has a variable focal length so that its field of view can be varied from wide angle, through normal to telephoto. Increasing the focal length is *'zooming in'* or taking a *'telephoto'* shot, while decreasing the focal length is *'zooming out'* or taking a *'wide-angle'* shot.

The range of focal length of a camera is measured in millimetres, while the range of a digital zoom is measured in multiplication factors.   Most models offer 2X or 3X, with the Sony CyberShot DSC-F505 offering 5X and the Mavica MVC-FD91 offering a 14X optical zoom.

NOTE:

The zoom factor measures the amount of <u>area</u> that is included in the captured image, not the vertical and horizontal dimensions.   So, if a camera was currently set to capture an image from an area that was 9m wide by 6m high, it would capture an area of 54 square meters.   If the zoom is then set to a factor of 3X, it will now capture an area that is one third of the previous size (i.e. 54/3 = 18 square metres).   It does not divide the dimensions down to 3m x 2m.   This would give an area of six square metres, which is a ninth of the original size, not a third of the size.

Typical figures for a digital camera's range are 28mm up to 115mm (expressed as 35mm film equivalents).

A camera with a stated focal length of 35-70mm has a zoom range of 2X.

Digital camcorders usually have a superior optical system to digital cameras.   A digital camcorder usually offers a zoom range of 10X or even 15X, while a typical digital camera has a 3X zoom.

Digital zoom

Some cameras also provide a further digital zoom factor. There is a great difference in how optical and digital zooms operate.   The optical zoom is used to fill the CCD area with light from a smaller or greater object area.   So, if the camcorder zooms in on an object, only the light reflected from that smaller area enters the lens and the full CCD area is used to capture the new image information. This maintains high quality pictures at all zoom settings.   Digital zoom, on the other hand, reads in the entire image information into the CCD and only uses the centre portion of the data, discarding the rest.   The data in the centre portion is then expanded to make it fill the camcorder's screen resolution.   The greater the digital zoom is advanced, the blockier the picture and high zoom settings result in unusable content. The optical zoom should be used at all times, unless a deliberately blocky effect is required.

Add-on lenses

If the camera's existing zoom range does meet all the photographer's needs, additional converter lenses are available. These screw into the front of the existing lens and range from a .45x wide-angle converter to a 5x telephoto converter. These ratios are applied to the existing zoom range. Therefore, a 3x optical zoom on a camera is extended to a 15x optical zoom when the 5x converter is fitted.   As the lens is zoomed in, less and less of the scene enters the lens.

From the opposite point of view, the wide-angle converter allows more of the scene to enter the camera lens. A 0.5X converter, for example, would double the area that is captured as an image. Wide-angle shots are particularly useful when the camera operator cannot get far enough back from the scene to be shot (e.g. filming in a small room, or wide panoramic scenes).   Wide-angle settings also exaggerate perspective.   This is sometimes used to achieve special effects (e.g. using a wide angle to shoot someone's head close up results in their nose and mouth being extra-prominent).

Aperture

The aperture of a lens controls the amount of light entering the camera.   The maximum aperture for a lens is set by the physical diameter of the lens.

The aperture is adjusted to suit the subject being shot and the prevailing light conditions.   In very bright sunlight, a lower aperture is required, while the aperture would be much greater for low-light conditions.

The setting of aperture sizes is on a scale of *'f numbers'*, such that each step on the f number scale lets in half the amount of light of the previous f number. This is not a linear scale so, for example, settings may be f2.8, f4, f5.6, f8, f11, f16 and f22 for a film camera. Digital cameras usually have only a five-stop range.

Moving from a setting f8 to f11 halves the amount of light, while moving from f5.6 to f4 doubles the amount of light.

This scale is not a set of absolute values, since different cameras have different lens diameters and hence allow different amounts of light in at their maximum setting.   Consequently, it is a relative scale that measures the ratio of the focal length to the diameter of the aperture.   So, a 50mm lens with a 12.5mm aperture = f4.

Depth of field

A camera is focussed on a particular subject, so that it is clearly captured within the camera.   The spot that produces the clear image is known as the *'plane of focus'*. Another object in the same focal plane will also be clearly focussed in the camera.   Objects that are positioned closer or further from the plane of focus distance may not be clearly focussed in the camera's image.

The *'depth of field'* describes the distance in front and behind the focal plane in which objects will still be sharply focussed. For a camcorder, it is also the amount of distance that an object can travel during a recording and remain clearly focussed.

The scope of the depth of field is determined by the camera's focal length, the lens aperture setting and the distance between the lens and the plane of focus. A shorter focal length and a smaller aperture (i.e. higher f-stop number) increases the depth of field.

The diagrams give some indication of the relationship between the various factors.   It shows, for example, that the depth of field is much smaller when shooting with a focal length set at telephoto, compared to shooting with a focal length set at wide angle.

It also shows the greater depth of field that is achieved with smaller aperture settings.

This limitation can be a problem in some situations.   At other times, the photographer takes advantage of this to deliberately have a defocused background (e.g. to concentrate on the foreground subject or to hide an unsightly background).

CCDs

Digital cameras do not use a roll of film.   The images are captured on to a magnetic storage medium. The camera's electronics carry out the conversion from light intensity to digital computer file.

Light passes through the camera lens and is converted into electrical signals by a CCD (charge-coupled device).   The CCD is a solid-state chip as small as 1/3" or 1/4" that contains a matrix of light sensors. Each sensor is a tiny photodiode that produces a value of electrical charge that varies according to the amount of light that hits it.   Each row and column of sensors corresponds to the picture's horizontal and vertical resolution.

The number of pixel sensors has a bearing on the final picture quality, with greater resolution being achieved by CCDs with a greater number of pixels.   This is not the only factor that determines picture quality as the quality of the lens, method of writing to tape, etc also have a significant impact.

When the user presses the button, a microchip reads the amount of charge in each cell.   The values from each row are read off and make up the serial image output stream. The electronics uses analogue shift registers to move the image data off the CCD and through the ADC.

The CCD specification fitted to different models varies and typical examples are:

Under 2 million pixels

The Agfa CL50 has 1.3 million pixels, the Kodak DC265 has 1.6 million, and the Epson PhotoPC 800 has 1.9 million.

Over 2 million pixels

The Toshiba PDR-M5 has 2.1 million, and the Ricoh RDC-500, FujiFilm MX-2700 and Kodak DC290 have 2.3 million pixels.   The Canon PowerShot S20 and Olympus C-3030 have 3.3 million pixels.

Film quality CCDs

The FujiFilm FinePix 4700 has 4.3 million pixels, while the Kodak Professional DCS560 has a 6 megapixel CCD. At the time of writing, FujiFilm were introducing the FinePix S1 Pro SLR, using a 6.1 megapixel Super CCD and IBM's microdrive for storage.

With the FinePix 4700 model, FujiFilm have introduced the *'Super CCD'* mentioned earlier.

Colour

As described, the camera would only produce a monochrome output, with the output signal varying purely in sympathy with the intensity of the incoming light.   The production of a colour camera is a little more complex.   Firstly, there are three sensors for each pixel, sitting next to each other in the horizontal row.   Each sensor is dedicated to producing an output that corresponds with the intensity of the red, green and blue components of the incoming light.   Colour filters are placed in front of the CCD to break down the incoming light into its components.   In this way, only the varying intensity of the red component reaches the sensors set aside for the red signal. Similarly, only the blue component of the light reaches the blue sensors and the green component of the light only reaches the sensors on the CCD set aside for handling green.

The camera has three colour outputs, one each for the red, green and blue components of the picture and their relative values are combined to produce the final colours stored for each pixel in the image.

Triple-CCD systems

Using three CCDs has been common in professional equipment for some time and is now being provided in some top-end consumer cameras and camcorders.

A separate CCD is dedicated to converting each colour component and a prism separates the incoming light from the lens into its red, green and blue components. The prisms direct each of these to a separate CCD. This provides improved sensitivity and colour reproduction, compared to single-CCD models.

Some triple-CCD systems use a technique known as *'pixel shift'*.   One of the CCDs is fixed slightly out of alignment with the others.   The summing of the three

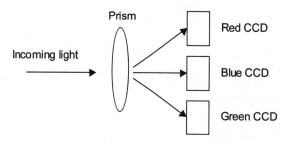

signals will produce a monochrome signal that has the same resolution as a system that is not using pixel shift. However, the overall effect is to improve low-light sensitivity.

Filters

Although photo-editing software can enhance the final graphic file contents, it cannot replace areas that have been completely darkened or washed out at the capture stage.   Therefore, digital cameras often require the use of filters.   Filters are additional optical devices that look like ordinary lenses.   Cameras that provide for filters have a fine thread machined in the barrel of the lens housing. The filter screws in this thread and fits over the lens.   This means that all light entering the camera has to pass through the filter and it can therefore affect the light in some way.   The filters themselves are threaded, allowing more than one filter to be fitted to a camera.

UV filter

This filter absorbs ultra-violet rays, preventing haziness and fogginess in distant landscapes.   Many owners keep this filter permanently attached to the camera as it is neutral in most situations and acts as a protector for the lens.   The lens fitted to a camera could be very expensive to replace if it became scratched or cracked, while a UV filter is a very cheap component.

Polarising filter

This is probably the most common filter that is used.   Light from the sun, a flash gun or a studio lamp are all unpolarised - the light travels in several different planes.   Sometimes, the light can reflect from a particular surface, such as water, glass or shiny surfaces apart from metal.   The reflection is at a shallow angle (around 30°) such that the light waves then all travel in the same plane. This makes it very difficult to shoot without interference from these reflections.   A good example is trying to shoot through a shop window; the reflections from the glass spoil the image.   Similarly, water scenes can be spoiled by reflections from the sky.   The polarising filter is fitted in front of the lens and rotated in its mount until the unwanted reflections are minimised or eliminated. Note, however, that some cameras rotate their barrel during auto-focus altering the setting of the polarising filter.

The polarising filter also increases the final colour saturation (the richness of the colours).   For example, the blue of the sky is deepened and the clouds are displayed more strongly.

Star filter

Sometimes called a *'cross screen filter'* it is available in 4-point, 6-point and 8-point versions.   A bright light in the picture is extended across the screen area in the shape of a star.   This is mostly used for night-time filming, where a sunset, traffic lights, car headlights, hotel neon sign, etc. are enhanced.

Soft focus filter

It removes any harshness from the lighting and gives a *'misty'* look to the scene.   It is often used for nostalgic or romantic photographs (e.g. the virginal heroine, the sleepy valley, etc)

Graduated filters

One end of the filter is clear, with a progressive tint towards the other end. It is used to overcome the extremes of contrast in sunny locations.   Normally, the camera's automatic exposure system averages out the incoming light.   This might leave the bright sky washed out and the foreground too dark.   Moving to manual exposure allows the foreground to be given more exposure, but this results in the sky becoming even further washed out.   The filter is fitted with the darker end at the top.   This reduces the amount of light from the bright sky, lowering the contrast ratio and preventing the scene contents from being driven into the extremes of darkness or washout.   These filters are effective with both automatic and manual exposure.   Graduated filters are produced with varying properties.

Graduated Filters and their uses	
Filter type	**Description**
Graduated blue filter	Minimises extreme light difference between sky and landscape. Does not affect the colour content of the scene.
Graduated grey filter	Minimises extreme light difference between different areas of a landscape. Does not affect the colour content of the scene.
Graduated tobacco filter	Used to enhance shots of sunsets and sunrises.

Other filters

Many filters that are available for film cameras fit on digital camera lens.   This allows a whole range of special effect filters to be used.   In addition to the filters mentioned above, other filter types include:
- Multi-image filters (multiple copies of the image are captured in a prism-like effect)
- Warm filters (have a slight orange tint to overcome some cold effects from harsh light. People look sun-tanned and locations appear to be bathed in an evening sunlight).

Storage problems

As digital cameras have developed, their CCDs have included more and more pixels. While this provides a great boost to the image's resolution, it also means that there is a greatly increased file size.

There is always a trade-off between the amount of storage, the resolution at which the image is captured and the number of pictures that can be stored.   Early digital cameras were sold with a fixed amount of built-in storage. This meant that the user had top either settle for low resolution image, or take less photographs. The arrival of removable storage eases the situation, but purchasing a collection of memory cards is expensive.

Colours

Photorealistic images are much larger than cartoons and clip art.   Clip art only uses a small number of different colours, while a real-world image is made up of millions of different colours and shades.   The amount of storage space for a photograph is therefore much higher than simple graphics.   Cartoons, logos, etc. use up to 256 different colours, while photographs use 16.7 million different colours. Cartoons only requires eight bits (i.e. a byte) to represent any individual pixel, while the digitised photograph uses 24 bits (i.e. three bytes).   This means that photorealistic images will always be three times larger than a 256-colour graphic.   It may be possible, in some circumstances, to reduce a photographic image to 256 colours. This reduction in colour depth (i.e. bit depth) may be used to create special effects.   Alternatively, it may be used to further shrink the storage needs of a small web image, where a reduction in colours may not be so noticeable.

Resolution and file size

The largest possible file size, for a single image, for a particular camera is produced by storing its highest resolution setting, at full 24-bit colour, without any compression.

The storage requirement of an uncompressed photo-realistic file is calculated thus:

File Size = Bit Depth x Screen Resolution / 1024

The bit depth for a photograph is always 16.7 million colours which requires 3 bytes of storage for each pixel in the picture (i.e. 24-bit colour divided by 8 to convert the figure to bytes). Dividing by 1024 converts the answer into kilobytes.   For very large files, the answer can be divided by a further 1024 to get the answer in megabytes.

Some example uncompressed file sizes are:

- A photograph intended to fill a VGA screen would require
  3 x 640 x 480 = 921,600 bytes
- A 1280 x 960 image requires
  3 x 1280 x 960 = 3,686,400 bytes or 3.515MB.
- The Ricoh RDC-5000 has a resolution of 1792x1200. This would require a huge
  3 x 1792 1200 / 1024 / 1024 = 6.152MB
- The FujiFilm FinePix 4700 has a maximum resolution of 2400x1800, requiring a massive
  3 x 2400 x 1800 /1024 / 1024 = 13MB of storage for each uncompressed image.

An alternative way to calculate the largest file size is to take a camera's CCD, multiply it by three and convert it into binary numbering.

So, if a camera states that it has 2.1 megapixels, the calculation is
  2,100,000 x 3 /1024 /1024 = 6MB

Compression

It is currently impractical to store many images of 6MB and 13MB on a removeable storage system, although the supply of digital cameras with miniature hard disks will ease the problem. Even then, the huge files will take a little time to download from the camera into the computer.

The current solution lies in compressing the image files down to a much smaller storage size.   This is usually some form of JPEG algorithm and files are saved with the .jpg extension.   More details on compression techniques are given in other chapters.

Since JPEG compression is a 'lossy' system, some degradation of the image results from this squashing of the file size. The greater the file compression, the greater the file degradation. Most cameras offer both a choice of resolution (e.g. standard, high) and level of compression (e.g. good, better or best).

For example, a 8MB storage card may hold 36 images at high compression, 18 images at medium compression and only two uncompressed images.

Storage media

Early models had permanent, built-in memory chips (of around 4MB or 8MB) and there was no means of adding extra storage. Some models still provide built-in memory but also allow the use of add-on memory cards (e.g. the Ricoh RDC-5000, the Musteck VDC-300 and the Trust range of cameras).

Most cameras use memory cards that are slotted into the camera. When the card is full, it is removed from the camera and another card is inserted. All forms of removable media have to be small, to match the small size of the cameras. Most are solid state devices, offering non-volatile flash memory. This means that they do not lose contents when the camera is switched off. The most popular devices currently in use are the SmartMedia and CompactFlash cards. The full range of devices used to store digital images is explained below.

SmartMedia

This storage medium is as thin as a credit card and shaped something like a small floppy disk, although a lot smaller at 45mm x 37mm x 0.78mm. It is available in capacities up to 32MB. It has a row of 22-pins for its connection.

CompactFlash

This card is roughly the same size but at 43mm x 36mm x 3.3mm it is about the size of a book of matches. It is available in capacities up to 64MB. It has a 50-pin connection that fits a PCMCIA type II 68-pin card adapter.

Sony Memory Stick

This is a relatively new technology developed by Sony. At 50mm x 21.5mm, it looks like half a stick of chewing gum. It is available in capacities up to 64MB and has a write-protect switch like a floppy disk. It is used in the Sony DSC-55E digital camera and is used to store still images in their DCR PC100-E camcorder.

Floppy disk

This is used in the Sony Mavica range of cameras. These cameras use standard 1.44MB floppy disks to store the images. Since the images are stored as standard JPEG files, the floppy can be placed in the floppy drive of any computer and immediately copied or imported into an application. This avoids the need for a separate hardware device or software driver to transfer files between the camera and computer. While it is convenient, the size of the floppy means that the cameras are large and the storage on any one floppy disk is limited.

Iomega Clik! Disks

This is a compromise solution using a miniature 40MB disk drive. It is currently used on the Agfa ePhoto CL30 Clik! The disks have much larger storage capacity than a floppy disk and can be inserted into any computer that has a Clik! drive.

IBM microdrive

An even greater storage capacity is offered by cameras that fit the tiny IBM microdrive hard disk. The drive has a capacity of 340MB and a uses a PC Card slot. It is currently used by the Kodak DCS560.

Videocassette

A growing number of camcorders provide facilities for capturing still pictures. The data from a single frame is taken from the CCDs and recorded as a still onto the videotape as a short video clip (of perhaps seven seconds), normally allowing a voiceover to accompany the still.

Connections to the computer

Once the images are stored to the camera's storage medium, the files need to be transferred or copied from the camera into the computer. There are a number of ways that the camera can connect with a computer, to transfer the images to the computer's hard disk.

Serial cable

All digital cameras provide the option of connecting the camera to the computer via the computer's serial port. The benefit of this method is cheapness. Since every computer has a serial post socket, there is no need to provide special hardware. The cable plugs into the camera at one end and the other end plugs into the computer's serial port. Providing that the software exists for the transfer (see the notes below on TWAIN) the files can be transferred at the relatively slow peak transfer rate of 115.2kbits per second. While this is fast enough for small files, the transfer of an entire microdrive's 340MB contents would be far too slow. All other transfer methods improve on this transfer rate, sometimes by a very large margin. Unfortunately, a few cameras still only offer a serial connection method.

USB cable

A cable connects the camera to an unused USB port on the computer.   Again, no other hardware is necessary, although the file transfer software has to be installed on the computer.   This connection method is not available on all cameras, but is found on models including the Kodak DC-240, DC-265 and DC280, Toshiba PDR-M4, Ricoh RDC-5000, AGFA CL30, Musteck VDC-300, Sony DSC-F505K, and the Nikon CoolPix 800.

The data transfer rate for USB peaks at 12Mbits per second, which is far faster than serial transfers. Of course, this method can only be used with newer computers, as older computers did not have USB connections.   To overcome this, an add-on card is available that provides USB facilities for older computers, as long as they have at least Windows 98 installed.

USB adapter

The USB adapter is a dedicated piece of hardware that connects to the computer's USB port.   The CompactFlash or Smartmedia card is removed from the camera and placed in the reader's card slot.

As above, the computer must have a USB port or an add-on USB port adapter.   Examples of USB card readers are the FujiFilm SM-R1 and the CardPort Swift models.   The Smartmedia card reader transfers images 40 times faster than a serial link.

Parallel adapter

The parallel adapter is a dedicated piece of hardware that connects to the computer's parallel port.   The CompactFlash or Smartmedia card is removed from the camera and placed in the reader's card slot. These are faster than serial connections but slower than USB transfers.   Examples are the CardPort Swift P/Port range of adapters for SmartMedia and CompactFlash cards and the Pico PC PhotoReader.

Floppy disk

As mentioned above, the Sony Mavica range of cameras uses standard 1.44MB floppy disks as the storage medium. No special hardware or drivers are needed. The images are already stored in normal file format and the images are read as with those on a normal floppy disk.

Floppy adapter

The SmartMedia card is removed from the camera and inserted in an adaptor which is designed to fit in a computer's floppy drive. As long as the software driver is installed, the images on the card can be read and copied onto the hard drive. An example is the FujiFilm FlashPath adaptor FD-A1.   At a transfer rate of 250KB per second, it is over twice faster than serial connection transfers. Sony also produces a floppy adaptor for its own Memory Sticks modules.

PC Card adapter

Most portable computers are fitted with PC card slots (also called PCMCIA slots).   These allow a range of add-on devices such as modems, drives and CD-ROMs to be added to the system by plugging them into spare PC Card slots.   Adapters are available for SmartMedia and CompactFlash cards and Sony Memory Sticks.   The cards are inserted in the adapter and the adapter plugs into the PC Card slot.

Infrared

A few cameras, such as the Kodak DC265 use infrared waves to transfer images between the camera and any computer with an infrared (IrDA) receiver.   There is no physical connection between the units and the medium is not removed from the camera.

TWAIN drivers

At one time, all manufacturers produced their own driver software for downloading files into the computer. The files were then brought into the graphics editing package as a separate operation. TWAIN is now an accepted standard used in data acquisition (e.g. cameras and scanners).   It defines the major operations that are required for image capture.   If all capture devices and all software used the same operations, then every piece of software could communicate with every device.   This allows TWAIN-compatible software, such as PhotoShop and Paint Shop Pro, to directly import images from any hardware device that is also TWAIN-compliant. TWAIN supports serial, USB and PC Card transfers. It allows photographs to be downloaded from the camera directly into the editing application.   It also allows the application programs to import images straight from a scanner, without leaving the application. Some cameras (e.g. the Olympus Camedia C-800L) are not TWAIN-compatible and the images still have to be downloaded into the computer using the supplied software, then brought into the editing application.

Other camera features

Additional features to consider when buying a digital camera include:

TV output

Many digital cameras provide a video output.   This does mean that they record video clips.   It just means that the photographic images can be shown on a television screen by connecting a cable to the television's *'video in'* sockets.   This is mainly a facility for camera owners to displays images to a group of people, without the need for a computer.   If the LCD viewing screen is not showing enough detail, this facility provides a useful way to examine photographs while on location.   For the UK, the video output should be in PAL format.   Some cameras, such as the Kodak DC280, have both PAL and NTSC outputs and this allows photographs to be displayed on televisions while on holiday in the USA, etc. The video output of cameras can often be fed into a video capture card and used as a video camera to capture movie clips.   This is a cheap alternative to purchasing a digital camcorder but, since the camera has to remain attached to the computer, it is not only suitable for studio recording.   A separate camcorder should be purchased, if possible, as it usually has a superior lens system, has built-in audio recording and other refinements.

Batteries

Digital camcorders are notorious for the heavy drain on their batteries.   Much of this is caused by illuminating the LCD viewing panel.   Some models use standard AA type NiCad batteries (Nickel Cadmium), whose regular replacement is a costly business.   Some models use proprietary rechargeable batteries, which are also expensive to replace after their useful life.   The most flexible choice are cameras that use normal rechargeable lithium ion or nickel metal hydride batteries.

Flash

Many cameras have a built-in flash.   This must be under the control of the operator. Flash must be able to be turned on and off by the user, as the automatic setting is not always suitable. There are occasions, for example, when it would be used in bright daylight to fill in shadows on a face or object.   At other times, it would be turned off even during light conditions that are poor. This would include situations when a flash would be intrusive e.g. a church service, shooting wildlife, surveillance, etc. On the other hand, an underexposed photograph might be required, for artistic effect.

LCD panel/optical viewfinder

Most cameras provide a rear LCD panel, to allow the camera operator to see exactly what image will be captured.   It also allows previous photographs to be recalled and examined or deleted.   As an alternative, or as an addition, it may provide an internal optical or electronic viewfinder.   The disadvantage of the LCD panel is that the screen is washed out when viewed in bright sunlight. It also consumes a fair amount of power from the battery pack.   The optical viewfinder saves on battery consumption and is much easier to view in brightly lit conditions. On the other hand, an LCD panel is useful for viewing awkward angles, where looking though an eyepiece is not practical.   Examples are recording a passing parade, where the camera is being held above the heads of the crowd, or turning the camera round so that the camera operator can photograph himself/herself.

The best film cameras use an SLR (single lens reflex) optical system that allows the operator to see exactly what will appear in the captured image.   This is rarely found in digital cameras.   The Olympus Camedia C-2599L uses an SLR optical system. This has the advantages of not having to use the LCD viewing panel (hence saving on battery drain) and always being able to see the content of the scene under the brightest light conditions.

Writing time

When taking posed or still-life photographs, the time taken to write the captured scene to the media does not pose any problems.   However, in capturing real-world events, the time delay makes the difference between capturing enough of the event - or spending more time waiting than shooting.   The writing time of digital cameras depends upon the medium.   Writing to a mechanical medium is slower than writing to memory chips.   The delay ranges from a few seconds up to 10 seconds or more. The Toshiba PDR-M4 saves photographs with around a one-second delay.

The Kodak DC290 has a time lapse mode. The user can set intervals of 1 minute up to 24 hours between taking photographs.   These images can be grouped together (using a package such as GIF animator) into a time-lapse video sequence showing a flower opening, the movement of clouds, etc.

Video capture option

Newer models now offer the facility to capture miniature video clips. These are all of small resolution and short duration, due to the even greater storage demands of video recording. This facility is not a serious alternative to recordings from a digital camcorder.   For hobbyists on a low budget, it is the ideal way of capturing web-sized video clips. Examples of video performances are given below.

The Sony DSC-55E and Sony Mavica MVC-FD88 capture up to 15 seconds of MPEG-1 at 160x112 or 320x240.   The Sony MVC-FD91 captures up to 60 seconds of MPEG-1 at 320x240.   The Sony CyberShot DCS-F505 captures up to 42 minutes of video on a 64MB memory stick.   The Casio QV-2000UX and QV-5500SX can capture AVI clips and the FujiFilm FinePix 4700 captures 320x240 AVIs.   The Nikon CoolPix 800 offers 40 shots at 320x240 in one and a half seconds.   It also offers continuous capture mode of one image every two-thirds of a second.   The Kodak CD290 captures 16 images at 720 x 480 at 3 images per second.

Sequence shots are also provided by the Toshiba PDR-M5, HP PhotoSmart C30, Agfa CL50, Casio QV 7000SX, Olympus C-900 and Kodak DC240.

Automatic/Manual Controls

Cameras usually automatically adjust their focus and exposure settings in response to the nature of the incoming light.   While this is satisfactory for *'point and shoot'* situations, the operator will often require more control than the default automatic settings. For example, the camcorder's auto focus allows the subject to remain in focus whether at close range or at long distance. The operator, however, may wish to have the foreground subject out of focus, with the background being in focus. The camera should allow the manual override of exposure, focussing and other settings.

Voice annotations

Some cameras provide a built-in microphone. This allows a brief audio description to be attached to an image file. This could be a useful aid for cataloguing shots.   Cameras that provide this facility include the Agfa CL50, Kodak DC265 and DC290, Canon PowerShot A50, Sony DSC-55E and DCS-F505.

DPOF support

DPOF (digital print order format) has no particular benefits for multimedia use. It is supported by Kodak, FujiFilm, Canon and others.   It allows normal prints to be created from the memory card, from chemists supporting this scheme..

Capturing digital images

The techniques involved in taking digital photographs differ little from using standard film cameras. With standard cameras, the steps are plan, prepare, shoot, develop and hope for the best.

The steps for capturing photographic images are:
- Plan the photographic session.
- Prepare all necessary resources.
- Shoot the pictures.
- Examine the captured images and reshoot if necessary.
- Download the images into the computer.

Digital photography provides more control over the process, as the results can be viewed as the shoot proceeds. Of course, the camera's results are determined by its operator's skill and experience.   Like video recording, digital photography is a creative process as well as a technical process.   This section does not provide all the knowledge and experience necessary for professional results. Readers interested in this area are invited to join a camera club or take an evening course at a local college.

This section, along with a section in the chapter on digital video, contains useful information on picture composition, lighting the subject, camera positioning, use of zoom, etc.   These pages reflect the conventional wisdom on the subject but, as in all creative work, breaking the rules can achieve special effects.

Orientation

Digital cameras usually have an aspect ratio of 4:3 (e.g. the image may be 640x480 or 800x 600) to match the aspect ratio of computer monitors.   This means that the camera takes a rectangular picture that can be shot in *'Portrait'* or *Landscape'* mode. The default orientation of the captured image is landscape format.

The camera has to be physically rotated 90° and held this way, to capture images in portrait format. With the camera in this position, it can sometimes be awkward to reach the camera controls.

The pictures on the next page illustrate images captured in both formats.

The picture on the left was taken in normal landscape format and there is a lot of wasted space in the image.   The second picture shows the same picture captured in portrait format.

Of course, the first picture can be cropped to produce exactly the same result - except that many of the pixels in the image have been discarded.   The picture has a lower resolution than the picture originally taken in portrait format.

The second set of pictures shows a view of the city of San Francisco, taken from a boat in the Bay, with a camera fitted with a wide-angle lens adaptor.

In this case, the default landscape view shown on the right is much more efficient, as it includes a wider content than that captured in portrait mode. It is also more natural, since the flow of content is in a horizontal plane.

Large sections of the panoramic view are lost in portrait format and, since the camera cannot be moved further back, there is no way to encompass the entire panorama in this format.

For photographs of groups (families, workmates, football team, etc) the landscape format uses the capture area to best advantage. It is also best for panoramic scenes.

The portrait format is best used for photographing individual portraits and tall objects such as full-body shots, high-rise buildings, etc.

NOTE:

When an image is captured in portrait mode and transferred to the computer, it is stored on its side. Fortunately, all image editing software has a *'rotate'* facility that will rotate the image through 90° so that it can be saved in the correct orientation for use in projects.

Composition

Composition is the term used to describe the two essential ingredients of a successful photograph - subject and context.   Since the images are for use in a multimedia project of some description, these are even more important questions than photographs taken for the family album (although the rules can be applied to good use in all photographic situations).

Each photograph should have a purpose and a list of shots might have been prepared by a storyboard or a shooting list drawn up from a web site plan.   Each shot in the list should specify the main content of the photograph.   This should not be listed in terms of *'picture of school'* or *'picture of footballer'*.   The photograph is intended to play a particular part of the final project and the context describes the location, activity, surroundings, or any other element that conveys the mood or meaning of the photograph.

Examples of shot descriptions may be *'picture of school with students playing'* or *'picture of school from a majestic angle'*.   The first picture conveys a *'feel good'* mood, while the second is more formal.

Similarly *'picture of footballer tackling an opponent'* and *'picture of footballer in pinstripe suit'* convey entirely different moods.

Most photographs can be improved by correctly balancing the subject and context. For example, a photographer of a watchmaker or a miner at work conveys more meaning than pictures of them standing next to their tools or machinery.   This means that the main subject is rarely positioned in the middle of the photograph, a common mistake among beginners.   The exception may be portraits of the bank manager or college principal.

Centres of Interest

Artists and photographers often use the *'Rule of Thirds'*. This divides the picture area into thirds, both horizontally and vertically.   The four points where the lines intersect are regarded as the *'centres of interest'* (i.e. the main spots where the eye is attracted in a scene).   Centres of interest are also known as *'hot spots'*. Many photographs are improved by avoiding having the main subject in the centre of the area.   The landscape picture of San Francisco placed the dark skyscraper in upper left hot spot.

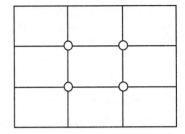

The main subject is often placed on a vertical axis, with a subsidiary object occupying the other axis.   An example is a Member of Parliament positioned on the right axis of the screen, while Big Ben is visible in the background on the left axis.   This is a good example of using context in a photograph.   The viewer may not recognise the individual but he/she is immediately identified with Parliament because of the background context.

Other useful composition points to note are:

* Secondary objects should be smaller than the subject or be placed well in the background.
* The primary subject should be the most prominent in the composition.   This may be achieved using the relative size of the subject compared to subordinate objets, or the main subject may be the most brightly coloured picture element.

Horizons and Lines

We generally think of horizons as being the area where the sea or land meets the sky, some way off in the distance. From a photographer's point of view, the horizon is any horizontal object that meets the sky to create separate picture areas. Therefore, the roofline, a wall or rows of trees are all examples of horizons. The horizon should not divide the picture exactly in half.   Dividing a picture into three-thirds is generally accepted (e.g. the beach, the sea and the sky).   The earlier San Francisco landscape photograph cut the picture into sea, cityscape and sky.   The rule can be relaxed to achieve particular effects. For example, a low horizon emphasises the expanse of sky and suggests spaciousness, while a high horizon draws the viewer into a more intimate foreground scene.

If possible, avoid major vertical or horizontal objects in the picture.   For example, a river or road is best shot running diagonally across the frame.

Professionals regularly use *'lines and paths'* within the compositions. These may be real or inferred lines that lead the viewer's eyes into and around the picture content.   These may be objects such as roads, rivers, fences, railway lines, overhead cables, etc. that meander naturally.   Alternatively, they may be the outlines of furniture, equipment, human limbs, etc., which lead or point around the picture.

Many photographs look flat and uninteresting. In some cases, this is due to a lack of perspective in the picture.   Viewers cannot grasp the relative dimensions of objects, as there are no reference points in image.   This is traditionally overcome by using *'vanishing points'*.   These are real or inferred lines that provide perspective to a composition.   The lines are parallel but run for such a long distance that they appear as if they will merge at some distant point.   The diagrams show two examples. The first shows two symmetrical lines. This would be achieved when the camera is placed looking down a street, airport runway, railway line, telephone lines, etc.   The second

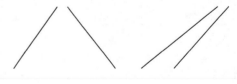

diagram shows that the camera can be offset from the lines and still achieve the same effect.   In both cases, depth has been added to the picture and the relative size of objects is easier to comprehend.

Framing

The framing technique is exactly what it sounds like. The main subject is in the centre of the image and a foreground object, or objects, provides a graphic frame around the image.   The chapter on computer graphics (*'Welcome to Naples'*) shows an image of a pool viewed through an archway. All sorts of objects can be used for frames (e.g. trees or bushes). Shooting the subject through a doorway or window is another more obvious framing technique. Frames add depth and interest to a picture and focus the viewer's attention on the subject being framed.

Use a sharp focussed foreground for photographing scenic images, as an out-of focus foreground distracts the viewer.   An out of focus foreground is acceptable, and desirable, for most portrait work.

Backgrounds

The photographer has to have an eye for the background content of an image and not just concentrate on the main subject being shot. The following points should be considered:

- A relatively uncluttered background helps concentrate the viewers' attention on the main subject.
- Avoid stark lines in the background. These attract the viewers' attention away from main subject.
- Avoid shooting a subject against a dark background. The camera adjusts to the overall level of incoming light (i.e. dark) and overexposes any lighter objects. In human subjects, this is seen as *'burnouts'* of the highlighted areas of the face such as cheeks and forehead.
- If a dark background is unavoidable, zoom further in on the subject. This reduces the ratio of dark in the overall picture. Alternatively, use lighting to illuminate the background and/or the subject.
- Be watchful of poles or trees sticking out of people's heads.

Camera height

Not all photographs are taken from a normal standing height. A kneeling position provides an alternative camera height and is ideal for photographing children, dogs, people who are seated and objects that are close to the ground. Filming at their own eye level produces a much more natural result than pointing the camera down at them.

For really low camera positions, even a mini-tripod is too tall. On other occasions, a normal tripod may be too small (e.g. trying to photograph a passing parade). Use a beanbag, small pillow or folded blanket. This can be sat on the ground for low shots. It can also be sat on a wall or bus shelter for recording high shots. This is preferable to the operator holding the camera above his/her head.

Importantly, the height of the camera in relation to the subject can be used to convey mood or status. Shooting upwards makes the subject tower over the frame and appear larger than life. Shooting down on the subject makes the subject appear smaller and less significant.

Portraits

Portraits of individuals is a common use for photographs and these appear in everything from family albums to company reports. Portraits range from formal (picture of the company chairperson, police mugshot, etc) to informal (holiday pictures).

These often have no broader context and are capturing the personality of the subject. There are exceptions, such as wedding pictures, graduations, and so on. One useful approach is to try to capture the person's personality through extending the formal setting of portraits. This might involve taking a portrait of the person at work, at play, or working on a hobby. Although a portrait only covers the person's head and shoulders, the image can still include elements that encapsulate the individual's personal traits. Examples are subjects holding a phone, listening to a Walkman, wearing a party hat, wearing their uniform, holding a fishing rod, and so on. These are all much better than the subject sitting on a chair, wearing new clothes and grimacing the word *"Cheese"*.

It is important to relax the subject. It is also best to avoid posing the subject. If they settle naturally, they usually strike a better pose. It is often best to photograph the subject with the camera slightly above eye level. Subjects often stare into some point in the distance when being photographed. However, a photograph where there is eye contact draws the viewer into the picture.

Composition issues with portraits include:

- Filling the frame with the subject is acceptable with portraits.
- Always use plain, or out of focus, backgrounds. Using a telephoto setting and a large aperture setting makes the background out of focus.
- Set the camera focus on the subject's eyes.
- Avoid wide-angle settings with portraits as they creates *'big nose'* facial distortions.

Lighting issues include:

- The lighting for portraits varies a little compared to scenic shots. While scenic shots benefit greatly from bright sunlight, this creates problems for outdoor portraits, as it makes the subject squint. Placing the subject with his/her back to the sun prevents squints but means that the camera is now shooting into the sun. It also means that the subject's face is hidden in deep shadows.
- If possible, shoot when the sky is overcast as this produces a much more even light.
- Otherwise, look for a shaded area.
- Always use the camera lens hood to minimise stray light from entering the lens.
- Use reflected light or a flash fill, to lighten the darkened shadow areas of the subject's face.
- Consider using a soft focus filter on the camera.

Red-eye

The curse of flash photography is the appearance of *'red-eye'*.   This is caused by light reflecting from the retinas at the back of the subject's eyes.   The effect seems to be more common among people with blue eyes and is mainly a problem in low light environments.   In dark conditions, the pupil of the eye dilates to allow in more light, thereby exposing more of the retina.   Some cameras provide red-eye reduction systems.   They all work based on presenting light to the subject, just before taking the photograph.   This is either by illuminating a small lamp or by emitting one or more low-power bursts from the flashlight.   These cause the pupil to contract just before the main flash goes off and the photograph is taken.   Alternatively, the red-eye can be eliminated at the editing stage.

Close-ups

Majestic panoramas, crowd scenes and human portraits are all large-scale images that make up the bulk of the images used in projects.   However, the miniature world can be captured for interest or impact.   An image of a single tear running down a cheek conveys an immense message.   Similarly, other close-up shots such as a bead of sweat, the petal of a flower, a train ticket, etc. can be used to convey mood or intent.

At an even more miniature level, the macro shot provides an unusual view of the world.   Examples of such shots are a bent paper clip, the mechanics of a watch, an insect's head, or the wording on a stamp or coin.

Capturing action

A still photograph can capture a moving subject and still display the sense of the original movement. There are two basic types of action shot - the *'freeze frame'* and the *'blurred motion'* shots.

The stop action shot, also known as a *'freeze frame'* shot, aims to capture a clear image of the moving subject, either through using a fast shutter speed or using flash.

Alternatively, an action can often be captured at a peak moment.   In many activities, there is an action, followed by a period when motion is almost suspended, followed by further action.   The photograph can be captured during the moment of suspended animation.   Examples of this are children on swings or with skipping ropes, carpenters sawing, athletics hurdling and pole vaulters.

Blur is also minimised if the action is shot from a distance rather than close up, as the closer the camera is to the action, the quicker the subject passes across the lens.   If possible, capture the subject moving diagonally or towards camera, rather than across camera view.

With freeze frame shots, the subject and the background are photographed free from any motion blur.

Blur, however, can be used to provide the feeling of moment.   Some element of blur is not only acceptable, but is desirable.   If the photograph is taken while the camera is panned to follow the subject's movement, the subject is captured clearly but the background is blurred.   This is a commonly used effect. Slow shutter speeds increase the background blur, making the action appear even faster.

Of course, motion blur can be introduced in an image at the editing stage.

Camera positioning

Before considering positioning, consideration should be given to ensuring that the camera is as stationary as possible during the taking of a photograph.   It is difficult to hold a camera steady while pressing its shutter button.   Pressing too hard can move the camera and blur the shot or capture a shot whose content is not placed as expected.   When a telephoto setting is used, the slight movement is even more exaggerated.   The solution lies in mounting the camera on a tripod.

The tripod has a ¼" bolt that screws into the base of the camcorder.   When the tripod's legs are spread, the camcorder is held in a very stable grip.   Of course, it is not always possible or practical to use a tripod, particularly when the camera has to move around a location quickly.   An alternative for these situations is the mini-tripod.   It provides many of benefits of the large tripod, but is small, easy to carry round and can be sat on wall or table to provide stability for the camera.

If all else fails, the camera operator can stabilise the camera by resting against a wall, a tree, a car or a lamppost.   The ideal shooting stance is legs apart, knees slightly bent, arms tucked into the sides of the body so that wrists are straight when holding the camera.

Lighting

Lighting is an extremely important factor in photography.   Please read the chapter on digital video for full details.

Scanners

The operation of a scanner is similar to that of the digital camera described earlier.

Consider the operation of a photocopier. It has two separate phases. The first phase is capturing the image from the document that is placed on the glass. The second phase is writing a copy of the image on to a sheet of paper. These operations can be also be carried out by two well-known computer peripherals - the scanner and the printer. Indeed, software is available to use them as a photocopier.

The scanner can be used to bring all kinds of images into the computer. Although this chapter is concerned with photographic images, the scanner can be used to capture line art, logos, hand-written signatures, diagrams and other flat objects such as a driving licence or bus pass. However, many flatbed scanners are not limited to flat objects and can provide a useable image from objects placed on the glass bed. This allows pages from books and magazines to be scanned, as well as 3-D objects such as a human hand, coins, and so on. Anything that is scanned on a photocopier at the office party is capable of being scanned on a flatbed scanner.

How a scanner works

The quality of the final image depends on the quality of the scanner components - and on the resolution of the scanning mechanism. The scan resolution is measured in dpi (dots per inch). Since many measurements are metric, conversions have to be done into inches to calculate file sizes (see below).

The most common type of scanner is the flatbed model and the description for this type follows, although the general principles apply to all scanner types.

The photograph (or other object) is placed face down on the scanner glass bed and the capture software is started. This can be a dedicated capture application, or can be any graphics package that has a capture facility through a TWAIN interface. A bright cold cathode light and a scanning head are mounted on a frame that is slowly moved down the photograph by a stepper motor. The light is shone on the surface to be scanned and the reflected light is focussed on to the scanning head. The scanning head consists of a CCD (see the earlier explanation of CCDs). The head only contains a single row of sensors, compared to the megapixel arrays of camera CCDs. The camera captures all the image data at the one time, while the scanner captures the photograph's detail one line at a time. This much simpler CCD assembly makes the scanner a very much cheaper device than a digital camera. Since most flatbed scanners handle an A4 sheet, the width of the scanned area is a minimum of 8.27", with most models having an 8.5" scanning width. If a scanner supports a maximum scanning resolution of 600dpi, the CCD in the scanning head will contain 8.5 x 600 = 5,100 sensors. Even a top-quality 2,400dpi optical resolution requires just over

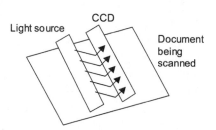

20,000 sensors. Current digital cameras now mostly contain CCDs with millions of sensors. Older scanners made three separate scanning passes, to gather the red, green and blue information in the photograph. Current mainstream models use a single-pass method, with colour filters in front of the sensors (as used in digital cameras).

Some scanners now use a CIS (Contact Image Sensor) system. This replaces the cold cathode light source with a LED array and allows the light and sensor to be very close together. It dispenses with the optics required with traditional systems and makes the final mechanism more compact.

Either way, the scanner gathers the image data as a series of pixel data and this is sent to the computer via the cable interface.

Controlling the scan

The scanner can record the entire area of the scanning bed. However, the user often only requires scanning a smaller photograph area, or even a part of a photograph. In addition, there may be some adjustment to be made to the resolution or colour settings for the scan.

The steps for scanning a photograph are:

- Run the scanner capture software, perhaps through a TWAIN-compliant application.
- Run the initial scan, to acquire a preview of the entire image placed on the glass.
- Set final desired area to be scanned.
- Set the desired resolution.
- Set the desired colour depth (including colour, greyscale, line art).
- Set any brightness, contrast, gamma correction, or sharpen settings.

- Perform a final scan
- Save the image - usually as a compressed JPEG file, or perhaps as a BMP, PCX, TIFF or GIF file.

Twain interface

See earlier in this chapter for a general description.   The interface controls how capture operations are carried out.   It does not specify what piece of software is required to interface with it.   A scanner manufacturer may supply its own software for operating the scanner and this software would communicate with the hardware through the Twain driver. Alternatively, the user may access the scanner through his/her existing application packages.   For example, in Paint Shop Pro, the scanner is accessed through the *'File'* drop-down menu.   Choosing *'Import'*, followed by *'TWAIN'* and *'Select Source'* displays a list of the TWAIN devices connected to the computer (e.g. a camera and a scanner).

There are more Twain interface controls for scanners than for cameras, as there are more factors to control in the capture process. The Twain interface gives instructions to the scanner, under the control of the user. In fact, the range is large enough for Agfa to distribute two versions of their Twain driver with their scanners . FotoSnap has a simple set of controls for beginners while FotoLook has more advanced controls for more experienced users.

Optical resolution

As explained above, the construction of the CCD determines the maximum scanning resolution. This is called the *'optical resolution'* and is usually 300dpi, 600dpi or 1200dpi in the horizontal plane.   The stepper motor moves the head in amounts set by the user. If the user chooses 600dpi for the vertical resolution, the head is moved 1/600th of an inch for each vertical scan. If the scanning head is moved down the bed in movements that are equal to the CCD sensor spacing, the final resolution is equal in both planes (e.g. 300dpi x 300dpi or 600dpi x 600dpi).   If the head assembly is moved in smaller steps, the vertical resolution becomes greater than the horizontal resolution (e.g. 600dpi x 1200dpi, 600dpi x 2400dpi or 1200dpi x 2400dpi).

Interpolated resolution

Most manufacturers also quote a figure for their scanner's *'interpolated resolution'*.   This is a much higher figure, up to 9600dpi, to make the specification appear more impressive.   Since the scanner cannot actually detect any more data than its number of CCD sensors, the *'extra'* data for the higher resolution is interpolated (i.e. estimated).   If, for example, a scanner has an optical resolution of 600dpi and an interpolated scan of 1200dpi is chosen, there is twice as much data to be stored in the file than is being physically scanned.   The scanner software looks at the actual readings on adjacent CCD sensors and works out the likely values of colour and contrast that would appear in between.   If the two sensors both detected the same colour, then the intermediate pixels would be saved as being the same colour.   If a colour value of 222 was detected in one sensor and 218 in the next sensor, the software saves 220 as the intermediate value.   The process would be applied to horizontal and vertical image data.   The image file contains twice as many pixels values in both the horizontal and vertical planes.   No extra original information has been extracted from the photograph, but the file size is four times larger. In addition, since the process averages out the values at edges, the final scanned image is slightly softened.

Improved techniques include *'bicubic interpolation'* (which uses all the values around the new pixel to estimate the pixel contents) or *'colour curve interpolation'* (which takes into account the rate of change of a colour along a run and fits in a new value which need not be a linear fit between the existing pixel values).   At the end of the day, however, an estimate is still an estimate.

Since interpolation can also be carried out within a graphics editing package (e.g. when using a *'resize'* option), there is little benefit in choosing an interpolated scan.   The extra time required to resize an image is a price worth paying compared to storing all images in a huge size.

Interpolation is generally more successful when used with line art scans, as they have clean outlines, sharp edges and are only black and white.

If a photograph is to be scanned at less than a scanner's maximum resolution, it is best to set the resolution to whole fractions of the maximum resolution. For example, if a scanner maximum optical resolution is 1200dpi, it has 1200 sensors in its CCD reader.   If a document is scanned at 600dpi, it only uses the reading from every second sensor, while a setting of 400dpi reads from every third sensor, and so on.   Setting to, for example, 500dpi, involves unnecessary interpolation of values, with a possible loss in quality.

Colour depth

The values from the scanner's CCD are read off into the electronics, where the ADC (analogue to digital converter) digitises the scanned red, green and blue values. Most scanners work in a final 24-bit colour depth. This provides 8 bits (i.e. one byte) to describe the amplitude of the image for each of the three (red, green and blue) sensors of each pixel. Since a byte can store 256 different levels (from zero to 255), the total number of colours that can be displayed is

$$256 \times 256 \times 256 = 16777216 = 16.78 \text{ millions colours}$$

This is the standard amount of colours used to represent all the colour shades necessary to reproduce a photo-realistic image. Darker areas of the photograph will reflect less light and are given lower values in the light level scale.

Oversampling

Many scanners are marketed as 30-bit or 36-bit models.   The Umax Astra 2200 even has a 42-bit mode. These models do not actually save the image file at this colour depth.   They are used to provide *'oversampling'*.   This is used to compensate for image noise that may be generated during the scanning process.   Increasing the dynamic range of a signal improves its signal-to-noise ratio.   With 36-bit sampling, the photograph is scanned at a greater colour depth than is required.   Each colour has a range of 4,096 possible values compared to only 256 values with 24-bit working.

The theoretical colour depth of the scanned image is now

$$4096 \times 4096 \times 4096 = 68,719,476,736 \text{ different colours}$$

However, this would result in vastly more colours than the eye is capable of discerning, not to mention impossibly large storage requirements (see later).

Therefore, the image data is subsequently converted to a 24-bit colour depth.   This reduces the total bits allocated to the image and reduces the noise proportionately.   The result is a cleaner sharper image than a normal 24-bit scan.

Although oversampling provides an improved image, the difference is often so slight as to be unnoticeable, especially with small, highly-compressed images for the web.

Line art

Line art describes all images where there is only black and white used in the composition. This may be a cartoon, a diagram, a map or a hand-written signature.   With colour images, each pixel used 24 bits to store the information for each individual pixel.   With line art images, each pixel requires a single bit to describe it. It is either black or white, it is either digital 'off' or digital 'on'.   Since a single bit can only have two values - zero or one, this corresponds to the two colours states.   So, the information about each pixel in a line art image can be stored in a single bit.   This means that a line art image only requires one twenty-fourth of the storage size of a full-colour image of the same size.   It would not make sense, therefore, to use a colour scan setting for monochrome image. Of course, the images that are used as the scanning source can be in colour and the line art setting will ensure that the scanned copy of the image is in black and white.

Greyscale images

Not all photographic images are in colour.   All old photographs are in shades of grey and even contemporary photographers use monochrome film for special effects.

The scanner has a setting for scanning in greyscale. Since there is not a separate red, green and blue component to the image, a single byte is sufficient to store 256 levels of greyscale (from black to white).

If a colour photograph is scanned with a greyscale setting, the scanned image will be in greyscale and be one-third the size of its colour equivalent.

The illustrations show the effect of scanning a colour

256-greyscale   line art

photograph in greyscale and in line art settings. The 256-greyscale image retains much of its clarity, while the line art settings has forced all pixels down to black level or up to white level.   This effect is often used in pop-art and advertising images.

Scanning printed images

There is a huge resource of existing graphic material in magazines, books, etc. and these can be scanned for use in multimedia projects (subject to obtaining permission, of course). The printed material is made up of millions of tiny dots. The scanner, in turn, wants to scan at a set rate of pixels. Since these will not neatly correspond, an interference pattern can be created between the two layouts - known as a Moiré pattern. Most modern scanners provide a *'descreen'* option to minimise this effect. Alternatively, the photograph can be scanned at a resolution that is higher than required, and the scanned image can be run through a blur filter in a graphics editing package. The image resolution is then reduced to the final size required, and run through the sharpen filter.

File sizes

The size of a scanned image is calculated by taking the screen area to be scanned and multiplying it by the number of dots per inch. This gives a file size for a monochrome scan. A 24-bit colour scan is three times the size of a monochrome scan.

An A4 sheet of paper is the size of this book and many magazines. The dimensions are 210mm x 297mm, or 11.69" x 8.27", when converted to inches.

If the entire page were to be scanned in colour, the file size for a range of different scanning resolutions is given in the table.

File sizes for various scanning resolutions (from an A4 sheet at 24-bit colour)	
Scanning resolution	Uncompressed File Size
300dpi	25MB
600dpi	100MB
1200dpi	398MB
2400dpi	1.56GB
4800dpi	6.22GB
9600dpi	24.89GB

Take the example of scanning at 600dpi. The page is 8.27" wide, so this requires 8.27 x 600 = 4962 dots of horizontal resolution. The page is 11.69" long, requiring 11.69 x 600 = 7014 dots of vertical resolution. The number of dots to represent the entire A4 sheet is then 4962 x 7014 = 34,803,468 dots. This represents the size for a monochrome image, each dot being either black or white. To store a colour image, each dot is represented by varying amounts of red, green or blue. A byte is required to store each of these colour values. The file size has then to be multiplied by three to get the final size in bytes. In the example, a staggering 100MB of storage space is required for an A4 image at a respectable 600dpi.

Since a photograph in a magazine can expect to be printed at a minimum of 4800dpi, a scanned A4 image would not even fit on an entire DVD disk.

If the 36-bit sampling mode discussed earlier was actually stored in that format, the files sizes shown in the table would have to be multiplied by a factor of 36/24 = 1.5. This would make the 9600dpi scan require a staggering 37.34GB of storage - greater than the capacity of most large hard drives!

Scanning for multimedia use

Fortunately, photograph images for multimedia are much less of a problem. This is for a number of reasons.

Most importantly, a monitor has a much poorer resolution than the range offered by scanners. A typical monitor may only have display around 72-90 pixels per inch of screen. This means that the scanning resolution can be turned down to this lower figure and massive savings can be made on file size.

Consider a full monitor screen of 1024 x 768 pixels, on a 17" monitor. The 1024 pixels are spread across a theoretical horizontal dimension of 12". In practice, only about 90% of the actual screen area is visible. The 1024 pixels are contained in a horizontal row of about 11.5". This equates to about 72 pixels for each inch and this is a common resolution to use for scanning.

To fill the screen at the full resolution of the monitor, only 1024 different pixels need to be scanned. If more pixels are scanned, the extra details cannot be physically displayed on the screen. The file is extra large, without providing any greater viewable information. If less pixels are scanned than the amount physically supported by the monitor, either the content of the unused pixels are interpolated (estimated) so that the full screen is still occupied - or the photograph is displayed at less than full screen size.

The table shows the size of photograph area that would be scanned to fill a 1024x768 screen, at various scanning resolution settings. At 90 dpi, an A4 photograph, taken in landscape, would almost match the monitor's full

Source sizes for various scanning resolutions (to fill a 1024x768 screen)	
Scanning resolution	Size of original
90dpi	11.38" x 8.53"
100dpi	10.24" x 7.68"
150dpi	6.83" x 5.12"
300dpi	3.41" x 2.56"
600dpi	1.71" x 1.28"
1200dpi	0.85" x 0.64"
2400dpi	0.43" x 0.32"
4800dpi	0.21" x 0.16"

screen. It can also be seen that high scanning resolutions are useful when a small area of a photograph is required to fill the screen. For example, scanning at 1200dpi allows a postage stamp to fill the monitor screen. In multimedia, a photograph is rarely used to fill a full monitor screen. While a background may sometimes require using an entire photograph, photographic images normally only occupy a part of the screen area.

Optical Character Recognition

This is not particularly applicable to photographic scanning but is included for completeness. It may be useful in other areas of multimedia, such as storyboarding, planning, correspondence, and other areas where text plays a part in the process.

If a source document contains text, it can be scanned and converted to a plain text file that can be read with any word-processing package. This is carried out in several steps by the OCR software. Firstly, it scans the document, detects where the individual lines are (by looking for the white space between lines). It then scans each line, breaking it into individual characters (by looking for the spaces between the characters).   At this stage, the software has a collection of little graphic images - one for each character in the text.   The software stores a set of known font descriptions and compares these with the characters that have been scanned.   It starts with the first scanned image and compares it to the font descriptions. When a match is found, that letter is added to the text output file.

While OCR software packages talk of achieving 98% accuracy, it is the few percent of errors that cause all the problems. While a package may include a spell-checker, other techniques are applied to improve the accuracy.   The interpretation of the scanned images are often made using neural network techniques. These learn from successful recognition and apply them to text has different fonts from the standard sets. They may also use POWR (Predictive Optical Word Recognition) which attempts to recognise whole words at a time.   With older techniques, there may be a problem knowing whether a letter is an *'e'* or an *'o'*, for example. This can lead to the word *'bite'* being read as *'bato'*. With POWR, placing all possible interpretations of an unknown letter in its context reduces any ambiguity. There is no such word as *'bato'* in the recognised list, while *'bite'* is a recognised word.

Scanner interfaces

There are three different ways that a scanner can be connected to a computer:

Parallel

There is a parallel port fitted on every computer and this is usually used for connecting a printer. Where a scanner has a parallel plug connector, the user can unplug the printer from the computer's parallel port and insert the scanner plug, or he/she can fit a parallel *'pass-through'* connector. This connector allows two parallel port devices to be connected at the same time and saves plugging and unplugging each time the scanner is to be used.

This parallel interface scanner is easily carried round for use on another computer. The scanner software is installed on the new computer, the scanner is plugged in and the system can be used. There is no internal connection, so the computer does not require to be opened up.

Care has to be taken with parallel systems, however, as most new scanners assume that the computer has a parallel port that operates to the EPP (Enhanced Parallel Port) standard.   This allows faster transfers than the standard parallel port, but is only fitter on newer computers.   If the scanner transfer system is EPP only, it will not work with an older, non-EPP, computer.

SCSI

This provides faster data transfers than the parallel port system and is useful where lots of photographs need to be scanned.   The SCSI interface card usually supplied with the scanner. With the introduction of fast USB scanner interfaces, SCSI scanners have become much less popular.

USB

This is now the most common way to connect a new scanner to a computer. It is easily connected - there is no special adapter card to fit, as with SCSI, or pass-through adapter, as with parallel. The cable from the scanner is simply plugged into the computer's USB socket, the scanner software is installed and the scanner is recognised when the computer is restarted.

Some of the Hewlett Packard and Umax ranges provide both SCSI and USB connections while the HP Scanjet 5300C provides both a parallel and USB connection.

Scanner types

Although flatbed scanners are by far the most popular models, other scanner types are marketed and these are explained below.

Handheld

This type of scanner looks like a large mouse and its small size was a selling point. There is no mechanism to move the scanning head or the image. The user has to roll the scanner over the surface of the object to be scanned, at a steady pace. If the hand movement is not steady and at a constant speed, the image is distorted. Unfortunately, as with a mouse, these scanners are difficult to push in a straight line. They never really caught on as they only covered a small width (3" to 4") and larger areas had to be constructed from patching together several smaller scans. It is difficult to scan objects smaller than the scanning head. For example, to scan a postage stamp or a small photograph, they would have to be glued or taped to a larger surface. It was used mainly for scanning small items for clip art, signatures and other small images. As flatbed scanners became ever cheaper, there was no financial reason to choose a handheld. HP CapShare 910 is a modern version of this device. It is a self-powered device and does not connect to the computer while scanning. Instead, it stores its scanned data in 4MB of internal memory. This means that the scanner can carried around and used anywhere, independently of the computer. Images can then be sent to the computer later, using its serial port or an infrared port (if one exists). The supplied software carries out the stitching of sections into a complete document.

Sheetfed

This type, also described as a page scanner or document scanner, looks and works in a similar way to a fax machine. It usually has a small footprint (i.e. it does not take up much desk space). It uses a roller to move the paper past the head and can be fitted with an automatic sheet feeder to hold multiple sheets. It is designed for handling A4 sheets, and some are unable to handle smaller sizes. It is commonly used with OCR software (see earlier) for archiving correspondence and documents.

A major drawback is its inability to scan book and real-world objects, as they will not pass through the rollers. The flatbed scanner is the only type that allows the scanning of thick documents or objects.

Examples of sheetfed scanners are the Logitech PageScan, the Fujitsu ScanPartner and the Avigramm MiniDoc.

Drum scanner

These types are used for high-resolution scanning of large original documents. With flatbed scanners, the image remains stationary, while the scanning head moves across it. The drum scanner takes the opposite approach. The document is attached to a glass drum that is then slowly spun past a scanning head. They provide excellent colour reproduction. However, they are expensive and are used mainly in high-end professional publishing and reprographic markets. They are able to scan very large sheets - up to A0 (an area that is sixteen times greater than an A4 sheet).

Slide scanner

These types are dedicated to scanning mounted slide transparencies or strips of negatives. Some also handle APS (Advanced Photo System) cartridges and others may supply adaptors to handle APS cartridges. Since they are used to digitise transparencies, they don't work on reflected light. The light is shone thorough the transparency. The method is said to be *'transmissive'* rather than *'reflective'*. They still use CCDs as their method of detecting light patterns and some provide an automatic slide feeder for batch work. Since the area being scanned is much smaller than that of an A4 flatbed scanner, the scanner requires a much higher scanning resolution, to produce a reasonably-sized digital image. Figures up to 4000dpi are typical.

Examples of slide scanners are:

- The Nikon LS-300 Coolscan III has an optical resolution of 2700dpi. For a 35mm slide, this produces an image that is 2592x3894, requiring almost 30MB of storage space for an uncompressed 24-bit image. The model has a SCSI interface.
- Another SCSI interface model is the CanoScan FS2710, which provides a cassette into which an APS roll is inserted.
- The FujiFilm AS-1 is designed specifically for handling APS rolls and has a parallel port interface. It provides a 835dpi resolution which equates to 512x896 for an APS frame. The Kodak FD 300 is another parallel-port, APS-only scanner.
- The Hewlett-Packard PhotoSmart S20 has a resolution of 2400dpi and has a USB interface.

Some flatbed scanner manufacturers sell an optional add-on to convert them to slide scanners.   This is a replacement lid with a built-in light source, to shine through the transparency.   These are much cheaper than buying a dedicated slide scanner, but the resolution is not good enough for many professional purposes. Their poorer performance is caused by the physical layout of the flatbed scanner's light sensors. The CCD sensors are spread over an 8.5" wide strip, while the slide is about 1" wide.   Since only one-eight of the sensors scan the slide, the effective resolution is lowered by this ratio (e.g. a 1200dpi scanner only uses 150 sensors to scan the 1" slide are - producing a 150dpi resolution).   This is still sufficient for multimedia use, where the image is displayed on a television screen, web site or television monitor. A publishing house would have to invest in a higher quality dedicated film scanner.   If this is not an affordable solution, the film can be developed and printed on A4 photographic paper, for scanning in the normal manner.

Photo-editing

Most digitised pictures, whether scanned or captured by camera, gain from editing.   Typical editing activities are:
- Removing scratches and dust marks from old film photographs.
- Compensating for problems with brightness and contrast in all types of photographs.
- Retouching images (e.g. removing scars or moles from a face, swapping one background for another).
- Creating photographic effects.

Before starting, please read the section on Paint Shop Pro's tools in the chapter on computer graphics. The rest of this chapter introduces some other Paint Shop Pro tools, although the principles (and many of the names) are identical in other packages.

Some general advice

There are many different adjustments and effects that can be applied to images and these often provide control over their attributes. Many of these activities can be carried out on the same image (e.g. an image can have its colours adjusted, have its dimensions distorted, have several filters applied to it, and so on). This provides a vast range of different potential configurations.   Some adjustments and effects have to be tried to test their effectiveness on a particular image.   Although Paint Shop Pro allows multiple undo's (including an undo history), once the file is saved the original contents are lost forever.   It is strongly recommended that all editing work should be carried out on a copy of the original image.   In that way, if it all goes horribly wrong, the original is still there to start all over again.   For the same reason, if a file is being worked on over several sessions, it is best to save copies of the edited work as it progresses. However, it should be noted that when a image is saved to a standard graphic format, such as JPEG or GIF, the layers and other elements of the composition are flattened into a single layered image.

For this reason, the best policy for ongoing work is saving in Paint Shop Pro's own PSP format.   This is not a format intended for distribution. Its importance lies in its ability to save all the layers and other information for future editing.   When the file is re-opened later, all the layers are available for manipulation.   So, when the editing is finally complete, it makes sense to save one copy with a PSP extension as well as one in the required final format of GIF or JPEG, etc.   This allows the image to be returned to for any future alterations.

Incidentally, it is best to view the image at the actual size it will be displayed before saving, to ensure that the details appear as good in small size as they did when edited full-screen.

Editing tools

The main tools for editing digital photographs are:

Tool	Description
Deformation tool	Used to rotate, resize, skew and distort a piece of text, image or selection.
Crop tool	Used to remove unwanted areas and borders from an image.
Selection tool	Used to select a particular part of an image for separate processing.
Freehand tool	As above but works with irregular shapes.
Magic Wand	Used to select an area from an image, based on its colour.
Clone Brush	Used to retouch photographic images
Color Replacer	Used to replace all pixels of a certain colour to a new colour.
Retouch tool	Used to retouch photographic images

These tools, when used in conjunction with layers and with the many extra utilities provided on the pull-down menus, provide a rich variety of editing and effects options.

Examples of utilities provided from the drop-down menus are colour adjustments, filters and special effects such as embossing, glowing edges, blinds, etc.

Rejuvenating old monochrome photographs

There are huge stocks of photographic images that encapsulate times past.   These may be of historical or family interest. They are monochrome images that show the signs of their age. They may have faded, browned, been scratched or folded, and may contain flaws from the photographic process (e.g. poor lighting, dust spots, etc). The techniques for restoring old monochrome images can be put to good use with colour photographs, although colour images provide extra problems as covered later.

The first task is to remove any tiny dust spots from the image by using the *'Despeckle'* tool from the *'Noise'* sub-menu of the *'Image'* drop-down menu.   It creates a mild blurring of the image, except for edges and areas of good contrast.   This has the effect of neutralising dust spots.   The *'Median Cut'* filter that is also available from the *'Noise'* sub-menu has a different approach. It examines each pixel in relation to the pixels surrounding it and alters the pixel's colour accordingly.   This has the effect of softening the image and any rogue pixels (e.g. a white dust spot in a dark area) are replaced by the median colour for the area.

Any larger blemishes, such as scratches, are tackled using the Dropper and Paint Brush tools.

The steps are:
- Zoom in on the affected area.
- Use the Dropper to pick up the shade from the surrounding pixels.
- Use the Paint Brush tool, with the brush size and hardness set low and opacity about midway.
- Paint over the affected pixels.

If it is a large blemish, do not paint out the whole area with the one shade, as it will look obvious. Keep using the Dropper to sample afresh from the surrounding area, so that a mix of the subtle shades is painted over the blemish.   Of course, if the blemish happens to appear on a solid shaded area, the painting is much easier.   For larger blemishes, particularly on areas with complex content, the Clone tool should be used, as detailed later.

Adjusting colour photographs

A digitised photograph may require having its colour components adjusted.   This may be due to imperfections in the camera or scanner, or imperfections in the camera operators' settings.   It may also be due to a colour cast on the subject, caused by light reflecting from a large brightly-coloured object (wall, side of a van, etc.).   There are different tools for tackling these problems.

To assist in deciding where the problems lie, Paint Shop Pro provides a Histogram window that shows the levels of each RGB component in the image. If the graph data gathers at the left of the horizontal scale, the image has a general low brightness, with less vivid colours.   If the data gathers at the top of the scale, it indicates that either a certain colour is over-saturated or the entire image is too light.

The histograms illustrated show the effect of adjusting an underexposed photograph.   The left illustration shows the original image with a high proportion of its content at the bottom of the scale. The right histogram is of the same image after having its brightness and contrast levels increased.   The image in generally brighter and the colours are now more vivid.

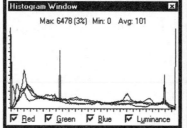 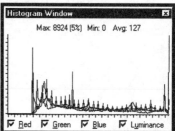

The *'Colors'* drop-down menu has an *'Adjust'* option whose sub-menu provides a range of tools. These tools provide sliders to make the adjustments and have two windows to examine the image content before and after an adjustment. If the *'Auto Proof'* box is checked, the results of an adjustment is visible in the main image ar.

The *'Brightness/Contrast'* option opens a dialog box with two sliders to set the levels of brightness and contrast. The 'Hue/saturation/Lightness' option opens a dialog box with three sliders to set the percentage levels of the hue, saturation and lightness in the image.

Many users find these utilities fiddly and hard to master and often rely on the *'Gamma Correction'* utility.

The illustration shows the dialog box of the *'Gamma Correction'* utility. It provides sliders to set the red, green and blue levels.

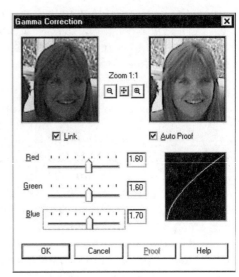

If the *'Link'* box is checked, all three sliders are locked so that moving one slider moves the other two by the same amount. This can be used to lighten or darken an image, without affecting the relative strengths of each colour. If the slider values are increased, the image is lightened, while lowering the slider darkens the image.

If the *'Link'* box is unchecked, each colour's strength can be independently set. This is ideal for making slight adjustments to a photograph that was captured a slight colour cast, due to a reflection from an a brightly-coloured object. Small, careful adjustments to the levels will remove the cast and restore the correct colour balance. This is sometimes referred to as *'colour correction'*.

The Gamma Correction utility can be used to help make a colour image look like an old photograph. The steps are:

- Load the image.
- Choose the *'Add'* option from the *'Noise'* sub-menu produced by the *'Image'* drop-down menu.
- Check the *'Random'* box, to apply random noise.
- Select a low percentage of noise.
- Draw a few white or grey lines to simulate scratches and folds.
- Convert the image to grey scale, to remove all colour components.
- Convert the image back to 24-bit colour.
- Open the *'Gamma Correction'* utility and ensure that the *'Link'* box is unchecked.
- Adjust the Blue value to zero or a small value.
- Adjust the Red and Green values to achieve the sepia colour of old phonographs.

Working with selections

The chapter on computer graphics explained that a selection was an area that can be defined and can then be treated separately from the rest of the image. The selection can be flood-filled, painted, deformed, and subjected to many other image manipulations. Once outlined, the selection can be dragged to any part of the active image area. The selection can also be cut from the frame and pasted into a new layer or as a new image. This facility is probably the most important editing tool. It can be used equally effectively on large or small areas of the image. Its most common uses are in adjusting colour and brightness levels, and as a tool for retouching images.

Many photographs have areas that require to be treated separately. Consider a photograph with one area darker than the rest. If the entire image has its brightness raised, the excessively dark is lightened - but so is all the rest of the image. This will probably result in some areas becoming washed out. The solution lies in only adjusting the brightness of the excessively dark area and ignoring the rest of the image.

Consider, for example, wishing to lighten both the sea and the sky in this image. Fortunately, the sea area is a perfect rectangle. To brighten this area, it is first selected using the rectangle selection tool. The *'Brightness/Contrast'* utility in the *'Colors'* drop-down menu is then adjusted for the desired effect.

The skyline poses a more difficult problem. It has a very irregular outline that would be slow to trace using the freehand or even the smart edge selection tool. For this area, the Magic Wand tool in the Tool Palette is used. As the sky is not a single block of colour, the tolerance level is increased to a point where it selects the entire sky area, without starting to include the buildings in the selection. The selection can then be adjusted independently of the rest of the image.

This technique has many uses in compensating for inadequate lighting or poor contrast in photographs. As long as the contrast was not so high as to push dark objects down to black level (and light objects up to white level), they can be at least partially recovered. If, however, an entire area was reduced to a single blob of black or white, the details are irrecoverable.

Another use for selections is in cutting, pasting and copying parts of an image. Once outlined, the selection can be dragged, or copied, to any part of the active image area. The selection can also be cut from the frame and pasted into a new layer or as a new image. This provides huge opportunities for doctoring photographs. This technique is sometimes used for comic effect (e.g. placing Cousin Bill's head on the body of Arnold Schwarzenneger). However, it is most commonly used to repair blemishes or make cosmetic improvements in an image.

A portrait can be improved by removing blemishes such as a wart, a tattoo or perhaps facial jewellery. The sets for such a task are;

- Look at the skin tone around the blemish and find another skin area with the same tone.
- Use the freehand selection tool, set to a small amount of feather.
- Select an area of the blemish-free skin, using an irregular shape. Do not draw a regular shape such as a rectangle or circle as it is more easily detected.
- Use the *'Copy'* option from the *'Edit'* menu (or use Ctrl-C).
- Use the *'Paste as a new selection'* from the *'Copy'* menu (or use Ctrl-E).
- Position the new selection over the blemish and click the right mouse button to fix on the image.

Example using selections

The photographs of the house front illustrate the use of various selections. The first task was to replace the dull sky for a brighter version with some clouds, to add interest. The house image was opened and an improved sky image was extracted from another photograph and placed on a separate layer of the house image. The house layer was then promoted to a layer and the order of the layers was swapped, to make the sky the background layer. The house image was made the active layer and the areas of sky were selected using the Magic Wand and deleted from the image. The Eraser was used to delete the telephone pole and wires from the left of the image and the top of the street lighting pole in the centre of the image. The sky is now visible through all the deleted areas.

The next step was the removal of the figure and the street lighting pole.

The bricks on the garden wall and the house facing brick were built to a regular pattern.

This allowed the selection of brick areas to be copied on

the areas obscured by the figure and the bottom of the pole.

A small section of the pavement surface was selected with the freehand tool and copied over the area obscured by the figure's foot.

A point-to-point selection of a section of the wooden roofline fascia was used to cover the section obscured by the street lighting pole.

The obscured area of the wooden seat was recovered using the Clone Brush (see below) although point-to-point selections would have achieved the same result.

The remaining wall area obscured by the human torso was recovered using a combination of the Clone Brush (see below) and the copying of freehand selections from the pebbledash wall surface.

Another example

A common technique, beloved by advertisers, is to create an image where the subject is in full colour while the background is in grey scale. Adobe Premiere provides a tool for achieving video sequences like these. The Paint Shop Pro method for still images is to create a selection around the figure or object. This can be a freehand or a smart edge selection, depending on the complexity of the outline. The *'Invert'* option is then chosen in the *'Selections'* drop-down menu. This results in everything except the subject being selected. The *'Hue/Saturation/Lightness'* option is then chosen from the *'Colors'* drop-down menu. The saturation level is reduced to zero and this removes all colour from the selection while leaving the subject in full colour.

The Clone Brush

The clone tool, as its name suggests, paints on an area of the image, using pixel information from another part of the image (or even from part of another image).   The area being chosen for copying is called the *'clone source'* and the area being painted over is called the *'clone target'*.   The content of the clone target is overwritten with the content picked up from the clone source.   If required, the cloning can be confined to a defined area by creating a selection before cloning, or an area can be cloned into a newly created layer.

Cloning is used for painting over dust marks, scratches and other imperfections in a photograph.   If the imperfection is in an otherwise plain image area, it can easily be remedied by picking up the surrounding colour with the dropper and painting over the blemish.   However, if the blemish sits in an area of varying shades or intricate detail, this is not a satisfactory method.   This is where cloning comes in.

Consider the photographs of the house front.   The pole for the streetlights obscured part of the house.   However, the house has an uneven pebbledash surface with many shades.   Painting over the pole, using the dropper and paintbrush, would leave an obvious vertical block of uniform colour.   With the clone brush, an area of the pebbledash texture is selected as the source and this texture is used to paint over the pole.   Similarly, the wooden seat under the window is obscured by the seated figure.   The Clone tool was used to extend the slats of the chair to cover the obscured part of the seat.   This approach is useful for copying any complex area, such as brickwork, clouds, foliage, skin, fur, scales, clothing, and so on.   The cloning is used for covering over blemishes, or for creating duplicates (adding extra clouds in the sky or turning someone's baby into twins).

The Clone tool is accessed by clicking its icon, the one with two paintbrushes, in the Tool Palette.   This brings up a dialog box that sets the brush size, density, opacity, etc.

The steps for cloning an area are:

*   Select the area to be copied, the source area, by right-clicking on it.
*   Select the image, layer or selection to be used as the target.
*   Hold down the left mouse button and paint over the area to be changed.   The crosshairs on the image indicate which pixels are being copied at any particular moment.

For best results, avoid painting in straight strokes, as this tends to leave noticeable edges.   It is often best to keep changing the spot being used as the source.

Finally, ensure that the source area has the same texture and shades as the potential target area.   For example, the texture on a jacket will vary depending upon whether it is a flat area or a curved area, flooded by light or in a darkened crease, and so on.   The characteristics of section chosen as the source should match those of the target area.

NOTES:

*   The Clone brush can be used only on a 24-bit or greyscale image.
*   When cloning from one image to another image, both must have the same colour depth.

Filters

Filters apply a process to all the pixels in an image, or in a selection.   Earlier use was made of the *'Despeckle'* and *'Add Noise'* filters.   A range of filters are accessed through the *'Filter Browser'* sub-menu of the *'Image'* drop-down menu, or from the *'Sharpen'* and *'Blur'* options on the *'Image'* menu.

The *'Blur'* filters smooth out the pixel contents and are used for removing blemishes and compensating for any patterns imposed on the image during filming or scanning.   There are six different varieties of Blur.   The *'Blur'* and *'Blur More'* filters work on the hard edges or boundaries of large colour changes in objects in the image, while ignoring the rest of the image.   The *'Soften'* and *'Soften More'* filters produce a smoothing effect across the entire selected area and are more subtle than the *'Blur'* filters.   The *'Gaussian Blur'* filter is the only variety to provide user control over its strength.   It produces a blur that is more dense at the centre, feathering out towards the edges of the image.

The last filter in this set is the menu is the *'Motion Blur'* filter which is used to add a sense of movement to an image by emulating the picture blur often resulting from photographing a fast car, a sprinter, a child on a swing, etc.   The user can set the angle of the blur movement and the intensity of the effect.

The *'Sharpen'* filters produce the opposite effect of the Blur filters, as they seek to accentuate the contrast differences on the boundaries between areas of the image.   Where a dark area meets a light area, the dark edge is further darkened, while the light edge is further lightened.   This highlights the image's edges providing the illusion of a sharper all-round picture.   There are three varieties of Sharpen.   The *'Sharpen'* and *'Sharpen More'* filters provide fixed levels of effect, while the *'Unsharp Mask'* filter provides user control over the intensity of the effect.   Remember, however, that since it highlights existing edges, it will make dust marks more prominent - so use Despeckle, etc to remove dust marks before applying this filter.   Anyway, in most cases this is the last tool to be used, before the image is finally saved.

Retouch

The filters mentioned above are applied to an entire image or to an entire selection. Many users want more precise control - even down to pixel level. Users with graphics tablets would also value the ability to use their pen in freehand mode to carry out fine adjustments in images.

The Retouch tool is accessed by clicking on its icon, the one that looks like a hand with a pointing finger, in the Tool Palette.   It provides a paint brush that applies effects to the image, rather than applying paint to the image.

The Retouch dialog box has a tab that provides options to set the brush size, opacity, density, etc.

The second tab provides options of retouch mode.   Modes include Lighten RGB, Darken RGB, Lightness Up, Lightness Down, Saturation Up, Saturation Down, Soften, Sharpen and Smudge (great for smoothing out those wrinkles).

Color Replacer

The Color Replacer tool was covered in the chapter on computer graphics.   It allows all instances of a colour to be replaced by a new colour in a single operation, or allows selected areas of a colour to be altered to the new colour.

Consider wishing to alter the sky colour behind the tree area of the house front image.   As can be seen, there are many isolated pockets of sky, in between the branches of the tree. While it is easy to flood fill the large area to the right, the small areas are best tackled with the Color Replacer tool.

The existing sky colour is picked up with the Dropper tool and the new colour is selected from the colour palette.   The dialog box provides options to set the brush size, opacity, density, tolerance, etc.   If the brush width is set too high, the new colour may creep over into areas of the house surface. Setting the tolerance high removes any feathering or anti-aliasing. If the new colour is vastly different from the old colour (e.g. replacing a grey sky with a magenta sky) the cleaner outline provided by a high tolerance value is preferred. If the new colour is broadly similar to the old colour, a low tolerance value leaves some of the edge detail which helps maintain a more natural look.

Special Effects

Paint Shop Pro, like many other image editing packages, provides extensive special effects that can be applied to images.

In Paint Shop Pro, these are accessed by the *'Effects'* choice on the *'Image'* drop-down menu.   This produces the list of effects shown in the illustration.

Some of these effects are more useful than others and they should all be used sparingly.   A special effect should remain special as the repeated use of these effects in a production will quickly annoy the viewer.

Nevertheless, used carefully and moderately, photographs that have had special effects applied to them can be very eye-catching and effective.

The image below was created using the *'Blinds'* effect.
The steps are:

- Crop the image to the desired size.
- Invoke the ellipse selection tool, with some feathering to obtain a fuzzy edge.
- Select an ellipse on the image that surrounds the eyes area.
- Choose the *'Invert'* option from the *'Selections'* drop-down menu. This selects all of the image, apart from the eyes are.
- Hit the *'Delete'* key to remove the outer area of the image.
- Choose the *'Blinds'* option from the *'Effects'* sub-menu.
- Check the *'Horizontal'* box.
- Set the width and opacity of the blinds to achieve the desired effect.

The *'Black Pencil'* effect seeks to translate a photograph into an image that looks like it had been hand-drawn with a pencil. The final effect can be very impressive indeed but getting the correct results is a little fiddly, as the settings for different images can vary substantially.

The image can simply be loaded and have the effect applied but this tends to give a slightly crude finish. If the line drawing and the original image are overlaid on each other, the effect is much more realistic.

The steps for this are:

- Load the image.
- Make a copy of the entire image into a new layer
- Call up the *'Black Pencil'* tool.
- Set the *'Detail'* and *'Opacity'* values for the most realistic effect for the image being used.
- Try the effect of using the *'Soft Light'* option in the Layer Blend Mode. Other options include Hard Light, Normal, Lighten and Darken.
- Adjust the layer opacity of the original image by adjusting the slider (see the illustration).

Obtaining the best results may require that the image brightness and contrast be adjusted before the effect is applied. In some cases,

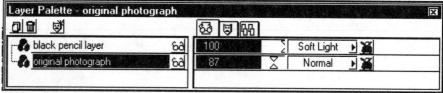

the final flattened image is improved by a little Gamma Correction. The final effect is worth the trouble.

These are only two of the effects that are in the Effects menu. Others, such as Emboss and Buttonize are useful and its worth spending a little time trying out various effects.

Finally, other effects are available from other packages, notably the warp and morph facilities provided by Elastic Reality and the 360° panoramic images from QuickTime Virtual Reality software. The latter package stitches together multiple images into a circular panorama that can be viewed by clicking and dragging the image.

Digital Watermarks

Piracy is common on the Internet. Computer software, games and music albums are all copied and placed on pirate web sites. Huge efforts are made by the software publishers and the record industry to combat this growing trend. Photographers and graphic artists are not immune from this piracy and their work is easily downloaded from a web site and re-used in another production. Most creative people wish to protect their intellectual property and one response has been the introduction of *'watermarks'* into image files. It has been given this name as it mimics the way a watermark is embedded into paper currency notes. The watermark on a pound note is not visible, unless the note is viewed in a certain light. Then the underlying pattern embedded in the paper becomes visible.

In the same way, electronic watermarking of files is designed to protect against illegal use of images or video material. The file has details embedded that do not affect the visible content of the image, but can be retrieved to prove ownership.

In Paint Shop Pro, the facility can be accessed from the *'Image'* drop-down menu by choosing *'Watermarking'* followed by *'Embed Watermark'*. The dialog box allows details such as the unique Creator ID (available free from Digimarc), image attributes (e.g. permission to copy, adult content. etc.) and watermark durability.

The technology is constantly developing and there is some debate about how durable the watermark is. Proponents of watermarking claim that the image can be scaled, cropped, rotated, requantized, compressed, etc - and still maintain the watermark content. Other claim that the watermark can be detected and removed. In many respects, it mirrors the virus race - someone invents a virus and someone else invents the virus detector. In this case, someone invents a watermarking system and someone else works out how to remove it. However, just as with viruses, the system with all its imperfections is better than no system at all.

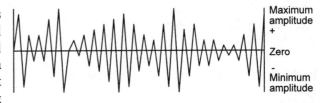

The Nature of Sound

The many uses of voice, music and sound effects in multimedia productions are covered in the chapter on design.   This chapter is concerned with the theory of digital audio and the practical tasks in capturing, editing and compressing sound clips.   Before considering digital sound, the composition of natural sounds needs examination.

Sound is produced and carried by the rapid variation of the pressure of the air surrounding the object that is creating the sound.

Consider listening to the sound from a computer's speaker system. The audio card's output drives the cone inside the speaker. The speaker cone vibrates in sympathy with the audio card signal. As the cone vibrates, the air next to it is alternately compressed and rarefied. This constant change of air pressure sets up sound waves, which travel through the air until they reach the listener's eardrum. The sound waves then vibrate the eardrum, producing the sensation of sound.

The air does not actually travel between the speaker and the ear.   As the air next to the speaker cone

moves back and forth, it passes on this movement to the air next to it - and so on.   It is similar to the water in a pool when a stone is dropped in it.   The waves move outwards but the water does not travel outwards.   The knock-on effects of the variations diminish as the waves travel outwards, resulting in sound becoming quieter the further away the listener is from the source. The air is alternating between a compressed and a rarefied state- i.e. at one point it is more compressed than its normal state, while

it is more rarefied than normal at another point.

This constant alteration of the state of the air is translated into the alteration of electrical signals within audio equipment, where the signal alternates between being above and below a quiescent figure. Often, the quiescent figure is at electrical potential zero, with the voltage swing positive and negative from this value.   These varying signals can be directly replayed through an amplifier or can be recorded to audio tape.   In the case of computer audio, the varying signal is digitised and saved to hard disk as an audio file.

The Hearing Process

The normal hearing process is described as being 'binaural' - i.e. the listener hears with the use of two ears that point in different directions and are a distance apart.   The brain processes the information received at these two receptors to identify the type of sound (e.g. car, voice, musical instrument) and its location within the surrounding three-dimensional space (e.g. to the left or right, in front or behind, above or below). In the real world, sounds are heard from all around the listener - often all at the same time.

This is a complex process and the output from the computer's sound card has to match these natural conditions as much as possible.

Sound Systems

Sound cards and audio reproduction software has developed greatly from the early editions.   They have followed much of technology used in hi-fi equipment, digital TV and in the movie industry.   The three most commonly used audio formats are:

MONO

The most basic audio signal is 'monophonic'. The sound sample is captured into a single audio channel, often using a single microphone to record the sound. The resultant audio waveform stores the essential information that allows the listener to identify the sample as a particular voice or musical instrument. It also provides some information regarding the volume of individual objects within the same (e.g. the drum is loud while the piccolo is quiet).

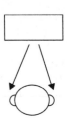

STEREO

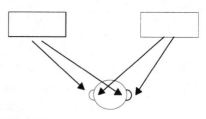

Stereophonic samples record the audio on to two separate channels, using a separate microphone for each channel.   If the microphones are spaced apart, then sound from objects on the left will record at greater amplitude on the left channel.   Similarly, sounds from the right hand side will record at greater amplitude on the right channel. Sounds that situated in between the microphones will record with equal amplitude on each channel.   When the sample is replayed through two speakers, the relative volumes from each speaker reproduce the relative positions of the original sound sources along a left-to-right plane (e.g. the bass guitar is on the left, the drums are on the right and the vocalist is in the middle).

SURROUND SOUND

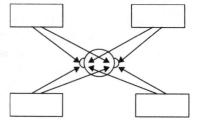

Basic Surround Sound, such as the Dolby Surround Pro Logic, uses four speakers (two in front of the listener and two behind), which creates a circle of sound around the listener. The most commonly used surround sound speaker layout is the 5:1 system provided by both Dolby Digital and the MPEG-2 systems. This process is explained later in more detail.

The Components of Sound

Sound has three essential elements:

- Frequency (the sound's pitch).
- Amplitude (the sound's volume).
- Harmonic content (the richness and uniqueness of the sound).

Frequency

This describes how often the amplitude of the signal changes over a given time period and is measured in complete cycles per second.   The unit of measurement is the Hertz (Hz), where 1Hz equals one complete cycle per second.

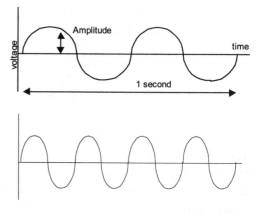

In the first example, two complete cycles of the audio signal have been completed within a one-second period, so the diagram shows a 2Hz signal.   The second example shows four cycles being completed in the same time, so it is a 4Hz signal.   The UK mains supply varies at 50Hz and the US mains supply runs at 60Hz.

The human ear often detects sounds down to about 100Hz, although some can detect lower frequencies (e.g. the hum from the fluctuating 50Hz power mains or even as low as 20Hz).

At the other extreme, the ear can detect frequencies as high as 20kHz, with the average person's upper limit being around 17kHz. These values steadily reduce with old age.

Most of the useful audible range is between 300Hz and 3000Hz (i.e. 3 kHz), a fact that is exploited in many telecommunications systems to reduce bandwidth and minimise costs.   The human voice can produce frequencies in the range 40Hz to 4kHz, with vowels producing low frequencies and consonant producing higher frequencies.

NOTE:

Computers measure capacity or speed in bits or bytes.   A byte is made of a collection of eight bits.   The upper case 'B' usually denotes bytes while the lower-case 'b' usually denotes bits, although there is sometimes confusion in the use of these suffixes.   A modem may transfer data at 56kbps.   The computer may have 128MB of memory installed. A hard disk may store 20GB of data.

In these examples, all values are in binary denominations.   So, a Kilo is 1,024, a Mega is 1024 kilos and a Giga is 1024 Mega.   Therefore, a 1MB memory chip stores 1024 x 1024 = 1,048,576 bytes, while the 56kbps modem is processing 57,344 bits (i.e. 56x1024 bits) every second.

With waveforms, a Kilo is 1000, a Mega is 1,000,000 and a Giga is 1,000,000,000.   Therefore, a 800Mhz CPU runs at 800,000,000 Hz

The Frequency Spectrum

Information is received through our sense of sight, sound, touch, taste and smell.   Much of the information is conveyed in the form of waves - sound waves, light waves and heat waves. In addition, waveforms such as ultrasonics, radio waves and microwaves are used as a vehicle to carry information.

We do not actually hear the radio waves, just the picture or sound information that was previously imposed on them. The table shows the frequency spectrum for the common carriers of information.

Description	Range	Typical Use
Sub-Audio	Up to 20Hz	Below the hearing threshold
Audio	20Hz to 20kHz	The entire range of sounds, speech and music
Ultrasonic devices	20kHz to 30kHz	'Silent' dog whistles, some remote control devices
Long wave	30kHz to 300kHz	Radio
Medium wave	300kHz to 3MHz	Radio
Short wave	3MHz to to 30MHz	Radio
VHF	30Mhz to 300MHz	Radio
UHF	300MHz to 3GHz	Television, aircraft landing systems
Microwaves	3GHz and above	Radar, satellites, TV and communication links

Other frequencies exist, such as heat and X-rays but are not used as information carriers.

The audio spectrum is not equally used by all objects and living things.   The male voice spans a lower range of frequencies than a female voice, while a bass tuba's fundamental range is much lower than that of a clarinet.

The table shows where some of the objects lie on the audio spectrum.

Source	Fundamental	Total range including harmonics
Bass Tuba	40Hz to 375Hz	40Hz to 7kHz
Trombone	80Hz to 500 Hz	80Hz to 8kHz
Cello	70Hz to 900Hz	70Hz to 14kHz
Speech (male)	---	100Hz to 8kHz
Speech (female)	---	180Hz to 10kHz
Soprano Clarinet	150Hz to 1.7kHz	150Hz to 14kHz
Violin	190Hz to 3kHz	190Hz to 15kHz
14" Cymbal	----	300Hz to 17kHz
Room Noise	----	30Hz to 18kHz

Amplitude

There are two measures of amplitude:

- the *'volume'* or *'intensity'* of a sound as heard by the human ear.
- the changing signal levels in equipment such as sound cards and amplifiers.

The intensity of sound is measured in decibels (dB). This is not a linear scale, as the human ear does not perceive volume changes in a linear way.   Doubling the sound energy arriving at the human ear is not perceived as being twice as loud.   The sound energy has to be increased tenfold before it is perceived as being twice as loud. The ear's response to sound changes is logarithmic and therefore audio volume controls are similarly logarithmic.   Turning up the audio volume results in logarithmic increases in output and not linear increases.   Doubling the volume is a 3dB increase, while quadrupling the volume is a 6dB increase.   Increasing the volume by eight times is a 9dB increase and a 30dB increase turns up the volume to 1,000 times its previous amplitude.

Absolute sound intensity decibel levels are calculated thus:

intensity in dB = 10 log (measured value/reference value)

where the measured value is expressed in watts per square metre and the reference value is 10^{-12} watts per square metre.   In practice, noise levels readouts are obtained from meters that are calibrated in decibels.

Examples of everyday audio levels, expressed in decibels are shown in the table.

Prolonged exposure to excessive noise results in permanent hearing impairment.   For example, daily exposure to 110dB for as little as 3 minutes per day presents a likely damage risk, while a level of 85dB risks damage at a daily rate of 4 hours per day.   The source of the excessive levels may be work-related (such as factory machinery or working on building sites or airports) or may be social (such as the over-zealous use of ghettoblasters, or attendance at loud concerts).   The first problem is a matter for Health & Safety procedures, while the latter is more difficult to resolve.   The damage is always permanent and losses are not restored with time.

In addition, increasing age results in declining hearing ability, particularly of the higher frequencies.   Elderly people commonly are unable to detect frequencies above 10kHz, no matter how high the volume is set.   Hearing loss commences at age 25 and declines steadily until aged

DB Level	Example
160	Jet engine
130	Large orchestra at full blast
120	Start of pain threshold
110	Power tools
100	Loud rock music
90	Subway
80	Car/Truck
70	Normal conversation
60	Background noise in busy store
50	Background noise in house or office
40	Quiet conversation
30	Whisper
20	Quiet living room
10	Background noise in recording studio
0	Hearing threshold

about 60.   Thereafter, the decline in women's hearing tends to tail off, while men's hearing continues to decline.   A male aged 60 may have a typical hearing loss of 7db for frequencies around 500Hz while the loss at 5000Hz might be around 35dB.   The corresponding figures for women may be 9dB and 18dB.

The decibel is also used to measure the voltage changes that an amplifier can achieve.   In this case, the decibel is not an actual value - it measures the <u>ratio</u> between a reference point on a logarithmic scale and the value that is actually measured.   It measures how far the signal deviates in any one direction (i.e. how high or how low).   Different electrical and electronic devices make use of the mean or average value of the signal, while others are concerned with the RMS (root-mean-square) value.

For audio digitisation, the maximum or peak value expresses the greatest range that the signal covers and determines the scale to be covered by the equipment handling the signal.

Harmonics

If a number of people were to sing exactly the same musical note, their voices would remain unique and identifiable.   This is because of the harmonic content of each person's voice.   Apart from sounding the basic frequency of the note, the human voice will introduce an individual collection of other sounds that are mixed with the basic frequency.   These other sounds are multiples of the original frequency and are known as *'harmonics'*.   It

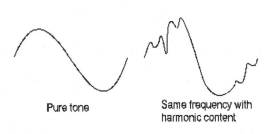

Pure tone   Same frequency with harmonic content

is the quantity and relative volumes of each of these harmonics that makes each person's voice different. In the same way, a piano is very rich in harmonics while a tin flute is devoid of harmonics.   The extra components give the piano its *'richness'* of tone in comparison to the purer sound of the flute.   A sound that is rich in harmonics contains much more detailed information than a purer simpler sound and this causes problems for their storage on computer, as explained later.

The diagrams show three waveforms.

The first diagram shows a basic waveform that carries out two complete cycles within a one-millisecond period.   It represents a pure sine wave with a frequency of 2kHz.   If this is the basic component of a particular sound, it is described as the *'fundamental'* frequency.   The second diagram shows the second harmonic of the sound.   It occurs at twice the frequency of the fundamental.   The third diagram shows the third harmonic, which occurs at three times the fundamental frequency.

The fundamental frequency provides the sound's pitch, while the harmonics provide the sound's tone (often called *'timbre'*).

Different musical instruments produce different mixes of harmonics.   They also produce harmonics at different amplitudes. To further complicate the issue, they often produce different harmonic mixes/amplitudes dependent upon how high the fundamental frequency is or how hard the instrument is plucked/struck/blown.   These intricacies give instruments their uniqueness and explain why real-world sampling produces more realistic results than synthesised sounds.

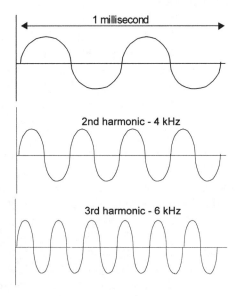

1 millisecond

2nd harmonic - 4 kHz

3rd harmonic - 6 kHz

Harmonics also impose demands on the overall system, if true audio reproduction is to be achieved. Consider a sound with a basic frequency of 4,500Hz and a 9,000Hz second harmonic and a 13,500Hz third harmonic (there is no *'first harmonic'* as this is the basic or *'fundamental'* frequency).   If the sound passes through a component that has a top handling frequency of say, 10,000Hz, then only the basic frequency and second harmonic will pass through.   The waveform will have been changed and the sound, although having the same pitch as before, will no longer sound the same.   Sources that may cause this loss of clarity include:

- Digitising the sound at too low a sample rate (see later).
- Using poor quality sound systems (e.g. playing tapes through an old tape deck) as the source for audio capture.
- Using cheap microphones with a limited frequency range.
- Playing the finished sound through poor quality loudspeakers or headphones.

Digitised Sound

Audio in the real world is analogue; it contains infinite variations in amplitude. However, the computer only stores data in digital format. Therefore, the circuitry on the sound card has to convert analogue sounds into a digital equivalent. These digital files can then be incorporated into web sites or into multimedia CD-ROMs.

Analogue-to-Digital Conversion

Sound is fed into a sound card in analogue format, usually from a microphone or other audio source.

The conversion is carried out by a chip in the sound card called the *'ADC'* - the *'Analogue-to-Digital-Converter'*. The ADC processes a sample of sound and generates a series of numbers that can be stored to disk for later replay. The numbers store the amplitude of the sound waveform at progressive points in time during the duration of the sound sample.

The diagram shows a waveform whose amplitude is varying with time.

The amplitude of the waveform is measured at regular time intervals and the value read at each time interval is stored. The set of sampled readings represents the changes in the waveform and can be used to recreate the original sound using a DAC.

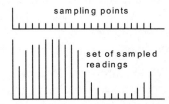

The DAC (*'Digital-to-Analogue Convertor'*) works in the reverse manner to an ADC. It accepts a digital input and uses the values to build a varying audio signal output. In most formats, the waveform swings above and below a reference point of zero. This means that low amplitude levels have a negative integer representing them while positive integer numbers represents high amplitude levels.

The diagram shows an ADC being fed with a sound source. The output shows the effects of digitisation. The ADC circuitry looks at the amplitude of the audio input at regular time intervals and converts the value that it finds at each moment into its nearest binary value. Since the input has an infinite number of possible amplitude levels, the ADC chooses the nearest binary level that the chip offers. This is known as *'quantisation'*. The chip carrying out the

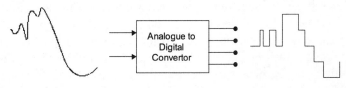

conversion has a binary output system. In this example, there are four output pins. This allows values from 0000 (i.e. decimal zero) to 1111 (decimal 16). If the chip had eight output pins (as in 8-bit sound cards), it would provide 256 different output levels. 16-bit sound cards have 16 output pins, allowing output resolution down to 65,536 different values.

The conversion process is called PCM (Pulse Code Modulation) and the raw data with no compression (e.g. a RAW or WAV file) is described as an LPCM (Linear PCM) file.

Two factors determine the quality of digitised sound:

- The dynamic range (i.e. the accuracy in terms of absolute amplitudes).
  The larger the range of values stored, the greater the accuracy of the sound's reproduction.
- The sampling rate (i.e. the accuracy of the amplitude at any one instant).
  The more samples taken in a time period, the greater the sound's fidelity.

Dynamic Range

The more complex the waveform to be stored, the greater total of different numbers required to store the sound. The span from the lowest amplitude to the greatest amplitude is known as the *'dynamic range'*. This is sometimes also described as *'resolution'* or *'bit-range'*.

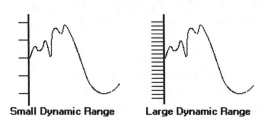

Small Dynamic Range   Large Dynamic Range

In the left diagram, only a small number of bits are allocated to store the waveform, so it is incapable of handling the small amplitude variations in the waveform and these details are averaged away.

In this case, the ADC produces a series of numbers that approximate to the overall waveform but the harmonics that make a piano sound different from a guitar are lost as are the harmonics that differentiate between different human voices.   The right-hand diagram shows a greater dynamic range allowing the same analogue signal to be converted into a greater number of digital levels.   This allows for a greater clarity of reproduction, as the replayed sound is closer to the original sound.

The early 8-bit sound card used 8 data bits to store each sound sample.   Eight bits allows a range of 256 different levels.   This is still sufficient for some purposes (e.g. voice samples and digital telephony) but does not provide a high quality sound sample.   Current 16-bit sound cards handle a range of 65,536 different sound levels, giving the quality expected from a domestic audio CD system.   This is not a professional quality, since each of the 65,536 levels is a linear step while the human ear responds to amplitude variations in a logarithmic way.   This means that many of the discrete stored levels do not store changes that can be detected by the ear and so are wasted. This is not a problem since only a few professionals use PCs for their audio work.   Given these limitations, 16-bit sound recordings have obvious quality advantages over 8-bit recordings. They do, of course, require twice as much disk storage space as their equivalent 8-bit sound samples.

The maximum dynamic range of a digital signal is the ratio between the smallest and the largest value that can be stored, with 0dB as the threshold of human hearing.   A 16-bit resolution card has a maximum range of 96dB, while an 8-bit resolution card has only a 48dB maximum range.   Since a 96dB range is the approximate range perceived by the human ear, it was the natural choice for CD audio and music.

While uniform PCM uses linear steps in its sampling range, mu-law files have a dynamic range that uses logarithmic steps for quantisation.   With logarithmic quantisation, an 8-bit file represents the same range of values that would require 14 bits with uniform quantisation.   This produces a compression ratio of 1.75 to 1, with the lower amplitudes being more accurately encoded than higher amplitudes.   This is particularly suitable for speech processing, where most of the voice information is low levels.
Cards are now available with 18-bit, 20-bit and 32-bit resolution, to provide greater quality output.

Sampling Rate
The dynamic range determines the accuracy of the amplitude reading at any one point in time. Of equal importance is the frequency of taking these readings.   If the readings are too infrequent, an amplitude change will pass undetected.   If the readings are too frequent, the conversion will produce a giant series of amplitude readings.   The timing of the conversions is known as the *'sampling rate'* and is measured in kilohertz (i.e. how many thousand amplitude conversions are carried out each second).
The left diagram shows the effects of a low sampling rate.   The sound sample is converted into six samples with varying amplitude levels.   When the sample is replayed, the sound card's DAC (Digital-to-Analogue Converter) uses the six levels to reconstruct the sound wave.   This sound wave is then amplified and sent to the loudspeakers.   As the diagram shows, the final output is an approximation of the original sound with a considerable loss of detail.   The inertia in the loudspeaker cones acts to smooth the transitions between different output voltage levels from the DAC.   The right-hand diagram shows the same sound sample with twice the sampling rate.   The

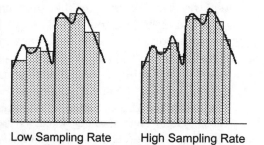

Low Sampling Rate   High Sampling Rate

audio is now stored in twelve different samples and this is much more representative of the original sound source.
Quality signal processing is based on the *'Nyquist Theorem'* which states that the sampling rate must be at least double the frequency of the highest frequency to be sampled.   If, for example, the sampling rate were exactly the same as the input frequency of a sine wave, the input source would be sampled at the exact same spot on the wave for every sample - the source would appear to be a constant value.
Since the average human ear can only hear frequencies up to about 20kHz, a sampling rate of 44kHz is adequate for most uses.   Indeed, the human voice itself does not produce useful sound information above much more than 3kHz.
The original Sound Blaster card was first introduced with a sampling rate of 11kHz.   Sound cards now usually operate up to 44.1kHz (the same rate as audio CD) and sampling rates are adjustable down to as low as 4kHz. DAT (Digital Audio Tape) for domestic use samples at 48kHz while professional studios use sampling rates up to 96kHz.

Noise

Noise is unwanted electrical signals that exist in the signal along with the original signal. As long as the noise stays at a low level there is no serious problem - but when the noise increases to the point where it is becomes noticeable, it detracts from the final sound.

The measure of sound quality is the *'signal-to-noise ratio'*. This compares the level of noise present in a signal to the amplitude of the wanted signal. This is measured as a ratio and expressed in decibels.

$$\text{S/N ratio} = \frac{\text{average signal power}}{\text{average noise power}}$$

This ratio is a better measure of quality than simply measuring the noise level.   The noise cannot be drowned out by turning up the volume level, as the amplifier will increase both the noise and the wanted signal by the same amount.   The sources of noise have to be minimised, so that the signal has little noise content.   Noise from poor installation can be corrected but all sound cards introduce some background noise.

The quality of the output from the budget sound cards is limited and higher quality cards have a much better performance. For example, the Creative SoundBlaster Live! card has a signal to noise ratio of 120dB compared to the average of 85dB for most cards (and only around 60dB for older cards).   Cards based on the Vortex 2 chipset produce a SNR of 100dB or better.

The main sources of noise are:

Quantisation Noise - caused by the nature of the sampling process, although much more pronounced with low bit-resolution.   The smooth analogue input waveform is converted into a squared off, stepped version as shown.   Signals with steep sides are rich in harmonics.   This way, extra unwanted signals have been introduced in the digitised waveform.   These are high in frequency and are heard as background noise.   Increasing the bit range results in more digital levels and reduces the larger steps.   For example, using 4-bit resolution results in a signal-to-noise ratio (SNR) of around 24dB, while 8-bit and 16-bit resolutions provide SNRs of around 48dB and 96dB.   In practice, the introduction of other noise reduces the system's overall SNR figure.   The worst effects can also be minimised by using filters to smooth the transition between each step.

Component Noise - caused by random or unwanted electron fluctuations within both inactive devices (such as resistors) and active devices (such as integrated circuits).   Professional and high-quality equipment uses gold-plated plugs and sockets for all audio and video connections to minimise bad and dirty connections.

External Interference - caused by everything from natural sources (such as cosmic radiation and electric thunderstorms) to manmade sources (such as radiation from electrical appliances).   This can be minimised by ensuring that all audio cables are adequately screened and ensuring that electrical apparatus is kept at a distance from the audio and PC equipment.

Crosstalk - caused by signals from one cable being picked up on another cable.   This occurs due to the effects of capacitive and inductive coupling between lines that run adjacently.   This can be minimised by ensuring that audio cables use screened cable and are not run alongside power cables, loudspeaker cables, etc.

Underdriving - caused by feeding a very low level of signal into an input that expects to be driven by a signal of greater amplitude.   The input signal level may be hardly any greater than the general noise level present in the amplifier.   In such a case, increasing the gain of the amplifier increases the noise by the same amount as the wanted signal.   This can be minimised by matching the output of the driving device (e.g. the output voltage from a CD player) to the range required to sufficiently drive the input device.

Hum loops - caused by inadequate earthing (grounding) arrangements.   Power supply cables to the various devices should be fed from the same mains socket, through a multiple outlet strip if necessary.   If not, a ground loop may exist between the PC and the other equipment.   This is caused by the devices' own earths not being at exactly the same potential.   The resulting voltage difference produces a small current to flow in the shielding of the audio cable and this can introduce a hum or buzz into the audio signal.

Distortion

The digitised version of the analogue signal would only never be accurate if the ADC was able to convert the signal to an infinite number of digital values. This would require an infinite number of samples taken every second and an infinite number of binary values to store the reading. This is unlikely to be achieved in the near future and the digitising process tolerates the present compromise between quality and practicality. Nevertheless, the current sampling rates and bit resolutions inevitably lead to distortion of the sound quality.

Another source of distortion is the mismatch between signal levels when devices are connected.

A sound card has two main audio inputs:

- The 'Microphone' input, designed for the connection of low voltage drives up to around 100mV (i.e. one tenth of a volt).
- The 'Line In' input, designed to be fed voltages up to around 1 volt from CD players, etc.

The diagrams below show the effects of connecting a 200mV input signal to both types of input connector. In the first case, the input signal is applied to the *'Line In'* socket. The input swing is within its operating range and it successfully handles the signal. It is passed on to the digitising circuits. In the second case, the signal is connected to the *'Microphone'* socket. This signal greatly overdrives the sound card amplifier circuitry. The signal is amplified to such an extent that it exceeds the maximum output signal swings of the amplifier. This effect is known as *'Clipping'* and introduces a great deal of distortion into the signal prior to digitising.

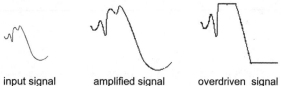

| input signal | amplified signal | overdriven signal |

Sound cards often employ *'AGC'* (Automatic Gain Control) circuitry to minimise clipping problems. The AGC components detect large input signals and reduce the gain of the amplifier to prevent it being overdriven.

Of course, the incoming signal should be fed from a high-quality source. Playing a high quality tape through an old tape recorder, for example, is certain to introduce distortion into the signal before it even arrives at the sound card.

Distortion can also arise within the sound card's circuitry. Even a good quality amplifier will introduce some distortion of the signal, as it is very difficult to design amplifiers that produce the same amount of amplification of the signal at every possible frequency and at every amplitude level. The output amplifiers that are built into the sound card - the one that drives the loudspeakers - are commonly of lesser quality than those found in stereo systems. Users often the *'Line Out'* socket of the sound card to connect to the domestic stereo system for better quality reproduction.

Storage Overheads

Current sound cards have stereo channels, allowing each channel to process independent contents. This improves the character of the reproduced sound but requires double the storage space. The table shows the amount of disk space required for even short digitised samples, when sampled at 44.1kHz. The storage figures in the table can

	bytes per sec	bytes per min
8-bit mono	44,100	2,646,000
8-bit stereo	88,200	5,292,000
16-bit mono	88,200	5,292,000
16-bit stereo	176,400	10,584,000

be halved if the sampling rate is dropped to 22.05kHz and can be halved again if an 11.025kHz sampling rate is used.

From the table, it can be seen that a four minute song in CD-quality stereo occupies over 40MB of disk space. A more detailed table is displayed later in this chapter.

A professional 24-bit multitrack system, using only eight tracks, and sampling at 96kHz, stores 2,304,000 bytes per second and requires over 500MB to store the same song!

The storage requirements of an uncompressed audio sample can be calculated thus:

Storage   = sampling rate   x sample duration   x   bit resolution   x number of channels   / 8
            (in samples per sec)   (in secs)   (i.e. mono/stereo)   (to convert to bytes)

Therefore, the calculation for a 1 minute stereo sample at 16-bit resolution and CD-quality is:

Storage = 44,100 X 60 X 16 X 2 / 8 = 10,584,000 bytes

This calculates the raw data, known as *'Linear PCM'*, as used by Red Book (i.e. audio) CDs.
Dividing the answer by 1024 will produce the value expressed in kilobytes.

Format Considerations

The table shows the generally accepted descriptions for some commonly used recording formats. Of course, many more permutations are available. Another common standard for speech is 8-bit mono at an 8kHz sampling rate.

Dynamic Range	Number of Channels	Sampling Rate	Quality Description
8-bit	mono	11,025	Telephone Quality
8-bit	mono	22,050	Radio Quality
16-bit	stereo	22,050	Most Home Audio
16-bit	stereo	44,100	CD/MiniDisc Quality
16-bit	Up to six (Dolby 5.1)	44,100, 48,000 or 96,000	DVD Quality
24-bit	multi	96,000	Recording Studio

There is a trade between the file's quality and the file size. These are vital considerations for recording audio files intended for use on a web site, as the person browsing the site is unlikely to wait for a long period just to listen to the site's opening jingle or the site author's words of welcome. Audio files are more easily accommodated on a CD-ROM, with its 650MB of capacity but even productions here can get tight for space. DVD-RAM disks with even greater capacity to accommodate larger files are already available.

The table shows the rate at which data would have to be supplied to the user playing back an audio file. While CD-ROMs can handle these data rates, the higher quality clips could not be sent in real time - even with current top-quality 56k modems.

Dynamic Range	Number of Channels	Sampling Rate	Data Rate per second
8-bit	mono	11,025	10.7kB
8-bit	mono	22,050	21.5kB
16-bit	stereo	44,100	172.3kB

Designers wishing to minimise the storage and data transfer rate problems have to consider the following options:

Dynamic Range

8-bit recordings are noisier than 16-bit recordings, as they introduce signal levels that were not present in the original audio signal. In addition, as described earlier, the poorer approximations in the final recording lose much of the fine harmonic detail. This results in *'flatter'* reproduction.

Nevertheless, 8-bit recordings are adequate for reproducing speech, feedback noises and low-quality music (particularly basic synthesised sounds).

For quality recordings of music, 16-bit recording is necessary. Professional studios require 24-bit or greater working.

Number of Channels

Stereo requires twice as much storage space on a CD-ROM, or twice the download time over the Internet. Only use where necessary:

- High-quality music
- Stereo sound effects (e.g. train or plane passing)

Examples where mono is satisfactory:

- Speech
- User feedback sounds (e.g. 'bleeps' or 'clicks')
- Most uses of music, particularly on the web.

Sampling Rate

As the sampling rate is reduced, the sound becomes more *'muddy'* as detail is filtered out. This is more pronounced at the lower end of the range of sampling rates. The difference between dropping from 44.1kHz to 22.05kHz is less noticeable than dropping from 22.05kHz down to 11.025kHz.

The best quality to be expected from domestic audio equipment, such as tape decks, is the equivalent of a 16-bit, 22.05kHz recording. Sampling such signals at higher than 22.05kHz increases the file size without producing any noticeable improvement in quality.

Compression

The large files required to store audio files, and the long times taken to download them over the web, encouraged the development of a range of storage methods that involved compressing the file on saving and decompressing again on playback. This means that the processed file is smaller and therefore requires less space to store, less time to load from hard disk or CD and less time to transmit over the Internet.

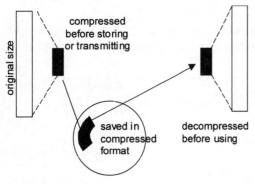

This can be achieved without any loss in the quality of the audio sample. If desired, the file can be made even smaller although this amount of compression results in some loss of quality.

Some systems offer a range of possible compression ratios, ranging from low-compression lossless samples to high-compression samples with loss of some detail.

Lossless compression may only reduce an audio clip to half its original size. Lossy compression, on the other hand, can reduce a clip to a tenth of its original size. Additional software can be installed (see MP3 later) that provides compression ratios of up to almost 100:1.

CODECS

The utility that carries out these transformations is known as a CODEC (compressor/decompressor).

The compression stage uses an algorithm (i.e. a certain set of rules) to shrink the file size. This means that when the file has to be enlarged again for use, it must use the same type of algorithm (in reverse!) to recover the file.

Most of the audio CODECs are implemented as software routines, although top-end equipment may use built-in hardware CODEC chips.

Carrying out the tasks in hardware speeds the process. Implementing the system in software used to be a problem, as the higher sampling rates required a very fast response from the processing software (which explains why some boards could only compress while recording at low sampling frequencies).

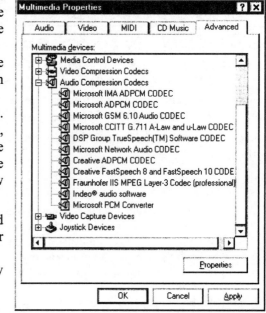

Windows installs a number of software CODECs and others may be installed as part of the installation of other hardware or software.

The CODECs present on a computer can be examined by selecting

Start/Settings/Control Panel/Multimedia

Clicking the 'Advanced' tab (in Windows 95) or the 'Devices' tab (in Windows 98) and opening the 'Audio Compression Codecs' folder displays a list of the CODECs installed on that computer.

The most significant CODECs supplied with Windows are:

Codec Name	File Extension	Description of Best Use
IMA ADPCM	.wav	4:1 compression of 16-bit 22.05kHz audio is used in QuickTime and the Sony MiniDisc recorder/player. Also supports 8kHz, 11.025kHz and 44.1kHz.
Microsoft ADPCM	.wav	4:1 compression of 22.05kHz mono or 11.025kHz stereo. See more below. Also supports 8kHz and 44.1kHz.
GSM 6.10	.gsm	10:1 compression of mono at 8kHz was originally developed for digital cellular telephones and is now used for Internet phone applications. Also supports 11.025kHz, 22.05kHz and 44.1kHz.
CCITT G.711	.au	2:1 compression of 16-bit audio is the standard for international telephony. Known as A-law in Europe and µ-law (pronounced mew-law) in the USA. Now also used for videoconferencing. Supports 8kHz, 11.025kHz, 22.05kHz and 44.1kHz.
DSP TrueSpeech	.wav	8:1 compression of 8-bit 8kHz mono only. Adopted by the ITU as the G.723 audio standard for videoconferencing.
MPEG Layer 3	.mp3	See later.

The table shows the top performance of each CODEC.   Each CODEC is able to provide user choice of a range of sampling rates and dynamic ranges and this is covered later.

ADPCM

The ADPCM CODEC shown is one of a range of standards based on the *'Adaptive Delta Pulse Code Modulation'* system.   This takes standard audio that has been encoded into its normal PCM values and compresses the data so that it requires less space than its raw .WAV equivalent.   By only storing the deltas (i.e. changes between samples), it requires about a quarter of the normal disk space.   Since a sample size does not vary greatly from the previous sample, its difference value can be stored in only four bits compared to the 16 bits required for storing the absolute value.   This method appears the in ITU (International Telecommunications Union) standards such as G.722 (for video phones/ videoconferencing) and G.726 (for noisy industrial / military environments).   Variations and sub-sets of ADPCM appear in manufacturers' own proprietary CODECs.   It is also used with CD-I disks.

ADPCM is offered in Windows 95/98 and the IMA variation is used by Sony for its Mini Disc recorders/players.

Speech Encoding

Particularly good compression rates are available obtained for speech-only encoding.   These are optimised for speech compression and are not suitable for other audio processing. These systems (known as *'vocoders'*) are designed for uses such as cellular telephones although they are also used for Internet phone applications.   They are not used with multimedia applications.   These methods are called LPC (Linear Predictive Coding) and CELP (Code Excited Linear Prediction) and they use an analytic model of the human vocal tract to optimise the encoding/compression process.   GSM 6.10 is a variation of the LPC system.

AC-3

This compression system is produced by Dolby Laboratories and produces high quality *'Surround Sound'* audio for DVD, cinema and HDTV.

Like most compression systems, AC-3 is *'lossy'*.   It divides the audio spectrum into narrow frequency bands that closely match the audio selectivity of human hearing.   A vigorous policy of noise reduction is applied to these bands, allowing bands with little or no information to be coded with fewer bits, thereby releasing the extra bits for bands with greater frequency content.

The AC-3 *'shared bitpool'* also allows bits to dynamically shared among various channels, allowing channels with greater frequency content to use more bits than channels with less content.   The result is that AC-3 coding provides multichannel audio surround sound while still requiring a much lower bit rate than that required by an ordinary stereo channel on an audio CD.

More details on surround sound systems are given later.

Playback CODECs

Many different audio files are available and these will have been saved using different compression methods.   Sometimes, the type of file compression is obvious from its extension.   For example, the .ra extension is used with RealAudio files. However, as the earlier table shows, the .wav extension is used for ADPCM, the IMA variation and True Speech and others.   In addition, each compression type supports a range of different sampling rates and dynamic ranges.

The playback process must be automatic.   When an audio file is played, the correct CODEC and the correct playback parameters must be chosen without user involvement.

There are three ways that a CODEC can be brought into use to decompress a file:

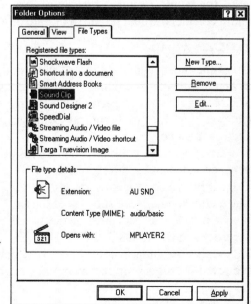

File Associations

In Windows, a file's extension can be linked to a corresponding application package.   As new applications are added to the computer, the file extensions used by the new application is added to the added to the database of associations.

Clicking on an audio file in Windows Explorer loads and runs the application that is associated with file, then the application loads the audio file. If the file association has been configured correctly, the application uses the CODEC that is appropriate to the audio file compression method.

Where more than one application can process a file with a particular extension, only one application can be the default association - i.e. the one activated when the file is double-clicked in Explorer.

These default associations can be viewed and altered within Windows Explorer by pulling down the *'View'* menu.

In Windows 95, the *'Options'* choice and in Windows 98, the *'Folder Options'* choice both provide a *'File Types'* tab as shown in the example.

In the example, files with the *'AU'* and *'SND'* extension are played using the *'MPLAYER2'* application. The *'Edit'* option allows the default application to be altered.

<u>Application-invoked</u>

Many applications will automatically use existing CODECs when required. Examples include Internet browsers, multimedia authoring packages and videoconferencing software.

<u>Standalone Players</u>

An application may be dedicated to handling a particular CODEC.   The best known of these is the range of applications to handle the MP3 format (see later).   These include software players that can be invoked from DOS or Windows (such as Winamp) and hardware players (such as the portable *'Diamond RIO'* player).

Playback Rates

Files must be played back using the same parameters as were used to compress the file during recording. If a file saved using a low sampling rate is played back at a high sampling rate, the audio playback will cease much earlier; the result is that the audio clip is heard at higher frequencies.

When a file is opened by a CODEC, it examines the information in the file's header (see the section on File Formats).   Embedded in the header is data on dynamic range and sampling rate.

Transmission Rates

Reference is often made to the *'Bit Rate'* of various compression systems.   Users have two conflicting demands.   On the one hand, they want audio files of the highest quality.   On the other hand, they want to be able to send these files over transmissions lines (e.g. telephone links, ISDN links) as quickly as possible - preferably in real time.

The final audio may be mono, stereo, or multi-channel (such as surround sound 5.1).   The designer is concerned with the <u>total</u> information that has to be sent in a given time.   Increasing the number of audio tracks increases the number of bits to be sent.   Providing greater compression reduces the number of bits to be sent.

As a result, the final demands are expressed in the bit rate.   This is usually the number of data bits that need to be sent in a single second.

So, for example, the stereo audio from a CD would require a data rate of 1378kbps while an equivalent MP3 file would require a bit rate of 384kbps and a Dolby Digital Surround Sound AC-3 file (with six audio channels) would require a bit rate of 448kbps.

MPEG Audio

On of the most significant recent audio compression systems is MPEG audio. It is used in a wide range of applications in communications, broadcasting (e.g. BSkyB), DVD and web music.

The Moving Picture Experts Group is directed by the ISO (International Standards Organisation) and IEC (International Electro-Technical Commission).   Despite its title, the group develops standards for both audio and video.

The chapter in this book on video discusses the MPEG video standards but it is important to distinguish between video and audio standards.

The MPEG video standards are MPEG-1, MPEG-2 and MPEG-4.

The audio standards are sub-sets of the MPEG-1 and MPEG-2 standards.

For MPEG-1, it is part three of the specification (IS-11172-3).   For MPEG-2, it is parts 3 and 7 of the specification (IS-13818-3 and IS13818-7).

Although this compression system is widely used, its Layer 3 variety, usually shortened to *'MP3'*, has produced the biggest impact on multimedia and web music.

The table shows the main standards and their capabilities.

MPEG Standard	ISO/IEC Reference	Capabilities
MPEG-1	11172-3	Mono and stereo compression at 32kHz, 44.1kHz and 48kHz.
MPEG-2 BC	13818-3	As above, plus: • Sampling rates of 16kHz, 22.05kHz and 24kHz • Support for 5.1 surround sound
MPEG-2 AAC	13818-7	Advanced Audio Coding. Also known as MPEG-2 NBC (Non Backward Compatible) as files are not interchangeable with the other standards. Supports 48 main audio channels plus 16 low frequency ('woofer') channels, 16 multilingual channels and 16 data streams.

The MPEG-2 BC (Backward Compatibility) audio specification allows for compatibility with the MPEG-1 audio specification.   This means that audio files sampled at any of 32kHz, 44.1kHz or 48kHz and encoded by an MPEG-2 encoder will be able to be processed by an MPEG-1 decoder, and vice versa. However, it also includes a *'low sample rate extension'* to the specification.   This provides for additional sampling rates of 16kHz, 22.05kHz and 24kHz, and MPEG-1 decoders cannot read files encoded this way.

These standards all support the same three main compression levels (known as Layers 1, 2 and 3).   Each higher Layer number denotes a compression algorithm of increased complexity and an increased sound quality per bit rate.

The MPEG-1 and MPEG-2 BC Audio Layers are:

Layer	Allowable Bit Rates	Typical Compression ratio	Typical Bit Rate	Typical Use
1	32kbps to 448kbps	4:1	384kbps	Digital Cassette
2	32kbps to 384kbps	6:1 up to 8:1	256kbps to 192kbps	Broadcasting
3	32kbps to 320kbps	10:1 up to 12:1	128kbps to 112kbps	DVD, portable music players, Web music

The *'Typical'* figures in the table are those that maintain CD stereo quality.   The highest layer number has the most complex algorithms but provide the best quality for the sample rate.

Layer-3 decoders can handle all layer types, while the Layer-2 decoder can handle files compressed in Layers 1 and 2. A Layer-1 decoder can only handle Layer-1 files.

These standards are public and, although generally not promoted or supported by commercial music interests, it is very popular among music and Internet enthusiasts.   This is because many applications such as MP3 encoders and players are freeware or shareware and anyone is free to write their own code for their own applications without incurring any licence fees or restrictions.

MPEG-2 AAC looks like being more business oriented and is already the means used by a2bmusic.com for playing its downloadable music.   It has a more complex compression algorithm and achieves a ratio of 20:1, resulting in a bit rate of only 64kbps per channel.

MP2

Layer 2, commonly known as MP2, is used in professional applications such as broadcasting and film. It has less loss than Layer 3 and provides a more dynamic sound as a result.   The lower compression means that the files are larger than their Layer 3 equivalents and consequently have a higher bit rate.

MP3

The most popular standard for general use is MP3, officially known as MPEG-1/2 Layer-3.

As the table shows, its files are compressed to bit rates as low as 112kbps. This means that for a user with an ISDN link to the network, as with the BT Highway, the two 64kbps channels can be combined to carry full CD quality transmissions in real time.   This has been used by radio stations for high-quality links to other sites, without incurring the much higher costs of renting noise-free dedicated broadcast links.   The encoding and decoding is carried out in this instance by studio equipment.   Layer 3 encoders/decoders for PCs are available as hardware (add-on PC cards) or as software (e.g. L3ENC, and AudioCatalyst from Xing).

Layer-3 can also compress using lossy algorithms, to achieve even smaller files at the expense of some quality.   The choice of compression ratio will depend upon the type of audio source being recorded.

Typical compression ratios are:

Sound Quality	Typical Compression ratio	Bit Rate	Bandwidth
Almost CD Quality	12:1 to 16:1	96kbps to 128kbps	15kHz or greater
FM Radio Quality	24:1	64kbps	11kHz
AM Radio Quality	48:1	16kbps	4.5kHz
Telephone Quality	96:1	8kbps	2.5kHz

Even at compression ratios of 24:1 and above, the finished product is still of much better quality than trying to reduce file size by reducing the sampling rate or the dynamic range.

MPEG audio compression uses *'perceptual audio coding'* to reduce file sizes. The amplitude and harmonic relationship between frequencies in the sample, along with the set of frequencies present in the sample at any one moment results in parts of the signal not being heard by the human ear. If a particular frequency is very loud at one point, the ear does not distinguish any nearby frequencies of lower amplitude. These lower frequencies can be filtered out without any loss of perceived quality. It is also common to filter out frequencies that are likely to be above the threshold of human hearing. Since the signal contains less detail, it occupies less space. A typical audio track may occupy around 50MB when stored as a WAV file and just over 4MB when stored as an MP3 file.

The MP3 format is now being supported by many software applications including Microsoft's Netshow, RealAudio, Director Multimedia Studio, and SoundEdit. It is also supported by Internet Explorer 5 (i.e. MP3 files can be called within HTML pages - see the chapter on web site creation)

MP3 Players

A huge range of MP3 players has appeared on the market, using PC-based software players or dedicated players (both portable and non-portable).

SOFTWARE PLAYERS

The most popular players are WinAmp (available from www.winamp.com), FreeAmp (from www.freeamp.org) and Sonique (available from www.sonique.com). These are all freeware products. Microsoft's Media Player handles all the major audio formats, but does not provide all the additional facilities that are available from dedicated MP3 players. Players such as Winamp can be enhanced by additional software. These are known as *'skins'* and *'plugins'*. Skins improve the appearance of the interface while plugins add extra functionality such as audio effects, track mixing, screen animations, light shows and the display of the track's frequency spectrum.

WINAMP

The diagram shows the main screen for Winamp, the most popular freeware MP3 player. Clicking on the *'PL'* button opens a dialog box for creating and modifying the *'playlist'*. The user can browse through a disk's folders and select a number of tracks to be played, or the list can be saved into a .PLS or .M3U, so that it can be easily fetched for playing again in the future.

Clicking the *'EQ'* button displays a graphics equaliser, to setting the output at different frequency bands to individual taste (e.g. being heavy on the bass). Hitting the Ctrl and P keys on the keyboard brings up a dialog box for setting the current skins, plugins and many other options.

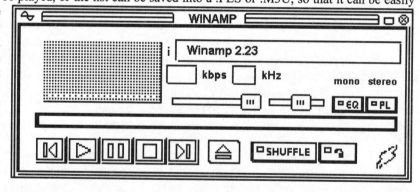

HARDWARE PLAYERS

Most players are portable and are designed to be carried in a pocket. Examples are Creative, Pine, Trust, LG or Samsung players that are based on storing MP3 files in memory. The Pine SM-200C is a portable CD player that handles both normal audio CDs and CDs containing MP3 tracks.

Other player systems are now beginning to appear, such as the *'Empeg Car'* car entertainment player. Casio has built an MP3 player into their palm PCs and even produce a watch with a built-in MP3 player. All these players, unlike a car tape deck or a Walkman, have no moving parts (with the exception of the new 'Rio', which uses a microdrive disk). To augment the built-in memory, most players use SmartMedia cards for extra file storage, with some products using CompactFlash, SD (Secure Digital) memory, or the Sony Memory Stick flash ram. Terratec make a hardware player, the M3PO, which is designed to sit on a desk or shelf. It can play MP3 files directly from CDs or can store MP3 files on its internal 9GB hard disk. A more portable version, Creative LAB'S Digital Audio Jukebox, uses 6GB to store in MP3 and normal CD format.

Details of MP3 encoders are covered later.

MP3 and the Music Industry

The Good...

The MPEG format was originally designed as a means of compressing video files, including both the video and audio components of the file.   It soon became apparent that the audio compression offered by MPEG Layer 3 had uses other than with video files.   It was soon used to compress audio files, particularly with music tracks.

MP3 has provided an ideal medium for up and coming bands to advertise their abilities.   They record their own material, convert the songs into MP3 format and place the files on their web site.   Since they are greatly compressed, a band can provide a good selection of their work on a moderately sized web site. With files in WAV format, they would have to decide between having fewer files on the site or renting out extra web site space and extra bandwidth from their Internet provider.   Many web sites now provide audio MP3 files of this type and even some major bands provide tracks for these sites.   Check out www.mp3.com, which is a web site with over 10 million downloadable tracks, mostly of unsigned bands. All of this is absolutely legal and is a great example of the Net being used for most people's benefit.   The only potential losers in this are the few giant music corporations that currently control the market through the traditional distribution of music media.

The Bad ...

However, MP3 has also become the chosen format for the distribution of pirate audio CDs.   The ability to store the contents of up to 12 normal commercial music CD's on a single disk has led to a mushrooming of this illegal industry.

And the ....

The potential breaking of the distribution monopoly - combined with piracy of existing artists - has produced widespread fear throughout the recording industry.   The turnover in the US music industry is immense and the UK music industry turnover is around £3 billion. Five giant music corporations, along with their many subsidiary labels, dominate the generation and distribution of the music media.

Critics point to the excessive amount of money floating round the industry, with high CD prices subsidising overpaid megabands and recording industry fat cats. They also point to the UK pricing policy (it is cheaper to buy a UK band's CD in the *'foreign import'* section of a US store than it is it buy it in a UK store).   These factors are used as the explanation for the rise in pirate copies.

Music industry spokespeople defend the status quo on the basis of the amount of people employed and the export gains provided to the country; they also point out that the law is on their side.   With vast amounts of money at stake, all the major music agencies have taken steps to limit the damage from pirate MP3 CDs.   The RIAA (Recording Industry Association of America) has pursued vigorous legal action, closing down web sites that offered free music that had not been authorised by the artist or the recording label.   The RIAA, along with the BPI (British Phonographic Industry) and the IFPI (International Federation of Phonographic Industries) made an unsuccessful legal bid to prevent Diamond Multimedia from marketing the Rio portable MP3 player.   In fact, the industry would dearly love to kill the entire MP3 distribution method, even for legally produced music, as it threatens the existing production, distribution, and control of music.   The UK copyright watchdog for music is the Mechanical Copyright Protection Society (see www.mcps.co.uk).

While the music manufacturers have nightmares over MP3, the artists themselves are less troubled by the medium. They are much more concerned that their work is heard and is properly paid for.   This is the attitude adopted by the Musician's Union in the UK.   From the artists' point of view, a combination of MP3 compression and file encryption would protect the performers' rights.   Fears that MP3 distribution will kill the music industry are not treated seriously as similar claims were made that the invention of cassette recorders and VCRs would kill the video industry.

The major players are now moving slowly towards marketing and distribution on the Internet.   EMI has started US sales of 100 titles using credit card transactions and this is likely to spread.

SDMI

Recognising that they are fighting a losing battle, manufacturers are coming round to the view that they have to embrace and control this medium.   SMDI (Secure Digital Music Initiative) is an attempt by the music, computer and consumer electronics industries to take control of the distribution and playback of commercial MP3 audio.   It proposes to encrypt MP3 files so that they cannot be played on the existing software decoders, both freeware and shareware.   The encrypted files will have to be played through dedicated hardware or commercial software players that will be sold through the normal retail outlets.

The players will be able to decrypt and play the MP3 files - if the encryption code that is embedded in the audio file matches that expected by the players.   This means that future audio media will be sold with unique codes for each purchaser, who can only play the material through their own matching players. The media is no longer truly portable; the music probably cannot be played at a friend's house, for instance.   While this system is intended to prevent illegal copying, it will probably also build up resentment against the restrictive nature of the media.   In the end, this may push even more users into piracy, as hackers will inevitably find ways to get round this protection system.

AT&T have developed *'PolicyMaker'* which provides a variety of playback arrangements.   The code embedded in an audio file can be sold with in-built restrictions such as the number of times the track can be played, the expiry date for the track, whether a set number of copies is allowed, etc.   This system is used by a2b Music.

MP3 and the Law

The law in the copyright area is generally based on common sense and fair play. For example, nobody calls for the abolition of VCRs because they can be used to illegally record films.   As with videotape and audiotape, a distinction has to be made between the medium and the content.   In the case of MP3, the medium is the CODEC and the content is the file that is compressed.

WHAT'S LEGAL

MP3 software decoders are legal.   They play back MP3 files.

MP3 hardware players are legal. These are many standalone devices such as the Creative Rio.

MP3 encoders are legal.   They create compressed MP3 files from WAV files.

MP3 rippers are legal. They grab the digital audio stream off a normal audio CD and convert the audio tracks into WAV or MP3 files.   This, of course, assumes that the manufacturer of the CD allows such copying (as in the case of royalty-free samples).

Most MP3 files from legal sites can be downloaded and stored for personal use. Such sites, at the time of writing, include:

www.mp3.com	www.mp3dda.com	mp3park.com
www.peoplesound.com	www.burbs.org.uk	mp3now.com
www.songs.com	www.mp3.lycos.com	mp3place.com
www.vitaminic.co.uk	www.popwire.com	

Sites, such as www.emusic.com, sell individual music tracks for downloading. The Virgin Entertainment Group are also planning a similar service.

WHAT'S ILLEGAL

The manufacture and distribution of copyright material without permission is illegal.   However, this is true of all media, not just MP3 files.   Copying copyright material onto tape or uncompressed audio CD is equally illegal.

The use of MP3 files for public performances (e.g. playing them at a public function or playing them on the radio/TV) is prohibited without the permission of the artist(s).

Most artists have copyright agreements with the record producers.   This means that both would have to agree that tracks be placed on the Internet.   While the artist or band might be happy to place material on the Net, record producers would almost certainly prevent this.   Exceptionally, they may allow a snatch of a song to be released as a marketing tactic.

Where there is any doubt about the copyright on material, the project manager must either clarify the material's status or capture a fresh sample (capturing with consent, of course).

MPEG-4

MPEG-4 Audio is set to find its way into mainstream applications.

It provides even lower bit rates and uses a range of different compression methods including CELP and an extended version of MPEG-2 AAC called MPEG-4 AAC (although MPEG-4 players will still be able to handle MPEG-2 AAC files).

Its bite rate of 2 to 24kbps at 8kHz sampling and 14 to 24kbps for 16kHz sampling compare very favourably to existing communications CODECs such as G.721 (32kbps), G.722 (48/56/64kbps), G.723 (5.3/6.3kbps), G.728 (16kbps) and G.729 (8kbps).   In particular, its *'communications quality'* rate of 2kbps has become the lowest international bit rate standard.   It is an ideal vehicle for communications systems, Internet telephony, video conferencing and a range of multimedia applications.

Streaming Audio

Files with a *'streaming'* format provide low bitrate encoding for transmitting in real time over the Internet. This allows the transmission of radio programs, etc in real time. For example, users in the UK can listen to US baseball match commentaries as they happen. The disadvantage is generally poorer audio quality. The main formats are Liquid Audio, a2b Music and Microsoft's ASF (Advanced Streaming Format) which includes MS Audio. Most of these files need their own special decompression software to play back the content, although ASF files can be played through Windows Media Player (at the moment through downloading the codec from Microsoft's web site; ASF support will be built in to future Windows releases).

More information on streaming audio formats is provided in later chapters on web site creation.

AUDIO FILE FORMATS

One of the first things a user notices is the bewildering array of file formats and acronyms. All elements of multimedia, even simple text, have several different formats, each with its own benefits and restrictions. Dredging through the morass of standards to find the one that is best suited may seem a huge task, but many of the file formats are either very specialised or just too old and inefficient to be of use.   For instance, sound samples may come with extensions like VOC, WAV, SND, SOU, AU, IFF, SAM, RAW, ULW; some may even have no extension at all. There are also many samples out there that are *'raw'* samples, and have completely arbitrarily extension names, such that they may appear to be separate file formats. However, there are only really a few ways to store digitised sound, and the rest is just dressing.   All the file formats below may be used to store the same audio content; only the manner of storage is different.

All audio file types, apart from RAW files, are called *'self-describing'* and comprise two information sections.

Header Also known as the *'wrapper'* or *'Format Chunk'*.

Header	Audio Data

The header information of different formats vary but generally contain: Name of the clip, size, duration, number of channels (e.g. mono/stereo), resolution, sample size (in bits), sampling rate (in kHz) and type of compression used.

The header of a WAV, for instance, provides the option for the inclusion of a whole range of additional information, such as:

Artist	the name of the artist appearing on the clip
Source	the source of the recording
Genre	the category of the sound (e.g. rock or classical)
Medium	the medium on which the original recording was made
Comments	general comments on the sound clip

If this information is added to a file, it can be viewed by carrying out these steps:

- Open Windows Explorer.
- Highlight the wanted WAV file.
- Click the right mouse button.
- Choose the *'Detail'* tab from the dialog box that is displayed.
- Choose the *'Other Information'* option.

Data Also known as the *'Data Chunk'*, this stores the audio information in binary format. This is the actual audio data stream that is used to reconstruct the original sound.

RAW files contain no header information.

The most important sound file formats are:

RAW : This extension indicates that the file's contents consist solely of the string of numeric data, with no special processing or headers. Its uses PCM (Pulse Code Modulation) to store the data and is the format used for audio CDs. Although raw sound samples may be stored on a PC with the extension .RAW, more often they have a less obvious name or sometimes no extension at all. .SOU, .PCM and some .SND files are raw files with a short header to tell the playback software information on what sampling speed to use for the playback. If the raw sample has no header storing the frequency of the sample, then the user has to calculate, or estimate, the sampling frequency (number of samples per second of digitised sound).   It should be obvious when the user hears the sound whether the frequency selected is correct.

WAV : Introduced along with Windows, the basic uncompressed WAV file is a linearly encoded sound sample with a short file header. The benefit of WAV files is that many Windows programs can play them using the same common Windows sound driver.   Of course, the Windows sound driver is not limited to WAV files, but Windows programs themselves tend to prefer WAV files since they are the native format for Windows sound. The WAV format offers a variety of encoding methods, with ADPCM being the most common, although encoded WAV files may not play on some non-PC systems and some older software.

VOC : A common digitised sound format on PCs is the VOC format, created for the Sound Blaster card. Other than the sampled data itself, a VOC file can contain other 'blocks', such as a loop, end-of-loop, or silence block. A silence block allows any length of silence in a sound sample without the comparatively data-hungry sampling of that silence. VOC files also allow compression of the sound sample, albeit usually with some noticeable loss of quality. The Sound Blaster software includes utilities to convert VOC files to the Windows-compatible WAV files, and vice versa.

MP3 : MPEG-1 Audio Layer 3 as previously discussed, while mp2 files are MPEG-1 Audio Layer 2.

MOD : Introduced by the Amiga, MOD files are small 8-bit, signed, headerless files. They are a hybrid of raw digital samples and MIDI-type control information. The file contains up to 31 digitised audio samples along with four information tracks dictating the order of playing of the samples. Since the same sample can be played in different parts of the playback, the overall file size is reduced. The ability to play four sounds simultaneously made the MOD format popular. There are various developments of the MOD format (e.g. the U69 format provides more tracks).

IFF : The Amiga's IFF format is used for many other things apart from sound samples. The Interchange File Format stores 8-bit sound samples in unsigned format - i.e. the wave is sampled from zero upwards, rather than from zero in either direction. The end result is the same, but this small peculiarity means that PC sample files will have to be converted to play on an Amiga, and vice versa. Can be identified by its .iff file extension. Some other digitised samples use the unsigned format but are not IFF files, bearing the extension .SMP or .SAM.

AIFF : The Audio Interchange File Format from Apple uses the .aif file extension and is most commonly found on Macintosh and Silicon Graphics (now renamed 'SGI') computers. Although it offers a range of sampling rates and channels, it is most commonly used for CD-quality samples. Apple also produced a compressed format known as AIFF-C or AIFC which compresses files up to a 6:1 ratio, with some loss of sound quality.

AU : This format is comparatively unusual on PCs, having been developed by SUN Microsystems for their workstations. Another, now extinct, version was produced for NeXT computers. Usually found in μ-law compressed format, although also supports compressed A-law and uncompressed PCM. Although supported by all software and browsers, it is a low quality file with poorer compression than MPEG files.

SOUND STANDARDS

Sound standards are intended as a guide for computer purchasers and as a spur for software developers. The audio specifications contained in the two currently accepted guides are:

MPC3

The MPC specifications were developed after wide discussion within the industry and set the expected performance levels of the individual components of the multimedia computer system. This includes the CPU speed, memory capacity, hard disk size, CD performance, etc.

The audio specification for MPC Level 3 is:
- 16-bit DAC and 16-bit ADC.
- Linear PCM encoding with a CODEC capable of 11.025kHz, 22.05kHz and 44.1kHz sampling rates.
- Multi-voice, multi-timbral wavetable synthesiser capable of 16 simultaneous melody voices plus 6 simultaneous percussive voices.
- Multi-voice, multi-timbral FM synthesiser capable of 6 simultaneous melody voices plus 2 simultaneous percussive voices.
- Internal mixing capability for three (preferably four) audio sources. The sources being Red Book CD (i.e. audio CD), synthesiser, DAC (waveform) and preferably also an auxiliary input source.

This is now quite an old standard and MPC Level 4 is awaited.

PC99

Intel and Microsoft jointly publish their views on PC specifications and these have a great influence on PC manufacturers.

The audio requirements for PC99 are not greatly upgraded from PC98, with 3-d Audio being removed from an earlier draft. The main changes are that future sound cards have PCI interfaces instead of ISA, and the inclusion of three USB connections on computer motherboards. These improvements pave the way for the future inclusion of surround sound using USB distribution.

SOUND CARDS

Early PCs used the internal speaker to provide a limited audio facility. This is still used to *'beep'* for a user's attention (e.g. to signal a hardware failure) but the size of the single internal speaker restricts the quality of the sound generated.   The solution rests in add-on cards dedicated to providing high quality stereo sound from a PC. All machines are now supplied equipped with at least a basic sound card.

SOUND CARD FUNCTIONS

The leader in the field of PC sound was the range of Sound Blaster cards from Creative Labs. It was not the first sound card on the market, but it balanced quality and effectiveness with a reasonable price tag. It handled input from many sources, through a variety of physical connections and competitors were forced to create 'SoundBlaster Compatible' models.   There are now a range of cards, from budget to professional, offering various functions and levels of quality.

THE BASIC SOUND CARD

The basic sound card performs the following elementary functions:

- Recording of audio.   An audio source, such a human speech or music is processed into digitised data for later re-processing.
- Playback of digitised audio.   The data is translated from data into audio.
- Playback of audio CDs.
- FM synthesis.   The sound card contains synthesiser chips that are capable of generating a sound that is broadly similar to that produced in the real world.   For example, the chips can produce the sound of a piano or guitar even although no musical instrument was involved in its creation.   The chips can also produce sounds that are intended to have no human equivalent - e.g. the electronic organ.   The sound card uses dedicated chips employing frequency modulation techniques (i.e. using one sine wave to modulate the amplitude of another sine wave) to produce a sound with the desired harmonic mix.   Each different synthetic sound is known as a *'voice'*.

  Synthesisers also have the following qualities:

  POLYPHONIC

  > The card is capable of outputting many different notes at the same time, allowing the playing of musical chords.

  MULTITIMBRAL

  > The card is capable of outputting several different voices at the same time, allowing the playing of multitrack music.   The Midi Manufacturers Association defines a multitimbral device as one that can play at least two different instruments and at least five different music notes simultaneously.   In practice, sound cards offer between 32 and 128 simultaneous voices.

  Although most audio cards still provide FM synthesis for compatibility with older software and games, newer software uses wavetable synthesis as explained below.

- MIDI equipment interfacing.   The sound card is able to communicate with an external MIDI device, such as a musician's electronic keyboard.   The sound card carries out the processing of the musical score but the MIDI device produces the actual sound from its own synthesiser chips.

MODERN SOUND CARDS

Modern sound cards add the following functions to the above list.

- Wavetable Synthesis. Synthesised sound output is not comparable with a natural sound.   The richer the sound source is in harmonics, the more difficult it is to reproduce synthetically.   That is why even expensive electronic keyboards have had difficulty in emulating the humble piano.   The solution lies in converting an actual sound into a set of digitised data and storing the sample in ROM on the sound card. This is called Wave Table Synthesis and produces greatly improved sound quality.   Wavetable cards normally also provide on-board RAM so that users can use their own captured samples. PCI cards take advantage of the fast speed of data transfers between card and the computer's own system memory to store samples in system RAM.   This results in less memory on the sound card and lowers the card's price.   The SoundBlaster Live!, for example, has 64 voices stored in ROM and up to another 448 voices can be stored in the computer memory.   Sets of SoundFont banks of samples can be pre-loaded into RAM for instant access.   To store a sample for every possible musical note for every possible instrument played in every possible way would require massive amounts of storage. The card stores a set of samples for each instrument (called *'multisampling'*) and slows or speeds the playing of a sample to generate lower or higher musical notes.   This involves complex processing as some instruments have different harmonic content at different pitches or at different playing volumes.
- Digital in/out.   This produces higher quality audio transfers, as the losses involved in the conversions between analogue and digital (and vice versa) are eliminated.

- Surround Sound, using up to eight separate speakers.
- Environmental effects to simulate sounds in a concert hall or under water, for example.
- Full-duplex working. This allows simultaneous recording and playback.   This is used for multi-track music recording and the provision of Internet telephony and videoconferencing.

All sound boards use ADCs and DACs. The ADC (Analogue-to-Digital Converter), as explained earlier, converts an incoming audio sample into its digital equivalent.   The DAC (Digital-to-Analogue Converter) circuitry converts the stream of digital audio data into a varying analogue signal that is fed out through the sound card's *'Line Out'* socket.

Most cards have a SDP (*'Digital Signal Processing'*) chip to carry out audio signal enhancements such as reverberation and chorus effects, as well as handling MIDI and sound file compression /decompression.

SOUND CARD CONNECTIONS
The diagram shows the essential connections of a basic sound card.

Input Connections
<u>MICROPHONE IN</u>
The *'Microphone Input'* connects live real world sounds to the sound card for digital storage. The maximum voltage drive to this socket is typically 100mV (100 millivolts - one tenth of a volt). Most microphones, in fact, produce a drive level much lower than the maximum input.

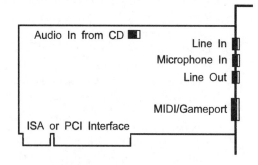

<u>LINE IN</u>
The *'Line Input'* connects other audio sources such as that from the *'audio out'* sockets of a cassette player, an audio CD player or a domestic video recorder. The maximum voltage drive to this socket is typically 1v rms.

The *'Audio In'* allows the internal connection of an audio source into the card.   This is most commonly connected to the *'Audio Out'* socket on a CD-ROM, allowing normal audio CDs to be played on the computer's CD player (with the appropriate software).

<u>GAMES PORT/MIDI</u>
The 15-pin *'Games Port'* allows the connection of a joystick or of a MIDI interface.

The MIDI input allows the real-time capture of a musician's work, for example from an electronic music keyboard. This is stored in the MIDI format as explained later.

Finally, audio cards can receive input via the normal bus connections to the computer.   This allows programs to directly send data to the sound card through the data bus.

Output Connections
<u>AUDIO OUT</u>
Most older ISA cards had an inbuilt amplifier capable of around 4 Watts of audio output power, usually with a volume control mounted on the card's plate.   Most PCI cards abandoned the use of internal amplifiers, as they were low power devices and users now demand higher wattage outputs.

<u>LINE OUT</u>
The *'Line Out'* socket connects the card's analogue audio output to external amplifiers, headphones or computer speakers. Manufacturers produce sets of external speakers for sound cards. These are generally mains-powered with some providing a battery option. One of these speaker cases usually houses an in-built amplifier and volume/tone/balance controls.   Alternatively, the *'Line Out'* connection can be taken to the input of another amplifier to achieve greater output wattage.   Connecting to a domestic hi-fi will boost the audio output to the maximum provided by the hi-fi amplifier.   The maximum voltage output from this socket is typically 1v rms.   The dropping of internal amplifiers also improves the quality of sound cards, as the amplifiers were generally built to a low budget and introduced unwanted noise. Removing the amplifier improved the cards' signal-to-noise ratio.

The MIDI output connects to a MIDI-compatible device such as an electronic music keyboard, synthesiser or drum machine.

Older sound cards were capable of directly interfacing with a CD-ROM.   The cable between the card and the CD-ROM took the control signals to the CD-ROM that carried out the usual drive functions such as moving the head, etc.   This was in addition to the normal data cable that carries the digital audio data on the CD into the sound card for translation into an analogue audio signal.

MODERN INTERFACES

The three major possible changes/additions to modern cards' connections are:

PCI BUS

All audio cards were initially designed to plug into the motherboard's ISA bus. ISA cards have now been replaced with PCI versions. These cards connect to the 32-bit PCI bus, offering simultaneous audio streams and 3D spatial sound effects. They also reduce the demand on the CPU's time. The card's extra DSP (digital signal processing) circuitry now carries out tasks previously undertaken by the CPU. An ISA sound card took 10% of CPU time when playing a WAV, while a PCI card takes 1%. The EMU10K1 chip (found on the SoundBlaster Live!) is reputed to be as fast as a 166MHz Pentium.

DIGITAL I/O

Better sound cards provide an auxiliary external input/output known as SPDIF (Sony/Philips Digital Interface). It is a digital output for direct connection to other digital recording devices such as DAT (Digital Audio Tape - a common standard for music professionals), Mini-Disc machines and some CD players. Direct digital connections maintain the sample in digital format and avoid the distortions introduced by digital/analogue/digital conversions. DAT, MiniDisc and CD systems should be connected to a 44.1kHz SPDIF connection. SPDIF connection types include RCA/coaxial and optical cable.

CONNECTIONS FOR DVD AUDIO

Allows the audio output of a DVD player to be reproduced in full Dolby Digital Surround (see later).

SOFTWARE INTERFACES

Sound cards are connected physically through plugging into the motherboard's ISA or PCI bus.

The computer's programs need to communicate with the sound card, passing on the information to be processed. The basic information is the digital waveform data that is to be converted back into an audio waveform.

Early computer games (and even some current games) were DOS-based and communicated directly with the sound card through DOS. The games software had to be able to work with a variety of software drivers that were specific to a manufacturer's own sound card. With the arrival of Windows 3.1 and 95/98, it became possible for any Windows application to utilise a sound card's basic benefits using a single sound driver. As long as the correct driver for the sound card was installed, all Windows programs could communicate with the sound card.

However, modern sound cards can now handle a variety of enhanced audio activities such as waveform synthesis, wavetable handling and 3D effects using multiple speakers. In addition, most card manufacturers still have their own hardware interface methods using their own brand's sound card device driver.

This would cause nightmares for the writers of applications and games if it were not for the use of APIs.

The API (Application Programmable Interface) is a piece of the application code that passes advanced audio instructions to the sound card. As long as the sound card's hardware or software is compatible with the API, it can understand and implement the instructions. In this way, the same program is able to work with a range of sounds cards, despite their different internal workings and different drivers.

In most cases, the sound card implements these API instructions through dedicated circuitry on the card.

EFFECTS APIs

Almost all new cards provide some form of three-dimensional effects.

Microsoft provides DirectSound and DirectSound3D (DS3D) as part of its DirectX APIs. Although DS3D can be implemented by the computer's own CPU, most cards handle DirectSound instructions through hardware.

Aureal Semiconductors introduced the A3D standard in 1997 and then A3D2. Some cards handle these instructions through their hardware (using Aureal's own Vortex II chipset), while others use slower software emulations. Many do not yet support this API at all.

Creative Audio introduced the EAX (Environmental Audio Extensions) and EAX2 API standards. Support for these standards is still very patchy with most cards not yet able to handle them. However, since the system comes from the manufacturers of the famous SoundBlaster range, compatible software drivers are continually being developed for other cards. EAX is now incorporated into Microsoft's DirectSound, making any software developer's job simpler. Similarly, the Sensaura standard can be accessed via Microsoft's API, although some effects currently remain proprietary.

Where a card cannot handle an optimised standard, it will usually revert to handling sound samples at the basic DirectSound3D standard (with some loss of quality).

SURROUND SOUND

The human brain and auditory system perceive their audio surroundings in terms of its frequency, harmonic content, amplitude, direction and time. The early sound cards adequately handled frequency, harmonics and amplitude. Mono audio samples gave the listener reasonable reproduction of the original sound but did not reproduce the normal listening process.   Although an improvement, even stereo samples do not provide the listener with a normal listening experience.

In the real world, the listener's brain processes a range of audio factors.

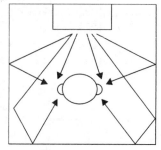

Consider listening to the sound of an orchestra.   The instruments are situated from left to right and from back to front. In addition, the acoustics of the hall in which the music is played affects the final sound. The listener will hear most sounds directly from the instruments. However, sound will also be reflected from the hall's walls, roof, etc. The listener will hear sounds from many different directions - from behind, above and from the side.   The shape of the human external ear canal receptors results in a slightly different frequency response to sounds picked up from the rear

A mono sample stores the sounds of all the instruments but provides little positional information. If a particular instrument is louder than another, the brain will generally consider it to be closer than a quieter instrument.   However, it does not indicate whether the instrument is to the left or the right of the listener.   A stereo sample provides further information. This requires the listener to be situated in a defined listening area, with the speakers placed to the listener's front-left and front-right. This effective listening area is smallish and is known as the 'sweet spot'.   Now, if one of the instruments were only recorded on to the left channel of the sample, its sound would reach the listener's left ear before if reached the right ear. The brain detects this small time delay (the 'inter-aural delay') and interprets it as a sound coming from the left.   If the audio sample recorded the instrument equally on both channels, the sound would reach each ear at the same time and be interpreted as coming from directly in front of the listener. Adjusting the relative volumes of the instrument on each channel can therefore place the sound in any part of the left-to-right plane.   In addition, of course, a sound could be initially recorded at high amplitude on the left channel and low amplitude on the right channel to make it appear to be positioned to the listener's left.   Then the volumes could be gradually reversed, lowering the amplitude in the left channel while raising the amplitude in the right channel. This way, the sound would appear to move across in front of the listener. This technique is known as 'panning'.

Although stereo techniques provide additional positional information, the listener requires further 'depth of image' information.

Sound cards normally implement three-dimensional sound effects by providing for the connection of four speakers. The traditional stereo speaker layout has a speaker at the front-left and front-right of the listener.   Improved 3D effects are achieved by also having a rear-left and rear-right speaker.   The listener is then placed within a defined listening area, which is significantly larger than the stereo sweet spot. By adjusting the amplitude of the audio signal sent to each speaker, the sound is perceived to be anywhere within that listening area.   In this way, listeners can hear a door opening behind them or can hear a bird or a plane circling around them (using panning).   This technique is not new and was employed for the film 'Fantasia' as early as 1940. It was further developed by Dolby in its four speaker 'Pro Logic' systems.

The surround sound system used with DVD videos has a 5.1 speaker layout (i.e. 5 speakers and 1 sub-woofer).   This is associated with the Dolby Digital system and the MPEG-2 audio system.

The four-speaker system has an additional speaker located directly in front of the listener. Since much of the sound from a DVD movie is in front of the viewer, a separate centre audio channel is used to feed a centrally positioned speaker. This provides more effective 'localisation' than using the left and right speakers to place sound in this central area.

Left	Centre	Right
	Sub-woofer	
Rear Left		Rear Right

The sub-woofer handles the lower audio frequencies (about 20Hz to 120Hz) and is particularly effective in reproducing bass guitars and low frequency effects such as thunder and explosions in movies and games.   The sub-woofer speaker needs no special positioning, as the human ear is poor at detecting the direction of lower frequencies.

FULL 3D EFFECTS

But, it is not only the relative volumes that provide positional information, since a quiet sound nearby can still be drowned out by a distant loud noise. Amplitude levels alone are insufficient to reproduce the normal listening experience. A listener also distinguishes local and distant sounds by the amount of reflected sound from that object. A quiet sound that is close to the listener has less reflected sound than that from a loud distant noise. The brain processes the ratio of reflected sound to the original sound to help estimate how far away the original sound source is.

In the acoustically dead recording studio, multi-track recordings are made with each channel independently recording each instrument. Since this loses all reflected information, it has to be re-inserted artificially, by adding reverberation effects.

While Surround Sound provides realism in two planes (i.e. left to right and front to back), the real world is three-dimensional; sounds also have a third plane (i.e. up and down). For example, the sound of a plane should appear to be above the head of the listener. The sound of someone climbing stairs should not only pan from left to right but should also be perceived as moving from a low level to a higher level.

Most 3D audio techniques use HRTFs (Head-Related Transfer Functions) which can employ up to a dozen audio filters mimic the effect of normal listening. The human outer ear acts as a filter that processes sound from different directions differently. Most sound arrives directly at the ear but some is also reflected from the listener's face, shoulders and ears. This information is used by the brain to help the listener pinpoint the direction that a sound comes from. Sound samples that have been rendered with HRTFs mimic the filtering of the ear and fool the brain into placing a sound in any position in a three-dimensional area surrounding the listener.

Aureal's A3D system uses this method to imitate the effect of multiple speakers positioned above, below and behind the listener - with only two speakers connected. The 3D2 system uses HRTF positional audio on a front pair of speakers and stereo panning on a rear pair of speakers. Sensaura uses HRTF on all four speakers.

OTHER EFFECTS

The APIs are capable of transforming the basic sound sample by adding echo, reverberation, ring modulation, flanging, distortion, vocal morphing and pitch-shifting effects. They also provide a range of *'environmental'* effects, where the sound sample is processed differently according to the scene in which it is played. For example, a sound sample of a footstep would be given added echo when placed in the setting of a large hall or empty rooms; the same sound would be muffled if the rooms were heavily carpeted. Similarly, the sound of music, gunshots, etc sound differently when heard underwater.

The listener also detects *'Doppler'* effects with some sounds. For example, the frequency of the sound of a passing train lowers as it moves past the listener. This effect cannot be reproduced using simple panning techniques.

Examples of sound card specifications

Card	Chipset	Max bit resolution	DirectSound3D	A3D	EAX	Wavetable voices *	MIDI channels	SNR
SoundBlaster Live!	EMU10K1	32-bit	Hardware	Emulation	Yes	448+64	32	-120db
SoundBlaster PCI 128	EMU10K1	32-bit	Hardware	Emulation	Yes	128+16	32	-79db
Diamond Monster Sound MX300	Vortex II	16-bit	Hardware	Hardware	Yes	320+64	16	-96db
Turtle Beach Montego A3DXStream	Vortex II	18-bit	Hardware	Hardware	No	32+32	16	-85db

* The table shows the number of wavetable voices implemented in software plus the number stored in hardware.

Sound on a DVD-Video

A DVD video is capable of storing up to eight separate audio streams along with the video data. The audio can be compressed or uncompressed. Each audio stream can contain from one (i.e. mono) up to six (i.e. surround sound) channels. The number of available audio streams will depend upon the number of channels placed in each stream, the audio encoding method used, and the video bit rate required.

The audio encoding methods for adding sound to a DVD video depend upon the television system in use in a particular country (e.g. the UK uses the PAL system while the USA uses the NTSC system) and are:

Disc Type	Required Provision
NTSC	Linear PCM or Dolby AC-3
PAL/SECAM	Linear PCM, MPEG-1, MPEG-2 or Dolby-3

Therefore, a DVD disk designed for the US market must have either LPCM tracks or Dolby AC-3 tracks (see below) but may also provide MPEG tracks. So, it may have LPCM and Dolby, it may have LPCM and MPEG, it may have Dolby and MPEG - or it may carry all three audio tracks.

Although LPCM provides the highest quality sound tracks, it requires a much higher data rate than compressed audio streams and most DVD disks use a compressed encoding method such as AC-3.

A typical DVD disk (DVD-5 type single sided) will hold 133 minutes of MPEG-2 video and three surround sound channels and four subtitle channels. The audio is currently sampled at 20-bit resolution, with a 48kHz sampling rate, although 24-bit, 96kHz sampling will become more common.

The possible options are:

Bit resolution	Sampling rate	Number of channels
16	48kHz	8
20	48kHz	6
24	48kHz	5
16	96kHz	4
20	96kHz	3
24	96kHz	2

Dolby Digital

This system is also known as Dolby Surround Digital or Dolby Surround AC-3 and is to be found in a growing number of applications.   These include multichannel digital cinema sound, HDTV (High Definition TV), satellite broadcasts, digital cable TV and DVD.

It is a 5.1 system using Dolby's **AC-3** (Audio Coding version 3) compression.

AC-3 is a very efficient compression system, resulting in very low bite rate as can be seen in the comparison table below.

System	Bit resolution	Sampling rate	Number of channels	Maximum Bit Rate
AC-3	20	48kHz	6	448kbps
MPEG-1	20	48kHz	2	384kbps
MPEG-2	20	48kHz	8	912kbps
LPCM	20	48kHz	6	5.76Mbps
Audio CD	16	44.1kHz	2	1378kbps

AC-3 encoding provides a six channel stream of audio at 20-bit resolution and yet only requires about one-third of the bit rate of a normal 16-bit stereo channel.   However, the provision of additional language streams will increase the required bit rate, or may require a reduction in the quality of some streams down to only stereo or mono. For example, a disk aimed at the English-speaking market may provide full 5:1 surround sound in English, while only providing Spanish, French and German streams in stereo.

DVD-Audio

Current music CDs can store a maximum amount of 74 minutes of audio. This is due to the use of the Red Book CD standard (uncompressed 44.1kHz, 16-bit encoding). This limitation is being tackled with the introduction of the DVD Forum's new 'DVD-Audio' specification.   The greatly increased storage capacity of DVD disks offers extended playing times, higher audio quality, multiple audio channels and additional features such as optional text and still pictures - along with some limited user interaction such as menu selection.   Audio disks that also contain some video are known as DVD-AudioV disks.

The DVD-Audio Specification provides for a range of encoding methods such as LPCM, AC-3, MPEG-1, MPEG-2, etc and a range of sampling frequencies (44.1, 48, 88.2, 96, 176.4, 192kHz). It also allows the bit resolution to be 16, 20 or 24-bit.   The playing times of DVD-Audio dics will range from 43 minutes (6 channel, 96kHz, 24 bit unpacked on a single layer disk) to 622 minutes (2 channel, 48kHz, 24 bit on a dual layer disk using Meridian Losssless Packing).

Music CDs will be encrypted and watermarked so that they only run on licensed players.

Sony and Philips are producing a rival standard known as the "Super Audio CD".

CAPTURING AUDIO

A wide range of digitised sound samples exists, covering music, sound effects and real world sounds (e.g. dogs barking, gun shots, etc.).   While these are very useful, there are many occasions when a specific sound or message is required.   Examples of this include:

- Voiceovers to accompany video clips, animations or photographs, explaining how something works or how useful an object is.
- Interviews with significant people (e.g. a products technical designer, a company's chairperson or a sports personality).   The content of such an interview is unique to the production and will not exist as an off the shelf clip.
- Specific background music, perhaps specially written to match the multimedia production.
- Sampling of specific sounds that would not be found on royalty-free disks of audio clips. This might include the sound of the company's new product, the crowd noise at a sports event or public demonstration, or an unusual sound effect.

Almost all computers now have sound cards fitted and these are mostly used to output audio, they are all capable of digitising an audio source.   The quality of the sound depends largely on the quality of the sound card, while the added features (e.g. editing facilities, adding echo, etc) depend on the software that is used to capture and manipulate the audio clip.

The steps for making a recording are:

- Connect the audio source to the sound card.
- Configure the computer for recording
- Make tests to adjust the incoming sound levels.
- Make the final recording.

Connecting the audio source

The first step is to check that all the necessary components are present. This will include ensuring that all source devices have a suitable output socket and that all the necessary cables for connecting the sound source to the sound card are available.   Most sound cards use 3.5mm sockets on the rear panel, although some also provide RCS phono sockets or even digital connections.   Most audio sources use RCA phono sockets on their rear panels.

Where to connect

The audio input can come from a microphone connected to the computer's *'Microphone'* socket, or the *'Line In'* socket of sound card can be connected by cable to the output socket of an audio player such as an audio CD player, cassette player, video recorder, etc.   This allows the sampling of music or voice from a variety of sources, although the provisions of copyright will apply to such samples.

Load matching

It is important that the load matching of the audio source and the sound card is correct.   The sound's card's *'Line In'* socket can handle larger voltage input swings than the microphone socket and should be used for all high input sources.   The output from a device is best taken from the *'Aux'* or *'Audio Out'* socket of the device, as this output is designed to be at the same line level as the sound card's *'Line In'* socket.   Do not use the headphones socket of a player as the audio source as this does not properly match the sound card's inputs and will produce disappointing results.   The headphone socket is sometimes used as a last resort, when the player has no other audio output socket.   Much better, however, is using another audio source with a proper audio output socket. Do not connect an audio player's *'Aux'* output to the sound card's microphone input, as it will almost certainly produce distortion.

Connect digitally where possible

It is always best to connect digitally, where at all possible.   For example, an audio track can be copied in digital format from the surface of a CD in to a file on the hard disk (see *'rippers'* later).   The CD is placed in the computer's CD caddy.   The same CD could be placed in an audio CD player and connected to the sound card's line input.   However, this would involve converting the audio track from digital into analogue format, then sending it to the sound card where it would be converted back to digital format. This method introduces all sorts of possible noise and quantisation errors.   Even worse would be to record the track by placing a microphone next to the CD player's loudspeaker.

The SPDIF connector discussed earlier provides an ideal format for audio transfers.   For example, an interview that was carried out on location might be recorded on a DAT recorder that has recorded and digitised the conversation onto digital tape.   The DAT recorder's digital output can be connected directly to the sound card's SPDIF socket, allowing the transfers to be carried on in digital format.

Minimising interference

Always use shielded cables for connection between the audio source and the sound card, to minimise any stray electrical pickup. Keep the mains cables and the audio cables apart.

Cables are available with gold-plated plugs to reduce contact resistance and the better soundcards also use gold-plated sockets.

When an audio source such as a cassette or CD player is used, the player and the computer should share the same mains wall socket. This prevents a ground loop from being set up, which might result in a hum or buzz being added to the recording. If necessary, connect the audio source and computer to the same trailing mains socket and connect this to the wall supply.

Configuring the computer

Before making recordings, the computer should be configured for the best performance. This generally involves optimising the hard disk used for storage and ensuring that the operating system and recording software are working together.

Configure the computer for recording (screen saver, volume control, and sufficient disk space, defrag)

Defragment the hard disk

Ideally, all files on a hard disk should be written to the disk surface as a continual block of data. However, over time, the continual deletion of old files and addition of new files leaves the available surface *'fragmented'*. The free space on the disk is spread over lots of little pockets, rather than being in large blocks. New files, especially large files, end up occupying several non-contiguous areas of the disk. The continual movement of the disk drive head from one area of the surface to another slows the writing of data and can cause loss of data in the file. The data rate of the audio sample is sometimes greater than the constantly diverted drive head can keep up with.

The solution is to regularly defragment the disk. The defragmenter is a piece of utility software that re-orders the allocation of the disk surface, to achieve contiguous space for files. The result of defragmenting is to have each existing file occupying consecutive disk clusters. More importantly, any new audio files written to the disk find themselves being written to a contiguous block of disk space.

If regular audio recordings are planned, it is best to have a hard disk set aside for the task, as it is easier to keep defragmented than a disk that is also used for other purposes.

Windows 95/98 have built-in defragmenters, reached through Start / Programs / Accessories / System Tools / Disk Defragmenter. The user chooses which disk to defragment, and the software gives a report on the current state of fragmentation (as shown opposite) and can show the details of the defragmenting process.

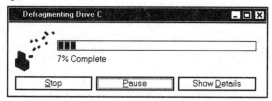

Check for free disk space

As mentioned before, although nowhere near as hungry as video, audio still consumes large amounts of disk space. The table shows the amount of disk space required for storing a single second of digitised, but uncompressed, audio.

	5.5kHz	11.025kHz	22.05kHz	44.1kHz	48kHz
8-bit mono	5.38kB	10.77kB	21.53kB	43.07kB	46.88kB
8-bit stereo	10.77kB	21.53kB	43.07kB	86.13kB	93.75kB
16-bit mono	10.77kB	21.53kB	43.07kB	86.13kB	93.75kB
16-bit stereo	21.53kB	43.07kB	86.13kB	172.27kB	183.11kB

At the top of the range, a five-minute audio clip requires over 53MB of disk space.

Before recording, a check on the available disk space should be made. The free space left on a hard disk can be checked with the following steps:

- Run Windows Explorer.
- Click on *'My Computer'* in the left pane.
- Look at the wanted drive letter in the right pane.
- Read the amount listed under *'Free Space'*.

Software settings

The operating system and the recording software must be set to recognise the recording inputs and to ensure that the recording process is not interrupted.

Turn off the screen saver

The first step is to turn off the screen saver, as this can produce a system interrupt that will cause a momentary break in the recording. The steps to turn off the screen saver are:

- Click on the *'Start'* button on the Windows lower menu bar.
- Choose *'Settings'* from the sub-menu.
- Choose *'Control Panel'* from the *'Settings'* sub-menu.
- Choose *'Display'* from the *'Control Panel'* options.
- Choose *'Screen Saver'* tab.
- Set the value to *'None'*.
- Click the *'OK'* button to return to the main screen.

Enable the input devices

The next step is to ensure that the chosen input device is enabled (i.e. not muted) and this uses Microsoft's *'Volume Control'* panel. With Windows 95, the *'Volume Control'* option is found in the *'Multimedia'* option of the *'Accessories'* menu within the *'Programs'* menu.   In Windows 98, it is found in the *'Entertainment'* option within *'Accessories'*.

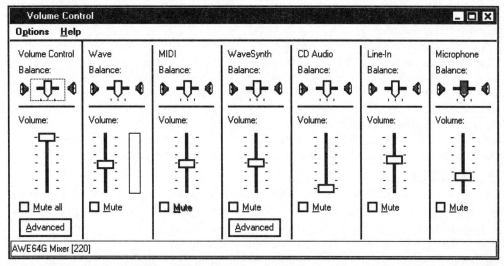

Each device has a *'Mute'* check box.   If the box is checked, the input from that source is not passed through to the sound card's digitising circuitry. All unchecked boxes are treated as valid inputs and any incoming level can be adjusted by moving the slider on the corresponding volume control.

Disable Power management

Finally, it is a wise precaution to disable the computer's Power Management system, to prevent the possibility of the computer shutting down during the recording.   Window's Power Management allows the setting of times before the system closes down after lack of use.
The steps are:

- Click on the *'Start'* button on the Windows lower menu bar.
- Choose *'Settings'* from the sub-menu.
- Choose *'Control Panel'* from the *'Settings'* sub-menu.
- Choose *'Power Management'* from the *'Control Panel'* options.
- Choose *'Power Schemes'* tab, as shown in the diagram.
- Set the values to *'Never'*.
- Click the *'OK'* button to return to the main screen.

The values can easily be returned to their original settings after the recording session.

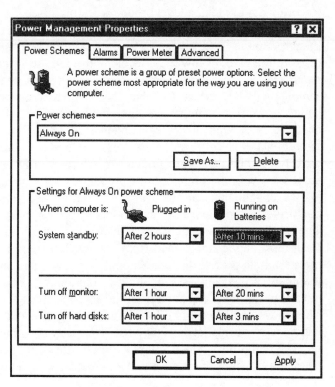

Using Sound Recorder

Many sound cards provide their own software to create audio samples and these recording applications have various advanced features. However, Microsoft's *'Sound Recorder'* is supplied with Windows and, although simple, is adequate for many purposes. With Windows 95, the Sound Recorder is found in the *'Multimedia'* option of the *'Accessories'* menu within the *'Programs'* menu.   In Windows 98, it is found in the *'Entertainment'* option within *'Accessories'*.

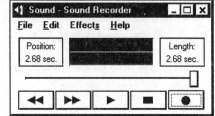

The interface is as shown in the diagram. The right hand button has a red circle and clicking on this icon starts the recording process that creates a digitised sample from the signals received at the currently active inputs.   The time of the sample is shown on screen as the recording is made. The middle window displays a real time oscilloscope representation of the incoming signal.

When the recording is finished, the user clicks on the button to the left of the record button (the button with the square on it).   The final sample length is displayed.   Clicking the middle button causes the newly recorded sample to be replayed.   The recommended sequence is:

- Make tests to adjust the incoming sound levels for optimum recording (see below).
- Make the final recording.
- Replay the clip to check its content and quality.
- Save the clip as digitised audio file, with meaningful file names being used.
- Enter the details of the new clip into a database of the sound files used for the project.

NOTE: There is a default limit of 60 seconds recording time. This can be overcome by creating a large empty file, which can then be used for recording.   First, a 60 second blank recording is made. When the 60 seconds recording is finished, click the record button again to add another 60 seconds to the file.   Repeat this until there is enough time available for the required recording. If required the blank recording can be saved for later re-use.   Drag the bar back to the 0 seconds mark and begin the actual recording.

SETTINGS LEVELS

The aim is to record at the highest possible level without affecting quality.   Two variable controls affect the recording level. The first is the output control of the source and this is normally the source's own manual volume control.   The second control is the input level control of the recording software (e.g. the microphone or line level control in Microsoft's *'Volume Control'*).

Recording at too low a level introduces noise into the sample, as the signal to noise ratio is lowered. Although the editing software can increase the sample's amplitude, it also increases the noise. It is also a mistake to set the output level from the source to a low level and try to compensate with a high recording level at the recording software.

Recording at too high a level produces clipping (see the earlier section on distortion).   If flattening of the higher amplitude signals is seen, this is a sure sign that the system is being overdriven.   The only cure is to lower the drive to the card, or lower the level controls in the software, whichever is the culprit.   Bear in mind, however, that the sample may be perfect and that the problem may be the audio amplifier overdriving the loudspeaker.   If, for

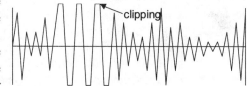

example, a 5 Watt amplifier is connected to 1 Watt speakers, the speakers are overdriven and the distortion is taking place at that spot.   Similarly, cheap loudspeakers systems are easily driven into distortion when their volume control is turned fully up.   If the distortion disappears when the audio amplifier's volume is reduced, the problem is with the hardware.   Alternatively, if the recording software allows examination of the waveform during recording, then the clipping can be confirmed as an overdriven sample or an overdriven loudspeaker system.

The level controls are adjusted while observing the effects on the display on the recording software.

With most applications, apart from *'Sound Recorder'*, the incoming signal is shown by the levels on VU meters that appear on the applications window. The incoming level is adjusted until the bars in the bar graph are at their highest amplitude without entering the red *'overload'* area.   This test should be carried at the loudest level expected from the audio source.   Better software will have a 'Record Pause' facility. This allows the levels to be set without having to actually record a sample. Note, however, that the level meters in some applications may not be entirely accurate and it is best to confirm the settings by listening to a test recording.   Since Sound Recorder does not have VU meters, a recording sample is created while watching for signs of clipping in the oscilloscope window - and adjusting the controls accordingly.

SETTINGS FORMATS

In many recording software applications, the quality of the sample is set before making the recording. With Microsoft's Sound Recorder, the sample is recorded and the sample's attributes are decided just before saving the file.

With Windows 95 and 98 the steps are:
- Make the recording.
- Click on 'File' in the top menu.
- Click on 'Save As' in the drop-down menu.
- If the reported Format is not suitable, click on the 'Change' button and select new properties.
- Enter the name of the file in the 'File name' dialog box.
- Click the 'Save' button.

Windows 95 also allows the properties to be set before making the recording.
- Click on 'Edit' in the top menu.
- Click on 'Audio Properties' in the drop-down menu.
- Click on the 'Customize' button.
- Click the 'OK' button.

There are two ways to select the settings for a recording:
1. Choosing from a named list.
2. Setting each parameter individually.

The named list

The 'Name' drop-down menu allows a choice from a well-known set of attributes (e.g. radio quality or telephone quality). The example shows CD Quality being selected. This displays the attributes for that choice at the top of the 'Attributes' list.

The attributes

Names, such as CD quality and radio quality, only apply to the most well known sets of attributes. There is not a name for every possible combination. Other sets of attributes can be selected from the list and the resulting data rate for each option is displayed. So, for example, CD quality will record at 172kB per sec.

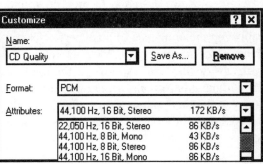

The attributes are made up of three elements:
- Sampling rate
- Dynamic Range
- Number of channels

The expected quality and storage overhead for each choice was discussed earlier in this chapter.

The Format

The 'Format' describes the way that the file is stored - either in uncompressed format or compressed by a CODEC.

The drop-down list of options includes all the CODECs that are installed on the computer and will vary between users. All computers with Windows will have the standard set, such as plain PCM, ADPCM and so on. In the example, the computer has additional CODECs installed and this allows the capture of sounds directly into MP3 format.

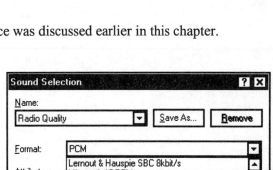

The desired CODEC is selected from the list.

Best practice

It is best to record a sample at a reasonable quality, even where that level of quality might not be the expected final quality. The audio editing software can convert a sample to lower sample rates and lower bit resolution, if the file is to be shrunk later. Although, the software can also increase the clip's sample rate and bit resolution, this produces no extra quality, although the file size has been considerably increased. It is not possible to add improved quality into a sample and so the sample should be saved at the best quality that can be achieved, with decisions on its final quality/size being taken later.

Microphones

All recordings of real world sounds, such as interviews, birds sounds, traffic noise, etc are captured using a microphone, also known as a *'mike'*. A microphone is a pressure transducer. That means that it aids the conversion of air pressure changes into changes in voltage. A variety of types are available and they have different uses.

There are two basic microphone transducer methods:

- Those that generate their own electrical signal, such as moving-coil, ribbon or crystal microphones. These are known as dynamic microphones.
- Those that vary an existing voltage signal, such as capacitor and carbon microphones.

They are available in the following formats:

HAND MIKES

These are the most common types and are designed to be held by the user. They can also be mounted on a mike stand or on a boom.

TIE CLIP MIKES

Also known as *'Lavalier'* mikes, these attach to someone's tie, lapel or other part of clothing. They are used by commentators for live filming, and for attachment to musical instruments.

RADIO MIKES

Radio mikes attach a mike to a transmitter and the modulated radio signal is picked up by a matching receiver and the demodulated audio is fed to the audio equipment (e.g. audio mixers, a camcorder's mike socket or a sound card's line input). They are widely used in TV studios and live concerts. The mike used can be a hand mike, a tie clip or a headset.

MICROPHONE CHARACTERISTICS

Microphones are designed to pick up sound in different ways. Some are best for up close recording while others are best for distance recording. Some are best for quiet interviews while others are best for capturing the ambience of a concert. The way mikes respond to the sounds around them is described as their *'polar diagram'*. Polar diagrams - also known as *'polar patterns'*, *'polar plots'* or *'directional patterns'* display the response of the microphone to audio signals coming from the front (*'on axis'*) and the comparable response from other directions (*'off axis'*).

A polar diagram shows a line that joins all points around the microphone that will produce the same microphone output from a given audio source.

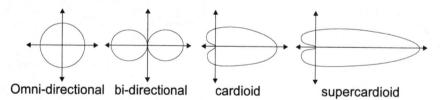

Omni-directional   bi-directional   cardioid   supercardioid

Omni-directional

The output from the microphone is equal from sound all round the microphone. Any sound of a particular amplitude will produce the same mike output when picked up from any point at the same distance from the mike. So, for instance, if a dog runs round the microphone barking, it will produce the same output whether it is in front of the mike, behind the mike, to the side of the mike, etc.

Bi-directional

The bi-directional microphone is constructed so that its corrugated ribbon diaphragm responds equally to air pressure changes from the front and from the rear.

Unidirectional

While some occasions require the benefits of omni-directional pickup (e.g. recording the crowd at a football match), the user will often require a more selective pickup. This requires a greater pickup at the front of the microphone compared to sounds at the sides or rear. The mike picks up sounds mostly from the direction in which it is pointed. The three varieties are:

Cardioid	This has the basic cardioid (i.e. heart-shaped) directional characteristic as shown.
Supercardioid,	Also known as *'shotgun'* mikes, these have a narrower pickup response area (i.e. more directional). They are usually bought to replace the camcorder's integral mike.
Hypercardioid	These have an even narrower pickup response area and are used in specialised areas.

MICROPHONE TYPES

In each case, the changes in air pressure vibrate a thin plate called the *'diaphragm'*. The diaphragm in turns varies either an inductive or capacitive value in the mike's circuitry and this varying value changes in sympathy with the audio being picked up. The varying signal is fed to the amplifier or the microphone input socket of the sound card.

CONDENSER

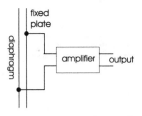

All electronic circuits use condensers (known in the UK as *'capacitors'*).
These components can be found in radios, televisions, computers, hi-fis, etc.
A condenser is made up of two metal plates that are separated by air or some insulating material. They are capable of storing an electrical charge. The capacitance (i.e. amount they can store) is determined by the size of the plates, the nature of the dialectric (i.e. the material between the plates) and the thickness of the dialectric. The condenser microphone uses a moveable diaphragm as one of the two plates. Changes in sound pressure move the diaphragm closer and further away from the fixed plate. As the capacitance alters, the voltage stored alters and this change is in proportion to the audio being picked up.

Professional versions use an electrostatically charged plate that is is powered by a separate 48 volt power supply or a voltage feed from a mixing desk or from a pro-level camera. A more down-market version uses a permanently charged plate powered by its own internal 1.5 volt battery. This is called an *'electret'* microphone and is the most common type used with camcorders. Capacitor mikes are usually unidirectional or omni-directional and are popular with professional users, due to their flat frequency response and tolerance of varying operating conditions.

MOVING COIL

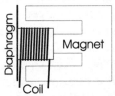

The moving coil mike works like a loudspeaker in reverse. In a loudspeaker voltage changes are applied to a coil that moves and vibrates the surrounding air. With a moving coil mike, the air fluctuations move the coil and induce a voltage change. As the diagram shows, a diaphragm is attached to a coil of wire. As the diaphragm fluctuates, it pushes and pulls the coil within a magnetic field provided by a permanent magnet. The moving coil has a voltage induced into it. The faster the movement of the coil, the greater the voltage. Hence, the mike's voltage output is proportional to the amplitude of the audio signal. The faster the coil vibrates the quicker the voltage changes and thus the frequency of the audio is detected. This construction is commonly used for omni-directional mikes. These are commonly found used on stage and are used by announcers and vocalists.

RIBBON

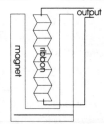

The bi-directional microphone is constructed so that its corrugated ribbon diaphragm responds to air pressure changes from the front and from the rear. The ribbon sits in a magnetic field and the ribbon's movement through the field induces a voltage across it in sympathy with the changes in air pressure.
It works on the *'pressure gradient'* principle. There is a pressure difference between the front and the rear of the ribbon. Loud sounds from the front push the ribbon towards the rear, while loud rear sounds push the ribbon towards the front. The mike responds equally to sounds from its front or rear. Since sounds at the sides of the ribbon do not create differences in air pressure between the front and rear, the mike does not detect these sounds. This gives the ribbon mike it characteristic polar diagram, often referred to as a *'figure of eight'*. This means that there is a phase difference between sounds from the front and sounds from the rear.

Others

Other types, such as crystal mikes and carbon mikes are no longer found in audio recording work.
The carbon microphone was widely used for telephone handsets and was a low quality device. The vibrating diaphragm altered the pressure on a cup of carbon granules. Increasing air pressure compressed the granules together and lowered the resistance of the microphone. This altering resistance was used to alter the current through the device. The crystal microphone works on the *'piezoelectric'* effect. The microphone contains a slice of crystal. Altering air pressure slightly bends the crystal and this causes an electric charge to be developed across the faces of the crystal. This altering charge is then amplified.

IMPEDANCE

Microphones are categorised into two impedance bands:

- Low impedance, typically between 600 ohms and 10,000 ohms.
- High impedance, typically 50,000 ohms and over. These are not normally used with sound cards.

Some degree of mismatch is acceptable and a device with a low input impedance usually accepts any low impedance mike. However, large variations from the manual's stated input impedance causes loss of power transfer and lowers the level of the incoming signal (resulting in a poor signal-to-noise ratio).

Summary of microphone types and their characteristics

Mike Type	Polar Diagram	Quality	Likely Use	Comments
Crystal	Omni-directional	Low	Speech, background sounds, sound effects	Fallen out of use.
Moving Coil	Omni-directional and Cardiod	Good	Speech, Vocals Music (drums, bass)	Can be used outdoors.
Ribbon	Figure of Eight	High	Speech Music (woodwind, strings)	For indoor use.
Condenser	Omni-directional and Cardioid	High	Speech Music (piano, brass)	Can be used outdoors (use with wind gag)

USE OF MIKES

Although most microphones can be used for all purposes at a pinch, the results will not be adequate for professional use. The characteristics of different microphones result in their use for specific purposes.

Omni-directional

These are often used as a general purpose hand mike, as the speaker does not need to be on-axis at all times. It is still common, and annoying, to see TV interviewers conducting street interviews with unidirectional mikes. They ask a question into the mike and are too slow in pointing the mike towards the interviewee. The result is that only parts of the conversation are intelligible. This problem is avoided with an omni-directional mike.

Another popular use is to record the proceedings at a meeting. The mike is placed on the table and is able to pick up each participant equally.

It is not for situations where public address systems are in use, as it will pick up the sound from the P.A. loudspeakers and create howl round feedback.

Bi-directional

While the cardioid mike reduces off-axis sounds, it also eliminates the echoes and reverberations that provide the characteristics of a recording (e.g. from a church or a sports stadium). The figure of eight pattern of a bi-directional mike provide the compromise, allowing both the presenter and the background ambience to be picked up.

Cardioid

This is the type fitted in most camcorders. Its selective pickup pattern makes it ideal for picking out one sound from a noisy environment. For example, it can be is used in an auditorium or other large gathering to record one speaker in an audience. While one member of the audience is being recorded, the coughs, sneezes and other unwanted sounds are minimised.

Hypercardiod mikes are often used when it is difficult to get close to the audio source. They are also useful in locations that produce lots of echo, as they will not pick up most of the reflected sounds.

Similarly, they are helpful in a commentating situation where there is lots of unwanted noise.

The more directional the mike, the more difficult it is to control the recording. So, for example, it is difficult to record an audio source that moves, since the source might easily move out of the angle over which the mike receives. Also, the more directional the mike the harder it is to maintain stereo.

POPPING

A mike is often held close to the presenter's mouth to help minimise background noises. During some sessions, the speaker's voice will project a quick puff of moist air into the mike aperture. Words with the letter 'p' or 'b', such as 'Pepper' or 'Bobby' are the worst offenders. This causes a 'popping' noise to be introduced to the recording. Ribbon mikes are the most affected by this problem. The effect is minimised by:

- Speaking further away from the mike
- Fitting a windshield or 'pop shield' to the mike.

WIND NOISE

When strong winds are present during an outdoor recording session, it is picked up by the mike as a roaring noise. This noise can be reduced at the post production stage. The computer's audio software can apply a low pass filter to the audio file. This reduces the roaring sound but it also removes some of the wanted signal. Prevention is better than cure and the best approach is to minimise the effect of wind on the mike. This is achieved by using a windshield, or wind gag. This is a *'furry sock'* that covers the microphone. The material is *'acoustically transparent'* and therefore does not impede the capture of audio. However, the fur reduces the air velocity around the mike. The cheaper sponge wind gags are only partially effective. In an emergency, any piece of sponge, or a woolly sock, is better then nothing.

SIBILANCE

Sibilance is the word used to describe the distortion that affects certain letters such as *'s'* and *'c'*. For example, the word *'yes'* is recorded as *'yesh'* or *'yessss'*. There are three solutions to the problem:

- Talk over the microphone rather than directly into it.
- Use a hardware de-esser processor (only an option for a studio)
- Use a software plug-in that can process the audio file.

MICROPHONE TECHNIQUES

Positioning mikes

A little thought and a little preparation can make a big difference to the quality of the final recording.

Position the mike as close to the source as is practical, as this minimises the pickup of unwanted surrounding noises. It does tend, however, to also accentuate the bass component of the sound (known as the *'proximity effect'*).

If the session is being taped with a camcorder, do not use the camcorder's internal mike. These are generally unsuitable for all but the closest of work. More often, they are too far back from source and even a cardioid mike will pick up sounds from the sides in these circumstances. Camcorder mikes are also notorious for picking up the sound of their own motors. In almost every situation, it is preferable to use an external mike and most camcorders have sockets for external connection. When taping a conversation or interview, the microphone should be located as close to the subjects as possible, without the mike being seen by the camera. This is usually achieved by:

- Using a boom mike. A mike is held on a long pole that is mounted on a stand. The boom is adjusted so that it is close to the subjects but is above their heads and out of camera view.
- Using a hidden mike. A mike hidden within a bunch of flowers, behind an object on the table, etc, so that it is close to the subjects without being obtrusive.

In general, it is preferable to use the mike on a stand, to avoid handling noise. For voiceovers, this prevents handling noise and leaves the speaker free to turn pages of notes.

For recording a meeting or a discussion panel, it is best to use multiple mikes where possible. This provides better results and more control than a single omni-directional mike.

Lastly, the public is generally scared of using a mike. They tend to either shy away from it, or shout into it from a very short distance. It pays to spend a few moments training someone in the handling of mikes. It is also useful to make a few test recordings to ensure that they are being used properly.

Room acoustics

Where recordings are made within a building, there is more control over the recording process. Often, there is time to prepare the location where the recording will take place. This includes mike placement and the spotting of any possible recording interruptions (e.g. does a train pass the window every two minutes, is the air conditioning noisy, has the switchboard been told to bar any incoming call, etc).

The biggest room problem is usually unwanted echoes from large unfurnished areas, such as large tiled areas and large window spaces. If possible, hang blankets or heavy curtains around the problem areas and cover large smooth tabletops with a cloth.

Monitoring the recording

Listen while recording, to prevent unwanted sounds slipping through undetected. Camcorders often have a headphone socket. If possible, a second person should listen to the recording, allowing the camera operator to concentrate on the filming. Bear in mind that camcorders also have automatic gain control - they adjust their amplifiers to match the incoming audio volume. A sudden unwanted local noise could result in the amplifier reducing its gain and the wanted signal being lost for a while.

SOUND MIXING

With sound mixing, two or more audio sources are combined in proportions that produce the desired balanced output. The sources can be speech, music, and sound effects and can be obtained via microphones, CDs, cassette tape, or pre-digitised computer files in WAV or other format. The amplitude of each input signal can be independently adjusted.

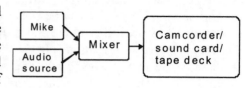

There are three types of mixing:

Live mixing

The live audio from the microphone is mixed in at recording time. The other audio sources can be live (e.g. a second mike) or pre-recorded (e.g. from a tape). This is most useful for situations where the background sound is a one-off; for example, an interview with a promoter while the band plays live in the background. This involves some careful setting of the levels before making the recording and can be tricky and prone to errors.

Studio mixing

Where resources allow, it is much better to record a separate audio track for each audio component and mix them later. Mixing desks provide electronic filters and tone controls to adjust, correct and augment individual signals. They also allow additional processing such as fade, panning, echo, etc. Unlike live mixing, all the sources are individually accessible at any time. So, for example, an adjustment or effect can be can be applied to a single component, leaving the others untouched. As a minimum, the foreground sound, the background ambience (such as crowd noise and sound effects) and background music should be stored separately. For music recordings, there may be many separate channels for different instruments, backing vocals, lead singer and so on.

The tracks are still being mixed in analogue format, although this is being replaced by digital processing.

Computer mixing

For those with more limited resources, similar facilities are provided by most respectable audio editing software packages. The audio components are copied from the storage device, such as tape deck or camcorder audio output, and are digitised into sound clips. These sound clips are then processed and mixed in digital format. For professional results, it pays to invest in a good multitrack sound editor. This provides separate tracks for speech, effects, music, etc and the software can cross-fade between the tracks. CoolEdit Pro is an example of a standalone audio editor that supports 64 tracks. Of course, multitrack facilities are already available in video editing software such as Adobe Premiere and Media Studio Pro.

EDITING AUDIO

A user-created sound sample is rarely immediately usable. It may contain unwanted pauses or noises, or require augmenting by special effects before it is used.

Editing software packages provide a variety of facilities and these may involve different steps in different packages. For example, one package may require the user to understand how to use of a set of tools to eliminate hiss, while another may have automated the process by having a *'Hiss Removal'* feature. Dart Pro, for example, has range of features such as *'DeClick'*, *'DeNoise'* and *'DeHiss'*.

Sample Re-ordering

These tools do not alter the quality of the audio sample. They are used to change the length and order of parts of the sample.

Cropping

Also known as *'Top and Tail'*, this removes periods of silence from the start and end of the wanted sound.

Cut/paste

A section can be cut from one point in the clip and placed in another point in the same clip - or in another clip. For example, a gunshot can be extracted and placed in a more appropriate point. It can also be used to delete unwanted sections, such as someone's coughing fit during interview. It can also be used to delete a pop or click that occurs during a period of silence.

Copying

Used to extract a sample from one part of the clip and insert it in another part as a duplicate sound. For example, the sound of a taxi horn could be repeated in various parts of a clip.

Looping

Used to repeat a section of the sound several times in succession. Commonly used to create music loops and to make a background atmosphere clip last longer.

Sample restoration

These facilities attempt to bring the quality of the sample back as close to the original sound as possible. This involves removing any blemishes that may have occurred during recording or digitising.

DC Offset

The signal should vary above and below a value of zero, where zero represents no output voltage and hence no audible signal. Zero represents silence and if the quiescent value of an audio clip sits above or below the zero line, then the signal is said to contain a *'DC Offset'*. This is often caused by equipment that is not properly earthed. It may introduce noise into the output and the DC Offset (or DC Bias) control exists to adjusts the signal so that it varies around the zero value.

Noise gate

The noise gate is used to remove background hiss from the quiet sections of a clip. The signal has to exceed the value set as the threshold before it is included in the output signal. This eliminates the smaller value signals from the clip. The usual controls are:

Threshold

Sets the amplitude level at which the gate opens and allows the sound to pass through. This value can be gradually increased until the hiss is removed from quiet sections of the clip. Increasing the threshold to too high a level results in parts of the wanted signal being lost. This is the reason that the noise gate cannot be used to remove background hiss from louder sections of the clip (see Noise Elimination below).

Decay time

Sets the time, in milliseconds, before the noise gate fully closes and prevents any sound from passing through. A very small value results in a sudden cut-off of the signal and the value should be set so that the signal quietens more naturally.

Noise Elimination

This is useful for eliminating broadband noise (noise that covers a wide frequency spectrum) as conventional filters cannot remove this noise without lowering the amplitude of the wanted signal. It is also useful for eliminating hiss where the noise gate cannot operate (see above). The technique is to highlight a section of noise, usually in a section where the main audio is silent or quiet. The application uses it as the sample for eliminating this noise throughout the file. A new profile should be sampled for each file, as the noise composition in a file is different for each clip.

CoolEdit also allows a sample of the inherent noise in the system to be tested before a recording is made. This noise profile is then applied to recorded signal in real time and carries out noise elimination before it is saved.

Interpolate

This facility uses linear interpolation to smooth out the content of a part of a clip marked by the user. So, for example, if the selected section had a starting value of 18 and a finishing value of 30, interpolation would replace all existing values within the marked area by values that rose from 18 up to 30. This is very useful when used on a small area that contains a pop or click, as their sudden amplitude increases are removed. It cannot be applied over a large area, as too much of the original signal would also be removed. The area to be marked should be selected after using zoom to view the section at close quarters.

Silence

This reduces the level of the marked section of the clip down to zero. This is a simple way to eliminate clicks, pops and hiss during quiet periods in the clip.

Low Pass

High frequencies are described as *'treble'* and low frequencies are described as *'bass'*. Many pieces of domestic hi-fi equipment are fitted with treble and bass controls. The application's high and low pass filters are the equivalent of these controls.

The low pass filter allows low frequencies (bass) to pass filters but progressively attenuate high frequencies (treble) above the assigned cut-off frequency. They are used to reduce high-end hiss noise or other unwanted high frequency sounds. Setting the cut-off frequency too low removes too much of the wanted signal, leaving the remaining signal sounding too deep and muffled.

High Pass

High pass filters progressively attenuate low frequencies below the assigned cut-off frequency, while allowing high frequencies to pass. They are used to remove deep rumbling noises (such as some motor noise and wind roar) or other unwanted low frequency sounds. Setting the cut-off frequency too high removes too much of the wanted signal, leaving the remaining signal sounding tinny and hollow.

Bandpass

A bandpass filter blocks all frequencies outside the specified range, and only allows frequencies within the specified range to pass. This can be used to pick out a particular sound from a clip, where the main content of the sound lies within an identifiable range.

Bandstop

A bandstop filter has the opposite effect to a bandpass filter. It blocks all frequencies within the specified range, and only allows frequencies outwith the specified range to pass. This can be used to suppress narrow band noise, such as a hum, within a clip.

Parametric EQ

Equalisation boosts or cuts the amplitude of certain frequency ranges within a signal. It was first introduced to compensate for losses in analogue signals that were sent long distances over a line. The aim was to restore all the frequency elements back to their original levels (hence the name *'equalisation'*). It now appears in hi- systems as *'graphic equalisers'* consisting of a panel of sliders used to adjust for room acoustics or for personal taste (e.g. turning up the bass).

Equalisation is now available with most computer audio software players (e.g. Winamp), where it acts on digital signals. It is now more often used to accentuate a particular frequency range, so that a particular feature of the audio clip (such as the speaker's voice or a particular musical instrument) is brought to the fore.

With standard equalisation, there is a set of filters, each covering a fixed band of the frequency spectrum. Since hearing is logarithmic, the bands' allocations are not linear but are spaced in octaves. The gain of each filter can be adjusted to boost or attenuate the amplitude of that band.

With parametric equalisation, the user can not only set the amplitude of each band, but also has control over the centre frequency of each band and the bandwidth of each band.

It is generally preferable to lower the gain in the unwanted bands, rather than boosting the wanted bands, to avoid boosting unwanted noise. So, for example, to improve the voice part of a clip, the frequencies that lie outside the main voice band (i.e. under 300Hz and above 3kHz) should be attenuated. It is very useful to correct the loss of treble that is common with streamed audio clips.

Normalise

This facility is used to improve the clip's quality by increasing its dynamic range. This is used where a signal has been recorded at a low level, such that its peaks never reach the maximum swing allowed by the dynamic range of the system (usually the sound card). The entire clip (or the section that is selected from a clip) is examined and the highest peaks of the signal are found. The clip's volume is then increased to the maximum percent possible without producing distortion through clipping. This is a useful tool for bringing up the level of all clips in a project to the same level, ironing out any differences in recording levels of clips. It is often the last process to be applied to a clip.

Changing amplitude levels

Normalising maintains the ratio between different sound components.

However, there are occasions when individual sections of the clip will require having their amplitude increased (e.g. where one person on a discussion is quieter than the rest). The section of the clip can be highlighted and have its volume increased relative to the rest of the clip's contents.

Compressing

Compression reduces the difference between the highest and lowest amplitudes in a signal. It should not be confused with file compression such as MP3s, which is covered later. The effect of compression is to raise the level of all sounds within the clip. This is useful where some of the components of the sound were recorded at too low a level. For example, it can bring up the voice of a member of an audience at a meeting. It is also used to even out a commentator's voice, where the amplitude has varied during the recording. Over-compressing will make the clip sound flat.

Sample augmentation

These alter the content of the original sound, known as *'sweetening'*.

Fade in

This facility gradually increases the volume of the highlighted section of the clip, from a prescribed percentage starting value (i.e. 0% fades up from complete silence, while 50% fades up from half volume).

Fade out

This facility gradually decreases the volume of the highlighted section of the clip, to a prescribed percentage value (i.e. 100% fades to silence, while 50% fades to half volume).

Cross-fade

A simple butting together of two audio clips usually causes a click at the point where they joint, unless clip 1 ends with a silence and clip 2 begins with a silence. On any other occasion, the content of both clips are at different voltage levels at the point of butting and the sudden change of voltage causes a clicking sound.

clip 1	clip2	butt edit

clip 1	clip2	cross-fade

When butting two audio files together, it is possible to fade out clip 1 and then fade in clip 2. However, this introduces a quiet section in the middle.

The cross-fade fades out clip 1 while simultaneously fading in clip 2. Initially clip 1 is at full volume and clip 2 is zero volume.   By the end of the cross-fade, clip 2 is at full volume with clip 1 at zero - with a seamless join.

Envelope shaping.

You are presented with Shape Controls. With these controls, you can define the amplitude envelope of a sound. The shape line is initially horizontal at 100. By bending/moving the line, you can dynamically change the volume of the selection.

Combining

This facility allows the addition of extra content to that already present in the clip.

Adding in extra audio

It is common to add to the original sound, to augment the effect. Often, an interview will take place in the absence of the sounds that normally provide the correct ambience for that setting. This is corrected by adding the extra material later. This may be music, background environment sounds (e.g. car traffic or pub sounds) or sounds off (e.g. gunshots or doors creaking open).   These are secondary sounds to the foreground content and must partially fade (known as *'dipping'*) during foreground speech. This prevents a sudden drop during speech. A likely setting is to fade for about half a second, then overlap the speech content by about quarter of a second.

Adding in effects

These may be of more use in a musical clip than spoken audio. A common effect is *'flanging'*, which mixes the original sound with delayed sound and feedback for a distinctive new sound.

Echo

This facility produces an echo to the source, to provide the effect of large acoustic spaces. So, for example, the effect of a sound being played in a football stadium or a church can be imposed on any audio being reproduced. The sound should always be initially recorded without any echo; the echo can always be added later whereas the echo cannot be removed from a clip pre-recorded with an echo. As the amount of echo is increased, the source appears to fade more into the background, so the effect should not be over-applied.

Strictly speaking, echo is a single repetition. In other words, if the speaker says *'Hello'* the word is repeated slightly later for a single time.   With reverberation, the word is repeated a number of times, getting fainter with each repetition.

The basic settings for echo are:

- Delay — - The time taken for the echo to bounce back. Long delays suggest larger locations.
- Volume — - The volume of the echoed content. Use low levels, unless the effect of standing in a large cavern is required.
- Reverb — - Whether a single or repeating echo is to be used.

Other controls are provided by some applications including reflection, diffusion, decay and pre-delay.   The provided preset values are a good way to get into using reverberation, until the controls are mastered.

Echo/Reverb is a very useful tool to brighten vocals but should not be overdone or applied to all clips.

Panning

This facility controls the balance between the volumes in the left and right channels of a stereo sample.

With panning, the volume of the sound in the left channel is decreased while the volume in the right channel is increased. Panning allows a mono signal to be positioned, or moved, anywhere within the stereo plane.

In multitracks, panning is used to position sounds in the stereo plane of the final file. With interviews, it may require placing the interviewer's sound to the left channel while the interviewee's sound is directed to the right channel.   With music tracks, it may be used to position the vocals in the middle and position the instruments (e.g. bass guitar to the left, lead guitar to the right).

Panning is more of a problem with stereo samples.

When the source has been recorded in mid-position between the stereo mikes, the Balance control is used to between channels with stereo. However, if the sound source was positioned closer to one mike than the other during recording, then changing the balance does not provide a panning effect; it simply reduces the overall volume of the source. For example, if the source is closer to the left mike, there is little signal recorded on the right channel.   So, fading the left channel reduces the audio output while increasing the right channel does not produce any appreciable increase in output.

If a panning effect is anticipated, then the source should be recorded in mono, or with the source in the middle of stereo mikes.

Transpose

This facility changes the musical pitch of the highlighted sound by resampling it at a different sampling rate. This is often used to convert a note recorded from a musical instrument into a set of samples covering the musical scales.

Reverse

Reverses the order of the data in the clip, so that it will play backwards.   The facility is of little practical use, apart from a few novelty effects.

Resample/Time stretching

This facility alters the sampling rate of the entire clip, so that it plays at a different speed without altering the pitch of the final sound. It re-calculates and interpolates all the clip's digital values, so that the pitch remains unchanged within the new time slot.   This is only effective with minor time alterations, as any large changes affect the quality of the final output.

Resampling is also useful for converting files down for use on the web. It makes file sizes considerably smaller and therefore speeds up the transfer of the files over the Internet.

Playback rate

This facility alters the rate at which the clip is played.   The sound will play faster (or slower) and its pitch will be higher (or lower).

Editing Software

Many competent applications packages are dedicated to the editing and processing of audio samples. These include Sound Forge, Goldwave, SoundEdit and CoolEdit.   The manufacturers of sound cards often bundle commercial editing packages with their products, or supply their own editing software.

The *'Sound Recorder'* utility provided with Windows provides some basic tools such as Top and Tail, echo, sample reversal and basic mixing. Sound Recorder is limited but is a useful starting point.

A useful additional facility is the ability to batch process - e.g. converting all sound clips to mono, resampling all files to the same sampling rate, etc.

File Compression/Conversion

The advantages and growing popularity of saving and distributing audio files in MP3 format were discussed earlier in this chapter.   New versions of software have support for MP3 included.   This includes authoring packages, CD-burners (such as CD Creator 4) and Windows itself (from 98 onwards). However, all older software requires add-on software to enable MP3 to be handled.   In addition, MP3 is not always the automatic choice of format.   This means that there is a need to convert audio files between formats. The following notes cover file conversion - and the conversion from CD audio into computer audio files.

MP3 Encoders

There are two basic operations that a user may wish to perform:

- Encoding from a WAV file to an MP3 file.
- Ripping tracks from an audio CD.

Ripping

Ripping is the term used for extracting the audio content from a CD track and saving it as a computer audio file, such as a WAV file. It is useful for converting samples from royalty-free CDs, which contain background music or sound effects, into compressed clips.   Although it is also widely used for reading off commercial audio CDs, this practice is illegal without permission.   There is some argument about whether anyone would be prosecuted for creating compilations from their own legally purchased music CDs, but these remain prohibited under the law.

Ripping requires the appropriate hardware and software.

Many older CD-ROM drives are unable to read from audio CDs, as the drive has to support the reading of RAW data.   In some cases, older CD-ROMs were capable of reading RAW data but the supplied drivers were incapable of providing the *'Read_Long'* service.   Most ripper software will report on the suitability of the CD-ROM installed on the computer. As a last resort, the audio source can be fed into the sound card and converted into a WAV file by Sound Recorder. This is not satisfactory, as distortions are introduced by the extra digital/analogue and analogue/digital conversions carried out by the CD player and the sound card..

Rippers maintain the sample in digital format and at the same quality as the original (assuming no downsampling). Many utilities are available that rip and encode in a single operation.   The track is copied straight from the CD and saved directly as an MP3 file, without first being converted to a WAV file.   Examples of combined rippers/encoders are Xing's AudioCatalyst, CDEX, MusicMatch Jukebox, and RealJukebox Plus.   Examples of simple rippers (i.e. audio to WAV only) are CDDA for use in MSDOS and plugins for Winamp.   Other rippers can be found on www.mp3.com

The diagram on the next page shows the screen layout of the CDEX freeware ripper/encoder.

When the audio CD is placed in the CD-ROM drive, the information on each track is displayed in the main panel.   This includes information on file size and playing time.   The user selects the files to be ripped by high-lighting them.   In the example, tracks four to seven have been chosen for processing, but all tracks on the CD can be highlighted if desired.

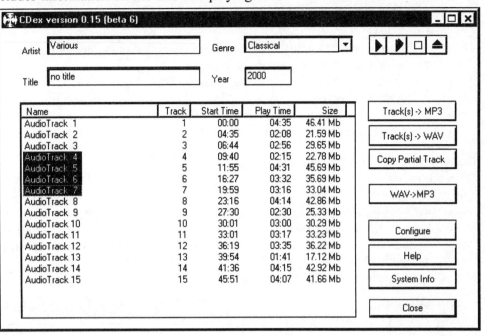

The buttons on the right side offers the option of ripping to WAV format or ripping directly to MP3 format.   The *'Configure'* button provides control over the encoding options.

Encoding

MP3 encoding can be built in to a ripper, as mentioned above, or can be provided by a dedicated piece of encoder software.   An example of a standalone encoder is the freeware BladeEnc encoder.   In either case, control over the encoding settings is provided.   The main decisions are:

Bit Rate Selection

Selection of bit rate.   This is normally set to 128kbps, although it can be lowered (to say 16kbps for Internet files) or raised (to say 320kbps for high-quality file archives).   BladeEnc supports up to 256kbps, while MusicMatch Jukebox and AudioCatalyst support up to 320kbps.

CBR/VBR Selection

By default, all encoding is carried out at CBR (constant bit rate).   If the usual bit rate of 128kbps is used, then 128kbits is used to encode a second of audio, 12.8kbits for a tenth of a second and 1.28kbits for a hundredth of a second, and so on.   The same amount of bits is allocated to encode a period of silence as is allocated to encode another equal period of time when there may be a great amount of audio detail in the recording.   An orchestra playing a dramatic background to a piece of dialogue, with included sound effects is a very complex piece of audio and requires more bits to encode it.   Since CBR runs at a constant rate, bits are wasted during quiet times and are in short supply during complex passages.   The result is a loss of quality during the complex passages and a consequent variation of quality throughout the clip.   The only solution is to use a bit rate that is high enough to cope with the most detailed audio passage. This would greatly enlarge the size of the audio file, to cope with a small proportion of the clip time.   This is only currently a viable option for broadcast systems.

VBR (variable bit rate) encoding tackles the problem by allocating the same average bit rate dynamically.   This means that a VBR setting of 128kbps would pass an average of 128kbits of data per second, and would allocate the bits as required - allocating less bits for quiet passages and more bits for complex passages. The overall effect is to provide a fixed quality throughout the sample.

MusicMatch Jukebox and AudioCatalyst, for example, both allow the selection of VBR.

Speed vs Quality

The encoding *'algorithm'* is the program's method of achieving the compression.   When many files are being processed in batch mode, the speed of encoding is an important factor.   But, even more important at the professional end of the market, is the quality of the completed file.   The record for the fastest encoding speed is currently held by AudioCatalyst.   However, AudioCatalyst is faster because it uses the *'Xing'* algorithm and this ignores all audio above 16kHz.   Most applications, such as MusicMatch Jukebox and MP3 Producer, use the *'Fraunhofer'* algorithm.   This is slightly slower because it processes up to 20kHz.   The trade between audio quality and encoding speed is a matter of preference. If the files are destined for web sites, they may already have had their sampling rate and dynamic range reduced to reduce file size and any small reduction in quality may be of no significance. If the files are destined for professional use, or for playing over high quality amplifiers, then the quality of the encoding algorithm is more important than final file size.

Other facilities
The extra facilities offered by different packages vary and may include options to:
- Play each track while compressing in real time.
- Convert between audio file formats, particularly WAV, MP3, WMA.
- Add lyrics to song files.
- Fetch song titles from the on-line database of CDs and their track details (CDDB at www.cddb.com).
- Encode audio direct from the computer's soundcard (e.g. as with AudioCatalyst).

Converting MP3s to WAVs
With the growth in the number of files that are now available in MP3 format, there is also a need to be able to convert them into other formats. Likely reasons for the conversion are:
- To integrate into multimedia packages that do not support MP3 files.
- To write to CD-R as CD audio tracks that can be read on any domestic or car CD player. Most CD writing software uses WAV files as the source for creating audio CDs, although CD Creator 4 can convert MP3 files directly into CD audio tracks for burning.

Most modern applications now provide facilities to convert between formats.

Using Winamp
The freeware Winamp MP3 player package can also be used to convert MP3 files into WAV files. The exact steps vary with the Winamp version, but the general steps are:
- Open Winamp's Playlist Editor.
- Load in the MP3 files to be converted.
- Select the *'Options'* from the main menu.
- Select the *'Preferences'* option and click on its *'Output'* tab, as shown..
- Set the *'Output Device'* to WAV (sometimes marked as *'Nullsoft Disk Writer'*).
- Select a destination folder for the new files.
- Click *'OK'* to return to the main screen.
- Click on the play control to convert the files.

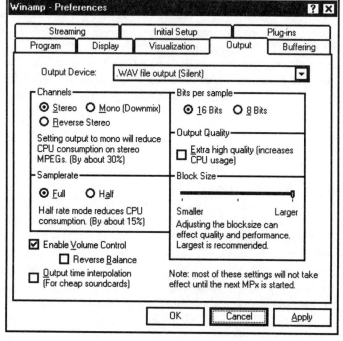

Other Conversions
Sound Recorder is capable of carrying out a range of file conversions. After a file is loaded, choose the *'Properties'* option from the *'File'* menu. Choose *'Recording Formats'* from the *'Format Conversion'* dialogue box. Click *'Convert Now'* and choose the new format from the drop-down list. Click *'OK'*, play the converted sound and save it if is satisfactory.

MUSIC
There are two distinct categories of music reproduction with the PC:
- Replaying pre-recorded music to liven up a presentation, impart information, or for personal pleasure.
- The creation of musical pieces.

The first category requires no knowledge of music theory as the *'artistic'* work has already been done. The user only requires to connect the correct equipment and to install and use the correct software. The creation of new musical pieces is not considered here.

A basic musical piece will, in general, contain a table of musical notes, played in sequence much like a musical score. Each note has a number of characteristics:

FREQUENCY
The table shows a range of musical notes and their corresponding frequencies. All instruments would produce the same frequency for a given note, even though the sound of the notes may be widely different. A saxophone and a piano, for example, would both produce exactly the same frequency for Middle C on the musical scale.

The notes are often referred to as having 'pitch' rather than frequency. A note may have a 'vibrato' effect superimposed upon it, with the note being swung above and below the original frequency. In such a case the frequency is always slightly altering but there remains a base frequency - the pitch.

Note	Frequency	Note	Frequency	Note	Frequency	Note	Frequency
C	65.41	C	130.81	C	261.63	C	523.25
C#	69.30	C#	138.59	C#	277.18	C#	554.37
D	73.42	D	146.83	D	293.66	D	587.33
D#	77.78	D#	155.56	D#	311.13	D#	622.25
E	82.41	E	164.81	E	329.63	E	659.26
F	87.31	F	174.61	F	349.23	F	698.46
F#	92.50	F#	185.00	F#	369.99	F#	739.99
G	98.00	G	196.00	G	392.00	G	783.99
G#	103.83	G#	207.65	G#	415.30	G#	830.61
A	110.00	A	220.00	A	440.00	A	880.00
A#	116.54	A#	233.08	A#	466.16	A#	932.33
B	123.47	B	246.94	B	493.88	B	987.77

TIMBRE

The difference between musical instruments lies in their different harmonic mixes, as explained earlier. The mix of harmonics and their relative strengths is referred to as the instrument's timbre (pronounced 'tamber'). Sound cards may refer to the 'voices' they support. These are usually the number of different instruments that the card's synthesiser is capable of playing concurrently. Each of these voices will correspond to an instrument timbre but it is likely that the card will handle more instruments (timbres) than it is capable of playing concurrently.

DURATION

Each note's length is considered relative to the other notes in the musical piece, since a musical work can be played at differing paces. The diagram shows the relative lengths of the commonly used durations. So, a Semi-Breve lasts 32 longer than a Demi-Semi-Quaver, regardless of the tempo of the piece being played. The note

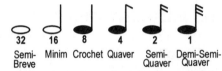

lengths would be supplemented by 'rests' of various durations. These are short periods of silence. A rest may be used as part of the overall composition or may be inserted between notes to make note distinct to the listener. This is more important where there is a long run of notes of the same frequency, as the listener must discern different notes rather than hear a continuous longer note.

OTHER ATTRIBUTES

The sound is often described in terms of its 'envelope' and this encompasses four different features - often called the ADSR.

ATTACK	The speed at which the note's initial volume increases.
DECAY	The speed at which the volume fades away.
SUSTAIN	The main amplitude that is maintained during the note (e.g. if a synthesiser keyboard key is held down).
RELEASE	The time it takes for the sound to completely stop.

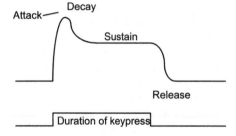

MUSIC FORMATS

Music formats vary with the following being the most common:

CMF : The Creative Music Format was introduced with the Sound Blaster card. It uses instruments defined in the file, or in .SBI Sound Blaster Instrument files, along with a note sequence, to play the music. CMF music is generally not as good as some other formats, but produces compact files.

ROL : Similar in basic idea to the CMF file, the ROL musical format was introduced with the Roland sound card. Again, it generally means small files, but slightly lesser quality.

MOD : Designed on the Amiga, the MODule format uses digitised instruments played at different sampling frequencies. Since each instrument is digitised, MOD files have a much more convincing, realistic feel, but are usually slightly larger files. MOD files are prolific on BBS services, and other than MIDI, it is probably the most used music format on PCs.

WAV : Introduced along with Windows, the WAV file format is a simple sound sample with a short file header. It is used for music as well as speech, sound effects, etc. The benefit of WAV files is that many Windows programs can use them with a single Windows sound driver. Of course, the Windows sound driver is not limited to WAV files, but Windows programs themselves tend to prefer WAV files since they are the native format for Windows sound.

MP3 : Uses a compression ratio of up to 12:1 to produce compact audio files for playing from a computer, or from a dedicated portable MP3 player such as the Rio. See earlier in the chapter for more details.

MIDI

The *'Musical Instrument Digital Interface'* was developed as a standard interface between different pieces of musical apparatus such as electronic keyboards, synthesisers, sequencers, drum machines, etc. These were initially produced by different manufacturers with different interfaces and were notoriously difficult to connect together.   As a response, the first MIDI standard was introduced in 1983 as an agreement between manufacturers.   This standard (The MIDI 1.0 Specification) specifically mentioned the use of home computers but MIDI-compatible items can be connected and used together without the need for a computer.   However, there are many benefits from using a computer in a MIDI music system. When music is played directly at a music keyboard, the keystrokes can be saved and manipulated.   The computer can be used to synchronise the notes more accurately, allow cut and paste of passages of music, etc.   The completed piece can be saved for later playing through a MIDI music device.   MIDI music can be played through computer sound cards, but is much better when used in conjunction with MIDI connected instruments such as keyboards. This allows the computer to read a .MID file and thereby tell the MIDI instrument which notes to play. The result is that the sound comes from a dedicated musical instrument rather than a simple wave modulator.   This usually provides a superior and more versatile result.   However, sound cards are available which incorporate the quality waveforms associated with external instruments.   GM (General MIDI) compatibility allows the playing of commercially produced MIDI music files. It is an extension of the MIDI specification, such that specific channels and voices are linked to specific pre-defined sounds (e.g. 26 is always an electric guitar).

THE MIDI INTERFACE

External connections to MIDI instruments require a dedicated MIDI port on the computer.   This is either directly available from a sound card or is supplied as an add-on to a sound card.   The MIDI standard specifies both the hardware and software requirements for the interface.

HARDWARE   The computer's MIDI connection will have both an input and an output socket.   The input connector (marked as 'MIDI IN') can be used to receive input from an electronic keyboard.   The output connector (marked as 'MIDI OUT') takes the messages from the computer to the external synthesisers, etc.   Many MIDI devices also support a MIDI THRU connector and this 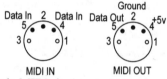 reproduces whatever appears on the device's MIDI IN socket.   This allows multiple MIDI devices to be connected together.   The connectors are of 180-degree 5-pin DIN type and pins 1 and 3 are not used and have no wired connections.   The connecting cable is twisted-pair wires with a protective shielding to prevent electrical interference to the signal.   It is important that this shield is only connected at the one end, to provide interference protection while maintaining the electrical isolation of both devices.

The messages are passed in serial format comprising byte-sized packets as shown in the diagram.   The signal is very similar to that used in the RS232 serial interface.   The signals are asynchronous and have a start bit, eight data bits and a stop bit.   The start and stop bits are used to ensure the proper synchronisation of the data (i.e. the receiving device is able to properly decode the status of each data bit at any one point in time.   No parity bit is used. The ten bits require a time of 320 microseconds.   This means that the MIDI messaging system runs at a 31.25Kbaud rate.   This is a relatively slow interface but it is a simple serial device saving the use of multicore cable or multi-wire ribbon cable to connect devices.   Cables must be a maximum of 50ft in length.

MESSAGES   Note the MIDI message does not contain any actual sounds embedded in it.   The message contains a <u>description</u> of each note in terms of its frequency, timing and timbre (which musical instrument).   Each message is spread over several bytes and typical information includes:

Message	Meaning		
Note on	indicates the start of information on a note.		
Channel number	indicates which of the 16 available channels to use. This is allocated to a particular instrument and acts like a single recording track on a conventional recording studio system. However, different devices may use a particular channel number for different instruments. So, a note intended for a guitar may be reproduced as a piccolo. Windows includes a *'MIDI Mapper'* utility to map the correct instruments for particular MIDI devices.		
Key	indicates the pitch of the note.	Duration	indicates the note's length.
Volume	indicates the note's amplitude.	Velocity	indicates how hard a key was struck.
Note off	indicates the end of the note information.		

These explanations simplify the process and interested readers are advised to read up on the more detailed issues of Omni Mode, Poly Mode, Channel and System Messages and the detailed content of the Data Bytes.   The use of sophisticated software for music score writing and printing is also beyond the scope of this chapter.

VIDEO - an introduction

Of all the multimedia components, video has the greatest impact. The message for the viewer may be adequately contained in the project's text but a picture commands more instant attention. A moving picture has yet even more appeal, where "seeing is believing". It provides an immediate perception and can convey feeling and influence attitudes. The viewer can see the effects of natural disasters or the plight of refugees, making the point much more vividly than words alone. This is well recognised and news reports and charities make good use of video to create the desired impression.

Video is also an important tool to further understanding of a situation or a process. A simple video clip, demonstrating how a car's spark plug is changed, is worth thousands of words of explanation.

For these reasons, video is now found in many applications - in information kiosks, on CD-R, on web sites, etc.

Video is a sequence of individual pictures which, when displayed on the screen at a fast enough rate, provide the illusion of movement. This technique is used to project movies in cinema theatres and transmit television pictures. It also used by camcorders to capture moving sequences.

Each picture is called a 'Frame' and the more frames that are displayed in each second, the smoother is the perceived motion. The 'frame rate' describes the number of individual frames that are displayed each second and is measured in frames per second (fps).

The chart shows the number of frames displayed per second in various systems, to maintain the illusion of continuous movement.

Typical frame rates and their uses	
0fps	Still frame
15fps	Minimum acceptable for motion
24fps	Motion pictures
25fps	British television
30fps	American television

Computer video is the term used to describe the set of pictures taken out of the camcorder and stored as a computer file on the hard disk. The audio that is recorded along with the video is included within the video file. It is not saved as a separate audio WAV file.

The early days

Video remained a specialist area for many years. Traditional cine cameras used rolls of film that had to be processed before they could be viewed or edited. Since film processing took time, there was no way of knowing that the scene had been properly recorded. Multiple takes had to be made to ensure that one clip would be usable. The editing of developed cine film was largely a job for experts. Apart from the simple cutting and splicing of pieces of filmstrip, all other editing tasks required studio facilities.

The introduction of analogue video cameras changed all that. The scene was recorded on to videotape and the tape could be instantly rewound and played back, to examine the scene. However the editing process was analogue based and very expensive. Editing consoles were cumbersome and used a process known as 'Linear Editing'. The editing equipment was based on the mechanical movement of videotape, with multiple players and recorders being used to copy clips back and forth. Putting special effects on a project required special electronic devices.

Benefits of digital editing

The breakthrough came with the arrival of the computer video capture card. Video footage taken from VCRs and camcorders could now be converted into computer files and these files could be edited within the computer. Transition effects and special effects were easily applied to provide professional results at a fraction of the price of previous methods. It uses 'Non-Linear Editing', where all the video content is stored digitally and processed digitally. Once the clips are taken off the tape, the camera equipment plays no further role in the editing process.

Like analogue, there is no reel of film, no processing and no waiting time. However, the computer software has the distinct advantage of easily manipulating the digital clips. Individual scenes can be deleted, cropped, optimised, re-ordered and have effects added. Every individual frame of the video clip can be cleaned up, sharpened, tinted, and so on, with all the work being carried out by the computer program. The computer's CPU is used to figure out all the changes necessary to achieve the special effects. This allows a whole range of special effects that were previously impossible or very expensive to achieve.

Current PC video editing software can quite easily provide such facilities as:
- Titles (fixed titles, scrolling credits, sub-titles, etc)
- Chroma key (a foreground object is superimposed on a different background scene)
- Fades (one scene is faded down as the next scene becomes visible)
- Dissolves (one scene merges into the next scene)
- Wipes (one scene moves on to the screen as another is pushed off)

These are discussed further in the chapter on video editing.

The initial limitation with NLE (non-linear editing) was the specification of computers. They did not have the processing power, data transfer rates or storage capacity required to handle large video files. Modern computers have fast processors, loads of spare memory and large fast hard disks and these have begun to alleviate the problem. However, there is still a long way to go before all users have computers that are capable of displaying full-screen, high resolution, fast-moving video.

Overview of the process

As the illustration shows, many different video sources may require to be incorporated into a multimedia project. The computer system has to be capable of dealing with some, or all, of these different sources.

A summary of the entire video process is:

Camcorder → link to computer → computer file → editing software → final output media.

The above stages are:
- The camcorder records the video scenes.
- The camcorder's output is fed to the computer's video capture device (usually a plug-in capture card or interface card).
- The computer hardware/software turn the video signal into a computer file that is saved to hard drive as a disk file. This is known as *'digitising'* and the file may also be compressed at this stage.
- The computer's editing software uses this file, along with others, to compose a complete video/audio/animation sequence.
- The completed project is output to one or more media formats. This could include outputting to video tape, uploading to a web site, or recording on a CD or DVD.

The block diagram below highlights the main features of creating digital video and each feature is briefly explained below.

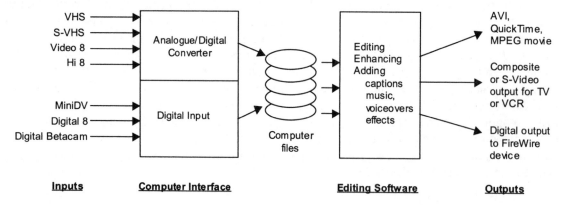

Inputs

The diagram shows the range of possible connections to a video capture card or interface card. Of course, not all are used at the same time.

There are two basic type of video input:

Analogue   These may be of different qualities (VHS, S-VHS, Video 8, Hi8) and may use different
            signal processing methods (composite, S-Video)
Digital   These may use different digital formats (MiniDV, Digital 8, Digital Betacam)

Computer Interface

The purpose of the computer interface is to get a copy of the video clip content held on the videotape into the computer as a disk file. Most older camcorders record on to the videotape in analogue format, while newer camcorders record the video content on to the tape as digital data.

As a result, there are two different types of interface, as shown in the diagram on the previous page.

Analogue   The electronics inside the video capture card converts the incoming analogue video clips to digital files (i.e. the Analogue to Digital Converter shown in the diagram).

Digital   Some camcorders record in digital format on to tape and the video data is transferred directly to computer in digital format.   They do not need to be converted from analogue format to digital format and so do not use the analogue/digital conversion system.   This digital interface is known as an IEEE 1394, or *'FireWire'*, connection.

Some interface cards provide both analogue and digital connections. In this case, the analogue signal is digitised while the digital connections bypass that circuitry.

Editing Software
The editing software is used to prepare the content. This involves activities such as trimming the clips, placing them in the required playing order and adding effects, transitions, titles, overlays and audio dubbing (see the chapter on video editing).

Outputs
The finished project consists of one or more video clips, stored on the computer's hard disk.   If the interface card has composite or S-Video output sockets, the disk files can be converted back into a television format, for feeding directly to a television set or to the inputs of a VCR.   This tape output would be in PAL format for UK VCRs or televisions. (See the video editing chapter for details of TV standards).

FireWire cards have *'digital out'* connections that allow the video files to be sent to other digital devices such as a camcorder's DV-in socket or a Sony MiniDisc recording input. The content remains digital throughout these data transfers, avoiding the losses and distortion associated with analogue/digital conversions.

More commonly, the files are held on disk in a file format that is easily integrated into larger multimedia productions.   Likely file types are AVI, QuickTime movie and MPEG (versions 1, 2 and 4).

Before saving the file, a number of decisions have to be made about the clips' characteristics.
These are:
- Choose the final desired screen resolution.
- Choose the file's data rate.
- Choose the compression method.
- Choosing a frame rate for the clip.

These characteristics and their effects are explained in this chapter and in the chapter on video editing.

Creating a project
The steps for creating a video project are:
- Plan the shoot.
- Prepare all necessary resources.
- Shoot the clips.
- Digitise and store the clips.
- Edit and compose the project
- Review the final project.

The steps surrounding the recording are often divided into two categories - pre-production and post production.   The pre-production phase includes issues such as research, scripting, storyboarding, scheduling, and logging.   They are all designed to save shooting time (the expensive bit) and wasted editing time (the other expensive bit).   This stage might also include resource gathering such as purchasing royalty free CDs, recording voiceovers and background music, etc.

The post-production phase covers the tasks of digitising, editing, formatting and outputting the project.

Recording Technology
The basic principle of the camcorder is simple.   The light reflected from the subject being recorded is converted from light variations into electrical variations. These electrical variations are then recorded on to a cassette tape.   For domestic use, the recorded video is played through a television set.   For multimedia use, the changing electrical content is converted into digital information on hard disk.

Light passes through the camcorder lens and is converted into electrical signals by one or more CCDs (charge-coupled devices). See the chapter on digital photography for more details. The CCD specification fitted to different camcorder models varies and typical examples are the Canon MV20i with 420,000 pixels, the Sony DCR-PC3 with 800k pixels and the Sony DCR-PC100 with over one million pixels.

Each row and column of the CCD's sensors corresponds to the picture's horizontal and vertical resolution. The values from each row are read off and make up the serial video output stream. The lines are read off in an 'interlaced' manner. First, all the odd lines are read followed by all the even lines being read. Each set of alternate lines is known as a 'field' and the two fields are combined to compose the complete picture, known as the 'frame'. Each field is read off in 1/50th of a second and a complete frame is built up every 1/25th of a second. This provides the 25fps (frames per second) associated with UK video. This speed was chosen to match the frame rate of UK television systems. In the USA, the frame rate is 30fps and so the lines are read 60 times per second. Interlacing is only used for television reproduction and the capture card converts the picture into a non-interlaced version for computer use (See the chapter on screen technology for more information).

The camera has three colour outputs, one each for the red, green and blue components of the picture. It also has an output that carries synchronisation information, so that the device receiving the signal knows when to start a new scan line or to return to the top of the screen.

Camera signal processing

Every camera works in the ways described above. With analogue systems, such as Composite Video, S-Video and Component Video, the output is kept in an analogue state while it is stored to a VCR or transmitted as a television picture. With digital systems, such as MiniDV camcorders and digital television, the signals are digitised before being stored or transmitted.

S-Video

The three colour signals store all the information about the picture's colour. They also, in total, store all the information about the brightness of the picture. The brightness (known as 'Luminance' and represented by the letter 'Y') can be separately extracted to supply, along with the synchronisation information, a monochrome picture. The remainder, the colour picture with the luminance removed, is

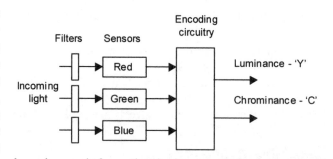

known as the 'Chrominance'. Put another way, chrominance information is the extra information that is

required to turn a monochrome picture into a colour picture. This system is used to provide the 'S-Video' output that is available on most decent camcorders. S-Video stands for Separate Video and it can be used with both PAL and NTSC systems.

The diagram shows the layout of the female S-Video connector. It is the same size as a PS/2 mini-DIN socket and has four pins. Pin 3 carries the luminance information and pin 4 carries the chrominance information. The other two pins are at ground potential. Although better quality than composite video, the picture is sometimes degraded due to 'chroma crosstalk' which is the leakage of chrominance information into the luminance channel. This produces some moiré effects on the final picture.

Composite Video

When all the signals are mixed together on to a single output socket, it is described as 'composite video'. This is the most common form of analogue output to be found on camcorders. Having a single output cable is convenient and the receiving device (the television set or the video capture card) is left to unscramble this information back into C and Y signals and from there back into RGB signals. However, there is a certain amount of mutual interference between signals when they are composited and this reduces the final picture quality. The most common artifact is the colour strobing that appears on moving patterns such as a presenter's tweed jacket. Highly saturated vertical edges can also result in dots crawling along the edge.

RGB

When all four signals are separately output, it is described as *'RGB'* output. This method does not create luminance and chrominance channels. It simply outputs the relative intensities of the red, green and blue components of the incoming picture at any point in time. This produces the highest quality output, as there are no processing losses associated with the other methods. Resolution is a direct function of the bandwidth of each channel. This type of output requires four sockets and four separate connecting leads. The fourth connection carries the timing and synchronisation information of the video signal.

Digital Video

The technique used with digital video is to convert the signal into luminance and two chroma channels. This is known as *'component video'*.

The DV circuitry records the picture as three separate components:

- The Luminance (the basic monochrome picture information) and the synchronisation pulses - known together as the *'Y'* signal.
- The Chrominance signal, which is broken into two component signals known as *'R-Y'* and *'B-Y'*. These are described as the *'colour difference'* signals, and the three analogue values are described as *'YUV'* signals. Once the colour difference signals are digitised, they are called the *'Cr'* and *'Cb'* components and the overall signal is described as *'YCbCr'*.

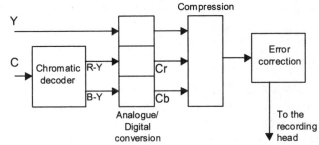

This is similar to the method used for television broadcasting, as the transmission of two colour difference signals requires less bandwidth than the three original red, green and blue channels.

The amplitude of each of the three component signals is represented by an 8-bit value.

All three analogue components have to be sampled to digitise them and the *'sampling rate'* of the various components is expressed as a ratio. DV uses a 4:1:1 system. This means that the luminance signal is sampled four times more often than the other two colour components. Professional formats, such as Digital Betacam (DB), use the ITU-R 601 standard of 4:2:2 as a sampling ratio to ensure higher resolution. The chrominance information is sampled less often, as the human eye does resolve chrominance information as effectively as luminance information, allowing for bandwidth savings.

With DV, the luminance signal is sampled at 13.5MHz, while each colour difference signal is sampled at 3.375MHz. Therefore, one second of a DV clip has 13.5m samples + 3.375m samples for each colour component. This gives a total of 20.25MB per second and a data rate of 162Mbits/sec. However, this signal contains the overheads that required for sending the signal to a television receiver. If these are removed, the data rate of the DV signal drops to around 124Mbits/sec.

The actual data rate for DV, excluding audio is:

Horizontal resolution x vertical resolution x 1.5 (for 4:1:1 sampling) x 8 bits per pixel

For PAL formats, the data rate is

720 x 576 x 25 x 1.5 x 8 = 124.4 Mbits/sec

The three signals are then passed through compression circuitry which achieves around 5:1 compression. The video is compressed, frame at a time, using the same DCT (Discrete Cosine Transform) method that is used with JPEG stills compression. The signal is then passed through very effective error correction circuitry before being sent through the camcorder's recording circuitry to the recording head.

The data rate is now 24.88Mbits/sec and a clip requires around 2.966MB of storage per second.

Adding in the audio brings the data rate of DV to around 3.6MB/sec.

Unlike other formats, DV is a fixed data rate. The compression, screen size and data rate are all fixed.

Progressive scan

Many digital camcorders now provide the ability to take still pictures. Having still and video capture in a single camera is a useful bonus and the facilities of the camcorder are usually better than those provided on digital cameras. For example, the lens on a camcorder is often of higher quality and the zoom range is greatly superior (usually around 10x compared to a still camera's 3x zoom).

The great problem with capturing stills from a camcorder is the way that the picture is constituted from two separate fields.   It takes a 1/50th of a second to complete the scan of the odd fields of an interlaced picture.   So, by the time the start of the even fields is started the adjacent lines are always separated in time by 1/50th of a second.   If the subject is moving, this will cause blurring of the combined picture. The solution rests in progressive scanning, where the entire picture is scanned as a single frame.   The frame is then broken up into single fields for recording in interlaced mode as normal.   When a still is required, the information is taken from the complete frame version that was captured before being split into fields.   To the video world, a progressive scan system has an identical output to an interlaced scan model.   But, for the still pictures, the best possible picture is saved, with minimum blurring.

Camcorder Specifications

A camcorder's specification is viewed in terms of its quality of recording and its variety of recording features.   The intrinsic quality of the construction reflects in the condition of the final recording. Construction issues include the quality of the lens, the quality of the electronic components, and the stability of the drive mechanism.   The optical and light gathering system in better camcorders results in sharper pictures and improved colours.   The better quality components result in less unwanted picture noise.   The better mechanism results in smoother sequences, with lessened jerkiness of the recorded clip. The ingenuity and skills of the camera operator or the video editor cannot adequately compensate for deficiencies in the camcorder equipment's components.   Camcorder manufacturers often emphasise the additional features that are supported by their models.   Some features, such as image stabilisation add to the quality of the recording.   Other features, such as built-in titlers, fades and effects, are aimed at hobbyists, as more control over such effects can be exerted during the editing process. Within limits, it is always best to obtain the highest-quality equipment that can be afforded.

Analogue and digital features

The following features and characteristics are available in models that are based on analogue recording or digital recording.   The additional features found on digital camcorders are covered separately.

Lens/Filters

These features are covered in the chapter on digital photography.

Zoom Range

The lens has a variable focal length so that can be varied from wide angle, through normal to telephoto. This is covered more fully in the chapter on digital photography.   The optical zoom range of a camcorder is typically up to 10X or 15X.   Most camcorders also provide a further digital zoom factor (e.g. some Sony models provide up to 180X digital zoom).   The optical zoom should be used at all times, unless a deliberately blocky effect is required (see chapter on digital photography).

Some camcorders also provide a 'Macro' facility.   This allows the camcorder to remain in focus while up close to very small objects, some positioned right up to the lens.   In this way, small objects such as insects, watch mechanisms, etc. can be shot.   In this mode, the depth of field is small and the subject is difficult to illuminate as the camcorder blocks the light.

Most camcorders provide a motorised zoom.   While a manual zoom is perfectly useful for framing a scene before shooting, it is less suitable for zooming while a recording is taking place.   The power zoom provides a smoother control.

Number of CCDs

Triple-chip CCDs produce improved light sensitivity and colour reproduction compared to single-chip CCDs, although the camcorder is significantly more expensive.

Image Stabilisation

The image stabiliser system keeps the image steady when using the telephoto zoom setting and prevents jitters from minor camera movements.   Optical stabilisation mechanically alters the lens to maintain a stable picture as the camera shakes.   This is the most expensive option.   Electronic stabilisation is cheaper but less effective. It does not allocate all the available sensors in its CCD array. Some are only used when the camera shakes and are not counted in the overall picture resolution. When the camera shakes, the electronics uses the light from these extra rows or columns to replace the rows or columns displaced by the camera movement. The result is that a picture area identical to the previous area is sent for storage.

Viewfinder

A camcorder may provide a foldout LCD panel, to allow the camera operator to see exactly what is being recorded. As an alternative, or as an addition, it may provide an internal optical or electronic viewfinder. The advantages of each method are discussed in the chapter on digital photography.

Remote Control

This is a handheld infrared remote control, similar to the type used to control a VCR. This allows control of the camera without the operator being close to the equipment. This is useful for the recording where the operator's presence is

- Obtrusive (e.g. recording wildlife). The camcorder is hidden in a bush or under branches and is operated from a distance.
- Dangerous (e.g. recording car racing). The camcorder is mounted on a tripod next to the track and operated from a safe distance.
- Impossible (e.g. recording in a small crevice, over a cliff edge). The camcorder is fixed to a pole that can be mounted where required and operated with the remote control.

Since the remote control also has playback buttons, it can be used with the camcorder connected to a television's video input sockets. In this mode, the camcorder acts like a VCR and the user operates the start, stop, rewind, fast forward and pause buttons in the same way as operating a TV remote control.

Time Code

This feature is mostly found in digital camcorders but is also available on top end analogue systems. Every frame of the video clip has included a value that denotes how far into the tape the frame appears. It is measured in hours, minutes, seconds and number of frames. So, for example a time code of 01:22:07:19 indicates that the frame appears 1 hour, 22 minutes, 7 seconds and 19 frames into the tape. This is very useful later for accurate video editing.

Automatic/Manual Controls

Camcorders usually automatically adjust their focus and exposure settings in response to the nature of the incoming light. While this is satisfactory for *'point and shoot'* situations, the operator will often require more control than the default automatic settings. For example, the camcorder's auto focus allows the subject to remain in focus whether at close range or at long distance. The operator, however, may wish to have the foreground subject out of focus, with the background being in focus. Similarly, special effects can be obtained by setting the white balance to a value other than the default.
The camcorder should provide a manual override on exposure, focussing and other settings.

Low Light Filming

There will be times when filming is carried out in less than ideal lighting conditions. If an event takes place in overcast weather conditions or at dusk, the camcorder should still be able to capture the scene with some degree of usefulness. Camcorders have varying abilities in this regard. Models with low *'lux'* values can record in lesser light conditions than models that demand a higher illumination. Typical current values range from 0 lux to 11 lux, with some models offering 0 lux for nightshots. This issue is covered later.

Shutter Speeds

The camera allows light in as a series of snapshots. The frequency of these snapshots is called the *'field rate',* while the time that the lens is opened for each shot is termed the *'shutter speed'.* Variable shutter speeds range from slow values (1/3, 1/6, 1/12 sec) for filming in low light conditions, to high values (1/50 to 1/10,000 sec) for filming fast moving objects. With fast shutter speeds, the camcorder still samples at 50 times per sec, but the sensor is exposed to the light source for a shorter time. Since the object moves less in the shorter time, there is less blur. The shortened exposure time means that high shutter speeds only work in good lighting.

Audio Features

The chapter on digital audio covers the types and uses of microphones. Nearly all camcorders provide some sort of built-in microphone. This is only of use for quick point and shoot recordings, where there is no time to set up a superior audio system. The microphone should at least face the direction that the lens is being pointed.   Some microphones point towards the sky and the mike in Sony PC100 actually faces away from the subject being recorded.   The camcorder should have provision for the connection of an external mike, usually a microphone socket and shoe mount.   The external mike is necessary to prevent the pickup of camera motor noise, the operator's breathing and to get closer to the source that actually needs to be recorded.   The camcorder should also provide a headphone socket, so that a set of headphones can be connected to monitor the quality of the incoming sound.

Digital only features:

The features mentioned above are all applicable to digital camcorders and the list below covers the additional features that would only be expected with a digital camcorder.

Digital Interface

Every digital camcorder has a DVi link, also known as an IEEE1394 or FireWire output. This enables the digital recording to be transferred to the computer via its FireWire connection.   Older and cheaper models only provide a digital out connection.   The camcorder should also have a connection that allows the digital output from the computer to be recorded back to the camcorder.   This is a separate FireWire connection and is marketed as *'DV-in'*.

Digital Stills

A growing number of camcorders now provide facilities for capturing still pictures.   The data from a single frame is taken from the CCDs and handled as a digital file that can be stored separately.   Most record a still onto the videotape as a short video clip (of perhaps seven seconds), normally allowing a voiceover to accompany the still.   Some Sony camcorders use a separate *'Sony Memory Stick'* to store still images.

Progressive Scan

Progressive scan CCD provides the best quality stills. These camcorders process images by the frame rather than the field (see earlier in this chapter).   Their output is not so good if it is going back to a television screen, but it is better for computer applications as the picture is improved (it contains no artifacts caused by the interlacing process).

Special Effects

Digital camcorders can easily incorporate special effects and scene transitions (wipes, dissolves, fades, titler, sepia, strobe, monochrome, mosaic, negative, pastel, etc) as the movie is being shot.   This is useful for amateur moviemakers but is mostly left unused by operators shooting for multimedia (as these effects and more can be added at the editing stage.   If the effects are applied at the editing stage, they can be removed or altered.   Effects embedded during video recording can not be removed later, to recover the original footage underneath.

Chroma Key.

A digital still picture is stored in memory to fill a blue background of a live image (e.g. Sony use their Memory Stick for purpose).

Typical camera connections	
Connection	**Description**
Power	Used to recharge batteries, or to run the camcorder directly.
Composite video	Used to connect to a video capture card, domestic VCR or television with composite input (usually RCA sockets). The yellow socket carries the video information while the stereo audio is carried by white (for left channel) and red (for right channel) sockets. The television sometimes only has a SCART socket (the standard European 21-pin connection) and a composite/SCART adapter would then be required
S-Video	Used to connect to a video capture card, S-Video recorder or a television that accepts S-Video in.
DV out	Used to connect to a FireWire card, digital recorder or another DV camcorder with a DV-in connection.
DV in	Used to connect to the output of the digital devices mentioned above.
External microphone in	Used to connect an external mike, in place of the camcorder's own internal mike.
Headphone socket	Used to connect a mike for monitoring the sound recording.
Edit control socket LAN-C	Used to connect to control circuitry for the automatic command of the camcorder functions such as play, fast forward and rewind.

Camcorder Video formats

While digital video is regarded as the future of all video recording and processing, there are a very large number of camcorders in use that still use analogue formats. The sheer size of the user base, and the vast amount of material that is already available in these formats, means that these formats have to be understood and given serious consideration.

Analogue Formats

The analogue camcorders are grouped into two quality bands:

Low-band types - VHS, VHS-C, 8mm

High-band types - S-VHS, SVHS-C and Hi8

The main characteristics of each type are considered below.

VHS

This was an early runner and is still the most popular format. It is the format used by almost all VCRs and is the distribution format for UK videotapes. It uses ½" tape (12.65mm) in a large cassette and each frame stores 250 lines of video. There is a huge existing base of source tapes, either commercial or from home taping.

VHS has been overtaken by formats with smaller cassettes, higher quality and higher resolution. In many cases, these higher formats are used for the captured, editing and storing of video. However, the popularity of VHS VCRs means that VHS format remains the most likely choice for distribution of a project in cassette form. After editing, a video project is recorded back to tape for distribution.

VHS-C

This format uses the same type of ½" tape as VHS but stores it in a smaller cassette. An adapter is used, so that the cassette can be played on a standard VHS VCR. It also stores 250 lines per picture.

S-VHS

Super-VHS is a superior format to VHS and manages to store 400 lines per picture. However, it never took off as a distribution medium, due to its large ½" tape cassette size and the fact that S-VHS tapes could not be played on existing VHS VCRs. Although it used the same cassette, it needs a S-VHS video player and these are very expensive. It remains a popular choice for the capture of analogue material.

Video 8 (8mm)

This is the most popular of the low-band types for domestic use. Its cassette is small and its tape is only 8mm wide. Although it only stores 250 lines per picture, it has an improved audio system.

The cassette will not play on a VHS player but the camera's output can be linked through composite leads.

Hi8

This is a better quality than both the 8mm and S-VHS formats. It uses metal evaporated tape and stores 400 lines per picture. It has the best audio system of the high-band types, with AFM and PCM tracks.

It uses a small cassette, which will not play on VHS VCRs.

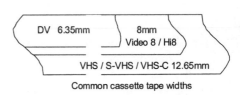

Common cassette tape widths

Digital Formats

The predominant digital format is known as *'MiniDV'*, although a new Sony format called *'Digital 8'* has been released.

DVC/ MiniDV

This format first appeared in 1995 as a standard developed by 55 manufacturers of consumer digital equipment, such as camcorders and VCRs.

All the formats discussed above record their information on to tape in analogue format (i.e. the amount that the tape is magnetised reflects the analogue level being recorded). Digital systems still record to tape but the information that is stored on the tape is purely digital (i.e. a series of '0's and '1's). This system is less prone to signal noise and level fluctuation.

Currently, MiniDV is primarily an acquisition system, not a distribution system. There are no domestic DV players and few DV decks are available. The Digital Video Cassette will not play on VHS players. Of course, the camcorder can be connected to a television's composite input, allowing the cassettes to be played (although this does not make the best use of the system's 500 line per picture capability).

MiniDV is designed for the serious amateur/semi-professional market and is the ideal format for computer and multimedia use.
It uses 6.35mm (1/4") metal evaporated tape, which is available in two cassette sizes:

Digital Video cassette sizes		
Type	**Cassette Size**	**Description**
Standard	125mm x 78mm x 14.6mm	Slightly larger than an audio cassette. Almost no models use this size. It is intended for long recordings of up to 4.5 hours.
MiniDV	66mm x 48mm x 12.4mm	This 3" x 2" cassette opened the way to a whole series of pocket-sized camcorders, with high specifications.

Digital camcorders also provide analogue outputs, so their composite or S-video outputs can be fed into an analogue video capture card, as already discussed.
The full benefit of digital camcorders is gained when the camcorder's FireWire output is connected to a computer's FireWire interface card.   This allows the data to be transferred in full 500-line digital format, without any signal degradation associated with analogue transfers. All analogue systems suffer from degradation when copying due to the losses, especially when copying from copies. There is likely to be a loss of up to 15% of the quality each generation (i.e. each time the tape is copied). Digital systems make perfect replicas time after time.
The video signal requires a bandwidth of around 3MHz to handle the 500 horizontal lines at a PAL resolution and 25fps. The system also supports a time-code capability.
The sound track is also recorded digitally, with either two pairs of 12-bit stereo tracks or one pair of 16-bit PCM stereo tracks.
As the diagram shows, the signal is recorded on to the tape as a set of diagonal tracks. A VHS tape would only require two tracks for each frame but DV requires much more because it contains much greater detail and requires greater bandwidth.   An NTSC tape, as used in the USA, requires 10 tracks to record a full frame. In the UK and other countries using PAL, each frame requires 12 tracks per frame.

One frame of 12 PAL tracks
(10 tracks for NTSC)

Each track is written as four separate areas of data.   The main areas store the video and audio data, while the Sub Code sector stores data such as the time code, and the ITI sector stores tracking information for later audio dubbing and editing.

Digital 8
The Digital 8 format was introduced by Sony in 1999.   It records digital video and audio on the analogue Hi8 tapes.   Digital 8 camcorders can play Digital 8, Hi8 and Video 8 recordings.   These camcorders can then digitise analogue tapes by sending the digitised version out through the *'digital out'* socket to a computer or DV edit deck.   American models also have analogue inputs and this allows analogue in/digital out conversion from VHS VCRs.   The claimed performance of 500 lines is equal to MiniDV.

MPEG
Most digital camcorders, like analogue models, record on to conventional videotapes. The difference is that the recording format is digital instead of analogue.   Now, MPEG digital camcorders are available with a range of different storage methods.   They all use some form of MPEG compression, but the video data is stored on a disk or SmartMedia cards.
The Hitachi MP-EG1 stores up to 20 minutes at 352x240 of MPEG-1 on a 260MB PC Card Type III hard disk.   Alternatively, it can store 3,000 JPEG still images. Currently, its composite video output is only NTSC.   The Sony DCM-M1 uses a 650MB MiniDisc to store up to 20 minutes of MPEG-2 video, 4½ hours of digital audio or 4,500 JPEG still images at 640x480.   However, it is spoiled by having no digital output (it only has S-video and composite outputs).
The Sharp VN-EZ1 uses MPEG-4 compression. It stores 10 minutes at 320x240, or 60 minutes at 160x120, on a 32MB card.   It is mainly intended for web use. It has no TV output and no serial port. A floppy disk adaptor is used to read its SmartMedia card.   Currently, ASF File players are still uncommon, although it works on IE5, Win98 and Win 2000. Other support is still awaited.

Professional formats

If regular high-quality shooting work is anticipated, consideration should be given to buying, or hiring, a BetaCam SP camera. This is a professional analogue format and requires subsequent digitising with a suitable capture card. It records between 600 and 850 lines and is the choice of broadcasters.

Other options are Pro DV systems, such as DVCAM and DVPRO, which are used for low end broadcast work. They use the same tape as standard MiniDV (i.e. the larger of the two DV cassette sizes) but record between 500 and 850 lines. They use a wider track pitch on the tape. This results in less recording time per DV tape, while allowing more accurate editing with editing decks. They also produce better results for chroma-key (also known as Bluescreen) effects. DVCPRO 50, or DV50, run at double the data rate of normal DV and record

Performance of different video standards		
Standard	Compression	Data Rate
VHS	9:1	2MB/sec
S-VHS	6:1	3MB/sec
DV	5:1	3.6MB/sec
BetaCam	3:1	6MB/sec

at 750 to 1000 lines. JVC produce their own standard - Digital S - it records on 750 lines on a tape that is the same size as a S-VHS cassette. Its data rata is 50Mb/sec, compared to DV's 25Mb/sec, the track pitch is greater, the tape speed is faster and it samples at 4:2:2 compared to DV's 4:1:1. It is by far the best digital video format. Along with the Sony BetaCam, it has received the approval of EBU for use for mainstream broadcast use.

Shooting Video

There are many excellent books that adequately cover the creative side of video filming and they are full of hints and tips on the art of scriptwriting, scouting, screen composition, direction and other related issues. This section covers the technical and practical considerations for video filming.

The first consideration is to understand the limits of the team's capabilities. Some jobs have special video demands (such as filming someone rock climbing or skydiving) or special audio knowledge (such as recording in a church or auditorium). If the job demands it, and there is any doubt over the ability to deliver, call in the professionals. The cost of hiring a team may be expensive but this should be compared to hiring a famous personality to promote a product or service then finding out that the recording was useless - after everyone has gone home. Apart from camera expertise, there are professionals who specialise in lighting or in audio capture. Bear in mind, however, there are differences between the video shot for eventual use on web sites, video streaming or any other situation where small file sizes are important. Normal video recordings remain on videotape, where there are no considerations of clip size and distribution.

Technical Considerations

Many questions on camera use are covered in the section of digital photography and that section should be read before carrying on. The following notes consider the additional factors that have to be considered for video filming compared to capturing still images.

Lighting

Precise lighting and camera settings are the key to video filming and this raises several related issues:

Colour Balancing

The *'colour temperature'* of a light source depends upon its wavelength and is measured in degrees Kelvin. Typical colour temperature readings are shown in the table. The daylight values will vary with time of day and weather conditions, from around 4000°K to 8000°K.

Typical Colour Temperatures	
6500°K	Arc light
5500°K	Average daylight
4500°K	Fluorescent lamp
3200°K	Studio floodlight
2000°K	Domestic light bulb

The camera has to be adjusted to match the *'colour temperature'* of the scene being recorded. Artificial light is warmer than daylight, while an overcast day produces light that is colder than direct sunlight. The human eye normally adjusts for these changing conditions, but the camera faithfully records what it sees. The resulting clip can have a perceived unnatural colour tinting. High colour temperatures produce a bluish tint, while lower colour temperatures produce an orange or reddish tint. This effect is seen most clearly on a white colour subject. Colour balancing is the task of adjusting the camera so that a white object is recorded as neutral white - without a cold or warm tint. Most cameras carry out this task automatically, but can be overridden for manual setting. Most cameras provide an Indoor/Outdoor option from their menus or, for older cameras, from a press button or switch. Try to avoid mixing natural and artificial light, as the camera cannot adjust for both tints simultaneously.

Light Levels

While degrees Kelvin measures the underline{wavelength} of the light, it does not measure the underline{amount} of available light. The measurement of light illuminating a specified object is in *'lux'*. A well-lit office might be lit to around 200 lux, while domestic lighting is always substantially lower. Natural daylight can vary from a few hundred lux up to over 10,000 lux in very sunny conditions.

The automatic exposure system in the camera adjusts the opening of the iris of the lens in response to the underline{average} level of incoming light. This means that the predominant level controls the iris. If the average level is high, the iris closes more to allow less light into the camera. In scenes that have mostly low light levels, the iris is opened further and the gain of the camera's internal video amplifier is turned up in an attempt to maintain the picture detail. Leaving the exposure setting on automatic can result in a number of practical problems that are covered below.

The exposure can be manually set by the operator for greater control, but the following factors have to be taken into consideration:

- Over-exposure - Allowing too much light into the camera drives all the video content levels high (towards white). All bright details of the scene end up at white level. Details washed out this way are irrecoverable.
- Under-exposure - Allowing too little light into the camera reduces all video content low (towards black level). The darker details end up at black level and are also irrecoverable. Since the entire video signal has a lower contrast ratio of lightest to darkest, the compression CODEC is examining a smaller dynamic range and outputs a lower range of video values. This results in excessive video noise.

Any details lost and any noise introduced during recording cannot be adequately dealt with during editing. Lighting levels of 1000 lux to 2000 lux for the foreground subject and roughly half these levels for the background will result in a lens that is stopped down and a signal that is lifted out of noise.

Low Light Level Filming

Of course, there are times when low level lighting is an integral part of the shoot (e.g. Shooting a night scene or inside a dark castle). Viewers expect to view murky pictures; that's all part of the atmosphere and is perfectly acceptable.

Manufacturer's specifications quote camcorders as recording at very low lux levels (e.g. the Sony PC100 works at only 7 lux). These are the underline{minimum} figures for achieving any kind of video signal and do not indicate the level for normal satisfactory recording. Nevertheless, there are advantages to cameras that work at low lux levels, as they allow recording of wildlife, surveillance recording, etc.

Some cameras offer *'NightShot'* facilities and these record scenes as low as zero lux. Since this level is complete darkness, the camera uses infra-red transmitters and filters to records these scenes. The output from these recordings is lacking in all colours, apart from a slight tinge of green (similar to that the monochrome display expected from using nightlights). The transmitters may be built round the front of the camera or may be sold as an infra-red spotlight attachment.

Backlighting

The camcorder's automatic exposure control adjusts itself to compensate for changes in incoming light. This causes problems where there is backlighting. For example, a person may be filmed in a seated position, with darks trees as a background. As the person stands up, he/she is gone from the dark background and now is silhouetted on a sunny sky as a background. Other examples are people walking in front of a window or patio doors, or sitting down next to a table light or candles. Other sources of backlighting are car headlights, street lamps, domestic lamps and office fluorescent strips.

When these situations occur, the camera adjusts to the increased average light by allowing less light into the lens. This dims the foreground subject.

It is best to either avoid these situations, or to switch to manual over-ride (some cameras provide a *'Back Light'* button). The aim is to sacrifice the background, which may be washed, so that the subject is adequately exposed. Sometimes backlighting is used for effect. A person standing against the sun has a halo effect around them, or a church, castle, hills or other objects can be silhouetted against the sky.

Outdoor Lighting

Filming outdoors is much easier than filming indoors, as there is usually an abundance of natural lighting, hitting the subject from all angles. Therefore, it's best to interview people outside, if possible.

The exception is bright sunlight, which can introduce deep unwanted shadows to a scene (e.g. around the human face).

These unwanted shadows can be filled in with reflectors (see below) or artificial lights (as a last resort).

Indoor Lighting

While outdoor shooting can often rely on plenty of light around a subject, indoor shooting requires more attention to providing adequate lighting.   If possible the subject should be shot with natural lighting. This may involve locating a subject next to a window, an open door or patio doors.   Larger scenes will almost certainly require supplementary lighting.   The benefit of understanding and owning artificial lights is that they can be used in any situation, or at any time of day or night.

Light sources

These vary from small lights that attach to the camcorder, to large studio lights.   Full descriptions are available in the product catalogues.

The simplest and cheapest option is a halogen-quartz video light that fits on to the camcorder. These are usually 10W to 30W, and can be mounted so that they point straight at the subject. This produces poor results compared to lighting a subject from a side angle.   For improved results, they should be used detached from the camcorder, or at least used with a diffuser. An alternative is to purchase a light that has an adjustable mount, so that the light can be pointed at the walls or ceiling for a deflected, more even lighting.

The next stage upwards is a photoflood bulb mounted on a tripod.   Again the light mount should be adjustable and the tripod's height is already adjustable.   This provides a variety of positions to achieve general even light fills.   For more serious work, halogen-quartz tubular with rectangular reflectors, or halogen-quartz bulbs in cans with *'barn doors'* can be purchased.   These can be mounted on canopies and the *'barn doors'* are hinged flaps that shape the beam and screen the camcorder from its direct light.

Light Diffusers/Filters

Direct sunlight or indoor lighting results in *'hard'* lighting, with high contrast, pronounced shadows and a feeling of depth.   It picks out the outlines on features, making them stand out (including facial wrinkles). Hazy or cloudy conditions result in *'soft'* lighting. Light is striking the object from many angles and this reduces the contrast around edges.   Wrinkles are minimised and the picture has a smoother warmer look. This can be achieved indoors by fitting translucent diffusers (known as *'scrims'* or *'gauzes'*) over the lighting units.   These scatter the light to achieve an effect similar to outdoor lighting.

In addition, lamp filters can be fitted to change the colour from the lights. These are most often used to change artificial light for mixing with natural light.   They are specially made to withstand the high temperatures of the lamps.

Placing Lights

Although the lighting demands of each location will vary, artificial lighting setups normally use three separate light sources - known as the keylight, the fill-light and the backlight.

The keylight is used as the main illumination source. It is placed to the side of the subject (by about 45° from the camera) and directed down on the subject (by about 20°).   The keylight is a hard light and provides depth to the picture.   It also creates pronounced shadows - both on the contours of the subject and also on the background.

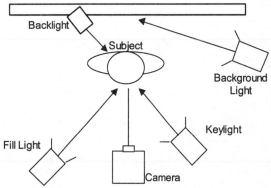

The fill-light is about quarter or half the wattage of the keylight and is placed about 45° from the camera in the opposite direction from the keylight.   It reduces the dark shadow on the subject and a soft light is best for this purpose.

The backlight is used to provide separation of the subject from the background and to provide any additional subject enhancement, such as providing highlights to the subject's hair or providing a halo effect).

The background light is used to illuminate the background by little more than half the level of the subject.   It can be used to bring a darkened background into the focus of the main picture, or it can be used to soften the shadows cast on a wall from the keylight and fill-light.

Notes
- The viewer has certain expectations in terms of lighting.   A modern office, hotel or kitchen is expected to be brightly lit, while drab surroundings are expected to be dimly lit.

- Scenes will not always require the use of all of these lights.   For example, an interviewee in a large workshop or auditorium may be standing 100 feet away from any background surface, removing the need for a background light.   On the other hand, for close up work, a reflector may prove more useful than a fill-light.   These lighting rules may be broken to achieve special effects.   Brightly lit and evenly lit scenes suggest normality, while light subjects shot against a dark background is perceived as being sinister, builds tension, and suggests danger.   Hard lighting on a face suggests an austere or menacing character while soft lighting suggests softness of character.

Reflected Light

A useful way to achieve soft lighting is to use *'Bounce lighting'*. This involves illuminating the subject with light that is reflected off walls and ceilings.   While this is less efficient than direct lighting, it provides a much more even and soft source of light and interviewees much prefer this to the direct glare of frontal lighting.   Walls can used as natural reflectors or a range of additional reflectors can be used. These can be professional reflector umbrellas, or can be improvised when required. For example, white sheets, aluminium foil that has been crumpled and straightened out again, and cine projector screens all make good reflectors.

Other scene considerations

The chapter looks later at the role of storyboarding in planning the content and nature of individual video scenes.   This tries to anticipate all likely problems. In practice, certain decisions have to be made upon arrival at the location.   These concern the positioning of the main subject to avoid recording problems and to optimise the video content for future editing.

Backgrounds

Where the recording is planned to be distributed on videotape, there is no concern about how the video content affects computer file sizes.   However, since most video clips will be used in conventional multimedia use, a little planning can ensure that the scene is adequately recorded, while the clip does not become too large for distribution.

The key consideration is that scenes that have a lot of detail, or are constantly changing, create larger file sizes when they are finally compressed for distribution. The following guidelines are useful:

- Keep the detail in the recorded picture to a minimum, to achieve best compression.
- Use plain backgrounds if possible, to maximise spatial compression.
- Avoid backgrounds that are constantly altering (crowd scenes, trees blowing in the wind, etc.) to maximise temporal compression.
- If a constantly altering background is unavoidable, make the background of focus, to avoid distracting the viewer's eye and to improve future compression.   This helps with both spatial and temporal compression.

At the end of the day, however, the above considerations must not outweigh the artistic needs for the screen content to adequately convey the required mood or information.

Avoiding moiré

A moiré pattern is seen as a shimmering or the appearance of unwanted colours in certain areas of the screen.   It is caused by the inability to handle fine detail in some picture elements such as some men's suits and ties with fine stripes. This effect was noticed in early television broadcasts and now the clothes worn by newscasters are chosen to avoid this effect.   This effect will not be seen through the viewfinder. They are artifacts produced during the processing of the signal.   The results cannot be removed from the picture. If in doubt, make a quick test recording and view the results.

Subject Positioning

Depending upon the final intended media for the footage, consideration should be given to the degree to which the subject fills the screen. The diagram shows the display screen with two inner areas marked off.   The outer area is the total screen size but this is not always visible on all screens, depending on the adjustment of the screen controls. This means that some content positioned at the edges may not be visible on some screens.

To ensure that all of the subject content is always visible, the area known as the *'action-safe zone'* should be considered as the main screen area for all subject recording.

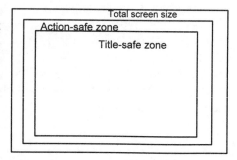

Likewise, the inner area, known as the *'title-safe zone'* should be used as the area in which all title text should be placed.   The camcorder operator should bear these zones in mind during filming.   Objects filmed outside these areas may not be visible on some screens, or suffer from the distortion that some screens have at the edges of the picture.

This problem mostly affects television screens and it only applies to full-screen footage. If video is being shot for display on a small area of the screen, these zones do not apply as the clip can be positioned on a safe area of the screen before being sent to videotape. If the footage is being used on a known system, such as a kiosk, the safe boundaries can quickly be confirmed by creating a test video clip.

Shot Sizes/Uses

The subject positioning discussed above was to avoid technical problems. Subject positioning also plays a major role in the artistic composition of a shot.   Shot size describes how fully an object fills the frame. It is usually applied to the human figure and the common shot sizes are shown in the table.

Shot sizes should reflect the use of the scene.   A tutorial on jewellery repairs would require a close-up shot, while a tutorial on constructing a bridge would require a medium long shot or long shot.   In practice, a clip would switch between shot sizes, as the content unfolds.

In some cases, viewers take their psychological cue from the positioning of people on screen.   If two people are having a heated argument, a mid shot or medium long shot indicates that the viewer is an observer of the argument.   If the participants are shown in close-up, the viewer is being drawn into the scene and this can disturb

Common Shot Sizes		
ECU/XCU	Extreme Close-Uo	Part of face
CU	Close-up	Head, maybe shoulders
MCU	Medium Close-up	Head and shoulders, maybe chest
MS	Mid-Shot	Head to waist
MLS	Medium Long Shot	Head to knees
LS	Long shot	Full body

the viewer (of course, that might be the dramatic intention of the scene!).   Similarly, if two lovers are having an intimate conversation, a long shot appears to be too aloof a setting.

Watch television programmes and notice that the subject is not always in the centre of the frame, especially if there is an interesting background. If the person on screen is looking to the left, leave some screen space on the left.   When a single head and shoulders is to appear on screen, do not leave too much free space above the head. It is better to move the camera closer or zoom in slightly.

Using the Camcorder

The operator's control of the camcorder contributes greatly to the effectiveness of the final recorded clip. Largely, it is a question of practice, although the following guidance should prove useful.

Camcorder Positioning

As with the still camera, a tripod is a great aid in video filming. The added stability greatly enhances the recording. There is nothing worse than viewing a recording that has obviously been made with a hand-held camcorder, complete with shakes, wobbles and jolts. In addition, small camcorder movements when recording at a fully zoomed setting result in large changes in the picture content.   The greater the zoom, the more obvious the wobble.

If the camcorder has to be moved during the recording, some form of image stabilisation should be used. This could either be within the camera (optical or electronic stabilisation), or be a physical device, such as a motion stabiliser (e.g. a Steadi-Cam or a Steadymate).   However, walking while filming is an art that has to be practised.

There remain the few occasions when the more *'natural'* effect of hand held recording is desirable. It gives an *'amateur'* or *'documentary'* feel. (as in *"The Blair Witch Project")*.

Focusing

The theory and problems with depth of focus are covered in the chapter on digital photography. It is best not bypass the automatic focus, wherever possible. The automatic system uses the centre of the image as its focus point and this need not always be where the centre of attention is in the picture. The result is that the wrong object is in focus.   A recent example involved filming the flight of a microlight aircraft, with the camera filming the scene from inside a screened porch.   The camcorder auto-focus decided to focus on the mesh of the screen and the aircraft was completely out of focus.

The automatic focus can be left in operation in situations where there is likely to be rapid changes in focus (e.g. filming a football match or a street demonstration).

Zooming

The zoom lens is a very useful tool, when used in the correct way. On most occasions, the zoom facility is used to frame the shot, but is can also be used while filming.

Zoom then shoot

The camera's zoom control alters the focal length of the lens and thereby alters the amount by which the subject is magnified. This also affects the depth of focus. Therefore, the best way to fill the frame is to move the camcorder closer to the subject, rather fill the frame using the zoom.

Its main use is to allow a subject to dominate the frame without the camera being moved where moving closer to the subject is not practical.   This could include dangerous situations (e.g. filming a burning building, or passing trains) or to avoid disturbing a natural situation (e.g. children at play, birds feeding, etc).

Another problem with recording scenes when zoomed in is the difficulty in keeping a moving object in focus if it moves towards or away from the camera.   The telephoto setting reduces the depth of field, so that the subject can easily move out of focus.

Zoom while shooting

Zooming can help place an object in its surroundings. For example, zooming out on a car might show that it is one of thousands sitting in a car park.   While this can be pretty dramatic, it is an effect that can quickly be overused.   Zooming in and out while shooting should be used very sparingly and only when the effect is planned in advance.

The manual zoom on camcorders is less smooth than the operation of the motorised zoom. Better cameras have progressive zoom. Pushing the zoom button slightly produces a slow zoom, while pushing the button further produces a faster zoom.   This produces a very smooth gradual slow zoom.

When the camcorder is set to manual focus, the zoom in operation can leave the subject out of focus. To prevent this, carry out the following steps:

- Zoom in on the subject.
- Adjust the manual focus, to get the subject in focus.
- Zoom out to the required starting zoom setting.
- Start recording the scene.
- Zoom in on the subject, while recording.

By ensuring that the subject is in focus at the end of the zoom, the zoom effect is successful.

Panning/Tilting

Some shots involve a stationary camcorder recording a fixed scene. All the subject's movement or content are contained within the area being recorded by the camcorder.   Other shots require the camera to be moved. This could be to follow a moving subject, or to bring into view another part of a scene that is too large to be fitted in a single frame.

'Panning' is the movement of the camera in a horizontal direction, while 'tilting' describes moving the camera in a vertical direction. If panning or tilting, use a tripod with a smooth fluid head, so that camera movement is smooth.

Panning involves the camera being rotated (preferably on a tripod's pan head) to follow the movement of the subject in a scene. Examples are following someone walking along a street, following a bird in flight, or following a horse at a racetrack. It is always useful to stop panning towards the end of the clip, so that the subject exits off the end of the frame.   Panning is also used to record a scene that will not fit into the frame, even using wide-angle attachments (e.g. wide panoramic scenes).

Poor panning results in jerky picture sequences. These look bad and result in poorer compression ratios. If no tripod is available, the camcorder should be held firmly against the body, elbows against the sides of the body, with the hips being swivelled to follow the movement.

A panning sequence should start and end with a stationary shot. This aids the audience in placing the background and prevents travel sickness!   If used with a telephoto converter, the rapid panning of a panoramic view produces a dramatic effect in the direction of the panning.

Tilting is used to follow vertical movement (e.g. a rocket taking off, a kite being launched, someone climbing a rock face).   It can also be used to scan a large vertical object (e.g. scanning the Empire State Building from ground level to the tip of the top tower).

Care has to be taken as the tilt may result in the lens being pointed directly at the sky, with the resulting problems with the camera's automatic exposure system as mentioned under 'Lighting'.

Tracking/Crabbing

Zooming is carried out with the camcorder remaining stationary, while it is rotated in a horizontal or vertical direction. Tracking involves physically moving the camera during the recording. Similarly, a crab is a movement of the camera to the left or right during a recording. These are regularly seen in movies and are powerful effects when carried out successfully.

Planning Considerations

The script for a multimedia video shoot is largely determined by the overall specification of the project. That does not mean that the content of the video shoot should not be planned in detail. The check list on the next page provides some suggestions for those planning a shoot at an external location. Some of the points are mundane, such as checking equipment, organising transport and checking that the people to be filmed will be present at the agreed time. However, consider the consequences if any of these checks failed.

The checklist looks at the mechanical and technical factors in preparing for a recording, but even more important is planning the content of the session. The storyboard is there to help prevent errors and to ensure that the final video content matches the needs of the larger project.

Storyboard

This subject is covered in the chapter on design, but some aspects also apply for video shooting. A simple recording of a two-minute interview seems straightforward enough. But, consider having to visit a factory hundreds of miles away, to shoot clips of their production process for an educational or promotional production. The visit has been specially arranged, so that a supervised visit with the safety officer and production manager is present. The visit involves general and close up shots of the equipment and structured interviews with the key operators and controllers. A storyboard is an essential part of the video shoot, as returning to shoot an overlooked piece of equipment or a forgotten question in an interview cannot easily be returned to.

The storyboard would also tell the camera operator details of the individual clips (e.g. factory in wide angle, drilling machine in close-up, finished product in macro, etc). Even smaller shoots benefit from a little planning. Even a two-minute interview with a rock star after a concert can go badly wrong, if you forget to ask the big question. As in other aspects of multimedia, it is not only about planning the look. The content is vital and may well involve some research before shooting. Other events, such as a birthday party or a wedding would benefit from having its video coverage planned.

The contribution of the storyboard to the technical performance of the file compression systems is covered later.

Software packages, such as *'Script Werx'* and *'Story Board Artist'* are designed for script and storyboard creation, while *'The Executive Producer'* also provides scene logging facilities.

Continuity

Continuity is ensuring that the finished product appears as a single cohesive piece of work. Everyone loves to spot the deliberate mistake in films and television plays. For example, the ones where the pirate has a patch over his left eye in one scene and over his right eye in the next scene.

This is an obvious continuity error and large productions hire staff to do nothing other than check for such possible errors. This may also be an issue for shooting video for multimedia, when the video recordings are spaced out over several days.

Continuity is also an issue at the editing stage, to maintain a smooth logical flow of clips. For example, it would be wrong to insert an interview with the company sales director in the middle of a set of clips detailing how a product is manufactured.

Again, viewer expectations shape the filming continuity. If a plane is leaving London for New York, it should fly off the left of the screen and not the right, as New York is to the west of London.

Some extra clips should be taken to aid the future editing process. These are particularly helpful for providing the sense of variety and perspective when filming is carried out with a single camera. This could include, for example, shots of an interviewee's hands (a *'cutaway'*), shots of an audience and general local ambience shots (broken windows, graffiti, local skyline, passing traffic, commuters, etc). Sometimes, extra shots can be recorded later such as the interviewer nodding wisely (a *'noddy'* shot) or giving a smile of encouragement.

Recording Check List

This is a suggestion list. Not all points need to carried out and not necessarily in the order given.

Checks before the shoot

Permission to shoot at the location (if required).	
Permission to shoot the subject(s), if appropriate.	
Confirmation that any person(s) appearing in a shoot will be present at the agreed time/date.	
Confirmation that the location is safe for the subject, camera operator and any equipment.	
Location identified of electrical wall outlets for lighting, camera and other equipment.	
Check that all the equipment works, including power extension cables, power strips, lighting, light meter, microphone, headphones, and a mobile phone (for emergencies)	
Confirm that likely ancillary materials (electrical tape, basic tools, tripod, stands, reflectors, diffusers, and spare bulbs) are packed.	
Clean the camera (use air brush cleaner to blow away dust and fibres, use anti-static cleaning cloth or lint free tissues to clean the lens, in worst cases use lens cleaning fluid)	
Check that the camcorder batteries are charged and there are adequate spares.	
With new cassettes, fast forward to the end of the tape and then rewind	
Transport for people and equipment is organised.	

On site activities

Check location for unexpected problems (crowds, weather, etc.)	
Screw camera to tripod and locate at best viewing point.	
If capturing direct to disk, connect the camera to the computer capture card and run capture software.	
Frame the subject according the specified storyboard shot size.	
Check the lighting. Set up any additional lighting required.	
Focus on the subject. Check if auto or manual focus will be required.	
Record the clips, according the storyboard instructions.	
Log each shot.	
When a cassette is full, rewind it, remove it, label it, and write protect it (DV cassettes have a write-protect lever).	
Store tapes in dust-free container in a condensation-free area. Store cassettes on their side or on their end, to minimise the risk of the tape slipping off the spools.	

Digitising Video

The video source material has to be converted into computer files that can be stored and manipulated. The video source will usually be a camera source (such as a camcorder or webcam) or a VCR. Their video outputs can sometimes be connected directly to the computer's parallel port or USB port, but all professional results are obtained by feeding their output into a special card designed for the purpose. This is called a *'video capture card'* and is an add-on card that is fitted into one the computer's expansion slots (ISA or PCI slots for older cards and AGP slots for newer cards). Some have analogue connections for use with composite and S-Video inputs, while others use digital connections to a FireWire source.

Video Sources

There are two sources of video material:

Live Capture

The video data is captured live from the camcorder or webcam to the computer, for storage to hard disk. The material does not require to be first recorded to cassette tape. The advantage of this method for analogue capture is improved quality, as the cassette recording is always inferior to the direct output from the camera. Live capture is at its best in controlled situations, where the recording can be repeated until the desired effect is obtained. Examples are studio footage and location footage where planning time and human resources are available. Since the computer equipment has to be set up on location, live capture has serious practical limitations.

Digitising Pre-recorded material

Most material will come in the form of pre-recorded camcorder cassette tape. This is essential for uncontrolled situations where a second take is impossible, or where it is impossible to set up computer equipment. Examples include sports events, concerts, holiday footage and vox pop interviews.

There is often a need to use previous footage that was recorded on older equipment and copied to VHS tape. Although digital video is becoming very popular, there will still be a large source of material being recorded for the foreseeable future in S-Video and BetacamSP format.

Capture Methods

There is a range of hardware/software options when capturing video:

Capture raw video without any compression

No compression is used and therefore the resulting files are very large but the data is of the highest quality. This is an ideal format for quality archives and provides the best material for further processing and editing, with the decision on the compression method being decided later. Indeed, the same source material may be required at different quality levels - perhaps one version for web site use and another version for CD distribution. Storing the uncompressed version allows flexibility in the later use of the clip. The down side, of course, is the amount of storage required even for short video clips. The falling price of large hard disks, CD-R, tape drives and DVD-RAM make this less of a problem than it once was.

Use this method for analogue systems, wherever possible.

Two-Step Digitisers

This was an older system where the video input was saved directly to disk in uncompressed form. The package's CODEC (compression/decompression) system then created a smaller version by compressing the saved file. The CODEC was implemented by a dedicated chip or by a software program. This two-step system was useful for less-powerful computers that could not cope with simultaneous reading and compression of data. It was a more laborious method and required more free disk space than single-step digitisers, as it had to store both the uncompressed version and the newly created compressed version. An example of this type of approach was the VideoSpigot capture card.

Capture and compress in real-time, using software compression.

Single-step digitisers convert the video input into a digitised form, compress it and save it - all in a single stage. There is no need to first store it in uncompressed form. Single-step compression is also known as *'On-the-Fly'* compression since it occurs in real time.

Using software compression means that the process is heavily dependent on the speed of the computer's CPU and the efficiency of the other system components such as the hard disk. If the computer cannot keep up with the amount of data coming from the capture card, some of the data is discarded and this results in dropped frames.

Capture and compress in real-time, using hardware compression.
An even more efficient system results from using hardware for single-step compression. The chip on the capture board does all the compression processing and relieves the computer's CPU of that work. These always produce better results than software implementations. Most capture cards provide hardware facilities for compression and examples are given later.   The most common hardware capture compression systems are the M-JPEG and MPEG formats.

Capture in all-digital format
A growing number of digital video cameras are providing FireWire outputs (see the chapter on computer technology).   These cameras carry out the analogue to digital conversion internally and pass on the digital information directly to the PC.   This conversion occurs in real time and removes a previous bandwidth bottleneck.   The stored video can remain in DV format or can be compressed. Manufacturers are working on high-performance VCRs that have FireWire connections, allowing them to record high-resolution material.   This will be a future source of pre-recorded material.
Use this digital system, if it can be afforded.

Capture connections
There has been an expanding market in devices to interface computers to camcorders.   They are of varying quality, power, features and price but are broadly of three interface designs.

Through the parallel port
The camcorder is connected to the device and the device is plugged into the computer's parallel port. The software supplied with the device allows it to read in the video data via the parallel port lines for digitisation.
Example devices are:
- The Pinnacle MP10, with composite and S-Video inputs. It captures as MPEG-1, with a converter to AVI. It also provides composite out, for connection to a VCR or television.
- Most older webcams.
- The FutureTel Video Shpinx Pro also captures directly (real-time compression) as MPEG-1.
- The Logitech QuickCam captures 352x288 at 15fps
- The Datek QuickVideo DVC1 captures at up to 30fps, using on the fly compression.

Through the USB port
The camcorder is connected to the device and the device connects to one of the computer's USB ports. Since most older computers do not have USB ports, they would have to be fitted with a USB adaptor card to uses these devices.
Example devices are:
- All newer webcams,
- The VideoBlaster WebCam III, captures VGA at 15fps, or 352x288 (MPEG-1) at 30fps.
- The VideoBlaster WebCamGo also captures VGA at 15fps, but has 4MB of onboard RAM so that it can also operate as a standalone handheld digital camera.
- The Philips PCA645VC CIF captures at 15fps and has a built-in mike.
- The Belkin adaptor, has both composite and S-Video inputs.

Through Capture Cards
Initially, capture cards were add-ons to the graphics card that fed the monitor. The two were usually connected by a ribbon cable through the *'feature connector'* extension port on many graphics cards. This is a pin-out on the internal circuitry of the card called the *'feature'* connector, which can be attached by a ribbon cable to other cards such as video capture cards, full-motion video cards and genlocking equipment.   Now, some cards function both as a normal graphics card and as a player/recorder of full-motion video.   These capture cards combine the capture facility with the normal 2D and 3D acceleration expected from a graphics card. Examples are the Matrox Marvel G400 and the 3dfx Voodoo3 3500 TV. The more professional end of the market (e.g. Pinnacle DV500, DC1000, MotoDV Studio) uses a separate card for the capture process.   Sometimes, as with the Pinnacle Studio DV, the separate card is used to achieve a low selling price.
There are three basic capture types - analogue only, digital only, and analogue + digital.

Analogue cards

The diagram shows the process of capturing via an analogue capture card.

The analogue signal is taken from the camcorder's composite or S-video output socket and fed into the capture card. The ADC (Analogue to Digital Converter) converts the varying analogue signal into a

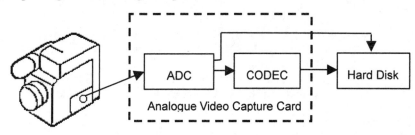

corresponding set of digital values. These values can then be stored directly to disk in uncompressed format. Alternatively, the digital signal can be fed through a CODEC where it is compressed before saving to disk.

Until the coming of digital camcorders, this was the dominant method of capture video footage. This system will remain in force for a long time, due to the number of analogue camcorders in use and the amount of footage already available in analogue format.

Example devices are:
- The ATI All-in-Wonder Pro 128 is a PCI bus device with a built-in TV tuner and TV/VCR output.
- The DATAVideo MJ600 has composite and S-Video in/out, and captures full PAL in M-JPEG.
- The Marvel G400 TV has a built in TV tuner and composite and S-Video in/out. It uses hardware capture to M-JPEG, with software compression to MPEG-1 and MPEG-2.
- The 3dfx Voodoo3 3500 TV provides real-time capture to AVI or MPEG-1 and MPEG-2, all limited to a resolution of 320x228.
- The Miro DC50 offers component video along with composite and S-Video, aiding use with BetaCam SP studio equipment.
- The Fast AV Master 2000 provides composite and S-Video in/out, and captures to M-JPEG at 4:1 compression with the superior 4:2:2 sampling.

FireWire digital connections

These cards can only be used with digital camcorders using FireWire (also known as *'iLink'*) connectors. For simplicity and cheapness, many FireWire cards only provide FireWire inputs, while some provide in and out. Since the data is always shifted round in digital format between the camcorder and card (and possibly back again), the card has no ADC chip. This vastly improves signal quality as explained earlier (see the section on camcorder formats).

Like the analogue cards, there is the option to save the video data in uncompressed or compressed format. Example devices are:
- The Pinnacle StudioDV can output as DV, AVI, MPEG-1 or RealVideo.
- The Pinnacle Studio DV captures as DV or using an Indeo 5.1 software codec. Outputs as AVI, RealVideo or MPEG.
- The MotoDV Studio has both in and out connections and saves as a QuickTime movie.
- The Digital Origin EditDV works in QuickTime rather than Video For Windows and overcomes the 2GB file size limit.
- The Digital Origin IntroDV is another QuickTime only version. It uses the same capture card but ptovides less powerful software. Neither model offers MPEG-1, MPEG-2 or AVI output.

Some cards have internal FireWire connectors, for connecting to future FireWire devices such as FireWire hard disks.

The Adaptec Ultra HotConnect 8945 has an Ultra-Wide SCSI connection on its card, so that SCSI hard drives can be connected directly to the capture card.

Digital/Analogue

Most cards are FireWire only or analogue only. Some handle both types of input. This supports the highest quality for new digital recordings, while maintaining the ability to digitise old VHS and S-Video footage. These cards have analogue to digital converters, but they are only used when an analogue signal is being processed.

Example devices are:
- The Pinnacle DC1000 captures straight to editable MPEG-2 (see later). It provides composite video, S-Video, audio and FireWire inputs.

- The Pinnacle DV500 captures and holds in native DV format, then data is output as DV, AVI 1 or AVI 1.1 with MPEG-2 compression. It provides composite video, S-Video, audio and FireWire inputs. The DV output connects to a camcorder's digital input or to a FireWire digital VCR (there are currently very few in circulation).
- The Matrox RT2000 provides composite video, S-Video, audio and FireWire inputs. It captures I-frame MPEG-2 up to 25Mbit/sec. It outputs as GOP (group of Pictures) MPEG-2 for DVD, VideoCD or streaming.
- The Fast DV Master provides composite video, S-Video, audio and FireWire inputs. It captures in native DV, with the ability to convert with any chosen codec.

Breakout Boxes

The problem with all add-on cards is that their sockets are located at the rear of the computer case. This is not a problem for connecting a mouse or a keyboard that is not removed or replaced very often. However, it is a big headache for users of capture cards, as they wish to plug and unplug various devices (camcorders, VCRs, video decks, audio equipment, etc) on a fairly regular basis. They do not wish to haul their computer out of its corner to access these rear sockets.

The solution lies in providing a breakout box. This is a box with a cable that connects to a socket on the capture card. The box is then brought round to the front of the computer where its sockets can handle the range of audio and video connections that it supports. The swapping of devices to the breakout box becomes an easy task.

Capture cards that supply breakout boxes include the Pinnacle DV500, Matrox G400 TV, Matrox RT2000, 3dfx Voodoo3 3500 TV, Fast DV Master, and Miro DC50.

Video Stills

Devices are produced that are dedicated to capturing a still picture from a movie clip. Examples are the Logitech *'Snappy'* and the *'Video Snapshot'*, which are both external models that connect to the parallel port.

It is difficult to capture a precise frame, as there is usually a delay between seeing the frame, clicking the mouse and getting a frozen image. This applies to video direct from the camcorder or coming from a VCR's videotape. Freezing the videotape usually makes matters worse, as most VCRs produce a very poor picture in frozen mode.

The principle of still capture is shown in the diagram. The image is stored in RAM chips within the video capture card before being fed to the monitor for display. The video RAM in the card has its contents automatically updated and the user has no control over this process. However, the software supplied with the video capture card allows the user to prevent its video RAM from being updated, thereby *'freezing'* the current stored picture. If the captured frame is satisfactory the user can store the image as a graphics file, in formats such as TIFF, BMP and PCX.

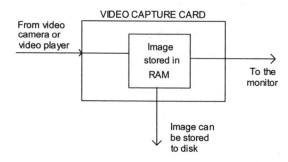

This method is satisfactory for hobby or general use.

A much more precise still capture is obtained during the editing process. Video editing software takes an entire video clip and can display every individual frame of the clip in a scrolling window. The user can then select the exact frame required and the software can save it in the chosen graphic format. This technique is covered in the chapter on video editing.

Dual Stream

Until now, transition effects and titling were usually rendered in the editing process (see next chapter). The new Dual Stream capture card has two hardware CODEC streams and this allows:

- A bitmap in one stream and the video in the other - real-time static titles.
- Video in both streams - blending two clips for real-time transitions, such as wipes and dissolves.
- Video in Video.

Since this merging is taking place during the digitising process, there are no long waits as occurs with rendering during the later editing process. This system was available a few years ago in the DPS Perception RT, at a cost of around £9,000 and the £10,000 Matrox DigiSuite (since reduced in price). This facility now appears in the Pinnacle DV500 Pinnacle CD1000, and the Matrox RT2000.

The Capture Process

When a video clip is being captured for use on the web, no great pressure is put upon the computer components.   The video clip will be of small resolution and will have a low frame rate.   This means that the amount of data being transferred around the computer is comparatively small.

Over time, users constantly demand improvements in multimedia performance -including bigger and smoother video clips.   The space required to store one minute of video is becoming ever larger. However, buying a larger disk drive does not solve the problem. The recording system still has only one minute to move around this larger set of data. This places greater demands on all components in the system.   The recording process involves a series of data transfers - from the camcorder to the capture card, to the computer's memory, through the CPU to the disk controller and finally to the disk. The system is only as powerful as its weakest link.   The *'data transfer rate'* of each component must be high enough to cope with the fastest demands placed upon it.   Temporary slowdowns in the data transfer rate, anywhere in this chain, would result in lost frames while recording

The selection of components for a multimedia computer system was covered in the first chapter.

There are two problem areas for video recording:

- The hardware may not be capable of handling the highest data rate.
- The software may not be optimised for recording.

Check the hardware

Check that the hard disk is fast enough to handle video transfers, especially with older hard disks. SCSI drives tend to have fewer problems with data rates, but UDMA disks are improving all the time.   Write to an AV disk if possible as they provide guaranteed uninterrupted data transfer rates.

The disk controller interface also has to be high performance, with IDE being replaced by UltraDMA or SCSI-2 or even SCSI-UW.

The computer's processor should be spending most of its time controlling the capture process.   Any unnecessary interruptions to this process could result in dropped frames.

The following steps should minimise unwanted interruptions:

- Use Scandisk to check and isolate any disk surface errors.   Once the disc surface has been checked, and any possible faulty sectors isolated, the Recycle Bin should be emptied.
- The disk should now be defragmented, to minimise the number of head movements occurring inside the drive.
- If possible, the captured data should be saved to an empty drive or partition.
- Put a disk, any disk, in the computer's floppy, CD-ROM and ZIP drives. This saves the computer checking the drives at regular intervals.
- Turn off the printer.
- Disable a network card, if one exists.

Use a sound card with a good SNR (see the chapter on audio). Avoid using sound facilities that are built in to computer motherboards, as they generally have inferior performances to add-on cards. Some video capture cards include audio capture on the card to aid the synchronisation of audio and video data.

When the hardware has been tested, the video source should be connected to the capture card.   This may be a camcorder, VCR, or MiniDisc player, as required.

Prepare the software

There are other software steps that can be taken to avoid unwanted computer activities that might interfere with the smooth flow of data during the capture process.

- Ensure that all devices are using the latest drivers.
  These can be downloaded from the manufacturer's web site on the Internet, if necessary.
- Close all applications, apart from those required for the capture process.
- Turn off screen saver.
- Turn off the clock.
- Set the virtual memory to off.
- Enable 32-bit addressing.
- Enable write caching on the drive, and disable read-ahead optimisation
- Disable write-behind caching for all drives.
- Set the monitor to full colour.
  This prevents the real time translation of the video stream to fewer colours from slowing down the CPU.

Run the capture software

The exact steps for capturing video clips depend upon the hardware and software in use. It is possible to capture through Video for Windows' VidCap, through the utility supplied with the capture card (e.g. the software supplied with the Matrox 400) or through the video editing package such Avid Cinema or Adobe Premiere. The capture format available depends upon the choices offered by the system but might include native DV, uncompressed video, M-JPEG, MPEG-1, MPEG-2, etc. Where the content is being used in the later editing process, an uncompressed option should be chose. Where a clip is being taken from a VCR, the content may already be in satisfactory condition and the capture process can chosen to digitise and store in a compressed format.

Batch capture

A videocassette will probably contain a collection of video clips and it is a common practice to keep back winding, looking for the start of a particular clip. The constant play and rewind gradually scratches the tape surface and degrades the signal. It also produces excessive wear on the heads.

Some capture software supports a batch capture facility where the software recognises the start and finish points of each clip and saves all the clips to hard drive in a continuous operation, without further operator intervention. This is a great time saver, but it assumes that there is plenty of disk drive space to store all the clips. Since disk drives are now cheap, this is an efficient way to carry out mundane tasks. The clips are easily deleted or clipped after they are saved as disk files. For more control, some software supports edit decision lists, where the operator can choose which clips to capture and only those are saved to disk.

Capture at highest resolution

The user has control over the resolution that the incoming video will be digitised to. The highest resolution should be chosen, as the final resolution can be chosen after editing. The disadvantage of this choice is the larger file size. This results in greater storage needs and slower editing, as there is more data to be moved around. The advantage is greater quality. The high quality clip can be archived for future use at any resolution. A high-resolution clip can always be converted to a lower-resolution clip for web or other use. In fact, the scaling down process averages out adjacent pixels reducing video noise and improving the compression ratio. Most video clips suffer from *'overscan'* (sometimes referred to as *'edge blanking'*). These video clips have to be cropped before use. If the clip were captured at the desired final size, the cropping would result in the clip being smaller than required. Scaling up to the desired size would introduce unnecessary picture degradation. Capturing at the higher resolution allows for cropping before scaling to the desired resolution, maintaining picture quality.

Capture at highest quality

The capture software provides user control over the capture settings. One control allows the compression ratio to be set. Often, there is a single *'Quality'* control slider that sets up the file resolution, frame rate and compression ratio in a single operation. There is often control over individual elements. The example shown is the compression control for the Matrox G400 TV capture software.

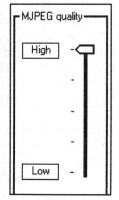

The highest quality possible should be selected, even if the final destination for the file is only the web. If possible, capture in uncompressed mode. Like the resolution mentioned above, the compression CODEC and compression ratio can always be decided after editing.

If a file is captured with an AVI CODEC, it introduces artifacts into the file. Subsequent MPEG compression is therefore less effective, resulting in larger file sizes and extra noise. So, always capture video uncompressed, if the intention is to have MPEG as the final destination.

The Data Rate

The *'Quality'* slider of a CODEC produces a range of options:

- The *'High'* end of scale produces low compression, high image quality and high data rates.
- The *'Low'* end of the scale produces highly compressed, poorer quality images at a lower data rate.
- Intermediate settings on the slider produce files with values between these extremes.

If the slider is set to, say, a compression value of 20:1, it will compress all parts of the video stream by that same amount. However, not all parts of the clip may require compression. Some scenes contain simple content detail while others contain complex content. The illustration shows the varying rate of a typical AVI file, displayed using a facility provided in Adobe Premiere. A fixed compression ratio could

easily result in one part of the clip being compressed unnecessarily, while other parts are not sufficiently compressed.   This degrades the picture in the sections with simple content and introduces artifacts in the sections with complex content.   Both parts of the clip are being treated inefficiently and producing a poorer quality final result than is possible.

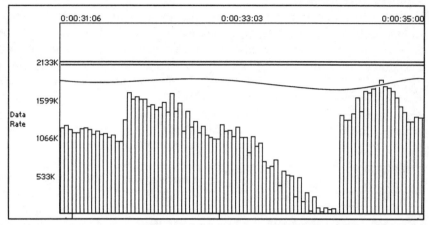

A better approach is to set the maximum data rate for the clip.   All parts of the clip with content that would fit within that limit are left untouched, while the other sections are compressed.   This improves the quality of the simple sections and minimises the introduction of artifacts in complex sections. If the chosen CODEC cannot compress to required data rate, the complex content sections will produce data rates in excess of the maximum set by the user.   The solution in that case, is to use another CODEC with a higher maximum compression ratio.   The alternative is to set a lower maximum and accept a lower quality than was originally anticipated.

2GB File Limit on AVI

One of the great obstacles to video editors is the limit of 2GB that is placed on saving AVI files.   This limit was initially due to the 16-bit FAT file system used by DOS. It was carried over into early versions of Windows.   Although Windows 95 onwards used a 32-bit FAT system and could handle beyond 2GB, the code for Video for Windows was not re-written to suit.   Therefore, the 2Gbyte file limit for AVIs is imposed by Video for Windows and does not apply to a non-AVI format such as native DV.

This is not a regular problem, as a project is often composed from a collection of smaller files, for ease of edit and assembly.   However, there are occasions when no editing is required, such as the simple copying of a videotape format to digital file format.

Various attempts have been made to get around this problem.

Some editing software can daisy chain lots of AVIs into an apparently seamless production when output to a VCR.   The Pinnacle DV300, for example, includes a Premiere plug-in that plays a seamless list of clips to screen or to DV out (for a DV recorder).

The software supplied with the Canopus DVRaptor allows the batch capture of a long videotape into a set of sub-2GB files and a scene list is automatically built for referencing individual file clips.

The new AVI 1.1 format uses OpenDML to provide for file sizes that extend to Terabytes.   However, there is some debate over whether the limitations of Windows 98 currently restricts this to 3.9GB. The Pinnacle DC1000 can save in AVI 1.1 format, as can the Pyro Digital Video card.   They both use Microsoft's DirectShow.

Test Captures

It is best to make a small test recording before committing to a long capture session. This checks the efficiency of the system and ensures that the capture settings are not greater than the ability of the computer. Problems are shown up as dropped frames. Most capture software will produce reports on the number of frames captured during a session and will report on any dropped frames. Playing back files with dropped frames shows up as jerks in the smooth playback.   The test also shows if the equipment is of sufficient quality (no algorithm artifacts, no excessive camera/capture card noise).

Backup

The chapter on Windows stressed the importance of backups.   This is true of all media but some are more important than others.   It may be possible to reconstruct correspondence, meeting notes, scripts, and even Director scripts. But, material that is time sensitive (e.g. a football match, an interview with an American personality while in the UK, etc) cannot be replaced.   Backups are even more important in these cases.   If possible, the original videocassette should be retained, labelled and stored.   The video files can be archived to tape drives, CD-R, or Zip drives.   See the chapter on Windows for more details.

Video Storage

Digitised full-motion video can easily occupy huge amounts of hard disk space. The chapter on screen technology covered the storage requirements for a single picture frame at different resolutions.   Video clips are stored (i.e. saved to disk) and played back between 15 and 30 individual screens per second.

The storage capacity per second of uncompressed video can be calculated thus:

File Size = Bit Depth x Screen Resolution x Frames/Sec

This is divided by 8 to get the answer in bytes, divided by 1024 to get the answer in KBs and divided again by 1024 to get the answer in MBs.

So, one second at 256-colour (i.e. 8 bits) VGA (i.e. 640x480) at a 15fps screen update would require

640 x 480 x 8 x 15 / 8 / 1024 / 1024 = 4.39MB

Number of colours	Screen Resolution	Frame Rate	Storage/Sec
256	640 x 480	15	4.39MB
256	800 x 600	15	6.86MB
256	1024 x 768	15	11.25MB
256	640 x 480	25	7.32MB
256	800 x 600	25	11.44MB
256	1024 x 768	25	18.75MB
16.78m	1024 x 768	30	67.5MB
16.78m	1600 x 1200	30	164.79MB
256	352 x 288	25	2.41MB
16.78m	352 x 288	25	7.25MB
16.78m	720 x 576	25	29.66MB

The chart shows the amount of storage required for a range of popular displays.

The smallest figure for a full screen image is 4.39MB, while the professional performance figure is around 165MB per second! The two bottom chart entries describe the resolution of MPEG-1 in its uncompressed form. The saving and playing back of live video involves not only the storage but also the transfer of huge amounts of data; this requires a fast hard disk, a fast CPU and a fast video system.

These storage figures are not practical and a number of methods are introduced to reduce this size:

- Using only a portion of the screen to display the video.   If the video occupies a quarter of the screen area, it only needs a quarter of the storage space.   This is commonly used on CDs to accommodate the low performance of most disks/CPUs/video cards.
- Reducing the colour palette to 256 colours may mean a barely noticeable loss of colour gradation, but would result in a video clip that is a third of the size of a 16.78m colour clip.
- Lowering the frame rate at which the picture is displayed. This makes savings but the picture is jerkier.
- Compressing the files for storage and decompressing them when they are to be played.   Unlike the other three methods, compression need not produce any deterioration in picture quality.   The user has the option to make even bigger savings at the expense of some picture quality.

Compression

Compression involves the restructuring and possible elimination of data to achieve a smaller file size. This restructuring is carried out by a CODEC (compressor/decompressor). This is an engine that shrinks the files on saving and expands them again when they are to be used.   CODECs can be implemented in either hardware or software.   Hardware CODECs are more expensive but, because they use dedicated chips instead of the computer's CPU time, they are significantly more efficient.

At its best, compression may result in a smaller file size with no loss in picture quality. If a file saved in a compressed format can be uncompressed to produce a picture that is identical bit-by-bit with the original, it is described as 'lossless compression'.   The GIF format for graphic files and the GIF89a format for animated GIFs are examples of lossless compression.

Files can be compressed to a greater degree if some loss of detail is acceptable.   Since the human eye cannot detect small detail changes, 'lossy compression' techniques are the types found in most compression systems.   Lossless compressed files are used for high-quality images or for archiving of quality original images.

If the degree of compression is not too great, the loss of quality will not be noticed.   This is termed 'perceptually lossless compression'.   The human eye is used to viewing objects from a variety of distances, from the side of the eye and through adverse conditions such as rain, fog and darkness.   The human brain adjusts to cope with these degraded images. So, if the compressed video results in images that correspond to the brain's ability to compensate, the losses are not perceived by the viewer. Indeed, sometimes a small degree of detail loss is perceived as an improvement in the picture.   The picture is seen to be 'cleaned up' with some of the 'grain' being removed.

Increasing the compression and lowering the image quality will eventually result in visual artifacts (e.g. blockiness, the removal of edges to objects, the creation of spurious edges, etc.) that will be identified by the viewer as a poor quality picture.

The degree of compression can be altered to suit the purpose of the final product. For example, a video file destined for placing on the web will be compressed further than a video for use on a CD. The poorer quality is traded for faster Internet transfer.

Noise and compression

The software cannot tell the difference between fine picture details and general unwanted video noise. It will process both through its compression algorithm.   Any fine picture detail lowers the compression ratio and this is often a price worth paying for picture quality. However, noise in the signal also lowers the compression ratio, without adding anything to the picture quality.   If test recordings produce significant levels of noise, the camcorder, cables, and capture card should be individually tested, usually with a temporary replacement.   The higher the quality of the original clip, the greater the compression (less noise).   BetaCam SP is best, followed by DV, then the high band analogues, the low band analogues and finally the webcams.   Darker pictures result in more noise and less compression.

Noise and Artifacts

Artifacts are unwanted visual elements that appear on the picture and are the result of applying the CODEC algorithm.   Some algorithms produce more artifacts than others, in given situations.   The inability to maintain picture quality under all picture contents is shown in problems around the edges of objects and blockiness of diagonal surfaces.

Noise is the result of unwanted elements produced by the electronics of the hardware.   These are usually unwanted electrical signals, signals introduced by the electronic components in the camera or the video capture board.   Their position in the picture is more random than algorithm artifacts and appear as *'snow'* in the picture in worst cases.   Noise also describes the unwanted video data that is produced when the camcorder is unable to properly resolve a picture in low light conditions.

Storyboards and compression

The camera operator can ensure that the video is shot in sufficient light to reduce noise and improve compression.   Where a particularly small video file is required, extra care has to be taken at the storyboard stage to prevent camera operations that result in poorer compression.   Compression algorithms work less efficiently with scenes that contain a lot of detail or a lot of movement.   Careful attention should be paid to the amount of unnecessary detail that will appear in a scene. This may result in removing a very leafy plant from an office scene, or changing the heavily patterned curtains for a plainer set.   Shooting the subject in front of a plain backdrop such as a matt painted wall is recommended.   Alternatively, the camera can be adjusted to make the background out of focus.   Similarly, prevent the subject wearing fussy clothes, such as a herringbone jacket, paisley pattern blouse, or striped suit.

The question of movement is a little more difficult.   The less movement in the scene, the higher is the compression ratio.   The movement may come from the camera (panning, zooming) or from the subject.   However, a clip with little or no movement soon becomes uninteresting.   A balance has to be struck that reflects the nature of the clip.   A busy factory shop floor may make an interesting background for an interview with the company manager, but if the interview is being conducted in the factory car park, avoid a background of moving cars, people walking, trees blowing in the wind, etc. If a particularly animated object is to be filmed, shoot from further back if possible, as this reduces overall scene movement in the frame.

Using *'hard cuts'* during editing in place of fades, wipes, pans and dissolves will also improve compression.   These effects produce constantly changing frame contents (that's their purpose!).

Keeping the exposure control on manual reduces the problems of people moving in front of/away from windows and changing the automatic exposure.   The camcorder operator should stay on manual, or plan to avoid these light changes which reduce compression.

At the end of the day, these technical considerations have to be balanced with the dynamism created by fast moving video clips.

Two basic approaches

Data compression schemes are mostly based on the following techniques:

INTRAFRAME (Spacial Compression)	This considers each individual frame and discards any trivial data. This is the method used by RLE, DCT, VQ, JPEG and M-JPEG compression systems.
INTERFRAME (Temporal Compression)	This considers the differences between successive frames, removes the unchanged parts of the information and applies JPEG type compression on what is left. This is also called *'difference compression'* or *'delta compression'* and is used by the MPEG system.

Compression Methods ,

A range of techniques is employed to achieve file compression. CODECs will often employ more than one of these methods in its algorithm.

Run Length Encoding

Run Length Encoding (RLE) is available as a Windows CODEC and as a standalone video CODEC. The techniques are also incorporated into the Discrete Cosine Transform method (see later).

A single video frame consists of a long series of pixels that are displayed as a set of rows on the screen. Often, adjacent pixels will have identical colours. For example, part of a background may consist of a horizontal run of 20 identical pixel colours. RLE stores the length of the band rather than the individual pixels. If the colour of the pixel was represented by the number 19 then the uncompressed file would have to store the same pixel colour value 20 times as below:

19 19 19 19 19 19 19 19 19 19 19 19 19 19 19 19 19 19 19 19

An RLE file would store it as:

20 19 (i.e. 20 pixels of the colour 19).

This technique works best with images that use relatively few colours and have little detail (such as cartoons and animations). 24-bit real-world images contain lots of detail and many colours. The constant change of colours means that a long run of the same colour rarely appears - and the compression is poor as a result.

Discrete Cosine Transform

This is the most widely used compression method and is found in JPEG, M-JPEG, MPEG-1, MPEG-2, MPEG-3 and the video conferencing standards such as H.261 and H.263.

A *'transform'* converts data to a form that that can be represented with less data. RLE analyses the colours of pixels in a sequence, looking for runs of the same colour. DCT recognises that there will also be great similarities between the <u>rows</u> that make up the completed picture. So, if there is a lot of blue sky in one row of the picture, there is also likely to lots of blue sky in the next row.

DCT, therefore, works on blocks of the picture that are 8 pixels by 8 pixels in size. The differences are then quantised and, since many of these produce a value of zero, the storage requirements are reduced. In addition, a higher quantisation factor is applied to the higher DCT coefficients (i.e. the ones representing the higher frequencies) as the human eye does not normally see these components. The resulting sets of coefficients is then Run Length Encoded before saving.

Vector Quantisation

This technique is found in Cinepak and Indeo 3.2 compression.

This system also divides the image up into blocks - in this case 4 pixels by 4 pixels. The make up of each block is examined (i.e. what colours are included and in what order). The aim is to find identical, or similar, block compositions. After scanning all the blocks in the picture, a lookup table is then created, containing the structure of the most commonly found pixel colours/layouts. Each individual block is then assigned the value of block in the lookup table that most closely resembles the actual block's makeup. In some cases (e.g. solid blocks of colour) there will be an exact match. In other cases, a block is given a lookup value that is closest to one in the table. Since there is not always an exact match, Vector Quantisation is inherently a lossy technique.

The analysis of the picture is CPU intensive (there is a lot of number crunching going on) and is therefore slow to encode. However, the existence of the lookup table in the saved file means that the decode algorithm works quickly.

Discrete Wavelet Transform

This technique is found in Intel Indeo versions 5.x and 5x, and in the VDOWave CODEC.

Each frame image is passed through a series of high pass and low pass filters to separate the basic low-resolution picture (the low frequency components) and the fine details (the high frequency components). This allows the CODEC to identify and remove redundant information. Vector quantisation is then applied to the resulting signal to achieve compression.

DWT does not produce the *'blocking'* or *'tiling'* artifacts common with other methods. However, like DCT, increasing compression leads to eventual blurring and ringing artifacts at sharp edges.

Motion Compensation

All lossy compression techniques assume that these will be some *'redundancy'* - detail within the picture that can be omitted without the viewer noticing. All the above methods search for *'spatial redundancy'* - areas of a single frame where adjacent pixels have the same colour.

Motion compensation also adds in the concept of *'temporal redundancy'* - that an area of a frame will be identical to the same area in subsequent frames.   This is a valid assumption for much of the time. Consider an average movie clip.   While there may be some movement in the foreground, the background often remains unchanged for longish periods.   If the background remained static for 10 seconds, then those areas of the screen will be storing the same colour information repeatedly for 250 frames.   This requires a lot of storage space for information that is static.

Motion compensation techniques seek out these unchanging areas and their values are not included in the frame being saved.   When an area's content is altered, this is detected and only the changes are included in the frame being saved.   This technique is used with QuickTime's *'Sorenson Video'* CODEC but the most well known system using motion compression is the MPEG format.

MPEG

The Moving Pictures Experts Group was founded in 1988 by the International Standards Association. Their remit was the production of standard covering the transmission of digital video and audio.

The MPEG-1 standard was published in 1990, the MPEG-2 standard was published in 1995 and MPEG-4 appeared in 1997.   With MPEG compression, the frames that make up the video picture are made up from three differently coded types:

I-Frames

The Key frame, or I-frame (Intracoded Frame), is always the first frame of a video clip.   As such, it has to store the entire picture information for the frame.   The only compression on the frame is spatial compression (using a form of DCT JPEG compression).

P-Frames

The Delta Frame, or P-Frame (Predictive-coded Frame) follows the first frame of the clip.   Its contents are dependent on the content of the previous frame.   It employs a combination of temporal and spatial redundancy, along with motion vectors that chart the movement of groups of pixels in a scene (e.g. a bouncing ball or a bird's flight).   Motion vectors work on the basis that a frame is often composed of the same elements as the previous frame, expect in slightly different positions.   The frame contents are examined as 16 x16 blocks.   The distance that an element has travelled, horizontally and vertically, is estimated and stored as vector information.   The total information is used to construct the new frame from the changes or *'deltas'* in the frame compared to the previous frame's contents.

The P-Frame does not store the detail of an entire picture - it stores the instructions that allow a frame to be constructed; the P-Frame uses the information stored in the previous frame to build a new frame.

The second frame of a clip will be a P-Frame that uses the data from the first (I-Frame) frame to construct the frame to be displayed.   The third frame will also be a P-Frame and it will alter the picture constructed by the previous P-Frame, and so on.

Since the P-Frames contain only data on the changed areas (and even this is compressed), the I-Frames are much smaller than an P-Frames.

Maintaining Quality

Ideally, a video file should contain only one large I-Frame, with all other frames being the much smaller P-Frames.   This would produce the greatest amount of compression possible under this system.

However, as the predictive element in each P-Frame introduces some small error, the effect is accumulative.   To maintain picture quality, it is necessary to include extra I-Frames in the video stream. This introduces a freshly sampled complete picture at regular intervals as below:

I P P P P P I P P P P P I P P P P P I

Increasing the number of I-Frames in a file increases the file size but also improves its quality.   In practice, the repetition rate for I-Frames can be set by the user and is often around every 12 to 15 frames.

B-Frames

B frames (bi-directional frame) are frames that search for data from both past and future frames.   As such, they contain fewer instructions than P-Frames and are even smaller, providing even better compression.   A typical sequence, known as *'IPB encoding'* might be:

I B B P B B P B B P B B P B B P B B I

GOP (Group of Pictures)

The total sequence of frames from one I-Frame to the next is known as a GOP (Group of Pictures).
The video encoding is carried out on a Group of Pictures at a time. First the I-Frames are encoded, followed by the intermediate P-Frames, and finally the B-Frames are constructed using the B-Frame data. Motion compression provides the best compression when there is little change in the video scene. Since there is less change, there is less error drift, requiring fewer I-Frames (i.e. the GOP becomes longer). Clips with little movement, can have key frames inserted every 30 frames.

Conversely, if the clip has rapid scene changes and other major changes to the image (e.g. a recording of a Formula One race), extra I-Frames are required to maintain picture quality.

The repetition rate for key frames can be set during MPEG encoding. Also, extra I-frames can be added to fast-moving scenes during MPEG encoding.

Editable MPEG

MPEG files are difficult to edit, as intermediate frames have to be constructed to create the sequence of frames necessary for editing. Files constructed using IBP encoding are currently not able to be edited with any accuracy. The currently available software is unable to efficiently handle this format, as any attempt to cut between two B-Frames loses the information that is required to maintain the picture sequence.

A number of editable MPEG systems are available, using differing approaches to get round the problem. The Matrox RT2000 (as an option) and the Fast 601 overcome the problem by saving their MPEG files solely as a set of I-Frames. The EBU recommends that MPEG-2 video should be stored in I-frame only format for editing, even though it has a much poorer compression ratio resulting in a 50Mb/sec storage requirement. The Pinnacle DC1000 saves files using only I-Frames and P-Frames. Since both DVD and digital television use the full IBP format, the clip has to encoded into IBP for exporting for use in these media.

MPEG Versions

The <u>M</u>oving <u>P</u>ictures <u>E</u>xperts <u>G</u>roup format uses a complicated set of compression methods including spatial compression, Huffman coding and predictive compression - based on only saving the <u>differences</u> (or *'deltas'*) between successive frames. Depending on the quality and speed required, it may sometimes require expensive hardware, but can achieve surprising compression rates. Compression ratios up to 50:1 can be achieved before the picture quality deteriorates noticeably.

MPEG-1 Most systems were initially designed around MPEG-1 with data rates of around 1.4Mbps and frame rates up to 30fps. Its maximum bit rate is 1.856Mbits/sec. It provides the lowest common format as it can produce 340x240 at 30fps for American NTSC TV (or 352x288 at 25fps for European PAL TV) from a standard CD-ROM player. This is sometimes referred to as SIF - the Standard Interchange Format. It is also a common multimedia format. It produces a result similar to television's VHS quality, although it does not support fully interlaced video. Many video clips on CDs are designed for this format and don't therefore take advantage of the significant hardware improvements that modern PCs contain.

MPEG-2 MPEG-2 is a standard for higher quality with a resultant increase in data rates. It can deliver a maximum screen resolution of 720x576 and a maximum frame rate of 60 fps. MPEG-2 is the basis of DVD products. It supports both interlaced and non-interlaced (progressive) scanning. The increased demands of MPEG-2 have led to further improvements in component specifications.

MPEG-4 This is an emerging standard and the video part of the standard is available for Windows - but currently only with the QCIF picture size of 176x144. Primarily targeted at web, telephone and cellular phone markets.

MPEG-2 applications

Level	Size	bit-rate	Application
Low	352 x 288	4Mbits/sec	Consumer (e.g. CD White Book films, video games, SIF clips in CDs
Main	720 x 576	15-20Mbits/sec	Studio TV
High 1440	1440 x 1152	60-80Mbits/sec	HDTV
High	1920 x 1152	80-100Mbits/sec	Film production

Other applications include DBS (Direct Broadcast Satellite), DVD (Digital Versatile Disk) and VOD (Video on Demand). In the UK, it is sused by Sky, On Digital and digital cable companies.

Symmetrical/Asymmetrical CODECs

Most software CODECs require a great deal of computational time to compress a video clip, due to the complexity of the algorithm involved. So, for example, a ten second video clip takes much longer than ten seconds to compress. In these instances, the compression is not taking place in real time.

The decompression section of the CODEC is always much faster, as it applies a set formula to every file, regardless of frame video content. This allows the playback to run in real-time. When a CODEC takes longer to compress than decompress it is described as *'asymmetrical'*.

A CODEC with a long compression time is no use in real time situations such as single-pass compression capture cards, streamed video and video-conferencing applications. The compress and decompress times do not need to be perfectly symmetrical but the compress time has to at least happen in real time.

File Architectures

When discussing video file formats there are two separate issues:

The CODEC	This describes the way that the data is compressed and decompressed.
The Architecture	This describes the way that the file is packaged for delivery. This includes file format, CODEC used, playback format and packaging details for multiple tracks.

This means that Video for Windows (AVI) and QuickTime are examples of architectures, while Indeo and Cinepak are examples of CODECs. Confusion arises because the AVI architecture can encompass many different CODECs. The type of CODEC used to compress the file is embedded in the AVI or QuickTime file's header, to indicate the type of CODEC required to decompress the file.

AVI and QuickTime are architectures designed for CD, kiosk, web and general use, while RealVideo is an architecture specifically designed for web video use.

Microsoft has decided to replace Video for Windows with *'DirectShow'* and phase out AVI in favour of their new ASF (Advanced Streaming Format). DirectShow is built on top of DirectX and uses the normal Windows Media Player. ASF support began with Windows 98.

AVI Codec Types

The AVI (Audio Video Interleave) format is the Windows standard and is so-called because it stores the audio and video information as a single file, with the video data and audio being divided into blocks and interleaved in the file. Since both streams of data are stored next to each other in time, it aids the synchronisation process. Where video and audio files are held separately, the delays in reading both sets of data from disk and interpreting the separate streams leads to severe problems of keep the sound synchronised to the picture. AVI files can be in compressed or uncompressed format depending whether one of the compression algorithms (see below) has been applied them.

No software CODECs were supplied with Windows 3.1 and these had to be installed by the user.

Windows 95/98 Video for Windows comes with four CODECs pre-installed. These all result in files with *'AVI'* extension and are:

Cinepak : Developed by Apple for their SuperMac computers and now licensed to Microsoft, it is currently the most popular of the Video for Windows CODECs. It is also supplied with Apple's QuickTime.
It handles 8-bit colour (for animations and cartoons) and 24-bit (for everything else). This is a good general purpose CODEC for CD ROM distribution but has been replaced by more efficient CODECs for slow web data rates (below 30kbps).

Indeo This system was initially developed by Intel as a CODEC for capture cards based on the Intel i750 video processor chip. Indeo 3.x had a slightly better compression ratio and compression time than Cinepak but introduced more artifacts. AVI files processed with the Indeo CODEC have had both interframe compression and run length encoding techniques applied (see earlier). Indeo 4.x, now renamed Video Interactive 4, took advantage of the new improvements in Pentium technology, such as MMX, to improve performance and quality. It also introduced transparency masks for their clips. This is the same technique as *'chroma key'* (see chapter on video editing). Version 5.0 is aimed at web video by including progressive download (see QuickTime for details).

MSVC : The Microsoft Video Compressor, also known as Video 1. It was developed to use algorithms that place less pressure on the CPU. Although supported by cards such as the Black Widow Media Master Plus, it has not found a place in general use. This is probably because it only supports 256 or 32k colours.

RLE : Run Length Encoding takes a horizontal area of a colour and stores the length of the band rather than the individual pixels. This is very effective in animations where backgrounds are plain but produces poor results as a video CODEC.

Another CODEC that produces an AVI file is the M-JPEG CODEC. This is not supplied with Video for Windows but is usually bundled with a capture card that produces M-JPEG compression.

M-JPEG

Motion-JPEG, called M-JPEG, is similar in basis to the JPEG graphic format.   Each individual frame is compressed using JPEG techniques and each frame is stored individually and separately. By concentrating on individual frame compression, it produces less spectacular compression ratios (around 8:1) but provides 24-bit depth, higher quality and easier manipulation and editing.   Its larger file size and subsequent increased data rate needs meant that it could not be supported by the slow speeds of early CD players and no mass-market M-JPEG players were produced. It is a popular storage and editing medium but is not used as a distribution medium. A M-JPEG clip would be converted into another format such as MPEG for distribution. It has the normal *'AVI'* file extension, eg. *'wedding.avi'*.

Non-AVI Codecs

Apart from the four CODECs supplied with Windows 95/98, there are some other very significant and popular CODECs that can be installed, such as MPEG, OpenDML M-JPEG and VDOWave..

QuickTime

Apple originally produced the QuickTime architecture for their range of Macintosh machines but it is now *'multi-platform'* - versions are also produced for Windows and NT. Its files have the extension *'MOV'*, e.g. *'racing.mov'*, and are referred to as QuickTime movies.   MOV files are *'cross platform'* - if, for example, a MOV file is placed on a web site, it can be downloaded and played by any hardware system that has a QuickTime player.

QuickTime Player

The QuickTime Player is free and can be downloaded from www.apple.com/quicktime/

It is a software based application and therefore requires some of the computer's CPU time.   The current version, QuickTime 4, has a free Player that handles a wide variety of media, being able to display or reproduce AVIs, MPEGs, WAVs, MP3s, Audio CDs, Flash, FLC/FLI animations, GIFs, JPEGs, MIDI, text and much more. Version 4 recognises over 60 different file types.   The MOV file contains a header that informs the computer about the format of the contents.

However, it is its ability to package a wide range of multimedia objects within a MOV file that has resulted in its adoption as the first choice for most multimedia developers.   It soon became the most common plug-in for the Netscape and Windows Explorer web browsers and has the major share of use on CD and kiosk projects.   It provides a comprehensive set of commands for embedding in HTML files. These allow control over the playback of MOV file from the web (see the chapter on web design).

MOV files also support multiple tracks, where each track can contain a different media type.   So, for example a MIDI track can play while a video file is being displayed, or a URL can be placed in a text track so that a web site is automatically opened at a certain point in the file.

QuickTime Pro

QuickTime Pro is the authoring version of the application and is not provided free.   It has much superior facilities to Video for Windows.   It provides tools to capture, edit, compress and package video. It can also be used as file converter, as it can import and export a wide range of common file formats.

Streaming

QuickTime Pro provides facilities to create files for the web that accommodate both *'Progressive Download'* and *'True Streaming'*.   Like all streaming files, the web site server has to be capable of handling the format.   Normal, non-streamed, files have to be downloaded then played. Streaming allows the movie to be watched while the file is being downloaded.

With progressive download, the user is provided with a file at a pre-determined level of speed/quality (see *'Scalability'* below). There may be a slight delay before playing, but thereafter the movie is played in real time.

With true streaming, the video is delivered in real time by the server. This is often used for live interviews, concerts, etc but can equally be used to transmit pre-recorded material.

If the effective transfer speed of the user's connection is reduced, through noise or congestion, the real time playback is maintained by dropping frames (reducing the playback quality of the video).

Scalability

QuickTime Pro is used by web site developers to create a number of different versions of the same video file for placing on a web site. Each version has a different compression/quality level.   The Internet user can set the computer's connection speed within the QuickTime settings, as shown.   When a video clip is selected for viewing, the clip that matches the user's Internet speed is selected.   This produces the best possible results for each user. Those with slow modems are given the smaller, poorer quality, file; those with fast connections are given the larger, higher quality version. The new Microsoft Advanced Streaming Format provides a similar facility although it is limited to handling just two (high bandwidth and low bandwidth) versions of files.

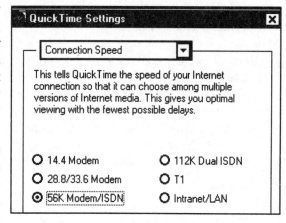

Editing
Although most editing of QuickTime movies will be carried using well-known editors such as Adobe Premiere or Macromedia Director, QuickTime Pro offers some basic editing facilities such as cut and paste. A range of video effects such as emboss, blur, lens flare and edge detection are also provided through the package's built-in filters.

The CODECs supplied with QuickTime include Cinepak, Sorenson Video, Video 1, Indeo 3.2/4.4/5.0, RLE, M-JPEG and Apple Video.

RealVideo
This is marketed as RealSystem 2, where is it is combined with the RealAudio application. It does not offer the wide range of facilities provided by QuickTime, as it is primarily aimed at Internet use. Its CODEC applies Fractal Image Compression, which provides high compression, resulting in very small file sizes. It is CPU-intensive but the quality of its files is superior to MPEG-1. It provides both progressive download and true streaming.

Determining the CODECs installed
Over time, different CODECs will be added to the default set provided with Windows. To see the list of CODECs on a particular computer, the following steps should be carried out:

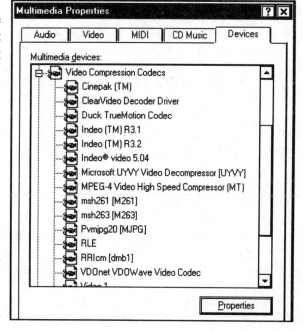

- Click the *'Start'* button on the main menu bar.
- Choose *'Settings'* from the pop-up menu.
- Choose *'Control Panel'* from the sub-menu.
- Choose *'Multimedia'* from the choices in the pop-up window.
- In Windows 95, click on the *'Advanced'* tab.
- In Windows 98, click on the *'Devices'* tab.
- Click on *'Video Compression Codecs'* in the displayed list of devices.

The list of CODECs that are installed on the computer are then displayed, as shown.

If a CODEC is highlighted and the *'Properties'* button is clicked, extra information on the codec may be displayed. If the *'Settings'* button is not greyed out, it can be clicked and individual CODEC features may be enabled.

Playback Systems
All compressed video files require to be played back using some type of CODEC. These CODEC routines are usually implemented in software although hardware implementations are also available and are more efficient.

Software Codecs
AVI
All AVI files compressed by a particular CODEC should be decompressed with that same CODEC. So, an AVI file with Cinepack compression should be run using Cinepack decompression software. AVI files can be played through the Windows Media Player, the QuickTime Player, through an

editing package such as Adobe Premiere, or through a host of smaller players that are available as freeware and shareware.

MPEG

Software MPEG CODECs became popular at one stage. The speed of CPUs and the general data transfer rates of computer systems had increased to a point where software MPEG decoding was possible, dispensing with the need for a dedicated decoder card. Software CODECs are supplied with some graphics cards and this results in cheaper card prices.   Currently, hardware implementations through dedicated chipsets are more popular, particularly for handling DVD.   Windows 98 supports the MPEG-1 software CODEC while Windows 3.1 and Windows 95 need an extra MPEG-1 driver to be installed.   Windows 98 can handle MPEG-2, once the DVD card's driver software is installed.

Hardware Codecs

AVI

These use dedicated chipsets to produce full screen playback of AVI files and are now widely used. The chipsets play AVI Indeo and Cinepak files full screen.   The use of a *'digital movie accelerator chipset'* provides an interpolated algorithm to estimate the extra pixels required to fill the full screen. This prevents *'blockiness'* and *'jagged edges'* on the image but tends to soften the picture. The smaller the original AVI file, the more marked will be this loss of contrast.

MPEG

Clips that were created and saved using MPEG compression require to be decompressed before the video information can be sent to the monitor.   The machine showing these clips has to be fitted with an MPEG playback card or have MPEG decoding software routines.   The hardware implementation is potentially faster as the card contains chips that are dedicated to MPEG decoding.   This saves much of the computer's CPU time.

MPEG cards are available in the following varieties:

- An add-on to an existing graphics card, usually via a plug-in daughterboard, such as offered by the Matrox *'Rainbow Runner'* card.
- An MPEG decoder card that plugs into the VESA *'feature connector'* of existing graphics card.   An example is the Aztech *'Galaxy Oscar'*.   The VideoLogic *'SonicStorm DVD Player'* connects to the existing video card using an analogue loop-through connector.
- Cards that completely replace existing graphics cards. They act both as a standard graphics card and as an MPEG decoder.   Examples are the ATI *'Rage Fury'* and the Diamond *'Speedstar DVD'* card, both for the AGP bus.

M-JPEG cards will not handle MPEG files and only play back M-JPEG files.   Converters are available which take the higher specification M-JPEG files and convert them into MPEG files for general use.

Determining the CODEC used on an AVI File

Since an AVI file may have been encoded using one of a variety of CODECS, Windows 95/98 provides a method to get a report on a file's configuration. If an AVI file is highlighted in *'Windows Explorer'* and the mouse right-hand button is clicked, the *'Properties'* option of the resulting menu produces the screen shown.

There are three main options:

- The *'General'* option shows file dates, size, etc.
- The *'Preview'* option runs the clip in miniature.
- The *'Details'* option shows that the file called *'Beatles'* is designed to be run in a quarter of a VGA screen at 15fps using a Cinepak CODEC. Its data rate is only 146kbps, allowing it to be

run directly from even the slowest CD-ROM drive.   This is a good example of how early AVI files were produced to match the lowest possible hardware performance.

Since even compressed video clips tend to be enormous, most clips found in the public domain are low resolution with a low frame rate. The result is below TV quality, but gets the message across effectively, which is the intention of multimedia in the first place.   The clips that are found in many magazines' *'free'* CDs are of larger size but they still have to be tailored to the lowest standards, to be compatible with the largest numbers of user machines.

Video Editing

Video Editing

Video editing is very much a creative as well as technical process.   The techniques for manipulating content can be learned as a mechanical process.   The ability to create a single, cohesive project requires a range of skills beyond the scope of this chapter.

For the hobbyist, video editing may be simply making the best use of the existing footage to create a wedding or holiday video.   The individual clips may have been recorded almost at random and the editing process involves selecting the shots and ordering them in a way that conveys the mood of the event.   For the multimedia editor, the footage was shot to meet the needs of the production.   The camcorder operator may have been given a list of required shots, arising from the development of the storyboard.   Even here, the operator may notice angles, views or content that would enhance the final project that would not have been known by the storyboard creators.   The team on location often uses its initiative to capture extra material.

As a result, even the best professionals shoot many times more hours of footage than is ever used.   The editor reviews the clips and will discard material for a number of reasons:

- The material at the start and finish of each clip is often too long.
- Shots that are redundant (e.g. multiple clips of crowd scenes may be recorded, so that the best clips can be selected).
- Shots that are unusable due to poor recording (poor sound, wind noise, bad lighting, etc). The ability of the operator to review footage on location and reshoot minimises the wasted footage reaching the editor.
- Shots where only part of the clip is used (e.g. extracting a 20-second clip from a five-minute speech).
- Shots from multiple different angles (e.g. a close-up shot may be passed over in favour of mid-shot).

The post-production phase involves the selection of clips, the editing of clips, the addition of special effects, audio dubbing and mixing.

In Camera editing

An old technique was to 'edit in camera'. The series of clips for the project was pre-planned and shot in the correct order.   The camera's own titling, fading and other effects were applied during the recording. The videotape was removed from the camera as a finished product.   These facilities still exist in camcorders and the synchronisation of digital camcorders means that the clip transitions are smooth (older cameras tend to exhibit a picture roll or picture break-up at the junction of two separately recorded clips).   Compared to editing in the computer, this is a much less flexible approach and one that does not tolerate errors. For example, when played back, an effect may look less effective than anticipated. Even worse, consider a wedding shot of the happy couple, with the in-camera titler being used to add the wrong spelling of the bride or groom's name.   The problem would not be discovered until it is too late to reshoot the scene.

Linear Editing

With linear editing, the video clips stored on the camcorder's tape are transferred to another tape. This may use the camcorder in conjunction with a VCR, or may involve using multiple VCRs.   This approach involves a lot of playing, fast forwarding, rewinding, replaying - to identify the clips to be used in the final project. The steps are:

- The VCR is set to record and left on pause.
- The camcorder is rewound to the start of the first clip.
- The camcorder is set to play and the VCR is taken off pause.
- At the end of the wanted clip, the VCR is put back on pause.
- The camcorder is moved to the start of the second clip and the process is repeated.

The process is made more efficient by connecting the camcorder to a computer and using a software package to automate the process. One such package is Pinnacle's Video Director. The user decides on the list of scenes to include in the final project and adds the information into the package's 'Event List'. The software then uses the LAN-C control of a camcorder to output the video clips named in the Events List to the VCR for recording the final master tape. LAN-C remains an option for DV camcorders.

Non Linear Editing

With non-linear editing, all the video is stored digitally and processed digitally. Once digitised from the tape, the source tape plays no further part in the editing process. The individual scenes are stored as separate computer video files that can be deleted, re-ordered, enhanced, modified and have effects added. This can be carried out with individual frame accuracy using a software package. Access to each element of the project is quickly accessible. Most of all, the output can be easily packaged for a range of distribution media such as CD, kiosk, web, as well as videotape. Some editing software packages use a flowchart view of the project, but most use a timeline view.

Timeline editing

Consider this analogy of editing cinema film. The processed cine film is one long strip, containing each frame shat was shot in a long sequence. The filmstrip is chopped up into a set of separate scenes and is assembled in the required order. Imagine all the pieces lying on a large table. The individual strips are placed in a row to create the new running order, with unwanted strips going in the bin. The remaining strips are positioned in the order that they are displayed in the final movie. This collection is ordered with respect to time. When the collection of end-to-end strips is joined together, they form the new film and the individual clips are viewed as a continuous movie.

This same approach is used with computerised editing. Clips are digitised and the wanted clips are placed on the editing table (Premier's Project Window). The clips are then placed in the required order as a continuous strip (Premiere's Timeline window). Since all the clips are stored on the hard disk, editing tasks are simpler and quicker. Titles may be altered, the order of scenes altered and different effects can be tried and discarded. This all takes place within the computer and only the chosen clips, titles and effects are composited into the finished product.

Rendering

The editing software can handle multiple video tracks and audio tracks at the same time. Additional effects, such as transitions, filters and titling may be added at this stage. When the project is completed, it is saved as a single computer file (AVI, MPEG, etc) or sent back to a video recorder. The editing software has to take all the clips and effects and merge them into a single video and audio stream, applying all the alterations to the frame contents. This process is known as 'rendering' and can be time-consuming if complicated transitions and effects have been used.

The editing suite

Post-production suite depends upon the intended output

Minimum equipment for editing

- A camcorder, preferably with a FireWire digital output.
- A VCR for older VHS footage.
- A computer with a video capture card and ample fast disk storage.
- As much computer memory as can be afforded. Premiere uses three image buffers to store the file at different stages. So the total memory required is three times the file size + the amount of memory to hold Windows and the editing software. For example, a 10MB clip would require around 33MB of memory. Even a well-endowed computer with 256MB of RAM can only directly handle a file of around 84MB. Larger files can be handled, but they are slower to process as they cannot all fit into memory at the same time.
- Video capture software (usually supplied with the capture card).
- Video editing software (e.g. QuickTime Pro, Avid Cinema, Adobe Premiere).
- A microphone, for voiceovers.
- The CODEC to be used for processing the final output (e.g. MPEG, Sorenson, RealVideo).

Useful additions

- A dual-monitor card, such as the Matrox 400. This allows two monitors to be connected to the computer and the various application windows can be distributed for display over the two windows. This allows more tools (even from different applications) to be seen at the one time, for greater clarity.
- LAN-C connections, to allow control of the camcorder from the computer keyboard. This sends timecode information to the camcorder, informing it where to start playing a clip and for what duration.
- Animation software (3D Studio Max, Poser, True Space).
- Image Manipulation software (e.g. PhotoShop, Paint Shop Pro).
- Royalty-free audio and music clips.
- Batch processing software such as Debabilizer and SmartCapture.
- Video enhancement software such as Adobe After Effects and Media Cleaner Pro.

VidEdit

This application was supplied by Microsoft along with Windows 3.1 and was accompanied by a package called *'VidCap'* for capturing video clips. It is an example of an early video editing package and looks decidedly lacking in features.

It only operated on a single clip at a time and did not provide any transition effects. It did not offer other special effects such as titling.

Nevertheless, it was a useful application for elementary video capture and some basic editing activities.

Personal AVI Editor

This application is currently being distributed as a shareware package. A copy is included on our CD (see the back pages of the book).

The package provides video capture facilities.

Significantly, it allows multiple clips to be worked on within the package. A separate channel is provided for storing video clips and audio clips. Several clips can be placed in a channel in a horizontal row.

As shown in the illustration, it provides five plug-in modules offering *'transitions'* between clips. This means, for example, that one clip can fade out as the next clip fades in.

It allows the independent editing of the audio and video tracks and can be saved in one of a variety of output formats.

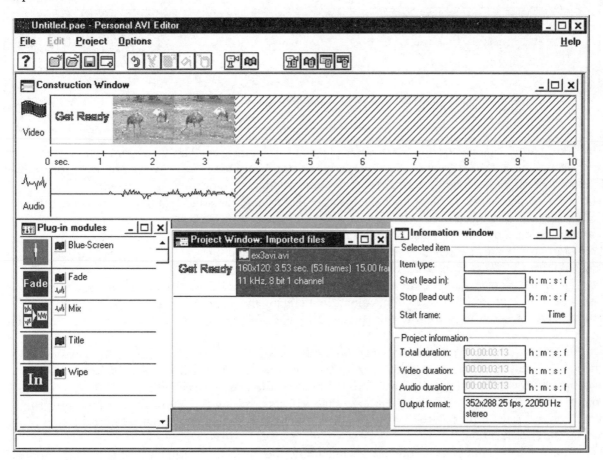

Avid Cinema

This application is currently bundled with a number of video capture cards and is aimed at the beginner and the amateur.   It has far fewer facilities and controls than a fully-blown editing package such as Adobe Premiere, but is easier to learn and is probably sufficient for the hobbyist.

As the diagram shows, the package guides the user through the four main stages of the process - planning, capture, editing and output.

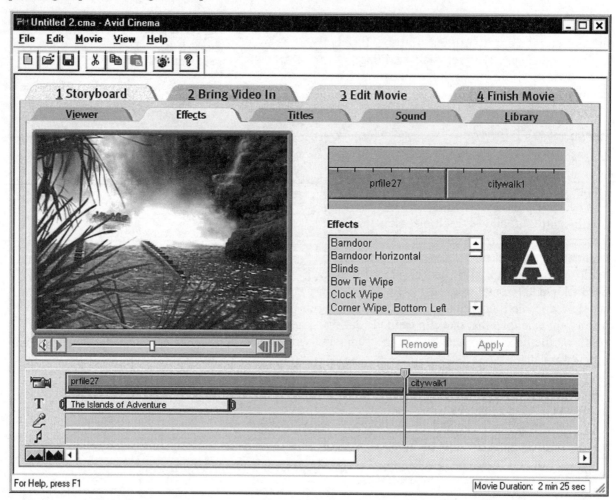

The *'Storyboard'* tab displays the list of shots planned for the project. The storyboard can be created by the user or can be loaded from over 25 pre-designed storyboard templates covering projects for Product Overview, Real Estate, Sales Training, Sports Events, weddings, graduations, and so on.

The *'Bring Video In'* tab invokes the video capture facility and links the captured video clips to the list designed in the storyboard.

The illustration shows the sub-tabs that are available when the *'Edit Movie'* tab is clicked.

The *'Library'* tab allows the importing of files from disc into the project.   These can then be added to the row with the camcorder icon, in the order that they are to be played.

The *'Titles'* tab provides facilities to add opening titles, closing credits, etc on top of the video footage.

The type face, font size, font style, font colour, font alignment can all be set and the text can be static or can be made to scroll up, down, left or right.   The title, *'Islands of Adventure'* has been added in the example.

The illustration shows the option provided under the *'Effects'* tab.   It shows that two files have been included in the list. The first is called *'prfile27.avi'* and the second is called *'citywalk1.avi'*.   Since the two files follow each other on the list, the box holding the entries is called the *'timeline'*.   This is a common way to display files during editing.   The effects scrolling box allows a transition effect to be used between the two files, such that the end of the first file does not simply butt against the start of the second file (see later).

The *'Finish Movie'* tab opens up options for outputting the video to a variety of formats (CD, the web, videotape).

Getting started in Adobe Premiere

Adobe Premiere is the most common professional choice of video editing software.   It provides a great many features and has provisions for add-ons from other software houses, to enhance its abilities.

Many excellent books go into detail on the subject of video editing in general and using Premiere in particular.   This section of the book covers the general techniques and looks at the most common editing activities.   The material is based on Premiere v5, although most of activities covered can be carried out in earlier versions.

Choosing a project format

When a new project is being created, the user is first provided with the opportunity to decide on how the file is treated within the editing software and the overall final output parameters of the file.

Premiere's project settings are grouped under the following headings:

- General Settings
- Video Settings
- Audio Settings
- Keyframe and Rendering Settings
- Capture Settings

This entails a lot of setting up before an editing project can be begun.   However, the settings can be saved (see the *'Save'* button in the illustration) and re-used in a future editing session (using the *'Load'* button).   Once a user's preferences for resolution, CODECs, etc, are set up they can be retrieved from the saved settings thus saving a lot of wasted time each session.

The main options for each group of settings are outlined below.

General Settings

This is the first window that is displayed when a new project is opened.

The dialog box is as shown in the illustration.

The main window displays all the current settings. If they are set to the desired characteristics, the *'OK'* button can be clicked.   Otherwise, the individual characteristics can be set.

The General options are:

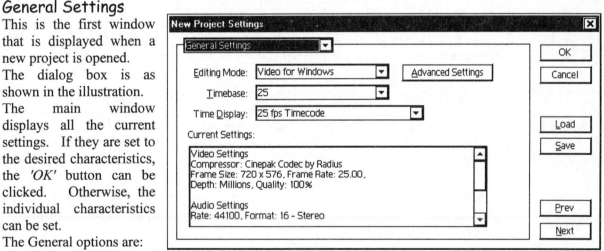

Premiere's General Settings	
Option	**Description**
Mode	Decides whether Video for Windows or QuickTime CODECs are offered in the *'Video Settings'* panel.
Timebase	Decides how each second of time is divided. An edit activity can only occur on one of these time divisions. Set to 25 for PAL video, 29.97 for NTSC video. This setting does not affect the final output rate but does affect the accuracy of the editing process
Time Display	Decides the manner in which time is displayed in the editing timeline. Set to 25fps for PAL video, 30fps for NTSC and *'Feet+Frames'* for motion-picture film.

For smoothest results, the frame rate of the video clips to be edited should be identical to the Timecode and the Timebase frequency.   The final destination of the clip should be borne in mind during shooting, so that the values match.   In practice, there are occasions when there is some mismatch. For example, clips at 30fps may need to be edited along with clips at 25fps, or clips at 25fps may need to be output at 15fps.   In these situations, excess frames are dropped, or extra frames are added, so that the final output needs are met.

If the video or audio settings displayed in the *'Current Settings'* window need changed, choose the required options from the drop-down menu containing *'General Settings'*.

Video/Audio/Keyframe and Rendering Settings

These settings are covered fully in the section of the chapter dealing with the outputting the final project. If the editor requires knowing precisely the effects of the settings on the final project, they can be set before editing, so that their effects are observed during the playback from the Timeline.

Capture Settings

Most capture cards use their own software routines for capturing video and most of these can be accessed through Premiere's capture facilities.

When all the desired parameters are all selected, click the 'OK' button.

Premiere Capture Settings	
Option	Description
Capture Format	Decides between CODECs for capturing, offering QuickTime, Video for Windows, or the options provided by the capture card manufacturer. Apart from the in-built set, the user's own video card may provide an additional compressor to match its hardware (e.g. the Matrox G400 TV adds a Matrox M-JPEG compressor in to the list. The option chosen may alter the options offered in the remaining settings and in the dialog boxes produced by clicking the 'Video', 'Audio', or 'Advanced' buttons.
Capture Video	Checking this box enables the capture of the video component of the incoming signal. If the box is left unchecked, and the 'Capture Audio' box is checked, only the audio component is digitised. This is useful when a camcorder has been used to capture some background atmosphere noises and the video content is not required.
Size	Decides the final resolution of the captured video and is input as pixels amounts. If the footage has been recorded on a camcorder, it normally records at a 4:3 aspect ratio. The values used will depend on the final destination of the file (e.g. set to 352x288 for an intended MPEG-1 file, smaller for web use and larger for CD and kiosk use). It is best to capture at the same size as the intended output, as re-scaling during editing deteriorates the picture quality.
Constrain	Checking this box maintains a 4:3 aspect ratio for the captured clip. Typing in a new value in one of the size boxes is then automatically calculated for the other box, to ensure that the correct vertical to horizontal relationship is maintained. Some camcorders can record in a widescreen 16:9 ratio and the vertical and horizontal values chosen in this case should maintain the ratio and avoid picture distortion. The box should remain unchecked if widescreen values are to be entered.
Capture Audio	Checking this box enables the capture of the audio component of the incoming signal. If the box is left unchecked, and the 'Capture Video' box is checked, only the video component is digitised. This is useful when a camcorder has been used to capture some scenes where the audio content is not required, as a voiceover or background music is planned to be dubbed during editing.
Report Dropped Frames	When the box is checked, Premiere will report when even a single frame is dropped during the capture process. The capture session is completed and the user can decide whether to use the digitised clip or alter the settings so that the hardware can cope with a repeat session.
Abort on Dropped Frames	When the box is checked, the capture process is automatically stopped if even a single frame is dropped during the capture process.
Decode Burned-In Timecode	Only applies to computers with the Macintosh operating system.
Capture Limit	Decides how much video is captured in a single session.
Device Control	These settings only apply to capturing video from a deck or camcorder that has an interface that allows control of the tape mechanism's play, rewind, etc.
Video button	If this button is not greyed out, it can be clicked to access options that have been provided by the software supplied with the video capture card. These should be set according to the recommendations supplied in the capture card's manual.
Audio button	See above.
Advanced button	See above.

Capture Hardware Settings

While Premiere uses the computer's memory to process editing changes, it is seldom enough to store the large projects that are being handled. When the memory becomes fill, it stores the remainder of the information on temporary files on the drive. It also uses hard disk space for storing captured video files. The user can control which drives are used to store the information. Premiere recommends that a separate disk drive to be used for storing the application, the video files and the audio files. It also recommends that the drives for storing video and audio information be AV types.

These disks are called *'scratch disks'* and they are set up using the following steps:

- Choose *'File'* from the main menu.
- Choose *'Preferences'* from the drop-down menu.
- Choose *'Scratch Disks'* from the sub-menu.
- Choose the drive for storing captured movie clips (this is both the video and audio data).
- Choose the drive for storing files while creating video preview data.
- Choose the drive for storing files while creating audio preview data.
- Click the *'OK'* button.

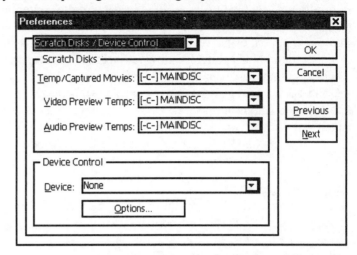

When all the settings are chosen, clicking the final *'OK'* button brings up the main Premiere interface.

The Interface for Premiere

The main Premiere window contains a collection of sub-windows, each dedicated to a part of the editing process. Together, they offer a wide range of tools to edit digital video. Each window can be displayed or hidden by clicking on its name in the *'Window'* drop-down menu.

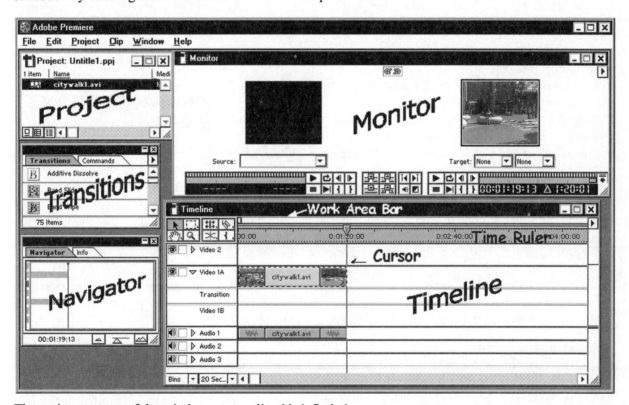

The main purposes of the windows are outlined briefly below:

Project Window

The source items to be used in constructing the final project are first imported into the project window. These may be video clips, audio clips or graphic files. From here, they are dragged and dropped into the timeline, where they may be chopped, altered or added to in many different ways.

Timeline window

The Timeline window (known as the *'Construction Window'* in earlier versions) has a number of horizontal containers. The illustration shows three containers that are capable of holding video streams, three containers capable of holding audio streams and a separate stream for storing transition effects. At the start of a project, these containers are empty.   The files are added to the timeline in their chronological running order, as the playback of the content is from left to right.   Video clips are dropped into the video containers on the timeline.   If the video clip contains an audio track, as in the example, the audio component of the file is automatically dropped into the audio container.   Separate audio files, such as background music, effects and voiceovers can also be dropped into the audio containers.

These containers are usually simply referred to as *'tracks'* (i.e. Audio 1 track or Video 1A track).   Track 1A and 1B are used to store movie clips and still-images.

Track 2 and higher are known as *'superimpose'* tracks.   Their contents can be superimposed on any video that may be contained in the other tracks.   These tracks have several other uses, as shown later.

Extra video and audio tracks can be added to the window, as Premiere supports up to 99 audio and 99 video tracks.

Monitor window

The Monitor window allows the video to be viewed during the editing process, without first having to render a complete movie.   It contains two viewing screens.   The *'Source'* screen shows the video clip currently being worked on and allows it to be edited.   The *'Target'* window allows the content of the entire timeline to be displayed and edited.

They also show the timecode value of each frame as it is displayed.   In the example shown above, the project consists of a single clip that is 1 minute, 30 seconds and 1 frame in length.   The player is currently displaying the frame that is 1 minute, 19 seconds and thirteen frames in from the start of the project.

It is best to reduce these windows to the smallest size that is still viewable, as the software creates a special file that is just used for displaying previews.   The preview file allows the effects of transitions, fades, etc to be seen.   A smaller preview window reduces the rendering time and disc space required for the preview file, allowing the editing process to run faster.

Navigator palette

The Navigator Palette provides an overview of the clips that are in the Timeline window, as shown in the illustration.

It is mostly used as a quick way to move around a project with a long duration.   The viewing window can be dragged with the mouse to any position in the timeline and the corresponding section of the timeline is displayed in the Timeline window.

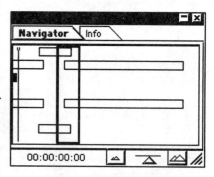

The controls at the bottom of the window provide a quick method of altering the amount of time shown in the Timeline window. Dragging the slider to the left shrinks the timeline so that more of the project's contents are visible without scrolling.   This also means that less detail is visible.   Clicking the button to the left of the slider has the same effect.

Dragging the slider to the right expands the timeline so that less of the projects total contents are visible in the timeline.   This requires more scrolling through the timeline but provides a greater level of detail in the timeline.   Clicking the button to the right has the same effect.

Transitions palette

Transitions are simply the way that one scene leads into another.   When two video clips are butted together in the timeline, the playback of the first clip content ends abruptly and the second clip start immediately after.   This window provides a range of transition effects that can be applied to the join between two clips, to provide a smoother visual move from one clip to the next.

Live Capture

Video scenes can be captured live from within the Premiere application, which uses the computer's video capture card and drivers.   Of course, this requires the camcorder to be connected to the capture card, the lighting to be set up and so on.   It is best to capture one clip for each separate scene.

The steps for capturing live video are:
- Choose *'File'* from the main menu.
- Choose *'Capture'* from the drop-down menu.
- Choose *'Movie Capture'* from the sub-menu.

Incoming video from the camcorder is displayed on a screen and clicking on the *'Record'* button starts the capture process. Clicking the mouse button ends the capture session and the clip can be previewed. The clip can then be named and saved as a video file, for later importing into the Project window.

It is best to make a test capture, to ensure that the equipment is capable of handling the video data rates. The performance of the test recording can be checked by highlighting the file in the Project window, right-clicking on the file and choosing *'Get Properties'* from the drop-down menu. This gives the average data rate for the file along with other useful information. Clicking the *'Data Rate'* button displays the changing data rata during the duration of the clip.

Where a controllable tape deck or camcorder is available, this can be connected to the computer via an add-on card or the control sockets on some capture

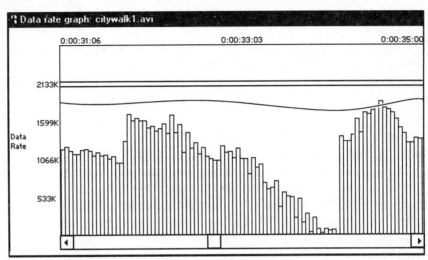

cards. This is set up through Device Control in File / Preferences. The process is accessed through the *'Batch Capture'* choice in the *'File'* menu's *'Capture'* option. This allows the user to set up Premiere to find a list of clips on a tape, capture them and store them to disc.

Importing files

There may be a need to rename some of the media files before they are imported. It is much easier to identify a file later if it is called *"interview.avi"* rather than *"file17a.avi"*. The ability to use long file names makes choosing meaningful file names easier (although it is best to check that this causes no conflicts with any other software that is being used).

The steps for importing a file into the Project window are:

- Choose *'File'* from the main menu.
- Choose *'Import'* from the drop-down menu.
- Choose *'File'* from the sub-menu.
- Navigate through the hard disc's folders to find the desired file.
- Highlight the desired file.
- Click the *'Open'* button, to add the file to the list in the Project window.

To delete a clip from the Project window, highlight the file and press the Delete key. If the clip is being used in the Timeline, this is reported and confirmation of the deletion is requested.

After a project is completed, it may be found that files were imported into the Project window but not used in the project. These files can be deleted from the Project window by choosing *'Remove Unused'* from the *'Project'* drop-down menu.

Adding files to the Timeline

Click on a file in the Project window and drag it into the timeline window. The default for Premiere is *'Snap to Edges'* which means that the new file will butt directly behind an existing file, without the need for any accurate positioning by the user. If a gap is required between clips, the clip can be dragged along the timeline until the left-hand edge of the clip aligns with the required point on the time ruler. If a clip is required to overlap an existing clip (e.g. for creating a transition), the new file would not be placed in the same video track as the existing file. It would then be dragged to sit at the required position on the timeline, using the time ruler for accurate positioning.

It is important to note that any changes made to a file within Premiere will not change the contents of the original file. The changes only apply to the copy of the file that is stored within Premiere and displayed on the timeline.

A file can be included in the timeline as many times as required. Any changes to one instance of the file (e.g. trimming or adding effects) applies only to that instance of the file and has no effect on the other copies of the file in the timeline.   They are treated as entirely separate files once they are brought into the timeline.

Viewing a single clip in the Source window

Highlight the Source window in the Monitor window.   Then click on the clip's icon in the Project window and drag it into the Source window. Click the Play button on the Source window controls, to view the video clip.

Each playback window has its own set of controls for play as shown in the illustration.

There is a slider bar above the time code. This can be grabbed by the mouse and moved to any part of the clip.   Clicking the left or right Nudge buttons moves the view one frame back or forward, giving control down to frame level. Clicking the letter 'a' on the keyboard returns the clip player to point to the start of the file.

Viewing any part of the project

If the vertical cursor in the Timeline window is grabbed by the mouse and dragged along a section of the time ruler, the video contained during that section of time is displayed in the Target window.   This process is known as 'scrubbing' and the section that is scrubbed could be part of a single file, or could encompass several adjacent files, or even be the set of files for the entire project. The cursor can be dragged to the left or the right and the video is played backwards or forwards. This is a quick way to get an appreciation of the running order and content of the clips. However, it does not give a feeling for the pace of the project, as the user's control of the mouse is not identical to the actual real-time playing speed of the clip

To view a part of the project in real time, the start of the section to be viewed should be identified by either positioning the cursor on the time ruler, or by moving the slider bar.

Viewing the entire project

Highlight the Target window in the Monitor window.   If necessary, click the letter 'a' on the keyboard to return the clip player to point to the start of the project. Click the Play button on the Target window's controls to view the set of video clips that are present on the timeline.   As a clip is played from the timeline, a vertical pointer, the 'cursor', moves along the time ruler, to indicate the progress through the playback.

Previewing the entire project

This is invoked from the 'Preview' option on the 'Project' menu and the project must be named and saved to disc before it can operate. This is because it creates a rendered copy of the entire project, including all transitions and effects.   This is different from viewing the timeline contents, which shows each clip in the running order but does not show the results of applying effects or transitions.

Before running a preview, ensure that the entire project's contents are within the Work Area Bar (see below).

The Work Area bar

The Work Area Bar controls how much of the timeline content is rendered as a Preview or as the final movie output. When editing, the user will often want to see the effects of particular changes applied to a section of the timeline. There is no point in rendering whole areas that are not being examined.

The bar is situated just above the Time Ruler (see the earlier illustration) and has an arrowhead on each side. These arrowhead pointers can be dragged by the mouse to each side of the area that to be viewed (e.g. to see the effects of a fade or transition). Double-clicking the bar extends the bar to cover the width of the current Timeline window.

A Rough Cut

Before beginning the time-consuming and detailed editing work, there is often a need to view the general run and feel of the project.   This allows the editor to see how the various clips fit into their sequence, whether the overall general effect has been achieved and what specific tasks need carried out that may not have been included in the storyboard.   The viewing of the sequence of clip, before any editing or application of filters, transitions and effects is called a 'rough cut'.   The editor can view a rough cut at any time during the editing process. Premiere's output options allow for a project to be created that ignores all these time-consuming processes. It does not act on these modifications and the raw footage can be examined.   The settings are then altered prior to the final project output being created.

Viewing in greater detail

The timeline is measured horizontally in units that were selected for *'Time Display'* and *'Timebase'* when choosing the *'General Settings'* at the start of the project. For the UK's PAL video, this is 25fps, requiring 25 separate time markings on the timeline for each second. If, for example, a set of clips totalled 30 minutes of shooting, there would have to be 30 x 60 x 25 = 45,000 separate time markings on the timeline. It is impossible to see them all in the window at any one time and so the user must control the amount of detail seen at any time. The user may wish to view the entire project in the window, so that an appreciation of the size and location of each file is quickly achieved. On the other hand, for accurate editing, the user has to work at individual frame level. The time ruler can be set to have its major markings displayed as frames, seconds or minutes. There is a drop-down box that can be accessed on the lower left of the timeline window. When clicked, the menu offers *'Time Unit'* values from a single frame per division up to eight minutes per division. The higher values display the way that individual elements are arranged in the Timeline window, while the smaller values provide a detailed examination of the files.

A video file can be displayed as a horizontal bar, or as a set of thumbnails. The choice is selected by right clicking on a video clip in the Timeline window and choosing *'Timeline Windows Options'* from the drop-down menu. When the option for displaying thumbnails is used in conjunction with a ruler resolution of a single frame per division, the timeline displays a set of individual frames. This allows great accuracy in editing and applying transitions.

Trimming Files

Camera operators usually shoot with spare footage at both ends of the usable material and these unwanted sections will both need to be removed. Enough footage must be left to allow for transitions, fades, etc. If clips are trimmed tightly (little opening or closing waste) it injects a feeling of pace (watch some pop music on TV).

A clip can be trimmed by various methods:

Dragging the clip

A clip can be shortened by clicking on and edge of the clip and dragging it inwards. The frames that have been removed from the timeline will not appear in any preview or in any final rendered output. During the editing process, however, they remain available, so that the clip can be dragged back to restore some or all of the hidden frames if required.

This method shortens the clip, leaving a gap in the timeline; the total project duration remains unchanged.

Using the ripple edit tool

At the top of the Timeline window, there is a set of tools as shown in the diagram. This displays a small sub-set from which the *'Ripple Edit'* option +|+ should be chosen. The edge of the clip can now be dragged to shorten the clip, as before.

This option shortens the clip and moves other clips along the timeline so that there is no gap. The total project duration is

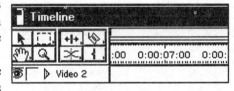

shortened by the amount of time removed from the clip. Like the previous method, the removed frames are available for any subsequent stretching of the clip. In both cases, the clip cannot be dragged to a duration that is larger than its original duration.

Using razor cuts

Select the *'Razor'* ✎ from the Timeline window tools. Click on the frame at which the clip should be shortened. This splits the clip into two smaller clips. Return to the *'Select'* tool, the one that is shaped like an arrow. Alternatively, move the cursor to the desired place on the timeline and choose the *'Razor at Edit Line'* from the top *'Edit'* sub-menu.

Use the Select tool to select the portion of the clip that is to be discarded. Once the sub-clip is highlighted, right-click the mouse and choose *'Ripple Delete'* from the menu that appears. This option removes the unwanted sub-clip and moves other clips along the timeline so that there is no time gap left. The total project duration is shortened by the amount of time used by the sub-clip. Unlike the other methods, the removed frames are no longer available for any subsequent stretching of the clip.

This method is also very useful for removing sections in the middle of a clip. In this case, the start and end frames for the cut should be marked with the Razor tool. This produces three sub-clips and the middle section can then be removed (i.e. ripple deleted).

Clipping/Cropping

The composite and S-Video outputs from a camcorder are designed for displaying on a television screen. However, televisions leave an area of the screen picture that is unseen. Only 576 out of the transmitted 625 lines are displayed on the screen. Likewise, a little of the screen edges are unseen. This is termed *'overscan'* or *'edge blanking'*. Television transmitters use the unseen lines to send Teletext and other signals. On some poorly set up televisions, the Teletext data is seen as a row of white dots at the top of the screen.

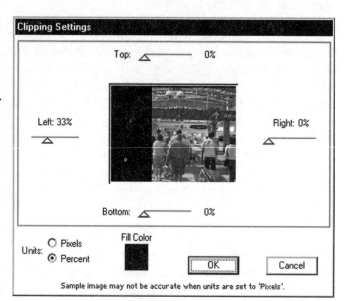

Since overscan techniques are not used with computer video, these extra borders are visible and produce ugly borders to the clip. They also consume file capacity.

Premiere provides two utilities - clipping and cropping - for overcoming overscan.

The steps for clipping a video clip are:

- Select the video clip in the Timeline window.
- Choose *'Filters'* from the *'Clip'* drop-down menu.
- Select the *'Clip'* filter from the displayed list and click the *'Add'* button.
- Click the *'Edit'* button to open the dialog box shown.
- Set the clipping to be as a percentage of the picture size, or measured in pixels.
- Adjust each value for the amount of clipping required.
- Click the *'OK'* button.
- Run a Preview to test the results and re-adjust if necessary.

The *'Crop'* utility works in exactly the same way as described above, except that it then resizes the clip to the original resolution. Bear in mind that altering one edge by a large margin will alter the scene's horizontal and vertical ratios. For example, setting the left slider to maximum, while leaving the rest untouched, results in a picture that is too tall compared to its width.

Premiere's Clip/Crop Filters	
Option	**Description**
Crop	This utility removes the edges from the video clip and resizes the clip to fill the original resolution of the clip. It results in the same size of file size, without the ugly borders.
Clip	This utility removes the edges but does not resize the clip. The result is a smaller file size, but it may not fit in with other material recorded at the original resolution. This is not a problem for a standalone clip, or for a set of clips from the same source that are all similarly clipped. It may also cause difficulties when it is intended to be output to videotape which expects a fixed resolution.

Splitting Files

A file may require to be split into two sections. This may be required for various reasons:

- So that one of the sections may be copied elsewhere.
- So that an effect can be applied to one section of the clip but not the other section.

Move the cursor to the desired place on the timeline and choose the *'Razor at Edit Line'* from the top *'Edit'* sub-menu. The clip will be split into two smaller clips that can be processed independently of each other.

Deleting from the timeline

To delete a clip and move the other clips to fill the gap, use *'Ripple Delete'* method explained in the earlier section on razor cuts. A clip can also be deleted by highlighting the clip and pressing the Delete key. This deletes the clip but leaves a gap in the timeline.

The clip is removed from the timeline but remains in the list in the Project Window.

Altering a clip's speed

Premiere allows the speed of an individual clip to be altered. This is achieved through the *'Speed'* option on the *'Clip'* drop-down menu. A dialog box is opened as shown in the illustration. It reports on the current duration of the clip and the clip speed, which is always initially 100%.

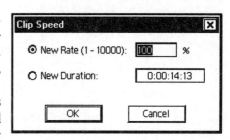

If the New Rate is set to 200%, the clip runs twice as fast, as every alternate frame is dropped. The clip's duration is halved and the clip has a jerky, high-speed appearance. Setting the New Rate to the maximum value drops most of the frames and provides a time-lapse photography effect that can be used to demonstrate how a slow moving process operates (e.g. a clock's mechanical movement, the construction of a building, etc).

If the New Rate is set to less than 100%, extra frames are inserted and the clip duration is lengthened. For example, a setting of 50% results in the repetition of each frame, doubling the clip duration. This can be used to create a slow-motion effect for dramatic effect (e.g. lovers running along a station platform to embrace) or to demonstrate fast-moving processes (e.g. to show the limb movements of a galloping horse or a ballerina).

An alternative method is to alter the duration of the file by setting a new value in the *'New Duration'* box. The value in the box is edited to enter the new value and the number of frames in the clip are increased or decreased to provide the new duration. This provides more precise control over the clip's final duration, but large variations will produce the slow-motion or speeded-up effects mentioned above.

Transitions

A *'hard cut'* describes the way that two files are butted together in the playback, such that the content of the first file ends abruptly and the content of the second file is displayed immediately afterwards.

An examination of footage in the cinema and on television reveals that many cuts are of this kind. A *'transition'* is a description of the way that the first clip changes over time into the second clip. For this to succeed, the two clips must have an overlap in the timeline window. That is one reason why Premiere provides extra video channels. The amount of overlap determines the length of the transition. For example, if the second clip overlaps the first clip by one second, then the transition should last one second. The Transitions window lists the range of transition types explained in the table below.

The desired effect should be chosen, clicked and dragged into the Transition track on the timeline.

The transition should be positioned and stretched so that it covers the overlapped area of the video files, as in the example.

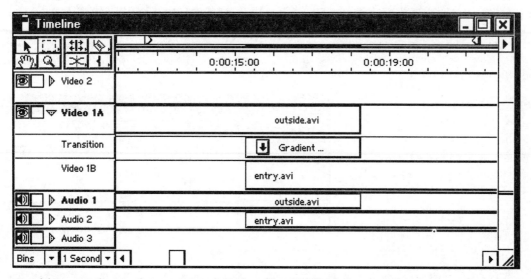

Some transitions can be used to convey a comic effect, while fades and dissolves can be used to indicate the passage of time, *'flashbacks'* in time, or even provide an effective pause in the project flow.

Transitions, fades and dissolves should not be overused. Too many detract from the video, require excessive rendering time and lower the compression ratio. Transitions should not just be used because they exist - they should be used where they add to the project (e.g. by pacing the project or by conveying extra meaning (see the table below).

Most transitions should last between half a second and about two seconds.   Excessively long transitions aggravate the viewer.

Typical Transitions		
Name	Action	Typical Purpose
Fade in	Displays a black screen, which gradually lightens to reveal the content of the clip.	Commonly used to open a project.
Fade out	Gradually darkens the screen content, until the last frame is completely black.	Commonly used at the end of a project.
Fade out / fade in	Two fades happening one after the other. The first scene fades completely to black, followed by the second scene lightening up from complete black. The two fades are separated in time. The fade in does not start until the fade out has completed.	Used to mark some significant break in the project flow. The darkened pause provides time for reflection on the contents of the previous scene.
Dissolve	The fade in and fade out happen at the same time. The picture never becomes black. Scene one is getting darker as scene two becomes brighter, maintaining screen brightness throughout the transition.	Used to mark scene changes or the passage of time, when the location in the two scenes does not change. Hard cuts are preferable where a more dynamic feel is required.
Wipe	The screen is divided into two sections by a line that can be horizontal, vertical or diagonal. At the beginning of the wipe, 100% of scene one is visible on one side of the line, while scene two occupies 0% of the screen. As the line moves, a smaller percentage of scene one is displayed, while more of scene two is visible. Eventually, scene one occupies 0% of the screen, while 100% of scene two is visible.	Horizontal wipes have a slow, deliberate, majestic effect that can control pacing of the project. Other wipes are used to indicate scene changes.
Ripple	The frame content appears as if it is a reflection on water.	Used at the start and end of a 'flashback' in time.
Page turn, also known as a peel	One corner of the first clip is progressively turned over, revealing the contents of the second clip.	This is used where a 'story' is being told, as it is an analogy of turning pages in a book.
Displacements	The second clip is brought into the picture as an animated object that pushes the first clip out of the picture and gradually replaces it. The second clip's path can be chosen from Push, Swap, Cross Stitch and Cube Spin. Unlike the other effects above, both clips are moved across the screen.	Attention grabbing method for scene changes.

NOTES

Premiere provides its own system for achieving fades and dissolves and these are covered later.   These transition effects do not appear as options in the Transitions window.

Hard cuts are by far the easiest transition to compress.   A simple vertical or horizontal wipe is relatively easily compressed.   Complex transitions such as page turns or rotary transitions produce the poorest compression and often result in unwanted artifacts.

Creating a Dissolve

The steps for creating a dissolve between video files are:

- Place one video file in the video track and another in the superimpose track.
- Click the triangle in the superimpose track
- This reveals a lower box along the video file displaying a horizontal red line. The red line has a starting handle and a finishing handle at each end of the line.
- Click on the red line, directly above the end of the first file, to add an additional handle to the line.
- Click on the red line, directly above the start of the third file, to add an extra handle to the line.

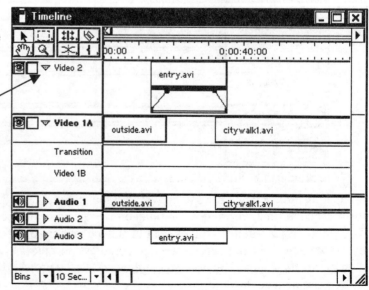

- Drag the outer handles low. At these points, the content of the second file is invisible/silent and the contents of the first and third files are fully visible/audible. Between the inner handles, the second's file's contents are fully visible/audible. On the line's slopes, the amounts of video/audio of each clip is somewhere between maximum and minimum.
- Ensure that the work area bar covers the section to be tested. Drag with the mouse if necessary.
- Run a preview.
- Adjust the settings, if necessary, to achieve the desired effect.

In the example, the video and audio content at the end of the file *'outside.avi'* is gradually reduced, while the content of the *'entry.avi'* is gradually increased.

Creating a Fade out/Fade in

A fade in/fade out is similar but there may be a gap in time between the clips, instead of them overlapping each other. During the gap time, there is no video output and the screen is black. For a shorter effect, the two clips can butt up to each other.

The steps for creating a fadeout/fade in between video files are:

- Place both clips in the superimpose track.
- Click the triangle in the superimpose track.
- This reveals lower boxes along the video clips, each displaying a horizontal red line. The red line has a starting handle and a finishing handle at each end of the line.
- Click on the red lines to add additional handles where the fades will start and end..
- Drag the handles low where the clips have to be invisible/silent.
- Ensure that the work area bar covers the section to be tested. Drag with the mouse if necessary.
- Run a preview.
- Adjust the settings, if necessary, to achieve the desired effect.

Creating a mid-fade

A mid-fade is applied to a single video clip. It is not a transition between clips, but a fade down/fade up within a clip.   The video scene is faded but the audio track continues to play over that period.   This might be used to simulate a temporary power cut affecting lights, a temporary fade while a voice from the audio track ponders a situation.

The steps for creating a mid-fade:

- Place the clip in the superimpose track.
- Click the triangle in the superimpose track, to reveal the lower box along the video clip, displaying a horizontal red line.
- Click on the red line to add additional handles where the fade will start and end..
- Drag these handles low. The distance between the points determines the duration of the fades and the angle of the diagonal lines determine the speed of the fades.
- Ensure that the work area bar covers the section to be tested. Drag with the mouse if necessary.
- Run a preview.
- Adjust the settings, if necessary, to achieve the desired effect.

Capturing a still from the video clip

A still picture can be captured from a video clip by placing the clip in the Source Monitor.   The tab should be slid and/or the nudge buttons clicked, until the desired frame is displayed in the Source Monitor window.   The *'Export'* option should be chosen from the *'File'* drop-down menu and choosing the *'Frame'* option from the sub-menu opens a dialog box to name and save the frame as a still image.

Capturing from a stationary or slow-moving clip will obviously produce better results than extracting from a fast-moving clip (unless a blurred image is required for effect - a speeding car or a sprint runner).

Adding a graphic
Designers may occasionally wish to include a static picture into their projects for purposes such as:
- To display a helpline number, while a voiceover reads out the details.
- To display an oil painting, while its merits are discussed.
- To display the static end credits with background music.
- To allow video players to get up to speed (see below).

If the end of the movie has a particularly dramatic feature, it is common that the action be frozen while the credits roll. This maintains an impact even after the moving footage has ended. It is wasteful of precious disc space and transmission time, to have a ten-second shot of video while the music or voices play over a static display. It is much more economical to take a graphic file and make it stretch over the ten-second period.   The graphic can be a digitised picture, a file created in a drawing package or a frame extracted from the video clip.   The graphic file is first imported into the Project window, and then dropped on to the video track.   By default, Premiere will display the graphic for one second.   This time can be extended by either:
- Dragging the file size wider.
- Right-clicking the file, choosing the 'Duration' option to open the duration dialog box, where a precise value can be entered.

If it is found that a video player, or Macromedia Director, jerks the content at the start of a video, extract a frame from the start of the video clip and place it in front of the video clip in the timeline. Extend the still frame to cover the time needed for the player to operate smoothly (adjust the length of time by trial and error the first time it is used).

Filters
Video filters are used to alter the content of each frame as it is rendered.   Unlike fades and other transitions, which only apply to a section of a clip, a filter is often applied to all of the frames in a clip.
There are two types of filter - those are used to enhance a clip's overall quality, and those impose special effects on the clip contents.   Any filter, like transition rendering, requires extra processing time. Most filters offer user control over the filter settings, to adjust the effect for the required purpose.   Premiere provides a good selection of filters and additional filters are sold as plug-ins to the Premiere application.

Filters for frame enhancement
The higher-quality construction of a computer monitor means that it can reproduce a greater colour range than is available from a television screen. Since videotape has been recorded with television in mind, it is designed to cater for the range handled by the TV screen.
Filters can be applied, before compression, to improve the colours in the movie. A small increase in contrast can produce significant improvements to the vividness of colours, as well as improving the black to white contrast.   The clip should be scrubbed through, to ensure that the changed settings have not adversely affected any part of the movie.   It is important to ensure that changes to contrast and brightness leave the blacks at true black level; otherwise it introduces noise and lowers compression.
Filters are commonly used to brighten up an under-exposed clip or to adjust colours to compensate for an incorrect white balance.
The filters supplied with Premiere include:
Brightness & Contrast, Color Balance, Color Offset, Hue and Saturation, and Gamma Correction
The Gamma Correction filter lightens or darkens a clip by changing the brightness levels of the midtones (the middle-grey levels) while leaving the dark and light areas unaffected.
The Levels filter manipulates the brightness and contrast of a clip. It combines the functions of the Color Balance, Gamma Correction, Brightness & Contrast, and Invert filters into one filter.

Effects Filters
Fancy effects filters can be very effective in the right situation. However, they tend introduce noise and artifacts and should only be used when necessary.
The filters supplied with Premiere include:
Alpha Glow, Anti-alias, Backwards (Video), Bend, Better Gaussian Blur, Blur and Blur More , Camera Blur, Camera View, Color Replace, Crystallize, Emboss, Gaussian Blur, Gaussian Sharpen, Horizontal Flip, Horizontal Hold, Image Pan, Invert, Lens Distortion, Lens Flare, Median, Mirror, Mosaic, Pinch, Pointillize, Polar, Posterize, Posterize Time, Radial Blur , Ripple, Roll, Sharpen and Sharpen More, Sharpen Edges, Shear, Solarize, Spherize, Twirl, Vertical Flip, Vertical Hold, Video Noise, Wave , Wind, Zig Zag.

Applying a Filter

Filters can be applied to a portion of a clip, an entire clip, or to a collection of clips. Premiere also allows the effects of a filter to be varied within a clip. So, for example a clip with the *'Lens Distortion'* filter applied to it may begin with a low level of distortion, have more distortion in the middle of the clip and have no distortion at the end of the clip. This would require the setting of three *'keyframes'*. A keyframe is a handle that appears on the clip's keyframe timeline, as shown in the illustration below. A keyframe contains all the information of the clip's filter settings that apply at that point in time. If multiple keyframes are added to the keyframe timeline, each can have different settings. Premiere then uses linear interpolation to work out the contents of each frame between the keyframes. This means that the filter's effect on the clip can be increased or decreased over different areas of the clip.

The alteration of filter settings during a clip is mostly used for special effects, while video enhancement filters are usually applied evenly to the entire clip.

The steps for applying a filter to a video clip are:

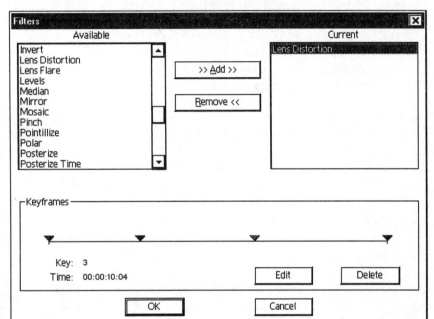

- Highlight the video clip in the Timeline window.
- Choose *'Filters'* from the *'Clip'* drop-down menu.
- Select the desired filter from the displayed list and click the *'Add'* button.
- Choose the filter settings in the dialog box that is displayed. These settings apply to the entire clip unless other keyframes are added, or the end keyframe settings are altered.
- Click the *'OK'* button to apply the settings to the first keyframe. The filter

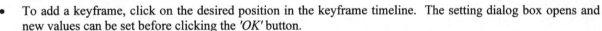

dialog box then displays the keyframe timeline, as shown. Initially, there are only keyframes at the beginning and end of the timeline.

- To add a keyframe, click on the desired position in the keyframe timeline. The setting dialog box opens and new values can be set before clicking the *'OK'* button.
- New keyframes can be dragged along the timeline to reposition them. As a keyframe moved, the *'Time'* reading below the timeline indicates the exact position of that keyframe along the timeline.
- To remove a keyframe, highlight it and click the *'Delete'* button. The first and last keyframes cannot be removed.
- The settings of any keyframe on the timeline (including the first and last keyframes) can be altered by highlighting the keyframe and clicking the *'Edit'* button. This opens the dialog box for that keyframe.
- When all the keyframes are entered, click the *'OK'* button at the bottom of the Filters dialog box.

If the keyframe timeline only contains the start and end keyframes, they can be set to different settings, for a gradual change of filter over the entire clip.

In the Timeline window, clips that have filters applied to them are displayed with a blue border at the top.

Applying multiple Filters

As can be seen in the above illustration, the *'Available'* window displays a list of all possible filters, while the *'Current'* window displays those filters that have been selected. More than one filter can be added to a clip, if more complex effects are required. The filters are applied in the order that they appear in the Current window and changing the order can change the final effect. The first effect is applied to the clip, then the second effect is applied to the result from the first filter, and so on. Each filter retains its own keyframe timeline and its own set of keyframes. Alterations to one filter's settings have no effect on the settings of another filter. The order of filters in the Current window can be changed by highlighting a filter and dragging it up or down the list.

The effects of a filter can be increased by adding it to the Current list more than once.

Applying multiple filters will result in much longer rendering times.

Black & White filter

This very simple filter converts a clip to greyscale.   There is no settings dialog box and the effect has to be applied to the entire clip, as no addition keyframes can be added.   For more control, see the Color Pass filter discussed next.

Color Pass filter

The Color Pass filter, like the *'Black & White'* filter, converts the content of each frame in a video clip to a greyscale.   However, this filter is adjusted to allow a specified colour to escape the greyscale conversion.   There are many examples of this technique in television adverts, where the entire world is grey is except for someone's bright red dress or lipstick. The filter does not attach itself to the object, just to the colour.   The planning of the project can take this into account and ensure that as much as possible of the object to be filmed for this treatment is in a colour that is not likely to be found in the surrounding area of the shot.   Examples are purple (e.g. someone wearing a purple dress), red (e.g. playing football with a bright red ball) and canary yellow (e.g. driving a yellow car).

The steps for applying this filter to a video clip are:

- Highlight the video clip in the timeline.
- Choose *'Filters'* from the *'Clip'* drop-down menu.
- Select *'Color Pass'* from the displayed list and click the *'Add'* button.
- Use the eyedropper to select the required colour in the *'Clip Sample'* window
- Dragging the *'Similarity'* slider sets the range of colours that allowed through the filter. So, for example, a blue sky will not be evenly blue across a frame or throughout a clip.   Increasing the similarity range ensures that more shades of blue are accepted to maintain the effect.   A range of 100% means that all colours in the scene are passed through the filter.
- Checking the *'Reverse'* box ensures that all colours <u>except</u> the chosen colour are preserved.

Ghosting

The Ghosting filter overlays transparencies of the immediately preceding frames on the current frame. This effect can be useful, for example, when you want to show the motion path of a moving object, such as a bouncing ball; the effect is best used with uncluttered scenes.   The effect can also be used to simulate the view of someone who is drunk, drugged or dazed from the effect of a punch or loss of memory. There is no settings dialog box and the effect has to be applied to the entire clip, as no addition keyframes can be added.

Replicate

The Replicate filter divides the screen into tiles and displays the whole image in miniature in each tile. The number of tiles is set by dragging the slider in the Replicate settings dialog box.   This filter supports additional keyframes.

Tiles

The *'Tiles'* filter divides the entire frame equally into a set of tiles, with each tile displaying a part of the frame content. The number of tiles is set by entering a value in the settings dialog box.   This filter supports additional keyframes.

Resize

The Resize filter resizes the clip to the output frame size using interpolated scaling. This provides better scaling than QuickTime or Video for Windows can achieve, adjusting the size when you export the final video project. There is no settings dialog box and the effect has to be applied to the entire clip, as no additional keyframes can be added.

Strobe

The Strobe filter is used to suggest a mood of hyperactivity or chaos (e.g. dance scenes or crowd scenes). The filter simulates a stroboscopic effect, or strobe light, by hiding frames at a regular rate as the clip plays. The regularity of the effect is set by specifying the number of visible and hidden frames in the settings dialog box. When the clip content is hidden, the frame is filled with a user-selectable colour.

Tint

The Tint filter applies a tint to the frame content.   The dialog box allows the tint colour and percentage of tint to be set.   This filter supports additional keyframes. It can be used along with the Black and White filter to simulate the sepia tones found in old films.

Picture in Picture

A basic *'picture in picture'* is deemed a high tech effect but is simple to achieve.

It can be used for a number of purposes, including:

- Displaying the commentator's head and shoulder in a corner of the frame, while the rest of the frame displays the content being discussed.
- Displaying a close-up of a process, while the main frame content displays the wider view.
- Displaying a set of sub-features of the main display (e.g. the main display shows a holiday resort, while the insert shows clips of the pool, the restaurants, the bedrooms, etc).
- Displaying special effects such as placing the insert in the area occupied by the main clip's television screen, computer monitor, videophone, etc.

The steps for achieving a picture in picture effect are:

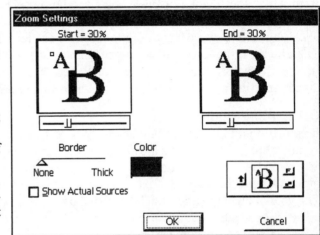

- Place main video clip in Track 1A.
- Place the clip to be inset in Track 1B.
- Select the *'Zoom'* transition from the Transitions window and drop it into the Transitions track.
- Extend the transition until it covers the duration of the clip being inserted.
- Double click on the transitions track to bring up the Zoom settings dialog box.
- Drag the left-hand slider to the proportion of the screen to be occupied by the insert clip.
- Drag the right-hand slider to the same value.
- Drag the handle in the middle of the left-hand window to the location where the insert clip is to be viewed in the final project.
- Set the colour and thickness of any border to be placed round the insert.
- Click the *'OK'* button.

Thought should be given at the storyboard stage to the use of picture in picture.   For example, if a scene involves two people having a conversation via a videophone, both clips should be recorded to reflect the eyelines of the participants.   Both people should be positioned for recording such that they appear to be looking at each other in the final video.   In addition, the quality of the inserted clip may be deliberately be downgraded, to give the impression of losses to the signal through travelling great distances.

Split Screen

A common effect is to split the screen into two horizontal sections, with a different video playing in each section.   It has the same uses as mentioned in picture-in-picture above and is also used for *'before and after'* situations (e.g. the garden before and after the makeover, the model's hair before and after using a particular brand of hair conditioner, etc).

The steps to achieve a split screen effect are:

- Place the 'left' video clip in Track 1A.
- Place the 'right' video in Track 1B.
- Select the *'Wipe'* transition from the Transitions window and drop it into the Transitions track.
- Extend the transition until it covers the duration of the clips being used.
- Double click on the transitions track to bring up the Wipe settings dialog box.
- Drag the left-hand slider to the proportion of the screen to be occupied by the left clip (e.g. 30%).
- Drag the right-hand slider to the value of 100% minus the size of the left screen (e.g. 70%).
- Click the *'OK'* button.

Chromakey

This is one of 15 transparency effects provided by Premiere. It provides the effect of the weather forecaster or holiday presenter in a studio, yet with all kinds of maps and exotic locations in the background.   Chromakey uses two clips. The foreground clip (e.g. the presenter) is recorded against a blue background (ensuring that no blue clothes are worn).   Then the blue area of the clip is made transparent.   The content of the second clip is now visible in all parts of the previously blue area. This is accessed through the *'Video'* option in the *'Clip'* drop-down menu, with *'Transparency'* chosen in the *'Video'* sub-menu.   The dialog box allows the transparent colour and the similarity level to be set.

Using extra audio tracks

Most video clips are recorded with a sound track and the *'Audio 1'* track will hold the audio track of the main video clip. The second video track will use the *'Audio 2'* track, if it contains audio information. Additional audio is often added to a project. This may consist of background music (for creating a mood), background effects (to provide atmosphere for the scene) or a voiceover (to explain a process, sell a product, etc).

Audio clips can be separately recorded. Many unusual sounds (e.g. a laughing hyena) or sounds that are difficult to record (e.g. the flight of a low-flying aircraft), can be purchased as royalty-free samples.

The clips are added to the Project window and are dragged and dropped into the *'Audio 3'* track. If a further audio track is required, it has to be added to the Timeline window. At the top right-hand corner of the Timeline, there is a rightward-pointing arrowhead. Clicking on the arrow produces a dialog box from which the *'Track Options'* choice should be selected. This results in a display of all the existing tracks on the timeline. From here, individual tracks can be named (e.g. Audio Track 3 can be renamed *'music'* or *'sound effects'*) and additional audio or video tracks can be added to the timeline.

The effect can be tested by highlighting the Timeline window and pressing the spacebar. The audio from both tracks is mixed together and played. Additional audio tracks should be at slightly less volume than might first be thought, as there is a tendency to set background tracks to excessive volumes.

Controlling audio levels

It is important to recognise that when separate audio clips appear in different tracks of the timeline, their volumes are additive. This means that at certain times, the combined peak volume is greater than can be accommodated by the range of the software, resulting in distortion. If distortion is detected during the preview stage, the volume of individual audio tracks will need to be reduced.

The gain of an entire track can be adjusted by the following steps:
- Highlight the audio clip in the timeline.
- Choose *'Clip'* from the main top menu.
- Choose *'Audio'* from the drop-down menu.
- Choose *'Gain'* from the sub-menu.
- Alter the percentage value in the *'Gain Value'* box (between 0% and 200%) and click the *'OK'* button.

There are also ways to lower the volume of a <u>section</u> of an audio clip. This allows, for example, a background music track to be faded during a voiceover, or allows the cross-fading of two music clips. The music should be faded slightly before the voiceover begins, so that the fade becomes less obvious. The voiceover should start about half way through the fade down and finish about half way through the fade up.

The steps for altering a section of an audio clip's volume are:
- Highlight the audio clip in the timeline.
- Click the triangle next to the audio track label, to reveal the lower box along the audio clip. This box displays a horizontal red line representing the audio clip's volume, and a blue clip representing the clip's panning between left and right (for stereo samples).
- Click on the red line to add additional handles where the fade will start and end..
- Drag these handles low. The distance between the points determines the duration of the fade and the angle of the diagonal lines determines the speed of the fades. If the sides of the fade are made vertical, the sound will cut off suddenly and be restored suddenly.
- Ensure that the work area bar covers the section to be tested. Drag with the mouse if necessary.
- Run a preview.
- Adjust the settings, if necessary, to achieve the desired effect.

The Boost and Compressor/Expander filters outlined below provide additional facilities for controlling the dynamic range of an audio clip.

Audio Filters

Ideally, the audio clip should have its quality optimised before bringing it into the Project window. This may involve increasing a quiet audio passage, removing unwanted noise, adding echo and so on, as explained in the chapter on audio. However, many audio processing facilities are provided by Premiere. Some filters enhance or correct a clip's characteristics. These include Bass & Treble, Boost, Compressor/Expander, Equalize, High Pass and Low Pass, Noise Gate, Notch/Hum, and Parametric Equalization. Other filters add special effects, such as the Auto Pan, Backwards, Chorus, Flanger, Multi-Effect, Multitap Delay, and Reverb filters.

Audio quality filters

Compressor/Expander

This filter alters the dynamic range of the audio clip, the ratio between the highest and lowest amplitudes in the signal.   The Compressor facility increases the amplitude of the quietest sounds while leaving the loudest sounds untouched.   This reduces the dynamic range and can "even out" the voices in a conversation, when one speaks more softly than the other.   The potential drawback is the possibility of increasing the amplitude of the unwanted signal noise along with the wanted audio signal.

The Expander increases the dynamic range of the clip.   This can be used to give emphasis to the louder sounds in the clip, or to reduce the noise level in a clip.   The total dynamic range is fixed by the computer's hardware and software handling capabilities.   Therefore, throughout the selected audio portion, increasing the dynamic range of one section of the audio amplitude range lowers the dynamic range in the remaining amplitude range.

The three controls are:

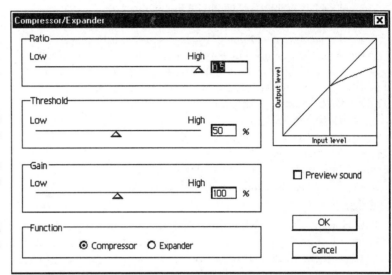

Threshold

Sets the level at which compression begins (or expansion ends). It is also known as 'the knee' and is the vertical line in the illustration.

Ratio

For the Compressor, it sets the expansion ratio to the right of the threshold.
For the Expander, it sets the compression ratio to the left of the threshold.

Gain

Sets the audio level at the threshold and therefore adjusts the overall output level.

Noise Gate

This filter removes the unwanted background noise that is present during quiet passages of an audio clip. It has two controls.   The 'Threshold' control sets the level below which noise is removed. If the setting is too low, there is little effect. If the setting is too high, it removes part of the wanted audio.

The 'Decay' control sets the speed at which the audio reduces to silence.   If it is set too low, the noise is still evident.   If it is set too high, it may cut off the end of wanted content or produce an unnatural effect.

Audio effects filters

Chorus

This filter takes a clip containing a single voice or instrument and adds a copy of the content after it has been slightly offset in frequency.   The aim is to create the impression of multiple voices or instruments (hence the name 'chorus') and create a more full-bodied audio clip.

Echo

This filter takes the sound clip and mixes in a copy of the clip after a slight time delay.   This produces the effect of the sound echoing off a distance surface.   If used with a small amount of echo, it adds greater depth to an otherwise flat voiceover.

Other audio considerations

The audio is often recorded along with the video track.   This is particularly important for ensuring proper synchronisation between the audio and video content.   Other audio recordings can be made to add to the effect.   An interview with a plant manager, for instance, may be recorded during a lunch break to ensure quiet recording conditions.   A separate recording of the factory machinery is made after the lunch break and the two sounds are mixed later. This allows the relative levels to be controlled during the editing stage and provides a much better result.   The second recording can be made with a separate tape recorder, such as a DAT recorder or MiniDisc recorder, or with the camcorder.   If the camcorder is used for audio recording, the video component is ignored during the editing process.

It is also common to repeat the playing of a clip of background atmosphere (e.g. street noise or office sounds). A single clip can be inserted several times to appear as a longer clip. For this to work smoothly, the edges where the clips butt must be at levels, and have content, that makes the join unnoticeable.

Another technique is to add variety by changing the video content during a longish narration. Instead of displaying the head and shoulders of the presenter, the project can cut away to a relevant video clip. The viewer then sees a variety of changing video shots during the single audio session. For best effect, the scene should be changed during a pause in the narration.

Titling

For most web and CD-ROM use, video clips will not require titles, as they are played by clicking a hyperlink or menu option. Some projects will benefit from titling and examples are:

- Projects designed to be output to videotape.
- Projects for the deaf, where sub-titles are of great benefit.
- Projects where a foreign language sub-title is displayed.
- Projects where a voiceover is not viable (e.g. a voiceover would spoil a video of a band and the additional information would be in written form as sub-titles).

The title text should be left on the screen long enough for it to be read twice.

The steps for creating a title are:

- Design the content.
- Create the title, using Premiere.
- Save the title.
- Import the title file into the Project window.
- Place the title clip in a superimpose track.

Design

The user should plan what should be included in the title. Care should be taken to achieve a balance in terms of content and of time. A title that flashes up for a second is too fast while nobody wants to watch screens of text slowly crawl up the screen for five minutes. The amount of necessary text should be included and the pace at which any moving text is animated should be considered before editing the title.

All the usual advice on use of type styles, font sizes and colours apply here. The title may also include drawings made with the Titler's drawing tools or items of clip art.

There is an additional consideration for titling on a video clip. The title may be opaque or transparent. With a transparent title, the title content is displayed over any video content that may be present in the main video track. In this case, the background content may be constantly changing. Care should be taken that the title contents remains visible over all changes in the video content. For example, black text would disappear if the video scene showed a train entering a tunnel, while blue text would become unreadable if the video content showed a plane taking off into a clear morning sky.

Creation

The title editing utility is accessed by clicking on the *'File'* menu, choosing *'New'* from the drop-down menu and *'Title'* from the sub-menu.

This opens a Title window, where the title content can be added. All content should be placed within the inner marker lines. These dotted lines mark out the *'title safe zone'* - the area that is visible on all viewing screens. Objects outside this are may not be visible on some screens, or suffer from the distortion that some screens have at the edges of the picture.

The set of tools at the left of window provide the facilities for adding and modifying the title contents.

Titles can incorporate both static text and scrolling text. Text can be scrolled upwards for opening and closing captions, while rightward scrolling text is useful for sub-titles.

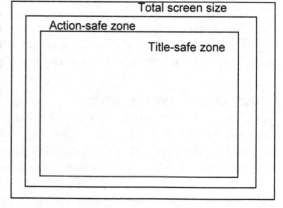

With scrolling text, consideration should be given to the spacing of the lines of text. Adding extra carriage returns before the opening line of text produces a pause before the title text lines scroll into view.   Adding carriage returns after the last line of text results in all the title text scrolling out of sight. Adding carriage returns between lines of text produces a time delay between individual lines in the title. To preview the title sequence, drag the small slider that is situated below the tool palette

Saving
When the title is completed, Click the *'Save As'* option from the *'File'* menu.   The file is named with a .ptl extension.

Using
The title should be imported into the Project window and dropped from there into the highest numbered unused superimpose track.   As the title is designed to superimpose on all other video content, it should be in the highest unused video superimpose track.

The effect of merging the title with other screen content can be viewed by carrying out a Preview.   If the animated content of the title is moving too fast, the clip's duration can be lengthened by dragging the right edge of the title clip along the timeline.

Another attractive effect is to play the title sequence over a static background that uses a graphic file or digitised picture.   The graphic is added to the Project window and brought into the timeline.   It is then stretched to cover the same time duration as the title sequence.

A digitised picture could usefully be the first frame of the video, or it could be another picture entirely. See the earlier section on *'Adding a Graphic'* for details.

Animating
The Title window allows some basic animation of text, using horizontal and vertical scrolling.   Once a title appears in the Timeline window, it can have much more complex animations imposed on it. While motion path animation can be applied to all video clips, it is particularly effective for title text, especially where the text is a static title.

Once the title clip has been clicked on in the timeline, the motion path dialog box is accessed by clicking on the *'Clip'* menu and choosing *'Video'* from the drop-down menu and *'Motion'* from the sub-menu.   The dialog box has the controls shown in the illustration.

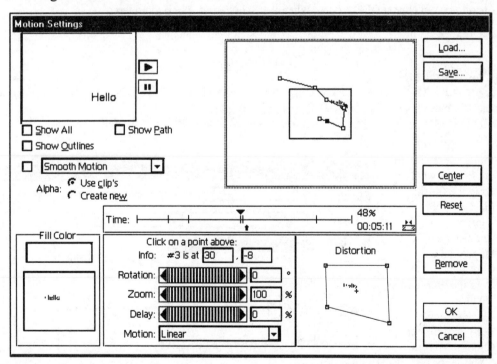

The right-hand window allows the path to be set, while the left-hand window displays an animation of the final effect.

Extra handles can be added to the path by clicking between the two existing handles.   All the handles can be dragged to the positions required for the desired effect.   As a handle's position is altered, the right-hand window displays the new animated path.

Other tools allow the text to be rotated or zoomed in or out, as its moves between particular handles on the path.

Working with multiple layers

On occasion, a very large project may require the inclusion of more video or audio tracks than is the maximum provided by Premiere. This requires the project to be built up in stages. The existing tracks are filled and the edited and the clip is saved to disc. It is then reloaded into the Video 1a track and additional tracks can then be added and the process repeated.

Test, test, test!!

Large projects using multiple clips and many effects and transitions will take a long time to render. As the project is built up, the time to render a full preview becomes ever longer. There may be a temptation to cut corners by assuming that each change and each alteration has produced the required effect. This could prove a costly mistake, as errors or unexpected results are only spotted after distribution. Like all software and authoring projects, the video editing process should be subject to continuous review. In a larger project, the completed video output may have to vetted by the rest of the authoring team or the project clients.

Rough cuts can be created using the *'Ignore Filters'* options in the output rendering options (see later). This will produce an output that is quick to create, since it does not render the transitions that have added during editing. While rough cuts are very useful in confirming the timing and order of the project's clips, they do not display the results of applying filters, transitions, etc - the processes that may also make or break a project.

The following points may prove useful for creating larger projects:

- Build up the project in stages.
- Use the Work Area Bar, so that only the area encompassing the effect, filter or transition is previewed. This will save a lot of wasted rendering time.
- Save each stage. That way, if a major blunder is made, the earlier version can be easily retrieved. This can be a time saver but supposes that the user has plenty of storage or backup capacity.
- Don't compress the material each time it is saved. Each time a clip is compressed, its quality is reduced and continued re-compression will further degrade the clip. If possible, always work with uncompressed clips up the moment when the final output is being rendered.
- Save project sections at hard cuts, as this makes them easier to re-integrate later.

Format Conversions

Premiere provides facilities for converting file types. For instance, a file that was imported as a QuickTime file can be saved as an AVI file, an vice versa.

QuickTime and AVI files can also be converted into Animated GIFs or FLC/FLI files.

The steps for achieving a file conversion are:

- Import the file in to the Project window.
- Drag the file into the Timeline window.
- Choose *'File'* from the main menu.
- Choose *'Export'* from the drop-down menu.
- Choose *'Movie'* from the sub-menu.
- Choose *'Settings'* from the dialog box.
- Choose the desired output file type

from the drop-down menu as shown in the illustration.
- Alter any advanced setting, if the box is not greyed out.
- Click the *'OK'* button.

If the QuickTime or AVI option is selected, the user is given the option to export only the video component, only the audio component, or both components. This provides an easy way to strip the audio from a video file, for example.

Converting to MPEG

Premiere does not have direct MPEG encoding facilities, although additional plug-ins can be added to carry out the task, For example, the program *'AVI2MPEG2'* that is on our CD is a freeware program that can be used as a standalone converter or as a Premiere plug-in.   The above illustration shows Premiere with this plug-in installed (it appears as the first choice in the drop-down menu).   Another application on the CD is *'MPEG Kit'* and it will convert AVIs to MPEGs and vice versa.   Xing MPEG Encoder and Ulead MPEG Converter are standalone commercial products that create MPEG streams from AVI files. VirtualDub is a freely distributable capture and processing program that can convert MPEGs into AVIs. It is available at www.geocities.com/virtualdub/

Converting to an animated GIF

Web sites commonly use animated GIFs as a means of adding animation or video content to a site.   This is an economic measure, as an animated GIF is much smaller than a comparative video clip.   This reduction in size is achieved because animated GIFs can:

- Use lower frame rates.
- Use loops.
- Use a clip in both forwards and backwards actions.

The section earlier on format conversions covers the steps to create an animated GIF from a video clip. Consider creating a web site home page with an animation of the author waving to the viewer.   The author's hand is moved up and down in a waving action and this is recorded as a video clip of relatively low resolution (say one eighth of a screen size).   This smaller size is perfectly acceptable in an animation and has already made a very substantial saving in size compared to a video clip.

An examination of the clip shows that the downward movement of the arm is simply a reverse of the upward movement.   This is a waste of footage and only one of these actions need remain in the clip. The section showing the arm being lowered is cut and the video footage has been reduced by a half.   The remaining section of the clip is copied and butted up itself.   There are now two clips of an arm being raised.   The second clip is now reversed, using the *'Backwards'* filter.   When played back, the arm is raised and lowered and the clip is the same duration as before it was edited.   However, since the exported version uses the same frames for both movements, the size of the clip is half as large.

The frame rate for the clip can now be reduced substantially compared to the original footage.   A frame rate of 6fps or 9fps is perfectly acceptable for an animated GIF and this reduces the file size by another factor compared to an original frame rate of 25fps.

The animated GIF option from the *'Export Movie'* settings provides an option to have the clip with a transparent background and an option to continuously loop the animation.   Choosing the looping option provides an animation that continuously repeats - which would be very large if implemented as a video clip. The Premiere controls for handling GIF animation are limited and the exported GIF can be brought into the *'Animation Shop'* in Paint Shop Pro, where greater control is available.

Other Packages

VidEdit, Personal AVI Editor, Avid Cinema and Adobe Premiere are among the many video editors that are available.   Other editing packages are Media Studio Pro, MGI VideoWave, SpeedRazor and Corel Lumiere.   They have varying degrees of sophistication and features, but they their main reason for existence is the amalgamation of video clips into a single production.   They are primarily time-oriented - getting clips trimmed to the correct length, assembling in the correct time sequence, aligning the content in separate layers for the correct synchronisation, and so on.

Although some of these packages also provide a large range of transitions and effects, they are not optimised for these purposes.   Consequently, other software products are available for handling the video footage after it has been edited.   Some of the most popular packages are covered below.

Adobe After Effects

This package is aimed at the top end of the market (it costs more than some PCs).   Adobe advertises the product as designed for the broadcast, film, video, multimedia and on-line production markets.

It can incorporate video clips, audio clips and graphics files that were produced in other packages.   Each is allocated to a separate layer and each can have effects applied to it.   The effects include animation, morphing, warping, masking, zooms, filters and flying layers.   It has a flowchart view to visualise complex projects, as it displays the relationship between the various objects (e.g. video clips, audio clips, graphics files) and the multiple effects that are being applied to them.

It can use other effects via extra plug-ins, such as the *'Eye Candy'* effects produced by Alien Skin Software. It also supports *'network rendering'* - the package is installed on a number of computers on a local area network and they then share the rendering tasks so that they complete much earlier. This is an example of *'parallel distributed processing'*.

Media Cleaner Pro

This package has more intelligent compression algorithms than those available with Premiere, providing better compression ratios. For example, it has algorithms that selectively blur the frame contents. Object edges are kept distinct, unlike when using Premiere's normal Blur filter. It also has a Black/White Restore function that ensures that black areas, such as backgrounds and shadows, are reduced to a more solid black.   This reduces noise and further improves compression.   So, many edit their clips in Premiere, then compress using Media Cleaner Pro.

Other Media Cleaner Pro facilities include batch processing and multiple conversions.   Multiple conversions, for example, converts a QuickTime move into a CD version and a variety of smaller and/or streamed versions in one activity (instead of the multiple separate conversions required with Premiere).

Other packages

Since Premiere imports any kind of AVI file, the output of 3D modelling and rendering packages can be directly included on the Premiere timeline.   Packages that produce such AVI files include 3D Studio Max, TrueSpace and Lightwave.

DeBabilizer is another useful tool for batch processing of graphics files and video clips. It can carry out file format conversions and convert AVIs to sets of still images.

AVI Constructor is a shareware package that constructs an AVI file from a set of bitmap pictures.   A trial version is included on the CD.

Pinnacle SmartCapture detects the join between shots in a videotape and creates a picture gallery of thumbnails from the first frame in each clip.   The thumbnails are dropped into the editing software in the final project running order and it then creates a set of video clips, without the user being in attendance.

Output

When the project is finally completed its editing stage, the material is output for distribution. The steps for this process in Premiere are covered below, along with suggested settings and approaches.

Generally, a videotape can store hours of footage and is therefore not subject to any physical restriction on the amount and length of video that appears in the final project.   The restriction is rather one of design and user reaction (does the audience really want to watch four hours of a wedding?).

Most output is designed for later computer use, through a kiosk, CD-ROM or web site and there are obviously much more restrictions in the amount of video that is included in these media.

How much video

The amount of video that is included in any multimedia project is largely determined by the purpose of the material.   A rock video must have full video content by definition, while a web site may still be very effective even with a video clip dropped in favour of an animated GIF or a Flash sequence.

Most CD-ROM and kiosk projects will mix live video with still photographs, graphics and animations. A CD advertising holiday homes in Florida may look impressive with a large amount of video clips but would soon run out of disc space.   In many situations, a still photograph (perhaps with music, audio or a voiceover) would be sufficient.   This balance should already have been addressed at the storyboard stage.

Preparing to output

The first steps are to remove any unwanted components that were brought into the Project window and were not included in the final project. This is achieved by choosing the *'Remove Unused'* option from the *'Project'* menu.   The project should then be saved using the *'Save As'* option from the *'File'* menu.   In fact, the *'Save'* option should be sufficient, as the project should have been already named and saved at many earlier stages of the editing process.

Premiere offers a wide range of output options and these are grouped in dialog boxes that are accessed via the *'File'* menu.   Choosing *'Export'* from the drop-down menu, followed by choosing *'Movie'* from the sub-menu, opens the first of the dialog boxes.

The opening screen is a menu for *'General Settings'* and this was illustrated in the earlier section of format conversions.

| Export Movie General Settings ||
Option	Description
File Type	Decides whether Video for Windows or QuickTime CODECs are offered in the *'Video Settings'* panel, or whether the video is exported as an Animated GIF, FLC file, etc.
Range	Decides how much of timeline content appears in the final output. Choosing *'Entire Project'* includes all material that appears on the timeline. Choosing *'Work Area'* only includes material that sits under the Work Area bar.
Export Audio/ Export Video	Checking the *'Export Video'* box ensures that the video content appears in the final output. Checking the *'Export Audio'* box ensures that the audio content appears in the final output. Checking both options ensures that the entire recording content appears in the final output. Checking only one option allows the audio or video component to be stripped from a recording.

Export Audio Settings

This dialog box is accessed via the *'File'* menu. Choosing *'Export'* from the drop-down menu, followed by choosing *'Movie'* from the sub-menu, opens the Movie Export Settings dialog boxes.

'Audio Settings' can then be accessed from the drop-down list available at the top-left of the window, as shown in the illustration.

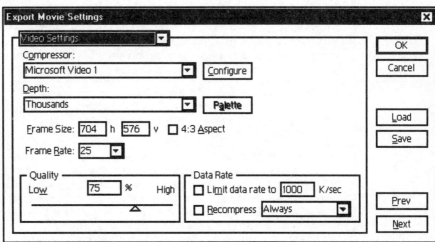

| Export Movie Audio Settings ||
Option	Description
Rate	Decides which sampling rate to use for the audio output. The range of options offered depends upon the compressor chosen in the *'Type'* selection below. For example, the *'TrueSpeech'* compressor only offers a 8000Hz rate, while *'Uncompressed'* offers a choice from 5KHz to 48KHz plus the option to type in any other sampling rate from the keyboard. This facility can be used to reduce the size of audio files recorded at 44KHz by outputting at a lower rate. This lowers the audio quality but produces files that are more efficient for web use.
Format	Decides the bit depth and number of channels for the final audio output. The options offered are controlled by the choice of audio compressor. The G.723.1 compressor, for example, only operates at 16-bit mono. ADPCM offers 16-bit mono or 16-bit stereo, while the uncompressed option offers a choice of both 8-bit or 16-bit in either mono or stereo. An 8-bit depth halves the storage size of a 16-bit clip but lowers the quality. A mono sample requires half the storage space of a stereo sample. It maintains the audio quality but loses the stereo effect.
Type	Decides what audio CODEC should be applied to the project's audio output. Read the chapter on audio for details of audio CODECs.
Interleave	Decides how audio content is merged with video content. The options are to insert audio data between every video frame or to have larger amounts of audio inserted between groups of video frames (up to two seconds worth of frames). The audio data is read into the computer's memory and played until the next section of audio data is read. If the computer has to process the audio data too often, the audio does not run smoothly and breaks up. Higher interleave values prevent this but require more memory to store the large audio chunks. The value chosen should reflect the expected specification of the computer playing the material.
Enhanced Rate Conversion	Decides the trade off between quality and speed when the sample in the timeline has to be resampled (i.e. either upsampled or downsampled from the current data rate to the new specified rate). There are three settings: • Off - quickest processing with poorest quality • Better - average speed and quality • Best - slowest processing with best quality The Best quality would be used in all but the largest of projects, and only where time is short.
Logarithmic Audio Fades	Decides how audio gain increases or decreases are perceived during playback. Checking this option produces a logarithmic change in volume, which is the way that the human ear perceives audio changes. This results in a more natural fade but takes longer to process. Leaving the box unchecked produces a linear fade. This is less realistic but takes less time to process.

Export Video Settings

This dialog box is accessed via the *'File'* menu.   Choosing *'Export'* from the drop-down menu, followed by choosing *'Movie'* from the sub-menu, opens the Movie Export Settings dialog boxes. *'Video Settings'* can then be accessed from the drop-down list available at the top-left of the window.

Export Movie Video Settings	
Option	**Description**
Compressor	Decides which CODECs to use for compressing the final output. The selections offered depend on the Editing Mode selected. With QuickTime as the editing mode, compressors such as Cinepak and Sorenson appear on the list. With Video for Windows as the chosen editing mode, the compressors offered include RLE, and Video 1. There is a *'None'* option that results in no compression to the output. This is useful to retain a high-quality archive copy, or to obtain intermediate files for re-insertion into the timeline. Some compressors (e.g. the Matrox MJPEG and the MPEG-4) also provide options to configure their data rates or compression ratios. In these cases the *'Configure'* button is not greyed out and can be clicked to access these controls.
Depth	Decides the colour depth of the final output. Sometimes this option is greyed out, while other CODECs allow the user choice of 256, thousands or millions of colours. Choosing *'None'* or *'Video 1'* for the compressor and 256 for Depth is a good way to reduce a clip to 256 colours for web use.
Frame Size	Decides the final resolution of the video output and is input as pixels amounts. The values chosen will depend on the final destination of the file (e.g. set to 352x288 for an intended MPEG-1 file, smaller for web use and larger for CD and kiosk use). If the footage has been recorded on a camcorder, it normally records at a 4:3 aspect ratio. In this case, the *'4:3 Aspect'* box should be checked, to ensure that the correct vertical to horizontal relationship is maintained. Some camcorders can record in a widescreen 16:9 ratio and the vertical and horizontal values chosen in this case should maintain the ratio and avoid picture distortion.
Frame Rate	Decides the number of frames per second that are used in the final output. If the value chosen is different from the rate used for clips in the timeline, Premiere compensates by dropping or inserting frames. Premiere offers a choice of rates between 1fps and 30fps.
Quality	Decides how lossy the compression is. More loss means greater compression but lower quality output. Some CODECs are tweaked via the *'Compressor'* option mentioned above. Most CODECs use the *'Quality'* slider to control the compression ratio. As expected, the *'None'* option does not provide compression controls.
Data Rate	Decides the maximum amount of data that is included in each second of the output. This is required to ensure that the amount of data does not overwhelm the system that it is intended to be used on. The *'Limit Data Rate'* box is checked and the maximum rate is entered. This is useful when outputting to videotape from the timeline, since the many of output options discussed only apply to outputting to disk files. A clip's current data rate can be determined by right-clicking on the clip in the Project window, choosing *'Get Properties'* from the drop-down menu and clicking the *'Data Rate'* button.
Recompress	Decides how clips are processed, to ensure that the final project is outputted within the above user specified maximum data rate. When the box remains unchecked, no compression is applied to clips (even previously compressed clips that have been imported) that have not been altered during editing. In practice, the editing process often results in significant alterations to frames through the use of filters and transitions, or the alteration of frame rates, CODEC options, etc. These alterations may significantly change the final data rate, thus requiring recompression of the final project. When the *'Recompress'* box is checked, there are two options. The *'Always'* option compresses every frame during the output processing, even if the contents have not been changed or the maximum date rate is not being exceeded. Since most compression systems are lossy, the recompression of previously compressed clips will reduce the picture quality. The *'Maintain Data Rate'* option only compresses frames when it is necessary to bring the output within the maximum data rate. This ensures a higher quality of output. If all files used in the project were imported as uncompressed clips, then they are all compressed at the output stage.

Keyframe and rendering options

This dialog box is accessed via the *'File'* menu.   Choosing *'Export'* from the drop-down menu, followed by choosing *'Movie'* from the sub-menu, opens the Movie Export Settings dialog boxes.
'Keyframe and Rendering Options' can then be accessed from the drop-down list available at the top-left of the window.

Export Movie Keyframe and Rendering Settings	
Option	**Description**
Ignore Audio Filters	Ignores any audio filtering options to produce a quick rough cut. Should be left unchecked for the final project output.
Ignore Video Filters	Ignores any video filtering options to produce a quick rough cut. Should be left unchecked for the final project output.
Ignore Audio Rubber Bands	Ignores any audio rubber band controls to produce a quick rough cut. Should be left unchecked for the final project output.
Optimize Stills	Decides whether long displays of still frames are processed as a series of frames. Checking the box results, for example, in a four-second display of a still being stored as a single frame being displayed for four seconds. Unchecking the box results in, for example, a four-second display of a still being stored as 100 separate frames (i.e. four seconds at 25fps). The optimised option saves storage space but may not replay properly on all systems. The non-optimised is a safer choice if there is any doubt about the capabilities of the computer that the final project may be used on.
Field Settings	Decides on the way that the video content is packaged. There are three options: • No Fields - provides a progressive scan as used by computers and motion-picture film. • Upper Field First or Lower Field First - provides an interlaced output as used by video recorders and television. See the chapter on screen technology for an explanation of interlacing.

The chapter on computer video discussed the use of keyframes during temporal compression. Some CODECs use keyframes and the user can maximise the picture quality and compression ratio by controlling where keyframes are inserted in the final video clip.   If the chosen CODEC does not support keyframes, keyframe options will not be able to be accessed.
In Premiere, the user can mark points on the timeline where keyframes should be inserted.   These can be additional to the set of keyframes inserted at regular intervals by Premiere, or the final clip can use only the keyframes inserted by the user.

Export Movie Keyframe Settings	
Option	**Description**
Keyframe Every _ Frames	The first box can be checked to allow a value to be inserted in to the adjacent box. The user enters the frequency of inserting keyframes. This value is the size of the Group of Pictures. For example, setting the value to 12 results in a keyframe being inserted after every 12 frames. When the CODEC exports the clip it inserts keyframes at the chosen rate.
Frames Only At Markers	This box is checked to only create keyframes at each point where a Marker has been added to the timeline by the user during editing.
Add Keyframes At Markers	Checking this box results in an output file that has a keyframe inserted at each marker on the Timeline.
Add Keyframes At Edits	Checking this box results in an output file that has a keyframe inserted at the beginning of each clip in the Timeline.

The first two options are mutually exclusive.   However, if the first option is chosen, there is still the opportunity to add additional keyframes using the last two options.
So, for example, a clip may have keyframes automatically inserted every so often, with the user adding additional keyframes at points of dramatic scene changes in the clip.

Special Processing

This dialog box is accessed via the *'File'* menu. Choosing *'Export'* from the drop-down menu, followed by choosing *'Movie'* from the sub-menu, opens the Movie Export Settings dialog boxes.

'Special Processing' can then be accessed from the drop-down list available at the top-left of the window. This dialog box has two sections - one for a final cropping of the video output and one for final tweaking of the quality.

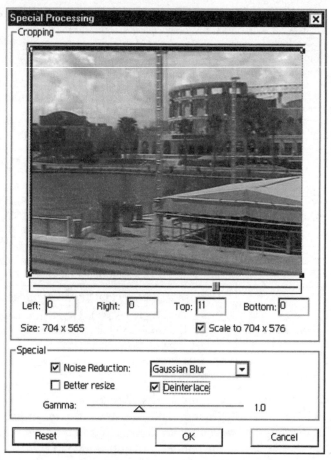

The cropping facility is similar to that provided in the Clip and Crop filters.

Four input boxes allow the frame to be cropped from any picture edge. The values are measured in pixels.

Alternatively, the handles on the screen can be dragged to any position and the boxes display the amount of each edge being cropped.

The *'Size'* reading below the picture displays the size of the frame after cropping.

If the *'Scale to ..'* box is not checked, the video is exported at the cropped size. In this case, it is best to choose an overall resolution whose dimensions are divisible by the pixel groups processed by the CODEC in use. For example, some CODECs examine the frame in blocks of 4x4 or 8x8 pixels and the dimensions should be divisible by 4 or 8 respectively, for the most efficient compression.

If the box is checked, the final output is scaled back to the frame size specified earlier in the Video Settings dialog box. Consult the notes on clipping and cropping. If the box is checked, the scaling may distort the final output.

The other options in this window are:

Export Movie Special Processing Settings	
Option	**Description**
Cropping	See above.
Noise Reduction	Decides what level of picture blurring should be set, to improve file compression. The drop-down menu provides three settings: • Blur - small amount of blurring, small file savings. • Gaussian - larger amounts of blurring, producing greater compression. • Median - blurring that tries to avoid blurs at the sharp edges between objects.
Better Resize	Decides what piece of software carries out any cropping or scaling. If the box is left unchecked, these activities are carried out by the CODEC selected earlier. If the box is checked, the activities are carried out by Premiere, at a slower processing pace but giving better quality.
Deinterlace	Decides what piece of software carries out any deinterlacing. If the box is left unchecked, these activities are carried out by the CODEC selected earlier. If the box is checked, the activities are carried out by Premiere at a better quality.
Gamma	Decides the level of gamma adjustment, to match different playback platforms (see the chapter on graphics). Dragging the slider sets the level of gamma, with a value of 1.0 leaving the picture unchanged. Premiere suggests a value of 0.7 or 0.8 for projects intended for cross-platform playback.

The slider that appears under the viewing window can be dragged, so that the effects of the alterations can be viewed across the range of frames in the project.

Choosing the output CODEC

The types of CODEC and their operation was covered in the chapter on digital video. The CODEC chosen for a particular project's output will depend upon the intended final use of the media. Apart from dedicated systems, such as kiosks, it is best to use software-based CODECs, as there is no guarantee that the end user has the appropriate hardware CODEC on his/her computer. The remainder of this chapter considers the factors that influence the choice of CODEC and their settings.

Media Type

CD

If the material is for general circulation on CD, a decision has to be made on the balance between the speed of CD players and the video quality. The clip size and frame rate could be sacrificed, so that the file will play on even the oldest CD ROM drive.   Alternatively, the better quality clips could be used, in the knowledge that older computers will not be able to reproduce them very effectively.   For reference, an old double-speed CD-ROM drive has a maximum data transfer rate of 300 KB per second, while a current 50x CD ROM drive has a maximum data rate of 7,500 KB/sec. Practical rates are a little less than these values.   A decision must also be made on how much of the disc space is allocated for video. Usually an AVI or QuickTime CODEC is used on CDs, as many computers still have no MPEG players.

DVD-ROM

The main development in video is the increased storage capacities offered by the DVD ('*Digital Versatile Disk'*), which can store 4.7GB on a single surface.   The future promises both double sided and multi-layer versions with ever-greater capacity.   This provides around eight times as much storage space than CD discs and there is a growing base of users with DVD players. This media allows high-quality full-screen MPEG-2 videos of about an hour's duration.   Future larger size DVD discs will provide an opportunity for even greater video storage.   Many multimedia products will not require that the video clip occupy the entire screen and this means that even more footage can be stored on the disc.

The output can be in any popular CODEC format and can include MPEG-2, since all DVD players are supplied with either hardware or software MPEG-2 CODECs.

Kiosk

The computer used for controlling kiosk presentations is known before the project is commenced. It is usually a high performance machine and can have as much fast hard drive storage space as is required. This imposes far fewer restrictions and output can be chosen for quality rather than file size. The output can even have no compression applied, for maximum quality.

Intranet

Universities, colleges and companies may run internal networks (intranets), where training or reference material is instantly available over the local cabling. Although local area networks may run at 10MHz or 100MHz (or even faster), this bandwidth is shared among large numbers of users. Generally, the faster networks are there because there are more users requiring services. Consequently, most systems do not have great spare capacity for each individual user.   The best that can be expected is 20KB up to around 100KB per second. Of course, this is still much faster than normal Internet speeds. The data rate of the intranet should be determined (the network supervisor should be able to supply this information) and the CODEC's video data rate should be matched to it.

Web site

This is the slowest medium for carrying video. Relatively few UK users have access to ISDN, ADSL or other fast connections to the Internet.   The vast majority of users are connecting with a 56k modem, or worse.   The speed of modem controls the effective transfer rate of the files.   A 56 kilobits per second modem has an effective maximum data transfer rate of around 5 Kilobytes per second (the Internet communications signals consume a chunk of the bits).   While scalability facilities (see earlier) cater for a range of sizes, even the best case is a large file.

Consideration should be given to:
- Reducing the clip resolution.
- Reducing the frame clip frame rate.
- Lowering the CODEC data rate.
- Converting a piece of video footage into an animated GIF.
- Converting the clip to a streamed file.

Back to tape

The only data rate restrictions are those imposed by the computer's hardware.   The computer system disk's, CPU, etc., should be capable of outputting the file to videotape without dropping any frames.

Frame Rate

PAL video runs at 25 fps.   NTSC videos run at 30fps.   These are high rates for some systems and it is common to package video for much smaller frame rates.   For example, a video clip at 5fps contains only a third of the video information of a PAL clip.   Therefore, it is only one fifth of the size and is suitable for low-end applications such as Internet video-conferencing.

At the other end of the quality scale, a video clip might require to run at the full PAL rate.

The frame rate trades file size for quality.   15fps is the minimum used to maintain any illusion of constant movement and is often found on videos clips supplied on CD-ROM with books and magazines. Sometimes, the jerkiness of a low frame rate is deliberately chosen for effect, such as simulating a security camera or an old movie.

Resolution

Video intended for videotape should be created at the frame rate and resolution of the intended tape format (see later). Video for CD-ROM, kiosk and web use does not suffer from these restrictions and can be a resolution that best fits the requirements.

In general, the highest resolution for video pictures is the first choice, where possible.   In practice, many compromises are forced on the designer by hardware and software restrictions.

High-resolution clips require more storage space and require fast transfer mechanisms. When a clip has both high resolution and high frame rates, it requires a high-performance software CODEC (such as Sorenson Video) running on a fast computer, or a hardware CODEC implementation such as an MPEG card.   In a multimedia product, there may not be so many requirements for full-screen video.   The nature of the content may require a smaller resolution to allow screen space for navigation buttons, menus, explanatory text, company logo, etc.   The hardware specification that can be expected from the end users' computers is rising all the time.   A screen of 240 x 180 was once a typical size, but larger sizes are now likely to be supported by most systems.   Of course, if a project is designed solely for use with a kiosk with a known high performance, the resolution can even be full screen.

I-Frame Setting

When a file is to be compressed with an MPEG CODEC, the user should control the size of the GOP (Group of Pictures).   In practice, this means setting the frequency of the key frames in the clip. Generally, an insertion frequency of every twelfth or fifteenth frame is used, with more insertions for clips with rapidly changing screen content.

If users have control over the playback, they wish to access the clip at random points.   If too few key frames are used, random access results in a delay while the CODEC reconstructs the current frame from a larger amount of P-frames.   If a clip is prepared to be played through uninterrupted, the number of key frames can be reduced, thereby achieving higher compression rates without sacrificing quality.

Target computer

The video must run on the minimum target computer that will be used to play the clips.   The CPU on older computers may not be fast enough to decode the video stream without dropping frames; the hard disk or CD player may be too slow to transfer the data in real time.   It can be decided that the user base must have a high minimum specification.   This ensures adequate performance but lowers the market for the product. This could also be a problem in an environment (e.g. college or university) where there is a mix of old and new computers.

The project should always be tested on the lowest target computer before it is finally packaged for distribution.

Typical considerations are:

- Does the target computer have the necessary CODEC installed?
- Should a well-known CODEC be used such as Cinepak be used in the knowledge that it is installed on all computers using Microsoft Windows?
- Can the video be packaged with its own software CODEC?   Does this raise legal or licensing problems?
- Can a user be reasonably expected to install a CODEC to watch the video?

Outputting to videotape

This requires a video card with a composite output - for domestic VHS distribution. The card contains a scan convertor that takes the video signal and ensures that the television scan rates and signal encoding are added to the output.

The steps for exporting a project to videotape are:

- Choose *'File'* from the main menu.
- Choose *'Export'* from the drop-down menu.
- Choose *'Print to Video'* from the sub-menu.
- Set the amount of seconds that a black output should be sent to the recorder, before the main project content begins to be exported.
- Check the *'Full Screen'* box, if the project screen size is smaller than the screen size supported by the video recorder.
- Press the record button on the video recorder and click the *'OK'* button.

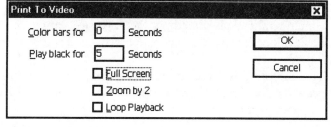

TV/VCR Video Standards

If a project is output to a videocassette, it should be in the format used by the intended country in which it will be distributed.

Different countries have different standards and they are not interchangeable - even when the cassette holding the tape might be the same size for some countries. It is the way that the video is recorded and the quality of the recording (resolution, etc) that creates the difference. For example, UK and US tapes are not interchangeable, although they are both described as VHS. Special video players are available that allow the playback of both types of recording - but normal VCRs cannot handle both types.

The terms NTSC, PAL and SECAM refer to the method of colour coding, but they are often referred to in terms of the expected resolution from each system. It is technically possible to make a 525 lines system using PAL or a 625 line system using NTSC. Its just that all the countries of the world have decided on a standard for their own transmissions and they are grouped around the three different specifications discussed.

The nature of colour analogue television signals was determined by the move from monochrome transmissions. When colour televisions were introduced, there was a huge base of black and white televisions in use. As there was not enough bandwidth available, a single transmission had to be used by both monochrome and colour television receivers.

As a result, even to this day, the analogue television signal is basically a monochrome (luminance) signal, with colour (chrominance) added as separate information (this part is ignored by mono TVs).

PAL

The PAL system (Phase Alternate Line) is used throughout the UK, most of Europe, Australia, China, most of Middle East and Africa.

It embodies 625 lines, with a 24-bit colour picture using a 50Hz interlaced field system (i.e. 50 fields per second), to produce a 25fps picture.

Books and magazines tend to give different resolutions for PAL including 736 x 560, 520 x 380, and 768 x 576. ITU-R 601 is the international standard for digitising component video for television. It defines the active area as 720 x 576. This is the standard used by most video software, such as Adobe Premiere. Note that although a UK television system works on 625 lines with a visible 576 lines, the domestic VHS recorder only records and plays back at 250 lines.

NTSC

The NTSC system (National Television Standards Committee) was introduced in the USA in 1952.

It is used in the US, Canada, most of Latin America, and Japan.

It embodies 525 lines, with a 24-bit colour picture using a 60Hz interlaced field system (i.. 60 fields per second), to produce a 30fps picture. The VGA computer resolution of 640 x 480 is based on the visible screen area of an American television picture tube.

SECAM

The SECAM system (Sequential Colour and Memory) is a 625 line, 50Hz system that is used throughout France, Russia, ex-French colonies in Africa, parts of Eastern Europe.

Authoring Systems

Having gathered the graphics, sound and music for the presentation, the developer's task is to integrate them and link them in the way laid down in his/her implementation plan.   While it is possible to write simple applications directly at the keyboard, larger and more complex projects require a careful plan to be developed, including navigation maps and screen layouts.   These issues are covered in the chapter on design.

The authoring software required depends upon the complexity of the project, the level of interactivity provided for the user, and the provision of additional facilities (such as linking to databases, animation, web tools, etc).

Multimedia development software is generally of two types:

Linear : The user watches a sequence that has already been determined by the designers and he/she has no influence over the presentation.   This approach is best suited to exhibitions, point of sale and other information providing situations.   Linear presentations can be achieved with simple software and there are many freeware and shareware packages to provide these development tools.   Although they use multiple forms of media, the finished projects are not full multimedia products as there is no real interaction with the user.   Simple multimedia presentations can also be easily constructed using a programming language such as Delphi or Visual Basic.

Interactive : The user controls the flow of the presentation, to explore particular areas, ignoring others and even returning to a particular area of the presentation.   The package may have built-in intelligence to know where a user keeps going wrong and giving targeted advice. This is suited to the learning environment where the user controls the pace and the content of the presentation. Computer Based Training programmes use this method, as each run of the presentation can be different, changing with the needs of the student.   CD-ROMs for the domestic market, such as encyclopaedias, use interactive techniques.   Interactive presentations require more sophisticated, and more expensive, software.   While some useful shareware packages can handle some interactivity, the top-end products provide the extra tools such as animations, layering, scripting and flexible packaging options that make the final project into an altogether different level of product.

All multimedia products can be written using conventional programming languages such as Pascal or C++, although they are time-consuming.   Using GUI-oriented (graphical user interface) programming languages such as Delphi and Visual Basic provide pre-written routines for buttons, user input, etc., and so speed the development process.   Best of all, multimedia authoring packages provide facilities to greatly speed up the development process.   Although programming and authoring methods both require analysis and design skill, some authoring packages can produce very useful results with no coding skills whatsoever. Most packages are able to produce run-time versions - executable files that do not require the use of the original package to display them. Packages range from hobbyist products to those with full-blown commercial aspirations.

Approaches to authoring

An authoring system is an application that provides pre-programmed elements to speed the development of multimedia applications (e.g. ready-made buttons, etc).   They create multimedia applications in a fraction of the time that would be required by script programming tools.   Buttons, dialog boxes, etc. can be brought onto the screen, positioned and linked to functions - without writing any code.   Interface design and screen editing are made much easier and quicker.   Animations can be complex and detailed and yet created in a relatively short time.

Of course, there is still the same amount of time required to plan, design and create the content. The designer still needs to know how programs work and have an appreciation of heuristic thinking and algorithm design.   Knowledge of module construction and basic screen construction skills are also still required.   Nevertheless, these packages are learned much more quickly than programming languages, especially for simpler projects.

Authoring methods

Designers and software engineers have developed a number of approaches to multimedia authoring. These are aimed at reducing the development time through the provision of design systems that are easily understood, coupled with a variety of useful tools. Their methods are designed around *'metaphors'*. A metaphor is a figure of speech where the description of one object is used to describe another object. For example, the designer can readily understand an authoring package that uses a *'page turning'* metaphor, even although there are no physical pages that are turned. The main systems are:

System	Typical products
Linear, frame-by-frame	PowerPoint, many freeware and shareware products.
Scripting language	Programming languages such as Pascal or C++, with Visual Basic and Delphi supplying improved interface tools.
Iconic/flow control	Authorware, Icon Author, Masterclass
Card/scripting	Toolbook
Cast/score/scripting	Director
Hypermedia Linkage	Any HTML editor, with packages such as Dreamweaver supplying increased functionality and less scripting knowledge.

Linear, frame-by-frame metaphor

This is the simplest metaphor of all. The project is designed to run in a linear fashion. That means that it has a beginning and an end and the viewer is intended to watch the project's contents unfold a page at a time. There is little or no user control of the project, apart from perhaps pausing or exiting. This method is best suited to unattended presentations at exhibitions and in supermarkets and for some product promotions. Since the flow material is determined for the viewer, there is only a single route to be followed and every piece of screen activity follows from the previous one in an orderly fashion.

Since the method is simple, the products are quickly assembled using basic authoring tools. There are a large number of freeware and shareware packages available for producing these kinds of projects and PowerPoint is the most common commercial product used for linear productions (although it can also offer some limited interactivity).

Programming

Programming requires scripts of code to be written by the developer. Early languages required complex scripts just to draw a box on the screen, while modern programming languages such as Delphi, Visual Basic and Visual C are blurring the boundaries between conventional programming and multimedia authoring. GUI-based development tools, such as Delphi and Visual Basic can bring in buttons, display graphics, and call up video and sound clips, etc. without resorting to heavy scripting.

Visual Basic, for example, uses a screen form (which can have a graphic image as a background), on which can be placed objects and controls. The developer then sets the properties that should apply to the controls. This is an *'event-driven'* system. Code is attached to a screen object and is only run when the object is activated. This allows some practical projects to be created without any coding. The package creates a compiled (i.e. self-running) product and provides comprehensive error checking and debugging facilities. In all, there are three types of scripting:

Scripting type	Example
Scripts to create the entire project.	GLPro is an authoring package that is entirely script-based, with no on-screen authoring.
Scripts that supplement authoring packages.	Director's Lingo script.
Internet advanced scripts.	JavaScript, Perl, etc.

Hypermedia linkage

This method covers the linking of any number of separate resources that allow user access. The most common implementation is a web site, although CD's can use hyperlinks for navigation and for linking to wider resources through the Internet. This system produces the widest possible navigation facilities and the most likely methods for implementing these systems are HTML scripts, JavaScript, CGI scripts, Perl scripts, etc.

Card/scripting

These are also sometimes called *'page-based'* systems. The project data is organised to simulate pages of a book, or a stack of cards. Each page has its own individual set of objects and its own layout. It can display graphics or play sounds, animations and video clips on any page.

It uses a book metaphor as its presentation format. Using navigation buttons, viewers can flick through the pages of the book in any order. This presentation method is best used when sets of sequences of pages are used, although viewers can also jump between pages. Examples of card-based authoring packages are Toolbook, Mediator and Illuminatus.

Iconic/flow control

This method makes the project's structure and links highly visible to the developer, as the main screens and user choices are represented on a flow chart.

These flow diagrams display the navigational links and flow of ideas. This aids the development of projects with complicated structures, as a top-down approach starts from the higher-level tasks and breaks them into lower levels tasks.

A flow chart plots the possible routes between activities; this is the *'navigation map'*. An activity is represented by an icon which could be a decision to be made, a user entry to be requested, a new screen of graphics to be shown, a video or sound clip to be run, and so on. At the design and implementation stages, groups of icons can be grouped together under a single icon - implementing a top-down design of sub-modules. Major points can be added to the flow line, and these can be returned to later to flesh out their sub-units and contents.

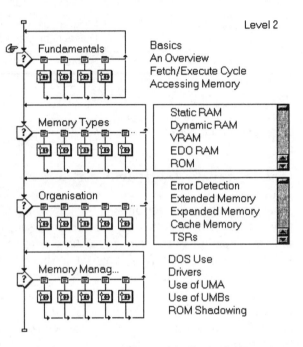

The example shows the second level of a package that displays a top menu with four choices (e.g. Memory Types, Organisation). Each choice produces a drop-down menu with other choices (e.g. Error Detection, Cache Memory). Examples of such authoring packages are Authorware and IconAuthor.

Cast/score/scripting

These packages often use the terminology of the film producer or theatrical producer, with a *'stage'*, a *'cast'* and a *'score'*. Little wonder, then, that the most used package of this type is called *'Director'*.

The package uses a cast (i.e. the elements such as text, graphics, sound clips, video clips, user entry buttons or dialog boxes, screen effects, etc.) and a score (e.g. a chart of all events and when they will occur in time).

It is based on a *'timeline'* as in the example, where each vertical frame stores all the objects that are used during that particular timeslot.

Each object can therefore be controlled down to the precision of a single frame (for a 25fps production, this means control down to 1/25th of a second). This allows animations to be set to precise durations, sound clips to be played at precise times that synchronise with other events, and so on.

All the project is laid out as a long chart of possible events (i.e. the timeline), navigation controls allow the user to jump to any point in the timeline.

There is no concept of individual pages; just what will be displayed on the screen at any one time.

Other considerations
Apart from the design method, there are many other considerations when choosing an authoring package:
- The range of drawing, animation, text manipulation facilities.
- The range of transitions and special effects.
- The range of packaging options (standalone executable, HTML file, Shockwave file, video clip, etc).
- Whether the package allows royalty-free distribution of the final project, or applies charges or conditions on the distribution. This may apply to a runtime module (a miniature version of the package used to create the project, with the development tools removed, leaving only the play functions).
- Whether the package can create cross-platform projects (e.g. can compile for PC or a Mac).

Scripting facilities
Some packages provide very simple navigation links but for greater control of navigation, and to support internal logic decisions, the author has to learn the programming language behind the package.   The examples show the minimum scripts used by the leading *'Director'* and *'Toolbook'* packages.

Director's Lingo	Toolbook
on mouseup 　　go to "quiz" end	TO HANDLE buttonClick 　　go to next page END buttonClick

Some authoring tools have no in-built scripting facilities (e.g. Illuminatus and Multimedia Fusion), some have very little (e.g. Mediator) and some have comprehensive facilities (e.g. Director and Toolbook).

Control facilities
In all multimedia presentations, the user approaches the application in an interactive way, expecting to be given control over the package.   The three most important elements are:

Buttons
The user has to control the flow of information in a package. Normally this is achieved by the user clicking the mouse on on-screen *'buttons'* that represent a particular choice. The choice may be from a selection of menu options (i.e. where to go next) or might be from a selection of possible data entries (e.g. choosing a correct answer or saving or loading a set of data).   Buttons can be the default grey variety provided in most authoring packages or can be user-defined such as pictures or shapes.
Alternatives to buttons are dialog boxes, where the user is asked to enter data (e.g. user name or age) and *'hot spots'* where areas of the screen act as equivalents of large buttons.   Clicking a hot spot has the same effect as clicking a button but a hot spot can be an irregular shape. For example, this allows the user to click anywhere on the Isle of Wight in a screen map of the UK to see more information about that island.   Other on-screen system controls are:
- Radio buttons (i.e. only one option can be active at a time).
- Check boxes (i.e. more than option can be active at the same time).
- Scroll bars.
- File/directory selection.

Events
Normal conventional programs are written to be mainly sequential. The program starts at the beginning of the code and finishes at the end of the code.   Multimedia products are explored in a different manner.   With event-driven systems, code is attached to objects and remains inactive until it is called.   Calls can be initiated by the user (e.g. clicking a mouse) or by the system (e.g. a timeout). The clicking of the button or hot spot is tied to a particular action.   So clicking the *'Show Interview'* button always plays the same video clip.   Clicking a *'More Details'* button may produce an entirely new screen with more information and a further set of buttons.   Clicking the *'Quit'* button should exit the user from the package. The navigation activities are called *'simple branching'*.

Control structures
For more control, *'conditional branching'* can be carried out.   So, a user when presented with six buttons representing six levels of difficulty may only be allowed to pursue a higher level if the lower level has been successfully completed.   The program has kept the user's previous performance in a set of variables and the branching allowed is a combination of what button the user pressed and what information is already stored.   In a multi-choice question, the user may only be allowed three attempts.   Control can be passed to internal code using constructs such as:
　　　　　IF ...　　　　　e.g. if a user score is less than 50% ....
　　　　　REPEAT ...　　e.g. repeat the question until the user chooses the correct answer.

Getting started in Director

The Macromedia Director package is one of the most powerful multimedia applications and is regularly used to produce the interfaces for the CDs that are given way with computer magazines, as well as creating countless commercial and educational products. Director provides many facilities within the one application. For example, it can create vector graphics, bitmap graphics, and animations. It also provides sound editing facilities and the final project can be packaged as a standalone program, or a Shockwave or Java-enclosed file for using on the web. Since all these facilities are built into the program, they can all be used without leaving the application to run lots of separate packages to do parts of the job. Of course, the professional user may still wish to use a full-blown graphics tool, such as PhotoShop, to create graphics images for use in Director. That is catered for, as Director can import a wide range of file formats such as Flash, animated GIFs, MP3s, PowerPoint presentations, etc, that will have been created on other packages.

The following pages look at Director 8, but the material covered applies to most versions of this package.

The quick tour

Director uses a list of resources (the cast) from which the developer chooses those elements that are used or seen on the screen. These are placed on a timeline (the score) at the points in time that they should be visible or active on the screen (the stage). These components (the sprites) can be animated to move around the screen, or can be text or static images. The Control Panel allows the developer to view the overall project, while the mouse can be used to place the playback head on any time slot on the timeline to display the screen contents at that moment. When the playback head sits on any one time slot, its screen contents are viewed in the stage window and the screen elements are viewed in the channels that have contents in that particular time slot.

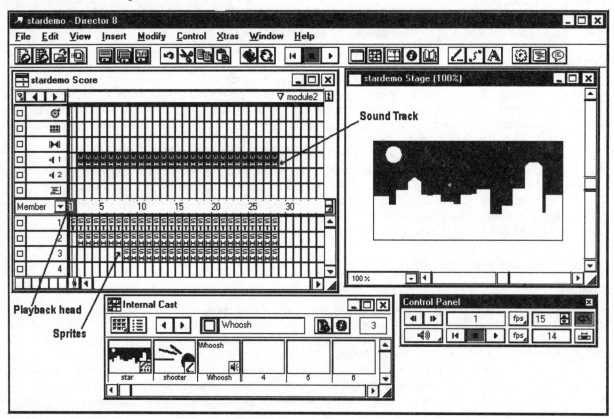

Movies

The projects created by Director are called 'movies' and are given the file extension .DIR (e.g. 'swimming.dir'). During development, the project should be saved as a .DIR file, as this stores all the project's components in a format that can be individually accessed later for subsequent alterations, amendments and maintenance. This also allows the project to be developed by another person. When complete, the project can be packaged for distribution in a variety of ways (e.g. standalone programs, web material, video clips, etc) and these are covered later.

Cast

The Cast is simply the list of resources (*'Cast members'*) that can be used in the multimedia project. Director can import a wide range of file formats into this database:

- Animations (Flash movie, animated GIF, FLC, FLI).
- Text (ASCII, RTF, HTML).
- Graphic images (BMP, GIF, JPEG, TIFF).
- PowerPoint presentations.
- Video movies (QuickTime, AVI).
- Sound files (WAV, MP3, AU).

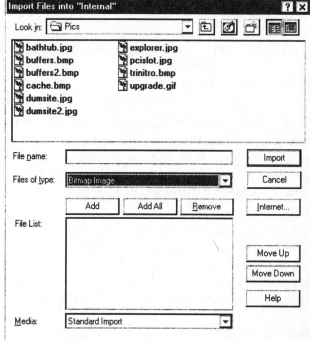

When a new project is started, the Cast window is empty and the resources are added by using the *'Import'* option from the *'File'* drop-down menu. This produces the dialog box shown in the illustration.

When a file, or set of files, is selected from the list, clicking the *'Import'* button adds the file to the cast list.

These files are treated as *'internal'*. That means that they are bundled into the final product and will not be seen as separate files. This creates a tidier final product and helps prevent the elements from being re-used without permission.

As the illustration shows, the *'Media'* menu default option is *'Standard Import'*, which is the internal option. Choosing the *'Link to External File'* option does not embed the elements into the project. Instead it provides links to them and these links fetch the file contents as the project runs. The external files obviously have to be supplied separately, along with the project that uses them. This allows the same components to be used in different projects. It also allows any one file to be updated or amended without altering the main project. This is useful for business (just change prices, photos) and different language versions (just change text files, audio files).

Adding cast members does not automatically include them in the project. They are equivalent to the crowd of hopeful actors waiting to be chosen to appear in a play. In both cases, they take no part in the production until they are brought onto the stage and told where to stand, what to do, etc. In Director, a cast member is brought into use by dragging it from the cast window into the timeline or the stage. For example, if a graphic file were dropped into time slot 10, it would only appear on screen during that one time period. If the project runs at 15fps, the graphic appears 0.6 seconds (9 slots of 1/15secs) into the playback and lasts for 0.0666 seconds, while a project running at 25fps would show the graphic for 0.04 seconds.

Director provides for the creation of multiple cast lists. For large projects, this organises separate casts for storing different resources, particularly if they are external. So, all video clips can be stored in one cast, all graphic images in another cast, Lingo scripts in another, and so on. Alternatively, all the resources for each section of a project could be stored in separate cast lists.

A single cast window is automatically provided when a new project is begun. The steps for creating a new cast are:

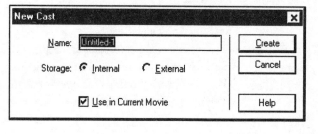

- Choose the *'New'* option from the *'File'* drop-down menu.
- Choose *'Cast'* from the sub-menu.
- Enter the name for the cast list in the *'Name'* entry box.
- Decide whether the cast list should contain internal or external components and check the appropriate radio button.
- Click on the *'Create'* button.

Sprites

When a cast member is dragged on to the stage or the score (the timeline), it is called a *'sprite'*.
Sprites follow these simple rules:

- A sprite is a single instance, a copy, of the cast member.
- There can be more than one instance of a cast member (i.e. there can be two or more sprites based on the same cast member).
- Each sprite has its own properties and actions.
- Altering (or even deleting) a sprite does not alter the original cast member, or any other sprite based on that cast member.
- Altering the cast member alters all sprites based on that cast member.
- Removing a cast member from the cast list makes all sprite instances of the cast member unusable.

Many sprites are a single instance of a cast member. For example, a heading, a piece of text or a video clip may only appear once in a project.

But sprites also allow multiple appearances of a cast member on the stage at the same time. So, for instance, a single drawing of a bird can become a flock of birds, or an image of a single person can be used to construct a crowd scene. Moreover, each bird or person can be moved independent of the rest.

The earlier illustration of Director shows a simple scene of a city night skyline, with the moon in the top left corner. Shooting stars will be animated across the screen from left to right (this same example is used later for demonstrating the creation of animated GIF and Flash versions). Note that two instances of the same cast member will be used. The shooting star graphic image has been placed twice on the timeline, allowing each of these to be independently controlled. So, changing the movement, speed or size of one of these sprite images will have no effect on any other sprite, or on the original cast member.

Score

The score is the most important tool of Director. It is the main construction window and it describes the movie frame by frame and shows the changes in the movie with time. The score is used to position sprites, add sounds and transitions, set timings and create the required navigation controls.

The score looks like a spreadsheet, with a grid of rows and columns. Each column is a time slot. The value of the time slot depends upon the playback rate set (e.g. 15fps or 25fps). For example, a movie set to 25fps allocates one twenty-fifth of a second to each time slot in the score's timeline.

Each row is known as a *'channel'* and version 8 of Director supports up to 1000 sprite channels. This allows a huge numbers of elements to be included in a project. In practice, however, developers strive to minimise the number of channels used as this improves performance and makes the development process easier to handle.

Members channels

The lower set is the *'members'* channels and each one holds a sprite. If a graphic image sprite is placed in a single *'cell'* (i.e. in one channel in a single time slot), it will flash on the screen for the short period that the playback head is over that time slot. If the sprite is copied across a range of cells in the channel, it will display for the amount of time that the playback head is over these cells.

Objects in higher channel numbers appear at the front of the stage and objects in lower channels are towards the rear of the stage. In the example, channel 1 holds the skyline image, while channels 2 and three hold sprites of the shooting stars. If the two sprites are animated so that their paths cross, sprite 3 will pass in front of sprite 2, since it has a higher channel number. When there are multiple sprites on the stage, altering channel numbers makes sprites pass in front or behind objects as required.

Effects channels

The upper set of six channels are the *'effects'* channels. These are:

- Two Sound channels.
- A Transitions channel (creates smooth fades and other transition effects between scenes).
- A Script channel (stores scripts for navigation, loops, and all other Lingo scripts).
- A Palette channel (controls the colour palette in use - Windows, Mac, Grayscale, Metallic, etc.)
- A Tempo channel (insert pauses, waits for sound or video to finish before moving on, etc)

NOTE:

Although the Director Score sets out all its activities in sequential time slots, users may jump around the timeline, to use different parts of the project as they see fit (see the section on navigation).

Stage

The Score is vital for setting out the objects in relation to time, but provides no help in positioning the objects on the screen.

The Stage therefore has two tasks:

- To allow the developer to place objects in their correct positions on the screen.
- To allow the developer to view the movie, or part of the movie.

The steps for setting up the Stage properties are:

- Select *'Movie'* from the *'Modify'* pull-down menu.
- Select *'Properties'* from the sub-menu. This will display the dialog box shown in the illustration.
- Set the stage size, background colour palette, number of sprite channels to be used for the project, etc.

NOTE:

If developing a project for use on the Internet, the colour palette should be set to *'Web21'*, as this is the set of *'browser-safe'* colours that is recognised by all computers using the web, whether PC-based, Mac-based or other.

Control Panel

The Control Panel is the tool the developer uses to switch between frames, to preview changes, to see the results of applying special effects, etc.

The explanations of each of the parts of the Control Panel are:

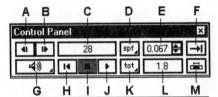

A	Steps backward one frame. The stage displays the previous frame's contents.
B	Steps forward one frame. The stage displays the next frame's contents.
C	Displays the number of the current frame being displayed on the stage (e.g. second frame, seventieth frame).
D	Tempo mode (frames per second, or seconds per frame).
E	Sets the tempo for playing the preview.
F	Sets the manner of a project playback. The setting shown above is *'single play'* and this plays the movie on the Stage, starting at frame 1 and ending on the last frame in the movie. If the setting is changed to *'loop'* (see the earlier illustration accompanying *'The Quick Tour'*), the playback head returns to frame 1 and plays the movie again and again until the stop control is pressed.
G	Set the volume for playback (from mute to loud). This value is used in the final movie or projector version. This means that if it is set to mute or a low setting for a more peaceful development environment, it must be returned to a higher setting before outputting the project. The maximum setting is usually best, as it leaves the volume control setting to the user at their end.
H	Rewind - move the playback head to the first frame in the project.
I	Stop playback. Leave the playback head at the current frame.
J	Play forward from the current frame.
K	Sets the type of measurement to be used for displaying the actual tempo achieved for preview (Running Total, Estimated Total, frames per second, seconds per frame).
L	Display the actual tempo achieved for the preview.
M	Only plays back the section of the timeline between selected frames. Frames are selected by highlighting a set of time slots. This is very useful, as the developer will not want to sit through a long project just to preview a change in a small section. This button can be used in conjunction with looping to allow the developer to continuously replay a selected section of the project, so that it can be thoroughly analysed.

There is no *'Fast Forward'* button. To play from a frame that is later on the timeline, the playback head can be dragged to that new position and play started from that point.

Adding sprites

A sprite is added to a project in one of two ways:

- By dragging a cast member from the cast list into a channel and dropping it at the required time slot.
- By moving the playback head to the required time slot and dragging the cast member from the cast list and dropping it into the stage.

In both methods, the sprite has to be placed in the correct timeslot(s) and, for visual information (i.e. text, graphics, animations, video), has to be placed in the correct screen position.

To assist in accurately placing sprites, the Stage can have a grid superimposed upon it. The grid will not appear in the final output and only acts as an alignment aid. The grid is turned on from the *'Guides and Grid'* option of the *'View'* drop-down menu, by checking the *'Show Grid'* option in the sub-menu. The same sub-menu has a *'Snap to Grid'* option. When this option is checked, it aligns any object placed on the Stage to the nearest grid line. The distance between grid lines, and therefore the amount of

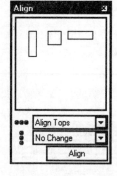

positioning control, is determined by the number of pixels entered in the *'Settings'* dialog box, accessed from the *'Guides and Grid'* sub-menu.

Another method of aligning sprites is to highlight a group of sprites in the Score. The sprites may be in the same frame or may cover a range of frames. Clicking the *'Align'* option from the *'Modify'* drop-down menu provides the dialog box shown in the illustration. The developer can choose from a range of alignments in both the vertical and horizontal axis. The illustration shows the option to align the tops of a set of objects. When the desired option is chosen, the *'Align'* button is pressed. This is a quick way to line up a set of navigation buttons, along the top or bottom of the screen or down the side of the screen.

There are some occasions when a sprite may only appear on the Score in a single cell. Examples are:

- When an introduction screen is displayed to the viewer and appears for a set amount of time (under the control of the Tempo channel - see later).
- When a set of instructions is displayed on the screen until the viewer clicks a mouse button to move on (see the Tempo channel later).
- When a menu is displayed on the screen until the viewer clicks on a menu choice button (see the MP3 player example later).

In many other instances, a sprite will have to appear many times across a channel. Examples are:

- A background image may have to be displayed throughout the project.
- A foreground image (e.g. a tree or a lamppost) may have to remain static during a scene, while other objects are moved around them.

Director allows a text or graphic sprite to be easily copied across many cells in a channel. The steps are:

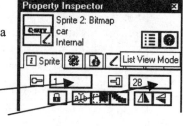

- Highlight the cell in the Score containing the cell to be copied.
- Right-click the mouse on the cell.
- Choose *'Properties'* from the menu that appears. This produces a dialog box as shown in the illustration.
- Click on the *'Sprite'* tab, to reveal two entry boxes as shown.
- Enter the number of the time slot when the object will start being displayed, into the left box.
- Enter the number of the time slot when the object will stop being displayed, into the right box.

Sprites can also be easily moved from one position on the Score to a new position. The cell(s) are highlight and dragged from their position and dropped in the new position. Care must be taken to ensure that the cells are not dropped over existing required sprites, as the new contents will replace what was there before.

Colour coding

Finally, it is good practice to colour code sections of the Score (e.g. part of a channel, or part of a group of channels) that carry out a distinct function in the project. This helps identify these sections later. For example, all help pages may be marked in yellow, all menus in cyan, and so on).

Colour coding is carried out by highlighting the required section of cells in the Score and clicking on one of the colour shading boxes that are displayed below the list of *'Members'* (i.e. sprites).

Text

Text can be imported, as previously explained, or can be directly added to the Stage, using the following steps:

- Move the playback head to the frame where the text is to appear.
- Click on the text icon (the one that looks a capital 'A') in the toolbar.
- Click the left mouse button on the place on the screen where the text is to sit.
- Enter the text into the text frame that appears.
- Re-position the text if necessary.

The above method is ideal for quickly adding headings and subheadings, whereas large amounts of text are best produced in a word processing package where the content can be spell checked and grammar checked before being imported into the cast window.

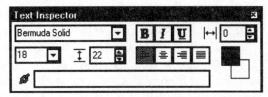

Any text sprites can have their properties altered at any point in the development of the project. The developer can decide to change the typeface, font size, etc. at any time and this is best carried out with the tools in the Text Inspector. This utility is activated by choosing the *'Text'* option from the *'Inspectors'* sub-menu of the *'Window'* pull-down menu. It produces the floating window shown in the illustration. Highlighting a text sprite in the Score displays its properties in this utility and these can be viewed and altered by the developer. It provides formatting functions such as choice of typeface, font size, alignment, kerning and line spacing.

The Property Inspector provides control over the anti-aliasing of text. If a text sprite is highlighted in the Score and is right-clicked, a drop-down menu appears. Choosing *'Properties'* displays the Property Inspector. Clicking the *'Text'* tab provides the developer with the choice of anti-aliasing text. Since small font sizes look better without anti-aliasing, the utility provides user control over the font size at which anti-aliasing is used.

Where many text sprites are going to be edited or formatted, Director provides a Text Window, as shown in the illustration. It is activated by choosing the *'Text'* option from the *'Window'* pull-down menu.

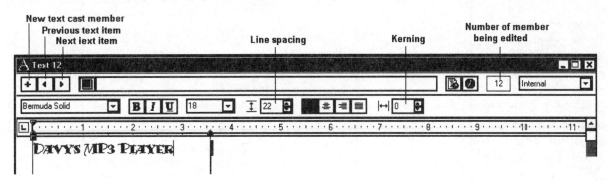

Its facilities are similar to the Text Inspector but provides additional facilities such as:

- The text can be entered or modified directly in the lower window, without touching the Stage window. Any amendments made within the Text Window are immediately seen on the Stage, if the playback head is sitting in the time slot storing the text sprite.
- New text cast members can be added within this utility (see the '+' button in the illustration).
- The arrow buttons in the top left corner are used to cycle through all the text sprites, to examine them or amend them.

NOTES:

Since text is regarded as a sprite, any text can be animated, rotated, etc. This allows flying headings, bullet points that move round obstacles, etc. This is in addition to any text effects that may be set up using the Transitions facility (see later).

Director's scripting language, Lingo, can be used to control text as the application runs. This provides personalised facilities. For example, the user may enter his/her name at the beginning of the program and this is used to display personal messages (e.g. *"Well Done, Dave")*. It can also be used to display a user's status in the application (e.g. *"Your score so far is 50")*. Lingo can also alter the typestyle or font size of a piece of text.

Fonts

Developers design projects with an overall look and feel. This includes the typefaces used, as they help to convey mood. This subject is covered in greater detail in the chapter on design.

The developer, therefore, wishes to ensure that the typefaces used in the creation of the application are the ones seen by the viewer, regardless of what fonts are installed on the user's computer. If no steps are taken, the finished application will use the viewer's own default system fonts at runtime.

The solution is to embed fonts in a movie, to ensure that the text appears in the specific typefaces intended. This is achieved by storing the fonts either in bitmap or vector format.

Bitmap Fonts

A bitmapped font is simply a vector font that was used for formatting a piece of text - converted into a bitmap graphic file. Since it is now a graphics file, it is totally independent of any font technology and is guaranteed to display correctly on every viewer's computer. Since the text is now a graphic file, it can be edited in Director's Paint Window. The steps for the conversion are:

- Highlight the text cast member in the Cast Window.
- Choose the 'Convert to Bitmap' option from the 'Modify' drop-down menu.

Once the text is converted to a bitmap, it cannot be reversed; there is no 'bitmap to text' utility'.

Although this method is quick and easy, it is not very versatile. For example, bitmaps don't rescale well and result in ugly ragged edges known as 'jaggies' when magnified (see the computer graphics chapter).

Embedding fonts

Director allows fonts on the developer's computer to be embedded within the movie. The font information is stored inside the movie and the font is only rendered (and anti-aliased) at playback time. This means that even the most obscure of fonts, or homemade fonts, can be included and will reproduce faithfully on the viewer's computer.

Embedded fonts are compressed and take up about 14KB to 25KB of extra file size and, because they are not separate-ly accessible, there are no copyright problems with distributing fonts in this way.

The steps for embedding a font are:

- Choose the 'Media Element' option from the 'Insert' drop-down menu.
- Choose the 'Font' option from the sub-menu.
- Use the 'Original Font' menu to choose the required font from the computer's installed list.
- Choose whether to include any bitmapped font sizes, by checking 'None' or 'Sizes'.
- If 'Sizes' is checked, enter the specific font sizes required for bitmapping, with a space or comma between each size.
- Check the 'Bold' and/or 'Italics' check boxes, if the bitmapped sizes are to include these variations. This option produces an improved outline but increases the final file size.
- Choose to embed the entire font (i.e. every letter, number, symbol and punctuation mark) by checking the 'Entire Set' button, or choose to embed only the characters required for the project, by checking the 'Partial Set' button.
- If the 'Partial Set' button is checked, choose the sub-set of characters to be embedded. The 'Other' option allows each individual character for embedding to be listed and provides the maximum optimisation.

At smaller font sizes (up to about 12 point), bitmapped fonts are usually clearer than anti-aliased vector fonts. This is why Director offers embedding of bitmap fonts, even though they take up extra file space.

Many developers decide on the fonts to be used in the project and embed them before any text is added to the project.   This is good practice, but Director allows files to be embedded at any time during development.

When a font is chosen from the list in the *'Original Font'* box, the font name is also displayed in the *'New Name'* box above it, with an asterisk added at the end.   This is now an additional font choice for developers.   In the example on the previous page, the *'Architecture'* font was embedded.   Any text that was previously added to the project with that font will now automatically use the embedded version instead, without the developer having to go back over every instance and amend it. Every new piece of text can also be formatted to use the embedded text. 'Architecture*' will appear on the Director font list and can be used just like any other font.

Embedded fonts are seen by Director as cast members and appear in the Cast Window.

Adding graphics

There are three options for adding a new piece of graphics to the cast:

- Import a graphic file.
- Draw a bitmap image in Director's Paint window (with very similar tools to Paint Shop Pro).
- Draw a vector image, using Director's Vector Shape tool.

Both drawing tools are available from the *'Window'* drop-down menu.

The import option is regularly used for bringing photographic images, stock clip art, previous drawings, etc. into a project, while the drawing options are best for creating new images.

Vector drawings are smaller, more scaleable and easier to alter at a later date, compared to bitmap images.

The Vector Shape tool is shown in the illustration and provides a reasonable set of vector drawing tools. The illustration shows an object with handles that can be manipulated to provide endless variations of a shape.

The Tool Palette

The tool Palette is activated by checking the *'Tool Palette'* option in the *'Window'* drop-down menu.
It provides the following facilities:

Left choice	Right choice
Selection tool.	Rotate and Skew.
Hand tool to move image around.	Magnifying glass.
Add text to the screen.	Draw a line.
Draw a filled rectangle.	Draw a rectangle outline.
Draw a filled rounded rectangle.	Draw a rounded rectangle.
Draw a filled ellipse.	Draw an ellipse outline.
Add a check box.	Add a radio button.
Add a piece of editable text (e.g. to capture data entered by the user).	
Add a button.	
Select the foreground and background colours.	
Select a fill pattern.	
Select a line width.	

The buttons are very basic and are frequently used to quickly assemble a working prototype of the project, replacing them with crafted graphic buttons later.

Transparent backgrounds

Most graphic files are intended to be laid on top of other objects on the screen. This can often lead to ugly superimpositions, with the background of an image obscuring other images. Consider the example below. The main screen is blue and a graphic file with a red circle on a yellow background is placed on

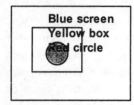

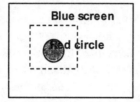

the screen. The left picture shows the result. If this is the wanted result then that's fine. However, it is more likely that the yellow background is undesirable and the effect on the right screen is the actual wanted result. In the right picture, the yellow background of the image has been declared transparent. This means that Director will not display this part of the image and all underlying content is visible. Only the red ball will obscure part of the background.

This was precisely the problem with the earlier example of moving shooting stars across a skyline. The skyline is black and the buildings are white. If the comet is drawn with a black background, it can cross the sky without a problem. When the comet wishes to pass in front of a building, however, it is seen as a moving black square with a comet in the middle. Drawing the comet with a white background simply reverses the problem. The image can cross the buildings happily but shows up as a moving white square against the skyline.

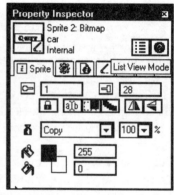

The only solution is to ensure that the background to the comet image is rendered invisible. Director will import a graphic file that already has its background colour set as transparent. For example, if the image of the comet had been drawn in Paint Shop Pro as a GIF image, its background colour could be made transparent before it is saved. It would then be imported with a transparent background straight into the cast list.

Director can also make the background of a vector or bitmap image drawn within Director be stored as transparent. If an image is right-clicked, it produces a menu from which *'Properties'* can be selected. This displays the Property Inspector as shown in the illustration. The illustration shows the inkpot with the *'Copy'* option selected. If the ink option is changed to *'Background Transparent'*, the background colour

chosen for that image is ignored when the image is displayed. All other instances of that colour in other objects are still displayed. Similarly, many images may use different background colours and the act of making the background transparent only applies to the display of that colour for that image only.

Alpha channels

Director also supports the use of alpha channels. These are 32-bit bitmap images, with 24 bits used for storing the colour depth information and an 8-bit greyscale bitmap that acts like a filter to control how much of the graphic is displayed. The black areas of the alpha channel prevent any of the picture from showing through, while the white areas allow all the picture content to show through. This means that an alpha channel with a graded fill from white at the top to black at the bottom results in a graphic display that gradually fades away towards the bottom of the screen.

Director provides transparency effects through the *'Ink'* option of Property Inspector shown above. To apply ink effects to a sprite, a copy of the sprite is placed in the next position in that cast list (i.e. if the original is cast member 5, the copy is cast member 6). This places the mask in front of the graphic image. The copy is then painted with black and white only and the *'Ink'* properties of the copy are set via the Property Inspector.

Sprite depth

Graphics in higher channel numbers appear at the front of the stage and may appear in front of graphic images with lower numbers. The order of layers can be altered to send an image further back or bring an image forward to a more prominent layer. The steps are:

- Highlight the sprite to be moved
- Choose the *'Arrange'* option from the *'Modify'* drop-down menu.
- Choose the *'Bring to front'*, *'Send to back'*, *'Bring forward'* or *'Move backward'* option, as required.
- Alternatively, use the Ctrl-Up arrow, Ctrl-Down arrow key combinations to move the sprite's order.

Moving the sprite on the Stage also changes its member number in the Score.

Adding video

A video clip can be imported into a cast list. QuickTime movies and AVI files are directly supported by Director and MPEG movies can be imported using an *'Extras'* add-on utility. A movie is added as a cast member that can be placed as a sprite on to the Score where required, in a sprite channel. As a sprite, it can be manipulated and controlled within the Score or by Lingo commands. It can even be animated, although the demand for a flying video clip may be a little limited!

A video clip starts to play when the playback head reaches the time slot where the video clip sprite is stored. If the sprite sits in a single time slot, the clip will only play for that amount of time before the playback head moves on. So, for example, if the Director movie is set to 25fps, then the video clip will only play for one twenty-fifth of a second.

There are three ways to ensure that the video clip plays to the end before the project moves on:

- Go to the timeslot where the video clip is stored and add an entry into the Temp channel. The *'Wait for Cue Point'* option in the Tempo dialog box should be chosen (see the section Tempo later, for more details). This option prevents the playback head from moving to the next frame until the video clip is fully played.
- Use a Lingo script to prevent the playback head from moving on until the video clip is fully played.
- Extend the video clip sprite across enough timeslots on the Score, to give the video clip sufficient time to finish playing. This method is particularly useful if there is to be any other activity going on (e.g. fresh text being displayed, animation, etc.) during the playing of the video clip. This requires the *'Direct to Stage'* option to be unchecked (see below).

Setting a video clip's properties

Director provides a range of controls over how the video clip is displayed. The following steps set up the controls:

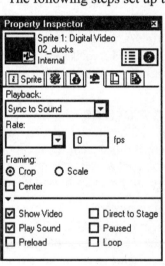

- Right-click on a video clip and choose the *'Cast Member Properties'* from the menu. This displays the dialog box shown in the illustration.
- Click the *'AVI'* tab of the Property Inspector.

The *'Framing'* options control how a video clip appears within the sprite's bounding rectangle when the video clip is rotated, scaled, etc.
The Framing options are:

- The *'Crop'* option displays the video clip at its default size. Any portions that extend beyond the sprite's rectangle are not displayed.
- If *'Crop'* is checked, then the *'Center'* option can be made active. If checked, this option centres the video cast member within the sprite; otherwise the video cast member's upper left corner is aligned with the sprite's upper left corner.
- The *'Scale'* fits the video clip inside the bounding rectangle.

The playback options are:

- Checking the *'Show Video'* option ensures that the video content of the clip is displayed.
- Checking the *'Play Sound'* option ensures that the audio content of the clip is to be included.
- Checking the *'Preload'* option loads the video clip into memory when the movie starts, so that it is immediately available when the clip is to be played. If the viewer's computer does not have sufficient memory to load the entire movie, Director loads as much as will fit in the existing memory. If this option is left unchecked, the video clip is played from the disk resulting in poorer video performance, as each frame has to be retrieved from the disk before being played.
- Checking the *'Direct to Stage'* option allows the QuickTime and AVI drivers installed on the viewing computer to control the video clip's playback. This is the most efficient option but has the potential disadvantage that the video clip always plays at the forefront of the stage, preventing other sprites from being overlaid on the video (e.g. captions, language translations).
- Checking the *'Paused'* option stops the video clip when it first appears on the Stage (while playing the Director movie).
- Checking the *'Loop'* option sets the video clip to play continuously. This is useful for displaying a welcoming video message until a key or mouse is pressed (e.g. for presentations at exhibitions).
- If the *'Direct to Stage'* option is enabled, the 'Playback' menu provides control over how the sound and video are synchronised. The *'Sync to Sound'* option will skip over some video frames, if necessary, to keep the video in step with the audio. The *'Play Every Frame (No Sound)'* option ensures that every frame in the video clip is played, at the expense of the sound in the clip.

Adding sound

A sound clip can be imported into the cast window as a new cast member and from there it can then be dropped into a time slot on the Score, in one of the audio channels.

Like the video clip discussed earlier, the audio clip will start to play when the playback head reaches the time slot where the audio sprite is stored. If the audio sprite is placed in a single time slot, then the clip will only play for that small single segment of time before the playback head moves on.

As with video clips, there are three ways to ensure that the audio clip plays to the end before the project moves on:

- Go to the timeslot where the audio clip is stored and add an entry into the Temp channel. The *'Wait for Cue Point'* option in the Tempo dialog box should be chosen (see the section Tempo later, for more details). This option prevents the playback head from moving to the next frame until the audio clip is fully played.
- Use a Lingo script to prevent the playback head from moving on until the audio clip is fully played.
- Extend the audio clip sprite across enough timeslots on the Score's audio channel, to give the audio clip sufficient time to finish playing.

The Property Inspector for a sound clip provides a *'Loop'* option that makes the audio clip play continuously.

Director's scripting language, Lingo, provides much more control for playing audio clips, with facilities such as:

- Controlling the clip's volume.
- Turning the sound off and on.
- Preloading the audio clip into the memory of the viewer's computer.
- Queuing multiple sounds.
- Creating accurate sound loops.
- Synchronising audio clips to animations.

The later section on navigation shows an example of audio clips being controlled by user buttons.

Animations

One of the most powerful utilities in Director is its set of animation tools. Animations are powerful in their ability to attract attention, focus attention and enrich the learning process. Animations can be as simple as a flying banner to a complex animation demonstrating mechanical or scientific processes. Director provides four methods for creating animations.

Cel Animation

Director describes this as *'frame-by-frame animation'* and *'multiple cast member animation'*, both describing the general process. At its simplest, this technique works exactly like an animated GIF. Each frame in the animated sequence is created as a separate graphic file and imported into the cast list. When these are placed into consecutive time slots, they play back as a continuous animation. For a 25fps movie, fifty separate graphic images would be required to be imported for a two second animation (assuming that no two frames were identical). This process consumes a lot of space but can achieve results that the other methods cannot. This is the only method that can use photographic image as the basis for the content's animation (as opposed to simply moving an image around). A photographic image may be used, with changes made to the image on successive frames. For example, a picture of a human head could be displayed with an eye winking, something that the other methods cannot handle.

Tweening

This term is taken from the language of the early film animators. The head animator would create a key drawing showing a cartoon character or an object in a certain position. He/she would then create another drawing indicating the next key position for that person or object. The animation assistants would then draw the cels that were required to take the animation from one key stage to the next, by breaking the movement into a set of frames that gradually altered the positions in the drawing. The process of creating the in-between frames is called *'tweening'*.

Tweening is a key utility for computer animators, as the computer is used to calculate and draw all the intermediate frames between key action frames. In Director, tweening can involve moving a sprite, resizing a sprite, rotating a sprite, altering colours in a sprite - or a combination of any, or all, of these effects. Since they commonly use vector-drawn sprites, they are also very economical in size.

The steps for animating a sprite are:

- Place the sprite in the first time slot on the Score.
- Extend the sprite across as many cells in the channel as required.
- Highlight the last cell in the sprite's set.
- Right-click the mouse and choose *'Insert Keyframe'* from the drop-down menu that is displayed.
- Drag the sprite across the Stage to the final resting place of the animation. This will produce a Stage similar to that in the illustration. The circle in the bottom right corner is the position of the sprite in the first time slot and the upper-left corner shows the final position of the sprite (i.e. as stored in the last time slot). The marks

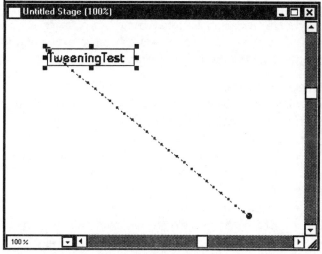

between these two points represent the time slot between the start and finish cells.   If there were 20 time slots between the start and finish cells, there would be 20 marks along the line.

- Hold down the 'Alt' key and use the mouse to drag one of the marks to a new position. This has created a new keyframe and the text sprite has an amended path to follow.
- Continue until the required path is created. The illustration shows a text sprite entering from the top-left of the screen and looping the loop before stopping in the middle of the screen.
- Run the animation and go back to make alterations, if required. Highlighting any cell along the row of animation cells displays the path on the Score and places the sprite on the position in the path that corresponds to the time slot being examined (e.g. if the seventh cell in the

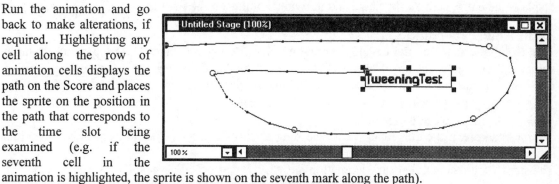

animation is highlighted, the sprite is shown on the seventh mark along the path).

The illustration shows the Tweening dialog box, accessed from the *'Tweening'* sub-menu choice of the *'Sprite'* drop-down menu of *'Modify'*. The lower set of controls alters the animation path.

Checking the *'Continuous at Endpoints'* box ensures that there is a smooth transition between the start and end positions of the sprite and is used with continuous loops.

The *'Curvature'* slider moves from *'Linear'* (with straight movements between points on the path), through *'Normal'* (with a curved path between the keyframes) to *'Extreme'* (with extended curves between keyframes).

The *'Speed'* options are *'Sharp'* or *'Smooth'* changes and they determine how abruptly the sprite changes direction (e.g. over a few frames or over many frames).

The *'Ease In'* and *'Ease Out'* sliders control the acceleration and deceleration of the sprites movement. Each slider is scaled to 100%, but the totals for the two must add up to 100% (e.g. the sprite cannot be accelerating 80% of the time and decelerating 60% of the time). Increasing one slider too high will reduce the other's value, to maintain a 100% maximum.

Of course, tweening is not restricted to changes in position of a sprite. For example, a sprite can be rotated (or even be rotated while being moved) and the Tweening utility will calculate and store the intermediate frames in the process.

Step Recording

Also known as Step Frame Recording, this technique builds up an animation one frame at a time. It provides better control for irregular animation paths.

The steps for creating a step-record animation are:

- Drag the cast member from the Cast window and place it as a sprite in the time slot in the Score that is the beginning of the animation.
- Position the sprite on the Stage to the starting position of the animation sequence.
- Highlight the starting cell in the Score.
- Choose the *'Step Recording'* option from the *'Control'* drop-down menu. A red arrow appears next to the channel, to indicate that recording is in operation.
- Click the *'Step Forward One Frame'* button on the Control Panel. This moves the animation forward to the next frame.
- Drag the sprite to the next position on the Stage.
- Repeat the above two steps until the animation sequence is complete.
- Choose the *'Step Recording'* option once more, to end the recording.

The animation can be returned to for alterations or fine-tuning. Clicking on any cell in the animation displays the entire path on the Stage and individual points on the path can be dragged to new positions.

Real-time recording

This technique involves the developer dragging a sprite on the stage while recording its motion. The software then creates the set of frames that comprise the animation. Since the recording is being made in real-time, the number of frames used for the animation depends upon:

- The speed at which the developer traces the movement.
- The frame rate of the recording.

So, for example, if the developer ran a recording at 25fps and took 2 seconds to trace the animation, the sequence would occupy 50 cells across the channel.

The steps for creating a real-time animation are:

- Highlight the cell containing the sprite to be animated.
- Choose the *'Real-Time Recording'* option from the *'Control'* drop-down menu. A circle appears next to the channel in which the animation frames will be created, and a red and white *'selection frame'* is displayed round the sprite.
- Drag the red and white selection frame to start recording the animation path.
- Release the mouse button to end the recording. The channel fills with the additional cells that make up the completed animation. These extra cells extend from the initial starting sprite along the same channel, so the developer has to ensure that there are sufficient free cells in the channel before starting the animation.

Many developers prefer to record at a slow tempo (i.e. reduce the number of frames per second), as this slow-motion recording gives them more control over the animation. The playback of the animation sequence is then speeded up to the normal tempo during playback. So, for example, if a developer requires a four second animation, he/she might half the tempo, recording the animation over eight seconds. When played back at the normal tempo, the animation takes four seconds to play. The required time span has been achieved but the longer tracing time provides more control of the mouse and hence a smoother animation path.

If a specific time is allocated for an allocation, that will equate to a specific number of frames (multiply the number of seconds by the tempo). Before the animation is recorded, the *'Selected Frames Only'* option on the Control Panel should be checked. This ensures that the animation completes within the allotted time span and prevents the possible overwriting of other sprites further along the channel.

This recording technique is useful for simulating the movement of a pointer (e.g. a pointing finger graphic is used as a moving sprite to point to key features in a piece of software, while a voiceover discusses their use). It is also used for quickly tracing a complex motion that can be tweaked later. Another use is to check the *'Trails'* option in the sprite's Property Inspector. This can provide special effects with photographic images or can be used to simulate handwriting.

Lingo

Lingo is Director's scripting language. This means that the developer moves away from using the mouse as the only means of controlling the project flow and activities and starts to use the keyboard to write *'scripts'*. Director Scripts are programs that are written in a language that Director understands and the developer has to learn the scripting language to write these scripts.   Scripts add much greater functionality to a project but may have a steep learning curve for many developers.

A project may have many scripts scattered throughout the project.   Some may be attached to objects on the screen (e.g. a script for a button sprite) and some may be embedded in a frame of the Score (e.g. for looping back to a certain time slot) or even attach to the entire movie.

A script may be very small (e.g. a script attached to a 'Quit' button may simply require the developer to enter a single line saying "go to exit") while others may be very complex (e.g. scripts for database handling).

Lingo is not like any other language and even those with some previous programming experience have to start from the beginning.   Their knowledge of constructing logic, decision-making and mathematical calculations is very useful but they will still have to learn Lingo commands.

The structure of a Lingo script is
>   on event
>   do something
>   end

Each script is known as a *'handler'*, as it is designed to respond to an event. The event might be a user activity (e.g. pressing a key or clicking on a button) or might be time-related (e.g. stop after 30 seconds) or logic-related (e.g. stop after five attempts).

The script for the project's quit button might be:
>   on mouseDown
>   go to exit
>   end

In this case, the event is mouseDown, one of the special events built into the Director language. Other examples of events are mouseUp, keyDown, keyUp, RightMouseDown and RightMouseUp.

The instructions to be followed are contained between the event and the word 'end'.   In this example, there is only a single command - to move the playback head to a specific point in the Score labelled as 'exit'.   Many scripts will use a list of commands, with each command appearing on a different line. When the handler is run, the commands are executed in sequential order (e.g. the first command is carried out first, the second command second, and so on).

Director provides a *'Lingo Dictionary'*, which is accessed from the *'Help'* pull-down menu. This lists all the Lingo commands and explains their purpose and their syntax (the order and manner in which they are written).   Lingo is not case-sensitive, so scripts can be written using upper and lower-case letters.

Variables

The Lingo language contains many commands but the developer will need to extend these commands by tweaking them to meet specific demands in the projects.   Examples would include:

- Using the viewer's name in the project (e.g. *'First Aid Test for Jim Smith'*).
- Making an animation repeat a set number of times.
- Keeping the score for a viewer's self-test.
- Providing messages that depend on the user's input (e.g. *'Too Old'* or *'Too Young'*).

There are many other examples of such tasks, but they all have the same requirement to have a temporary store to hold a value (i.e. a name, the number of times round the animation loop so far, the running total, or an age). Each variable has a name (e.g *'name'*, *'loopcount'*, *'score'*, *'age'*, etc).

This temporary store is called a variable and there are two types in Lingo.

Global variables	The values stored in these variables can be accessed and altered from anywhere within the movie. If the finished projector contains multiple movies, then the values are available across all the movies. So, for example, the viewer's total score in a test or in a game can be updated as the viewer tackles different parts of the project.
Local variables	The values stored in these variables are only accessible within the handler. This is useful for the temporary storage of values that will not be required by any other part of the project. Examples are loop counters and temporary storage for mathematical calculations.

Navigation

A major use for Lingo scripts is in allowing the viewer to navigate through the project.

A simple project, such as a standalone exhibition presentation can be created as a sequential set of events, with text appearing and disappearing, graphics flashing up, videos and sound playing, etc. All this can be very effective and is achieved without any scripting (apart from getting the playback head back to the beginning to repeat looping).

For all other projects, there is a need for user interactivity. This means that the user controls where to go in the project and this requires two things:

- Navigation controls (buttons, menu choices, etc).
- Scripts attached to the controls.

The controls are the parts that the viewer sees and the scripts control what happens when the viewer presses a button or menu choice.

Navigation scripts are usually quite straightforward and mainly jump the playback to another frame on the Score or to another frame in another project. Occasionally, navigation scripts can be more complex, using logic as part of the navigation choice. So, for example, an educational project may have a button to move the viewer on to the next lesson but the section jumped to may depend on the score achieved by the user in the previous section.

An 'Iconic/Flow Control' authoring system has the advantage of dividing up a project into manageable modules and these are easily recognised and the links between them are readily understood.

Since Director uses a 'Cast/Score/Script' technique, the entire project spreads across the Score window and can be a bit awkward to create, visualise and amend. This is why Director is often the choice for creating linear projects, or projects that contain long linear sequences.

To aid recognition and to allow navigation, markers can be added to the Score. Each marker has a name to describe the contents of the following frames and this marker name is also used as a reference for navigation. A marker is added to the Score by left-clicking the mouse in the bar above the six effects channels and entering a name for the marker. A marker can be removed by dragging it out of the Score.

MP3 player example

This simple example shows a cast list of twelve items made up of 5 items that appear on the screen (one heading and four buttons), four scripts (one for each button and one to create a loop) and three MP3 sound files.

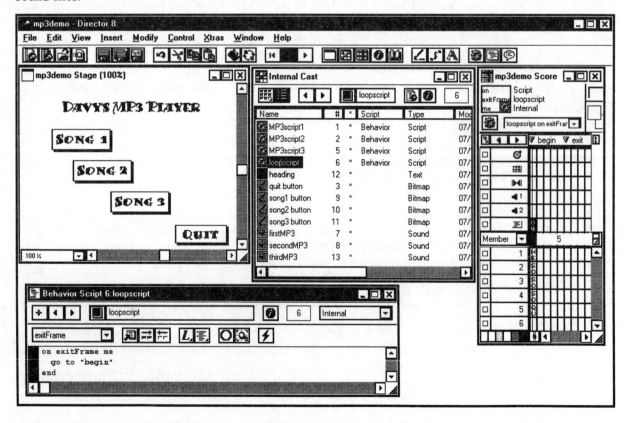

The first frame has a marker that names the time slot *'begin'* and there is another marker titled *'exit'*. The script channel has a script in the first, as shown in the illustration, with the contents

```
go to "begin"
```

At the end of the frame, the script is run and this returns the playback head to the start of the frame, creating a tiny endless loop that simply displays the text and the buttons.

Each button has a script attached to it, which plays one of the MP3 files. For example, the script attached to the 'Song 1' button uses the Lingo 'PuppetSound' command:

```
PuppetSound "firstMP3"
```

When a song button is pressed, the script plays the MP3 file, and this will play to the end if no further buttons are pressed.   If another song button is pressed the new script is run and this plays the new MP3 file instead of the previous file.   The *'Quit'* button has the following script attached to it:

```
go to "exit"
```

When the *'Quit'* button is pressed, the script moves the playback head to the time slot marked as *'exit'* and this jumps the program out of the loop and terminates the application.

Creating sub-modules

The simple menu system in the MP3 player only required a single frame in the Score. For larger projects, clicking a menu option would result in a set of actions being carried out rather than a single activity. Each menu option would wish to run a different section of the Score contents before returning to the main menu.

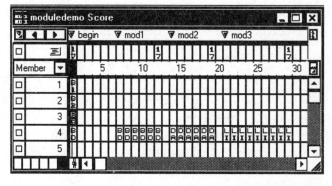

The illustration shows a miniature menu system. The first time slot contains four cast members. One is a screen background image and the other three are menu buttons.

The first button has a script attached that contains the command

```
go to "mod1"
```

This moves the playback head to the *'mod1'* marker (i.e. to the seventh frame) and the playback would continue stepping through frames from that point.   When the playback head reaches the end of the section (i.e. the twelfth frame in the example), it runs the script in the script channel and this contains the command

```
go to "begin"
```

This takes the playback head back to the first frame where it displays the menu again and waits once more for user input.

A similar process occurs when the viewer clicks the other menu buttons. Of course, there is no reason why a sub-module should not contain another level of menu, which takes the playback head to yet another range of sub-modules.

The illustration shows the very minimum necessary to explain the technique. In practice, a sub-module will make use of sprites in many channels. For example, the *'mod1'* section of the Score could have animations, text, graphics, sounds, and so on, as part of its playback - as long as these components were stored between frames 7 and 12.

Behaviors

To simplify scripting, Director provides *'behaviors'*. These are pre-written scripts that reside in a Director library and can be selected and attached to a sprite or frame by dragging the behavior on to it.

The behavior library is accessed through the *'Library Palette'* option on the *'Window'* drop-down menu. This produces the dialog box shown in the illustration. There is a drop-down menu at the top of box, offering sets of behavior scripts covering areas such as animation, controls, internet, etc.

The illustration shows the scripts available in the navigation section of the library.

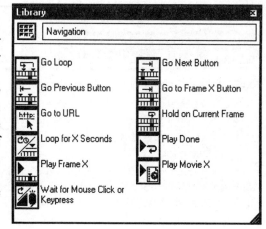

Some of the behavior scripts require parameters (information need to complete the process).
The illustration shows the dialog box that is produced when the

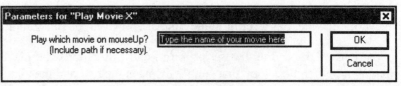

'Play Movie X' script is dropped onto a sprite. The developer enters the parameter (i.e. the name of the video clip) and that particular video will play when the button sprite is clicked. The behavior script is included as a new cast member in the project and the script attached to the button is an 'instance' of that script. This is exactly the same method as used with, say, a graphics sprite. This, of course, means that the same script can be dropped on another button and a different video file name entered.

Parameters are also required for some navigation scripts. For instance, the 'Go To Frame X Button' will ask the developer to enter the frame number to be jumped to. This behavior script can be attached to as many sprites as required, using different parameters for each instance of the behavior script.

Although Director supplies ready-made behaviors, these can be amended by the developer, or completely new behaviour scripts can be written by the developer.

Right-clicking on a sprite brings up a menu and choosing the 'Script' option displays the dialog box shown in the illustration. It shows the script attached to that sprite and allows alterations to be entered. The '+' button in the top-left corner of the window allows the developer to add a new behaviour script, while the arrow buttons are used to cycle through all the scripts to examine them or amend them.

Transitions

Director provides a range of transition effects that can be applied to a sprite when it is first due to appear in a frame. The abrupt change of background image can be avoided by gradually blending the content of one frame into the next frame. It can also be used to reveal text, one line at a time.

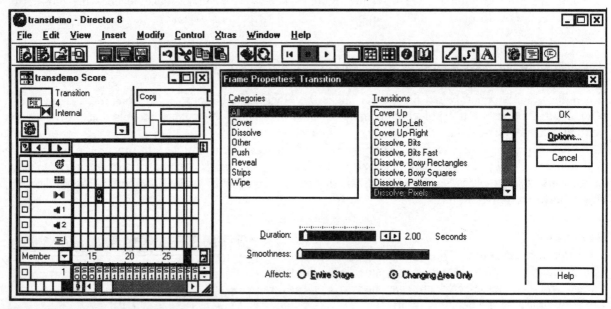

The steps for creating a transition are:
- Go to the time slot where the transition is to take place.
- Choose the 'Frame' option from the 'Modify' drop-down menu.
- Choose 'Transitions' from the sub-menu. This brings up the transitions dialog box shown in the illustration.
- Choose the desired transition and click the 'OK' button. The transition becomes a cast member.

An alternative method is to double-click on the appropriate cell on the transition channel.
The illustration shows the transition in the Score window and shows the transition options on the right.

Tempo

Tempo is the number of frames per second at which the movie is set to play back.   It only controls the sprites in the frames.   It cannot be used to make videos or audio clips play faster or slower and the settings have no effect on the time taken for transitions.

The tempo can be altered along the timeline. It will run at one tempo until it meets another setting in the Tempo channel and will then run at the new tempo.

The steps for setting the tempo are:

- Highlight the tempo cell in the score's time slot where the setting is to be inserted.
- Right-click on the cell, to display a drop-down menu.
- Choose *'Tempo'* from the drop-down menu, to display the dialog box shown in the illustration.
- Choose the setting required.
- Click the *'OK'* button.

The four settings are:

Choice	Activity	Example use
Tempo	Adjusts the maximum playback rate.	Controlling recording speed for the recording and playback of animations.
Wait	Keeps the playback head in the selected time slot for the amount of time set on the slider, before moving on.	Make a heading appear for a set time (e.g. opening credits, splash screens, etc).
Wait for Mouse Click, etc	Keeps the playback head in the selected time slot until the mouse is clicked or a key is pressed.	As above, except the user decides when to move on (e.g. providing a *'click anywhere to start'* message).
Wait for Cue Point	Keeps the playback head in the selected time slot, until the system tells it to move on.	Wait until a sound clip or video clip finishes, or wait until a cue point embedded in a video clip.

NOTES:

- Cue points can be inserted into QuickTime movies, but not AVIs, so this option only works with MOV files.
- The fps value used in the Tempo is the <u>maximum</u> playback speed.   The actual playback speed may be slower, depending upon the efficiency of the computer playing the project or the complexity of the sprites and animations used in the project.

Packaging projects

Projects created by Director are called *'movies'* and are given the file extension .DIR (e.g. *'firstaid.dir'*). Projects are stored in this format during development, as this format keeps all the elements used in the project fully accessible and alterable by the developer.   Projects should also be stored in this format, to allow later access for maintenance. Movies in .DIR format are not suitable for distribution, as they allow anyone with Director to edit them.

When the finished movie is ready for distribution, there are a number of ways that the movie can be packaged.

- They may be compiled into standalone applications - called *'projectors'*. This method is designed for CD and kiosk uses.
- They may be exported as AVI or QuickTime MOV files (e.g. *'firstaid.avi'* or *'firstaid.mov'*).   The finished video clip can be used in other applications, or imported into a Director movie.
- All, or parts, of the movie may be converted into a set of graphic images.
- They may be saved as Shockwave files, with the extension .DCR (e.g. *'firstaid.dcr'*), for playing on the web. The person viewing the Shockwave file needs a Shockwave plug-in with older browsers (this is already supplied in newer browsers).
- They may be saved as Java applets. This requires no extra plug-in, but needs JavaScript to be enabled on the user's browser.   It works best with simple banners and animations, as it does not support all of Director's features.

Standalone projectors

A projector is designed for use on CDs and kiosks.   It contains all the project's internal and external components, packaged as a stand-alone application (e.g. *'firstaid.exe'*).   The components include external files, external casts, any Xtras, and a player (called the Standard player).   It can also include several different movies, played one after the other, or linked by Lingo commands. If all the project's resources are internal, a single self-sufficient application file is created.   Since the projector is self-contained, all the components are secure from tampering and the file will play on any PC, without any special adjustments or add-ons.

If the project contains external components, such as linked music files, these will not be embedded in the final projector file and have to be distributed along with the projector.   When a projector is played, it will expect to access all external linked files in the same way it accessed them during authoring. This means that all linked media must be stored on a distribution CD, or kiosk hard disk, in the same relative locations as during authoring.   These problems can be minimised, if all external files are stored in a single folder - and this folder is also used to store the final projector.   This may not be convenient for very large projects, in which case great care must be taken over the way that external files are located on the final distribution media.

Another option, the Shockwave projector, is to have a standalone projector file that uses the Shockwave player installed on the viewer's computer.   Since this does not require any player code inside the projector, the finished file is smaller. Of course, if the viewer does not have a Shockwave player he/she will have to download and install a copy to view the projector.   This is recommended for web distribution, with the actual playback ignoring the browser software and using the Shockwave player directly.

Creating a projector

The dialog box for creating a projector is accessed from the *'Create Projector'* option of the *'File'* drop-down menu.   This allows the developer to select the movie and external casts that are to be included in the projector.   Clicking the *'Options'* button displays the dialog box shown in the illustration.
The options are:

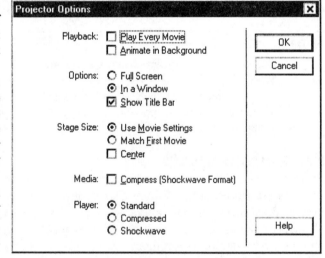

- If the *'Play Every Movie'* box is checked, the projector plays all its movies in order. If unchecked, the projector only plays the first movie, unless Lingo commands in the first movie call other movies.

- If the *'Animate in Background'* box is checked, the movie continues to play in the background when the user switches to another application.   If unchecked, the movie pauses when the user runs to another application and resumes when the user switches back to the projector application.

- Checking the *'Full Screen'* radio button displays the movie over the entire monitor screen.

- Checking the *'In a Window'* radio button displays the movie in a normal window.

- The *'Show Title Bar'* option is only available if the *'In a Window'* radio button is checked. If this option is checked, the movie window has a title bar and the viewer can move the window.

Some projectors will consist of several movies and each movie may have a different Stage size.

- Checking the *'Use Movie Settings'* radio button results in each movie occupying its own Stage size.

- Checking the *'Match First Movie'* radio button results in all movies conforming to the Stage size of the first movie.

- An option to centre the Stage on the screen. In Windows, projectors are always centred.

- Checking the *'Media'* box compresses the movie data into the Shockwave format, making the projector smaller.

The last options decide what player code is included in the projector.

- Checking the *'Standard'* radio button includes the uncompressed player code in the final projector. This starts the movie fastest, but creates the largest projector file.

- Checking the *'Compressed'* radio button includes a compressed version of the player code in the final projector. This reduces size of the projector file, but slightly increases the startup time of the movie, while the player code decompresses.
- Checking the *'Shockwave'* radio button does not include any player code in the final projector, expecting the projector to be viewed with a Shockwave player installed in the viewer's computer.

When all the projector options are set, clicking the *'OK'* button returns the developer back to the Projector dialog box. Clicking the *'Create'* button creates a standalone projector file with the name and folder location specified by the developer.

Macromedia make no charge for the distribution of compiled applications and movies, but require that a *'Made with Macromedia'* credit be placed on the products.

Shockwave

Shockwave is Macromedia's own playback system for the Internet and these movies are intended for viewing in a web browser that has a Shockwave player installed as a plug-in. Consequently, it does not have its own player code built in and this makes the final file size much smaller. The movie data is also compressed, further shrinking the final file size.

The creation of a Shockwave version of the project creates two files:

- The Shockwave movie, stored as a .DCR file.
- The HTML code containing all the tags necessary to run the .DCR file.

Where there are external casts, these are stored as a .CTT file.

Create a Shockwave movie

The conversion to a Shockwave movie can be as simple as choosing the *'Publish'* option from the *'File'* drop-down menu. The Shockwave version of the movie is based on the Publish settings and these are available by choosing the *'Publish Settings'* from the *'File'* drop-down menu. It displays a dialog box as shown in the illustration.

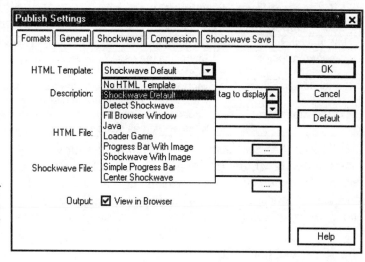

The settings are divided into five main categories:

- Formats
- General
- Shockwave
- Compression
- Shockwave Save

Another tab, the *'Image'* tab, appears if the *'Shockwave with Image'* choice is selected from the *'HTML Template'* menu.

The 'Formats' tab options

The *'HTML Template'* drop-down menu on this tab has the following options:

Option	Result
No HTML Template	Creates a Shockwave file without an HTML file.
Shockwave Default	Uses OBJECT and EMBED parameters in the HTML file to display the Shockwave file.
Detect Shockwave	JavaScript and VB Script determines whether the correct version of the Shockwave plug-in or ActiveX is on the viewer's computer and advises on an update if necessary.
Fill Browser Window	Expands the Shockwave file to fill the browser window.
Java	Displays a Java applet created using the *'Save as Java'* utility.
Loader Game	Displays a game with a progress bar while the Shockwave file loads.
Progress Bar with Image	Displays a progress bar and image while the Shockwave file downloads.
Shockwave with Image	Automatically detects and uses the Shockwave player or Active X control on the viewer's browser. If Shockwave is not on the viewer's computer, and the viewer is using Internet Explorer, the browser automatically installs the Active X control. Otherwise, the image specified in the *'Image'* tab is displayed..
Simple Progress Bar	Display a progress bar while the Shockwave file downloads.
Center Shockwave	Centres the Shockwave movie in the browser window.

The *'HTML File'* option specifies the folder in which to save the HTML file.

The *'Shockwave File'* option specifies the folder in which to save the Shockwave file.

The *'View in Browser'* option displays the Shockwave file in the developer's browser, on completion of the file's creation.

The 'General' tab options

The *'Dimensions'* menu provides three ways to specify the Shockwave movie screen size.

Option	Result
Match Movie	Makes the Shockwave movie the same size as the DIR movie. The width and height values of the movie are included in the OBJECT and EMBED tags in the HTML file.
Pixels	Allows the developer to specify the Shockwave movie's dimensions by entering values in the *'height'* and *'width'* boxes below the menu.
Percent of Browser Window	Allows the developer to specify the movie's dimensions in terms of the browser window size (e.g. 90% or 100% of the browser window).

The *'Page Background'* option specifies the background colour for insertion in the HTML code.

The 'Shockwave' tab options

The *'Volume Control'* option allows viewer's to adjust the volume of the movie's audio.

The *'Transport Control'* option allows the viewer to start, stop and rewind the movie.

The *'Zooming'* option allows the viewer to stretch the Shockwave display.

The *'Save Local'* option allows the viewer to save the movie.

The *'Display Progress Bar'* option displays the download progress bar while the file downloads.

The *'Display Logo'* option displays the logo while the file downloads.

The *'Stretch Style'* options determine how the movie displays when the *'width'* and *'height'* values in the HTML file are different from the movie's size.

Option	Result
No Stretching	Displays the movie plays at its original size.
Preserve Proportions	Maintains the movie's aspect ratio when the viewer changes the size of the browser window.
Stretch to Fill	Stretches the movie to fill the height and width values specified in the HTML file, even if this produces some distortion.
Expand Stage Size	Expands the Stage size to the size of the height and width values in the HTML file, while leaving all stage sprites at their original size.

The *'Stretch Position'* settings specify how the movie is positioned within the OBJECT or EMBED values in the HTML file (i.e. Top/Bottom, Left/Right, Centred).

The *'Background Color'* option lets the developer specify the colour that appears in the rectangular area in which the movie will play, while the movie is downloading.

The *'JavaScript'* box must be checked if any Lingo in the movie calls any JavaScript.

The 'Compression' tab options

The settings under this tab control the bitmap compression for all cast members in the movie.

Checking the *'Standard'* radio button produces a fixed compression level and is best suited for graphics that contain relatively few colours.

Checking the *'JPEG'* radio button allows the developer to set the level of compression using the slider. Higher figures mean less compression and greater image quality.

Checking the *'Compression Enabled'* box for Shockwave audio allows the developer to set the audio data rate and convert a stereo signal to a mono signal.

The 'Shockwave Save' tab options

These settings are for playing back movies with Macromedia's Shockmachine.

The 'Image' tab options

These settings choose the image to be used when the *'Shockwave with Image'* option was chosen in the *'Formats'* tab.

Java applets
Director can also export a movie as a Java applet. Java applets do not require the Shockwave player and may be an alternative packaging method for playing movies.   However, since not all features are available when converting to Java applets, this method is only useful with simple movies.

Shockwave streaming
A Shockwave movie can be configured for streamed playback over the Internet. When the viewer chooses to look at a Shockwave movie, the browser's Shockwave player loads the components required to display a screen. While the viewer is examining the first screen, the following frames are being loaded.   This means that the viewer does not wait until the entire file is downloaded before beginning to watch the movie.   This results in much reduced time before the viewer sees results and this increases the viewer's satisfaction with the project.

The dialog box for setting the options is accessed from the *'Playback'* option of the *'Movie'* sub-menu that is reached from the *'Modify'* drop-down menu. This displays the dialog box shown in the illustration.

Movie Playback Properties
General: ☐ Lock Frame Durations
☐ Pause When Window Inactive
Streaming: ☑ Play While Downloading Movie
Download 1 Frames Before Playing
☐ Show Placeholders
OK   Cancel   Help

Checking the *'Lock Frame Durations'* box locks the Shockwave movie speed to the project's tempo settings.

Checking the *'Pause When Windows Inactive'* box pauses the movie when another window is opened in the foreground.

Checking the *'Streaming'* box turns on the streaming facility.

The *'Download __ Frames Before Playing'* box should be set to match the needs of the project. The default setting is to begin playback as soon as the first frame is downloaded. However, sometimes there are a lot of cast members, or a number of linked elements, appearing early in the playback. In this situation, it may be better to wait until these are all loaded before beginning playback. The value entered should reflect the time needed to load these elements.

Checking the *'Show Placeholders'* box results in the movie displaying placeholders, in the shape of rectangles, for those media elements that have not yet been downloaded.

NOTES:
- These settings are used in conjunction with the settings available in the *'Publish Settings'* dialog box.
- When played, Shockwave movies loop by default. To make the movie play only once, the last frame of the movie should have the *'Hold on Current Frame'* behavior added to it.

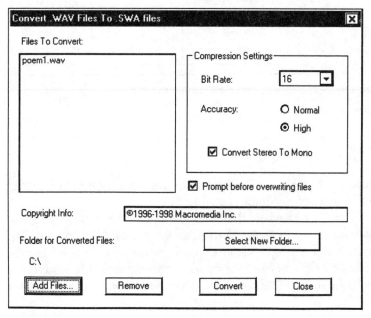

Streaming audio
Director can also create streamed audio over the Internet. The files have the extension .SWA (ShockWave Audio). The file cannot be transmitted on its own. It is not intended as a competitor to audio streaming formats such as RealAudio.   It is intended as a compressed audio file that is bundled with a Shockwave movie. As such, it is a cast member in the movie's score.

The first step is to compress the file. A WAV file is imported as a cast member. Then the conversion utility is accessed from the *'Convert WAV to SWA'* option in the *'Xtras'* drop-down menu. This displays the dialog box shown in the illustration.

The dialog box allows control over the bit rate of the audio, with 16kbps being the recommended rate for normal modem transmission and higher rates being achievable with ISDN and ADSL links. The more the file is compressed, the lower is its bit rate and the quicker it is streamed.   Of course, higher compression also results in lower quality.   Stereo audio clips with bit rates below 48kbps are automatically converted by the utility into mono clips.

The utility can compress internal audio cast members as long as they are in WAV format, while MP3 files or files already compressed into SWA format cannot be compressed further.

A Shockwave Audio Player is included in the final compiled Shockwave file.

Exporting as digital video

All, or part of a Director movie can be exported as a digital video file. This file can be used with other applications or it can be imported back into a project as a single video clip.

The export functions allow the movie to be exported in AVI format, or in QuickTime format if QuickTime is installed on the developer's computer. Each frame of the Score can be converted into a graphic image of the Stage, thus building up the video sequence.

There are serious limitations to these conversions that have to considered:

- All interactivity in the movie is lost.
- Sprites that are solely animated by a Lingo script are ignored.
- Video clips are not exported.
- When exporting to an AVI file, the audio content is ignored.

To export a movie, first choose the *'Export'* option from the *'File'* drop-down menu. This displays the dialog box shown in the illustration on the next page.

The options in the dialog box are:

- Checking the *'Current Frame'* radio button exports the current frame on the Stage.
- Checking the *'Selected Frames'* radio button exports the selected frames in the Score.
- Checking the *'All Frames'* radio button exports all the frames in the movie.
- Checking the *'Frame Range'* radio button exports only the range of frames entered in the *'Begin'* and *'End'* boxes.
- Checking the *'Every Frame'* radio button exports all the frames in the range chosen above.
- Checking the *'One in Every __ Frames'* radio button exports frames at the interval set in the data entry box (e.g. entering 5 in the box results in every fifth frame being used in the exported video clip).
- Checking the *'Frames with Markers'* radio button exports those frames that have a marker in the Score.
- Checking the *'Frames with Artwork Changes in Channel ___'* radio button exports only those

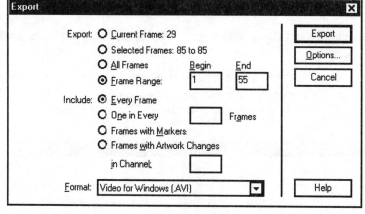

frames where has been a change in cast member in the channel number entered in the data entry box.

The Format menu allows the developer to choose to export as:

- An AVI file.
- A QuickTime file.
- A series of BMP graphic images.

The *'Options'* button allows the AVI options (simply setting the frame rate for the exported video) and the QuickTime options (type of compression, compression quality, etc.) to be set.

Clicking the *'Export'* button produces a small dialog box where the developer enters the name to be given to the exported movie. When the file is named, clicking the *'Save'* button creates the exported file. Exporting to an AVI or QuickTime file produces a single video clip. Exporting as a set of bitmap graphic files produces a numbered set of files. For example, if the name of the exported file is given as *'Davy'*, the first frame is saved as *'Davy0001'*, the second frame as *'Davy0002'* and so on.

CD Production

Multimedia productions including images and sound can easily run into several megabytes. When digital video or very high-resolution images are included, it can reach into the hundreds of megabytes, even after compression. This is not a problem for productions intended for a kiosk, or a presentation using the same computer on which it was created.

However, if the product is to be used by other systems, distribution of such a large amount of material becomes an important consideration. There are several methods of distributing material, including the Internet, floppy disks, and removable drives. Each of these is suitable for distributing certain types of data.

Distribution media

The Internet is a powerful tool for distributing up-to-date information. E-mail and web pages are excellent ways of providing fast, frequent updates. However, bandwidth is limited, and a large data file will take a long time to download. With streaming audio and video, the problem is eased, but the average modem can only download at most 5KB of streaming data per second, seriously limiting the quality of such material. In the UK, many Internet users also pay by the minute for Internet access, which could cause potential consumers to avoid downloading or streaming large files. CDs and DVDs are not as convenient as Internet downloads, but they are capable of storing a large amount of high-quality video, sound and graphics that would take many hours to download from an Internet site.

Floppy disks are used less and less in distribution, to such a degree that virtually nothing is distributed on floppy any more except device drivers and operating system installation disks. Floppy disks simply don't have the storage capacity distributors required, and also have extremely slow access times. CD-ROMs do not suffer from either of these problems. However, CD-ROMs, unlike floppies, require that the system is already able to access a CD drive. Hence the reason for distributing drivers and boot disks on floppy.

Removable drives, such as the Iomega Zip disk or Jaz drive, vary greatly in their capabilities. In general, they store between 100MB and 2GB, and access speeds vary even further. Some of these drives are noticeably superior to CD-ROMs, and offer read/write access instead of read-only. This makes for an excellent backup facility or in-house data transfer system. However, as a distribution media they are less useful – the cartridges are generally expensive, and not all end users can be assumed to have access to a drive capable of reading the media.

Even the humble VHS tape is no longer the most efficient method of distributing video. Video CD and DVD provide digital quality and additional functionality. If the video can fit on a single CD, then Video CD is also the cheaper option; VHS duplication is normally from £1-£2 per unit, while a blank CD-R costs well under £1, and if large numbers of stamped CDs are printed the cost drops to just a few pence each.

In the audio market, CD already dominates. Magnetic Cassettes are still available but suffer from degradation after time, something that is not a problem with digital media. The MiniDisc from Sony is an impressive technology, but currently it has nowhere near the market penetration that CD can claim.

Advantages of using CDs

- Large storage capacity. CD-ROMs can potentially store up to 650MB of computer data, or 741MB of digital video. At the time of writing, only extremely large or video-intensive products need more capacity than a single CD-ROM can provide.
- Widely supported. With the exception of floppy disks, no other computer media has such a large user base. Productions on CD-ROM can be used by virtually all PCs – anywhere in the world (unlike VHS tapes). Because of their popularity, DVD drives also support the reading of CD-ROMs, further extending their life into the foreseeable future.
- Low cost. Due to the sharp rise in sales of CD writers for PCs, their prices have fallen greatly since their first appearance, both for the CD writer and the blank CDs themselves.
- Long storage life. CD-ROMs are digital media, and as long as the disc is kept safe, a recordable disc will have a shelf life of 50 to 100 years. Manufactured CDs have a shorter lifespan of 10 to 15 years.

- Compact. While an individual CD might not seem particularly compact in comparison to an audio cassette, it is lighter and more easily stacked for distribution. When CDs are used for data or video, the space savings are even more marked.
- Convenience. A modern CD writer can be used to *'burn'* a disc in under an hour, using only a standard desktop PC equipped with a CD-R drive.

Disadvantages of using CDs

- Slow access times. CD-ROM drives have become much faster since they first appeared, but they are still very slow compared to hard disks and even some other removable media. Data that requires fast data transfer, such as video or high quality sound, may not run at an acceptable speed on some CD drives.
- Slow to create. Building a master disc to press large quantities of CDs makes CD production faster by an order of magnitude, but unless many hundreds of CDs are to be pressed it will prove to be an expensive proposition. If fewer CDs are to be created, the most cost-effective method is to use a CD writer to *'burn'* copies of discs. Even with newer eight speed and even twelve speed writers, the process can take up to half an hour per disc. This is due to the overheads of testing the writer, building an image, fixing the disc and so on. While this is quite acceptable for occasional convenient use, it is less useful for mass production.
- Large number of standards. An audio CD is playable on any CD unit, and a basic Yellow Book Mode 1 CD-ROM is readable on any computer CD drive. Beyond that, however, there are a large and often confusing number of standards, any one of which might not work on some of the systems of the target audience. A producer must consider the options carefully before deciding on which standard to use.
- Static. CD-ROMs cannot be updated once created; if a new version of the CD is designed, then the old CD can only be discarded. Furthermore, if the CD is to be distributed widely, it means that consumers have to be kept abreast of updates by other means or by additional CD updates.

How CD-ROM works

The simplified diagram shows the basic layout of a side view of a section of a CD ROM disc. The plastic disc has an embossed surface consisting of areas of normal thickness (*'lands'* or *'hills'*) and sunken areas (*'pits'*). The discs are stamped out from a master disc. After the high initial costs of creating the

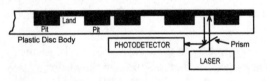

master disc, individual CDs can be stamped out very cheaply as can be seen by the number of computer magazines that include free CDs of shareware and program demonstrations. The changes of height along the track represent the data on the disc, although the

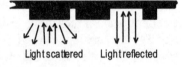

coding method is more complex than the simple storage of the data's 1's and 0's. The top surface of the disc is coated with a layer of reflective aluminium (the shaded area of the diagram) and this is covered with a protective plastic layer; the total disc thickness is 1.2mm. Pressed CD-ROMs are known as *'silver discs'* due to the colour of the aluminium used.

The disc is read from its underside by firing a laser beam at the revolving surface. The beam reflects from the aluminium coating and is diverted to a photo sensor by a prism. The normal depth areas - the *'lands'* - reflect back most of the laser beam while the *'pitted'* areas scatter the beam as shown in the diagram. So, the photo sensor will detect different reflected strengths from the two different surface areas. The laser beam passes through focusing lenses so that the beam is a tiny spot at the point of contact with the disc surface.

The spot is only 1 micron in size - one millionth of a metre. This means that much more data can be packed on to the disc surface compared to standard magnetising methods. This explains the ability to pack up to 650MB of data on to a single disc. Since the head does not require being close to the disc surface, it does not suffer the risk of head crashes associated with normal floppy and hard discs.

The disc contains only a single track, organised as single spiral similar to a long-playing record, except that the disc is read from the centre outwards. The laser, prism, lenses and photodetector are all enclosed in a single unit that is moved between the inner and outer parts of the spiral. It is the equivalent of the ordinary read/write head of a hard disc. Reaching a wanted sector requires the head to be moved to the approximate location on the spiral track. The head then follows the track until it reaches a sector header; this header information is then used to locate the wanted sector.

Although CDs use a number of error detection and correction techniques, they should still be handled with care. Grease from a fingerprint diffuses the laser beam while surface scratches deflect the beam.

Disc organisation

The disc is 120mm in diameter with a 15mm hole is punched in the centre.   A 6mm area of the surface, next to the hole, is used by the drive mechanism to clamp the disc while rotating.   The next 4mm area is used to store information regarding the disc's contents; this is known as the VTOC (volume table of contents).   The data area width is 33mm and comprises a single track spiralling outward about 20,000 times and totalling around 3 miles in length.

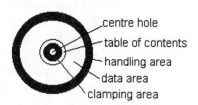

centre hole
table of contents
handling area
data area
clamping area

The outer area of 3mm is used for handling the disc.

A single-speed drive reads 75 of these sectors per second, giving a transfer rate of 150kb/s.   A double-speed drive reads 150 sectors/sec while a 32x drive reads 2400 sectors/sec, giving transfer rates of 300kb/s and 4,800kb/s respectively.   The original single speed model spins at 300rpm and other models are multiples of this - i.e. a quad speed rotates at 1,200 rpm and a 6x rotates at 1,800rpm.

Most CDs have a 2352 byte sector size of which 2k or over is used for data and the remaining bytes for error-detection and synchronisation information.

Hard discs specify a particular disc area in terms of track and sector. CD ROMs, showing their origins as audio discs, specify areas in terms of minutes, seconds, and sectors within each second.   Thus, a 74 minute CD has a capacity of: 74 x 60(secs) x 75(sectors) x 2k = 650MB of user data area.

A standard CD stores a maximum total of 333,000 sectors. These sectors are evenly spread throughout the spiral on the disc.

There are several methods of reading the data on the disc:

CLV - Constant Linear Velocity.

Using this method, the disc is rotated faster when reading the inner spirals than when reading the outer spirals.   This ensures a constant data rate, but requires a more expensive drive motor.

CAV - Constant Angular Velocity - also known as Full CAV.

With this method, the disc is rotated at the same speed throughout, meaning cheaper manufacture.   However, since the spiral is smaller near the centre of the CD, the data rate is slower there than near the edge of the CD.   Thus, a CAV CD-ROM drive might be described as being *'14/32x'* speed: it reads at 14 speed near the centre but 32 speed near the edge.   Since CDs only use the outermost spirals if they are completely filled, CAV drives may not even reach the full speed on many CDs.

PCAV - Partial Constant Angular Velocity.

Many CD drives are now a CLV/CAV hybrid, using CLV (i.e. changing speeds) on the outer tracks and CAV (i.e. constant speeds) on the inner tracks.

CD-ROM performance

The performance of a CD-ROM is determined by the following factors:

- The access time of the drive.

  These times vary from 65ms to 100ms for newer models and 350ms to 900ms for older models.   Compared to hard disc speeds, these are very slow times.   That is because there is one single continuous spiral track.   The read head cannot first go to the exact track and wait for the wanted sector to come round.   It has to make an approximation to the correct distance in then wait for the first sector header to tell the system where the head is positioned.   It then makes a second seek to get to the correct position.   This slows down the sector access times.

- The data transfer rate of the drive.

  The most common rates are:

Data Rate	Description	Data Rate	Description
150kbs	single-speed	1500kbs	10x
300kbs	double-speed or 2x	2400kbs	16x
450kbs	triple-speed or 3x	3600kbs	24x
600kbs	quad speed or 4x	4800kbs	32x
1200kbs	8x	6000kbs	40x

These figures do not give a complete picture since a quad speed drive will not provide double the throughput of a double speed, and so on.

This is for a number of reasons:

- The higher transfer rates only apply to long sequential reads. If the head has to make a number of random access seeks, the faster transfers are offset by the substantial individual access times.   The result is an average figure somewhat less than the performance suggested by the 2x, 3x, 4x, 6x, 8x and 10x ratings.

- With CLV models, there is an additional time delay while the motor changes speed when moving between inner and outer tracks.
- For the same reasons above, the sustained data rate shows up better with bigger files.
- AVI video files are often designed for double or quad speed and drives with faster rates have to work at the slower rate to be compatible with the data being presented.

- <u>The detection and elimination of read errors.</u>
  Errors occur due to slight imperfections in the boundaries of cells or from fingerprints or scratches obscuring the data read. For small data losses, the error detection system also has an error correction system that alters the read data to the original information. This is an improvement on normal discs and provides a more secure storage medium.

- <u>The size of the drive's buffers.</u>
  The current drive cache sizes vary from 16k to 1024k, mostly available in 128k or 256k. The cache size can have a significant influence on the smooth performance of multimedia presentations. SmartDrive can be used to gain a reasonably useful improvement in CD-ROM performance and utilities such as CD-Speed copy the CD's most commonly used files to the hard disc to speed up their access.

CD Standards

Many of the standards are named after the colour of cover used to report on the new standard. So, the standard for audio on CD became known as the Red Book standard because it had a red cover.

Broadly speaking, standards for CDs can be separated into two categories: physical standards and logical standards. In other words, standards such as Red Book and Yellow Book define how information is physically stored on the CD, while data standards such as

Standard	Purpose
Red Book	Audio CDs
Yellow Book	Computer data (e.g. application installation CDs)
Green Book	CD-Interactive applications, games and, entertainment
White Book	Video CDs
Blue Book	Music CDs with text
Orange Book	Recordable CDs
Photo CD	Kodak's multi-session picture storage

ISO 9660 and Joliet define how that information is logically organised into a computer readable format.

ISO 9660

Often known as *'High Sierra'*, since it was first discussed in the High Sierra Hotel in Nevada in 1985. By 1987, a superset of High Sierra, known as ISO 9600, was agreed as the common standard for computer CD ROMs. ISO 9660 is a logical standard, defining the way files may be stored on a disc. ISO 9660 is designed for use with a variety of computer systems including DOS, Unix and Macintosh, and thus has to cater to the lowest common denominator.

It comes in three *'levels'*, but only level 1 is used to any real extent, and the other levels may not even be catered for by all systems. In level 1, filenames are very similar to DOS filenames, with an eight-character name and three-character extension. However, filenames are further restricted in their choice of characters, allowing only upper case letters, numerals, and the underscore character. Directory names are restricted to eight characters with no extension, and any CD is allowed a maximum of eight levels of directories. These restrictions must be taken into consideration when creating an ISO 9660 CD-ROM.

All computer CD systems are capable of dealing with this logical standard for handling files and directories. The PC version is implemented with the MSCDEX or CDFS driver software. If the CD itself is to be truly cross-platform, then any executable or other machine-specific data should be stored in separate directories for different computer systems. For example many CD-ROMs have a directory on the root of the CD called 'DOS', one called 'MAC' and one called 'UNIX', each containing executable code for that system.

The ISO 9660 standard is built upon by most other CD file standards, such as Joliet.

JOLIET

With the advent of Windows 95, PC users had access to filenames longer than the previous 8+3 specification, something that was already available to Mac and Unix users. The ISO 9660 standard became very restrictive for PC users, and so the newer Joliet standard was introduced to provide more flexibility. It allows up to 64 characters in a filename (which is however still less than Windows 95 can handle), and is less restricted in the choice of characters, since it uses the international *'Unicode'* character set and allows the use of spaces.

However, Joliet discs cannot be read by any non-Windows system. For that reason, the Joliet specification states that discs should also contain an ISO 9660 file system that points to the same data.

Filenames longer than the normal 8.3 standard are truncated in the same way as Windows truncates files for DOS. For example *'Staff Memo 99.Doc'* would be stored on the ISO 9660 section as *'STAFFM~1.DOC'*.

ROMEO

The Romeo standard, like Joliet, is a logical standard that allows for long filenames, this time of up to 128 characters. However, Romeo does not use the Unicode character set, and all filenames are converted to upper case to increase backwards compatibility. Romeo filenames are also stored in a truncated format for ISO 9660 readers, but the truncation is much simpler.

For example *'Staff Memo 99.Doc'* would be stored on the ISO 9660 section as *'STAFFMEM.DOC'*.

This can potentially cause problems if several similar filenames are used, which are truncated to the same ISO 9660 filename. Further complications arise when the disc is used in a Macintosh, where the disc is readable only if all filenames are of 31 characters or less.

Due at least in part to these complications, Romeo has not seen as widespread use as Joliet.

Macintosh HFS

The Hierarchical File System used on Macintosh computers can also be used as the filing system on a CD-ROM. PC users cannot access Mac HFS discs, though, so a number of CD-ROMs have been produced as *'Hybrids'*, combining a Mac HFS filing system and an ISO 9660 filing system on the same disc. This works by having an HFS volume in the first 17 blocks, which are ignored by ISO 9660 CD readers.

Rock Ridge Extensions

This system is another logical format that, like Joliet, encompasses ISO 9660 for backwards compatibility but also provides further functions. In this case, the Rock Ridge extensions provide for more detailed file handling as demanded by UNIX systems.

Red Book

Established in 1980, this physical standard is also known as CD-DA (Digital Audio). The *'Red Book'* standard was the first of the series and defined the specification for the audio CD currently in use. It specified that the audio would be stored in digital format and be subject to error detection and correction. All CD drives are capable of reading Red Book audio CDs.

The Red Book standard specifies that an audio CD should contain up to 74 minutes of audio. It also specifies that this audio should be stored uncompressed in Pulse Code Modulated (PCM) format in stereo, 16-bit samples at a sampling rate of 44.1KHz. Thus, each sample consists of two channels of two bytes each, or four bytes per sample. At 44.1KHz (i.e. 44,100 samples per second), that means 176,400 bytes of data per second of audio.

The standard also specifies that audio data is to be stored in sectors each containing 1/75th of a second of digitised audio. Therefore, each sector (also sometimes called a *'large frame'*) contains 1/75th of 176,400 bytes, or 2532 bytes. This is further split into 98 frames of 24 bytes each. Since each sector stores 1/75th of a second, a full 74-minute CD stores 783,216,000 bytes of audio, or nearly 747MB.

Finally, the Red Book standard allows for 99 audio tracks per CD, with the disc's TOC (Table Of Contents) containing the starting point of each track.

Since Red Book is an audio standard, measurements are normally expressed in terms of minutes, seconds and sectors. Nearly all common CD standards are built upon the Red Book as a basis, and it is therefore not uncommon for other standards to refer to minutes or seconds of storage space rather than kilobytes or megabytes.

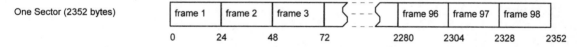

The Red Book audio specification includes a number of error detection and correction techniques. One form of error detection is called *Cross-Interleaved Reed-Solomon Code* (CIRC), and is often able to fix several bad frames in any sector. A method of error correction involves the insertion of sound values interpolated between surrounding values or repeated from the previous value. A single error corrected this way will not be noticed because individual frames contain less than a thousandth of a second of sound each.

In addition to the normal audio data in a Red Book CD, there are additional bits that normally remain hidden to the user, and which are only available in Red Book CDs. Most of these contain the error detection and correction data mentioned above, but there are also 8 bits per frame that can sometimes be accessed for use. These are called *'subchannels'* and are assigned letters from P through W.

The 'P' subchannel is used to indicate the beginning of each track.

The 'Q' subchannel is where the Table Of Contents is stored during the Lead-in, and gives time information during the music tracks. In addition to being available only to Red Book CDs, the 'P' and 'Q' subchannels are only available to the CD producer when the disc is created in Disc-At-Once mode.

The 'R through W' subchannel (The remaining 6 subchannels are combined because they are used for the same data) can store additional information such as graphics or MIDI information. These discs are sometimes referred to as CD+G (Graphics) and CD+MIDI discs, but are uncommon.

Yellow Book

The *'Yellow Book'* standard of 1985 defined the computer data CD specification that is now commonly described simply as CD-ROM.   This standard is based on the Red Book format, but uses the 2352 byte sector for other purposes than pure audio.

It has three modes:

Mode 1 is used to store computer data. If a few bytes of audio data are corrupted, it will make next to no difference to the overall sound. However, if a single data bit is incorrect in a computer program, it could cause it to crash. To reduce such errors, Mode 1 uses just 2k (2048 bytes) of each sector for data, with 16 bytes used for synchronisation and 288 bytes used for Error Detection Codes (EDC) and Error Correction Codes (ECC). This is in addition to some of the error correction techniques provided by the Red Book standard.

Mode 2 was the original attempt at CD-I and provided for compression of audio and graphic information. It offered a 741MB maximum capacity since it dropped the 288 error correction bytes, allowing each sector to store 2336 bytes of data.   Since the disc was spinning at the same speed, its data transfer rate was also greater - 170kb/s instead of the normal 150kb/s.   Mode 2, however, was unable to access computer data and audio/visual data at the same time, since they were stored on different tracks of the disc (only one mode is allowed per track).   This limited its usefulness and Mode 2 was never developed.

Mode 3 was termed Mixed Mode as it allowed computer data tracks and audio tracks to be placed on the same disc. Usually, the first track contains the computer data with the remaining tracks containing audio data. The audio tracks could be played through a domestic audio CD player in which case the player would require to be manually stepped over the data track.   A CD ROM drive would recognise the computer data tracks and would be able to play the audio through its audio output. However, it could not do both at the same time.

Some references to Mixed Mode refer to a drive that can handle both Mode 1 and Mode 2.

CD XA

It is possible for audio and graphic information to be stored in different CD tracks.   When each of these data items is used separately there is no problem but multimedia demands that both audio and graphic information be presented in a synchronised manner and this is not easily achieved.   The Extended Architecture (XA) specification allows both audio, video and computer data to be stored in the same track in an interleaved fashion, thus allowing greatly improved synchronisation.

CD XA is based on the Yellow Book Mode 2, but specifies two *'Forms'* of storing data. Form 1 is for computer data, and Form 2 for audio or video data. Since they are both based on Yellow Book Mode 2, they both require 16 bytes for synchronisation, and both Form 1 and Form 2 allocate an additional 8 bytes for the same purpose. Form 1, being for computer data, required extensive error detection and correction, for which 280 bytes are allocated. This leaves 2k (2048 bytes) for user data per sector. Form 2 does not require such rigorous checking, allocating just 4 bytes to error detection and none for error correction. This leaves 2324 bytes for audio or video data per sector.

Since Form 1 and Form 2 work under the same XA Mode, they can both be placed on the same track. This allows Form 1 sectors containing computer data to be interleaved seamlessly with Form 2 video or audio data sectors. CD drives can then read these sequentially, ensuring proper synchronisation of data, audio and video.   XA also saved space in the storage of audio by using a method called ADPCM (Adaptive Delta Pulse Code Modulation).   This stores the difference between sound samples rather than the values themselves and results in smaller values being produced and saved.

Green Book

This is also an extension of the Mode 2 of the Yellow Book, and this is designed for playing CD-I interactive applications.   It stores files compressed to the MPEG format and interleaves the picture and sound elements. All CD-I tracks are in Mode 2 XA format, and as such can use Form 1 data (such as foreign language text) and Form 2 video and audio.

Unlike White Book, it does not provide the standard ISO 9660 access and requires a special CD-I player, a PC upgrade such as ReelMagic, or a special device driver, since a normal CD ROM drive cannot handle the format. Dedicated CD-I players are available with their own CPU and video memory and these connect to a monitor or television.

One other capability provided by Green Book is the ability to write data into the gap before the TOC. Since audio CD players never try to access this area, it can be safely used for data, without any possibility of the track being accidentally played as audio, which could potentially damage the sound output device.

CD-Bridge

As the name implies, this standard allows a drive to handle CDs that were both XA and CD-I compatible.   This special bridge CD disc is really a CD-I disc with extra XA information added to it.   The Photo CD disc explained below is an example of a bridge disc.   The disc has more than one disc label and this allows the same disc to be played in a CD-I player or an XA capable CD drive.

White Book

Used for Video CD - i.e. the storing of full-motion MPEG-1 video. The output cannot be taken directly to any ordinary video card. It has to be decompressed through special hardware or software to restore MPEG files to their original size. MPEG-1 compression results in a CD with up to 74 minutes of VHS-quality video and stereo sound track. Videos that are longer than 74 minutes have to be split up over two discs. MPEG-1 handling now appears on many video cards, with software or hardware decompression. Video CD is now overshadowed by DVD, but there are a far larger number of CD-R drives available in comparison to DVD-RAM, and the price of DVDs is high compared to CDs.

White Book has seen a number of versions, of which the most widely supported have been version 1.1 and version 2.0. A disc created in White Book version 2.0 consists of a CD XA Form 1 track for computer data such as the program used to play back the video, and a CD XA Form 2 track containing the video data itself.

Blue Book

Also known as CD Plus, Enhanced CD or CD Extra, this is designed to provide multiple sessions on a disc. The first session contains Red Book audio tracks and the second session contains computer data. The main TOC (table of contents) contains information on audio tracks and points to a further TOC storing data tracks. If the disc is used in a normal hi-fi CD audio player, it will not attempt to play the data tracks as it will not recognise the second TOC. A blue book drive will recognise and use both TOCs. The most likely use for Blue Book systems appears to be in the music industry where a CD can be played both in a standard audio CD player and in a computer CD drive. In the latter, photographs and text about the performers can then augment the music. This, along with White Book covers most manufacturers' approaches to multimedia CDs.

Orange Book

Also known as CD-R (CD-Recordable), this describes the writing of CD discs, instead of the physical layout of sectors on the disc. The three parts to the standard are:

I. The use of Magneto Optical (CD-MO) drives which allow data to be written to disc, then erased or overwritten.

II. The use of the *'Write Once'* (called CD-WO, essentially the same as CD-R) format, where the data is written in a single session or multiple sessions but cannot be altered after it is written.

III. The Rewritable format (CD-RW) which allows the disc to be re-written up to 1,000 times. This requires a Multi-Read CD drive or a DVD drive to read discs written by a CD-RW writer.

CD Writers can produce discs in CD-ROM, CD-DA, Mixed Mode, XA and CD-I format and a quad-speed drive will record an entire disc in about 18mins. However, this bare recording speed does not take into account fixing the disc, creating an image, or gathering the material for the disc in the first place. See the *'Recordable CD'* section below for further details.

Kodak Photo CD

CDs are capable of storing large graphics files and the Kodak Photo CD system allows photographs taken with an ordinary camera to be placed on CD discs. When the film is taken to the developer, the images can be reproduced in both standard photographic print format and in CD format. Such photographs can be viewed in the same way as any other graphics file stored on a CD. A standard CD can store 100 photographs and the full 100 may be built up over a period of time with additional photographs being added at later dates. This is not a problem as Kodak can add any new photographs to the CD. However, an older CD is not capable of reading any added data since each new additional group has its own unique storage key and this cannot be accessed by the old technology. If this extra facility is required, a *'Multi-session'* model must be purchased, as this is capable of reading any subsequent additions. Almost all models currently on the market are now multi-session. CD-I players or CD drives that support XA Mode 2/Form 1 are capable of reading these files.

Universal Disc Format

Universal Disc Format, or UDF, is a format designed to allow easier and more efficient recording of CD-ROMs. It was developed by the Optical Storage Technology Association (OSTA), which is a group of hardware and software vendors, and its current version is 1.50. UDF supports a technology called *'incremental packet writing'*, (see *'CD Recording technologies'* below) which means that data can be written to CD-Rs in packets without having to create a disc image. Using UDF, a CD-R can be formatted, at which point any system equipped with a CD-R drive and UDF compliant CD writing software can send packets to record on the disc. Drivers using UDF can allow a CD-R disc to appear as a drive letter, which can be read from and written to in a similar fashion to hard disks or floppies. UDF, however, is not compatible with ISO 9660. In order for other systems to read a UDF disc, there are two options. The reading system can have a UDF driver installed – note that any system which is capable of writing UDF discs can also read them. Alternatively, a UDF disc can be *'finalised'* by writing an ISO 9660 readable volume, which consumes approximately 20MB of CD space. Even when the disc is finalised, a CD-R drive can still write to the disc. However, further changes will require to be finalised once again, consuming another 20MB, if they are to be ISO 9660 compatible.

Standards Hierarchy

The diagram shows how the various physical standards described previously relate to each other. Those standards with a double box around them are fully writable CD formats; the others are standards used as a basis for other formats and cannot be used on their own to create CDs. The diagram does not include Orange Book, as this standard simply defines how to create Recordable CDs of any type.

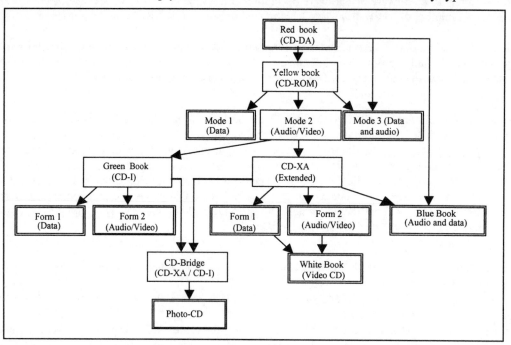

Recordable CD

For large quantity production of CDs, a master copy is laser cut into a glass master copy, which in turn is utilised to create metallic *'stampers'* that are used to stamp out the lands and pits on the reflective layers of each blank CD.   The master copy costs around £500 to produce but subsequent stamped CDs are extremely cheap by comparison, at just a few pence (which is why they are given away with computer magazines and audio magazines).   For small quantities, this is an expensive option.   CD-R (CD-Recordable) systems utilise a CD writer that uses discs of a different construction from the standard pressed discs.   Recordable CD blanks have a layer of dye that can be spot heated by a laser beam to create the 'pits' (technically, they create small mounds, but because the end result is identical to a pit, the terminology remains the same).   The blank discs, known as *'gold discs'*, are supplied with a *'pre-groove'* moulded on its surface, into which

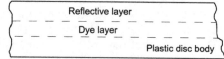

these pits are burned.   The groove provides tracking information for the drive's head servo and provides a cheap way to ensure quality tracking.   The individual blank disc is more expensive than a pressed disc but there is no expensive master to create. CD-R discs read normally on any normal CD drive, and CD Writers are also capable of reading normal CDs.   The dramatic fall in the price of CD writers has led to their widespread use as a backup device.   Current models can record at up to eight-speed, although depending on the manufacturing quality of the blank discs it might be advisable to use slower speeds than the drive is capable of using.

Preparing to write a CD-Rom

Before the CD-ROM writing software is even loaded up, a CD designer must prepare their material thoroughly. Ordinary CD-R or pressed CDs are not erasable, so any important mistakes will require the whole production process to be restarted.

The process of gathering material for a CD involves a number of activities:

- Deciding on material for the CD.
- Selecting the system on which the material should be available.
- Designing and testing the material.
- Creating an installation method for users.
- Writing and distributing the discs.

Deciding on material for the CD

Generally, the CD producer will already have at least a basic concept of what the CD should contain. In many cases, by the time it is decided to create a CD, the contents may already be largely or even completely decided. This especially applies to bespoke productions, audio CDs, video CDs or *'shovelware'* CD-ROMs.

However, that is not always the case. A producer who believes there is a niche in the market for, say, a surgical procedures CD-ROM including video footage of how to perform certain procedures, may have a concept but no material. At the other end of the scale, there may be a large amount of acquired material but no cohesive structure for collecting it onto a CD.

Storage concerns can play a large part in deciding what material to include on a CD. Some literature quotes inflated storage capacities for CD-ROMs such as 765MB. These numbers do not take into account such things as lead-ins, track gaps, the TOC, error correction codes, synchronisation and so on. A more reasonable limit for storage capacity is around 630MB, and this should be borne in mind when designing material. There is nothing wrong with supplying material on multiple CDs, but to require a second CD for just a few megabytes of material that didn't fit into the first disc hints at poor project management. For more information on CD storage space, see *'Storage Concerns'* below.

Selecting the system on which the material should be available

There are a number of options for consideration when it comes to selecting system availability of a CD to be produced, unless a plain audio CD is the target. These are technical or marketing considerations, rather than design issues.

Target System

First of all, the target computer system should be selected. If the project involves a lot of machine-specific executable code (for example a computer game, or a complex interactive multimedia CD on a highly technical subject) then it is highly likely that development time and space considerations will limit the project to one type of computer. For example an .EXE program for a PC cannot normally run on a Macintosh or UNIX system.

However, if the disc comprises mainly machine-nonspecific data such as images, sound, and/or video, then a cross-platform CD could be considered. For example, a CD containing scanned historical documents could be written as a CD-ROM full of TIFF images. In this case, a directory could be included for DOS, Windows, Mac and UNIX, each containing programs able to view, catalog and export such images on that system.

However, PCs are not the only systems that use CD-ROMs. Audio discs are generally compatible with all CD players. CD-I discs run on some computer systems, but otherwise require special CD-I players. Photo-CD discs are also readable by computer systems with appropriate software, but are also useable by consumers without computers at all, via computer-equipped photographic developers.

Finally, there is the option of DVD. Although DVD is superior to CD-ROM, there are currently far fewer systems equipped to read DVD discs. For that reason, even projects that span several gigabytes might currently prove more viable when produced as multiple CDs than as a single DVD.

Target Specification

However, even once the system is selected, the selection of target system may not be complete. For CD-ROMs that are designed for computer use, the producer must also decide on a minimum specification of computer to design for. In some cases this may not be a problem; for example Photo-CDs have no executable code and any system capable of reading Photo-CD discs will be able to read the final CD.

Even basic discs containing little more than, say, a catalog of images, will require some means of accessing that data, however. Expecting the end user to already own software capable of dealing with the files is bad practice and could limit the product's appeal. Even the most basic of file viewers has some form of minimum specification, although some may have a minimum specification so low that no modern PC would fail it. The specification should set a *'target'* for hardware as a minimum, including such things as display capabilities, system memory, CD-ROM speed, audio capabilities and any hard disk storage requirements if the CD installs to disk.

CD Standard

The physical and logical standard that the CD is to follow must then be selected. In many cases it is immediately obvious which type of CD to create. For example a CD of Beethoven's symphony is definitely best printed as a Red Book audio disc, unless it is to contain additional video footage or other multimedia information on the life and times of the composer.

In some cases it may not be so obvious which standard to use. For example, a virtual product demonstration that occupies 200MB of a disc has ample room for a standard CD audio score as background music. Alternatively, the music can be stored in the same data track as the program (as compressed MP3 files) to make space for more detailed graphics and video.

If the CD is to contain computer data, then the logical standard that the data is to conform to must be chosen. For maximum cross-platform readability, ISO 9660 is the best option. However, if the target audience is PC users running Windows 95, as many projects are, then Joliet provides better functionality while its drawbacks are not a concern in this case. Other standards might also be considered depending on the circumstances.

Designing and testing the material

- The chapter on *'Multimedia Design'* goes into detail about the kind of considerations that must be dealt with when designing and testing multimedia material. Similar guidelines apply to creating software for CD-ROM. However, there are additional factors to consider for CD production.
- File formats. CD-ROM, with its large storage capacity, often makes use of large amounts of media files. It is a good idea to decide on a common file format wherever possible. Supplying a catalog of images with various images in GIF, TIFF, JPEG and PCX format is not terribly impressive.
- Hard disk installation. Although it is often quite possible to run multimedia files or even executable code directly from CD-ROM, many manufacturers implement a hard disk installation routine (See *'Creating an installation method for users', below*). Some users resent having to give up hard disk space to something that is already stored elsewhere, so careful thought should be given to just how much of the project should be installed on the local hard drive, and how much remains on the CD.
- Data Rates. It is a temptation to go for high-quality video in multimedia projects due to the capacities offered by CD-ROM. This is not a problem if the target specification is high enough, but if the target CD drive is slow then this limits the use of video, or indeed any files that require fast throughput. An option is to cache the video files to hard disk, but this can be messy and/or use up a lot of hard disk space unnecessarily.
- Updates. CD-ROM is a static media – ROM means *'Read Only Memory'* and as such ordinary CD-ROMs cannot be changed at a later date, though they may be replaced. Replacing CD-ROMs may or may not be an expensive option, but it is likely that much of that update is duplicated material, and the logistics of the whole operation can sometimes be infuriating. Another option is to include a utility on the CD that will access a web site on the Internet to download updates to the local hard drive.

Creating an installation method for users

CD-ROMs that run fully from the disc without installation are the exception rather than the rule. Nearly all products provide some kind of installation feature. This is to facilitate future updates, as well as providing writeable configuration files on the hard disk.

The IMA (Interactive Multimedia Association) has produced a set of standards concerning installation procedures, known as the IMA Recommended Practices for Developers. It is a good idea to follow these guidelines, to provide a more recognisable installation method for users. It recommends the following:

- Perform system checks to ensure that the target system is capable of running the software <u>before</u> beginning the installation. This means checking that there is sufficient hard disk space for the installation, as well as checking that the system is capable of running the project adequately.
- Installation paths and drives should be able to be customised. In particular, the user should be able to specify the CD-ROM drive letter for cases where it differs from that expected by the software.
- When writing files to the hard disk, existing files should not be over-written without the permission of the user. If possible the option should be offered of backing up existing files. For safer installation, IMA recommends installing as many files as possible in an entirely new folder. Again, the user should be able to change the path of this folder, and it should not be created without the user's knowledge and consent. This is a particular problem with Windows DLLs (Dynamic Link Library files, which contain snippets of reusable program code). Microsoft recommends that DLLs are written to the C:\WINDOWS\SYSTEM directory, but this can cause serious problems if one package's DLL overwrites another package's DLL, and the new DLL does not perform the same functions as the previous version. The IMA recommendation would have DLL's in an entirely separate folder, which is non-standard but safer.
- Avoid making changes to the target system where possible. If the software absolutely must make changes, then display a dialog box explaining the changes and asking the user for approval before committing those changes. Any changes might require the installer to reboot, or at the very least ask the user to manually reboot, in order for the changes to take effect. All such changes made should be tracked and stored in a file in case of later uninstallation.
- An uninstall procedure should also be supplied that is capable of removing all files created by the application, and removing any modifications made to system files by the installation. However, any files that might be

shared with other applications (such as DLL files) should not be deleted until and unless the user has agreed to do so. In Windows machines, this criterion is fulfilled by complying with the *'Add/Remove Programs'* utility found Control Panel. When uninstalling, any changes made to system files should be undone.

Additional features that are desirable in an installer include:

* A splash screen, to display the company or software logo.
* The ability to abort the installation at any point.
* Options for a minimum installation, full installation, or custom installation. This will vary the amount of files copied to the hard disk, but also might affect functionality and/or speed.
* Looking for existing versions of the software, and offering to update them, over-write them, or back them up before continuing.
* Checking that the user has a valid license, for example by asking for a serial number and checking its validity.
* Licensing requirements. Many packages now include a licensing screen as part of the installation procedure, thus theoretically ensuring that the user has read and understood the terms of the license.
* Tutorials and help. If the install procedure takes a long time, it is common to display minor hints and tips during the install procedure. Also, the last thing many installers do is to load up a document explaining the basics of the program, any changes from the previous version, troubleshooting information and so on.
* Supplementary software and files. Some products might include, for example, PDF documentation, which will require the installation of Adobe Acrobat Reader to display the files. Another example might require new fonts to be installed, which the package will use when it runs.
* Compression. While CDs can hold a large amount of data, developers tend to squeeze as much performance out of their product as possible. Compression of data allows in some cases over 1GB of data on a single disc. The installer has to be able to uncompress files directly to hard disk in this case.

While it is possible to write an in-house installation tool for all products, or even a separate tool for each product, this takes time and provides an interface to the user that he or she is likely to be unfamiliar with. To help provide a more intuitive, familiar interface, several installer packages are available commercially. For Windows, the most common installation product is the *'Installshield'* program.

Using Installshield

This package provides all of the above functions, and provides a common interface that users will be able to instantly recognise. There is now a version of Installshield designed specifically for the enhanced installation tracking used by Windows 2000, although the more conventional Windows 95/98 installation routines can still be used.

Installshield includes a wizard to aid in the creation of installation routines, but creating a proper installation routine can still be a difficult task for large, complex programs, and even simpler routines can appear daunting to the uninitiated.

At its heart, Installshield uses a script, usually named SETUP.RUL, which appears very similar to a source code file for the C++ programming language. Despite this, it is entirely possible to create reliable setup routines for small software packages without even touching this code (which can be difficult to understand to those who have never done programming).

The install script is basically a set of rules governing how the finished SETUP.EXE program supplied with the finished CD product will go about the installation procedure. It performs a number of functions, such as telling the finished installer which screens are displayed in what order, which files are part of the installation types, and how to deal with user interaction and even error checking. The SETUP.RUL file can be very complex, and its precise structure is beyond the scope of this book.

However, the wizard can be used to create a basic script file from scratch, after asking the user a number of questions about the desired setup routine. This way, the user can manage the setup files and resources with a minimum of programming knowledge.

In addition to the script file, there is one or more *'setup types'*. This allows, for example, the commonly provided option in install procedures whereby the user is given a choice of Minimum, Typical, or Custom installations. At this point, each setup type should be associated with one or more *'components'*, describing which features should be installed as part of each installation type.

For example, the *'Minimum'* installation could install only the *'Program Files'* component and the *'Shared DLLs'* component, while the *'Full'* installation will also install the *'Sample files'* and *'Help files'* components. It is possible to specify that a certain component can only be installed if another component is also installed. For example, the user may specify that the email component should only be allowed if the communications component is also selected.

Each of these components is further divided into 'File groups'. Each component can specify one or more file groups, and two components may specify any of the same file groups as another component. However, the file groups in a component should be chosen to accurately describe what that type of install includes. For example the *'Program Files'* component could include the *'Program DLLs'* file group and the *'Program Executable files'* file group.

The file groups themselves contain *'links'*, which basically specify which individual files fall into that file group. Again, each file group is allowed to specify files that overlap with the files in any other file group.

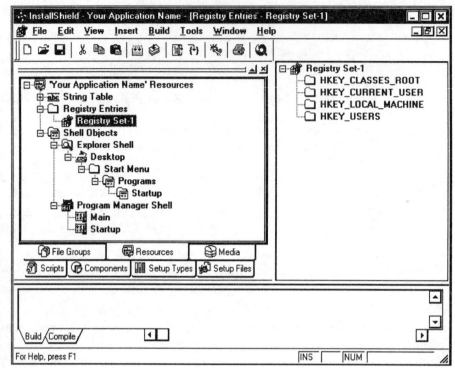

Besides these, there are a few other files associated with each installation routine. These include splash screens, (which can be dependent on language just like string tables), licensing information text files which are displayed during the install, and 'README' notes. These should be edited to provide new versions for the individual project, as the standard files provided with the wizard do not project a professional feel to the install procedure

Installshield also deals with *'Resources'*, which is a general heading for anything other than files that are installed on the system by the installation routine being created. In other words, this includes registry entries, links to be added to the start menu, desktop, or program manager shell, and string tables. String tables are collections of short messages that are used by the installation procedure (such as error messages, product keys, and version names), and they are grouped together by language so that multiple language installations can be created.

Once all the resources are gathered in an appropriate manner, the installation media can be generated using the *'Media Build Wizard'*. This allows various installation sets to be created including several forms of floppy disk, web install, and of course CD-ROM.

Creating an Autorun CD

Finally, there is the option of autorunning the disc on target machines. In Windows 95 and later, the operating system includes the ability to detect the insertion of a CD, and run software if it is specified on that CD. This is done through a file called AUTORUN.INF, which is located in the root folder on an individual CD-ROM disc. At its simplest, it consists of a header, and a line to tell the operating system which program or data file to load up. The only other setting that is particularly frequently used is a setting that assigns an icon (located in a file on the CD) to the CD when it appears in Explorer. An example file might look like the one shown in the illustration.

```
[autorun]
OPEN=INSTALL.EXE
ICON=MEDIA.ICO
```

A CD with this AUTORUN.INF file in its root folder will, upon insertion into the CD drive, tell the Windows operating system to run the INSTALL.EXE program, beginning the install procedure automatically. The filename here need not be a program. Autorun can be configured to load up the default HTML browser by specifying a .HTM file instead, for example. The 'ICON' setting lets Windows Explorer know which .ICO file to use when displaying an icon for the CD-ROM drive while it contains that CD. In this case, both the INSTALL.EXE and MEDIA.ICO files are also located in the root folder of the CD-ROM disc.

Storage Concerns

Depending on the recording software, the system may already take into account all recording overheads and simply present the user with a simplified drag-and-drop interface. However, if not, then the user must be aware of several factors affecting storage capacity of CDs.

As stated earlier, CD-ROMs do not use their full capacity for storing user data. A large portion of CD storage space is used in low-level error detection and correction, as well as data modulation. However, these cannot be removed under any circumstances and so they are of no concern to CD producers.

After these, the CD is left with 74 minutes of audio, or nearly 747MB of data as explained under the *'Red Book'* explanation. Red Book is the only standard that can use all 747MB of storage space for user data. All other standards use at least some of that space for synchronisation and additional error correction codes.

The table below shows how the storage space in each sector is divided up under each standard.

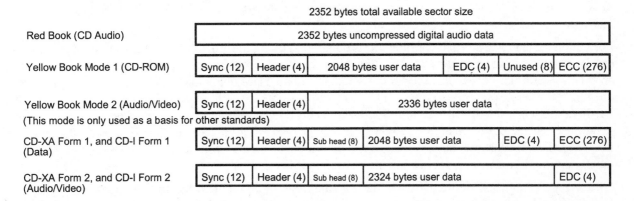

CDs are normally manufactured with a maximum of 74 minutes capacity, giving a total of 333,000 sectors. Some manufacturers are capable of producing CDs of up to 81 minutes length by compressing the spiral greater than normally. However, these are not standard CDs and do not follow the Red Book format. As such they are not guaranteed to work on all CD players, and are best avoided where possible. On the other hand, shorter CDs can be played in any standard CD player – 60 minute CDs are not uncommon, and there is a special *'mini'* CD just over 3 inches wide. These smaller discs can still be played in almost all CD players, because data is recorded from the inner spiral outwards.

From a standard CD with up to 333 thousand sectors, the following <u>theoretical maximum</u> storage capacities can be calculated:

Red Book	333,000 sectors x 2352 bytes = 783,216,000 bytes (approx 747MB)
Yellow Book Mode 1	333,000 sectors x 2048 bytes = 681,984,000 bytes (approx 650MB)
Yellow Book Mode 2	333,000 sectors x 2336 bytes = 777,888,000 bytes (approx 742MB)
XA or CD-I Form 1	333,000 sectors x 2048 bytes = 681,984,000 bytes (approx 650MB)
XA or CD-I Form 2	333,000 sectors x 2324 bytes = 773,892,000 bytes (approx 738MB)

Unfortunately, storage on a CD is not just a simple matter of just writing sectors away to disc. CD has its roots in audio, and so each disc is split up into *'tracks'*. In an audio disc, each track normally does represent one musical piece, and the Volume Table Of Contents lists up to 99 track locations. If a basic computer CD-ROM is produced, without additional music or video tracks, then the entire CD-ROM will comprise a single data track, either in Yellow Book Mode 1 or CD XA Form 1.

Things get more complicated, however, when other types of discs are produced. Generally, all data within a track must be of the same mode. However, a CD-XA or CD-I track will allow each sector to be either Form 1 or Form 2, so that data of both types can be interleaved to improve synchronisation. That means that, for example, a CD-XA video and data track could have 25 sectors of computer data and 25 sectors of video data, then back to computer data and so on. The storage capacity can only be calculated then by understanding just how many sectors will be Form 1 and how many will be Form 2.

Then there is the case of multiple tracks. Red Book CDs containing nothing but audio, and written in a single session, are the only type that can have tracks back to back. Every other type of CD must have a gap between each track. That gap is 2 seconds before audio tracks, and 3 seconds before every other type of track. Three seconds is 225 sectors, or 450KB in Yellow Book Mode 1, which is no longer available for recording data.

Finally, there is the consideration of multiple sessions. CDs written in a single session have an area called a *'lead-in'* before the tracks, and a *'lead-out'* area after the tracks in that session. If the CD is recorded in more than one session (see *'Tracks and sessions'* below) then each individual session must have its own lead-in and lead-out.

Each lead-in area occupies 4500 sectors, while the lead-out area occupies 6750 sectors for the first session and 2250 for each subsequent session. These overheads can seriously eat into the storage capacity of a CD, so for any distributable CD it may be wise to have as few sessions as possible.

For example, an often-used CD format is to have a single Red Book session of audio, followed by a second session of CD-ROM data. This format allows most computers to access the data, while normal audio units will only recognise the audio session. The audio in the Red Book session can be written back to back, and if it takes up say 45 minutes, then that corresponds to 202,500 sectors. Add to this the 4500 sector lead-in and the 6750 sector lead-out. The Red Book session would therefore consume 213,750 sectors, leaving 119,250 sectors for the second session. With the lead-in of 4500 sectors and lead-out of 2250 sectors, the data session has a maximum useable data area of 112,500 sectors, or approximately 219MB.

For computer data, the storage considerations do not end there, unfortunately. While audio or video data can be stored 'as-is', computer data requires a logical format in order to access the data. This might be an ISO 9660 format, Joliet, or some similar standard. In all cases, the logical standard requires some data on folders, filenames, and so on. ISO 9660 also stores a path table, and a root folder record. Furthermore, each folder will require disc space, and there is additional wastage when storage of a file leaves the last sector less than fully utilised. It is impossible to give hard and fast figures on the amount of space this will consume, but CD images should always be created with these additional overheads very much in mind, in order to avoid last minute trimming of files.

CDs written using packets in UDF have the added burden of a table that has to keep track of all packets and the files they belong to. This means a UDF packet written CD-R is reduced to around 600MB of space. CD-RWs written using UDF also use *'sparing'* techniques to prevent over-using areas of the disc, which further reduces available space to about 500MB.

CD recording technology

As mentioned previously, a CD has one or more sessions, with each session being further divided into tracks. Each session's lead-in contains the TOC for that session, listing up to 99 tracks in the session. If the recording has not been finalised then the TOC also contains the location where the next session recording can begin.

Each track can be of any mode. For example *'mixed mode'* CDs often have CD-ROM computer data in track 1 and up to 98 audio tracks following it. A Video CD might have up to 99 different MPEG clips, each in a separate track. For CD-ROM however, there is almost never more than one CD-ROM track per session.

Disc Images

Generally, CD creation software allows for the user to make *'CD images'*. This makes use of one large, and preferably contiguous, file located on a hard disk. The file is used as an exact replica of the data that is to be written to the CD. Since the reading of the file can be done easily and quickly in serial, this makes for good data throughput. Also, a disc image is useful when recording an entire disc in one go. (see *'disc-at-once recording'*, below)

Alternatively, most packages also provide for *'virtual images'*. Like a normal CD image, the virtual image is used to provide data for writing to CD. However, virtual images do not store an exact replica of the data to put on CD. Instead, they store a database of filenames and information on them such as their size, and where to put them on the CD. The software must then look through this database when writing CDs, and load the files into memory before sending them to the recording device. This method is sometimes called *'on-the-fly'* CD writing.

Virtual images have one major benefit, which is their convenience. This method does not require the slow and disk-hungry creation of a full CD image. However, care must be taken to ensure that the data is available on time to be written to CD. (See *'Preparing a system for writing'*, below)

A disc image is described as a *'raw'* file, because it stores the raw data that is to be placed on the CD. Audio tracks that contain basic 16-bit stereo PCM wave samples are also raw files, because they contain the exact data that can constitute a single audio track on a CD.

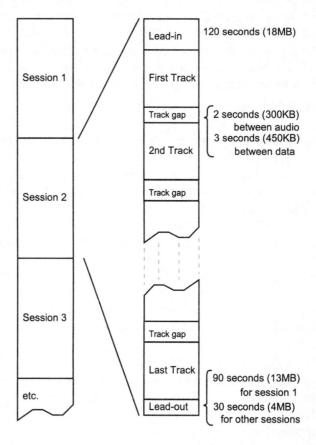

Disc-at-once and track-at-once recording

Both of these methods of CD creation use only a single session. Disc-at-once recording involves writing the entire CD from start to finish in one go, while track-at-once recording involves writing individual tracks separately, generally with a pause in between to assemble the next track. Some CD recorders do not support disc-at-once, while some others do not support track-at-once recording.

Using Disc-at-once recording means that the entire CD has to be assembled before writing, so that the Table Of Contents can be written at the start of the disc, and also so that the recording process is not interrupted. However, Disc-at-once allows the gap between tracks to be of any length, including zero. It also allows access to the 'P' and 'Q' subchannels. Disc-at-once recorded CDs may be used as masters to create batches of pressed CDs, but require careful planning to ensure that a buffer underrun does not ruin the disc during recording.

Track-at-once recording, on the other hand, creates the TOC after all the tracks have been written, meaning that it has to go back to write the lead-in after all the tracks have been created. Furthermore, because the system is paused between writing tracks, a track gap is required, as explained earlier. This gap is of two or three seconds depending on the type of track, or equivalent to 300 to 450KB of CD-ROM data. The gap creates an audible clicking sound when played on audio CD players, and as such is unsuitable to be used as a master to press CDs. However, under some circumstances a track-at-once recorder can partially recover from buffer underrun errors and write the rest of the tracks successfully. It can then leave the affected track(s) out of the TOC when it writes the lead-in.

Track-at-once allows other processing to be carried out between tracks, for example reading in another track from a source CD to copy into the new CD.

When creating a Yellow Book CD-ROM or CD-XA without audio, there is essentially no difference between disc-at-once and track-at-once recording. Barring the track gaps, which are an almost insignificant 300KB out of 650MB, the CD-ROM will appear identical to the end user when recorded in either method.

Multi-session recording

There are various circumstances where it is not desirable or not possible to write an entire CD is one go. Multi-session recording was introduced in the Orange Book, and allows users to write data to CD in one session, and come back to add more sessions at a later date. In order to use multi-session recording, every session must be recorded in multisession mode, even the first session.

Care should be taken when considering multisession recording. Audio CD players can only read the first session, and some older CD drives do not support reading of multi-session discs. There is also more than one implementation of multisession recording, and so there may be compatibility issues with discs recorded as multisession discs. Finally, reading of multi-session discs is even more problematic if the disc is still open for new sessions to be added. Until the last session is added, there is no TOC and only drivers that are written to handle open multisession discs can read them.

On the other hand, multiple sessions are instrumental in certain other situations. Kodak's Photo-CD system relies heavily on multisessions, for example. Since one set of photographs will not take up the full space on the CD, the CD session is written in multisession mode and left open. That way, when the user wishes to add new photos, the developer simply continues to append new sessions until the CD no longer has room, at which point the disc can be finalised.

Another standard which requires multisession mode is CD Extra, which relies on the added session to prevent accidental playing of computer data on CD players.

CD-ROM data can also be written in multiple sessions. For example, if company finance spreadsheets are to be archived at the end of each month, a new session could be created every time the archiving is to take place. This works by having the directory structure in the most recently written session point to both new files, and files in previous sessions. Drives which can read multisession discs will use the most up-to-date volume data. In this way, data can actually be 'deleted' from a CD-ROM – the file is not removed from the disc but the most up-to-date volume descriptor contains no reference to the file and so it does not show up for users to access.

Once the last session has been written, the disc must be *'fixed'* (also called *'fixating'* or *'closing'* the disc). Fixation of a disc involves writing a lead-in, including a Table of Contents, so that normal CD drives may access it. Another benefit of multisessions is that an individual session can be written in Disc-At-Once mode, with the benefits that this entails (See below).

Alternatives to multisession recording have been created to reduce the space overheads taken up by session lead-ins and lead-outs. These include recording data track-by-track (i.e. track-at-once), or sector-by sector (also called *'incremental packet writing'*).

Incremental Packet Writing

This is a useful alternative to multisession discs. Data is written to the CD in *'packets'*. Depending on the implementation, these packets might be one or more sectors long. At best, then, the minimum size of data that can be written to CD-R at one time is 2048 bytes. This is significantly smaller than the multi-megabyte overheads required by each session of a multi-session CD.

Incremental Packet Writing is normally used with UDF (see above), and so can provide convenient drive-letter access to the device, but needs to be *'closed'* before it can work in a normal CD-ROM system. Like multisession discs, files can be 'deleted' from CD-Rs, though no space will be freed in doing so. Packet writing can also prevent buffer underruns, because of the much smaller amount of data that the software needs to access in order to write to the CD.

Bootable CDs

For specialised purposes, a CD-ROM can be made *'bootable'*. That is, a computer whose BIOS allows it to boot up from CD-ROM instead of hard disk or floppy, can boot up, loading its operating system entirely from such a CD. Of course, the target machine's BIOS must support booting from CD-Drives for this to be useful. Some versions of Windows CDs are bootable, allowing that operating system to be installed with less fuss. However, in order to maximise the target audience, producers should take into consideration the option of supplying a boot floppy for users whose machine does not support this capability.

The standard which defines the operation of bootable CDs is, like the High Sierra standard, named after the place where it was drafted - the El Torito Grill. The *'El Torito'* standard is supported by nearly all modern BIOS systems.

When creating a bootable CD, it should be borne in mind that the media on which the program resides is read-only. For example, the Windows 95 operating system needs to read and write to and from the media that it is boots from, and so it is unsuitable for a bootable CD. In general, virtually the only use to date for bootable CDs is in the installation of operating systems.

An El Torito CD-ROM contains a standard ISO9660 area, but also a separate boot image. The boot image is a direct copy of the system files from an existing bootable media, which can be a floppy or hard disk. A bit image is made of these system files, which is then written to the CD-ROM.

Recording a CD

Once the material for a CD is available, and has been appropriately tested, preparations can be made to begin recording. For an existing setup that is already known to work sufficiently, there may be little or no preparation involved. However, every system has to be set up the first time, and CD writing requires fast access in order to make sure the writer is kept supplied with data to place on the CD as it spins by.

Preparing a system for writing

Many of the same factors are involved in ensuring steady data rates for CD recording, as with video capturing. The recording hardware maintains a *'buffer'* area of memory, which is used to load data from disk and store it until it is needed by the recorder. If there were no buffer, or if the buffer is empty when data is required (known as an *'underrun'*), then the recorder will want to write data when there is none there. During this period the CD will still be spinning, and so an area on the finished CD will not store readable data. This will under normal circumstances ruin an entire CD.

The data rate required by the recording hardware varies depending on its recording speed, and the amount of data per sector (sector size). A single speed drive needs to write 75 sectors per second, which equates to 150KB of computer data per second, or 172KB of audio data, for example. Thus, due to the larger sector size, audio and video CD writing requires even higher data rates than CD-ROM writing. Writing at double speed or higher will increase the required data rate even more.

Most CD-R drives have between 512KB and 2MB of buffer space. If this is filled up before the recording begins, then it gives some capability to recover from periods of interruption. This *'interruption time'* is based on the buffer size and writer speed. For example if a 1MB buffer is full, and the CD-R drive is writing a CD-ROM at double speed when an interruption occurs, it can continue to write for just over three seconds before an underrun occurs. (1024KB buffer / 300KB required data rate = 3.41 seconds)

The components that are relied upon to keep things going smoothly include the hard disk, the processor, the writer itself and the recording software. Some of these are covered in more detail in the *'Digital Video'* chapter.

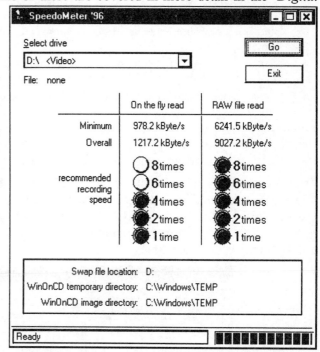

Hard disk speed. The software needs fast access to the disk image, to pass the data on to the drive. For slower requirements, a UDMA IDE hard disk might suffice but for higher data rates a SCSI-2 or SCSI-UW might be required and an AV classification disk would be preferable. Many CD recording packages include a hard disk speed tester, which will check that the system's hard disks are suitable. The screen shot shows the *'SpeedoMeter 96'* software, which performs this function. This software is supplied with WinOnCD OEM version 3.5. It can be used on any hard drive, and indicates suitable CD recording speeds using either a raw or virtual (on-the-fly) image on that disk.

Furthermore, defragmenting the hard disk before writing CDs may improve its performance. Using a full CD image rather than a virtual image may also help.

Processor availability. While the speed of the processor is rarely an issue except in older PCs, the recording software must have the processor's full attention. It is the processor that must supply the recorder with data, and if it is busy servicing another application it cannot do this. To this end, all other packages should be shut down, including any software in the system tray that could affect performance.

The CD Recording hardware and software. Modern CD-R units are capable of writing CDs at eight-speed or even faster. However, less modern units will not record so fast. In either case, the CD producer has to make sure that the recording speed set in the recording software matches the speed the drive is capable of handling.

Testing Recording Speed

Before writing CDs, most recording software has a facility whereby the writing of CDs can be simulated. Data is passed to the CD-R drive as if a CD is to be created, and the CD spins in exactly the manner it would if creating the CD, but the laser is not fully powered, and so no data is actually written to the CD. At slower speeds, this is a lengthy process, but it is well worth checking if more than one CD is to be created.

Recording a CD-Rom

There is a variety of CD Recording software available, but the basic functions are generally very similar. These examples show how to create a CD using WinOnCD OEM 3.5 by CeQuadrat.

When the user first loads WinOnCD, the opening screen is as shown in the illustration. The software deals with 'projects', which are essentially just a description of the track types and track contents to be recorded.

WinOnCD offers several CD creation options:

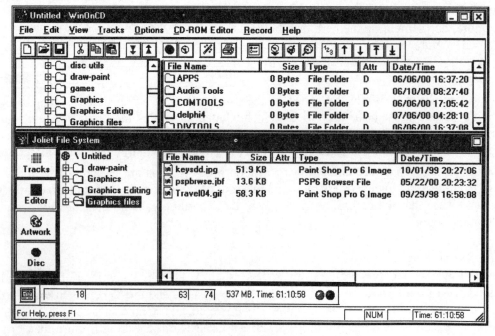

- "CD-ROM ISO 9660 / Joliet" creates a project with a single CD-XA Form 1 track. This track can form either a single session CD, or the first session of a multisession CD. As its names suggests, this option creates a CD-ROM track in the Joliet format, with backwards compatibility for ISO 9660 only systems.
- "Append Session" is the option that allows additional sessions to be added. The software will detect a disc in the drive, and examine it to find whether it is still open for writing, and how much space is left.
- "CD Copy", as should be obvious, will perform a direct copy of a CD. Of course, normal copyright laws apply.
- "CD Digital Audio" creates a Red Book project.
- "CD Extra" creates a Blue Book CD. WinOnCD Blue Book discs are made up of one or more Red Book audio tracks, and a CD-XA Form 1 track in Joliet format.
- "Video CD 2.0" projects consist of a CD-I portion not normally visible to PCs, a Joliet-based CD-XA Form 1 track containing the Video CD runtime files, and one or more CD-XA Form 2 tracks for the video data.
- "Track Image" opens a project into which one or more previously created track images can be loaded to form a complete session image.

Finally, the "Custom Project" option will open a completely blank project, allowing the user to customise the track types to be put on the CD. This option should be used with caution, as extravagant use of multiple track formats can create an unreadable CD.

Once a project type has been chosen, the user can place data into the tracks. If the CD to be created is a CD-ROM, then the default project will have just a single CD-XA track, as can be seen by viewing the tracks. This is sufficient for many CD-ROM products, but additional tracks can be added if required. By selecting *Edit / Insert* from the menubar, a CD-ROM project can add a Red Book digital audio track, a CD-Extra track, or a track image.

There are four large buttons on the left edge of the application window.

In the example, the *'Tracks'* button is depressed, and so the main view shows the number and format of all tracks in the project.

The *'Artwork'* button provides very basic functions for creating CD covers, such as placing text, indices, or bitmaps.

The *'Disc'* button is used to actually write the CD (see later).

To put the contents of the CD-XA track together, the *'Editor'* button should be used. This will take the user into a representation of the actual file system that will be on the finished CD. Since the project has just been created, it is blank. Dragging and dropping files or folders from the upper left window adds these files added to the track. If folders are created in the disc image, then the user can drag and drop files or folders inside that folder as well.

This means, then, that the project file in this case is just a virtual image, to be written on the fly.

The bar at the bottom indicates the amount of data the project is currently storing. Markers indicate the 18, 63 and 74 minutes, the common CD maximum sizes. WinOnCD keeps track of the amount of all data put into the project, so the user need only glance at this bar to see how much space is left in their CD project.

Once all the files for the CD-ROM are in the project, the disc can be recorded. Clicking on the *'Disc'* button changes the display to the *'Disc Properties and Recording Settings'* page, as shown.

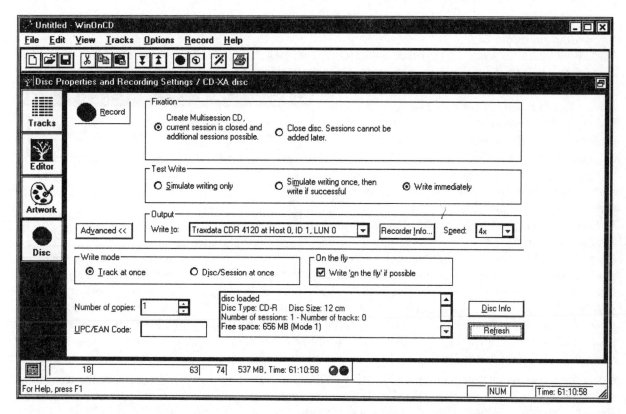

From this screen, the recording options are selected. The first option is a radio box, giving the option of either creating a multisession disc, or closing the disc and making it single session. Depending on the amount of data written to the disc, the user may wish to keep the disc open in order to make use of the remaining space at a later date. However, open discs may not be read by many normal CD-ROM drives.

The next option is *'Test Write'*. This option can be used to simulate writing to CD, to check that data throughput is fast enough to provide a constant supply of data to the CD writer.

The *'Output'* option allows the user to choose which CD-R unit to use if more than one is available. The drop-down box also gives the option of sending the data to an image file instead of a CD-R drive. These image files can be used later by creating a CD Image project, or inserting a CD image track into a project. Additionally, the *'Output'* box allows the user to choose which speed to record at – the driver knows the maximum speed the installed CD-R can cope with and will not allow this setting to go any higher than it can handle. The *'Recorder Info'* button simply displays a few tabs of information about the recording device, such as its SCSI details, driver files, the capabilities of the CD-R drive, and so on.

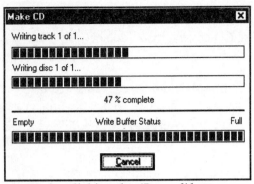

In the *'Advanced'* options, the *'Write mode'* box allows the user to choose whether to record in track-at-once mode or disc-at-once mode. Since this is a CD-ROM disc, there is next to no difference between the two options.

The *'Advanced'* part of the screen also gives options to choose to write on-the-fly where possible, select the number of copies of the CD project to create, and so on. For home users creating a basic CD-ROM to backup their hard disk or such, the advanced options will probably not be needed.

Once the recording is ready to begin, the user can start the process by clicking the *'Record'* button.

Then, a window appears, containing two progress bars and a *'Write Buffer Status'* bar. The buffer goes from empty up to full as the CD-R's buffer is filled, and then the writing begins. The track progress bar shows how much of each individual track has been written, while the disc progress bar shows how much of the complete CD has been written. Even if the CD consists of a single track, the track and disc progress bars will not be identical, because the disc progress bar includes the writing of the lead-in and lead-out.

Recording an audio CD

With WinOnCD, an audio CD is made by selecting the *'CD Digital Audio'* option instead of *'CD-ROM ISO 9660 / Joliet'*. At this point the user is shown the track editing screen, and a new project will have no tracks. In the track view, a placeholder will appear to show that it expects CD-DA tracks to be added, but the placeholder will have a yellow exclamation point beside it to show that there are currently no tracks in the project. Use Edit / Insert to insert new tracks. Since there are no defined tracks so far, any type of track can be added via the *'Insert track'* dialog box.

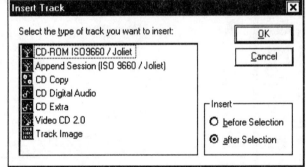

For an audio CD, nothing but *'CD Digital Audio'* tracks should be added.

Once a CD-DA track is added, the options to add new tracks are reduced to a single CD-ROM track at the start (making it a mixed-mode CD), a single CD-Extra track at the end (making it a Blue Book CD), or more digital audio tracks. Track images can also be selected, but in order to conform to the standards these images should be made of audio, CD-XA or CD-Extra tracks. Furthermore, a disc may not combine mixed-mode with Blue Book – only one data track per session is allowed. CD-ROM tracks, whether CD-XA or CD-Extra, are all edited in the same manner as described previously.

CD audio tracks are just very large, high-quality sound samples. The *'Editor'* button takes the user to the audio track editing screen. Here, WinOnCD provides some basic sound recording and editing functions, such as inserting silence, fades, loading waveforms, ripping CD audio, and selecting and deleting portions of the waveform. A few features are available here that normal audio editors would not have, such as detecting, inserting and deleting track marks, editing CD-Extra track properties and so on.

Although the WinOnCD editor cannot edit individual sound channels, it can display the left and right stereo channels separately or as one combined waveform. It also displays a volume indicator below the waveforms, showing the volume as a percentage of the original wave after any fades have been used.

Once each track has an appropriate waveform, the CD can be created in the same manner as a data CD-ROM. In this case, however, there is a noticeable difference between disc-at-once and track-at-once CD writing – track-at-once usually inserts a two-second gap between tracks, and only disc-at-once CDs can contain track marks.

Track marks are used to split one audio track into several audio tracks. This is useful when a single recording has been made, instead of each track being recorded separately. For example, a live recording of a concert would require track marks to indicate where each song ends and a new song begins. WinOnCD can load in a single waveform and use track marks to separate tracks, but it still sees them as a single continuous waveform.

Recording a video CD

A CD producer can use WinOnCD to create Video CDs by the White Book version 2.0 standard. Using this method, the first track <u>must</u> be a CD-XA Form 1 track containing video CD application files, as well as an ISO 9660 / Joliet file system that can contain any additional user files. All other tracks on that disc must be CD-XA form 2 tracks containing MPEG video. The finished disc can be played on a video CD deck, a home PC with appropriate hardware and software, or a DVD player.

For MPEG video tracks, the 'Editor' button simply brings up a dialog box, which allows the user to specify the file to use as a source for that track. This is done by clicking the button with the ellipsis in it, and then specifying the input file. The source file in a basic Video CD track must be an multiplexed MPEG-1 file, and the video data must be at a bit rate of 1.152Mbit/s, while the audio must have a bit rate of 224 kBit/s. These limitations make it difficult to create an appropriate MPEG file.

Fortunately, WinOnCD can also be used to select an AVI file, which will then be encoded into an appropriate bit-rate MPEG file for Video CD. It will display the video in a small window as it is encoded, along with the speed of encoding and the time remaining.

Adaptec's Easy CD Creator Deluxe 3.01 is not able to convert AVI files in this manner, but can create Video CDs that use a menu system. This makes use of stills in MPEG format to display a menu. The PC keyboard or the Video CD player controls select an option, and a different MPEG track is played for each option.

WinOnCD cannot handle menus on a Video CD or the more complex interactive videos, but CeQuadrat supply a separate package called VideoPack 4.0 that can do so.

Re-writable CDs

The Orange Book specification defines three CD recording methods. Of these, two methods involve re-writable CD media. These are MO (Magneto-Optical) and CD-RW (CD Read/Write).

Magneto-Optical discs operate differently from conventional CDs. The laser beam heats the alloy on the CD surface, to such a temperature that its magnetic properties are lost. Then, an electromagnet on the other side of the write head is able to change the area's magnetic polarity before it cools. Later, when a low power laser beam is used to read the data back, the light in the laser beam is influenced by the magnetic field of the alloy, allowing the reader to detect these changes and interpret them as data. Obviously, conventional CD drives do not have the circuitry to do this, and so cannot read MO drives.

The Sony MiniDisc operates on a magneto-optical basis, but it does not follow any of the standards defined in this chapter, not even the MO section of the Orange Book. It is not as yet used as a computer data storage medium, being almost entirely restricted to audio.

CD-RW systems are more correctly called CD-E (CD Erasable) drives. They operate using a phase change technology, but there are a number of compatibility problems between CD-RW writers and conventional CD-ROM drives.

Firstly, the original PCR (Phase Change Recordable) discs were larger than normal CDs. Later, Panasonic's PD discs were introduced, which were physically similar to CD size, but were logically incompatible due to a much smaller sector size on the PD disc.

When Orange Book was introduced, it defined a CD-RW standard for phase change discs, which could potentially be used by conventional CD-ROM drives with a little modification. Normal CD discs reflect 65 to 70 percent of light, while CD-RW discs only reflect 15 to 25 percent. This means that the read head on a normal CD drive requires additional circuitry (called *'automatic gain control'*) in order to detect the reflected light.

This is one major problem for distribution of CD-RW. While modern CD-ROM drives generally have the gain control built in now, not everybody can be expected to have a modern CD-ROM drive. Furthermore, because CD-RW is not created using sessions, it makes use of the UDF system. The discs need to undergo a process called *'freezing'*, similar to closing a CD-R disc, which makes it readable in a standard CD drive. CD-RW discs are also expensive compared to CD-Rs, and have even more limited space than CD-R discs due to the specification of 14KB of slack space after each 64KB block. This leaves just 530MB useable space on a CD-RW disc.

All of these problems may well make DVD distribution a more attractive option.

Future technology

A range of techniques is being developed to improve both the capacity and speed of CD ROMs. The main areas are:

- Creating multiple levels of disc.
  IBM is developing a sandwich of ten CD-R discs. By changing the beam's point of focus, different discs in the sandwich are used.
- Using higher frequency lasers.
  Blue violet lasers have a higher frequency (i.e. shorter wavelength) than red lasers and so smaller pits can be cut. This results in more data per spiral - up to 10GB per disc.
- Reading multiple bits simultaneously.
  Data from a normal CD drive is read sequentially, one data bit at a time. Several manufacturers are looking at the possibility of having multiple read heads, potentially increasing the throughput of the drive by a noticeable factor but not affecting its total storage capacity. This technique could even be applied to existing CD-ROM discs.

More speculative technologies that could potentially succeed the CD-ROM and DVD include:

- MFD (Multi-layered Fluorescent Disk), a disc that allows laser light to travel right through in a similar manner to a prism, and the varying wavelengths received at the other end can represent several bits at a time instead of the single bit of a CD-ROM.
- AFM (Atomic Force Microscopy), a technology that is reminiscent in operation to phonograph recordings. A microscopic 'needle' touches the track as it passes by, sensing minute changes in height and interpreting them as data.
- GMR (Giant Magneto-Resistive) is a media type that is already available to buy, and offers decent storage sizes (2.2GB) at speeds much faster than conventional CD-ROM or even DVD. It comes in cartridge form, and is yet to find a firm foothold in the market.

DVD

The current CDs have the following capacity limitations:

- Most hard disks are now much larger than the 650MB storage of a CD. So, backing up drives involves writing to several CDs per drive.
- A full-length movie stores on two CDs and requires the disc to be changed during viewing.

The response is the high-capacity *'Digital Versatile Disk'* (previously known as the 'Digital Video Disc'). It is mainly viewed as a mechanism for distributing films and the first DVD discs are of this type. It also provides an ideal medium for a wide variety of applications ranging from training material to encyclopaedias. Their large storage capacity makes the writeable versions a good choice of backup medium, and with the number of DVD players in use rising all the time, it is becoming a more attractive distribution option.

The disc retains the conventional CD diameter of 120mm but can be double sided and can have two separate layers capable of storing data. The largest capacity types have a sandwich of two layers (i.e. four storage surfaces). With double-sided versions, the disc is flipped over to use the other side.

Single layer discs, both single and double sided, are manufactured in a very similar way to current CD-ROMs. The second layer comprises a resin layer with partially transmissive qualities. The reflections from both layers vary only slightly in intensity requiring a particularly sensitive detection system.

Book	Specification
A	DVD-ROM
B	DVD-Video
C	DVD-Audio
D	DVD-R (Write Once)
E	DVD-RAM (Erasable)

The DVD specifications are known as *'books'* and are shown in the table. Aimed at the production of quality video discs, they support both the original MPEG-1 (i.e. 352x 240 at 30 fields per second) and the current MPEG-2 (i.e. up to 720x480 at 60 fields per second) video standards.

DVD discs interleave the video and audio streams. The planned range of products is shown in the table. A 4.7GB disc stores the equivalent of around 133 minutes of video and three audio streams. DVD5 drives are the models that are currently available.

Product	Capacity	No of layers	No of sides	Mode
DVD5	4.7GB	1	1	Playback
DVD9	8.5GB	2	1	Playback
DVD10	9.4GB	1	2	Playback
DVD18	17GB	2	2	Playback
DVD-R	7.6GB	1	2	Record-once
DVD-RAM	5.2GB	1	2	Record-many

Video standards

The DVD Book A standard supports a range of screen aspect ratios, from 1.33:1 (the 4/3 standard of normal TVs and monitors) to 2.25:1 (wide screen movies).

Most movies are produced at 1.85:1 and domestic wide-screen TV's display at 1.78:1 (usually advertised as 16:9 sets). When movies are played in DVD players, users can control how they are displayed, including *'squeezing'* the image (everyone looks tall and thin) and *'letterbox viewing'* (all the movie is displayed but the upper and lower portions of the screen are black). Discs and players are now appearing which make use of *'pan and scan'* technology. This uses a substream of data to indicate which portion of the widescreen picture to display on a normal 16:9 display. Pan and scan, as its name might suggest, allows 16:9 displays to pan and scan around inside the wide screen display, showing the most important parts of the action at any time.

Each DVD movie disc has a *'country lock'* - a code specific to a region of the world. DVD discs will only run in players that have the same zone code. Region 1 is USA while Europe is Region 2. This attempts to prevent US discs being played on European DVD drives. Already, though, *'region-less'* DVD systems are available, while some consumers in Europe have become disgruntled with the comparatively small number of Region 2 releases and purchased a Region 1 system, bypassing the problem entirely.

DVD Video discs consist of a TOC and any number of video tracks. Each track contains up to 9 VOB (Video Object) files of just under 1GB length, containing the digital video information. The video data itself consists of one MPEG-2 stream at a Variable Bit Rate (VBR), up to 8 audio streams in either Linear PCM uncompressed, Dolby AC-3 or MPEG-2, and up to 32 run-length encoded 4-colour 'subpicture' streams for captions etc. The video stream is at a resolution and frame rate depending on the output type. PAL video is at 720x576 resolution with 25 fps, while NTSC video is at 720x480 resolution with 30 fps. Like Video CD, DVD is fully capable of employing interactivity in its videos, in fact that is one of its major selling points.

DVD Movies employ a Content Scrambling System (CSS) in an attempt to prevent illegal copying. This CSS method, however, makes DVD videos impossible to use in a Linux system, and so a program called DeCSS has become available to bypass the system. Due to the obvious piracy implications, the DVD Forum is trying hard to make the program illegal.

A technology built on DVD is Divx, developed by Digital Video Express. On top of the normal encoding in a DVD, Divx has additional DES encryption for a specific purpose, namely video rental. Divx discs are not hired, but purchased. However, they will only allow the video to be played for a certain timespan. After that, any attempt to play the video will cause the Divx system to automatically dial up the vendor to inform them. At this point additional hire time can be purchased, or the disc can be upgraded to unlimited viewing. Divx, however, is even more expensive than DVD, and drops much of the additional functions DVD allows, in favor of plain DVD videos much like normal VHS videos.

With the adoption of HDTV (High-Definition TV) in the US, the standard 4.7GB DVD has inadequate storage capacity to hold an entire 90 minute film on one side. While dual-sided or dual-layered discs could alleviate the situation, Sony is developing an entirely new disc, slightly larger than CD and DVD, capable of storing 20GB per side.

Audio standards

DVD supports three *'theatre quality'* sound formats - Dolby AC-3 surround sound, MPEG-1 audio and MPEG-2 audio. Europe favours MPEG-2 surround sound, while the USA, Japan and the rest of the world use Dolby AC-3. MPEG-1 is described as *'2.0'* (i.e. two channel stereo) while AC-3 is *'5.1'* and MPEG-2 is either *'5.1'* or *'7.1'*. The number after the dot indicates whether the sound includes support for a low-frequency effects sub-woofer. The numbers before the dot indicate how many main sound channels are supported. So a 5:1 has a centre sound channel, a channel at all four corners of the sound room, and a sub-woofer.

MPEG-1 samples at 44.1 kbps while MPEG-2 and AC-3 sample at 48 kbps (see chapter on multimedia for an explanation).

Book C of the DVD specification allows for CD-quality audio to be stored on a DVD, i.e. 16-bit samples in stereo at 44.1KHz. However Book C also specifies the option of 20-bit samples in 8 channels at 48KHz, or 16-bit samples in 8 channels at 96KHz.

How DVD stores 4.7GB on a single side

A CD's basic capacity is 746MB, although 650MB is left for the user after error correction overheads are deducted.   DVD uses a combination of more precise engineering, higher laser frequency, and improved modulation and error correction techniques, to dramatically improve the capacity of a single disc side.

	Standard CD layout	DVD layout	Improvement Factor	New Capacity
Smaller pit length	0.972 microns	0.4 microns	2.4300	1.82 GB
Narrower track pitch	1.6 microns	0.74 microns	2.1622	3.93 GB
More surface used for storing data	86 sq cms	87.6 sq cms	1.0186	4.00 GB
Better error correction	25% of data area	13% of data area	1.1062	4.42 GB
More efficient channel bit modulation	08:14+3	08:16	1.0625	4.70 GB

Advantages of DVD drives
- Choice of up to eight language tracks.
- Choice of up to 32 tracks for subtitles and menus.
- Newer DVD drives can read all formats (i.e. all DVD modes and CD-ROM, CD-R and CD-RW discs).

Disadvantages
- Requires an MPEG-2 decoder and a sound card that can handle the disc's audio formats.   These cards are available separately as upgrade kits or are available bundled with DVD drives.   Software implementations are available (e.g. CompCore's SoftDVD) although their performance is poorer since they use CPU resources rather than dedicated hardware.
- Older DVD drives cannot read CD-R and CD-RW discs.
- Normal CD drives cannot read DVD discs.

Recordable DVD

Like CD-ROM, there is more than one option when considering production of DVDs. Pressing of DVDs is similarly expensive unless large numbers are pressed, and so there are DVD-R and DVD-RAM drives available to create single discs or small runs.

DVD-R

Book D of the DVD specification is DVD recordable, or DVD-R. The DVD-R format uses incremental writing, and defines two methods. The first is ISO9660 compliant, using the UDF bridge system, and the second is designed for drag and drop file transfer, using UDF but without ISO9660 compatibility.

While DVD-R can utilise both sides of a DVD, the technology involved makes it extremely difficult even in theory for DVD-R drives to create discs using dual layers. At present DVD-R drives can store 3.85GB per side, but plans are to extend that to match the 4.7GB per side of pressed DVDs.

DVD-RAM and DVD+RW

Book E specifies DVD-RAM principles. It operates on Phase Change technology similar to CD-RW discs, and again dual-layer writing seems improbable to be implemented in the foreseeable future. DVD-RAM systems are already in production, with Panasonic selling a model that handles both 2.6GB single-sided and 5.2GB double-sided cartridge-based rewriteable discs.   These discs require to be turned manually, but a 4.7GB single-sided version is due for release. DVD-RAM is based on the original agreed specifications of the DVD Forum (the major manufacturers) and will likely form the basis for future models from Toshiba, Hitachi and Pioneer.   However, Sony and Philips have broken from the Forum and are bringing out their own 3GB per side specification called 'DVD+RW'.   The discs written under DVD+RW will be readable in a DVD-ROM drive, while taking DVD-RAM discs out of their cartridge voids their warranty.   The Forum also produced a rewriteable standard, known as DVD-R/RW, with an expected 4.7GB disc capacity. Time will tell which format becomes the most popular, although DVD-RAM appears to have the head start.

DVD Recording Software

DVD recording is still in its infancy compared to CD-R recording, and both the hardware and software involved are currently rather expensive. Due to the fact that DVD drives are far outnumbered by CD-ROM drives in the installed PC base, few producers will use the format for anything other than video at the moment. DVD creation software, then is also geared towards video. As such, most software will offer capabilities such as video editing, titling, looping, menus and so on. On the technical side, the video stream still has to match the MPEG-2 specification, and multiplexing is offered by many products to ease the burden on the user in that regard.

Web Site Creation

There is a spectacular expansion in the number of web sites on the Internet.   Many are personal sites but there is also a rapid growth of commercial sites.   Until a few years ago, only the largest companies tended to have web sites. Now, many small companies have their own site.

Web site uses

It is estimated that over 80 million EU citizens and over 130 million American citizens are on the Internet.   Reaching that amount of people by conventional means (e.g. TV adverts, newspapers, leaflets, circulars, catalogues, etc) is a very expensive business.   The creation of private or commercial web sites opens up new and improved forms of communication across the globe.   The variety of existing sites is immense but the most common categories are:

e-commerce (promoting products or services, on-line stores).
- Public information (e.g. Inland Revenue, weather, etc).
- Private sites promoting ideas (e.g. politics, religion, music, art).
- Leisure (e.g. sports, hobbies, entertainment, radio stations).
- Reference (e.g. publications, dictionaries).
- Education (on-line learning).
- Support for products (e.g. on-line documentation, FAQs, software updates, drivers).

This chapter covers the essential stages in web site creation:
- Web site design.
- Gathering the resources.
- Implementation of the site pages.
- Uploading to the server.
- Publicising the site.

Web sites and multimedia

The production of multimedia presentations and the creation of web sites share many common areas. They both use text, graphics, audio and video in sets of screens that allow the absorption of information in a manner controlled by the viewer.   They both use similar equipment (still cameras, video cameras, video capture cards, scanners) and the raw material for integration often uses the same file formats (graphic, video and sound formats).   They differ in how they integrate and package these resources. More importantly, they differ greatly on how they <u>deliver</u> their final product.   Most multimedia, due to the large size of the files, is delivered on CD-ROM.

All the features of a multimedia CD-ROM are available as web site material but their widespread use is held back by the very slow rates of transferring data on the Internet.

Download problems

The single greatest problem with the Internet is the speed of access to web pages.   In part, this is due to the popularity of the medium.   The congestion on the Internet results in times when transfer rates fall well below the capability of users' modems; sometimes data transfer rates fall to zero.   Even during a quiet(ish) period on the Net, the speed at which users can download pages is governed by the speed of their modems.   Telephone lines have a limited capacity and many users are using older slower modems. This table shows the best possible page download times for a range of modems and different file sizes.

Modem speed (in bits /sec)	Max theoretical transfer rate (in kilobytes/sec)	Fastest theoretical download time for a 40k web page	Fastest theoretical download time for a 400k web page
14.4kbps	1.31KB	30 secs	300 secs
28.8kbps	2.62KB	15 secs	150 secs
33.6kbps	3.05KB	13 secs	130 secs
56kbps	5.09KB	7.9 secs	79 secs
ISDN	11.64kB	2.5 secs	25 secs

These figures take into account the transmission overheads but are still optimistic, as few users achieve an average transfer rate that is close to the modem's maximum figure.   Downloading of large files is usually acceptable when using ftp, since users are storing the file contents and can carry on with another computer activity.   This is not the case with web browsing, as users expect to see page contents appear within a reasonable time.

The consequence for web site designers is that they have to design for the lowest reasonable modem speed of 14.4kbps.   If a new, all-featured, site only performed adequately for users with ISDN or ADSL lines, then the site would have a very limited appeal indeed.   This then is the starting point for web site design.   Site builders do not have a free hand; they have to design with these severe restrictions in mind.

Site components
The main elements of a web site are:

Web Server
This is the computer connected to the Internet that stores the organisation's web pages.   The server may be the property of a single organisation and only store the single web site.   The majority of servers act as the host for many different users.   The users may rent out space on the server or, in the case of many ISPs, a certain amount of web space may be provided to users as part of their normal rental agreement. Extra web space can usually be rented for an extra fee.

Web Site
Strictly speaking, the server location is termed the *'web site'* but it is now customary to refer to each user's set of web pages as a web site.   The diagram shows a web server that is the host for two separate web sites.   A web site is the property of the person or organisation that owns and maintains the collection of files.   Passwords are used to prevent unauthorised access and tampering with web site contents.

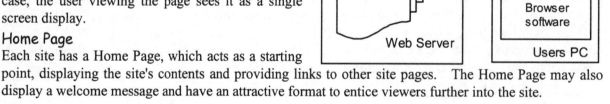

Web Page
This is a single page on the site.   It may consist of a single text file, or may be made up of several files, each occupying parts of the screen, combined with other files storing graphics, sound or video. In either case, the user viewing the page sees it as a single screen display.

Home Page
Each site has a Home Page, which acts as a starting point, displaying the site's contents and providing links to other site pages.   The Home Page may also display a welcome message and have an attractive format to entice viewers further into the site.

Technical characteristics
The main characteristics of web sites are:

Cross-platform
The script for every single web page on the entire Internet is stored in plain ASCII text and can therefore be read by every computer attached to the Internet.   This means that a script written using a PC can be read by the browser software sitting on a Macintosh, a UNIX system, etc.   This maximises the potential readership of sites and allows for easy interchange of documents between different hardware platforms.

Hyperlinking
The main benefit of web browsing is that users can navigate within sites and between sites by clicking on a piece of text or a graphic icon.   Users are presented with page contents that include underlined words or phrases or icons. These highlighted areas are the *'hyperlinks'* and they link information in one document with information in another part of the document - or an entirely different document.   The

other documents may reside anywhere on the Internet.   So, clicking on a hyperlink area (the highlighted text or icon) takes the user to another retrieved document - the one pointed to by the hyperlink.   This other document may consist of further text with further links, or it may even contain a video clip, an audio clip, a small Java program, etc.

This is a powerful tool and the site must be designed to take maximum advantage of these facilities.

Dynamic
The page can display contents that vary and this can be implemented in two ways:
- The contents of pages can be automatically altered as an organisation's prices or specifications change, with each viewer seeing the altered contents.
- The web page can be structured so that the same URL will return different content to different users, depending on a variety of factors such as geographical location (e.g. displaying prices in pounds instead of dollars), time of day (e.g. the TV programme schedules) and reader profiles (e.g. using previously gathered data to review arcade games for younger users and car road tests for older users).

Interactive
On the Internet, the user is not necessarily a passive viewer but can use the site for two-way communication.   Sites may provide order forms, voting slips, comments boxes, questions, etc to take input from site viewers.   (See chapter on developing web sites).

Intelligent
The system knows where the user has been!   It displays hypertext in two colours - one for links that a user has visited and another colour for unvisited links.

'Cookies' can also be used to store information on a user's previous usage, to guide that user's future usage of the site.   Cookies are files that are stored on the user's own local machine and can be accessed by the remote site when the user logs into that site.

Proactive
Traditional web access to information has been through browsing the millions of pages and *'pulling'* out the content that was required.   Since the web is vast and the content is constantly changing, a great deal of time is wasted through browsing and pulling.   An alternative, known as *'Push Technology'* has emerged.   This software allows users to specify the type of content that they prefer (e.g. news, share prices, sport).   The software then automatically finds the required information and places it on the users hard disk for off-line browsing at the user's convenience.   Because this process occurs at regular intervals, the user is kept up to date with their subject area.

Multimedia
The original web page carried little more than text.   Now, the basic page can deliver a wide variety of file formats.   Graphics, sound, animations and video are now commonplace.   Files created in other packages (e.g. Paintshop graphics, Director movies, Premiere videos, Voyetra MIDI music, etc) are easily integrated into web sites.   The introduction of the JavaScript programming language into the Internet also provides platform-independent applets (little programs) that are downloaded from the server and run on the local computer.   The one piece of code plays the same game or runs the same animation on PCs, UNIX boxes and Macintoshes.

Design
Like software and multimedia projects, the impact of the final web site depends upon the amount of preparation that goes into the design.   For all but the smallest of sites, a systematic approach to both content and design pays dividends.

Design characteristics
An effective web site is the result of effective design and this is characterised by two factors.
- Content   - what the site will contain and how it its pitched.
- Presentation   - how the contents will be displayed (see the chapter on Design).

Content
Users don't log in to a site to marvel at the overall presentation. They only stay, and return, if the content is valuable to them.   Soon, millions of students and hobbyists will have the ability to create reasonably advanced web pages.   What will distinguish one site from another is the impact made by the page

contents.   In that respect, it is identical to writing for any publication.   The site designer must understand the site content.   A thorough appreciation of the overall site flavour, down to the detail on each page is necessary to structure the contents to the best advantage.   If the creator is not the site owner, the site contents must be fully discussed prior to design planning.

Presentation structures

A web site consists of many linked pages. The design of the page contents is accompanied by the design of the structure of the site.   The isssue of structures is discussed in the chapter on 'Design'.

Presentation

The contents are the main purpose for creating the site but the presentation of the site's pages has a great impact on drawing users into browsing its contents.   Most users decide their impression of a site within the first 10 seconds of viewing.

This highlights two factors:
- The site should be aesthetically pleasing.
- Pages should not take too long to download.

The following design characteristics should be studied before the final page contents and their presentation are decided.

Universality

The site has to be viewable by the maximum readership.   A decision must be reached on the balance between implementing the features of the newest HTML standards and latest browsers - and the effect of viewing numbers.   More functionality is offered by newer standards but, since not all viewers have browsers meeting these standards, this reduces the numbers capable of viewing the site.   As time goes by more viewers will update their software - but by that time, even newer features will have been added!

Page Size

Pages will be read on Macs with browsers whose screens are 465 pixels wide as well as PC's with 640x480 screens. What looks good when designed on a 1024x768 screen may not look so good on these.

Scanability

Web site authors can learn from newspaper publishers. They know that readers don't read a page from top to bottom.   They scan the page, looking first at eye-catching components such as headlines, photographs and lists.   They only look at text after this initial scan.

For best results:
- Keep the most important points at the top of the page - like newspapers.
- Use headings and subheadings.
- Use bulleted lists.
- Use link menus as this improves scanability.

Simplicity

KISS - keep it simple, stupid!   Don't overdo the number of elements (lines, text, graphics, frames, and headings) on a page.   A fussy page is confusing and lacks clear navigation.

Style

Many sites revolve around the creator's flair or personality. Some of the best sites are not the most polished, but those showing the most vitality/originality.

Readability

The many tips for maximising readability include:
- Use 'white space'.   These are not necessarily white, but are clear screen areas designed to rest the eye - and focus the eye on important objects.
- The text content of links should be explicit (e.g. not 'important' or 'file57').
- If links are embedded within a sentence, they should be part of the text, not just stuck in
  eg do not use -   "click here to read about my new video camera"
  instead use -   "My video camera provides the raw material for the ..."
- It is OK to use links within the main body text but don't use whole sentences as links.
- Use lines to split the page into discrete areas by topic.
- Above all, spellcheck and grammar check text content

- Use a consistent layout throughout the pages. Use the same size of heading fonts, same method of navigation, same frame sizes, etc.
- Use margins, frames, tables and lists to break blocks of text into manageable chunks.

Colours

Colour monitors screens are covered in red, green and blue phosphor dots. Each dot can be lit to varying intensities to produce different colours (see the chapter on display technology for more details).

Maximum colours

24-bit

A 24-bit graphics card can vary the intensity of each dot to 256 different levels.   This produces 256 x 256 x 256 = 16,777,216 different colours.   It uses 256 different values for each colour and needs three bytes (i.e. 24-bits) to store the colour of a single dot on the screen.   24-bit graphics are high quality but result in large file sizes, a problem on the Internet.

8-bit

The approach used by GIF and other low colour range images, is to use a pre-defined set of colour values, stored in a table. Each colour has a colour number or *'index'*. This table is called a *'CLUT'* (Colour Look-Up Table) and it stores a maximum of 256 values and these values are used to set the proportions of red, green and blue to be used in each colour.   256 values (ie 0 to 255) can be stored in a single byte, hence the name *'8-bit'*. Of course, an image may not use all of the colours in the table or it may use a different set of colour combinations. The range of colours currently stored in the table is called the *'palette'*.   If an image contains colours not in the table, the extra colours are obtained by *'dithering'*. The browser produces a pattern consisting of some of the available colours.   The result approximates to the wanted colour and often produces unwanted *'hatching'* or *'dotty'* effects.

It is important to know that two GIF images may have different colours within their palettes.   One image may be a scanned photograph of a seascape.   This palette will be made up mainly of shades of blue.   Another image may be of a wood and have a palette mainly of green colours.   In each case, when the GIF image is saved, the palette details are saved inside the file.   When an application views the image, it reads the palette and uses it to set up the CLUT.   If the two images are displayed on the screen at the same time, more colours require to be displayed than can be stored in the colour table and large parts of the image are dithered.   That explains why some images appear very strange when loaded.

Conclusions

Leave 24-bit images to kiosk and CD use, or to images designed to be downloaded rather than displayed on-line. Larger palettes on the Internet are often a waste of capacity (they need more web site disk space), time (they take longer to download) and quality (most of the colours will be dithered).   Use 8-bit images for the Internet.   In fact, some users may only have 16-colour graphics cards and therefore it may be best to use the 16 primary colours for text, backgrounds, clipart, etc, to minimise dithering with older video cards.

Browser-safe colours

The Netscape Navigator and Internet Explorer browsers use the same colour table and this stores six levels for each colour, i.e. 6 red x 6 green x 6 blue = 216 different colours. All other colours not in this 216 colour table are dithered.

The six levels for each colour are shown in the table.

Hex	Decimal	Percentage
00	0	0%
33	51	20%
66	102	40%
99	153	60%
CC	204	80%
FF	255	100%

The percentage value shows the relative saturation while the decimal value expresses the RGB level.

HTML uses the hex values for each colour. So, for example, 000000 has all three colours turned off to produce black while FFFFFF has each colour at full saturation, producing white.

PCs and Macintosh computers can both use these 216 colours in their system palettes. However, of the standard Windows palette of 16 colours, only eight appear in the 216-colour palette.

CONCLUSIONS

Wherever possible, use the standard 216-colour table to minimise dithering.

Convert existing GIF files to this table's palette, using a graphics package such as Paintshop. This technique works best with clipart, graphs and other non-photographic images. Since photographs have a wide range of colours and many colours in the same range (e.g. lots of blues or lots of greens), converting to 216 colours will degrade the quality of the final display. The 216-colour palette may not already exist in a graphics package but all packages allow for the importing of new palettes. The palette can be downloaded from the Internet and stored in the graphics package. Search the web for *'216 colours'* or use the graphic file offered in:

> http://www.onr.com/user/lights/netcol.html

The site provides a graphics file that contains the palette. Resources are also available on the CD that accompanies this book.

The issue of designing with colour is covered in the chapter on Design.

Graphics

Graphics play an important, even primary, role in making a site more attractive. They can also be used to make navigation easier (i.e. by using navigation icons) and can impart information (e.g. displaying photographs, maps, graphs, etc).

Nevertheless, there are a few rules on the use of graphics.

- Do not place too many images on one page, as this is both distracting for the viewer, as well as producing long download times. There are exceptions where the user expects/wants to wait - e.g. to view goods or property, fanzine sites, etc. In general, the purpose of every image should be questioned with unnecessary graphics being ruthlessly eliminated.
- Don't let the page background overpower the content. The background image must not obscure the foreground text or dominate the page.
- Use the <ALT> attribute on all <IMG> tags. This provides a text alternative for graphic images and is useful for browsers set to read pages in text-only mode. It also ensures the maximum readership of the site.
- Use thumbnail graphics (i.e. miniatures) on the page, with links to downloading the larger version. This speeds up the page download. Users can see the draft of the graphics and decide whether it is worth the extra time to download the larger version.
- Use graphics for bullets. This looks better than standard bullets. Keep the same graphic (e.g. a red ball) for all other page bullets. The graphic will be loaded into the local PC's browser cache and this reduces subsequent download times.
- Reuse other images in the same way. The download time overhead only happens once.
- Use image libraries. Graphic files are installed on many web servers. These can be used for the server's web sites, reducing the space used by each site. Since the server also provides more effective caching of its own graphics, this results in speedier access.
- Scanned images should be scanned at the average of 72dpi. Monitors range from about 70dpi to 100dpi. Scanning at greater resolutions increases file space and provides no extra resolution quality.

GRAPHIC TYPES

The most common graphics formats are GIF and JPEG. They both use compression to minimise file size and download times.

JPEG should be used for photographic images. These are in 24-bit colour but offer increased levels of compression with decreased picture quality.

GIFs should be used for non-photographic images (e.g. clipart, logos, and banners). These files can be reduced to 8-colour or even B&W (although B&W images save little space and are used mainly for aesthetic reasons). The big advantage of GIFs is that they can be organised in a variety of ways (transparent images, animated images and interlaced images - see later).

HTML implementation

When the design is complete and all the resources (text, graphics, etc) are gathered, the elements can be combined in the set of web pages to comprise the web site. These are implemented using HTML and are given the extension .HTM with the home page usually being called *'index.htm'*.

The HyperText Markup Language is the language used for all web pages, although some other languages build round an HTML framework.   An HTML script is written in plain ASCII, using any plain text editor (e.g. NotePad or EDIT) or word processor with the document saved a plain text file.   Since ASCII characters are readable by all types of computer (UNIX, PC, Mac, etc) on the Internet, it forms the foundation of a platform-free language.   One script is used for all machines, with each translating the script into its own machine-specific tasks.

A web page is simply a text file (known as a *'script'*) containing a list of commands.   The script lines are used to display text and graphics, check whether the user has clicked on a particular object and jump to other parts of the script (or even other scripts).   In these respects, an HTML page script is similar to a DOS batch file or the script for a program written in interpreted Basic.

However, the script may also contain information about what font style to use for text, which pieces of text are to be checked for user input and so on.   This information is embedded in the HTML file as additional sets of ASCII characters.   These are called *'tags'* and are similar to the codes in Microsoft Word that turn italics or bold face off and on.   With Word, these tags are normally hidden from the user; with HTML, the tags appear as part of the ASCII script.   As long as all browsers know that the tag <I> turns on italics and </I> turns off italics, they can all make sense of the script file.   How each machine displays and prints italics is nothing to do with the web page writer - the translation is up to the user's browser and operating system.   Similarly, HTML may describe a piece of text as having a certain 'header' size, not as 24-point Arial.   Each machine will decide what font size and style it will use as a header.   This makes the entire HTML language completely machine-independent and explains its popularity as a means of exchanging information between different computer systems.

Apart from all the text to be displayed on the screen, the HTML script file contains:
- tags which tell the browser how to display the various parts of the text (font size, underlining, etc).
- tags which instruct the browser to fetch an image and place it on a particular area of the screen.
- hyperlinks which take the user to another part of the document or to another HTML document.

There are many applications that are dedicated to simplifying the process.   These vary from add-ons to Microsoft Word through to full-blown design packages.   These packages still produce an HTML ASCII file as their final products.

NB: HTML pages using simple commands can be read by all browsers.   If the latest HTML innovation or add-ons for animations, audio, video, etc are used, then only browsers equipped with these facilities will be able to make use of all the site's features.   Various brands of browser, and even different versions of the same brand, may produce different screen results while executing the same HTML command.   Due to constant changes and additions, no browser software faithfully implements every available command.

Basic structure

The illustration shows the minimum layout of an HTML script.   Note that all the tags start with the '<' (i.e. the less than symbol) and end with the '>' (i.e. the greater than symbol).   Repeating a tag reverses the earlier tag's effects, if the second tag is prefaced with a forward slash character.   The effects of some tags need to be cancelled (e.g. turning on and off italics around a word or phrase).   Other tags, such as drawing a line, need only appear once.   Tags are not case sensitive; they can be entered in upper or lower case, although most writers use upper case for easier recognition.

```
<HTML>
<HEAD>
<TITLE>
    title text goes here
</TITLE>
</HEAD>
<BODY>
    main script goes here
    ...
    ...
</BODY>
</HTML>
```

The tags used in this basic script are:
- The 'HTML' tags are placed at the beginning and end of all HTML documents to tell browsers that the information enclosed is the valid section for translation.
- The 'HEAD' tag contains the title of the web page, as it will appear in the browser's title bar.
- The words placed between the 'TITLE' tags are those that are used when the page is added to a user's bookmark.   It is also the text that is examined and displayed as the header in search engine results.
- The HEAD section can also contain 'META' tags that hold key words to help identify the site to search engines.
- Material placed between the two 'BODY' tags influences the contents displayed in the user's browser window.

Example script
This is a sample of a basic HTML script and its output, as seen by a browser.

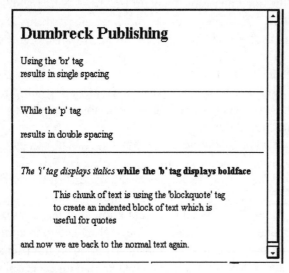

```
<HTML>
<HEAD>
<TITLE>A sample script</TITLE>
</HEAD>
<BODY BGCOLOR="#00FFFF" TEXT="BLUE">
<H1>Dumbreck Publishing</H1>
Using the 'br' tag<BR>
results in
single spacing
<HR>
While the 'p' tag<P>
results in double spacing
<HR>
<I>The 'i' tag displays italics</I>
<B>while the 'b' tag displays boldface</B>
<BLOCKQUOTE>This chunk of text is using the
'blockquote' tag to create an indented block of text which
is useful for quotes
</BLOCKQUOTE>
and now we are back to the normal text again.
</BODY>
</HTML>
```

Most tags also provide additional refinements. These are known as the tag's *'attributes'* and they may provide control over an object's size, colour and screen position.   The inclusion of attributes is optional, although non-inclusion usually results in the adoption of the current or default values.   For example, objects may be positioned on the left margin by default, while an attribute may be included in a tag to make that particular object right justified.

The various tags used in the above example are:

<I>   All text between this tag and a </I> tag is displayed in italics.

<B>   All text between this tag and a </B> tag is displayed in boldface.

BGCOLOR   This, along with 'TEXT' are optional attributes within the <BODY> tag.
The BGCOLOR attribute sets the colour of the screen background and the TEXT attribute sets the colour of the all the text in the document (unless overruled).
Colours values can be specified in two ways:

1.   By naming the colour - eg   TEXT="BLUE" or BGCOLOR="YELLOW".   This is the simplest method when one of the sixteen colour names understood by browsers is required (see later for the full list).   The default text colour is black and the default background colour is white.

2.   When subtle colours, without any given name are required, values are set by giving the hex value of the amount of red, green and blue in the mix.   In the example above, the red value is 00, while the green and blue values are both FF. This is entered as BGCOLOUR="#00FFFF" and results in a cyan background.   To obtain blue text, the text attribute could have been specified as "TEXT=#00FF00" - ie red fully off, blue fully on and green fully off.   The hash symbol '#' should be included to ensure that all browsers recognise the values as hexadecimal amounts.

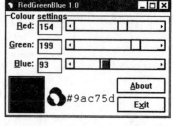

Software utilities such as RGB and RGB2WEB allow the writer to move sliders to mix the colours. When the desired colour is viewed in the colour box, the decimal and hex values for that colour are displayed.   The values can be noted and included in the page script or, in some utilities, the values can be copied straight from the utility and pasted directly into the page script.

   Provides the equivalent of a carriage return in word processing.   The remaining text is displayed on the next line.

<P>   The P tag is seen as the start of a new paragraph and an extra line of white space is inserted.
It provides the equivalent of two carriage returns.

<BLOCKQUOTE>   Any text enclosed between this tag and the </BLOCKQUOTE> tag is treated as a quote and is indented from both sides of the page. The <BR> tag can also be used between these tags.

<HR>   Draws a horizontal line, called the *'rule'*, across the page and is used to separate out or emphasise sections of text.   Without any attributes (i.e. used by itself as in the above example) it displays a line that is the width of the browser window.

Optional attributes for the <HR> tag are:

ALIGN=	Use LEFT, RIGHT or CENTER to position the rule on the screen.
NOSHADE	Draws the rule as a solid block. The default is a 3-D shaded rule.
SIZE=	Sets the height of the rule in pixels.
WIDTH=	Sets the rule width in pixels or as a percentage of the window width eg WIDTH=50%

As many of the attributes as required can be used together as in this example:
<HR ALIGN=CENTER NOSHADE   SIZE=15   WIDTH=300>

Text formatting

Note that there is no set width to a line of text.   Browsers word wrap the text into as many lines as its screen allows.   This, in turn, depends on the resolution of the monitor and font size used.   Lower screen resolutions screens and larger fonts result in more lines being displayed.

Also note that in the earlier example, separate script lines were used for the words *"results in"* and *"single spacing"* but the final output displayed it on the same line.   That is because normal carriage returns entered by an ASCII editor are ignored by browsers.   Browsers only respond to specific tag commands to move to a new line (apart from the word wrapping mentioned earlier).

Adding extra spaces between words or lines, for formatting and indentation purposes, are also ignored. All words are assembled into one giant paragraph unless formatting tags are used.

Font formats

Other font formats are <U> which turns on underlined text and <S> which turns on strikethrough text (eg ~~strikethrough~~).   Another tag called <TT> for *'teletype text'* is used to switch into a non-proportional font such as Courier.   It is used to display numeric tables as all columns can be guaranteed to align vertically. It can also be used to give a different appearance to programme listings of Pascal, Delphi, C, etc.

Other formatting tags are <SUP> which displays in superscript and <SUB> which displays in subscript.

The <SMALL> tag will display the content in a smaller than normal font until it is switched off with the </SMALL> tag.   Similarly, the <BIG> tag displays the content in a larger than normal font.   The actual size of the BIG and SMALL fonts will depend on the body font chosen by the user.

Heading tags

HTML provides a set of heading tags.   These are <H1> through to <H6> and are used to provide headings and sub-headings to improve the document's formatting.   All text enclosed by the <H1> and </H1> tags is displayed in the largest font size, with <H6> displaying the smallest font size.   As the example shows, cancelling a heading tag also results in a paragraph break.

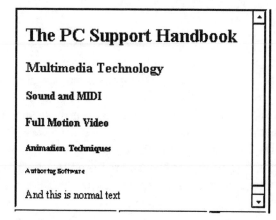

```
<HTML>
<HEAD>
<TITLE>Example heading sizes</TITLE>
</HEAD>
<BODY BGCOLOR="WHITE" TEXT="BLACK">
<H1>The PC Support Handbook</H1>
<H2>Multimedia Technology</H2>
<H3>Sound and MIDI</H3>
<H4>Full Motion Video</H4>
<H5>Animation Techniques</H5>
<H6>Authoring Software</H6>
<P>
And this is normal text
</BODY>
</HTML>
```

Headings should not be used to replace the <B> tag to emphasise parts of the text.   Many search tools use the headings of a page to extract important information from a site.   The tools assume that if the writer found the text to be significant enough to be used as a heading, then it is important enough for search purposes.   While a subject heading is a good choice for extraction, an individual word or phrase - emphasised with a heading tag - devalues the site search if it not of any significance.   For example the phrase "this should **NOT** be tried at home" should use the <B> tag to embolden the word 'NOT'.   If the word was emphasised using a heading tag, search engines would place an unwarranted significance to the word for search results.

Font faces

The viewer is able to set the typestyle that the browser uses to display web pages. This is set from the *'Fonts'* button on the *'Internet options'* choice in Internet Explorer's *'Tools'* menu. Users can choose from Times New Roman, Arial, Verdana, Georgia, etc. The webs site designer, however, may prefer that the viewer see the pages with a particular font. The pages, for example, may have been designed to look best with a sans serif font such as Arial or Verdana. There are a number of ways to influence what the user sees on his/screen and these are discussed below.

FACE

The FONT tag has a FACE attribute that specifies what font or style should be displayed. At it simplest, the lines

                                                                                  <FONT FACE="serif">   or   <FONT FACE="sans-serif">

can be included in the script. This ensures that the viewer will see the main class of type, but does not specifies the actual font to be used. The line

                                <FONT FACE="Verdana, Arial, Helvetica">

specifies that the Verdana font should be used as a first option. If the font is not present on the user's computer, the Arial font should be used, followed by Helvetica as the third option. If none of the fonts are installed on the user's machine, the default font will be used.

This is a very simple way of specifying fonts but it has two major drawbacks:

- Not every browser supports this attribute.
- Different computer systems use different names for their fonts (one system might have a Times font, while another has a Times Roman or a Times New Roman font).

Although the method is simple, it does not guarantee the required results for all those viewing the site.

Embedding Fonts

Bitstream have introduced a scheme to store their own TrueDoc fonts on their site. The designer creates links to their site at truedoc.com and these fonts can be displayed on a users web page. This requires a little JavaScript and either the <FONT FACE= > tag using Cascading Style Sheets. The user does not require to download these fonts, as Navigator 4 onwards, and Explorer with a free Bitstream Active X control installed, can read the font elements from the TrueDoc site and display them. This allows designers to choose fonts in the knowledge that the user will see them the way the designer planed. Microsoft, of course, has developed a competing standard known as *'TrueType font embedding'*.

Cascading Style Sheets

See the next chapter for details.

Graphic Text

There may be times when no existing font will do for a screen. For example, the letters of a heading may be required to be constructed from real world objects such as straws, pencils or even human bodies. Alternatively, a special font shape may be required to create the mood for the web site. For example, an oil company may wish the letters of the heading to look like drops of oil. Since none of these shapes will appear in any existing font, the only way to ensure that the user sees the text in the required way is to create the words as a graphic file. This results in a graphics file which, although not too large for use as a heading, could not be used as the entire body text. If the same type of text is required to appear in different headings throughout the web site, a graphic image can be created for each character that appears, so that these can be re-used throughout the pages.

Flash

Macromedia Flash (see the next chapter) can embed any font into a Flash screen, which can then be displayed on any viewer's computer. Since the Flash file contains vector data, only the descriptions of character shapes are sent and therefore the viewers computer can reproduce it. The Flash screen can have rollovers, sounds, animations, fades, etc. and can also have links that jump to other Flash files. This means that an entire web site could be created without the use of a single installed font. The problems with this method are that the Flash files are not searched by search engines and are not readable by text readers. Additionally, older browsers need a plug-in of around 118kB to be downloaded and installed in order to read Flash files and this is likely to put many viewers off.

Colours

Internet Explorer and Netscape recognise the following sixteen colour names:

- BLACK
- WHITE
- GRAY
- SILVER
- GREEN
- RED
- BLUE
- YELLOW
- MAROON
- OLIVE
- NAVY
- PURPLE
- LIME
- TEAL
- AQUA
- FUCHSIA

These colour values can be used to set the colour of the screen background, the main text, the borders and shading of objects and the various hyperlink states (e.g. unexplored or explored).

An alternative that is accepted by all browsers is using hex numbers for the RGB values.

To display white text on a black background use either:

    \<BODY BGCOLOR="BLACK" TEXT="WHITE"> or   \<BODY BGCOLOR="#000000" TEXT="#FFFFFF">

The text of unexplored links is blue by default.   This can be changed with LINK="colour"

    \<BODY BGCOLOR="BLACK" TEXT="WHITE" LINK="YELLOW">

The text of explored links is purple/red by default. This can be changed with VLINK="colour"

    \<BODY BGCOLOR="BLACK" TEXT="WHITE" VLINK="LIME">

The \<BODY TEXT=colour> tag changes the colour of the default text on a page.   To change the colour of a particular paragraph, sentence, word or even a single letter, the \<FONT> tag can be used with a COLOR attribute as in this example:

    Do \<FONT COLOR="RED"> NOT \</FONT> try this at home

The word 'Do' is displayed in the default text colour while the word 'NOT' is displayed in red.   When the browser reads the \</FONT> it again displays all text in the original default colour.   Again, the colour values can be entered as one of the given sixteen text values or can be entered as hex numbers.

Escape characters

There are times when the page has to display characters that are already used for formatting commands, such as & and > and <. Using them inside a normal text line may produce unexpected results in some browsers. In addition, some characters are not available in the standard ASCII set and can't be directly typed in from the keyboard.

```
Bonnie & Clyde

If x³ > y² then say " Thats big! "

© Dumbreck Publishing

What chemical has H² SO₄ as its formula?

¾ = ½ + ¼

8 × 5 ÷ 4 = 10
```

```
<HTML>
<HEAD>
<TITLE>Dumbreck Publishing</TITLE>
</HEAD>
<BODY BGCOLOR="YELLOW" TEXT="BLACK">
Bonnie &amp Clyde<P>
If x &#179 &#62 y &#178 then say &quot Thats big! &quot<P>
&#169 Dumbreck Publishing<P>
What chemical has H
<SMALL><SUP>2</SMALL></SUP>
SO<SUB><SMALL>4</SUB></SMALL>
as its formula?<P>
&#190 = &#189 + &#188<P>
8 &#215 5 &#247 4 = 10<P>
</BODY>
</HTML>
```

HTML provides escape sequences to overcome these problems.

All escape characters begin with an ampersand character and are either followed by a text sequence or by a numeric sequence.

The range of text escape sequences includes:

Sequence	Displayed character	Sequence	Displayed character
&gt	>	&amp	&
&lt	<	&quot	"

The numeric sequence places a hash symbol between the ampersand and the number and the range includes:

Sequence	Displayed character	Sequence	Displayed character
&#153	™	&#179	³
&#169	©	&#188	¼
&#174	®	&#189	½
&#176	°	&#190	¾
&#178	²	&#247	÷

Creating lists

Most visitors to a web site dislike having to scroll through long paragraphs of text, trying to extract the main points.   Often, the information can be displayed more effectively as a list of main points. HTML supports three types of lists and these are shown in the example below.

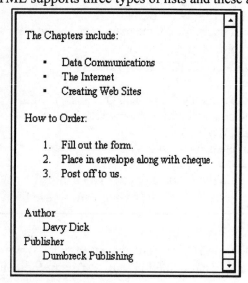

```
<HTML>
<HEAD>
<TITLE>Creating lists example</TITLE>
</HEAD>
<BODY BGCOLOR="WHITE" TEXT="BLACK">
The Chapters include:
<!--                     here is a bulleted list -->
<UL>
<LI>Data Communications
<LI>The Internet
<LI>Creating Web Sites
</UL>
How to Order:
<!--                     here is an ordered list -->
<OL>
<LI>Fill out the form.
<LI>Place in envelope along with cheque.
<LI>Post off to us.
</OL>
<!--                     here is a definition list -->
<DL>
<DT>Author
<DD>Davy Dick
<DT>Publisher
<DD>Dumbreck Publishing
</DL>
</BODY>
</HTML>
```

Unordered list

This is used when numbering the items has no relevance.   The items appear as a bulleted list as shown in the example.   The <UL> and </UL> tags indicate that the enclosed items are list items. Each individual list item has a <LI> tag.   The general layout is:

```
<UL>
<LI> first item to display
<LI> second item
<LI> third item
</UL>
```

The <UL> tag has a number of options, although the final effect may depend upon the browser used.

Use	Explanation	Example
TYPE="DISC"	The bullets are filled circles (this is the default)	●
TYPE="SQUARE"	The bullets are square	■
TYPE="CIRCLE"	The bulleted are unfilled circles	○

So, for example   <UL TYPE="SQUARE">   displays an unordered list with square bullets.

Ordered list

This is used when numbering the items is significant, such a set of instructions.   The items appear as a bulleted list as shown in the example.   The general layout is:

```
<OL>
<LI> first item to display
<LI> second item
<LI> third item
</OL>
```

The <OL> tag has a number of attribute options:

Use	Explanation	Example
TYPE="1"	Standard Arabic numerals will number the list	1, 2, 3, 4, 5, 6, 7
TYPE="A"	Upper case letters will number the list	A, B, C, D, E, F
TYPE="a"	Lower case letters will number the list	a, b, c, d, e, f
TYPE="I"	Upper case Roman numerals will number the list	I, II, III, IV, V, VI, VII
TYPE="I"	Lower case Roman numerals will number the list	i, ii, iii, iv, v, vi, vii
START=	Alters the default starting point for numbering	See below

So,   <OL TYPE="A" START=G">   displays an ordered list with the items listed as G, H, I, J, etc.
While   <OL TYPE="1" START="10"> displays an ordered list numbered as 10, 11, 12, 13, 14, etc.

Definition list

Definition lists, sometimes called *'glossary lists'*, produce a list of terms and their descriptions.

The general layout is:
```
<DL>
<DT>  first term
<DD> first definition
<DT> second term
<DD> second definition
</DL>
```

The <DT> tag places the text in the left of the screen and the following <DD> tag indents the next line.

Nesting lists

Lists can be nested - one list is embedded within another list.   The example also shows the <BR> tag being used within a list to move to a new line without inserting another bullet.

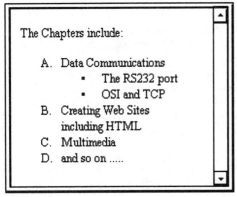

```
<HTML>
<HEAD>
<TITLE>Nested lists example</TITLE>
</HEAD>
<BODY BGCOLOR="WHITE" TEXT="BLUE">
The Chapters include:
<OL TYPE = "A" >
<LI> Data Communications
<UL>
     <LI> The RS232 port
     <LI> OSI and TCP
</UL>
<LI> Creating Web Sites
<BR>
including HTML
<LI> Multimedia
<LI> and so on .....
</OL>
</BODY>
</HTML>
```

Comments

The script on the previous page inserted comments using the <!-- *comment* --> tag.   Comments make the script easier to understand but their content is ignored by browsers and is not displayed.

Aligning objects

By default, text and other objects such as graphics, tables etc, are aligned down the left of the screen.

An individual heading or paragraph can be positioned using the ALIGN attribute. For example:

<H2 ALIGN=CENTER> blah blah blah </H2>	aligns the text in the centre of the screen
<H2 ALIGN=RIGHT> blah blah blah </H2>	aligns the text to the right edge of the screen
<H2 ALIGN=LEFT> blah blah blah </H2>	aligns the text to the left edge of the screen

With this method, each item has its own individual ALIGN attribute.   Where a larger section of items share the same alignment, the entire section is enclosed by a set of <DIV> tags as in this example:

```
<DIV ALIGN=CENTER>
<H1> My Name </H1>
<H2> My address </H2>
</DIV>
```

The <DIV> tag has the advantage that it can enclose all kinds of objects such as paragraphs of text, headings, images, tables, etc.   When a <DIV> tag is used it alters that section's alignment, but the software remembers the previous alignment.   When the </DIV> tag is reached, the alignment reverts to this previous value.   To ensure that the script will work with all browser versions, always cancel a <DIV> tag before issuing another <DIV> tag.

Order of tags

Tags may be *'nested'* - i.e. a new tag or set of tags may be placed within an existing set of tags. To ensure that the script produces the expected results in all browsers, cancellation tags should be placed in reverse order to the order of declaring them.

So,   <BLOCKQUOTE><I><B> blah blah blah </B></I><BLOCKQUOTE> is correct while

<BLOCKQUOTE><I><B> blah blah blah <BLOCKQUOTE><<I><B> is bad practice.

While some browsers may be more tolerant than others, failure to observe this rule may result in page formatting not looking the way that was anticipated.

Navigating the web site

So far, this chapter has considered:

- Web site contents.
- Design structures.
- Formatting of web page text.

The completed site consists of a collection of web pages held together by a set of *'hyperlinks'*.   The links are another set of HTML tags and they are used to:

- Take the user to another part of the same web page
- Take the user to another web page in the same web site
- Take the user to another web site altogether.

The basis of all web navigation is the *'anchor tag'* or *'link tag'*.   The format of a link tag is:

<A HREF="where to jump"> Text for the hyperlink </A>

The tag comprises several sections:

<A HREF="where to jump">	The 'A' indicates that it is an anchor tag - i.e. treat the tag as a link. The 'HREF' indicates that is a hyperlink reference (other options can be placed here as can be seen later). The text part indicates what document or part of the document to jump to. This may point to another document using either: • The URL (full hostname and filename) of a document on the WWW. • The name of another document inside the same web site. It can also point to a 'label' within the currently displayed document.
Text for the hyperlink	The text that appears underlined on the screen waiting to be clicked.
</A>	The closing tag to indicate the end of the link definition.

Example link tags are:

<A HREF="order.htm"> Ordering Information</A>
<A HREF="http://www.dumbreck.demon.co.uk/index.html"> Dumbreck Publishing </A>
<A HREF="#mboard"> Testing the motherboard </A>

Jumping within a web page

This is commonly used with large linear web pages such as FAQ pages and other technical pages.   The link tag points to a particular section of the document that is specially labelled.   The label is embedded in the document and is known as the *'anchor'* with its own anchor tag.   Labels can be spread throughout the document, allowing jumping both up and down through the document.   This technique is similar to the GOTO command used in DOS batch files and some programming languages.   The link tag has a hash symbol before the name of the label to indicate that what follows is a label and not a URL.   So, "#Chapter1" points to an anchor within the document.   The format of the anchor tag is:

<A NAME="anchor name"> The text to be displayed at the anchor point </A>

NOTE: In the example, all the text is displayed on a single screen and clicking the hyperlinks has no apparent effect.   To test this page, the text sections have to be expanded so that the document requires several pages to display.

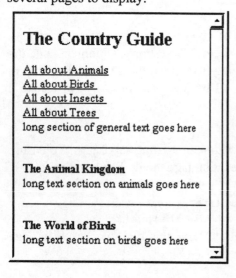

```
<HTML>
<HEAD> <TITLE>Dumbreck Publishing</TITLE> </HEAD>
<BODY BGCOLOR="WHITE" TEXT="BLACK">
<H2>The Country Guide</H2>
<A HREF="#Chapter1">All about Animals </A> <BR>
<A HREF="#Chapter2">All about Birds     </A> <BR>
<A HREF="#Chapter2">All about Insects   </A> <BR>
<A HREF="#Chapter2">All about Trees     </A> <BR>
long section of general text goes here      <BR>  <HR>
<B><A NAME = "Chapter1"> The Animal Kingdom</A></B><BR>
long text section on animals goes here      <BR> <HR>
<B><A NAME = "Chapter2"> The World of Birds</A><BR></B>
long text section on birds goes here <BR>
the other chapters go in here  <BR>
</BODY>
</HTML>
```

Jumping to another page

A web site usually consists of many pages and the user is encouraged to jump between the pages by clicking the hypertext links.

Consider the following hypertext link:

<A HREF="order.htm"> Ordering Information</A>

The words *'Ordering Information'* will appear on the screen as the hypertext link.   Clicking on that text makes the browser load the web page called *'order.htm'*.   This assumes that the file called *'order.htm'* is in the same directory as the web page that is pointing to it.   This is the most common case for small to medium web sites.   It also simplifies the command since only the file name need be supplied.

Where the site's files are held in a number of directories, relative paths may can be specified as shown.

HREF="finance/order.htm"	The web page can be found in the directory called *'finance'* and the 'finance' directory is a sub-directory of the current directory.
HREF="book/finance/order.htm"	The web page can be found in the directory called *'finance'* which is a sub-directory of the *'book'* directory which, in turn, is a sub-directory of the current directory.
HREF="../order.htm"	The web page can be found in the directory above the current directory.
HREF="../../order.htm"	The web page can be found in the directory two levels above the current directory.
HREF="/d|/mysite/order.htm"	The web can be found in the *'mysite'* directory of the D: drive. Note that a vertical bar replaces the semi-colon normally found after a drive letter.

Keep all the site's resources in the same directory - or use relative paths.   This simplifies site maintenance, since the site can be moved to different disk directories without changing all the link references.

NOTE: While tags are not case sensitive, the directory and file functions of some operating systems are case sensitive.   So, for example, entering *'Order.htm'* or *'ORDER.HTM'* will result in the file not being found.

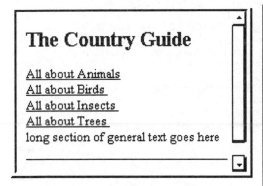

```
<HTML>
<HEAD>
<TITLE>Dumbreck Publishing</TITLE>
</HEAD>
<BODY BGCOLOR="WHITE" TEXT="BLACK">
<H2>The Country Guide</H2>
<A HREF="animals.htm">All about Animals </A> <BR>
<A HREF="birds.htm">All about Birds        </A> <BR>
<A HREF="insects.htm">All about Insects   </A> <BR>
<A HREF="trees.htm">All about Trees      </A> <BR>
long section of general text goes here      <BR>  <HR>
 </BODY>
</HTML>
```

This is the earlier example altered from one large web document into a set of linked web pages.   Clicking a hypertext link now loads the new web page instead of jumping to another part of the same document.   The list of hypertext links at the top of the document is called a *'link menu'*.

Jumping to an anchor in another page

In the above example, a link loads a new web page and the user sees the top of that web page.   It is possible to link not just to the top of the page but to any anchor within that new page.   The opening tag has to contain both the name of the new page and the name of the anchor as in this example:

<A HREF="birds.htm#robins"> All about robins </A>

Jumping to another site

The link can take the user to any page on any site on the World Wide Web, just by placing the URL in the tag.   This example takes the user to Dumbreck's home page:

<A HREF="http://www.dumbreck.demon.co.uk/index.html"> Dumbreck Publishing </A>

Graphic images

Graphics can make a huge impact on the effectiveness of a web page.

This section looks at *'Inline Graphics'* which are images that are loaded along with the web page (*'External Graphics'* are only loaded when the user asks for it, usually by clicking a link).

The image tag allows a GIF or JPEG image to be displayed on the web page.

The tag's basic format is:

<IMG SRC="filename">

A number of additional attributes provide for additional formatting of the image.   These are:

ALIGN=	Places the next line of text next to the TOP, MIDDLE or BOTTOM of the image. The first example below shows the result of using MIDDLE. Only one line of the text appears in the middle, with the remaining lines appearing under the graphic. The graphic, by default, is placed at the left margin of the page. If ALIGN=LEFT is used, as in the second example, the graphics is still on the left but the text flows down its right-hand side. Similarly, ALIGN=RIGHT places the graphic on the right margin.
BORDER=	Enlarges the border round the image, if require. The number entered is in pixels.
ALT=	Display a piece of text when the mouse hovers over the image. This is useful when users turn off the facility for viewing graphic images, as they can still get a description of the content.

An example image tag is:

<IMG SRC="world.gif" ALIGN=MIDDLE BORDER=10 ALT="World Map">

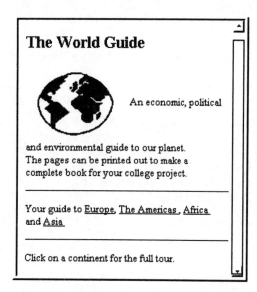

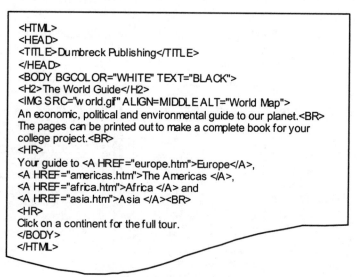

Changing the ALIGN setting to LEFT produces the result shown on the right.

CLEAR

In the example on the right, the first two sentences were both aligned down the side of the graphic image.

Inserting a <P> or a <BR> after the first sentence will still leave the second sentence aligned down the graphic.

If the second sentence is required to appear below the graphic, the effects of the ALIGN=LEFT attribute can be cancelled by using the <BR CLEAR=LEFT> tag.   After this tag, the formatting of text resorts to normal.

Similarly, a <BR CLEAR=RIGHT> tag is used to cancel the effects of a previous ALIGN=RIGHT.

Using a graphic as a hyperlink

Many hyperlinks display underlined text that can be clicked to activate the link. It is also possible to use a graphic image as the hyperlink object, where they are often known as *'Hotspots'*.

If an <IMG> tag is embedded inside a link tag, that graphic image becomes a clickable hotspot link. In this example

                    <A HREF="worlddb.htm" > <IMG SRC="world.gif"> </A>

the graphic tag has simply replaced the hyperlink text.   When run, the globe graphic appears with a box outline round it to indicate that it is a clickable object.   The width of this outline is set, in pixels, with the BORDER attribute.

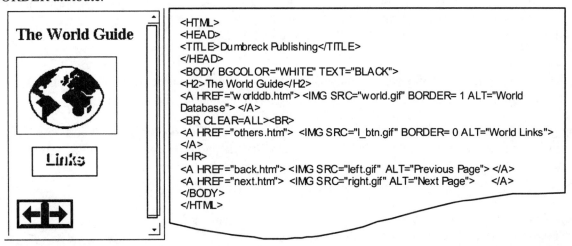

When viewers look at a web page, it is common for many of them fail to appreciate that some of the graphics are hyperlink objects.   To avoid this, images can be created in the shape of a text button, as in the second part of the example. In this case, its use is more obvious and the box outline is removed by setting the BORDER value to zero.

The third part of the above example shows graphics images in the shape of direction arrows (i.e. navigation icons).   These, and UP and DOWN arrows, are very useful for linear structures.

Labels can be attached to each, to explain its function if this is required:

This example shows how a graphic can be placed in the middle of a sentence if required.   The script entry for this is:

        Read the section on tool handling<A HREF="back.htm"> <IMG SRC="tools2.gif">
        </A> before you start.

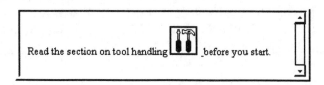

Height/Width
The <IMG> tag has HEIGHT and WIDTH attributes and these have two uses.
- If the size of the image is known (most graphic editing packages such as Paint Shop Pro or Photoshop provide this information) its dimensions can be included in the <IMG> tag.
  This reduces display times in some browsers as they load each image and identify their dimensions before displaying the text.   If the files' dimensions are supplied to the browser, it can make space for them and allow the user to read the text while the graphics are loading.
- If the HEIGHT and WIDTH dimensions are different from the actual dimensions of the graphic, the browser will scale the graphic display proportionately. The displayed image can be smaller or larger than the original.   However, too much enlargement will make the image look too 'blocky' while shrinking an image is wasteful (create a smaller original version as it downloads faster).

Example use: <IMG SRC="file.gif HEIGHT=250 WIDTH=200>

Backgrounds
The background can be a solid colour using BGCOLOR="value" or can consist of a graphic file. A graphic background is introduced using the BACKGROUND attribute in the <BODY> tag.

<BODY BACKGROUND="virago.gif">

A single large graphic designed to cover the entire background is too large and takes too long to download.   The browser overcomes this by taking a smaller file and *'tiling'* it.   With tiling, the image is repeated vertically and horizontally to fill the screen. This saves the overheads of using large files.

The example shows the effect.   In this case, the background image has only been tiled into the right hand frame as the BACKGROUND attribute has been inserted into the <TD> tag (explained later).

<TD WIDTH=200 BACKGROUND="virago.gif">

The graphic used has white space round the picture's edges and there is no visible 'join'.   Where a pattern is used as a background, the design will require seamless joins on edges - i.e. the edges of the pattern should be designed to create a continuous pattern when tiles are butted together as a background.

A useful method is to create one narrow but wide strip of a pattern.   This will cover the width of the screen and will be repeated down the screen.   This graphic file will be of small size and will be quick to download.

Marquees
Internet Explorer introduced a moving band of text that scrolls across the screen.   The default is to continually scroll from the right, disappearing off the left side and reappearing on the right side.

<MARQUEE>your message goes here </MARQUEE>

Its attributes are:

BEHAVIOR   The default value is SCROLL.   A value of SLIDE causes the text to move to the opposite margin and stop. A value of ALTERNATE causes the text to 'bounce' between the left and right margins.

DIRECTION   The default value is RIGHT but a value of LEFT causes the text to appear from the left and move rightwards.

LOOP   Sets the number of times the marquee scrolls.   A value of INFINITE causes the marquee to repeat continuously.

BGCOLOR   Sets the background colour of the marquee.

SCROLLAMOUNT   Sets the number of pixels that the marquee is moved with each step.

SCROLLDELAY   Sets the time, in milliseconds, between each step of the marquee's animation.

High values of SCROLLAMOUNT and small values of SCROLLDELAY result in marquees that are too fast to read while low SCROLLAMOUNT and high SCROLLDELAY values result in jerky animations.

Additionally, the font formatting <H> tags can be added to set the size of the scrolling text.

Example of use:
      <H2> <MARQUEE BEHAVIOR=ALTERNATE SCROLLAMOUNT=2 SCROLLDELAY=3
            LOOP=5 BGCOLOR="RED"> Bargain Offers Today </MARQUEE> </H2>

External graphics

Inline graphics are loaded as part of the web page.   This consumes downloading time even when the user is only idly browsing.   On the other hand, users are reluctant to switch off the display of graphics since many hyperlinks are made from graphic images. The most user-friendly approach is to allow larger sized graphics to be loaded only upon the specific request of the user.   These are termed *'external graphics'* since they are not part of the normal web page.   External graphics can be called up by clicking on a hyperlink.   This can be a conventional hyperlink or, more helpfully, can be a thumbnail (i.e. a miniature version of the graphic).   This allows users to click for more detail if they want.   For example, a web site for an estate agent wishes to entice users to view as many pages as possible.   Users can browse through many properties and only call up large graphic files for the properties that interest them.

```
<P>This <A HREF="kitchen.gif"> luxury kitchen </A> has to be seen to be believed<P>
```

The above script using a hyperlink to load and display the graphic if the user clicks it.

```
<A HREF="bigkitchen.gif"><IMG SRC="littlekitchen.gif"></A>
```

The above script shows a thumbnail view of the graphic. Clicking on the thumbnail view loads and displays the file storing the larger version.

Interlaced GIFs

A normal file is *'non-interlaced'* - the image is drawn one line at a time until the entire graphic is visible. It can be frustrating for the user to wait until there is enough of the file displayed before appreciating the graphic's contents.   The header inside a GIF can be set to display in this normal non-interlaced mode or display in interlaced mode.   In interlaced mode, the picture is built up in a couple of passes. On the first pass, alternate lines of the graphic are displayed with the other lines being filled in the next pass.   The user then sees most of the picture and can decide whether to wait for the rest or jump to another page.

Transparent GIFs

When a graphic file is loaded, its display area occupies a rectangle on the screen. An example is shown opposite.   The grey background area around the face spoils the look of the page.   The grey area can be made transparent, allowing the screen content underneath to be seen.   This is known as a *'transparent GIF'* and it stores all the colours of the image, with one colour nominated as the transparent colour.   Anywhere the transparent colour exists in the image, no pixels are displayed and the underlying screen content shows through. Transparent GIFs are created in image editing software by:

*   Selecting the required transparent colour, ensuring that the colour does not already appear in the foreground part of the image. Use the colour selector to find out the palette index number.
*   Ensuring that the entire background is painted to that colour.
*   Use the Colors/Set Color Transparency options in PaintShop Pro 5 or the File/Save As/Options in earlier versions to set the transparency value to the palette index number noted earlier.

Multimedia

These are many facilities that are not yet built into browsers.   Browsers are either configured to use the computer's existing facilities (sound card, video drivers, etc) or use browser add-ons such as Shockwave, Real Audio, etc.   However, even the standard browsers are capable of handling basic multimedia formats such as AU and WAV audio files and MPEG, AVI and MOV video files.

Sound

The <A> tag is capable of playing a sound file.   For example,

```
<A HREF="message.wav"> A word from our sponsors> </A>
```

displays a hypertext link that plays the message.wav file when clicked.
Internet Explorer inline sounds play automatically when the page is loaded, using the <BGSOUND> tag.

```
<BGSOUND SRC="message.wav">   or    <BGSOUND SRC="sun.mid">
```

BGSOUND has a LOOP attribute that sets the number of times the file is played.   If the value is set to INFINITE, the file plays continuously until the page is exited.   This setting should be used carefully as continuous messages or music can be very annoying for users.

AU, MID and WAV files can be used with either of the two methods above.

The equivalent command for Netscape browsers is <EMBED SRC="message.wav">

Video

The <A> tag is also capable of playing a video file.   For example,

<A HREF="heaven.mov"> The winning goal> </A>

displays a hypertext link that plays the heaven.mov file when clicked.   AVI, MPG and MOV files can be used with this method. Like inline sounds, inline AVI videos can play automatically when the page is loaded using the Internet Explorer DYNSRC attribute in the <IMG> tag.

<IMG DYNSRC="heaven.mov">

The LOOP attribute sets the number of times the file is played.   If the value is set to INFINITE, the file plays continuously, although this value would not normally be used.   The SRC="*file*" is used to display a static graphic for browsers that do not support DYNSRC.

The START attribute determines how the video file is activated.   If it is given the value of FILEOPEN, it plays as soon as the page is loaded.   If the value is MOUSEOVER, it does not play until the mouse passes over the blank playing screen.   The CONTROLS attribute adds the stop/start button and position slider.

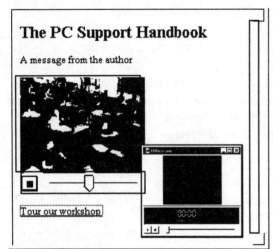

```
<HTML>
<HEAD><TITLE>Dumbreck Publishing</TITLE></HEAD>
<BODY BGCOLOR="#FFFFFF" FONT="BLACK">
<H2>The PC Support Handbook</H2>
<P>A message from the author<P>
<IMG DYNSRC="davy.avi" SRC="dave.gif"
         START=MOUSEOVER CONTROLS> <P>
<A HREF="office.avi" >Tour our workshop </A><P>
</BODY>
</HTML>
```

The above script shows both methods, with the left-hand video screen being the result of using DYNSRC.

Creating tables

The <TABLE> tag allows sets of data to be laid out in a structured and readable way.

Its general format is:

```
<TABLE>                                    <TABLE>
<CAPTION> Caption for the table </CAPTION>  <CAPTION> Caption for the table </CAPTION>
   <TR>                                        <TR>
       <TH> Heading</TH>                           <TH> Heading for the first column </TH>
       <TD> Data for cell </TD>                    <TH> Heading for the second column </TH>
       <TD> Data for cell </TD>                    ....
   </TR>                                        </TR>
   <TR>                                        <TR>
       <TH> Heading</TH>                           <TD> Data </TD>
       <TD> Data  </TD>                            <TD> Data </TD>
       <TD> Data </TD>                             <TD> Data </TD>
   </TR>                                           <TD> Data </TD>
       ....                                        ....
       ....                                    </TR>
</TABLE>                                    </TABLE>
```

Tables are defined row by row.   The definition on the left is used when the headings are to appear down the first column of the table (as in the example below).   The other definition is used when the headings are to appear at the top of each column.   Headings are displayed in a bold typeface.

The other main components are:

The optional <CAPTION> tag displays a centred heading for the table.

The text between the optional <TH> and </TH> tags specifies the contents of the heading for the table.

The <TR> and </TR> tags enclose the definition of a row and these sets would be repeated for each row required in the table.

The <TD> and </TD> tags enclose the data that will appear in a cell in the row. A set of these is required for each cell definition.

The contents of a cell can be text, a graphic image or a hyperlink.

```
<HTML>
<HEAD><TITLE>Dumbreck Publishing</TITLE></HEAD>
<BODY BGCOLOR="#FFFFFF" TEXT="#000000">
<TABLE BORDER=2>
<CAPTION><H2>Screen Resolutions</H2></CAPTION>
<TR ALIGN=CENTER>
  <TH> Standard</TH>
  <TD> <B>Resolution</B> </TD>
  <TD> <BR> </TD>
</TR>
<TR ALIGN=CENTER>
  <TH> CGA </TH>
  <TD> 640 x 200  </TD>
  <TD> <A HREF="cga.htm"> CGA details </TD>
</TR>
<TR ALIGN=CENTER>
  <TH> VGA </TH>
  <TD> 640 x 480 </TD>
  <TD> <A HREF="vga.htm"> VGA details </TD>
</TR>
<TR ALIGN= CENTER>
  <TH> SVGA </TH>
  <TD> 800 x 600 </TD>
  <TD> <A HREF="svga.htm"> SVGA details </TD>
</TR>
</TABLE>
</BODY>
</HTML>
```

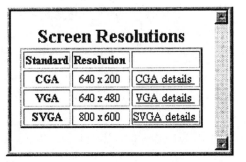

In the example, the cell in the top right corner is empty and this is achieved by:
<TD>
</TD>.

Formatting tables

The default positions for table components is:

	Vertical position	Horizontal position
ENTIRE TABLE	Defined by the script	At left of screen
HEADING CELLS	Centred	Centred
DATA CELLS	Centred	Left of cell

The table described so far leaves all table and cell formatting to the browser. A range of alterations can be made to the basic table definition to create more interest or to provide for irregular table shapes. This example shows the result of a number of these extra attributes and they are described below.

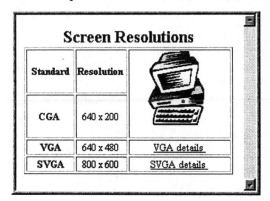

```
<HTML>
<HEAD><TITLE>Dumbreck Publishing</TITLE></HEAD>
<BODY BGCOLOR="#FFFFFF" TEXT="#000000">
<TABLE BORDER=1 WIDTH=100% >
<CAPTION><H2>Screen Resolutions</H2></CAPTION>
<TR ALIGN=CENTER>
  <TH WIDTH=25%> Standard</TH>
  <TD WIDTH=25%> <B>Resolution</B> </TD>
  <TD ROWSPAN=2 WIDTH=50% > <IMG SRC="monitor.gif">
</TD>
</TR>
<TR ALIGN=CENTER>
  <TH> CGA </TH>
  <TD> 640 x 200  </TD>
</TR>
<TR ALIGN=CENTER>
  <TH> VGA</TH>
  <TD > 640 x 480 </TD>
  <TD COLSPAN=2>  <A HREF=vga.htm"> VGA details </TD>
</TR>
<TR ALIGN=CENTER>
  <TH> SVGA</TH>
  <TD BGCOLOR="#DDDDDD" > 800 x 600 </TD>
  <TD ALIGN=CENTER    <A HREF=svga.htm"> SVGA  details
</TD>
</TR>
</TABLE></CENTER>
</BODY>
</HTML>
```

Border

The BORDER attribute determines the width of the border round each cell. A zero border values suppresses box drawing and is used to improve general screen formatting as described later.

The BORDERCOLOR attribute sets the colour around a particular cell as below:
<TH BORDERCOLOR="RED"> VGA</TH>

The background colour of a cell can be set using the BGCOLOR attribute in the <TD> tag,
e.g.   <TD BGCOLOR="#DDDDDD" > cell data </TD>

Table alignment

By default, tables are displayed on the left of the screen, with text appearing above and below the table. As in the case of graph images discussed earlier, ALIGN=LEFT and ALIGN=RIGHT alters the default positioning.   To place the table in the centre of the screen, the tag <CENTER> is placed before the <TABLE> tag and </CENTER> is placed after the </TABLE> tag.

Cell alignment

The ALIGN attributes of LEFT, RIGHT and CENTER, along with VALIGN, are used to place the cell's contents in the required position within the cell.   The CELLPADDING attribute is placed in the <TABLE> tag and determines the spacing between the cell walls and the text. The value is specified in pixels, e.g.

<TABLE CELLPADDING= 6>

The CELLSPACING attribute determines the width of the space between the cells, e.g.

<TABLE CELLSPACING=5>

The VALIGN attribute can be set to equal TOP, MIDDLE or BOTTOM, to position the cell contents in the vertical direction.

Table widths

The WIDTH attribute is added to the <TABLE> tag to specify how wide the table will appear on the screen.   The value can be set in pixels or as a percentage of the screen.   Using pixel values displays a table that does not alter its width when the user's screen is resized.   The percentage value ensures that the table width grows or shrinks depending on the screen resolution of the viewer's browser.

Column widths

The width of each column can be individually set using the WIDTH attribute in either the <TH> or <TD> tag.   Again, it can be specified as a fixed amount of pixels or a percentage of the screen width.

In the above example, the first two columns always occupy a quarter of the screen each, with the third column occupying the remainder of the screen width.   The column widths shrink or expand as the user's screen is resized but the columns always maintain the same ratio with respect to each other and to the overall screen width.

Merging cells

Many tables do not use a layout where there is a symmetrical matrix of cells (e.g. 5x5 or 8x7).

The examples on the next page show tables where cells have been merged - i.e. the data 'spans' more than a single cell. The first example shows a piece of data spanning the entire top row of cells.   The third example shows an entire column of cells being spanned by a single data item.   The middle example shows the first column being split into two separate vertical areas: the first data item spans the two upper rows of that column, while the second data item spans the two bottom rows.

Projected Sales		
	UK	USA
1999	8000	12000
2000	9000	18000

Male	Deaths	Injuries
	23	267
Female	Deaths	Injuries
	18	120

1998	750	
1999	1100	Web Site
2000	2100	
2001	5000	

To achieve the first effect, the COLSPAN or ROWSPAN attribute is embedded in the <TD> tag. So, if the data has to span the three cells, the value is set to three - e.g. <TD COLSPAN=3> or <TD ROWSPAN=3> The scripts for the above three layouts are:

```
<table border=1>
<tr>
<td colspan=3>Projected Sales</td>
</tr>
<td> </td><td>UK</td>
<td>USA</td></tr>
<tr><td>1999</td>
<td>8000</td>
<td>12000</td></tr>
<tr><td>2000</td>
<td>9000</td><td>18000</td></tr>
</table>
```

```
<table border=1>
<tr><td rowspan=2>Male</td>
<td>Deaths</td>
<td>Injuries</td></tr>
<tr><td>23</td>
<td>267</td></tr>
<tr><td rowspan=2>Female</td>
<td>Deaths</td>
<td>Injuries</td></tr>
<tr><td>18</td>
<td>120</td></tr>
</table>
```

```
<table border=1>
<tr><td>1998</td><td>750</td></tr>
<td rowspan=4>
<a href="www.somesite.com">Web Site
</td></tr>
<tr><td>1999</td><td>1100</td>
</tr>
<tr><td>2000</td><td>2100</td>
</tr>
<tr><td>2001</td><td>5000</td>
</tr>
</table>
```

Screen layouts

Tables are also commonly used to lay out data on the screen.   The example layout on the right is widely used. The data is laid out in two columns.   The left column displays a page headline, a graphic and a set of menu hyperlinks.   The right column displays the main text. When the user clicks a hyperlink, the new page is in the same style, with the same content in the left column.

So, as the user navigates round the site, there is a constant unchanging menu on the left.

The size of each column is set with the WIDTH attribute.

CELLPADDING is used to create a space between the two columns.   However, this also pushes the data down from the top of the column. An alternative is to insert a third column between the existing columns and adjust its width to the desired margin.

The example below shows the same script with the BORDER value set to 1.

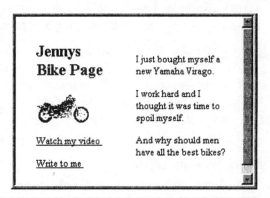

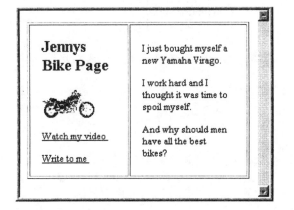

```
<HTML>
<HEAD><TITLE>Dumbreck Publishing</TITLE></HEAD>
<BODY BGCOLOR="#FFFFFF">
<TABLE BORDER=0 WIDTH=300 CELLPADDING=16>
<TR>
  <TD WIDTH=150>
    <FONT COLOR="RED">
    <H2>Jennys<BR> Bike Page</H2>
    </FONT>
    <IMG SRC="virago.gif">  <P>
    <A HREF="mybike.avi"> Watch my video </A><P>
    <A HREF="mailto:jenny@bikers.com"> Write to me </A>
  </TD>
  <TD WIDTH=200  cellpadding=5>
    <FONT COLOR="OLIVE">
    I just bought myself a new Yamaha Virago. <P>
    I work hard and I thought it was time to spoil myself.<P>
    And why should men have all the best bikes?
  </TD>
</TR>
</TABLE>
</BODY>
</HTML>
```

Graphic images

To insert a graphic image into a table cell, alter the TD (Table Data) tag to
                        <TD> <IMG SRC="filename.htm"></TD>

Frames

Frames are supported on all browsers from Netscape 2 and Internet Explorer 3 onwards.

The *'Jenny's Bike Page'* example used a table to create two distinct window areas and the *'World Guide'* site could be re-written using tables to create the display shown.

The aim was to display a menu of links on the left edge of the screen. Clicking a link alters the display on the right while the left column always displays the menu.

With tables, the <u>whole</u> screen is redrawn and the menu column is redrawn every time the right column displays new contents.   The contents of each left column are identical for all pages yet have to be re-displayed after each hyperlink jump.

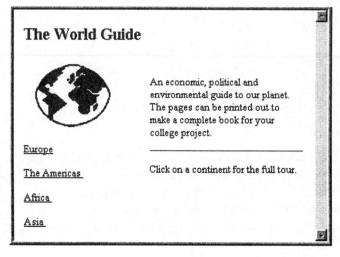

A more efficient way is to create distinct window areas called *'frames'*.   Frames still produce the same visual display as before but the left frame's contents would not be refreshed when the right frame was redrawn.   In the example, clicking a hyperlink only changes the contents of the right hand frame.

This technique can be extended so that several different frames are present on the screen at the same time.   For example, long documents may have a menu of links at the top of the document and a duplicate copy at the bottom of the document.   For a user who is somewhere in the middle of a document, there is no menu or help in sight.   With frames, a permanent menu can be placed at the bottom of the screen. The user can scroll the larger window's contents but the menu remains on screen at all times. Alternatively, a top frame can be used as a window to permanently display the web site banner and logo.

How frames work

The *'frame document'* is an HTML page that defines the size and position of each frame on the screen.   The frame document does not contain any normal screen data such as text or graphics; it purely defines the screen layout.   The screen data is supplied from other HTML pages whose contents fill the screen frames.   Each frame is given a name and this name is used to link frames and files.

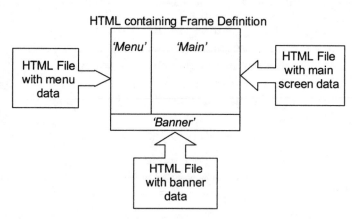

In the example, there are three frames called   *'Main'*,   *'Menu'* and   *'Banner'*.
Hyperlinks are used to load different files into the *'Main'* or even *'Menu'* frames as the user navigates the site.

Defining frames

The basic format of a frame document is:

```
<HTML>
<HEAD><TITLE>Dumbreck Publishing</TITLE></HEAD>
<FRAMESET
    The frame definition ..... >
</FRAMESET>
</HTML>
```

The usual <BODY> tags are replaced by <FRAMESET> tags.   These tags enclose the definition of the rows and columns that comprise the screen layout.

A basic layout may simply consist of only two columns or it may simply consist of two rows.

On the other hand, the layout may consist of a variety of frame combinations comprising both row and column shaped frames.   Like tables, dimensions can be expressed either in pixel amounts or in percentages of the screen size.

Simple frame definitions are:

Two-column layout

```
<HTML>
<HEAD><TITLE>Dumbreck Publishing</TITLE></HEAD>
<FRAMESET COLS="30%,70%">
    <FRAME    NAME="frame1"    SRC= "f1.htm" >
    <FRAME    NAME="frame2 "   SRC= "f2.htm" >
</FRAMESET>
</HTML>
```

Two row layout

```
<HTML>
<HEAD><TITLE>Dumbreck Publishing</TITLE></HEAD>
<FRAMESET  ROWS="50%,50%">
    <FRAME    NAME="frame1"    SRC= "f1.htm" >
    <FRAME    NAME="frame2 "   SRC= "f2.htm" >
<FRAMESET>
</HTML>
```

The FRAME tag provides specific information on each frame that will be displayed.

The NAME attribute provides each frame with a unique label for linking purposes (see later).

The SRC= attribute specifies what web page will load into the frame when the frame document is first loaded.   Of course, the frame contents can subsequently be changed as will be outlined shortly.

If a two-column definition were used for *'The World Guide'* it would produce the displays shown on the next page.

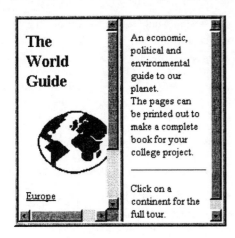 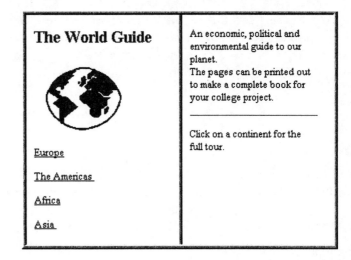

The right-hand screen is similar to the *'Jennys Bike Page'* example using a table shown on a previous page.

The left hand screen is the result of the user resizing the screen area and clearly shows that the display consists of two separate screen areas.

Complex definitions

More complex definitions are achieved by nesting a FRAMESET specification with another FRAMESET specification.   Example scripts for splitting rows and columns are shown below, along with the screen displays that are achieved.

```
<HTML>
<HEAD><TITLE>Dumbreck Publishing</TITLE></HEAD>
<FRAMESET ROWS="90%,10%">
        <FRAMESET COLS="90%,90%">
                <FRAME SRC= "f1.htm" >
                <FRAME  SRC= "f2.htm" >
        </FRAMESET>
        <FRAME  SRC= "f3.htm" >
</FRAMESET>
</HTML>
```

```
<HTML>
<HEAD><TITLE>Dumbreck Publishing</TITLE></HEAD>
<FRAMESET COLS="40%,70%">
        <FRAME NAME="MENU" SRC= "f1.htm" >
        <FRAMESET ROWS="90%,90%">
                <FRAME  NAME="MAIN" SRC= "f2.htm" >
                <FRAME  NAME="BANNER" SRC= "f3.htm" >
        </FRAMESET>
</FRAMESET>
</HTML>
```

NOTES

- The script lines are only indented for clarity. The browser ignores the spaces.
- Percentage values for ROWS and COLS don't necessarily add up to 100%.   In the example, both column widths are set to 90%.   Netscape and Internet Explorer add up the column percentages and distribute them proportionate to the screen. So, in the example, each column is allocated half of the users screen window width.   Specifications of 40% and 120% would result in the first column occupying a quarter of the screen.
- NAMEs have been added to the FRAME definition in the second example.
- In these examples, the MAIN area's contents alter every time a new page is selected from the menu. The BANNER area would probably only be loaded once and remain on-screen at all times.
- The MENU area, like the BANNER area, may never be updated.   Alternatively, it may be used to display sub-menus.   The left display shows the opening menu frame. Clicking on the DISK hyperlink loads the page shown on the right into the MENU frame. Clicking any disk hyperlink option loads the

matching data file into the MAIN frame.   When the user clicks on the Main Menu hyperlink, the original page shown on the left is loaded into the MENU frame once again.

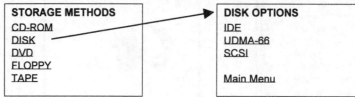

Attributes

The attributes available for FRAMESET definition are:

FRAMEBORDER	Setting the value to zero stops the display of the 3D border round frames. However, the space allocated for the border displays on the screen as a grey band.
FRAMESPACING	Setting the value to zero makes each frame butt on to the next frame, with no gaps.

Example:
<FRAMESET FRAMEBORDER="NO" FRAMESPACING=0>

Results in no borders being displayed around any frames and the screen appearing as a single display. Earlier versions of Explorer may need FRAMEBORDER to be set to zero instead of "NO".

The attributes available for FRAME definition are:

NORESIZE	The default, as with most Windows applications, allows the user to grab a window border and resize it. The NORESIZE attribute prevents the user from altering frame sizes.
MARGINHEIGHT	Sets the margin, in pixels, above and below the document.
MARGINWIDTH	Sets the margin, in pixels, between the document and the sides of the frame.
SCROLLING	Controls the user's ability to scroll through a frame's document, and has three settings: NO: The user cannot scroll through the document. This should be used with caution. If the screen is small size and the user cannot resize the window, then some screen content will be prevented from displaying. YES: Vertical and horizontal scrollbars are also displayed in the frame, even when the document is too small to need scrolling facilities. AUTO: The scrollbars are only displayed if the document is too large for the size of the frame window.

Example:
<FRAME MARGINWIDTH=10 MARGINHEIGHT=15 NAME="MAIN" SRC="file5.htm">

results in a 15 pixel margin above and below the document and 10 pixels of space between the document and the frame's vertical sides.   By default, scrolling facilities are automatically triggered by large documents and the user is allowed to alter frame sizes by dragging them with the mouse.

Noframes

If a browser does not support frames, it won't recognise the frame script and will display a blank page. To maximise the number of viewers to the site, a non-frame version of the site can be set up.   This uses the Netscape NOFRAMES attribute as shown below.

```
<HTML>
<HEAD><TITLE>Dumbreck Publishing</TITLE></HEAD>
<FRAMESET >
    The frame definition .....
<NOFRAMES>
    The same contents (e.g. text, graphics, and links) without using frames
</FRAMESET>
</HTML>
```

Browsers that can handle frames simply ignore the NOFRAMES section.   As users upgrade to more modern browsers, the need for this technique will diminish.

Floating frames

Many sites now use the technique of *'floating frames'*, also known as *'inline frames'*.   With normal sites, a window may be split into different areas (usually frames) but only one window is viewable at any one time.   Users click hyperlinks to change the whole page or parts of the page.   With floating frames, clicking a hyperlink brings up <u>another</u> window that pops up within the existing window.   It may also load up another copy of the browser to view the new contents. Closing a floating frame reveals the entire contents of the previous window (without having to be reloaded first).

The basic format of a floating frame is

```
<HTML>
<HEAD><TITLE>Dumbreck Publishing</TITLE></HEAD>
<BODY >
      Content, if any for the main screen .....
         <IFRAME  SRC="filename.htm">  </IFRAME>
</BODY>
</HTML>
```

Several IFRAME definitions can be inserted with the <BODY> tags, if required.

The attributes for IFRAME are:

WIDTH   Sets the width of the floating frame window (in pixels or as a percentage).

HEIGHT   Sets the height of the floating frame window.

ALIGN   By default, floating frames are displayed on the left of the screen, with text appearing above and below the table.   ALIGN=LEFT and ALIGN=RIGHT alters the default positioning, as explained earlier for graphics and tables.   CLEAR also has the same effect as explained earlier.

FRAMEBORDER   If set to zero, it inhibits the display of borders round the frame.

HSPACE   Sets the horizontal margin in pixels between the frame and other screen contents.

VSPACE   Sets the vertical margin between the frame and other screen contents.

SCROLLING   Same as the earlier definition given for FRAMESET attributes.

NAME   Attaches a label to the frame for linking purposes (see next section).

In addition, the attributes TOPMARGIN and LEFTMARGIN can be inserted into the <BODY> tag. TOPMARGIN sets the space, in pixels, between the top of the page and start of the display of the page contents.   LEFTMARGIN sets the space between the left-hand side of the screen and the start of the display of the page contents.

Example:

```
<IFRAME NAME="prices"  SRC="filename.htm" WIDTH=300  HEIGHT=300
     FRAMEBORDER=1  HSPACE=5  VSPACE=5 >  </IFRAME>
```

Results in a floating frame called *'prices'* with the contents of the *'filename.htm'* displayed in a 300 pixel by 300 pixel window.   The frame displays its border and has a 5 pixel spacing between it and other screen content.   By default, the scrolling facility automatically initiates when required and the window is left aligned.

Linking frames

The use of frames allows one frame's contents to loaded and displayed without altering the other frames on the screen.   Since each frame has been given a

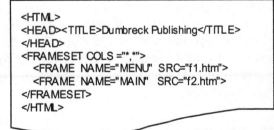

```
<HTML>
<HEAD><TITLE>Dumbreck Publishing</TITLE>
</HEAD>
<FRAMESET COLS ="*,*">
   <FRAME  NAME="MENU"  SRC="f1.htm">
   <FRAME  NAME="MAIN"  SRC="f2.htm">
</FRAMESET>
</HTML>
```

The World Guide

<u>Europe</u>

<u>The Americas</u>

<u>Africa</u>

<u>Asia</u>

An economic, political and environmental guide to our planet.
The pages can be printed out to make a complete book for your college project.

Click on a continent for the full tour.

unique name, the data that is loaded can be directed (*'targetted'*) towards that named frame. Since only a part of the screen is being updated, the transition is smoother.   More importantly, less of the screen being updated means that less data has to be downloaded.   This results in smaller files being fetched and navigation is therefore faster.

The first script shown creates a screen with two column frame areas.   The first column is called MENU and has the contents of file *'f1.htm'* displayed in it.   The second column is called MAIN and initially displays the contents of the *'f2.htm'* file.

The contents of the f1.htm file are shown on the right.   The HREF tags have a TARGET= attribute added to them.   This points to the name of the frame to be updated with the file being loaded.

```
<HTML>
<HEAD>
<TITLE>Dumbreck Publishing</TITLE></HEAD>
<BODY BGCOLOR="#FFFFFF" FONT="BLACK">
<H2>The World Guide</H2>
<IMG SRC="world.gif" ALIGN = MIDDLE ALT="World Map"> <P>
<A HREF="europe.htm"    TARGET="MAIN" >Europe</A><P>
<A HREF="americas.htm" TARGET="MAIN" >The Americas </A><P>
<A HREF="africa.htm"       TARGET="MAIN" >Africa</A><P>
<A HREF="asia.htm"         TARGET="MAIN" >Asia </A><P>
</BODY>
<.HTML>
```

The example file has four hyperlinks.   If the first link is clicked, it loads the *'europe.htm'* file. Since its target is the MAIN frame, the file's contents are displayed in that frame (i.e. the second column).

The left column's contents remain unaltered while a click on any of the hyperlinks in the menu results in the contents of the second frame being altered.

In the example, the one frame was the common target for all updating.   In this case the TARGET= attribute can be removed from each HREF line and be replaced by the single line:

<BASE TARGET="MAIN">

This line is inserted between the <HEAD> tags.   Where different frames are being updated, this method cannot be used.

The technique of targeted frames can be used to refine the menu system shown earlier.   In the example on the right, the top-left corner box permanently displays a main menu.   Clicking on a menu option displays its corresponding sub-menu options in the lower-left corner box. Clicking on any sub-menu option then displays its contents in the main screen area.   This way, the main menu and sub-menu are visible at all times.

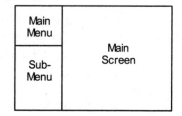

It is possible to make a single click update two frames simultaneously, but this involves the use of JavaScript.

MAILTO

This is a very simple single line of script that allows a user to send an e-mail to the site owner while still inside the site.   The user does not have to leave the browser and enter his/her e-mail program to send the message.   The format is

<A HREF ="MAILTO: address"> hyperlink message</A>

A typical example is

<A HREF= MAILTO:sales@dumbreck.demon.co.uk> Send us your comments </A>

When the hyperlink is clicked, the user is asked to provide a subject name for the e-mail and to provide the main text of the message.   When the user completes the details, the software sends the message and returns the user to the previously loaded web page.   An example of its use was seen in the *'Jennys Bike Page'* site earlier.

Resources

While a perfectly acceptable web site can be created armed with only a text editor and knowledge of HTML, a range of hardware and software tools can speed up and broaden a web site's development.
The hardware tools are

- Scanners
- Audio recording equipment
- digital still cameras
- digital video cameras

The software tools include:

- HTML editors
- HTML syntax checkers
- HTML generators
- Site performance testers

HTML editors/generators

The most basic editing tool is an ASCII editor such as Notepad or DOS EDIT. The author requires knowledge of the entire scripting language and layout, as there is no in-built assistance.

The next step up is an add-on to an existing word-processing package, such as Word. These can be as simple as a set of macros that provide on-screen buttons to embed tags into the document (e.g. GT_HTML.DOT) or can offer further facilities such as an add-on browser (e.g. Internet Assistant for Word). Since they are within a word-processing package, all the package's facilities, such as spell checking and text formatting, are available to the author.

The current trend is to use software packages that are dedicated to the production of web pages and entire web sites. These packages use two approaches:

- Text-based HTML editors.
- WYSIWYG-based HTML generators.

Text editors

An example of a text-based editor is shown in the illustration. The main work area is a text screen and the script entries are placed in this text area. The cursor is placed where the item is to be added and the desired icon or menu option is selected. This method speeds up page development but the effect of the script is not seen until it is viewed from the computer's browser (called up via an on-screen icon). This method involves an amount of trial-and-error - changing the script and viewing the result are separate operations. These packages are continually increasingly their features and the example package shown, 'Coffee Cup', also allows simple integration of graphics and Java applets into the script.

These editors are popular choices with writers with some previous HTML knowledge, who use them to get greater control over the site.

The drawback with the packages is that the writer is continually switching between the edit window and the viewing window. To overcome this, other packages, such as Hippie 97, display both windows on screen at the same time. Writers can edit their entries and view the script and the web page at the same time.

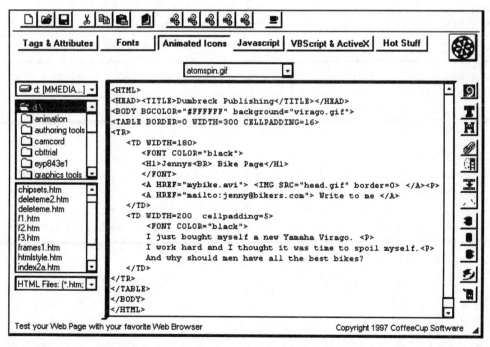

Graphics editors

These are the most popular packages, as the main work area is the web page rather than the HTML script. The writer can concentrate on the design and the package converts the screen layout into an HTML script. The script can still be edited directly for more complex work. All the elements such as text, tables, images and buttons can be dragged from menus and dropped into the page editor (i.e. the design screen).

There are facilities for both beginners and experienced authors.

- For novices, the packages provide *'templates'*. These are pre-designed layouts for both personal and business pages.   Once loaded into the editor, a template is then edited to personalise the content.   Templates offer comprehensive features such as *'Whats New'*, Table of Contents, Feedback forms and search forms.   Beginners can also use *'Wizards'* which creates a layout that results from answers to questions to the author.
- Advanced authors benefit from the simplification of tasks (e.g. resizing table widths or frame sizes by dragging with the mouse, or creating image map links simply by drawing an outline using the mouse cursor).

The packages also integrate some of the graphic functions of other packages, such as providing a clipart library, a catalogue of image thumbnails, or image editing and animation facilities.

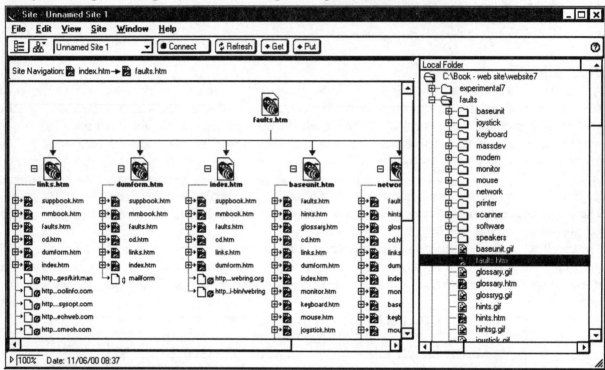

The illustration shows the Macromedia Dreamweaver package being used to display a site map.   The left panel shows some of the contents of the fault-finding system from the Dumbreck web site. Dreamweaver shows the resources that are included on each web page, including internal links, external links and graphics files.

Site management

As a site expands, there are increasing problems of managing the project, resulting in unfinished pages going unnoticed or inadequate navigation (e.g. pages with no links, links pointing to non-existent pages, etc).   The best editors provide not only page creation tools, but tools for managing the overall site.   This could include the graphical display of all pages and links, so that the author sees the overall structure. The package may also allow the author to create a *'To Do'* list.   The author creates the basic structure and the To Do list reminds him/her of the tasks still to be completed.

Site management tools could also include improved uploading facilities and database tools.

Validation checkers

These facilities may be built in to editors and are also available as separate utilities.   They check the page documents prior to them being uploaded.   They report on any syntax errors (e.g. missing tags) and check for any browser versions that cannot handle all the commands in the page scripts.   Examples are the freeware Xenu and Spyglass validators.

Site performance testers

This software reports on the time taken to load pages and the number of links that currently point to a page.   These facilities can be obtained on-line from tester sites on the Internet.

Maximising promotion

The later section discusses the methods to promote the completed site by contacting the press, Internet directories, newsgroups, etc. But the site can be augmented to maximise its drawing power to users, even before it is uploaded on to the server.

Search engines

Every day, large numbers of Internet users employ search facilities to find sites relating to their needs. Many software packages, called *'search engines'*, are available to aid these searches. The most famous is Alta Vista and others include HotBot, UK Plus, GOD and Excite.

Search engines use software packages known as *'spiders'* or *'robots'* to search the Internet for new sites and alterations to existing sites. These packages all note the content of web pages to compile indexes for user searches. The way that each package uses the information will vary with some giving greater emphasis to a particular feature than others.

Keywords

Keywords are the words that most distinguish the site's contents and the ones mostly likely to be used by someone searching the Internet for the site. Do not rely solely on keywords such as *'computer'*, *'car'* and *'employment'* as these are used by many existing sites and produce hundreds of thousands of matches for users of search engines. Use descriptive words such as *'fragmentation'*, *'Mercedes'* and *'welder'*.

<TITLE>

The text enclosed by the <TITLE> tags is not displayed on the screen but is the common starting point for text gathered by search engines. Therefore, the text should be as descriptive as possible, using keywords. This text is also used when a user decides to add the page as a bookmark in his/her browser. So, *"Great Bargains for All"* is useless while *"Printer Supplies"* is much more meaningful.

Page text

When analysing page content, search engines assume that writers place their most important information at the top of a page. Accordingly, search engines give greater weight to words at the top of the page. A web page, therefore should have a significant statement at the top of each page.

<META> tags

The <META> tag allows the site's description and associated keywords to be embedded in the web page, so that they can be automatically picked up by many of the search engine spiders. The script lines are located between the <HEAD> tags and have the following formats:

<META NAME="description" CONTENT="*description of the site goes here*">
<META NAME="keywords" CONTENT="*list of keywords goes here*">

Repeatedly inserting a single word in the keywords list used to ensure a higher ranking in search results but modern search engines penalise this abuse by ignoring the entire keywords list. META keywords are particularly useful with sites whose main file uses frames. A page with frames contains a <FRAMESET> and little else, so a keywords list informs the spiders about the page's purpose.

ALT attributes

```
<HTML>
<HEAD>
<TITLE>The PC Support Handbook</TITLE>
<META name="description" content="Computer textbook for college and university students">
<META name="keywords" content="student textbook, technician handbook, computer basics,
software & data, operating systems & environments, computer architecture, computer video,
pc configuration, batch files, computer memory, windows configuration, disks & drives,
computer viruses, pc support, upgrading, system selection, data communications, the internet,
web site creation, local area networks, multimedia" >
</HEAD>
```

Some search engines use ALT attribute text in their calculations. So ALT text helps promote the site as well as being helpful to users who have turned off their *'load images'* option.

<NOFRAMES> tags

Placing a site description between the <NOFRAMES> and </NOFRAMES> tags allows users with older browsers (i.e. ones not supporting frames) to view the page. The text is also included in search results.

Uploading

Large organisations may decide that it is cost-effective to establish their own web server at their own site, incurring the expense of establishing, preparing and maintaining a permanent server connection to the Internet.   Most organisations and individuals choose to use space on an existing web server.   In most cases, an ISP (Internet Service Provider) provides a fixed amount (around 5MB) of disk space as part of the standard user's rental.   Additional web site space can be rented at an extra cost.

When the site contents are written and tested, they have to be copied from the local hard disk to the remote server's disk system.

The transfer is known as *'uploading'* and the stages of the process are:

- Packaging the elements in a suitable uploading format.
- Testing the site before uploading.
- Transferring the files.
- Testing the final server version.

Format

Each server provider has different conditions and these should be checked before completing the site. Better still, check the conditions out before even starting the site design.

The issues to be considered are:

- The name of the server sub-directory allocated for the new site. This may be already created by the provider.   In this case, providing the correct password at the ftp logon automatically directs uploading to the allocated directory.
- Avoid using absolute pathnames for graphic images, since the paths used to store them on the server disk will be different and the files will not be accessible.   Using relative pathnames avoids this problem, as does having all the sites files stored in a single directory.
- The most common name for the main site file is expected to be index.htm, but some expect default.htm or other name.   The required main filename will be supplied by the ISP.
- Some providers support CGI scripting and offer image libraries and usage counters.
- The final site must fit within the maximum space allocated by the provider.

Pre-testing

Test all the links within the site to ensure that all the pages in structure function as expected.   Equally important, test the site with different browsers before uploading.   Some activities are peculiar to Netscape or Explorer and newer versions of the same browser support extra features not found in older versions.   To maximise the site's readership, a balance has to be struck between the utilising the latest technological innovations and the ability of users to view the pages.

Transferring

The site is uploaded using an FTP session.   When the FTP application is run, it produces a screen similar to that below.

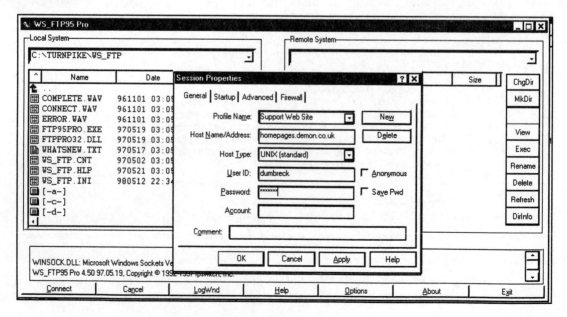

The details to be set up for an upload session are:

Profile Name:

A number of different profiles can be set up; one for uploading to the host server, others for downloading from particular sites, and so on.   The upload details can be saved as a profile and this can be called up each time the site needs to be updated.   The example entry is *'Support Web Site'* but this can be any name as it is purely for local use; it is not sent to the host server.

Host Details:

These are supplied by the server provider. The example uses a UNIX server and initially connects to the homepages area of the demon site.

User Details:

The user ID and the user password will have previously been agreed with the provider.

Initial Directories:

The Local Initial Directory is the directory on the hard drive that stores the web site files.

The Remote Initial Directory is the directory used for storing the files on the remote server.   This is usually left blank, as the correct password usually automatically directs uploading to the allocated directory.

Clicking *'OK'* and *'Connect'* produces the following results
- The local computer connects to the remote site.
- The remote server returns a message to the local system. This appears at the bottom of the ftp screen.
- The left window displays all the files in the local disk's web site directory.
- The right window displays the receiving directory on the remote server.   This directory will be empty.   On subsequent visits to update the site's contents, the complete set of site files is displayed in this window.

Between the two window columns are two buttons. One displays an arrow going from the local window to the remote window (i.e. from the local site to the remote server). The other arrow points from the server to the local computer.   These buttons are used to copy files between the two computers.

Below the windows is a set of radio buttons. These allow the files to be transferred in ASCII or Binary mode.

To upload the entire site:
- Set the transfer mode to ASCII.
- Highlight the HTML files in the local window.
- Click the right-pointing arrow to upload the text files.
- Set the transfer mode to Binary
- Highlight the non-text files (e.g. graphics, audio, video, executables).
- Click the right-pointing arrow to upload these files.

As an alternate, some ftp packages allow a drag-and-drop method where files are highlighted by the mouse and *'dropped'* into the server window.

In either case, the files will appear in the right window. This means that the entire population of Internet users can access them.

Final testing

After the site is uploaded, it should be tested.   This involves logging on to the Internet as a normal user and entering the site address in the browser.   The main page of the site should appear and each link should be tested, to see whether the expected pages appear and the text and graphics are displayed as expected.

Test the site with the *'display graphics'* option disabled to ensure that <ALT> tags work.

Test the site with different browsers, to ensure that the site appearance is satisfactory on a range of browser packages.

Test the site with different versions of the same browser.   For example, an older browser may not have the facility for displaying frames and this checks whether the <NOFRAMES> text works.

If possible, the site should also be tested on different platforms.   Many Internet users are not PC users and the site may not appear on other machines in quite the way that was planned.

Advertising the site

At this stage, the site is available to the wider Internet and has been designed to respond to search engines.   Traffic from search engines, however, only generates a minority of the visits to sites. There is much more that can be done to promote the site.   The amount of time and money invested in publicising the site depends upon the nature of the site.   Individuals and organisations will build a promotion strategy from the techniques listed below.   Hobby sites may decide to generate extra hits using cost-free methods such as obtaining directory entries or hosting regular site events.   Commercial sites may decide to embark on a range of advertising methods.   Charities and special interest groups may decide upon publicity in the media. There is no 'correct' way to promote a site.   Site owners will choose the mix of activities that produces the best results for their particular product/message.

Target Audience

The potential audience for the web site does not reflect all of society.   Some countries have very low numbers on the Internet, while richer countries such as the USA have large numbers of Net users.   There are far more young people on the Net than there are older users.   Within each country, Net usage is largely concentrated in the better-off and professional sections of the population.   Net users are still predominantly male, although female participation is growing rapidly.   The potential audience, therefore, is what actually exists and not what a site would wish to exist.   The site's expectations have to reflect this reality.   Sites for the unemployed, travelling people, pensioners, etc can expect fewer hits than sites for youth culture, consumer products, holidays, etc.

Newspapers/Magazines/Radio

It is worth contacting newspapers (both national and local), relevant magazines and radio stations about the launch of a new site.   This method only produces results if the site itself is newsworthy in some way (e.g. a charity site, a topical site, covering a niche market, etc).   Coverage is free and widespread but may not be targeting the desired audience.   This may work better for launching a helpline than launching a specialist site.

Press Releases

In addition to the printed press, sites can be publicised through on-line press releases.   Several sites provide on-line daily or weekly information on new sites.   Press releases should be short and sharp, using small paragraphs, if they are to be considered for inclusion.   Organisations may consider using an on-line distribution service. This is a commercial company that already has the knowledge and contacts and will process press releases for a fee.   Their experience can be a benefit as targeting is the key - not just maximising hits.

Site Reviews

There are two types of reviews for web sites - *'Guides'* and *'Cool Sites'*.   A *'Guide'* provides a review of a selected number of sites and provides a site rating.   The *'Cool Site'* usually reviews and recommends a different site each day.   These both provide a high volume of extra traffic for a short time.

Magazine Adverts

The impact of paid advertising depends on the nature of the site and ensuring that the advertising matches the target group.   There will be fewer hits from groups who normally do not own/use a computer and advertising costs may determine whether to proceed.   On the other hand, adverts placed in magazines for computer users, electronic technicians, educationalists, government users and the IT industry can expect a better return.

Directories

These sites use categories to direct viewers, via menu options, to their chosen topics. They are often described as the *'Yellow Pages'* of the Internet.   The menus have many categories and sub-categories. Inclusion on the directory, therefore, specifically targets those requiring the new site's information/product.   Directory providers provide forms for site registration and these gather details on the URL, directory category (e.g. sport, travel, computers) and key details of the site contents.   Not all sites are automatically accepted by a directory provider. Yahoo, for example, rejects a third of all submissions.   The most popular directories are Yahoo, Lycos, Webcrawler and Infoseek.

In addition to directory services, most directory sites also provide search engine facilities.

Newsgroups

There are over 30,000 newsgroups on the Internet and those with topics relevant to the site's contents can be selected for mailing.   This is a sensitive area, as some newsgroups do not allow advertising.   A posting to a newsgroup should not consist solely of the advert but should bring in the advert as part of a general contribution or answer to another's query.   So *"buy my product"* is counterproductive while *"...I hope that answers your question. For more details see my web site ....."* is acceptable.

Posting to newsgroups is a useful method, in as much as the audience reached have all chosen to read in the newsgroup topic and are therefore potentially more receptive to the new site's message. On the other hand, abuse of the newsgroup through blatant adverts and repeated postings will produce a hostile reaction.

Links from other web sites

Other web sites may promote similar interests or products and have an interest in providing links between sites.   An academic or hobby site may be very happy to provide a one-way link to the new site.   Their link may point to the main page or directly to a page that contains their specific interest.   Other sites may swap links, with both sites providing links to the other site.   The hits arising from web links is almost as high as that from search engines.

There is no special procedure for attracting links: an e-mail request to the other sites soon produces their responses.

Banner campaigns

Many sites are run by enthusiastic, and knowledgeable, amateurs.   If they have a costly server, they often are keen to get financial sponsors for their sites.   This can be a cost-effective method of advertising for commercial sites, as many sites attract large numbers of viewers.   Usually, the sponsorship results in advertising banners being placed on the other's site.   For larger companies, the extra expense of having a banner on a larger commercial site may be more attractive. The cost of advertising on popular directories and search engines is greater than on smaller non-commercial sites.

The site owners can be e-mailed for more information.   Be aware that only about 1% of users seeing a banner actually click on it to jump to the new site (known as *'clickthrough'*).   The impact of a banner depends on some crucial factors such as professional banner design, the use of animation, the use of bright colours and banner content appropriate to the user being targeted.

Electronic Newsletters

These aim to draw users into regular contact with the site, by inviting them to sign up to an e-mailing list for a regular newsletter.   The list is used to send regular e-mails outlining site changes, special offers, events, etc.   Before proceeding, there should be clear procedures that allow users to unsubscribe.

Site Events

These are designed to encourage users to pay regular visits to the site.   Events will depend on the nature of the site but could be competitions, games, surveys, on-line interviews with celebrities or experts, pre-recorder audio broadcasts, 'issue of the month', FAQ series.   These are all time-consuming as they require regular updating of the site contents but they make the site more attractive for repeat visits. Where the site is updated regularly, say so as *"Last updated ... ..."* messages encourages viewing.

Measuring Results

One simple measure of a site's success is the extra sales/donations/members/enquiries that are generated. Then again, a site's purpose might be as an information provider.   Sites providing tax or weather information, music charts, train or TV timetables and so on are intended mainly to provide one-way traffic.   For these sites, the best measure of success is the *'hit rate'* - the number of times pages have been viewed.   These figures can be gathered using *'counters'*.   Counters can provide information on the origins of traffic, the total visits to the site and the number of hits on particular pages.   The ISP can be checked for these services.   The hit rate for sites is used in the same way as viewing figures for TV channels.   Increased viewers results in increased fees for advertising on these sites.   This provides an incentive for sites to inflate their visitors' figures.   Reputable sites can pay a fee to non-profit agencies for *'web auditing'*.   These agencies monitor the site, its procedures and its results and pronounce on the accuracy of the figures.

Developing Web Sites

This chapter looks beyond the steps needed for creating a basic website.
It looks at three interlinked areas:
- Web programming.
- Browser enhancements.
- Commercial web sites.

The extensions covered in this chapter are designed to either add extra functionality to the site, or enhance page content.

Web programming

As the last chapter showed, perfectly useful web sites can be created with just the use of HTML.
However, to produce the extra functionality and looks, developers look to new and emerging technologies. This might be in the form of animations or audio and video streaming. Or it might be through the use of programming languages, many designed especially for web use. Web programming is considered as having two realms of activity - those involved with the clients (i.e. those who browse the web site contents) and those involved with servers (those who provide the web site contents).

Client side programming

This concentrates mainly on <u>how</u> the browser presents information (i.e. layout, style, animation, etc).
Client side programming means that all the program code is run at <u>browser</u> end. This has always been the case, for example, with HTML, but this has now been joined with a range of additional programs such as Java applets, JavaScript, Active X components, VBScript, APIs, DHTML, XML, and plug-ins.
Because they run purely within the viewer's own computer, they have the following advantages:
- They do not require a special server setup.
- They perform quickly once they are downloaded.

On the other hand, they have the following disadvantages:
- The browser has to download the code in order to run it, resulting in slower page downloads.
- The code may contain commands that only work on certain browsers, or browser versions.
- There may be browser compatibility issues with some client-side software. Most notably, Active X and VBScript only work on the Windows platforms and only with Internet Explorer.

Server side programming

This concentrates mainly on <u>what</u> information is communicated between the server and browser. It can involve CGI scripts, Perl scripts, Server Side Includes, Active Server Pages, etc. In this case, the program code is run at <u>server</u> end and can be used to store, process and package information for display at the browser end. This supports, for example, databases and on-line purchasing.
Consider the operations required when a user is choosing holiday options at a travel agent's web site.
The user completes a selection of criteria (e.g. dates, places, preferences, number travelling, etc). This information is sent to the server and is used to consult a database containing flight information, hotel vacancies, etc. The server then constructs a web page that displays the various holiday options that meet the users criteria, complete with costs.   The server has carried out user requests, consulted databases, carried out calculations and prepared an individual web page just for that viewer.   And all this has taken place within the server end.
Server side programming provides benefits such as:
- Processing takes place at server end, so program speed is not dependent on the age of the computer used for browsing.
- A huge range of facilities (search engines, database handling, maintaining site statistics, etc) are available.

The disadvantages are:
- It relies on what facilities are allowed by an ISP.   Internet providers are reluctant to allow user-programs that might introduce delays or system crashes and place limitations on what languages are allowed.
- Many facilities will only be available through an extra payment to the ISP.
- The program performance is dependent on how busy an ISP is at any time.

CGI scripts

CGI (Common Gateway Interface) scripts are the most common method of running programs on a server, based on the input from the user's web browser. The scripts are triggered by the input from a browser. CGI is not a specific language - it is more a specification for transferring information between a server and a CGI program.

There are a variety of modes that can be achieved by running a CGI script:

- It can be information passed from the user to the server (e.g. completing a form, or clicking a link).
- It can be information passed from the server to the browser (e.g. counter hits, time of day).
- It can be a two-way interchange of information (e.g. ask for a database search, get user-specific pages as a reply).

How CGI scripts work

The diagram shows the normal chain of activities that are involved in initiating and processing a CGI script. The steps are:

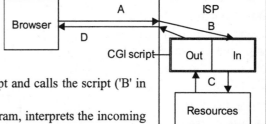

- The user's browser points to a URL. This could be from filling in a form or just from clicking an image or piece of hypertext.
- The URL is passed to the ISP ('A' in the diagram). The URL may be accompanied by user data (e.g. when sending in a form) or may not have any data attached (e.g. when calling for the current date or time).
- The ISP recognises that the URL is for a CGI script and calls the script ('B' in the diagram).
- The CGI script, drawn with double line in the diagram, interprets the incoming lines of script ('In' in the diagram).
- This usually involves accessing other resources ('C' in the diagram). The resources could be system data (e.g. the time), user's data (e.g. the user's hit counter or bandwidth statistics), databases, or other applications.
- The requested resources are taken by the CGI script and any processing that may be required is carried out (e.g. calculating prices) before the data is formatted into browser pages (see 'Out' in diagram).
- These pages are sent back to the browser ('D' in the diagram).

The user initiates the call to the CGI script and all the subsequent processing takes place within the server. The final output is in the form of a web page that is sent back to the browser for viewing.

The scripts contain plain ASCII text and can be in any programming language such as C, Perl, Pascal, Delphi, or Visual Basic. The choice of language is not decisive. What is important is the interface between the server and the script. If the syntax and methods are known, then any programming language can be used to write the CGI scripts.

In practice, however, Perl (Practical Extraction and Reporting Language) is by far the most common language used for CGI scripting and it is available free. Many Unix servers use Perl interpreters. The CGI script is a text file and this is passed to the interpreter, which translates each script line and carries it out. In most cases, servers keep the CGI scripts in a folder called CGI-BIN or BIN. Libraries of Perl and C scripts are available free on the Internet.

Perl programming is beyond the scope of the current book, but the two most commonly used CGI scripts are examined - those for handling browser forms and for proving traffic counters.

Forms

Forms are the standard method of getting information from a browser to a server. Forms are constructed from HTML and are used to call a CGI script at the server end. The CGI script then carries out the processing of the data passed to it.

Forms can sit anywhere on a web site, on any web page. They can be placed on a separate web page or can be part of a web page.

A form can contain a single entry (e.g. What is your favourite girl band?), have relatively few entries (e.g. name and address for joining a newsletter mailing list) or can contain many entries (e.g. filling in questionnaires or for entering data for on-line credit card purchases).

The illustration shows the variety of options for entering data into a Form. The script for this web page is described on the following pages.

Radio Buttons
The first two questions use radio buttons to extract a user response.   Only a single answer is expected (i.e. the book cannot be expensive and cheap at the same time).   A radio button method ensures that only one response can be entered. If a second button is selected, the previous button becomes unselected.

Multiple selections
The third question allows more than one box to be checked, so the user can check none, some, or all of them.

Selection from a list
The fourth question provides a drop-down menu from which a user can select a single choice.

Text entry
There are a variety of ways that a user can enter text into a form. The simplest way is to provide a single box, allowing a single line of text to be entered.   The

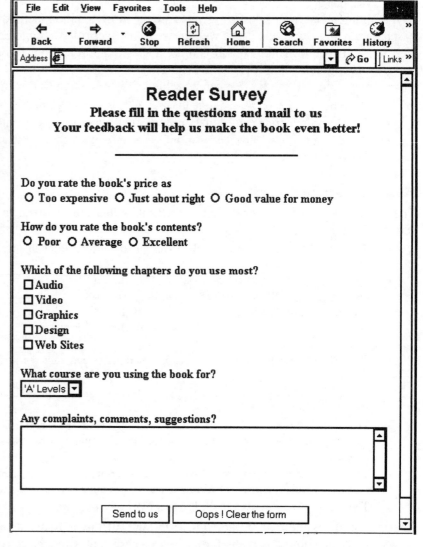

box may initially be empty or may contain an initial value. Providing an initial value is useful when the response for a field is often the same for different users (e.g. a field requesting a delivery address for goods may supply an initial value of *'Same as Invoice Address'*).

A text entry box can also be designed, as in the illustration, to allow multiple lines to be entered. While most other entry boxes are specific, this box allows the user more freedom to enter data in their own words.

Implementing Forms

The script for a form is described in the following pages. The script is placed between <FORM> and </FORM> tags and the script can contain fields for entering information and normal text for headings, explanations and notes. All the rules on fonts and alignment apply within the form's script area in the same way as any other part of the HTML script.

The CGI script will be sent a number of items of information from a form and has to be able to distinguish between one item and the next. Therefore, every data entry field on the form has to be given its own name. The form is then submitted to the CGI script as a named item with the value given to it by the user. For example, if fields were called *'name'* and *'age'*, the values would be sent to the script as

        Name=Davy and age=21

These are referred to as *'name/value pairs'*.

Text entry options
The simplest entry method for a form is

        What is your Post Code ? <INPUT NAME="postcode">

The first part is the text that will appear on the screen.   The INPUT tag places a text entry box on the screen next to the text.   The developer gives the field a name (*'postcode'* in our example).   When the user types information into the box, it is associated with the *'postcode'* field for sending to the CGI script.

What is your Post Code ? [   ]

In the above example, the default entry box is far too long, since a Post Code only requires a maximum of eight characters, including the middle space.   The SIZE attribute can be added to specify the size of the text box, as in the following line of code:

```
What is your Post Code ? <INPUT NAME="postcode" SIZE=8>
```

This produces a smaller box but still allows the user to type in more than eight characters.   To limit the characters accepted in a box, the attribute MAXLENGTH can be used, as below:

```
What is your Post Code ? <INPUT NAME="postcode" SIZE=8 MAXLENGTH=8>
```

An initial content can be placed into a text box, using the VALUE tag, as in this example:

```
Address for delivery <INPUT NAME="deladdress"
       VALUE="Same as the Invoice Address">
```

Address for delivery [Same as the Invoice Address]

The screen display would look as in the illustration.

Where large sections of text input is expected from the user, the TEXTAREA tag is used.   It has ROWS and COLS attributes that define the size of the text box.   The results can be seen in the earlier *'Reader Survey'* illustration.   The tag's format is:

```
Any suggestions:<br>
<TEXTAREA name="comments" rows=5 cols=60></TEXTAREA>
```

The INPUT tag also supports a PASSWORD attribute, as in this example:

```
Enter your personal ID number <INPUT TYPE=password NAME="ID">
```

The text entered at the keyboard appears in the box as a row of asterisks, preventing anyone from looking over the user's shoulder to note the ID.   The data entered into the field is sent to the CGI script as the original text typed at the keyboard.

Multiple selections

The INPUT tag allows the user to enter text for sending to the CGI script.   The use of the TYPE attribute allows the user to select from pre-written options.

The form can be displayed with set of check boxes. This allows the user to select multiple options from a displayed list.

The following code was used to create the checkboxes in the earlier *'Reader Survey'* illustration:

```
Which of the following chapters do you use most?<br>
<INPUT TYPE="checkbox" NAME="audio"    VALUE="ON"> Audio    <br>
<INPUT TYPE="checkbox" NAME="video"    VALUE="ON"> Video    <br>
<INPUT TYPE="checkbox" NAME="graphics" VALUE="ON"> Graphics <br>
<INPUT TYPE="checkbox" NAME="design"   VALUE="ON"> Design   <br>
<INPUT TYPE="checkbox" NAME="websites" VALUE="ON"> Web Sites<p>
```

The INPUT tag is using a TYPE attribute.   If this attribute is not included in an INPUT tag it is assumed to be the same as entering 'TYPE="text"' (i.e. the input is assumed to be text).

The above code uses 'TYPE="checkbox"' and this and each field has a NAME and a VALUE that depends upon whether the box is checked.   In the example, VALUE="ON" is used, so checking the first box results in audio=ON being sent to the CGI script.   In fact, the default value that is given to a checked field is 'ON', but other values could be substituted.

If required, some of the boxes could be displayed checked by default.   This could be employed where users often choose these boxes from the list.   An example of use is:

```
Click any other facilities you require<br>
<INPUT TYPE="checkbox" NAME="catalogue"  CHECKED> Catalogue  <br>
<INPUT TYPE="checkbox" NAME="newsletter" CHECKED> Newsletter <br>
```

Radio Buttons

Radio buttons display a range of options to the user.   The user can only choose one option and so only one name/value pair is used. This means that all the radio buttons are given the same name.
The syntax for this code is:

```
How do you rate the book's contents?<br>
<INPUT TYPE="radio" NAME="content" VALUE="poor">    Poor
<INPUT TYPE="radio" NAME="content" VALUE="average"> Average
<INPUT TYPE="radio" NAME="content" VALUE="good">    Excellent
```

Again, the CHECKED attribute can be added, so that one option is initially selected.

Selecting from a list

Where a long set of options is to be chosen from, the screen may look cluttered with too many checkboxes or radio buttons. As an alternative, the SELECT tag allows a drop-down menu to be created, to save screen space.

The syntax is as shown in this example:

```
What course are you using the book for?<br>
<SELECT NAME="course" SIZE="1">
        <OPTION>  'A' Levels
        <OPTION>  C&G
        <OPTION>  HNC
        <OPTION>  HND
        <OPTION>  BSc
        <OPTION>  MSc
</SELECT>
```

The field has a single NAME and, when the user chooses from the menu, that particular entry after the OPTION attribute is associated with the NAME as the name/value pair for sending to the CGI script.

The MULTIPLE attribute allows the user to select more than one option from the list, but that results in several values being associated with the NAME and this should only be used where the CGI script supports this method.

The SIZE attribute specifies how many lines of options are seen when the page is first displayed. The Up and Down arrow at the edge of the box allow the user to browse through the options.

Submitting the Form

When the user has completed the entries on the form, it can be submitted to the server by clinking on a *'submit'* button. The basic syntax to produce this button is:

```
<INPUT TYPE="submit ">
```

This produces an on-screen button with the words *'Submit Query'* on it.

The text in the button can be changed by specifying a new value for it, as in the following example script code:

```
<INPUT TYPE="submit" VALUE="Click to send">
```

If the user wishes to clear the entries and start over before submitting the form, the line:

```
<INPUT TYPE="reset">
```

clears all existing data from the forms' fields.   The default text in this button is 'Reset' and this can also be altered by using the VALUE attribute, as in the example below:

```
<INPUT TYPE="reset" VALUE="Oops ! Clear the form">
```

The user sends the form to the server with the ACTION attribute of the FORM tag. This dictates what action will be taken when the submit button is pressed.   In the example below, the action is to send the form's data to the CGI script that is stored in the URL given in quotes.

```
<FORM ACTION="/cgi-bin/mailform" METHOD="POST">
```

The example line is for a form running with Demon. Demon stores a cgi script called *'mailform'*. This is Demon's own script and its purpose is to receive the input from the form's fields and send them as an e-mail to the web site owner.   The CGI script may well have another name with another ISP.

The 'ACTION' attribute points to the URL where the script is stored (in this case the cgi-bin folder of the server).

The URL address could equally have been entered in full as

```
http://demon.co.uk/cgi-bin/mailform
```

The METHOD attribute determines the manner in which data is sent to the URL pointed to by the ACTION attribute.   It can either have the value 'GET' or 'POST'.

If the GET attribute is used, the user entries are attached to the end of the CGI script's URL (a process known as *'URL encoding'*).

For the 'Reader Survey' example, the final URL might be:

```
http://demon.co.uk/cgi-bin/mailform?value=good&content=fair&audio=ON&video=ON&....
```

A question mark separates the script URL from the data and each field's name/value pair is separated by an ampersand. This operates more quickly than the processing of POST data, but the reliable length of a URL is only 255 characters.

The POST method is the preferred method as the data is sent separately and has no limit to its size.

The complete script for producing the web page form shown in the earlier *'Reader Survey'* example is:

```
<HTML>
<HEAD><TITLE>Survey Form</TITLE></HEAD>
<BODY BGCOLOR="cyan"><FONT FACE="ARIAL,HELVETICA" SIZE="5">
<center><B>Reader Survey<br></font>
<font size=4>Please fill in the questions and mail to us<br>
Your feedback will help us make the book even better!</B></center></FONT><P>

<FORM ACTION="/cgi-bin/mailform"  METHOD="POST">

<hr width=250 align=center><p><b>

Do you rate the book's price as<br>
<INPUT TYPE="radio" NAME="value" VALUE="poor">     Too expensive
<INPUT TYPE="radio" NAME="value" VALUE="average"> Just about right
<INPUT TYPE="radio" NAME="value" VALUE="good">     Good value for money<br>
<p>

How do you rate the book's contents?<br>
<INPUT TYPE="radio" NAME="content" VALUE="poor">     Poor
<INPUT TYPE="radio" NAME="content" VALUE="average">  Average
<INPUT TYPE="radio" NAME="content" VALUE="good">     Excellent
<p>

Which of the following chapters do you use most?<br>
<INPUT TYPE="checkbox" NAME="audio"    VALUE="ON"> Audio    <br>
<INPUT TYPE="checkbox" NAME="video"    VALUE="ON"> Video    <br>
<INPUT TYPE="checkbox" NAME="graphics" VALUE="ON"> Graphics <br>
<INPUT TYPE="checkbox" NAME="design"   VALUE="ON"> Design   <br>
<INPUT TYPE="checkbox" NAME="websites" VALUE="ON"> Web Sites<p>

What course are you using the book for?<br>
<SELECT NAME="course" SIZE="1">
   <OPTION>  'A' Levels
   <OPTION>  C&G
   <OPTION>  HNC
   <OPTION>  HND
   <OPTION>  BSc
   <OPTION>  MSc
</SELECT>p>


Any complaints, comments, suggestions?</b><br>
<TEXTAREA name="comments" rows=5 cols=60></TEXTAREA>
<p align=center>


<INPUT TYPE="submit" VALUE="Send to us">
<INPUT TYPE="reset"  VALUE="Oops ! Clear the form"></center><P>

</FORM>
</BODY>
</HTML>
```

Counters

The one thing that occupies the minds of most web site administrators is the success of the site. Commercial sites can measure their success in terms of sales, numbers added to mailing lists and so on. Sites promoting charities, hobbies, clubs, etc. may measure their success in terms of new members, the growth in the newsletter circulation, donations, etc.   Sites that provide information (e.g. news, weather, travel, TV schedules, etc.) are designed for one-way traffic and there is little or no information going from viewers to the web site. One measure that most sites pay great attention to is the *'hit rate'*.   At its simplest, this counts the number of times a web site has been accessed in a given period.

There is huge interest in viewing figures among the commercial portals and directory services, as increasing viewing figures results in increased advertising revenue.

The simplest counting system requires a small text file to be stored on the web site, often called *'count.txt'*. This is a simple ASCII text file that can be read by any word processor. For example, it may contain the contents "2753" and these are made up of four text characters. A counter CGI script sits on the ISP's site and is activated by a call to its URL. It reads the site's count file, converts it from text into an integer number, adds one to the number, converts it back into a text representation, and stores it back in the site. This piece of text can then be sent to the browser and the user can see a caption saying something like *"Total visitors since December 1999 : 2754"*. The number has to be stored as text so that it can be easily incorporated into the HTML page that is sent to the browser.

Most counter scripts compose the individual characters of the hit rate into graphics characters. In the example, the graphic image of the number two is followed by the graphic image of the number seven, followed by five's image and four's image. This is composited into a single image that is sent to the browser for display.

The web page that requests a hit counter update will be something like:

```
<img src="/cgi-bin/count>
```

This is a demon counter script. A script from Tripod is very similar, with <img src=/bin/counter>

The HTML line uses a 'display graphic' tag and this calls the CGI script URL to obtain the graphic. The web site developer can leave the line above as it is, and this results in the site's visitors seeing the hit count. If the count is only for the site administrator's use, the output can be hidden from the visitors' view. In the case of Demon's script, adding sh=F to the script sets the sh (show) attribute to F (FALSE) disables the screen display of the count.

```
<img src="/cgi-bin/count sh=F>
```

Sources of counters

If the ISP provides a counter script, this is the easiest and best option. It is easiest because it saves writing a CGI script for the job. It is also the best option, as using a third party's counter involves giving up some of the privacy of visitors to the third party.

If the ISP makes no provision for counters or the storage of user CGI scripts, the developer can use counters provided by third parties. These are 'free', in the sense that there is no charge for the service. These third parties often provide comprehensive information about site usage. The downside, of course, is that all the information that it has gathered on visitors to the site can also be used by the third party for targeted e-mail.

Examples of third party counters are

www.pagecount.com - this provides lots of usage statistics but demands a largish advert on the web page.

www.thecounter.com - this also provides lots of statistics, and has options for the web display (counter hits can be displayed with third party logo, logo on its own, or no display).

Counter accuracy

Image counters are unreliable. They can be used as a general indication of the site's usage but have the limitation listed below:

- If a viewer sets the browser not to display graphic images, the HTML line containing the IMG tag is ignored and the CGI script is not called. A viewer has visited the site, but the counter has not been incremented.

- If a viewer hits the *'refresh'* or *'reload'* option on their browser, the counter script is called again and a an extra visitor may be recorded on some counters.

- The viewer may get the graphic image from cache, due to a previous visit. The counter script is not called and the visit is not recorded.

- A viewer may enter directly into a lower part of the web site's structure. This may be the result of a link from another site, or the result of a search. If the counter script is on the main page, the visit is not recorded.

- If the web site has a single counter script, sitting in the main page, the script may be called every time the viewer returns to the main page.

- If the same counter call code is placed on every page of the web site, then every page that is accessed counts as a hit. This gives a figure for the total usage of the site, but does not indicate how the site was used. For example, a hit count of 1000 may be 1000 people accessing the main page or just 20 people each accessing 50 pages.

The approaches for overcoming these problems include:
- Use an ISP that allows user-defined CGI scripts.
- Use an ISP that provides a counter CGI script (or even full viewer statistics).
- Use a counter script that maintains a list of recent URLs that accessed the counter and ignores refreshes and revisits.
- Use a third party counter if extra statistics are required (e.g. usage by day/hour, how many resulted from search engines).
- Use a third party supplier who allows multiple counters to be installed. This provides details on hits on individual web pages (e.g. how many viewers read the help page or the glossary page).
- With a single counter, place it on a 'splash page'. This is an opening introductory page that links to the main page. The site provides no links back to the splash page. This means that the counter is only incremented when the visitor first accesses the site.
- With a single counter, place in the frameset page. Again, a visitor only accesses this page once, with all subsequent navigation changes taking place within the frame areas.

Where the counter contents are hidden from visitors, there are two ways that the web site administrator can access the contents of the *'count.txt'* file to view the hit rate:
- Use FTP to access the ISP, and view the file.
- Create a page on the web site that displays the counter contents. The page has no links from anywhere on the site and the address is only known to the administrator. To prevent the administrator incrementing the counter every time he/she looks at the page, the script can often have an added attribute to prevent unwanted incrementing of the hit counter.
  For example, in Demon the script is changed to:
  <img src="/cgi-bin/count incr=F>

Using Javascript

What it is
JavaScript is a simple programming language that has many uses and has become popular on web sites. By learning this language, web designers make web sites more useful and decorative.

Netscape Communications invented JavaScript under the name *'Livescript',* along with Netscape 2. JavaScript became popular and a 1.1 version was released with Netscape 3.   Microsoft released a similar version of JavaScript, referred to as JScript, for Internet Explorer.

JavaScript is heavily influenced by other languages (C, Perl) but is not the same as Java.   Java is a more powerful language that requires a compiler. JavaScript is used exclusively on the web, whereas Java is used to create powerful software programs.

What it is used for
Using JavaScript, it is possible to:
- Customise HTML documents on the fly (e.g. adding current date and time).
- Write event handlers for elements on a page (e.g. rollover buttons).
- Validate data at the client side (e.g. checking that a form is only submitted when all fields have been entered).
- Perform other client-side computations (e.g. passwords, calculators).
- Detect what browser is being used and take the viewer to pages designed to work with that browser.

How it works
The JavaScript code is embedded within the HTML file and is interpreted by the client browser.
The only necessary tools are a web browser (from Netscape 3+, IE 3+ onwards) and a plain editor.

Pre-defined functions
The JavaScript interpreter that is built into Netscape, Explorer, etc, understand a range of pre-written functions.

The following example uses the onMouseOver and onMouseOut functions that are built in to the browser's JavaScript interpreter. It needs two graphics files and gives the familiar *'rollover'* effect. The screen will normally display the image called *'view2.gif'*.   When the mouse hovers over the image, the onMouseOver function changes the graphic to display *'view1.gif'*.   When the mouse is moved away from the graphic, the onMouseOut function changes the graphic back to *'view2.gif'*.

The code for the script is:

```
<HTML>
<HEAD>Usual header text in here</HEAD>
<BODY>
        <A HREF="index.htm" onMouseOver="s.src='view1.gif'" onMouseOut="s.src='view2.gif'">
        <IMG SRC="view2.gif" name="s"> </a>
</BODY>
</HTML>
```

User-created functions

There is a long list of commands that are available in the JavaScript language and they can be used to create a script that is tailored to the site's needs. Also, the various pre-written functions can be combined to write a more complex program.

The JavaScript commands are placed within <SCRIPT> and </SCRIPT> tags as shown below:

```
<HTML>
<SCRIPT LANGUAGE="JavaScript">
JavaScript goes in here
</SCRIPT><HEAD>Usual header text in here</HEAD>
<BODY>
Usual HTML can go here
Usual HTML can go here
</BODY>
</HTML>
```

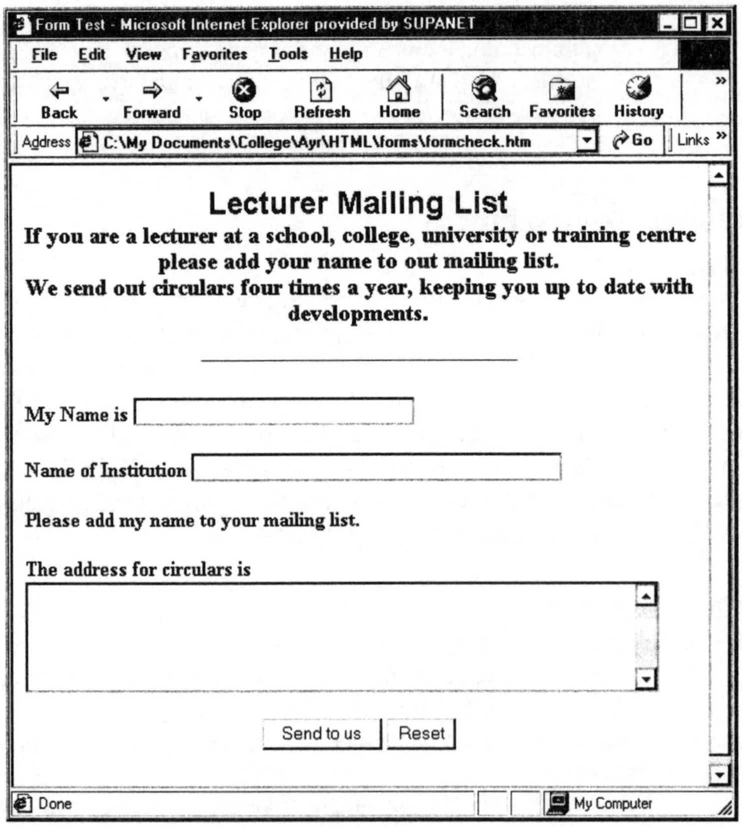

The example shown is for a simple three field form that uses JavaScript to ensure that the form is not submitted if any of the fields have been left empty.

If a field is left empty, the user is given an error message indicating the problem.

When the three fields are given contents, clicking the *'submit'* button posts the form.

The script for creating this web page is shown on the following page. All material relating to the JavaScript action is printed in bold.

The three entry boxes are created in the manner discussed previously.

The extra features are:

The form has to be given a name. This is not required with a form that is purely HTML-based, but is required by JavaScript.

The form is named during the FORM declaration as shown in this line of code:

```
<FORM NAME="maillist" ACTION="/cgi-bin/mailform" METHOD="POST"  onSubmit="return fieldcheck();">
```

In the example, the form has been given the name *'maillist'*. The other addition is the last few words in the line. The onSubmit command is activated when the submit button is pressed. It calls a function called *'fieldcheck'* that is written in JavaScript. While *'onSubmit'* is a command taken from the JavaScript language, *'fieldcheck'* is not a pre-written function. This means that it can be given any name (except those already used by the Javascript language).

The function is intended to return a value that is either *'true'* or *'false'*. It should return the value *'true'* if all the fields are found to contain some content; otherwise it should return the value *'false'*. The form will only be posted when the onSubmit call gets a return that is *'true'*.

The function used in the example appears at the top of the HTML page and its lines of code are wrapped in the <SCRIPT LANGUAGE="JavaScript"> and </SCRIPT> tags. Every function has to have a name so that it can be called from within the HTML script (*'fieldcheck'* in the example.

The function's code lines are surrounded by braces, as shown below.

```
{                                              This set of code takes the form:
  if (document.maillist.name.value.length < 1)    If something is found to be the case
    {alert ("The name box must have an entry.");     tell the user
     return false;}                                  and send the value 'false' back
  return true;                                   Otherwise send the value 'true' back
}
```

The *'something'* that is being tested in the example is how many characters are found to be in the form's *'name'* field.

The document that is being tested is the *'name'* field used in the *'maillist'* form. One of the values that this field possesses is the length of the text contained in it. If this length is less than one character (i.e. the field is empty) then the results of the test trigger the error message and the return of the *'false'* value. If the field contains characters, its length is greater than zero, no error message is given and the *'true'* value is returned. This results in the form being posted.

The complete script for displaying the *'Lecturer Mailing List'* page, complete with all field validations is:

```html
<HTML>
<SCRIPT LANGUAGE=" JavaScript">
function fieldcheck()
{
  if (document.maillist.name.value.length < 1)
    {alert ("The name box must have an entry.");
     return false;}
  if (document.maillist.institution.value.length<1)
    {alert("The name of the institution must be entered.");
     return false;}
  if (document.maillist.address.value.length <1)
    {alert("The address must be entered.");
     return false;}
  return true;
}
</SCRIPT>

<HEAD><TITLE>Form Test</TITLE></HEAD>
<BODY BGCOLOR="white"><FONT FACE="ARIAL,HELVETICA" SIZE="5">
<center><B>Lecturer Mailing List<br></font>
<font size=4>If you are a lecturer at a school, college, university or training centre<br>
please add your name to out mailing list.<br>
We send out circulars four times a year, keeping you up to date with developments</B></center></FONT><P>

<FORM NAME="maillist" ACTION="/cgi-bin/mailform" METHOD="POST" onSubmit="return fieldcheck();">
<hr width=250 align=center><p><b>
My Name is            <INPUT TYPE=text NAME=name SIZE=30><p>
Name of Institution    <INPUT TYPE=text NAME=institution SIZE=40><p>
Please add my name to your mailing list.<p>
The address for circulars is<br>
              <TEXTAREA name="address" rows=5 cols=60></TEXTAREA><br>
<p align=center>

<INPUT TYPE="submit" VALUE="Send to us">
<INPUT TYPE="reset" ></center><P>

</FORM>
</BODY>
</HTML>
```

NOTE:

Some older browsers were written before the advent of JavaScript and will not understand what to do with the lines of script. If the lines of script are enclosed with the usual comment tags, as shown below, they are ignored by older browsers while still working with JavaScript-aware browsers.

```html
<SCRIPT LANGUAGE="JavaScript">
<!--
JavaScript goes in here
//-->
</SCRIPT>
```

Dynamic HTML

When *'dynamic HTML'* is spelled with a lower-case *'d'*, it refers to the contents of a page being dependent upon the circumstances of the user who wishes to view the page, e.g. through use of CGI scripts. DHTML or *'Dynamic HTML'* with an upper-case *'D'* refers to the coming together of HTML, CSS and JavaScript (or VBScript), plus some add-on browser properties and Java applets. It provides these main functions:

- The absolute positioning of every object on the web page, using x and y co-ordinates. This can be achieved through CSS, as explained later. Furthermore, the concept of 'z-indexing' is introduced: this adds a 'depth' to the web page, so that objects can be placed on top of other objects, perhaps dynamically changing their z co-ordinate at a later stage to make them closer to the front.

- Data binding, which is a method whereby part of the data within an HTML page is downloaded directly from a web database, rather than being part of the original HTML source. Controls on the web page can allow browsing of different records in the database, without changing the HTML content. This is not supported by Netscape's DHTML model. Microsoft's model uses Data Source Objects (DSOs), which contain specifications on how to retrieve and use each data object.

- Data awareness, the counterpart to data binding, which allows an HTML object to be aware of the database on which the data lies, enabling it to be downloaded or even uploaded. Again, only Microsoft's DHTML model handles data awareness.

- The alteration of page content <u>after</u> the page is downloaded. This is carried out through the scripting language, and Microsoft's ActiveX controls give even greater flexibility at lower bandwidth to dynamic content.

This is a problem area since the inherent difficulty is worsened by the fact that Netscape and Explorer use different techniques.

The Dynamic Object Model

At the heart of DHTML is the Dynamic Object Model (DOM). In this model, every item on a web page is treated as an object, be it an image, a paragraph, an anchor or any such entity. The model is hierarchical, starting with the *'window'* object representing the browser window. This object has several children, such as the *'location'* object which represents the current URL, and the *'document'* object which represents the HTML document currently residing in memory. Each of these objects can then have further children.

Some objects are, in fact, *'collections'*. These are groups of objects of the same type, for example the *'document'* object contains a *'links'* collection (among other things) that refers to all link objects in the document.

Each object can have *'properties'*, which often correspond to HTML attributes and/or CSS properties, which define how the object behaves. Objects also have *'methods'*, which are ways for the web page designer to make use of the code driving the object.

It is this object model that is used by the scripting language to create the dynamic aspect of DHTML. For example a page could be written so that hovering the mouse over one of several text objects will change the contents of an image object elsewhere on the page to display an image appropriate to the item that the mouse is hovering over.

This is handled through *'events'* that are associated with objects and scripting code. When an event (such as hovering the mouse over the object or clicking on it), happens to an object, the browser will check to see if there is code written for such an occasion, and carries out the code. Microsoft's version of DHTML also supports *'bubbling'*, which is where an event which is not handled by one object 'bubbles up' to the parent object within which it is contained.

XML

The eXtensible Markup Language is based on the extremely flexible Standard Generalised Markup Language (SGML), like HTML and other less well known mark-up languages. Where HTML uses a standard set of tags, however, XML is capable of creating user-defined tags. Furthermore, rather than being a document in itself, an XML file is more like a document description, laying out how the final document is made up.

At its most basic, an XML file consists of a DTD (Document Template Definition) and the actual document. The DTD may be included inside the XML file or can be a separate file, allowing for multiple documents fitting the same document template for greater standardisation.

The DTD describes a *'document'*, called a DOCTYPE. This document consists of one or more *'ELEMENTs'*, and in turn each element may contain attribute lists, or *'ATTLISTs'*. There are a few other items that can be included in a DOCTYPE definition, and all of these are described using the standard markup declaration format, which encloses declarations within '<!' and '>' delimiters. The DOCTYPE describes the basic parts that make up the final document in this way, and the content of each document uses tags that match the ELEMENTs of the DTD.

XML also allows extended linking capabilities through the XLL language. For example HTML gives designers the ability to link to a portion of another HTML page by using the '#' symbol. XML uses the '|' symbol for a similar function, but this indicates that the rest of the document outwith the specified region is not to be downloaded.

XML also has its own stylesheet language, called XSL (XML Stylesheet Language). Like CSS, it can be used on individual tags or applied to an entire document by using an external file. XSL can perform similar functions to CSS, such as text formatting, positioning etc. Of course, the language syntax is different.

While XML has more powerful facilities than HTML built in, it unfortunately has far less browser support. As a result, one of the most reliable methods of using XML is to use it on the server only, and use XSL to transform XML document definitions and server-side data into HTML documents to be sent to the client. In this way the browser need never know that XML was ever involved in generating the web page.

Active Server Pages

Another method of making dynamic web pages is Microsoft's ASP (Active Server Pages) extension for their servers based on their IIS (Internet Information Server) software, sitting on an NT server or Windows Personal Web Server. Of course, this would mean that ASP facilities could only be used on IIS servers and these are a small minority on the web (most servers use the free *'Apache'* web server software). Third party providers supply extensions that attempt to make ASP compatible with other operating systems.

An ASP file is written in plain ASCII text and is saved with the extension .asp (e.g. *'testing.asp'*). The ASP file is essentially a normal HTML file with additional tags used to perform scripting. ASP tags begin with <% and end with %>, and are there only to be interpreted by the server. The end user never sees these tags even if he or she views the page source, assuming of course that the page code is working properly.

Those brackets are placed around ASPScript code, which is very similar to VBScript. HTML is parsed sequentially, and so is ASP script, so placement of script code within the HTML document can be very important.

ASP scripting has several built-in objects that it can access. The 'Request' object gives the ASP script details of the user's request. This includes much more than just any form data that might be used. From this object the ASP script can garner information about cookies, the web server, and the browser that is being used for that request.

ASP scripts normally use the 'Response' object to create objects in the HTML output, giving options to build up the page in a buffer before sending, or redirect the user to another page. The 'Application' object allows the script to access application-specific items, such as using application memory space to store variables from one instance of a script to another, while the 'Session' object is used to maintain information about a persistent connection. This is when user information needs to be retained, and if the user does not access the server within a specified timeout period the session will be removed.

Finally, the 'Server' object provides additional functionality by allowing ASP scripts to access COM objects stored on the server. COM objects can thus be used to carry out the majority of the processing, leaving the ASP scripts relatively easy to understand and maintain while providing a wider range of functions.

Cascading Style sheets

While HTML is a powerful tool, its major drawback from the start has been its lack of control. It is impossible to set a standard style for the various types of content in all web pages within a site, under standard HTML. Approaches involving lengthy, complicated scripts tend to work only under certain circumstances, and are difficult to maintain. Some HTML creation software has capabilities built in for version management, but this may involve extra expense, and is really a workaround rather than a solution.

An alternative is to use Cascading Style Sheets (CSS). This allows page styles (including fonts, background images, borders and so on) to be specified for various classes of objects on the web pages. These definitions cascade down through the various types – for example a font that falls into two categories as described in the Style Sheet will have the settings from both, with the type that is defined last in the Style Sheet having precedence wherever there may be a conflict in style.

CSS is supported to varying degrees by Internet Explorer 3 and onwards, as well as Netscape Navigator 4 onwards. Browsers that do not support CSS will ignore the style part and continue to read the rest of the file, meaning that the HTML page will still display (albeit somewhat less attractively) on an old machine.

Inline Styles

The simplest way to use CSS is simply as an attribute of any text tag. For example the <H1> tag, the <P> tag, the <A> tag and so on can all use style definitions built in to the tag. This can give some greater control, and is useful to over-ride previously defined styles, but misses out on a lot of the power of CSS if it is the sole method used. A simple inline style might look as follows:

```
<P STYLE="color: red">Red text</P>
```

Style Blocks

One way of using style sheets is to specify them inside the web page. In this method, the style sheet is placed inside the HEAD portion of the page source. The Style Sheet is specified within a <STYLE> tag.

Unfortunately, older browsers do not recognise the <STYLE> tag, and so will instead display the source text within that tag instead of using it as a style. Therefore, in order to preserve backwards compatibility, the contents of the <STYLE> tag should also be within an HTML comment block, so that older browsers are told to ignore it if they cannot handle CSS. The comment block begins with '<!==' and ends with '-->', and so the general structure of such an HTML file is as shown.

```
<HTML>
<HEAD>
<TITLE>Page title</TITLE>
<STYLE>
<!--
Style Sheet definitions
-->
</STYLE>
</HEAD>
<BODY>Page text</BODY>
</HTML>
```

Linked Style Sheets

However, style sheets can be even more useful when they are used outwith a web page's source. If a CSS sheet is stored separately, then each page on an entire site can use a single stylesheet. In this way, the style of all web pages will be the same, presenting a more consistent web site. Also, it means that changes of style require just one file to be updated rather than every single web page. Finally, having a linked style sheet can slightly reduce the size of individual HTML files.

An HTML file can link to a style sheet using the <LINK> tag, as shown. The HREF attribute is a URL to find the linked file, just like in an anchor, while the REL attribute indicates the relation of the link – in this case, a style sheet. The TYPE attribute indicates the type of style sheet; there are a very few types of style sheets other than CSS, and they are not widely supported.

In this case, the browser will expect to see a CSS style sheet called "style.css" in the same directory as the HTML page. This external style sheet is an ASCII text file containing style

```
<HTML>
<HEAD>
<TITLE>Page title</TITLE>
<LINK HREF="style.css" REL=stylesheet
TYPE=text/css>
</HEAD>
<BODY>Page text</BODY>
</HTML>
```

definitions exactly as they would appear within the <STYLE> tags if they were inside the web page itself (see below).

Alternatively, external style sheets can be imported into style blocks within a web page. This is done within the style block, using the '@import' statement, followed by the URL. To do this, though, the browser needs to know what kind of Stylesheet it is, so the <STYLE> tag itself should contain this information as an attribute.

The import statement could look as follows:

```
<STYLE TYPE="text/css">
@import URL("style.css");
</STYLE>
```

Note: for both methods of using external style sheets, it is possible to use multiple links or imports, as well as style blocks, and even inline styles – this is the cascading aspect of CSS. If a type selector is defined multiple times, then the most recent values for any properties that are specified over-ride previous values. However, any properties that are left undefined in more recent style definitions retain their previous values.

For example, it is possible to have an external style sheet, an internal style block, and an inline style, all with properties applying to the <P> tag. The external sheet might make it indented and define a font face and font size, while the style block specifies an indent and a colour. The inline style might make the font bold and change the font face. In such a case, the resulting text will have the style block's indentation and colour, the inline style's bold weight and font face, and the style sheet's font size.

Fonts in Style Sheets

While <FONT> tags specify a single font that must be used if available, CSS allows the web page designer to suggest a group of fonts, and allow the browser to choose which of those fonts to use, or even override them entirely.

In addition, CSS stylesheets provide greater control over font types. This is achieved by having a number of *'selectors'* defined in the stylesheet, followed in braces by the style that should be applied to the selector when used within the web page. The most common kind of selector is a *'type selector'*, which simply applies a style to all text of a given type. For example, to embolden all text that is specified as being of Header 1 (H1) type, the following style definition might be used:

```
<STYLE>
H1 {font-weight: bold}
</STYLE>
```

Any text within an <H1> tag will now be bold. The details within the braces (the '{' and '}' symbols) are the *'properties'* of the selector. If the selector is to have multiple properties defined then these should be separated by a semi-colon (;). Furthermore, note that each definition is separated from its value by a colon (:). Some browsers will allow web pages to use an equal sign (=) instead of a colon, but this is contrary to the CSS standard and is not supported by all browsers. Consequently, it is recommended that designers use a colon.

Additionally, a property set can be applied to more than one type selector by separating the type selectors with a comma. For example if you wish H1, H2 and H3 text to be both bold and italicised, the following style definition will do that:

```
<STYLE>
H1, H2, H3 {font-weight: bold; font-style: italic}
</STYLE>
```

Some properties are able to specify several sub-properties within them. For example, the 'font' property can be used to contain the font-style, font-size, and font-family properties, in that order. If the properties are accessed individually then they can be put in any order. A font definition can thus be done in one of two ways:

```
<STYLE>
P {font-size: 50px; font-family: sans-serif; font-style: italic}
P {font: italic 50px sans-serif}
</STYLE>
```

For type selectors that apply to text, there are a number of possible properties. The most common and widely-supported options are as follows:

Property	Usage
font-family	Defines the set of fonts that may be used. They should be separated by a comma, and the browser is allowed to use any font from the list that it has available. This includes Windows fonts, but there are also a number of generic fonts that indicate only a general type, most notably 'serif', 'sans-serif' and 'monospace'.
font-style	The style of font to use. eg: 'normal', 'italic' or 'oblique'.
font-size	The size of the font. As well as a size value, it can be specified as 'small', 'medium', 'large' and other such values.
font-weight	The weight (boldness) of the font. For example 'lighter', 'normal' or 'bold'.

color	The colour of the font. Like most HTML colour attributes, it can be defined as a string-value (eg 'red') or as RGB values from zero to 255, such as 'rgb(255,0,0)'
text-decoration	This property can specify 'underline', 'overline', or 'line-through' for text decoration.
text-indent	Indents are very hard to handle in basic HTML; this style sheet attribute makes it much easier.
text-align	Specifies the alignment of the text, using the keywords 'left', 'right', 'center' or 'justify'.
letter-spacing	The spacing between each letter in the text. Spacing can be set to zero or even negative values.

Where a size is specified (such as in font-size, or text-indent for example), the default measurement is in pixels but it can also be specified in points (eg. '20pt'), inches (eg. '1in'), millimetres (eg. '15mm') and other measurements.

Other options in Style Sheets

Style sheets are not all about fonts and text. Web site style includes background images, tables, borders and so on. The following properties can apply to almost any object in a CSS sheet.

Property	Usage
border	This property places a border round an object. The designer can specify the size of the border, and the border style and colour. For example {border: 3px double RGB(0,0,255)} would produce a 3 pixel blue double border. Other keywords include 'solid', 'dotted', and 'dashed'. Individual edges of the border can be specified using the properties 'border-top', 'border-left', 'border-bottom' and 'border-right'.
position	By choosing 'absolute' for the position, the exact position of the object within the window can be specified via the 'top' and 'left' properties. The 'relative' option for position specifies a location relative to the current location on the web page.
width, height	These are separate properties, and they can be used to specify how much space (in percentage or absolute terms) in the window they should occupy.
float	This property can accept the values 'none', 'left' or 'right', specifying whether an object is to be placed 'floating' on the left or right side of the window with text wrapping around.

Furthermore, there are some useful properties that can only be applied to certain HTML tags. For example:

Property	Usage
background	This property applies to the BODY tag. It allows the designer to specify a colour, an image, whether the image is to repeat if it does not fill the window, whether it should scroll along with the page or stay fixed behind the page contents, and where the image should be positioned.
list-style	For the various types of lists, this property can set the style of bullet, images to be used as bullets, and the positioning of bullets.

The above lists are far from exhaustive, but the designer should be wary that CSS compatibility is sketchy at the best of times. While major properties such as font-styles and colour are relatively safe, the more in-depth CSS is used the more the web page will need to be tested on other browser platforms to ensure readability.

Both *'background'* and *'list-style'* properties are made up of other properties, in the same way as the *'font'* property discussed earlier. A style sheet that makes use of these properties might contain the following definitions:

```
BODY {background: url(santa.jpg) no-repeat top right}
LI {list-style: url(bullet.gif) inside}
```

Class Selectors

The type selector can be a powerful tool for ensuring consistency in a web site. However, CSS also provides greater flexibility than standard HTML, by allowing *'class selectors'*. Like type selectors, these are used to cascade style properties down onto objects shown in the browser window. However, while types apply to all instances of an object type, classes are more like sub-types that can be chosen within the body text. Each class is attached to a type, by placing a period between the type and the class. If no type is specified, then the class is not associated with any single tag, and can be used with whichever tags are desired.

For example, the style sheet in the page shown defines the 'sans' class of <P> tagged text as being displayed in sans serif font, and the 'big' class as being a generic class with adjusted font size. Note that in order to use two classes with one object, the classes must be enclosed in quotes, which are not necessary when only a single class is needed. Since the link is an <A> tag, it may not use the 'P.sans' class, but can use the generic '.big' class.

```
<HTML>
<HEAD>
<TITLE>Page title</TITLE>
<STYLE>
P.sans {font-family: sans-serif}
.big {font-size: 25px}
</STYLE>
</HEAD>
<BODY>
<P CLASS="big sans">This text is 25 pixel high Sans Serif</P>
<P CLASS=big>This text is 25 pixel high default font</P>
<P CLASS=sans>This text is default size sans serif</P>
<A HREF="link.htm" CLASS=big> This is a link which has been made 25 pixels high.</A>
</BODY>
</HTML>
```

Further CSS functions

In addition to type selectors and class selectors, there are a few other selectors. The ID selector is indicated in the style sheet by its preface of a '#' character. ID selectors should be unique, so using an ID selector with more than one object in any given web page is not recommended. There are more forms of selectors but they are rarely used.

Furthermore, CSS can use 'pseudo-elements' and 'pseudo-classes'. Currently, the only pseudo-elements that are defined apply to the <A> tag, and the only pseudo-classes defined apply to text classes.

The pseudo-elements are 'link', 'active' and 'visited'. Since they apply only to anchors, they allow an anchor to apply different styles depending on whether the link within is inactive, active, or has been previously visited. This includes changing colour, font size etc.

Similarly, the pseudo-classes are 'first-letter' and 'first-line'. As the name suggests, these classes can be used to alter only the style of the first letter and first line of the text respectively.

Image maps

An image can be turned into a link simply by putting it within an anchor tag. However, if it is a complex image representing multiple items, the designer may wish to link to more than one URL with a single image. If the graphical areas to be used as links are all rectangular, then it is possible to divide the image up into several boxes (usually placed in the cells of a frame), some or all of which will point to different URLs. However, this is a fussy process, and it is easy to produce a result that does not look as good on some browsers as it does on others. Furthermore, it is impossible to faithfully reproduce an area that is not rectangular as an area to be used as a link.

With an image map, the image is not cut up into chunks in this way; rather, it is a single image, and where the user's mouse is inside the image when he/she clicks the button determines which link to use. For example an image map showing demographic regions of the UK could link to a page of population figures for each region.

There are two methods of implementing image maps: server-side image maps and client-side image maps. Both of these use geometric shapes to define areas on the image map. Each geometric area corresponds to a portion of the image displayed, and mathematical routines can work out from the mouse x and y co-ordinates which region the pointer lies over when the mouse button is clicked.

The table shows the considerations when choosing between client-side and server-side image maps.

Client-side image map	Server-side image map
No special map script is required on the server.	The server needs to have scripting software to handle the mapping service.
When the mouse hovers over a region in the image, the appropriate link is displayed.	Wherever the mouse is in the image, only the x and y co-ordinates are displayed.
Area processing is carried out by the browser, instantly deciding on the URL to download.	Area processing is carried out by the server, resulting in delays.
Only implemented on newer browsers.	Implemented on most browsers.
For very complex maps, can significantly increase the HTML file size and thus download time.	The map is stored on the server, and so does not need to be downloaded at all.

Although both client-side and server-side image maps have advantages and disadvantages, to most private users client-side mapping may be the only option as they are unlikely to have the rights to install mapping software on their web server.

Creating an image map

The steps in creating an image map can be broken down as follows:

- If the image map is to be a server-side image, check that the server is capable of handling image maps and which standard it uses. If it does not handle image maps then additional CGI software will need to be installed to do so.

- Create a suitable image. Some images, complex digitised pictures in particular, do not lend themselves easily to geometric image mapping with its distinct areas. Suitable material for image maps might include: demographic maps, computer-generated art, or a photo-retouched image of a car engine for a tutorial on how to fix cars.

- Generate the image map. While this can be done by hand, it is unlikely that any desired image map will be simplistic enough for this to be feasible. There are a number of software packages available, such as Macromedia's Fireworks, which can be used as an interface to generate image maps.

- Create the HTML page. The image tag requires a special attribute in order to turn the image into an image map. If it is a client-side image map then the image map itself must either be included in a tag in the HTML or linked to as an exterior file.

Client-side image maps

A client-side image map consists of two parts: the image, and the map. The image is just a normal <IMG> tag, pointing at a URL to download an image from. However, it also contains the USEMAP attribute, which points to a map containing the areas and URLs to link to. This map can be an external file, or it can be within the HTML file. If it is a map defined within the same HTML page, then it can be referenced by a '#' character, followed by the name defined within the appropriate map definition.

The <MAP> tag itself has a NAME attribute that defines the name as referred to by the image tag. Between the <MAP> and the </MAP>, lie the area definitions. These are <AREA> tags, which has several attributes, as follows:

ALT	As with the ALT tag in a normal image, this tells the browser what to display if it is incapable of displaying graphics or the graphics have been turned off.
SHAPE	This attribute can be either 'RECT' for rectangles, 'POLY' for irregular polygons, or 'CIRCLE' for circles.
COORDS	These are the co-ordinates that define the dimensions of the shape. They are relative to the top left corner of the image.
HREF	Just as the HREF in an anchor tag points to a URL to use when the content within is clicked upon, the same attribute in an area tag defines a URL to use when the user clicks within the area defined in that tag.

The most important part is the SHAPE attribute, because it defines how the shape is represented on the image map. For example, a 'RECT' shape has two pairs of co-ordinates, corresponding to the two diagonally opposite corners of the rectangle. The 'CIRCLE' shape has three co-ordinates, defining the x and y co-ordinates of the centre of the circle and then the radius of the circle. Finally, the 'POLY' shape can have any number of co-ordinate pairs, each representing a point along the polygon. The polygon is always a filled shape, so the last point is automatically joined to the first point.

The following example shows a simple web page using a very basic image map. Note that the 'default' shape is listed last: areas defined first take precedence over areas defined later when it comes to capturing the mouse x and y co-ordinates and converting them into a URL. In this way the designer can ensure that every point on the image map will result in a URL of some kind.

```
<HTML>
<BODY>
<IMG SRC="image.gif" USEMAP="#imagemap">

<MAP NAME="imagemap">
<AREA SHAPE="CIRCLE" COORDS="113,115,81" HREF="circle.htm" ALT="This is the circle">
<AREA SHAPE="POLY" COORDS="305,45,399,193,214,193" HREF="triangle.htm" ALT="This is the triangle">
<AREA SHAPE="RECT" COORDS="431,44,612,191" HREF="rect.htm" ALT="This is the rectangle">
<AREA SHAPE="RECT" COORDS="0,0,700,200" HREF="default.htm" ALT="This is the region outside th
shapes">
</MAP>

</BODY>
</HTML>
```

Server-side image maps

An image map on a server is usually a file with a .map extension, which is a text file containing the same types of geometric instructions on which areas should link to which URLs. However, the syntax is different when compared with client-side image maps, and indeed different server systems have different syntaxes. What's more, a complex CGI script is needed on the web server to handle the image map processing, although in many cases this script comes with the web server software. However, the web page itself is much simpler; the image map is simply an <IMG> object embedded in a normal anchor tag. The anchor points to the CGI script that handles the mapping, while the image tag only needs to add an ISMAP attribute.

So, the image map portion of the web page might look as follows:

```
<A HREF="www.website.com/cgi-bin/imagemap/maps/uk-demo.map">
<IMG SRC="ukmap.gif" ISMAP>
</A>
```

Meanwhile, the map file on the server will look similar to a map definition within a client-side <MAP> tag. For example, in the NCSA image map standard, the options included are *'circle'*, *'poly'*, *'rect'*, *'point'* and *'default'*. However, the syntax of that standard means that the .map file for the previous example would look as follows:

```
default default.htm
circle circle.htm 113,115,81
poly triangle.htm 305,45,399,193,214,193
rect rect.htm 431,44,612,191
```

Animated GIFs

While images can brighten up a web page when properly used, animated images can bring even more interest to a page. However, they should be used sparingly, as they can detract from the actual content of the page. They are best used on 'splash' pages, or on the first page displayed. If animated images are overused on a web site, the viewer will likely become irritated by the excessive motion, as well as by increased download times.

GIF89a is the format used for virtually all animations embedded within web pages, because most browsers support this format. Animation Shop 2, which comes with Paint Shop Pro 6, is an application that can be used to create GIF89a animations. It is similar to other animated GIF software, such as Microsoft GIF animator or the GIF construction set.

Animation with GIF98a

GIF animations consist of a set of graphic images (or *'frames'*), which can be created with any drawing or painting package. Each successive frame is slightly different from the previous frame, and the images are displayed in succession to give the illusion of movement.

The GIF89a format contains a number of optimisation options that can be used to reduce the size of animations created. For example, if little changes from one frame to the next, the second frame can make extensive use of transparency, and browsers will understand that to mean that the transparent areas do not change in that frame. This saves having to store the contents of the unchanged area in each frame.

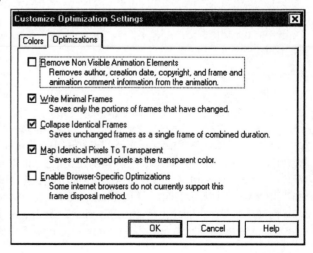

There are other similar options, and in Animation Shop these can be customised when saving the animation, by clicking *'Customize'* after giving a filename. The Customize Optimisations dialog box appears, and the *'Optimizations'* tab contains the options shown in the illustration.

In addition to this, animated GIFs often save a little space by requiring only one CLUT table for their palette. When using all of these optimisations a GIF89a can be surprisingly compact. The animation created below consists of eight frames each of approximately 1.6kB each, but the resulting animation is under 5kB.

Using Animation Shop

Animation Shop provides an *'Animation wizard'* that allows the user to import a string of existing images into animation frames, and a *'Banner wizard'* to create typical banner animations out of text supplied by the user. Animations can also be created from scratch, using some very simple built-in image editing tools. Fortunately, Animation Shop is linked to Paint Shop Pro, so images can be exported and edited using that package's superior tools, and the animation can be automatically updated without the need to constantly save and load images.

Most simple web animations consist of simple low-colour images generated using computer graphics packages, and/or some simple text, perhaps moving or blinking. However, it is entirely possible to create animations from photographic quality images, or even a series of stills taken from a full video clip. When dealing with these more detailed images, though, it should be remembered that GIF compression generally results in both a lower number of colours (256 colours instead of up to 16 million colours) and a worse compression ratio than a series of JPEG images. Also, editing photographic images is usually a longer and more difficult process than creating a simple animation from scratch, although the results may look better.

Creating a simple GIF animation

In this example, an animation is to be created, which shows a shooting star crossing the night sky over a

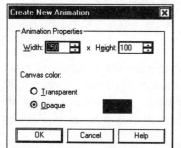

city skyline. The initial image created was the basic skyline, with the moon appearing in the corner. The shooting star is to be added later, in order that it does not obscure parts of the image (requiring them to be re-created later).

In Animation Shop, clicking the *'File'* menu and selecting the *'New'* option, displays the dialog box shown in the illustration. Since this image is to be a landscape, it should be wider than it is tall. A width of 250 pixels and a height of 100 pixels are appropriate. An opaque background is suited to this type of animation, as we do not want any interference from background images.

Among the basic painting tools provided in Animation Shop are:

- Paintbrush, which is useful for irregular shapes such as a shooting star. (see later)
- Shape, which can draw outlined or filled shapes such as a circle for the moon.
- Line, which can be used repeatedly in order to create irregular but straight objects, e.g. The skyline.
- Fill, which can then fill in the shape created by the lines with any chosen colour.

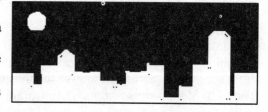

It may be useful to zoom in, by clicking on the magnifying glass icon, in order to draw such objects more precisely.

Adding New Frames

A GIF89a file with a single frame is nothing more than an image file. In order to turn it into an animation, more frames must be added. This can be done in several different ways. A new blank frame can be inserted by clicking *Animation / Insert Frames / Empty*. Alternatively, it is possible to create frames out of image files on disk, by clicking *Animation / Insert Frames / From File*. Animation Shop can import a wide range of both graphic and animation file formats, including GIF, JPEG, BMP, IFF, Flick, AVI etc.

However, the most useful method in many circumstances is to copy existing frames, and paste them into new frames.

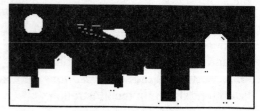

From there, minor changes can be made, thus saving the work of creating a whole new frame from scratch. For example, the second skyline illustration shows the same frame, with the addition of the shooting star.

Of course, more frames still need to be added before the animation becomes useful. Animation Shop can be used to create many new frames out of the existing frame containing the shooting star. These frames can then be edited in Paint Shop Pro by clicking *File / Export Frames to Paint Shop Pro*. Here the shooting star can be selected using the selection tool, and moved into new positions as appropriate to each frame.

Note that the first appearance of the shooting star was in the middle of blank space; this was done so that there were no problems such as accidentally selecting parts of the moon or buildings when moving the star image.

Arranging the Animation

Animation shop can display several frames at one time, as shown below. This allows editing to continue, while giving the designer some idea of how the animation might look when completed. Alternatively, the animation can be viewed as it might appear on a web page, simply by clicking *View / Animation*.

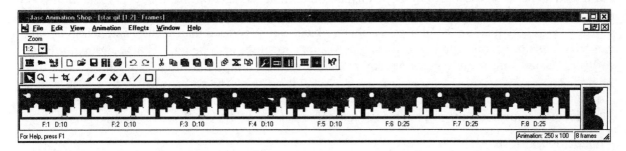

Using a GIF89a animation in a website

Paint Shop Pro can import a variety of image formats for use in animations. When saving the file there are also a number of options, namely AVI, GIF89a, Autodesk Flick, and Animation Shop's own MNG format. When using Animation Shop for web work, however, files should always be saved in GIF89a format, as this is the format that is accessible by the largest number of browser configurations.

The GIF animation can be referenced in a web site in the same way as any normal image, simply by using the <IMG> tag. If the browser is not capable of displaying animated GIFs, then it will simply display the first frame of the GIF. This is preferable to using AVIs or MPEGs, which simply will not display as part of the web page unless the correct plugins are installed.

The HTML source below will generate the web page shown.

Flash and Shockwave

Shockwave began life as a way to distribute Macromedia Director files. It was soon realised that it had great potential for web use, and Flash was created for that purpose. Shockwave Flash files, sometimes referred to as *'Shocked Flash'* files, are becoming more commonplace due to the wide range of facilities and impressive download times offered by this technology.

At its heart, Flash is a vector-based imaging technology. However, it is unlike most other vector-based file formats, in that it has no ordering. With a typical vector design package, each object is given a place in the display order, which tells the system whether other objects are displayed on top of or underneath that object. With Flash, however, the objects are allowed to simply displace one another. For example if a red box is drawn, and then a blue circle is drawn that overlaps it, the part of the square is over-written by the circle. If the red shape is selected and moved, it will have a chunk missing where the circle overlapped into it.

This can cause problems in designing layouts. Fortunately, Flash allows several layers in one file. So, the red box can be drawn on one layer, and the blue circle on another. The order of the layers determines which appears on top when the file is displayed.

Flash also stores a *'Library'* of objects, which are re-useable. Each object can be a graphic, a button or such. Every *'instance'* of the object that appears in the Flash file thus takes up very little space since the object is already defined in the library. A library object can be re-used many times, and a graphic object can have transformations applied to it such as scaling, rotating, or flipping. The Macromedia Flash 4 software comes with some objects already available in the library, and the user is able to add to the library.

However, Flash is much more than simply an image file format. The many things that can be done with Flash include animations, menus, interactive tutorials and games.

Animation in Flash

Like all animation formats, Flash deals with frames. Animation is handled by using *'keyframes'* which define important points in the animation along the *'timeline'*. At each keyframe, the contents of the layer can be modified. Note that the existence of a keyframe in one layer at any point in the timeline does not necessarily mean that there is a similar keyframe in any other layer at that point in the timeline.

In this way, major changes such as a complete change of background will happen instantaneously in the final animation. While this is useful for some purposes, most animations require the appearance of continuous motion. One solution is to have a keyframe in every frame, and modify the contents of the frame by hand. This is the only way to deal with more intricate animations, but is comparatively hungry on storage space. Macromedia Flash 4 has facilities for *'onion skinning'*, which displays all keyframes simultaneously at varying levels of opacity. This technique is useful to trace the motion of objects through each frame.

The real power of Flash animations is in using *'tweening'*. This involves defining the screen location of an object at keyframes, and letting Flash work out its location at the frames in between. While a raster image format such as GIF would need to store each frame individually, the vector format of Flash allows it to simply define the object and its location at each keyframe, making a great saving on space.

Furthermore, movement of objects by tweening need not be in a straight line. Special layers called *'motion guides'* are used to trace a route for an object once a tween has been created. This allows the animator to move objects in curves, wobbly lines, or spiralling patterns, for example, as well as define how quickly the object follows the motion guide.

Flash versus Animated GIFs

Flash's popularity is due to several factors, not the least of which is the small size of Shocked Flash files. The GIF89a animation created above weighs in at 4188 bytes, while a similar animation in Flash is just 623 bytes, with a greater number of frames. Larger resolutions will result in even greater savings by comparison.

Furthermore, Flash introduces a far more dynamic aspect than normal HTML with animated GIFs. It can be used to navigate the web, for example, meaning that an entire website could be written in Flash. It can also produce moving buttons and similar effects without the developer having to worry about Java applets or JavaScript compatibility.

Another advantage of Flash, which stems from its vector base, is that of scalability. Flash objects can be scaled to fit any web page, without the pixellation that a scaled-up bitmap would suffer from.

However, Flash files are not native to HTML. That means that the viewer requires a browser that is capable either of specifically dealing with Flash files, or of downloading and installing plug-ins to cope with the Flash format. While this places a burden on the viewer, the Flash plug-in is relatively small at just over 100kB, and many up-to-date browsers come with this plug-in pre-installed. A recent survey showed that 77% of Internet users had browsers that could handle Flash files, and another 10% had browsers capable of downloading plug-ins for such files. All browsers on the other hand support GIF files, and even if a browser does not support animated GIF it can still display the first frame as a still instead.

Some users find it too cumbersome to wait for a graphically intensive Flash page to load. Developers should give serious thought before deciding on a Flash website. If it is practical to do so, the site should give viewers the option of a Flash page or a standard HTML page. Furthermore, a fancy animated page may not be suitable for certain sites. While it is an excellent choice for an entertainment page, a business page is expected to have a more serious look.

Using Flash 4

The unusual vector format of Flash can take some getting used to. However, the interface is fairly straightforward. Like most drawing packages, it has a toolbar with all the standard tools and icons.

These include selection tools (The Arrow and Lasso); shape tools (Line, Oval and Rectangle); a text tool; Drawing tools (Pencil, Brush, Ink Bottle and Paint Bucket); editing tools (Dropper and Eraser); and view tools (Hand and Magnifier). These generally function in the same way as most other paint packages.

Each tool has a set of '*modifiers*'; these appear just below the toolbar as shown in the diagram. Modifiers include thickness of lines, width of paintbrushes, fill colours and so on.

Flash also has a timeline window, which shows the frames in the movie along the top, and the layers used along the left hand side. Along the timeline it also shows the existence of keyframes, empty keyframes, tweens, text comments called '*labels*', and special items called '*actions*' which handle the interactivity of Flash files. Each of these items is indicated by a symbol in the appropriate layer along the timeline, as shown.

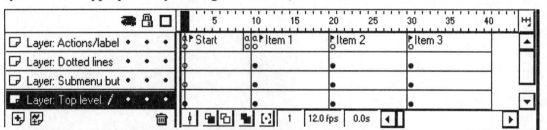

The black dots along the timeline indicate keyframes, while the outlined dots indicate empty keyframes. The small letter 'a' indicates an action, while a red flag indicates a text label. Tweens are represented by an arrow going from the first frame of the tween to the last frame.

Creating a simple Flash animation

When Macromedia Flash 4 is loaded up, it starts with a blank animation, or "*Movie*". It is unlikely that the movie to be created has exactly the size and settings of this default movie, so it may be best to change such settings immediately. Choosing *Modify / Movie* or pressing Ctrl-M will bring up the Movie Properties dialog box.

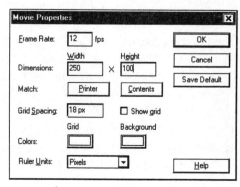

From here the developer set the size, frame rate and so on that will be used in the movie. To match the GIF animation created earlier, the width is set to 250 pixels, and the height is set to 100 pixels.

The only other setting that needs to be changed in this example is the background colour. It would save time and space if the background were set to black, so that the skyline, moon and shooting star can be drawn against it rather than have the black sky as another object in our movie.

Creating Objects in Flash

In this animation, three objects are required: the skyline, the moon, and the shooting star. The first object to be created should be the skyline, as it will determine the movement of the shooting star later.

First of all, the size of the animation is such that it will appear quite small on most monitors. The magnifier tool can be used to zoom in or out depending on which option is chosen from that tool's modifiers.

When the animation is zoomed in enough to work on, choose the '*Line*' tool in the toolbar. It might be necessary to ensure that the correct modifiers are chosen for the Line tool. The skyline should be drawn in white, and an appropriate line size and style should be chosen, for example 1-point solid lines.

The snap-to grid is often very useful for drawing irregular geometric shapes. It can be activated by clicking *View / Snap*, and if the grid squares are too wide then the Movie Properties box shown earlier can be used to change the grid spacing.

The skyline can be drawn as a series of lines. However, if the skyline is to be made a solid colour, the lines need to define an enclosed shape. This can be done simply by drawing lines from the edges of the skyline to the bottom of the frame and around to the other edge of the skyline, as shown.

To fill in this shape, the fill tool is selected, which is called the Paint Bucket in Flash 4. In its modifiers, the colour for the fill can be chosen. Clicking inside the shape that has just been drawn will fill it with that colour.

Adding New Layers

The moon should be created in a separate layer from the skyline, as a simple way of making the shooting star pass in front of the moon but behind the skyline. A new layer can be inserted by choosing *Insert / Layer*. The layer can be renamed by double-clicking on the current layer name. The moon can be created with the Oval tool – again, the snap-to grid may be useful.

Another layer is needed, however, for the shooting star. The star can be drawn by using an Oval for the head of the star, and the Brush to draw it's tail. The Brush size may need to be adjusted in order to do this accurately. For the star's trails the Line tool can be used, but in this case the snap-to grid should be turned off as they should not be horizontal or vertical lines.

When drawing objects that are to be moved, care should be taken to ensure that they are placed properly. In this example, the shooting star should enter from the left of the screen, and finish behind the tall building on the right. So, its starting position should actually be outside the animation area.

Using tweens

To animate the star, the easiest and most efficient method is to use a tween. In order to tween an object, however, there have to be frames in which to do the tweening. Frames can be inserted by selecting *Insert / Frame* or pressing f5. This should be repeated until enough frames are created for the tween.

The tween is created by selecting the keyframe containing the shooting star, and choosing *Insert / Create Motion Tween*. A dotted line appears from this frame to the last frame before the next keyframe. In this case there are no other keyframes so the tween goes from start to finish. The tweening line is shown as a broken line; this indicates some kind of problem with the tween. The problem is simply that the location of the star at the end of the tween is undefined.

This can be fixed by selecting the last frame of the tween, and dragging the shooting star to its final position: hiding behind the large building. If the star appears in front of the building rather than behind it, then the order of the layers should be changed until the star appears behind the building.

Similarly, it should be checked that the star passes in front of the moon. This can be done by selecting intermediate frames along the tween, following the motion of the star until it passes over the moon. Alternatively, pressing the Enter key will view the animation from the current selected frame right through to the end. If the star passes behind the moon, then the layer ordering needs changed.

Publishing the animation

By choosing *File / Save*, Macromedia Flash saves the animation as a .FLA file. This file can be loaded back into Flash and edited, but it cannot be viewed on the web. In order to publish the file, choose *File / Publish*. With the default settings, this creates an HTML file and a Shocked Flash .SWF file. The resulting file contains little more than some skeleton HTML tags, and an embedded object. This embedded object includes details that the browser needs to know, such as the filename to load, and where to get the plug-in for the object if it is not already installed. It also defines the height and width occupied by the object. Like images, embedded object sizes can be in pixels or in percentages of the viewable window. In this way a Flash object can be re-sized to fill an entire web page simply by changing the WIDTH and HEIGHT attributes to 100%.

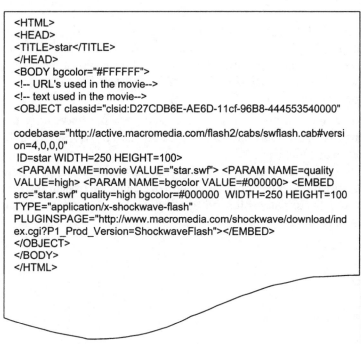

```
<HTML>
<HEAD>
<TITLE>star</TITLE>
</HEAD>
<BODY bgcolor="#FFFFFF">
<!-- URL's used in the movie-->
<!-- text used in the movie-->
<OBJECT classid="clsid:D27CDB6E-AE6D-11cf-96B8-444553540000"

codebase="http://active.macromedia.com/flash2/cabs/swflash.cab#versi
on=4,0,0,0"
 ID=star WIDTH=250 HEIGHT=100>
 <PARAM NAME=movie VALUE="star.swf"> <PARAM NAME=quality
VALUE=high> <PARAM NAME=bgcolor VALUE=#000000> <EMBED
src="star.swf" quality=high bgcolor=#000000  WIDTH=250 HEIGHT=100
TYPE="application/x-shockwave-flash"
PLUGINSPAGE="http://www.macromedia.com/shockwave/download/ind
ex.cgi?P1_Prod_Version=ShockwaveFlash"></EMBED>
</OBJECT>
</BODY>
</HTML>
```

Now, the additional text for the website can be added in the appropriate place, and the page is ready to be placed on the web.

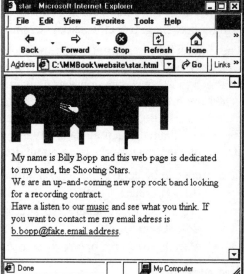

Streaming

Downloading audio or video files from the Internet is all very well, but in some circumstances it is desirable to be able to show such media instantly. This is achieved by *'streaming'*. Streaming is used almost exclusively for audio and video data, although there are streaming systems available for VR and even email.

Streaming generally requires special server software or at least a modification to the MIME types on the server software in order to supply the streamed data. However, there are some types of streaming (Such as VivoActive) which *'embed'* the streamed file into an object in an HTML page, almost as an image would be. Additionally, the server requires a new Internet protocol to handle the real-time transmissions, for example RTP (Real-time Transport Protocol), which is now a recognised standard.

On the client's side, the system needs to have software or plug-ins that are capable of understanding the particular streamed file format that is supplied. The software will generally download a few seconds of data into a buffer before beginning to play back the streamed data. If the buffer is used up before the next part of the data stream is downloaded then the software must pause while it continues to download. This means that the data rate of streamed files must match the user's modem speed if it is to avoid jerky or stalled playback in streamed data.

Most server streaming software works using UDP (User Datagram Protocol) rather than TCP/IP (Transfer Control Protocol / Internet Protocol). This is because UDP is capable of higher transmission speeds, at the cost of some reliability. Because streamed data normally consists of error-tolerant data such as video or audio, the shortcomings of UDP are rarely a concern. The main problem with UDP streaming is that most corporate firewalls do not allow UDP traffic, precisely because of its lack of control.

How streaming works

Servers, whether UNIX or NT, operate on the Internet (or an internal intranet) through 'ports'. In the early days of the Internet, almost every computer on the system was UNIX based, and had a large number of actual physical ports, each of which handled different types of information. For example, email often went through port 21. In today's world of ADSL and ISDN lines, there need not be more than one physical port, but the scheme is still useful logically.

Streaming data can use one of those ports, or it can be accessed directly if access is given to a file streamed file via HTTP. The URL which points to streamed data need not specify a filename in the URL, but instead may supply a port number or folder path after the server name. The server can usually be configured either to use ports, or to supply streamed data to anyone who tries to access a specified folder name.

Streaming data is not always supplied via the HTTP transfer protocol. If a URL is included in a web page that directly leads to, say, a RealAudio file, then the default action of the browser will be to download the file and either save it or activate a helper application to view it. In order to prevent this, 'pointer files' (or 'meta files') are often used. These are small text files with a different file extension to differentiate them from the actual streaming data files.

The pointer file is normally nothing more than one or more lines of text, each of which indicating the URL to receive streaming data. This means that more than one stream can be started by a single link, although they are shown consecutively rather than concurrently.

When the browser is sent to a pointer file, it will notice the file extension and, assuming an appropriate plug-in is installed, will start up the helper application. The application, however, will be passed the text file rather than the actual data stream. From the pointer file, the application knows where to read streaming data from, and can go about doing so properly.

Streaming can be done in one of a number of ways:

- Live streaming.
- Tape-delayed, or 'almost live' streaming.
- File streaming.
- Pseudo-streaming, or 'progressive downloading'.

Live streaming

Because the output is software-controlled, it is possible to send dynamic data, rather than being restricted to the files stored on the server. In this way it is possible to stream data as it is generated. Streaming uncompressed data is not a realistic option, so the server's software or hardware in must carry out compression in real-time. This can require expensive compression hardware for MPEG videos.

The software on the server has to be constantly fed with the data to be streamed, and it will encode the data to the appropriate format and provide it to whoever accesses the specified port, or folder name.

Almost-live streaming

Because of the burden of compression, many so-called 'live' systems are actually delayed by a set time period while the data is compressed. This is the basis of 'almost-live' streaming methods. Since the data is still dynamic, and is supplied in the same manner as live streams, it appears no different to the user, unless the time delay can somehow be detected. (for example, calling a friend's mobile phone and watching him answer it on web-cam 3 seconds after you hear his voice on the phone)

File streaming

Perhaps the most common form of streaming, file streaming (also called streaming 'on-demand') involves transmission of a pre-encoded file. This completely removes the burden of real-time compression, and can also give the supplier the option to provide many version of the same streamed file, that are each encoded at varying data rates to cater for faster and slower client hardware.

Pseudo-streaming

This method involves downloading a file normally, but having software on the client PC use the data as it is downloaded. Often, the pseudo-streamed files can be optimised to make things easier for the client software – for example *'fast-start'* movies that contain extra header information to facilitate viewing the parts of the movie that has downloaded so far. In this way, for example, the viewer can display some parts of an MPEG movie after just 15 percent of the file has been downloaded.

Since pseudo-streaming is exactly the same as a simple download as far as the server is concerned, the server does not require any additional software to be installed.

Streaming Audio formats

The uses for streaming audio include Internet radio broadcasts, commercial music distribution, and samples of audio available elsewhere.

The most common streaming audio formats include:

- Liquid Audio is a commercial system designed specifically for online distribution of music. The client software has built in capabilities to handle purchase of CDs, and download of music samples as well as streaming.

- RealAudio was among the first streaming audio formats, and along with its partner RealVideo, now accounts for the majority of streaming content on the web. While offering superb compression rates, the sound quality is not the best.

  However, with streaming, it is important that enough data is received that the stream can be played back without stalling, and RealAudio performs that function well. RealNetworks' RealPlayer software handles RealAudio as well as RealVideo. The pointer file in a RealAudio system is a .RAM file, which specifies the internet location of the stream, and also the protocol to use if other than HTTP.

- MP3 is not a format that was originally intended for streaming audio. However, at lower bit-rates MP3 offers decent quality sound that is still capable of streaming on basic modems. The pointer file for MP3 streaming is an .M3U file, which is nothing more than a collection of locations where the MP3 files reside, or servers and ports configured for streaming. The Audioactive player by Telos systems is one example of client software that handles M3U and MP3 files.

Streaming Video formats

Streaming video is useful for product demonstrations, entertainment, or video conferencing.

The most common video streaming format include:

- Vivo videos play through a browser plug-in, inside the browser window. While Vivo movies gain very good compression, it is at the expense of frame rates and video quality in general. However, Vivo does have one important advantage, which is that it is possibly the easiest form of video streaming around. It operates via HTTP, meaning that the .VIV file will be embedded in an HTML page – requiring no additional server software, and no editing of MIME types on the server at all. It is a so-called *'server-less'* system.

  HTTP also uses the TCP/IP transmission checking that UDP streaming lacks, and can operate through most firewalls. On the down side, because it is HTTP based, there is no control over how many users are allowed access to the file at one time, possibly leading to network congestion. Vivo was recently purchased by RealNetworks.

- VDO is a client/server streaming video method, meaning that both the client and server must install additional software. The VDOLive software, despite its name, can handle on-demand streaming as well, depending on the type of software installed on the server. VDO is in fact a type of AVI compression. This system can use .VDO pointer files, or can be embedded in HTML files and streamed using HTTP streaming.

- RealVideo, part of the RealMedia system along with RealAudio and other software, is a client/server system capable of normal streaming or HTTP streaming, and can handle on-demand or live streaming. It uses .RAM pointer files to point to .RM media files.

- Microsoft's ASF format is relatively new but already gaining popularity. ASF files can be interactive, and have other functions as well as having a choice of codecs. The pointer files used are .ASX files, which bear a remarkable resemblance to .INI files. Microsoft NetShow is the server software, which can handle live broadcasts as well as on-demand streaming.

- StreamWorks is Xing Technology's MPEG streaming platform. It is aimed at high-end systems with very fast transfer rates, and works well on intranets, but not so well on the Internet where 56k modems and even 28.8k modems are common.

Scalability

While most users may have a 56k modem, some still have 28.8k modems, and others have access to faster digital links. A good streaming server will be able to detect the speed of the client, and cater for it by providing an appropriately sized and compressed video stream. This capability is known as *'scalability'*. Some software can perform this on the fly, downscaling files for use when access is slower; but in many cases the only option is to save several files at varying compression rates to cater for the wider audience.

Embedding streamed data in HTML pages

At its worst, streaming can be a complex system, where files have to be encoded on the fly, ports have to be arranged, MIME types set up on the server, and software has to be installed and configured. At its simplest, however, anyone can set up a simple streaming system on an ordinary web server. Vivo videos, for example, can be put on the web server easily, and the only concern is whether the end user will have a Vivo player.

With RealAudio and RealVideo, a little more work is involved, as well as access to a streaming server. The following general steps apply to RealMedia, but equally apply to most other forms of client/server streaming.

- Ensure that the correct protocols are installed and set up correctly. The web designers should have already decided on a protocol to use for streaming, for example UDP or RTSP.

- Install the streaming software on the server. In the case of RealMedia this software is called RealServer, and is able to handle either live or on-demand streams through TCP/IP, UDP or HTTP. Configure a port on the server to provide the streamed data, if necessary.

- Capture and encode the streamed data, or set up hardware and software to provide live input and encoding. Again, it should already have been decided to which speed(s) of connection the streaming server will cater to.

- Add the streaming file format's MIME type to the server software.

- Create a web page that links to the pointer file, or embed the object directly into a web page. It is advisable that the web page containing the streaming also contains details of the format of the stream so that appropriate plugins can be downloaded and installed at the client end.

Push technology

While there are *'server-less'* systems that have no special software installed on the server in order to perform streaming, there are also *'client-less'* systems in operation. Conversely, this means that the client does not install software in order to read streamed data.

This works because the server *'pushes'* the software down from the server to the client as the stream is requested. The most common way of doing this is using Java. A user can click on a link, and a Java applet will download and run. This Java applet will then proceed to stream the data from the source. For example, as explained in the Authoring Systems chapter, Director is able to save files as Java applets.

This method involves an extra burden on the client; that of downloading the applet before streaming will even begin. However, it means that the client need not install any software, and this in turn means that the producers need not be concerned with which format to use, and how many users have installed a client for that format.

E-Commerce

The growth of products sales and services via the Internet has been phenomenal. Although, it only represents a small proportion of total sales and services, it is still a huge amount in cash terms. More importantly, the projections are for continued growth and many companies are examining their web sales strategies. This section does not look at all the planning, marketing, engineering, security, confidentiality, delivery and other practical and resource implications of such a move. It simply gives an overview of the commercial considerations in transaction processing.

To carry out credit card processing for internet sales, the supplier's web site has to have the following:

Security

The transactions between the customer and the retailer are routed through many intermediary computers, which threatens the security and privacy of individuals' and companies' bank details. The SET (Secure Electronic Transaction) specification encrypts these messages according to electronic locks and keys that are only held by the two parties involved in the transaction. In addition, a security firewall should be installed, to prohibit illegal access to the site's confidential data on customers and their credit card details.

Merchant server

The web site has to be hosted by a server that can handle credit card transaction (known as a *'merchant server'*). The server does not actually underwrite any buyer's liquidity. It only acts as the link between the customer, the supplier and both their banks.   The activities of the merchant server are explained below. The merchant server will make a setup charge, for getting the supplier into its system.   It will also levy a charge on each credit card transaction. This figures reduces with volume and is usually in the region of 5% to 10% of the item price.   This is in addition to the charges levied by the customer's bank.

Merchant Agreement

The seller of the goods will require the services of a *'merchant bank'*. This is a bank that is able to receive and process credit card transactions. The retailer reaches a *'merchant agreement'* with the bank. New companies, or small companies moving into credit card transactions, require an agreement to be set up with a bank for credit card transactions. Others already have this facility and wish a further account to be set up to cover Internet trading, in addition to its current over-the-counter trading or CNP (Customer Not Present) telephone ordering system.

The bank only concludes an agreement when it is satisfied that the supplier has a sound financial track record and has adequate site security.   The agreement will include charges for handling credit card transactions.   This is usually dependent upon the number of transactions, often with a minimum standing charge.

How a transaction is processed

The visitor to the site indicates a wish to make a purchase. This may be a simple activity, where the site sells a single product.   Alternatively, it may be a complex dynamic activity with the buyer using a *'shopping cart'* to choose goods and the web site calculating total costs including taxes and delivery charges. This requires a *'Secure Electronic Transaction',* known as *'SET'.*

The steps in the SET process are:

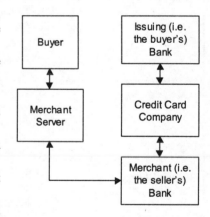

- When the buyer completes the purchase details (type of goods, quantity, name, address, credit card details), these are sent to the merchant server.
- The merchant server requests confirmation to process with the transaction.
- The user clicks the button to confirm.
- The merchant server then sends the credit card details to the seller's own merchant bank.
- The merchant bank contacts the buyer's credit card company for a transaction authorisation.
- The credit card company contacts the buyer's bank, to confirm that he/she has sufficient funds to cover the transaction.
- Assuming that the buyer is financially solvent, the credit card company issues a transaction code back through the chain.
- The buyer is informed of the successful transaction.

Extra code is added to the web site to send the details to the online transaction system.

A large number of software products are available, to enable users to set up on-line stores. These range from hundreds to thousands of pounds, depending upon the facilities required.

Many service companies also provide set up services for suppliers, at an appropriate price.

The total costs of connecting, plus the regular maintenance charges mean that suppliers have to have an expectation of reasonable amounts of extra sales to justify the cost of entering the area of credit card transactions.

Electronic Presentations

What are Presentations

People throughout history have used the power of speech to communicate ideas.   Some famous speeches were made spontaneously.   In other cases, speeches were carefully planned in advance.

The effect of speech making on the audience was later enhanced by using visual aids.   This combination of speech and visual material produces presentations that are currently used for a variety of purposes, including:

- Selling products
- Promoting ideas
- Training staff
- Making reports

The Old Ways ....

Before the advent of computer/digital projector systems, presenters used a variety of methods to display visual information to an audience.   These all had limitations as listed below.

Method	Drawbacks
Blackboard/Whiteboard	Not portable. Messy. All content has to be slowly hand drawn. Since each item is wiped off the board to draw the next item, there is no quick review of past material. Restricted to text and some simple diagrams. Relies on the presenter's writing and drawing skills. The cheapest method but also the slowest and poorest quality.
Flip Charts	A flip chart is essentially a large book of blank sheets, usually resting on its own stand. The presenter flips each sheet over as the presentation progresses. This has most of the problems of blackboards, although some sheets can be drawn in advance and the presenter can always flip back to a previous sheet if required.
35mm Slides	Slides allow the presentation of full colour and photographs but are expensive. They take more time to prepare and have to be developed at a bureau. This means that it is impossible to add new slide material at short notice and extra material would need to provided in some other form (verbal, handouts, or even using a whiteboard or flip chart!). The presentation often requires a darkened room, making it difficult for the audience to take notes. While previous slides can be reviewed, it is often a slow process to mechanically step the carousel on the slide projector. The audience seating and the projector stand have to be positioned so that the audience does not block the projected image. As the highest quality system of its time, it developed sophisticated systems of multiple projectors, many being controlled by computer systems to create dissolves between slide, add audio, etc.
Overhead Projectors	Light is shown through a transparent acetate sheet on which is written/printed the content of a single slide. This is then focussed by a lens and projected on to a wall-mounted or stand-mounted screen. Requires a darkened room and preferably a specially designed reflective projector screen. Like 35mm slide projectors, the audience seating and projector stand have to be positioned so that the audience does not block the projected image. Material is prepared in advance and the arrival of computers allowed special acetate sheets to be printed directly from a laser printer, allowing a range of fonts, colours, clip art and drawing tools to be used. Alterations (e.g. changing a date or the presenter's name) require new acetate sheets to be printed.

Differences between traditional presentations and electronic presentations
The effectiveness of early presentations (blackboard/whiteboard/flip charts) were heavily dependent on the artistic skills of the presenter, since all material was written and drawn as the presentation progressed. Unreadable handwriting and hastily drawn diagrams often spoiled a presentation.

Later systems, such as 35mm slides and OHP slides, allowed material to be prepared in advance.   Since presentation software was not available, the task of creating the slides was often assigned to graphics professionals.   This made slide creation slower, more expensive and difficult to update.

Electronic presentations rely on the benefits of computer software to create the presentation material. Each slide is prepared on the computer, providing the inclusion of text fonts, clip art, colours, photographs, animations, effects (such as dissolve), sound and video.   With a little training, the presenter is able to produce his/her own material.

The completed project is saved as a computer file and can be played back at any time through a monitor, LCD panel or digital projector.   The file can easily be accessed to add or make changes to the content.

Differences between multimedia presentations and presentation software.
With multimedia presentations, the full content of the presentation is packaged within the final application. All the arguments, facts, explanations and suggestions are contained within the material being viewed by the user.

With most electronic presentations, the screen display is only part of the presentation, with the major contribution coming from the accompanying speech of the presenter.   It is <u>people</u> who make presentations, aided by the software.

Presentation software - what it is
As previously mentioned, people recall 20% of what they hear, 30% of what they see and 60% of what they both see and hear.   Presentation software aids the easy organisation and preparation of the screen material for the presentation. This chapter discusses the design and integration of the spoken and visual information.   At its simplest, a student may make a presentation as part of a communications subject. The presentation may last only 10 minutes and be used to test the student's ability to prepare and present ideas.   General abilities are being examined.   For an honours degree student, the presentation will be longer and be used to test the student's in-depth knowledge of a subject.   Specific content is being examined.   No matter whether the presentation is being prepared for academic or corporate purposes, it follows the same design and creation system.

Presentation software, then, is a means to create an electronic slideshow.   Each displayed page is called a 'slide' and the final product is called a 'slideshow'.   This originates from the earliest software that was used to control a projector that contained 35mm slides.

What it does
The finished presentation can be used in a number of ways
- A presentation to an audience, controlled by the presenter, is the most common use.
- An unattended slideshow (e.g. in a shop window, at an exhibition, etc)
- As a distributed product for those who cannot attend the presentation.
- As a set of web pages for mounting on a web site.

The first three methods take advantage of the presenter's speech, knowledge and ability to answer any questions that arise.   The other three methods, although using presentation software, do not have the presenter on hand and therefore all knowledge has to be embedded in the finished product.   In this way, it is entirely similar to designing any other multimedia product.

What it does not do
The software provides a useful variety of visual tools to improve the overall look of the presentation, but it does not supply the flair, the imagination, and - above all - the content and the message.

Remember, the best speeches ever made (the Gettysburg address, Martin Luther King's *"I Had a Dream"*, Winston Churchill's *"We will fight them on the beaches"* and so on) were made without any visuals aids whatsoever.

Presentation software improves the quality of a message; it is not a substitute for the message.

Presentation hardware

The most commonly used types of hardware for displaying presentations are compared below.

	Viewer Numbers	Viewing Area	Typical Lighting	Typical Use
Small monitor	1-4	15"	Normal	Information kiosk, personal training, web site
Large Monitor	5-10	37"	Normal	Small presentations, exhibitions
Plasma Display	10-20	42"	Normal	Airport departure boards
OHP	8-30	Up to 5'	Low	Internal training
OHP+LCD Panel	8-30	Up to 5'	Low	Smaller presentations
Digital Projector	10-50	Up to 25'	Normal/Low	Larger, prestige presentations
CRT Projector	Large	Up to 30'	Low	Boardrooms, pubs
Video Wall	Large	Large	Normal	Conferences, Concerts
Back Projection	Large	Large	Low	Conferences, Concerts

NOTES:

Many companies will have invested in one of these products and may use it for all their needs. There is some overlap in the above table. For example, a plasma display would make an excellent display for a small to medium scale presentation. Bear in mind, however, that a plasma display - although having a bright image, wide viewing angle and a slim profile - is mainly designed for permanent displays and is not easily transported.

An alternative to a single large display is a number of monitors placed around the audience. This involves the use of video splitters, so that one computer video port can feed several monitors. The result is that every member of the audience is close to a display. The drawback with this system is that the attention of the audience may be focussed on the local monitor and not on the delivery of the presenter.

Finally, for presentations to a small group, the presenter may dispense with all of the above and simply use the display on his/her notebook computer.

LCD Panels

An LCD panel, sometimes called an *'OHP Tablet'*, rests on the glass of an overhead projector and is plugged into a computer's video output port. All the content on the computer's screen is also passed to the panel. The light from the overhead projector is directed through the panel and the panel's image is then projected to a screen. Since there are greater losses in an LCD panel than an overhead transparency, this system requires an extra bright bulb in the projector. Although it provides all the benefits of modern presentation software, it is often awkward to interface and set up. The system has now been replaced by digital projectors.

Digital Projectors

These are currently the most popular display system and two main technologies are used in projector construction.

LCD

The LCD projector uses a similar construction to the LCD monitor (see the chapter on hardware for more details). A lamp shines through the panels via a set of mirrors and the output is combined through a prism before passing through the lens for projection. The example shows a *'triple path'* system, with a separate light path for each panel. The light from the lamp is separated into its red, green and blue components by a set of diachroic mirrors. Each beam is modulated by a monochrome LCD panel and the three resultant beams are combined in a prism before being passed to the lens.

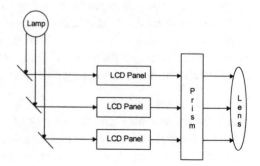

A *'single panel'* type is also produced. This uses three coloured LCD panels and a single light beam passes through each panel in turn. This is easier to produce and is cheaper. However, this construction often results in a dimmer image at the edges of the projected display.

This LCD system is known as *'transmissive'* and produces a contrast ratio of between 200:1 and 300:1. This system is widely used in both older and current projectors.

DLP

The DLP (Digital Light Processing) system was developed by Texas Instruments
It is a *'reflective'* system and uses DMDs (Digital MicroMirror Devices). This is a single chip that supports a matrix of tiny aluminium mirrors, each 16 microns in size, with three mirrors allocated for each pixel. Each mirror is pivoted and can be moved by electrostatic attraction into an *'on'* or *'off'* position. In the *'off'* position, the light beam from the lamp is deflected away from the lens into an absorption area. In the *'on'* position, the mirror reflects the light out through the lens.

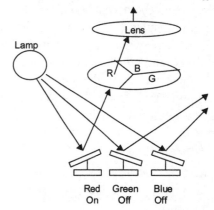

An RGB colour wheel is placed in front of the lens. The spinning of the wheel is synchronised to the DMD output, so that the wheel's red filter is in front of the lens when the reflection from the *'red'* mirror is due. Similarly, the green and blue filters are lined up with the lens when the green and blue pixel's mirrors may direct their beams towards the lens. Since only one beam is passing through the filter and lens at any one time, the viewer's own visual system (i.e. eye and brain) constructs a single full-colour image from the sequential colour information.

Since the mirrors are either *'on'* or *'off'*, they are either reflecting the beam towards the lens or towards the absorption area. So, either a colour is displayed at total brightness or is not displayed at all. Since there is a need to have each colour displayed at different levels of intensity, the time that the mirror is flipped into the *'on'* position is varied. A long *'on'* time produces a high level of intensity while a short *'on'* time produces a short burst of that high level and this is perceived as a lower intensity level.

The gaps between the mirrors are smaller than the gaps between cells on an LCD device. This reduces the *'grid of dots'* effect that is visible when the projected image is examined from close range.

Three-chip projectors are produced using diachroic mirrors to produce separate red, green and blue beams. There is a separate chip with mirrors for each beam. This system does not use the colour wheel and each chip has a light beam reflecting off during the entire frame time. This reduces the light losses and makes their output brighter. DLP projectors usually have a 400:1 contrast ratio, although there have been reports of poor colour uniformity.

Projector Characteristics

The main factors when selecting a projector are:

Noise

The bulbs used in projectors range from 120W to 400W. These bulbs run very hot and are positioned in an enclosed space. Powerful fans are required to keep the bulbs from overheating (and the case from melting) and these fans can be noisy. Fan noise may not be a problem for projectors with a throwing distance of 30m, as most of the audience will be seated far from the projector. However, in a compact space with a small audience, the fan noise can easily distract from the presentation.

Brightness

The brightness of the projector output is measured in ANSI Lumens; the larger the Lumens value, the brighter the picture. Typical outputs for current projectors are between 600 and 1200 Lumens.

Of course, if a projector is moved further back from a screen to obtain a larger display area, the resultant image is dimmer. Similarly, presentations that are made in a bright room will require a brighter bulb output. If the subject is one where audience is likely to take notes, jot down comments, questions, etc, then the room has to be sufficiently bright for that task and a brighter bulb is essential.

The heavy demands placed on bulbs to produce the highest possible light output in an overheated environment take their toll in terms of shortened bulb life. The claimed bulb life for most projectors is between 1,000 and 4,000 hours. Replacement bulbs are costly, usually around £300-£400 each.

Philips has developed an ultra-high-performance (UHP) bulb, aimed at boosting performance and increasing bulb life. Metal-halide bulbs create light by striking an arc between two electrodes. The UHP version reduces the gap between the electrodes, thereby reducing the power requirements and increasing lamp life.

Resolution

Most projectors have a maximum resolution of either SVGA (800 x 600 pixels) or XGA (1024 x 768 pixels).   SVGA is satisfactory for all but detailed diagrams and displays containing fine details.   This need not be a problem, since electronic presentations should not contain fine detail anyway, since it would not be visible to those viewers at the rear of the audience.

Projectors can accept signals of different resolution from their native resolution (the resolution they were built to display).   The circuitry in the projector will detect the different resolution and attempt to make it fit the display resolution.   This will involve scaling (interpolation) of the incoming signal to either shrink it or expand before using it to drive the display.   This is not the best option as it gives varying results. On most occasions, the incoming signal is of a higher resolution than the projector (computer technology is progressing faster than projector technology) and the reduction in resolution may result in the loss of some important detail.   If in doubt, the projector should be fed with its own native resolution where possible.   Newer projectors minimise this problem using intelligent compression to achieve the shrinking of incoming video signals.

Picture quality

The quality of the final projected image depends upon many factors, including:

Uniformity

> This describes the screen's ability to display a uniform area of colour, without tainted areas or blotches.

Contrast

> This describes the ratio between the darkest part of the image (i.e. black) and the brightest part of the image.   Current LCD projectors can have a ratio as low as 100:1 (e.g. the Sanyo PLC 9005BA) but most have values between 200:1 and 300:1. DLP projectors can exceed 400:1.

Keystone

> When the projector is pointed upwards or downwards on to a vertical surface, the image is distorted.   The example shows the resulting image from a projector that is directed onto a screen that is mounted higher than the projector.   This is known as the *'keystone effect'* and some projectors apply *'keystone correction'* which distorts the image in the opposite direction to produce a correct final screen shape.

Inputs

All projectors have the basic input connection to a computer's video output port and many accept video input.   The range of projector inputs currently offered is:

Input Type	Typical Source
VGA	Output from a computer's video output port.
S-Video	Output from a camcorder or video recorder.
Composite	Output from a camcorder or video recorder.
DFP	Output from a computer with a VESA Digital Flat Panel (DFP) Port.
DVI (Digital Video Interface)	Output from a camcorder with a digital interface.
PC Card	Stores the presentation as a set of PowerPoint slides or graphic files.

Projector Types

Projectors are available in a range of sizes, weights, features and performances.   For convenience, they are generally categorised into three headings.

Ultra-portable

These are lightweight models, usually weighing around 2.2kg.   As the name implies, they are popular for mobile presentations and are often used with notebooks.   The projector is usually carried around along with the notebook that stores the presentation.   These models are usually more basic in the set of features and have limited performance.   An example of this category is the Compaq MP1600.   It is a DLP model and weighs in at 1.9kg. Its light output is low at 600 Lumens and it has no optical zoom, no remote control, and the display of video clips is only available through the purchase of an extra adapter).

Transportable

These models are larger, heavier and are generally used within a building.   They have a better specification (e.g. higher resolution, brighter output, longer zoom) and extra inputs (e.g. video input, PC card slots).

An example is the Sanyo PLC-XU22.   It weighs 3.9kg and has a light output of 1200 Lumens.   Its features include remote control, zoom and PC card slot.

Fixed

These are much larger and much more powerful. They are usually screwed to the ceiling in fixed venues. Their performance is excellent, producing large, bright, high-resolution displays. An example is the Eiki Powerhouse. It has a light output of 2100 Lumens and can produce 600" images at a resolution of 1280x1024. It also has a large range of inputs. At the top end, ILA (image light amplifier) projectors produce even higher resolution displays (typically 2000 x 1340) and have a light output of 12,000 Lumens and a contrast ratio of 1000:1.

Other Devices

Other projectors and display aids are available and these are briefly explained below.

CRT Projectors

An alternative for permanent locations is the 3-gun CRT projector. It contains three Cathode Ray Tubes that project the red, green and blue components of the display onto the screen where they are viewed as a single picture. It is large, heavy and difficult to set up but is commonly used both in front and back projection systems due to its large projected display. Front projection units are mostly used in pubs, to show football and other sporting events but are not commonly used devices for other electronic presentations. Groups of CRT projectors are used to build up the rear projected 'video walls' that regularly seen at music concerts, political rallies and major government and corporate presentations.

Gas Plasma Displays

This is a flat screen with a depth of around 15cm. Two glass panes enclose a matrix of closed cells, each containing a mixture of neon and xenon gas. Just like a shop neon sign, when a high enough voltage is applied to the cell, the gas glows and light is emitted.

They are produced in sizes up to 42" and their quality is comparable to, or better than, normal CRT monitors. They have a wide viewing angle and the decay time of the gas means that the screen displays are virtually flicker-free. They are unaffected by magnetic interference and can be sited next to large loudspeakers, electric motors, etc., where normal monitors displays might be disturbed.

However, the high voltage required to fire the cells results in high power consumption and this hinders their use as portable computer screens. They are mainly found permanently sited in public display areas such as airports and railway stations. Despite their high price, they have poor resolution. Most models are either 604 x 480 or 852 x 480 (for widescreen reproduction). This is overcome (e.g. in the NEC PlasmaSync 42PD1) by allowing four or more monitors to built into a single screen (i.e. a 'video wall'). In this way, a signal of higher resolution is split into a number of smaller lower resolution displays.

Electronic Whiteboards

Intelligent whiteboards are made touch sensitive devices that are made from two conductive sheets that are held slightly apart. One sheet is the outer whiteboard screen, while the other is a solid backplate. The whiteboard is connected to the computer's serial port. The presenter can touch the screen with a finger or draw with special pens. Touching the screen makes the two sheets touch at that point and the information is sent back to the presentation software in the computer. This provides the presenter with two benefits:

- There is no need to constantly return to the computer to move the mouse or add annotations to the presentation. Navigation through the presentation can be achieved by using finger control. An example is the SMARTBoard range.
- Material that is added to the board is also captured at the computer end and can be printed out and distributed to the audience. An example is the Ibid Electronic Whiteboard range.

Scan Converters

Presentations may sometimes be made in locations where it is difficult to set up projectors (e.g. in a house) or where a 'quick and dirty' presentation is permissible (e.g. a school may only have 14" monitors but may have a 30" television on a trolley). Scan converters were designed to meet these situations at the low end of the market. A scan converter is a free-standing unit that connects to the computer's video output port and supplies a signal for connection to a normal domestic television's composite video, S-Video or SCART input ports. Some models include a modulator that translates the computer data into a radio frequency signal that connects to a television's aerial socket. This is a cheap system and a convenient alternative but the translation from the computer's video signals to those of TV result in poor image quality, particularly of text.

Presentation software

Most people who use presentation software are not graphics professionals. They are from other professions (e.g. teachers, lecturers, sales people, civil servants) who use the software as a tool to put over their ideas or reports.

Presentation software, therefore, has to be simple to learn, easy to use, provide a range of fonts, graphic and other design facilities, be easy to amend and result in a fuss-free final presentation.

The large range of presentation software has gradually shrunk to a few major players such as PowerPoint (Microsoft), Freelance (Lotus SmartSuite), Corel Presentations and some less well known products including shareware applications. At a basic level, they all work in a similar fashion and produce similar final presentations. They offer different facilities and PowerPoint is the most popular application.

Presentation software is mainly used to create on-screen presentations, but it can also create:

- Overhead slides, printing directly on to specially designed acetate sheets.
- 35mm slides produced by a film bureau from your disk files.
- Graphic files for inclusion in other applications.
- Speakers notes.
- Audience handouts.
- HTML pages.

All packages will create basic slide shows – the rest is up to the designer.

However, other facilities may be available:

- Easier navigation – not just progressing from one slide to the next in a linear fashion, but jumping to offshoot sets of slides justifying a topic or answering potential identified problem areas that may arise.
- Linking to other applications, allowing the slideshow to take a temporary detour and run another program.
- The selection of a pre-defined range of templates.
- The provision of clip art libraries.
- The ability to import a wide range of graphic formats, sounds and video clips.
- The provision of transition effects between slides.
- The ability to visualise the entire presentation and see the design in different ways (views).
- The ability to spell check the text.
- The provision of an *'Undo'* facility to correct mistakes.

Designing a Presentation - an overview

An electronic presentation is approached in a similar way to all multimedia and software projects.

The main phases are:
- Plan
- Create
- Present
- Review

Planning

An electronic presentation has to be planned before sitting down at the keyboard. The plan starts with ideas, the format and specific content such as artwork, sounds, etc, following later. Most presentation software packages provide an *'outliner'* facility (see later) to help sketch out a basic structure that can then be developed. Of course, a structure can even be sketched out on paper.

The traditional, and worthwhile, approach to a presentation's contents is to think of it as having three main components:

Beginning

The first minute of the presentation is most important, as all of the audience is guaranteed to listen for this first minute. This is perhaps the only time when a little attention-grabbing gimmick is permissible. Depending upon the nature of the presentation, this may be a video clip, dramatic music, the handing out of freebies or promises of free samples.

In the main, however, the purpose of this section is summed up in the first part of this old but true adage:

"Tell them what you are going to say, say it, then tell them what you just said".

In other words, this is the time to set the scene for the presentation. The presenter introduces himself/herself, mentions any important background to the event and introduces the subject and the issues being covered. The audience should also be informed of the length of the presentation and the format being used.

Middle

The middle section covers the main points of the presentation and explains/argues the case.   The use of headings and sub headings helps show the relative importance and linkage of various parts of the display. Charts and tables may help to better describe complicated sets of figures.

For students using the software to present university projects, this section should also identify problem areas in the project and discuss further possible options for the project.   For other presentations, this is the section where the main sell takes place.

End

This section is used to summarise the presentation and to make any recommendations.   These conclusions should not introduce fresh ideas.

If you tell the audience you are entering your last minute of the presentation, they will pay attention once again, providing an opportunity to stress the presentation's main points.   This section should also thank the audience for their attendance and invite questions.

Prepare for the worst

The presenter's motto should be *"hope for the best, prepare for the worst"*.

No matter how much preparation is made, there is always scope for a disaster!   The disaster may come from the hardware or it may come from the audience.

The biggest possible problem is the breakdown of equipment.   The presenter should prepare for system crashes and hardware failure - and have a strategy for handling the situation.   For example, the complex sets of graphs and tables on the slides can be printed out for distribution in the event of projector breakdown.   The printing of lecturer's notes are also invaluable, since they allow the presenter to carry on speaking without the prompts he/she normally reads from the screen display.   In other words, the presenter should be able to make the entire presentation without the aid of the screen display, although it may be less impressive.   Consideration of these problems enforces the realisation that the equipment's display is the secondary part of the presentation and the audience really came to hear the speaker.

The audience is another possible source of difficulty.   The awkward question is the presenter's nightmare.   The best preparation is to anticipate any contentious areas in the presentation and develop answers in advance.   These points should not be used in the presentation.   Answering problems in advance only draws the audience's attention to the problem.   However, having reasonable answers to hand gives the presenter added confidence in handling the situation.   Members of the audience often want more detail on a particular topic (e.g. clarification of a fact, more detail on a product specification, etc).   Again, the likely detailed questions can be anticipated and extra slides created to provide more information.   These extra slides would not be part of the main presentation and would only be displayed if the question is asked.   This technique avoids confusing the audience with too much detail.

Creating presentations

Before considering the detailed points on slide content, the presenter must consider three overall issues -
WHY, WHO, WHAT

Other considerations, such as WHEN, WHERE and HOW may have some influence over these issues but remain secondary to the project.

Why ...

This examines the overall goals of the presentation. It goes to the heart of the matter and asks questions such as:

Why are we making this presentation?   (e.g. to launch a new product)
What is the object of the presentation?   (e.g. to sell to an identified new market)
What are hoping to achieve by the presentation? (e.g. to increase awareness of the brand)
What is the presentation's main message?   (e.g. the product's price, facilities and support)
Can the same effect be achieved another way?   (e.g. using mail shots, advertising, internal circulars,
                                                                                     company magazines, etc).

These questions clarify the aims and content of the presentation; they also uncover the relative importance of the presentation and control how much resources (research, time, money) are spent on its creation.

Who ...

It is important to know the audience that are attending the presentation. This determines both the approach and the content of the presentation. For example, the technical content of a product launch will be different for consumers compared to support staff. Similarly, a health conference will present the same material in an entirely different way if it is aimed at doctors, compared to an audience of school children. And, of course, hype and razzmatazz may be useful at a music industry presentation, but would be less appropriate at an undertakers' convention! Knowing the composition, knowledge, experience, buying-power, etc of the invited audience shapes both the content and manner of the final presentation.

What ...

Obviously, the presenter should be knowledgeable on the subject being presented. The presenter should, in fact, know more than appears in the presentation - so that questions and requests for additional facts are easily handled. Stumbling over questions can lose the audience's confidence in the main presentation. The presenter also has to consider the final product from the point of view of audience. The general *'dumbing down'* of the media has resulted in ever shortening attention spans from the average consumer. While the academic, scientific and professional community might be happy to sit for long periods absorbing mountains of facts, this is not the case for the majority of the population. Information overload will switch these listeners into sleep mode, since - unlike multimedia productions - they are not in control. They have no *'quit'* icon and are forced to accept the presentation in purely linear format.

General Content

At the presentation, the audience is receiving information from two sources. The main content is the presenter's voice and the visual display supports this spoken word. The words on the screen are there for the audience to read. Therefore, the screen words and the spoken words must not be the same. The presenter may sometimes repeat words from the screen to emphasise a point and this can be effective. However, the presenter constantly reading from the screen is perceived as a sign of poor preparation and a lack of knowledge on the subject. It is also annoying to the audience, which has already read the text ahead of the presenter.

Simplicity is the key to a presentation. After all, nobody will sign a multi-million pound contract on the strength of a half-hour presentation. The presentation's job is to educate the audience and whet its appetite for more. Generally, therefore, the presentation should try to *'paint a picture'* and avoid losing the main points in a mass of supporting facts.

The presentation should contain only key points (often known as *'key messages'*). The presentation should aim to develop only relatively few key messages, perhaps no more than three in all.

Other content tips are:

- Don't use jargon
- If jargon has to be used, explain it
- Don't use unsupported statements
- Don't use vague statements
- Don't use abstract statements
- Use specific examples

In developing presentations, it is beneficial to learn from others – both good and bad examples. Learn what worked in other cases. See what flopped - and why.

Layout Style

The following approaches to layout have proven to be effective.

- Begin with a main heading/introduction, followed by the presenter's name.
- Only introduce one concept per slide.
- Use consistent page layouts. This covers the colour scheme used (i.e. background colour, text colour), where objects (such as company logos) are placed on the screen, the animation method used (e.g. always slide in from left)
- There does not always have to be new material on the screen at all times. It is effective to leave a dark slide or a simple logo up while a point is elaborated; this concentrates the audience's attention towards the presenter.

Text slides

Most slides in a presentation are text only slides and the main types of text slide are:

Title Large, bold text to introduce the presentation.

Body These slides present the main content of the presentation. The screen should not be crammed with text. If there is a lot to be said, it should be spoken rather than projected. If a lot of text is essential, avoid reducing the point size to make it fit a single screen, since the audience will not be able to read it. Instead, split the text over extra screens.

Lists/Bullets Lists are an efficient way of presenting a set of factors. This allows the audience to more quickly identify a collection of related ideas, compared to extracting the points from a long paragraph of text. Individual items on a list can be separated using bullets, although its best to avoid creating a presentation that consists entirely of a set of bulleted slides.

Quotes As long as they are short, a slide displaying a quote can be very effective. The quote may be an endorsement from a satisfied customer, a sound bite from a government spin doctor, a short extract from a report, and so on. These give added authority to a presentation and can be used to motivate an audience. Quotes should be displayed in italics, surrounded by quote marks and should include the name of the person at the foot of the quote.

Layout tips

The recommendations for text layout are:

- Headings, subheadings and main points in a slide should be highlighted, to draw the audience's attention to the importance of that particular item. This may be achieved by formatting the text to be bold, italicised or displayed in a prominent colour, or the text may be placed in a filled box.
- Avoid having more than 6 or 8 lines per slide.
- Avoid having more than 6 to 8 words for each line.
- Use a sans serif font for the text (i.e. fonts that do not have curly features, feet, etc). Plain, unadorned text is easier to read and fonts such as Arial, Univers or Verdana are ideal.
- Use serifed typefaces for quotes.
- Font sizes for projected images should be much larger than those used for printed output.
- If it is essential that an unusual font be displayed (e.g. using special foreign language characters or using fonts that embody a mood), it can be embedded into the presentation. This allows the distribution of the presentation on disk, CD, etc to viewers who may not have that particular font on their computers.
- Avoid using upper case letters, as lower case letters are easier to read.
- Use underlining sparingly, as overuse makes reading difficult.
- Don't use underlines on headings; instead, use a bold heading to summarise the slide.

Grammar tips

A well thought out presentation can be spoiled if it contains typing errors, grammatical errors or other inconsistencies that detract from a professional feel. Points to bear in mind are:

- Always spell check the text.
- Always grammar check sentences.
- Use active verbs.
- Always use the same tense within and between slides.
- Avoid propositions, adverbs and adjectives. If something is really, really good then say it, don't display it. The audience will accept excessive praise from a presenter more readily than a text version.

Tables

Tables are difficult to read from a distance and should therefore be made up of no more than about four columns and four or five rows. Making each column a different colour aids recognition. If trends in numeric data are being displayed, it is best to use a graph than a table. If a table has to be used, it is best to expose one row at a time, so that the information is explained as it is built up.

Colours

See the other chapters for general advice on the use of colours. In the simplified, quick-moving environment of the electronic presentation, some simple rules apply.

- Colour should be used for accentuating a point, not for adornment.
- There should be a maximum of 4 or 5 colours on each slide, except for embedded graphics/photographs. Consideration should be given to just having three colours, for the background, heading and body text.
- Since presentations are often made in darkened conditions, avoid using overbright colours such as bright yellow, particularly for large areas such as backgrounds.
- Don't use red on green or green on red, since around 10% of the population have colour confusion.

Templates

Presentation software often simplifies the designer's task by providing pre-written templates. These can be pre-defined master layouts that place headings, text areas and clip art areas on specific places on the slide. The designer uses that master to produce extra slides in that same image. Alternatively, templates may consist of complete sets of slides where the designer only needs to change the text of the sub-headings and bullets of the various slides.

The practical use of templates is covered later in the section on PowerPoint.

Backgrounds

Normally, the software applies the background design to all slides in the presentation, unless instructed otherwise. The backgrounds supplied with some templates are very elaborate and, although effective for an introductory slide that uses large bold headings, it obscures the text message when used for all the subsequent slides. Since backgrounds can be designed separately from the individual slide contents, it is best to use plainer backgrounds with the main presentation slides. Dark, cool background colours with light, warm text works best for projectors, particularly in rooms with subdued lighting. Avoid using white text on a black background, as this is perceived as being *'low tech'*. Graduated tints also make effective backgrounds. The gradient fill should be light at bottom and dark at top.

The final slide in a presentation should always be a black slide or a darkened logo. This prevents the text from the last slide remaining on screen while the presenter makes his/her wind up speech. Since there is nothing on the screen to distract the audience, they will concentrate more fully on the speech.

Charts

Presentations may wish to inform the audience about the progress of a particular project (e.g. how sales have increased or the how world's population has grown). Alternatively, it may wish to compare certain statistics (e.g. how much of the price of a gallon of petrol is taken in tax, how much goes to the oil producer, how much to the distributor). While these figures could be displayed as a list or as a table, the most effective way to represent them is in the form of graphs. With sets of numbers, the audience has to read the numbers and carry out some mental calculations. With charts, they instantly see that one figure is the same or larger than another figure. However, to be effective, graphs should contain the minimum detail necessary. Where there are several slides with graphs, the scales used for the axes should be consistent (e.g. one graph should not be measured in grams while another is measured in ounces).

The suggested use for each graph type is:

Flow charts	Useful for explaining processes (e.g. outlining the options and solutions for purchasing a house). Most flow charts are quite complicated and they should be spread over extra slides to accommodate the detail.
Organisational charts	Useful for explaining structures (e.g. how a company's management structure functions). Avoid unnecessary detail and create sub-charts if required.
Bar charts	The most commonly used type and the easiest to see from a distance. Vertical bar charts follow values over a period (eg monthly unemployment figures). Stacked bar charts show the total change over a period, while showing percentages within each bar (e.g. showing monthly employment changes per month and each bar showing unemployment amongst different age groups). Horizontal bars are often used when comparing different values (eg car prices). Display less than 8 separate bars on any one chart, otherwise the chart is too cluttered to read.
Pie charts	Useful to show the relative percentages of a whole (e.g. how many of the population are infants, teenagers, middle aged and seniors). The chart should contain no more than 5 or 6 slices. Extra sub-charts should be created if required. All the sectors should be clearly labelled, and contrasting colours should be used for adjacent slices. To highlight a particular detail, use a pullout slice from the pie, but never pull out more than two slices. Place most important slice in upper right of the pie. Creating 3D pie charts can result in a more attractive and readable chart.
Area Chart	Useful to show how the relative proportions of different items have altered over a period of time (a pie chart only demonstrates relative values at a fixed period in time).
Line charts	Useful to show how absolute values have altered over time. There should be no more than 3 or 4 lines per chart. Make the data lines bolder than the axis lines.

Existing graphs can be imported into a slide from Excel or other spreadsheets.

Use of multimedia
Never attempt to use flashy multimedia effects to mask a flawed presentation.   The presentation's aim is simplicity and effectiveness.   Too many gimmicks distract the audience, removing the simplicity and diminishing the effectiveness.   However, in certain circumstances, the addition of various multimedia elements can enliven or extend the presentation.   The possibilities are:

Graphics
The inclusion of graphics can be very useful, if it is not overdone.   Above all, the graphics used must add to the slide's message and not simply be added for adornment.   Excessive use, or the inappropriate use, of graphics can trivialise a serious message.

On the other hand, the inclusion of the company logo, product photographs and explanatory diagrams will add to presentation's content and give the presentation a more professional feel.

Usually, a selection of clip art is provided by the presentation software application.   While this allows for the easy inclusion of graphics, consideration should be given to fact that every other user of the package has access to the same clip art.   This means that a presentation with such clip art is recognisable to other I.T. professionals and will detract from the presentation's authority.

Other sources of clip art are readily available, although they should only be used where they have been confirmed as being copyright free.   Larger organisations may have their own graphic artists and smaller organisations may decide to secure the service of artists to create their own artwork.   This ensures that the artwork is of high quality and provides artwork that is more tailored to the needs of the presentation.

Animation
Generally, the use of animations in presentations is discouraged as being distracting while adding nothing to the knowledge of the audience.   Such examples include fireworks displays and moving banners, which attract the viewers' eyes away from the text towards the screen movement.   Sometimes, they may be regarded as essential and examples might be flybys, walkthroughs, and demonstrating processes (e.g. demonstrating the working of the combustion engine).

Consideration must be given to their expected extra effect compared to the large amount of time that is required to create most animations.

Sound
Music clips may sometimes be used at the beginning or end of a presentation, to indicate these significant events.   Music throughout a presentation is particularly annoying to an audience and should be avoided. Similarly, clips of speech can be effective when used in moderation.   The speech, of course, should not be played while the presenter is speaking.   Speech clips should be limited to significant contributions. These might include contributions from people who are known to the audience (e.g. the message from the company chairperson or endorsements from famous individuals).   Occasional clips from others, such as customer reactions, street interviews and clips from radio or television, can be effective if not overused. Once again, all clips must only be used with permission.

Video
Sound and video clips are slow to load before they can be played and the presenter has to ensure that the production takes those delays into account so that there are no pauses in the delivery.

Even compressed low resolution video clips can occupy large amounts of disk space and require powerful equipment.   Typical considerations are:
- Is the computer powerful enough to process the video files without frame dropout?
- Has the computer enough disk space to store all the presentation's files?
- Can the projector handle the fast data rates of video?
- Does the software support video file types such as AVI and MPEG, or will existing files have to be converted from their native format to the format that the software expects?
- Is the extra work involved in capturing/digitising/editing video worth the effort?

Examples of effective use might be an important interview or a stunning clip of a new product in use.

Another effective technique is to interview and videotape members of the audience as they arrive. The most appropriate clips can quickly be chosen and integrated into the presentation. This method has an impact on the audience but requires forethought about how/where/when in the script such an interview might be placed to maximise the impact. This, in turn, shapes the questions used in the interviews.

Getting started with PowerPoint

This section of the chapter introduces the practical steps in using PowerPoint, the industry's most successful presentation software package.   This section is only a starter and is not intended to replace a full manual or training guide.   The material covers using the main features of PowerPoint 97.   There may be some slight differences in other versions of PowerPoint and these can be looked up in the comprehensive Help system built in to the package.

A quick start

When in a hurry or when using the package for the first time, the AutoContent wizard assists in creating a presentation.

When PowerPoint is first opened, a dialog box is displayed as shown.

Selecting the AutoContent wizard opens a selection of options that takes the user through the creation process in easy stages. It allows the selection from pre-defined presentation types, with the user answering questions to select the required type.

The presentation types cover a range of personal, business, sales and promotional presentations.

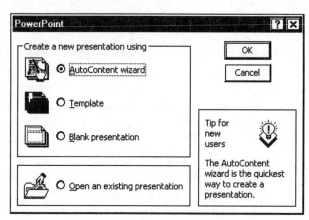

After selecting the presentation type, the Wizard offers output options covering screen output, OHP slide output, 35mm slide output and printed output.

After the details are entered, the wizard creates a set of slides with suggested headings. It also provides suggestions for the content of each slide.   The user need only edit the content of each slide to insert his/her own material and the presentation is complete and can be saved.

The items that can be edited are located in *'Placeholders'*.   Each placeholder is a dotted box that holds some content such as the title, some text, or a graphic.   The contents of placeholders can be altered as often as required.   It is easy to return to the presentation to alter its content or its look.

Viewing the presentation

There are different ways of viewing the presentation content.

These views can be examined and modified while creating a new presentation.   They can also be used to modify an existing presentation.

The bottom left of the screen displays a set of options as shown.   These are the five viewing options of PowerPoint.

The designer can only see one of these views at any one time, unless he/she is using PowerPoint 2000.   PowerPoint 2000 allows multiple

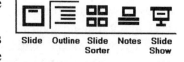

panes on the screen, with each pane containing a different view of the presentation.   This is a useful improvement, especially if you have a large enough monitor to comfortably view them all.

Slide view

This view displays a single slide on the screen, allowing it to be edited. Activities in this view include adding text, photographic images, graphics (objects that you draw), pre-defined shapes, clip art, graphs, sound, video, and hyperlinks (to other presentations, to Word or Excel documents or to an Internet address). This view is also used to edit existing text and objects and to change object colours.

Outliner

This view displays all the text of the entire presentation, in the order and indented levels that they appear on individual slides.   This allows text additions and editing over multiple slides, without having to keep displaying individual slides. This is covered more fully later.

Slide sorter

This view displays miniatures of each slide, allowing their order to be changed and transitions to be added.   This is the best mode for copying and deleting slides.   Cut and paste or drag and drop techniques are used to move the thumbnails of the presentation into the desired order.

Notes view

This view displays an individual slide, with an area below for adding speaker's notes.

These notes do not appear on the screen during any presentation.

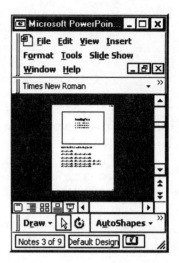

They are used to create the extra material that the presenter will use during the presentation and are intended to be outputted as printed sheets. Unlike conventional printed notes, these should be printed in a font that is large enough to be seen at a glance without peering.   Remember, the presenter may be working in subdued light, or having to refer back to previous pages in a hurry.

Examples of the contents are:

- The arguments that the speaker wishes to make
- Supporting facts and figures
- Theatrical timings. These are reminders to carry out certain events at that point in the presentation. These could include holding up an object, passing round a handout, or pointing out the presence of a particular individual at the presentation.

SLIDE SHOW

This view displays the slides in the chosen running order.   They are displayed on the computer's monitor without any of the software's tools being visible; the slides are displayed exactly as they would in the final presentation.

This allows an evaluation of the effectiveness of the overall project, as well as checking on the effect of various timings, transitions, etc.   The Slide Show View can be run at any time during the creation of the presentation, to check on individual items.

ADDING A SLIDE

An extra slide can always be added to a presentation at any time.

The steps are:

- Get into either Outline or Slide Sorter view.
- Highlight the slide to the right of where the new slide is to be inserted.
- Choose 'Insert' from the main menu bar.
- Choose 'New Slide' from the drop down menu.
- A choice of AutoLayout is then offered.
- Highlight the required AutoLayout and then click the 'OK' button.

The options as shown in the illustration are:

Title slide	Bulleted List	2 Column Text	Table
Text & Chart	Chart & Text	Organisational Chart	Chart
Text & Clip Art	Clip Art & Text	Title Only	Blank

Other options are available by pulling down the side scroll bar and these include:

Text & Object	Object & Text	Large Object	Object
Text & Media Clip	Media Clip & Text	Object Over Text	Text Over Object
Text & 2 Objects	2 Objects & Text	2 Objects Over Text	4 Objects

The layout of a slide can be altered at any time.

The steps are:

- Get into Slide View.
- Choose 'Format' from the menu bar.
- Choose 'Slide Layout' from the drop-down menu.
- Choose a new layout from the options displayed and click the 'OK' button.

No content is lost when a different layout is selected, although the size of the text or graphics placeholders may need to be resized to improve the appearance, or to prevent a graphic being superimposed over some text.

Deleting a slide

The steps for deleting a slide from a presentation are:
- Highlight the desired slide
- Choose 'Edit' from the main menu bar.
- If in Slide Sorter or Outline View, click the *'Clear'* option from the drop-down menu.
- If in Slide View, click the *'Delete Slide'* option from the drop-down menu.

Changing the order

During the development stage, the content and the running order of slides is often altered.

To change the order of slides in a presentation, the following steps are required:
- Get into Outline or Slide Sorter View.
- Click on the icon of slide to be moved and hold down the mouse button.
- Drag the icon to the new position (a horizontal rule is displayed as the mouse is moved up or down and this indicates where the slide would be placed if the mouse button were to be released).
- Release the mouse button when the icon is in the new desired position.

Adding text

Users of Microsoft Word and Microsoft Publisher will be familiar with the techniques of adding text, WordArt and graphics to a document. These additions are made with the Drawing Toolbar.

To add extra text (i.e. beyond those already provided in the existing placeholders supplied with the template being used) use the following steps:
- Click on the Text Box tool on the drawing tool bar
  or
  Choose *'Insert'* from the main menu bar and choose *'New Slide'* from the drop down menu.
- Move to the desired starting position for the new text.
- Enter the new text into the text placeholder.

Shadow effects

The slide's text can have shadow effects added. This is not recommended for small body text, as it makes the text difficult to read from a distance. However, it is often effective with slide titles and headings.

To add a shadow to a piece of text, highlight the piece of text and click the Shadow On/Shadow Off button on the formatting toolbar. This is located next to the Bold, Italics and Underline buttons as shown.

Adding clip art

To add a graphic from the package's clip art collection:
- Choose *'Insert'* from the main menu bar.
- Choose *'Clip Art'* from the drop down menu.
- Choose a category (e.g. *'Business'*, *'Household'* or *'Cartoon'*).
- Choose the desired graphic from the collection of thumbnails that are displayed.
- Drag the graphic to the desired position on the slide.
- Resize the graphic size, if necessary.

Adding graphics

PowerPoint provides a variety of tools for drawing directly on to a slide. Apart from basic line, circle and box drawing facilities, the package provides the same collection of pre-defined shapes. These are obtained from the Drawing Toolbar's *'Autoshapes'* option.

Shapes include flowchart symbols, arrows, stars and banners, as shown.

The steps for adding an AutoShape are:
- Choose the AutoShapes option from the Drawing Toolbar.
- Choose the category of shape required.
- Choose the shape from those displayed.
- Move to the top left of where the graphic will sit on the slid.
- Hold down the mouse button and drag the placeholder size.

Drawing Tools

The Drawing Toolbar provides the following other drawing facilities:

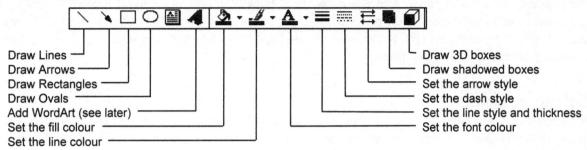

The other tools on the Drawing Toolbar are used to manipulate an item.

Choosing *'Draw'* opens a sub-menu that includes the ability to flip an item horizontally or vertically; in other words to convert an item into its own mirror image.

The *'Free Rotate'* tool allows an item to be rotated to any angle.

The steps are:

- Highlight an item
- Click on the rotate icon, rotate handles will appear round the item
- Click on a handle, hold down the mouse button and drag the item round to the desired angle.
- Release the mouse button.

Word art

WordArt creates text with special effects, as shown in the example.

The steps for adding Word Art text are:

- Click on the Word Art tool on the drawing tool bar

    or

    Choose *'Insert'* from the main menu bar, choose *'Picture'* from the drop down menu and *'Word Art'* from the Picture options.
- Choose a style from the shapes displayed.
- Enter the new text in the dialog box.
- Choose the font, size, and style for the new text.
- Click the *'OK'* button.
- Drag the Word Art to the desired position on the slide.
- Resize the Word Art object, if necessary.

Templates

As explained earlier, templates are pre-defined master layouts that place headings, text areas and clip art areas on specific places on the slide.   The designer uses that master to produce extra slides in that same image.   These are known as *'Presentation Designs'* in PowerPoint 97 and as *'Design Templates'* in PowerPoint 2000).   Alternatively, templates may consist of complete sets of slides where the designer only needs to change the text of the sub-headings and bullets of the various slides. These are known as *'Presentations'* in both PowerPoint 97 and PowerPoint 2000.   Examples of the complete presentations that are available are *'Company Meeting'*, *'Marketing Plan'* and *'Presenting a Technical Report'*.

Templates contain slide masters, fonts and colour schemes that are designed to produce an overall effect or *'feel'*.   When a new template is applied to a presentation, the new formatting details replace the existing details. The new template's characteristics apply to all slides in the presentation and each new slide that is added thereafter will also have the new look.

A presentation design template can be applied to a presentation at the start of its construction, it can be applied during the process, or it can be applied even after all the content has been completed.

Earlier versions, up to v4, did not provide an *'undo'* for templates.

The steps to apply a Template are:

- Choose *'Format'* from the main menu bar.
- Choose *'Apply Design'* from the drop-down menu.
- Choose *'Presentations'* or *'Presentation Designs'*, as required.
- Choose from the templates offered and click the *'OK'* button.

In addition to the supplied templates, users can design as save their own screen characteristics as a new template for use in future presentations.

For beginners or those requiring a speedy production, PowerPoint offers an AutoContent Wizard. This is offered as an option when a new presentation is requested. It guides the designer through decisions such as type of presentation (e.g. report, meeting, etc) and type of output (e.g. screen, slides, etc), before creating a set of slides for amendment.

Colour schemes

A slide uses a set of eight colours. These are used for the background colour, text colour, etc, as shown in the diagram below. PowerPoint provides sets of these of these colours, known as *'Colour Schemes'*.

A Colour Scheme consists of a set of eight colours that has been chosen to contain complimentary colours – i.e. colours that do not clash with each other.

The general choice of colours has been covered earlier.

In PowerPoint, each template stores a colour scheme as part of its set of characteristics. Altering a template will alter the set of colours used.

PowerPoint allows each slide to use a different colour scheme. Most presentations use the same colour scheme throughout the presentation for a consistent look, although different colour schemes are sometimes used to indicate different areas of the presentation. One scheme can be used, for example, for the main body of the presentation, while other colour schemes are used for the slides presenting financial, technical or sales information. Alternatively, different schemes can be used for different departments of an organisation or different product lines.

Altering the colour scheme

To alter a presentation's colour scheme from one pre-set scheme to another pre-set scheme, carry out the following steps:
- Choose *'Format'* from the main menu bar.
- Choose *'Slide Colour Scheme'* from the drop-down menu.
- Choose the *'Standard'* tab in the dialog box that opens.
- Choose a new scheme from the options displayed
- Choose *'Apply'* to only change the colour scheme for the currently highlighted slide or *'Apply to All'* to change the colour scheme for the entire set of slides in the presentation.

Customising a colour scheme

If none of the pre-set colour schemes are suitable, the designer can create and save his/her own preferred colour scheme.

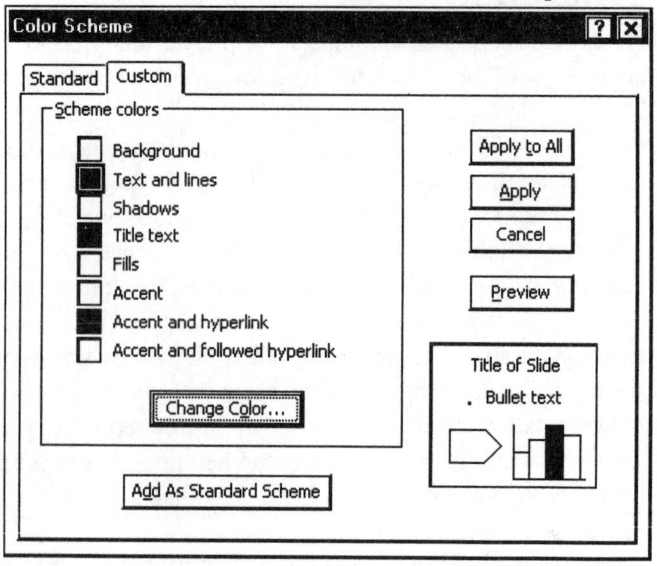

The steps to creating a new colour scheme are:
- Choose *'Format'* from the main menu bar.
- Choose *'Slide Colour Scheme'* from the drop-down menu.
- Choose the *'Custom'* tab in the dialog box that opens. This displays the screen shown.
- Choose the scheme colour to be altered and click the *'Change Colour'* button.
- Choose the desired colour from the displayed set and click *'OK'*.
- Choose *'Apply'* to only apply the changes to the currently highlighted slide or *'Apply to All'* to apply the changes to the entire set of slides in the presentation.

This method can change just a single colour or change all colours in the scheme.

If the scheme might be used again for a future presentation, it can be added to the list of schemes offered when the *'Standard'* tab is clicked. When the scheme is completed, the *'Add as Standard Scheme'* button is pressed.

Any objects that are added to a slide, such as graphs or items of clip art, can have their colours altered so that they match the slide's colour scheme.
The steps are:

- Highlight the item to be treated.
- Choose *'Format'* from the main menu bar.
- Choose *'Picture'* from the drop-down menu.
- Choose the *'Picture'* tab in the dialog box that appears.
- Choose the *'Recolor'* button.

While this is usually better than having the software create a dithered area to represent the colour that is outside its scheme, the option does not always work as hoped.

CHANGING THE BACKGROUND

The background colour of a slide can be altered to display:

- Any colour from the current colour scheme.
- A colour that is not in the current colour scheme.
- A more customised background, using fill effects.

The steps are:

- Highlight the slide to be altered.
- Choose *'Format'* from the main menu bar.
- Choose *'Background'* from the drop-down menu.
- From the *'Background'* dialog box that appears choose a colour from the current colour scheme, or select the *'More Colors'* or *'Fill Effects'* option.

FILL EFFECTS

Choosing the *'Fill Effects'* option within the Format/Background options displays the dialog box shown.
Its four tabs provide the following options:

Gradient   The example in the diagram shows the selection of two colours and a gradient fill extending from the top left-hand corner.   The user controls the colours selected and the direction of the fill.   Choosing the *'Preset'* option displays a selection of fills such as *'Nightfall'*, *'Chrome'* and *'Calm Water'*.

Texture   Clicking on the *'Texture'* tab results in the display of a range of textures designed for use as screen backgrounds.   These include background textures such as *'Parchment'*, *'Tissue Paper'* and *'Canvas'*.   While some textures provide an improvement over a plain background, other textures are quite prominent and could easily make it difficult to read the slide's body text.   The use of a texture background should be checked by viewing a projected version of the slide.   An alternative method is to find a clip art texture and alter its brightness and contrast using a package such as Paint Shop Pro or PhotoShop, to fade the texture before using it as a background, using the *'Picture'* option described below.

Pattern   This provides a selection of patterns such as *'Zig Zag'*, *'Horizontal Brick'*, *'Solid Diamond'* and *'Plaid'*.   The patterns are constructed using a foreground and a background colour that is chosen from the colour scheme.   Most designers find these patterns a little limiting and too bland.

Picture   This allows a piece of clip art or a digitised photograph to be used as the background.
The designer can use any graphic file that is on his/her disk and the following graphic formats are supported - wmf, jpg, cdr and pcx.
Generally, background images should remain in the background, so that the message is clearly seen.   Like prominent textures, background pictures can dominate a slide and distract the audience.   However, occasional slides can use pictures to great effect.   For example, imagine a slide showing a full screen display of a new product while bullet points describing its features gradually built up on the screen.

Using outliner

As explained earlier, the Outline view displays all the text of the entire presentation, in the order and in the indented levels that they appear on individual slides.

Each slide is numbered and has a heading.   Under each heading is the text used in the slide. Each text entry has a level that reflects whether it is a title, heading, subheading or lower level (perhaps appearing as indents or as bullets).

The Outline View does not display any graphics, although an icon on a slide indicates that the slide contains graphics.

Any text additions or alterations that are made in the Outliner will automatically be altered in the Slide View. Similarly, any text changes made in the Slide View are reflected in the Outline View.

Designers should always start a new presentation by using the Outliner. The content of a presentation does not spring from the designer's brain fully developed. Ideas, arguments, examples, supporting points, etc will come to mind and can be immediately entered into the Outliner as slide contents. The Outliner can then be used to assemble these points in a logical order and develop a rational presentation structure. Individual lines of text can be promoted, demoted or re-ordered within a slide, by dragging and dropping. Similarly, lines of text can be dragged from one slide and dropped into another slide. Finally, a slide can be dragged from its present position in the linear list and dropped into a new position in the order.   This allows the easy alteration of the content, as the designer develops the presentation.

The ability to edit one slide's contents while seeing the overall presentation's contents is also a great advantage.   It is easy to change the text content of many slides at the one session, without having to open each slide individually just to recall their contents.   It also allows text additions and editing over multiple slides, without having to keep displaying individual slides.

Masters

PowerPoint is installed with a default choice of type styles, colour scheme, etc.   This information is stored in the file default.ppt and is the set used when *'Blank Presentation'* is chosen.   If a company style is required for presentations, a presentation with the required settings can be stored as default.ppt and in this way, the default settings are changed to the preferred set.

Each presentation has a set of masters.   There is a master for slides, handouts, outlines, and speaker's notes.   All the slides in the presentation follow the content held in the master, unless the designer decides that a particular slide should use all, some or none of a master's attributes. PowerPoint will have provided placeholders for items such as the slide title and text areas.   These placeholders will appear on every slide.   However, the designer can add extra items to the Slide Master and these will also appear on every slide.   So, for example, a logo or graphic placed in the slide master will appear on every slide.

An individual slide can still be altered, to look different from the master.   For example, the text colour may be altered or the font's size may be changed.   These text characteristics only apply to the single slide – all others conform to the characteristics stored in the Slide Master.   If any subsequent changes are made to the Slide Master, they are seen in all slides, including any slides that have been altered from the Slide Master set. However, PowerPoint notices the changed parts of the slide and does not alter these changed areas.

Using slide master

To alter the characteristics stored in the Slide Master, carry out the following steps:
- Choose *'View'* from the main menu bar.
- Choose *'Master'* from the drop-down menu.
- Choose *'Slide Master'* from the secondary drop-down menu.
- Make any alterations/additions
- Click the *'Close'* button.

To create a slide that is different from the Slide Master set:
- Use Slide View to look at the chosen slide.
- Make any alterations/additions.
- These changes only affect that particular slide.

You cannot apply a Template to a single slide, only to an entire presentation.

Transitions

Presentations are normally run to display one slide after another. PowerPoint, like many other packages, provides facilities to bridge the gap between slides. These are called *'transitions'* and a typical transition would be one slide dissolving into the next slide.

Useful though they are, the aim is to minimise transitions between slides, as too many irritates the audience. All transitions should be fast. They are there to provide a smooth movement from one slide to the next. They are not intended to draw attention to themselves.

To add a transition:

- Get into Slide Sorter View.
- Click on the slide to which the opening transition is to be applied.
- Choose *'Slide Show'* from main menu bar.
- Choose *'Slide Transition'* from the drop-down menu.
- Choose the type of transition.
- Choose the speed of transition.
- Choose whether to proceed to the next slide on clicking the mouse or on waiting a set time. Setting specific times between slide changes saves the presenter being near the mouse, allowing him/her more free movement. However, set timings do not allow for unplanned for events (e.g. someone asks a question or the presenter temporarily loses his/her place in the speaker's notes.
- Choose whether to have silent transitions, or to mark the transition by playing a sound (e.g. a camera click). Bear in mind that hearing the sound for the hundredth time during a presentation may not be the best way to impress the audience.

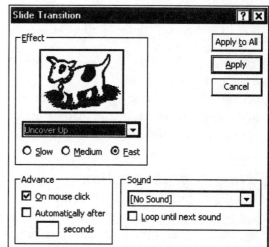

Build slides

Build slides are effects that are applied to the body text within a slide.

A set of text items is displayed on the screen one at a time, as the presenter clicks the mouse. Since the screen does not initially display all the slide's points, the audience is not able to read ahead of the presenter and has to wait until new points are added. This build up of a theme tends to maintain audience interest. The available effects include dissolve, dropping in and appearing to be typed by a typewriter. The effect can be applied to an individual line of text, the text of an entire slide, the text of a set of slides, or even all the body text in a presentation. While the build effect can have an impact (e.g. outlining the five reasons to quit smoking) it should not be overused, as it can quickly become annoying.

The steps to create build slides are:

- Go to Slide Sorter View.
- Highlight the slide(s) that are to have the effect applied to them.
- Choose *'Slide Show'* from the main menu bar.
- Choose *'Preset Animation'* from the drop-down menu.
- Choose the desired effect from the displayed list.

Preset Animations can also be applied to graphic objects.

Animation effects

In addition to slide transition and text build slides, PowerPoint provides the ability to create customised animation effects that can be applied to both text and graphics. So, for example, a piece of clip art can drop into the display or a photograph can gradually be revealed.

The steps to create animation effects are:

- Highlight the item that is to have the effect applied.
- Click on the Animation Effects tool on the main menu bar.
- Click on the desired effect from those displayed on the sub-menu shown.

The effects available include Drive In Effect, Flying Effect, Camera Effect and Flash Once.

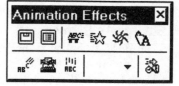

If animation effects are to be regularly used, the icons can be added to the package's toolbar by selecting *'Animation Effects'* from within the *'Toolbars'* sub-menu of *'View'* on the main menu bar.

If greater control over an effect is required, PowerPoint provides user control over the effect's parameters. The steps to create customised animation effects are:

- Highlight the item that is to have the effect applied.
- Choose *'Slide Show'* from the main menu bar.
- Choose *'Custom Animation'* from the drop-down menu.
- Choose the desired effect from the displayed list.

A range of effects, timings, sound effects, etc are available for selection.

Clicking the *'Preview'* button displays a miniature of the animation, so that the effects of changes can be instantly evaluated.

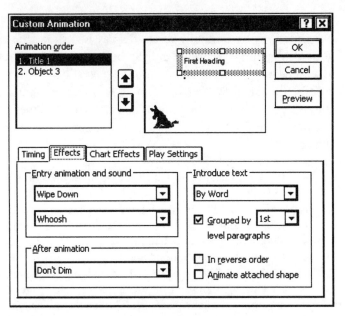

Saving a presentation

When the presentation is finally created, it is stored on the computer's hard disk. Before any decision is taken regarding the final packaging of the product, check the spelling and style used in the slides. This is essential, as an otherwise excellent production could be spoiled. Spell checking is achieved by clicking on the *'Spelling'* option on the drop-down menu that appears when the *'Tools'* option is chosen from the main menu bar. Choosing *'Style Checker'* from the same drop-down menu, results in reports of any detected problems (such as too many fonts on a slide, too many lines of text on a slide, etc).

The completed, spell-checked presentation can simply be stored on a hard disk or other storage medium, for use in the normal way - i.e. displayed to an audience, controlled by the presenter. While this is appropriate for management meetings, staff training, etc., it does not get the message out to those who are unable to attend a presentation. With some extra work, a presentation can be created for general distribution on floppy disk, CD, company internal network (an *'intranet'*) or over the Internet. This opens new markets for the presentation, such as

- an unattended presentation in a shop window or at an exhibition
- a distributed product for use in mail shots.
- a web site promotion.

NOTE: The presentation cannot be distributed without addition material. Since much of the message is contained in the presenter's voice, this material has to be added into the presentation. While a quick fix is to add the speaker's voice as a set of audio files, this is unsatisfactory due to the large file sizes and the reduced viewer impact. Additionally, viewers are now accustomed to hyperlinking around material and the presentation is linear. The entire material has to be revamped as a standalone, hyperlinked, fully documented presentation. See the chapters on web site design and multimedia design for details.

Output types

While the material can be used on a computer with PowerPoint, other output options are available.

Pack And Go

The *'Pack and Go'* facility compresses files and can include a PowerPoint Viewer, so that the presentation can be used by those who do not have PowerPoint installed on their computers. It is available from the *'File'* drop-down menu on the main menu bar.

Saving As Web Pages

The presentation can be output for uploading to a web site, using the *'Save As HTML'* for PowerPoint 97 or *'Save As Web Page'* from PowerPoint 2000. These are available from the *'File'* option on the main menu bar.

Saving As Bitmaps

The *'Save As'* option in the *'File'* sub-menu allows a single slide, or the entire presentation, to be converted into one or more .wmf files in PowerPoint 97 (plus .jpg, .bmp, .gif, .png in PowerPoint 2000).

These files can then be loaded into a PC card, inserted in a projector and shown without any additional software.

Delivering the presentation

Final preparations

When the electronic presentation is complete, the presenter has to prepare for its delivery.
The preparations revolve around:

- The readiness of the venue.
- The confidence of the presenter in the presentation's material.

The Venue

Where a presentation is being made within an organisation, there is more control over the preparation of the venue.   Where the presentation is made at different premises, e.g. at a client's office, an early arrival is essential to allow for basic checks and tests to be made.

In both cases, all the equipment has to be checked before the presentation.

Typical technical considerations are:

- Are there enough power points for equipment?
- Are multipoint adaptors required?
- Can the adaptors be safely used (check Health & Safety regulations)?
- Does the PC work with the projector supplied?
- Should the organisation's own projector be brought to the venue?
- Is the projector's output sufficiently bright to cope with the size of the audience?
- Can the presenter's voice be heard at rear of the venue?
- Is a Public Address system required?
- Is a radio mike available?

Typical venue layout considerations are:

- Is the seating adequate?
- Are the 'sight lines' correct:
  do the front audience block the view of the rear audience?
  do the seats need to be re-arranged or raised at the rear?
  do the loudspeakers, display screen and presenter need to be
  placed on a raised front platform?
- Are there any lighting problems (e.g. no shades on the windows)?
- Is it safe for the audience to move around OK in the dark (e.g. no blocked passageways)?
- Is it safe for the presenter to move around in the dark (e.g. no obstacles, steps or loose cables)?

Typical operator considerations are:

- Knowing where the presentation and its resources are stored on the disk's folders.
- Knowing how to reboot the computer if it hangs up.
- Knowing how to turn the projector back on if it switches into 'sleep' mode.
- Remembering to reboot the computer just before making the presentation. Computers might use up memory resources as they proceed and prolonged practice runs may have brought the system to near overload.

The Rehearsal

A great amount of time and resources will have been spent on creating the electronic presentation. An appropriate amount of time should be spent by the presenter in polishing the spoken part of the presentation. This is where many presentations fall down, as the audience soon spots an obviously ill-prepared speech.

Rehearsal is the key to the spoken presentation.   Rehearsal means going over the content and how it is delivered.   This does NOT mean writing a speech and trying to remember it word for word. That is the worst thing to do, as the entire speech will come to a halt if a word or a sentence is forgotten.   The speaker's notes should highlight the main points to be said but should not be printed on the sheet as complete sentences.   Rehearsals should cover both the content and the timing of slides.   The speech should be spoken aloud, as mentally rehearsing the speech provides an inaccurate estimate of time.

Rehearsals could be carried out in front of a mirror, or in front of colleagues, friends or family members.

If possible, rehearse in the room where the presentation is to be made, as this provides familiarity with both the surroundings and the equipment.

Presentation technique

There is a useful adage, which notes that

"You only get one chance to make a first impression"

While some are gifted speakers, others have to learn and practice the skill. The guidelines below may seem common sense but are often overlooked.

Appearance

The first thing that the audience will notice, even before a word is spoken or a slide is displayed, is the presenter's appearance and demeanour. A relaxed, confident presenter inspires confidence in the audience.

The list of appearance tips is:

- Make sure that all the speaker's notes are in the correct order before entering the rooms; shuffling sheets of paper does not give the appearance of being in control.
- Dress anonymously - the audience comes to hear the speech, not to be distracted by the presenter's dress code.
- Stay balanced – don't rock back and forth.
- Try to walk around, as this induces relaxation.
- Keep your hands out of your pockets.
- Face the audience, not the screen
- Talk to the audience, not to a fixed spot on the wall.
- If you have to point to something on the screen, stand to the side of the screen and continue facing and talking to the audience.
- Don't fidget.
- Avoid distracting mannerisms (e.g. running your fingers through your hair or tapping your pen)

Projection

Once the presentation is under way, the audience will focus on the slides and on the spoken presentation. The quality of the slides has already been determined. The quality of the spoken presentation can be improved with these approaches:

- Stand with your head up and shoulders back.
- Take a few deep breaths before starting opening the presentation.
- Don't talk too fast. In fact, it is usually a good idea to speak slightly more slowly than normal.
- Don't mumble.
- Speak clearly. The audience may include members with differing regional dialects from your own.
- Avoid monotone speech.
- Practice the use of inflection - use the tone of your voice to add extra meaning to certain parts of your speech (e.g. to denote urgency, importance, humour, irony, etc).
- Don't read from a script.
- Don't lower your voice at end of a sentence.
- Vary the pace.
- Keep sentences short, to save the audience having to maintain the thread of the argument.

Other presentation tips are:

- Don't overdo catch phrases.
- Make jokes, if you are able. A little humour relaxes the audience.
- If you are not able to tell a joke - don't. Save yourself and the audience the embarrassment.
- Use anecdotes, illustrations, endorsements.
- Use natural mannerisms and body language to add emphasis to certain points (e.g. using open arms to denote honesty, using hand-chopping movements to mark out items in a list).
- Let your enthusiasm and energy show through. If the audience sense that you approve of, or are motivated by, the content then they are more inclined to a positive view of the content.
- Don't repeat everything displayed on the screen, although repeating a heading or a particular bullet point might be useful to give emphasis to that item.
- Use a pointer to maintain the audience's focus on the screen. This may be a laser pointer or a remote mouse. A mouse connected to the computer can also be used but it ties the presenter to staying close to the computer.
- Annotate slides using a tablet and stylus or a mouse. Text can be added to a slide during the presentation, or a particular item may be circled or underlined. This prevents the presentation from being too static and also impresses a particular fact in the mind of the audience.

Interaction
A good presenter will learn how to involve an audience in the presentation and will know how to judge audience reactions.

The involvement of the audience starts right at the beginning of the presentation.   The opening material should introduce the speaker and explain why he/she is qualified to make the presentation.

During the presentation, the following techniques should be practised:

- Make eye contact with the audience.   Nobody trusts a speaker who looks at his/her feet or looks over the head of the audience.   Eye contact, although vital, should not be maintained for too long a time (not more than a few seconds) or it might be perceived as being aggressive or threatening.
- Maintain multiple eye contact.   Look around the room, so that all participants feel part of the presentation.   Some books recommend maintaining eye contact with only one individual, as a means of overcoming the speaker's nerves.   Consider, on the other hand, the nerves of the poor victim who feels picked upon or victimised.   This is particularly true if the presentation is imparting bad news.
- Learn to read the audience's reaction during the presentation.   Look for signs of interest, boredom, cynicism, restlessness, puzzlement, etc.
- Respond to the audience's reaction.   If an audience looks puzzled, for example, take the time to explain the point from another angle.
- Look for points of support.   It is useful if someone in the audience nods vigorously or states their agreement, as this boosts the impact of the message.
- Look for possible opposition (e.g. someone frowning, desperate to ask a question, scribbling furiously and aggressively).
- Ask rhetorical questions. Ask a question and then answer it yourself (e.g. *"How is this price made up?"*, *"What do all these facts mean?"*, *"Why is only available in the U.K.?"*).   This gives the impression (correctly) that you have considered all the implications of your presentation and have sought answers for all possible questions.

Handling questions
Every presentation should provide time at the end for questions. A good presenter will not wait for questions, but will actively invite questions or points of view; this inspires confidence.

Recommended techniques are:

- Anticipate questions and prepare answers (perhaps using extra hidden slides).
- Treat questioners with respect.   Brushing aside a point of view or ridiculing a questioner will justifiably produce a hostile reaction from the audience and result in serious damage.
- Keep answers short.
- Admit if you don't know an answer, but offer to find the answer and get back to them.
- Reply to the entire audience – looking at the questioner at the end of the reply encourages a follow-on question.

Using a pen
When answering questions, it is often useful to underline an item, circle a figure in a table, etc.   This is achieved in PowerPoint by the following steps:

- Right click on the slide.
- Choose *'Pen'* from the popup menu.
- Draw on the slide.
- Hit the right cursor key to move on to the next slide.

Handouts
Don't give away any printed copies until the end of the presentation, otherwise many in the audience will read ahead and miss much of the spoken material.   Sometimes, handouts are distributed with the slide at the top and a box for the audience to write notes.   It is also sometimes useful to distribute technical specifications, diagrams, etc to overcome detailed technical questions that might otherwise bog down the question session.   Another technique is to print the slide at the top, followed by the main points of the speech. This provides useful summaries for those who attended, but may appear as gibberish to others.

Post mortem
No one makes a perfect presentation at first.   The secret is to learn from mistakes.   This requires feedback from the presentation sessions.   Ask colleagues who were in the audience to inform you about the weaknesses and strengths in the session and adapt future presentations accordingly.

Corporate presentations

With student presentations, the difference between a mediocre presentation and a brilliant one may result in a credit grade instead of a pass. With corporate presentations, the difference may be measured in millions of pounds. The persuasive power of the presentation may win or lose a contract, or the launch of a new product line may be harmed. Consequently, much more preparation of message, content and presentation is expected. The event should be planned in great detail.

Such presentations often require far greater administrative effort, over and above the presentation itself.

Administrative Considerations

Organising a presentation for staff members may only require the issue of a memo or a notice on the notice board. Public presentations require much more effort, involving the following tasks:

- Deciding on the composition of the audience. The aim is not to achieve the biggest possible turnout; the aim is to get suitable people along. The content has been designed with a specific group in mind and only these should be invited.
- Deciding on the method of reaching the intended audience. Advertising in professional or trade papers may be suitable for reaching new clients, while an existing contact list may be used for more specialised presentations.
- Drawing up an invitation list. Very few presentations allow the audience to simply walk in from the street. All advertising and correspondence will include a method of registering for the presentation. They may have to return a form, or fax, telephone or e-mail their intention to attend. This allows organisers to estimate attendance numbers and this may determine technical factors (size of room, number of seats, need for public address, etc) and other factors (e.g. how many buns to order).
- Issuing credentials to attendees. Sufficient notice of the details must be given. If a presentation involves an attendance from a scattered geographical area, consideration should be given to a 10am rather than a 9am start.
- Organising resources. This may include hiring a room, PA equipment, and securing any technical assistance that may be required to set up and test the equipment. For high prestige events, consideration should also be given to having duplicate equipment, so that the show can still go on in case of a computer or projector breakdown.
- Abiding by Health and Safety regulations, such as the location of fire exits, maintaining unobstructed passageways, avoiding trailing cables, and ensuring that the audience is protected from all possible physical dangers (e.g. the hot projector).
- Ensuring adequate facilities. This should include parking places, toilet facilities. Disabled facilities (such as parking, ramps, elevators and toilets). Catering facilities should also be organised, so that early attendees can have a coffee, etc while waiting for the presentation to commence. For long seminars, there may also be refreshment breaks or even lunch breaks.
- Creating an organised welcome for attendees. Staff should greet arrivals, register their names and hand out name badges (to identify people during breaks). The welcome stage may also involve the handing out of support material, catalogues, specifications, or any freebies (such as CDs or umbrellas, pens, etc bearing the company logo).

The list is demanding and may require a logistics plan and a budget.

Creative Considerations

Although all presentations deserve proper presentation, large prestige events such as product launches, ministerial announcements, etc, require extra planning. The person who designs the presentation, the person who writes the speech and the person who makes the presentation are probably all different people. This requires some degree of co-ordination. Usually, someone has the overall responsibility or organising and liasing between the interested parties. The organiser would normally prepare a 'brief' before any detailed work is undertaken. The brief outlines the main message and the treatment of the presentation and may involve the use of storyboards (see other chapters). The organiser must protect against the danger of over complicating the presentation. The speechwriter is liable to include too many issues and the designer may wish to include too many high tech gimmicks. The organiser must ensure that the content is designed for the sole benefit of the audience (e.g. is it primarily an information session or a sales pitch, is it facts for techies or hype for buyers, and so on).

Once agreement is reached, the script should be signed for by the most senior member (e.g. a board member, politician, etc). Then the presentation would move on to integrating the input from professional photographers and graphics artists.

Index

Also available from the same author

The Computing Reference for Students

The PC Support Handbook is the UK's most popular computing textbook for students training in computing, IT and PC Support.

It is released in August of each year to coincide with the start of college/university terms.

It is of A4 size (210mm x 297mm) and contains 568 pages of explanations, tables and diagrams.

The nineteen chapters cover:

- Computer Basics
- Computer Architecture
- Memory
- Viruses
- System Selection
- Web Site Publishing
- Unix
- Using DOS and Windows
- Computer Video
- Installing/Configuring Windows
- PC Support
- Data Communications
- Multimedia
- Computer Software
- PC Configuration
- Discs & Drives
- Upgrading a Computer
- The Internet
- Local Area Networks

The book costs £29 per copy.   Where five or more copies are purchased, the price is reduced to £20 per copy. There is no extra charge for post and packing.

Dumbreck Publishing
8A Woodland Avenue, Kirkintilloch, Glasgow, G66 1AS
Tel/Fax: 0141-775-2889
E-mail: sales@dumbreck.demon.co.uk
Web site: www.dumbreck.demon.co.uk

Supporting Shareware CD

A CD has been specially prepared to accompany this book, in conjunction with the *'PC Support Handbook'*. The best programs, utilities and reference material have been included in a single CD that is designed to further assist the reader. The CD contains hundreds of programs that are directly linked with the subjects of the books.

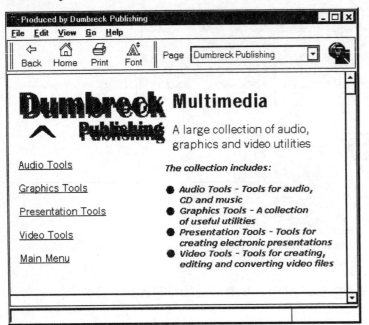

OTHER CONTENTS

INTERNET
Web authoring tools, browsing tools, call timers and FAX and modem utilities.

WINDOWS
Screensavers, font organisers, swap file monitor, emergency recovery, desktop utilities, etc.

DISKS
Disk and CD utilities, including cataloguers, backup and file editors.

VIRUSES
Virus scanners, anti-virus encyclopaedia, etc.

PC SUPPORT
System diagnostics, help desk utilities, card and cable connection references.

ARCHITECTURE
Assembler tools, reference material thousands of source code examples

LANS
Analysers, LAN glossary, Pascal source code, etc.

Plus ...
Useful utilities for students and lecturers.
Glossaries, tutors and tips.

The CD will autoplay or can be run under Windows 3.1, Windows 95 and Windows 98.

These programs and are distributed complete and unmodified, according to the distributor's wishes and methods.

The CD is menu-driven as shown above. Some programs run from the CD and each program has the following details
- Program description.
- Licensing details (e.g. freeware, shareware).
- Platform (i.e. DOS, Windows 3.1 or Windows 95/98).
- Installation details.

LEGAL PROVISIONS
The price paid for the CD purchases only the physical media. Payment to the original author is required if shareware is used beyond the specified trial period.
All software is intended to be virus-free. However, we recommend that the files be checked before being installed, as new viruses are continually being developed. Consequently, Dumbreck Publishing assumes no responsibility for any consequences of using these files.

HOW TO ORDER
The CD is available in the UK for £5.50 per copy, including post and packing. Two or more copies are supplied at £5 per copy. VISA and MasterCard transactions are an extra 20p per CD.
Cheques or postal orders should be sent to:

Dumbreck Publishing
8A Woodland Avenue, Kirkintilloch, Glasgow, G66 1AS
Tel/Fax: 0141-775-2889
E-mail: sales @ dumbreck.demon.co.uk
Web site: www.dumbreck.demon.co.uk